"While other companions provide scholarly summary-context and assessment-as a starting place for further research, this companion seems more individualized . . . *A Companion to Jane Austen* offers the useful charms of knowledge, stimulation, judgment."

1650–1850: Ideas, Aesthetics, and Inquiries in the Early Modern Era

"The advantage is that the chapters tend to be manageable, clear, and focused – perfect, in fact, for assigning to undergraduate and beginning graduate students. I for one certainly plan on doing that. After all, one of the charms of enchantment is that it can be contagious."

Notes and Queries

"How is it that fresh perspectives on Austen and her writing are still being thought up? Johnson and Tuite answer that the study of Austen today is a "diverse, expansive, excitable and critical life-form", growing and changing with new audiences and approaches to literary criticism. Arranged in five parts, this *Companion* covers the style and genre of her novels, including the history of manuscripts, editions and illustrations (with 13 black-and-white facsimiles); individual readings of the main texts, looking at how Austen was initially received by critics and readers alike and the success of *Pride and Prejudice*; Austen's literary style and technique, showing how the author used language and who she was influenced by; the political, social and cultural settings of her novels, discussing the French Revolution and feminism; and how Austen has been "reinvented" by different generations, from the "silver fork" novel of the Victorian era to "sexed-up" television adaptations of our screens today."

Reference Reviews

A Companion to
Jane Austen

Blackwell Companions to Literature and Culture

This series offers comprehensive, newly written surveys of key periods and movements and certain major authors, in English literary culture and history. Extensive volumes provide new perspectives and positions on contexts and on canonical and post-canonical texts, orientating the beginning student in new fields of study and providing the experienced undergraduate and new graduate with current and new directions, as pioneered and developed by leading scholars in the field.

Published Recently

For a full list of titles available in the *Blackwell Companions to Literature and Culture* series, please visit www.blackwellpublishing.com/literature

A COMPANION TO

JANE AUSTEN

EDITED BY

CLAUDIA L. JOHNSON AND CLARA TUITE

A John Wiley & Sons, Ltd., Publication

Library of Congress Cataloging-in-Publication Data

A companion to Jane Austen / edited by Claudia L. Johnson and Clara Tuite.
        p. cm.—(Blackwell companions to literature and culture ; 56)
    Includes bibliographical references and index.
    ISBN 978-1-4051-4909-9 (cloth) – 978-0-470-67238-9 (pbk.)
    1. Austen, Jane, 1775–1817—Criticism and interpretation—Handbooks, manuals, etc.
I. Johnson, Claudia L.   II. Tuite, Clara
    PR4037.C65 2009
    823′.7—dc22

                          2008019513

A catalogue record for this book is available from the British Library.

This book is published in the following electronic formats: ePDFs 9781444305975; Wiley Online Library 9781444305968; ePub 9781444354904; Mobi 9781444321562.

Set in 11/13 pt Garamond 3 by Toppan Best-set Premedia Limited
Printed in Singapore by Ho Printing Singapore Pte Ltd

1   2012

Contents

List of Figures

Notes on Contributors

Nancy Armstrong is Nancy Duke Lewis Professor of English, Comparative Literature, and Modern Culture and Media at Brown University. She is the author of *Desire and Domestic Fiction: A Political History of the Novel*; *Fiction in the Age of Photography: The Legacy of British Realism*; *How Novels Think: The Limits of Individualism 1719–1900*, and (with Leonard Tennenhouse), *The Imaginary Puritan: Literature, Intellectual Labor, and the History of Personal Life*. She is also the editor of the journal *NOVEL: A Forum on Fiction*.

Barbara M. Benedict is the Charles A. Dana Professor of English Literature at Trinity College, CT. She has written three monographs: *Framing Feeling: Sentiment and Style in English Prose Fiction, 1745–1800* (1994); *Making the Modern Reader: Cultural Mediation in Early Modern Literary Anthologies* (1996); and *Curiosity: A Cultural History of Early Modern Enquiry* (2001). She has edited *Eighteenth-Century British Erotica, 1700–1800, Vol. 4: Wilkes and the Late Eighteenth Century*, and coedited (with Deidre LeFaye) Jane Austen's *Northanger Abbey* (2006).

Linda Bree is the Literature Publisher at Cambridge University Press and author of a number of books and articles on eighteenth-century writers. She is editor of *Persuasion* (1998), and coeditor (with Janet Todd) of the *Later Manuscripts* volume (2008) in *The Cambridge Edition of the Works of Jane Austen*.

Fiona Brideoake is a Research Fellow in English Literary Studies at the University of Melbourne. Her current research includes work on Bluestocking sociability, Austen fan cultures, and queer historiography. She has published on the Ladies of Llangollen and Shakespearean filmmaking, and is revising a book entitled *"The Future Arrives Late": Queering the Ladies of Llangollen*.

Miranda Burgess is Associate Professor of English at the University of British Columbia. She works on Romantic-period literary history and on the histories of genre, print culture, and reading. Her book *British Fiction and the Production of Social*

Order, 1740–1830 (2000) traced the uses of genre change in developing theories of British society and nationhood across the eighteenth century. She is completing a manuscript titled *Romantic Transport: Printing, Reading, and Feeling, 1790–1830*, which explores the media contexts of Romantic affect and their sources in contemporary problems of transnational exchange, with a special focus on Ireland.

Laura Carroll teaches English at La Trobe University, Melbourne. Her research interests include literary adaptation, the afterlife of Jane Austen, and representations of animals in literature and film. She has published essays on Austen, Shakespeare, James Thurber, and Australian cinema.

E. J. Clery is Professor of Eighteenth-Century Literature at the University of Southampton, UK. She is the author of *The Rise of Supernatural Fiction 1762–1800* (1995), *Women's Gothic from Clara Reeve to Mary Shelley* (2000), and *The Feminization Debate in Eighteenth-Century England: Literature, Commerce and Luxury* (2004).

Deirdre Coleman is Robert Wallace Chair of English at the University of Melbourne. Her research centers on eighteenth-century literature and cultural history, focusing in particular on racial ideology, colonialism, natural history, and the antislavery movement. She has published in *ELH*, *Eighteenth-Century Life*, and *Eighteenth-Century Studies*, and is the author of *Romantic Colonization and British Anti-Slavery* (2005).

Edward Copeland is Professor Emeritus of English, Pomona College, Claremont, CA. He is the author of *Women Writing About Money: Women's Fiction in England, 1790–1820* (1995), and editor of Jane Austen's *Sense and Sensibility* (2006). He is currently preparing a book-length study of the silver fork novel and its cultural and political presence in the reform years.

Nicholas Dames is Theodore Kahan Professor in the Humanities at Columbia University, where he specializes in British and French fiction of the nineteenth century. He is the author of *Amnesiac Selves: Nostalgia, Forgetting, and British Fiction, 1810–1870* (2001) and *The Physiology of the Novel: Reading, Neural Science, and the Form of Victorian Fiction* (2007).

Margaret Anne Doody was educated at Dalhousie University in Nova Scotia and Oxford University. She has taught at Berkeley, Princeton, and Vanderbilt Universities, and is currently John and Barbara Glynn Family Professor of Literature at the University of Notre Dame. She is author of *A Natural Passion: A Study of the Novels of Samuel Richardson*, *The True Story of the Novel*, *The Daring Muse*, and a literary biography of Frances Burney. Her most recent book is *Tropic of Venice* (2006). She is also well known as the author of a series of mystery stories set in ancient Greece, featuring the philosopher Aristotle as the presiding detective.

Mary A. Favret is Associate Professor of English at Indiana University-Bloomington, where she teaches courses on a variety of subjects, especially in eighteenth and nineteenth-century literature. The author of *Romantic Correspondence: Women, Politics* *and the Fiction of Letters* (1993), she has written extensively on Austen and other Romantic-era writers. Currently she is completing a book titled *War at a Distance: Romanticism and the Creation of Modern Wartime.*

Jan Fergus is Professor of English at Lehigh University, PA. She has published two book-length works on Austen as well as articles on her novels and on the provincial reading public in her time. Her most recent book is *Provincial Readers in Eighteenth-Century England* (2006).

William Galperin is Professor of English at Rutgers University, New Brunswick. He is the author of several books including *The Historical Austen* (2003) and has recently edited *Persuasion* (2007).

Susan C. Greenfield is Associate Professor of English at Fordham University. She is author of *Mothering Daughters: Novels and the Politics of Family Romance, Frances Burney to Jane Austen* (2002), and of numerous articles on late eighteenth and early nineteenth-century English novels.

Sonia Hofkosh teaches in the English Department at Tufts University, MA. She is the author of *Sexual Politics and the Romantic Author* (1998) and coeditor (with Alan Richardson) of *Romanticism, Race, & Imperial Culture 1780–1834* (1996). Her current project explores the function of objects within Romantic discourses of subjectivity.

Claudia L. Johnson joined the faculty at Princeton in 1994 and now serves as Department Chair. She specializes in eighteenth and early nineteenth-century literature, with a particular emphasis on the novel. Her books include *Jane Austen: Women, Politics, and the Novel* (1988), *Equivocal Beings: Politics, Gender and Sentimentality in the 1790s* (1995), and *The Cambridge Companion to Mary Wollstonecraft* (2002), along with editions of Jane Austen's *Mansfield Park* (1998), *Sense and Sensibility* (2002), and *Northanger Abbey* (2003). She is now finishing a book about author-love, called *Jane Austen's Cults and Cultures*, which traces permutations of "Jane mania" from 1817 to the present, and is also working on another called *Raising the Novel*, which explores modern efforts to create a novelistic canon by elevating novels to keystones of high culture.

Vivien Jones is Professor of Eighteenth-Century Gender and Culture at the University of Leeds, UK. Her many publications in the field include *Women in the Eighteenth-Century: Constructions of Femininity* (1990) and *Women and Literature in Britain 1700–1800* (2000). She has edited *Pride and Prejudice* and *Jane Austen's Selected Letters* and is General Editor of Austen's novels in Oxford World's Classics.

George Justice is Associate Dean of the Graduate School and Associate Professor of English at the University of Missouri. He is the author of *The Manufacturers of Literature: Writing and the Literary Marketplace in Eighteenth-Century England* and coeditor of *Women's Writing and the Circulation of Ideas: Manuscript Publication in England, 1550–1800*, as well as the author of essays on Addison, Johnson, Austen, and other eighteenth-century literary figures.

Claire Lamont is Professor of English Romantic Literature at Newcastle University, UK. She specializes in English and Scottish Literature, especially the Romantic poets, Austen, Scott, and the literary representation of architecture. Her edition of Walter Scott's *Chronicles of the Canongate* for the Edinburgh Edition of the Waverley Novels appeared in 2000. She was Textual Adviser to the new edition of Austen's works in Penguin Classics (1995–98).

Devoney Looser is Associate Professor of English at the University of Missouri. She is the author of *Women Writers and Old Age in Great Britain, 1750–1850* (2008) and *British Women Writers and the Writing of History, 1670–1820* (2000), the coeditor (with E. Ann Kaplan) of *Generations: Academic Feminists in Dialogue* (1997), and the editor of *Jane Austen and Discourses of Feminism* (1995). She is a former member of the board of directors of the Jane Austen Society of North America.

Deidre Lynch is Chancellor Jackman Professor at the University of Toronto. Her books include *The Economy of Character: Novels, Market Culture, and the Business of Inner Meaning* (1998), which won the Modern Language Association's Prize for a First Book. She is also the author of many essays on eighteenth and nineteenth-century literature and culture, and is an editor of Austen and Wollstonecraft. She is currently completing a book entitled *At Home in English: A Cultural History of the Love of Literature*.

Robert L. Mack was educated at Columbia, Oxford, and Princeton; he is currently a Senior Lecturer at the University of Exeter, UK. His publications include a biography of the poet Thomas Gray, *Thomas Gray: A Life* (2000), a study of the literary mode of parody, *The Genius of Parody* (2007), and a history of the urban legends surrounding the figure of London's Sweeney Todd, *The Wonderful and Surprising History of Sweeney Todd* (2008). He has edited a number of texts for Oxford World's Classics and has also produced the first modern edition of the Austen family's periodical, *The Loiterer* (2006).

Anthony Mandal is Lecturer in English Literature at Cardiff University, UK. His research interests include Jane Austen, nineteenth-century fiction, the Gothic, book history, and digital humanities. He is the author of *Jane Austen and the Popular Novel: The Determined Author* (2007); coeditor (with Peter Garside) of *The English Novel, 1830–1836* (2003) and (with Brian Southam) *The Reception of Jane Austen in Europe* (2007); and developer of *British Fiction, 1800–1829: A Database of Production, Circulation & Reception* (2004) and *A Database of Mid-Victorian Wood-Engraved Illustrations* (2007). He is also the editor of the online journal *Romantic Textualities: Literature and Print Culture, 1780–1840*.

Juliet McMaster, University Professor Emerita of the University of Alberta and Fellow of the Royal Society of Canada, is the author of *Jane Austen on Love, Jane Austen the Novelist*, and of books on Thackeray, Trollope, Dickens, and the eighteenth-century novel. She is also the coeditor (with Bruce Stovel) of *Jane Austen's Business* and (with Edward Copeland) *The Cambridge Companion to Jane Austen*. She is illustrator-editor of

Austen's *The Beautifull Cassandra*, and founder and first General Editor of the Juvenilia Press. She is currently working on a biography of the Victorian painter James Clarke Hook, and was involved in curating an exhibit of his work at Tate Britain.

Roger E. Moore is Senior Lecturer in English and Director of Undergraduate Writing at Vanderbilt University, TN. The author of essays on Chaucer, Marlowe, and Sidney, he is presently working on a book project on the literary response to the dissolution of the monasteries, titled *Bare Ruined Choirs: The Cloister and the English Imagination from the Reformation to Romanticism*.

Mary Ann O'Farrell is Associate Professor of English at Texas A&M University. She is the author of *Telling Complexions: The Nineteenth-Century English Novel and the Blush* (1997) and coeditor (with Lynne Vallone) of *Virtual Gender: Fantasies of Subjectivity and Embodiment* (1999). Her current project examines Austen's uses in contemporary cultural and political discourse.

Daniel O'Quinn is an Associate Professor in the School of English and Theatre Studies at the University of Guelph, Ontario. He is the author of *Staging Governance: Theatrical Imperialism in London, 1770–1800* (2005). He has coedited (with Jane Moody) the *Cambridge Companion to British Theatre, 1737–1840* (2007) and has prepared an edition of the *Travels of Mirza Abu Taleb Khan* (forthcoming). His articles on the intersection of race, sexuality, and class in Romantic culture have appeared in various journals including *ELH, Studies in Romanticism, Texas Studies in Literature and Language, European Romantic Review*, and *Romantic Praxis*.

Ruth Perry, Professor of Literature at the Massachusetts Institute of Technology, is the author of many books and articles on eighteenth-century English literature and culture. Her most recent book is an edition (with Susan Carlile) of Charlotte Lennox's *Henrietta* (1758). It is her fondest wish to publish a volume of essays on Jane Austen.

Mary Poovey is the Samuel Rudin University Professor in the Humanities and Professor of English at New York University. She has written on subjects as diverse as feminist theory and the reform of government in nineteenth-century Britain. Her most recent books, *A History of the Modern Fact* and *Genres of the Credit Economy*, trace the history of some of modernity's foundational categories and institutions.

Gillian Russell is Reader in English in the School of Humanities, Australian National University, Canberra. She is author of *The Theatres of War: Performance, Politics and Society, 1793–1815* (1995) and *Women, Sociability and Theatre in Georgian London* (2007).

Diego Saglia is Associate Professor of English Literature at the University of Parma, Italy, and his main research area is British literature of the Romantic period. He has contributed to *Jane Austen oggi e ieri* (2002) and *Jane Austen in Context* (2005), and is coeditor (with Beatrice Battaglia) of *Re-Drawing Austen: Picturesque Travels in Austenland* (2004).

Harry E. Shaw has taught at Cornell University since 1978, where he has served as Chair of the Department of English and Senior Associate Dean of the College of Arts and Sciences. His main scholarly interests are the British novel and narrative poetics. He is author of *Narrating Reality: Austen, Scott, Eliot* (1999) and (with Alison Case) *Reading the Nineteenth-Century Novel: Austen to Eliot*, a book for students and teachers (2008).

Judy Simons is Professor of English and Pro-Vice-Chancellor at De Montfort University, Leicester, UK. She has published widely on women's writing, including numerous articles on Austen. Among her books are *Fanny Burney* (1987), *Diaries and Journals of Literary Women from Fanny Burney to Virginia Woolf* (1990), and *What Katy Read: Feminist Re-readings of Classic Stories for Girls* (1995). She edited *Mansfield Park and Persuasion: Contemporary Critical Essays, A Casebook* (1997) and has written student guides to *Sense and Sensibility* and *Persuasion*. She is deeply committed to developing English as a subject and has held a number of national positions. She was Chair of the Council for College and University English (1996–2000), Chair of the UK Council for University Deans of Arts and Humanities (2000–3) and Chair of the UK Subject Centre for English (2000–7).

Brian Southam's most recent publications are a revised and enlarged second edition of *Jane Austen and the Navy* (2005), *Jane Austen: A Students' Guide to the Later Manuscript Works* (2007), and (coedited with Anthony Mandal) *The Reception of Jane Austen in Europe* (2007). He is presently working on a study of Jane Austen and the professions.

Jane Spencer is Professor of English at the University of Exeter, UK. She has published widely on the novel in the eighteenth and early nineteenth centuries, and on women's literary history from the Restoration to the nineteenth century. Her latest book is *Literary Relations: Kinship and the Canon, 1660–1830* (2005). She is currently working on animals in eighteenth-century writing.

Mary Spongberg is head of the Department of Modern History at Macquarie University, Sydney, and the editor of *Australian Feminist Studies*. She recently coedited (with Barbara Caine and Ann Curthoys) the *Companion to Women's Historical Writing* (2005), and is the author of *Writing Women's History Since the Renaissance* (2002).

Fiona Stafford is a Reader in English at the University of Oxford and a Fellow of Somerville College. She has edited *Pride and Prejudice* and *Emma*, and is the author of *Jane Austen: A Brief Life* (2008) and editor of *Jane Austen's* Emma: *A Casebook in Criticism* (2007).

Kathryn Sutherland is Professor of Bibliography and Textual Criticism at the University of Oxford. She is author of *Jane Austen's Textual Lives: from Aeschylus to Bollywood* (2005) and coauthor (with Marilyn Deegan) of *Digital Technology and the Cultures of Print* (2008). She is currently working on a digital and print edition of Jane Austen's fiction manuscripts.

Katie Trumpener is Emily Sanford Professor of English and Comparative Literature at Yale University. Her *Bardic Nationalism: The Romantic Novel and the British Empire* (1997) reads *Mansfield Park* against contemporary abolition discourse, while her "The Virago Jane Austen" (in *Janeites*, 2000) traces Austen reception among Anglo-American women modernists. She is currently working on Romantic children's literature, and recently coedited (with Richard Maxwell) *The Cambridge Companion to Fiction in the Romantic Period* (2007).

Clara Tuite is Senior Lecturer in English at the University of Melbourne. She is the author of *Romantic Austen: Sexual Politics and the Literary Canon* (2002), as well as several essays on Austen, and is coeditor (with Gillian Russell) of *Romantic Sociability: Social Networks and Literary Culture in Britain, 1770–1840* (2002).

John Wiltshire has recently retired as Professor of English at La Trobe University, Melbourne. He is the author of *Jane Austen and the Body* (1992) and *Recreating Jane Austen* (2001), and has edited *Mansfield Park*. With David Monaghan and Ariane Hudulet, he is writing a book provisionally titled *The Cinematic Jane Austen*.

Susan J. Wolfson, Professor of English, Princeton University, is a specialist in the British Romantic era, and author of *Borderlines: The Shiftings of Gender in British Romanticism* (2006) and *Romantic Interactions: Social Being and the Turns of Imagination* (forthcoming). Her work on Austen includes "Boxing Emma: The Reader's Dilemma at Box Hill" (in *Re-reading Box Hill*, 2000) and (with Claudia L. Johnson) *Jane Austen's Pride and Prejudice: A Longman Cultural Edition* (2003).

Gillen D'Arcy Wood is associate professor of English at the University of Illinois, Urbana-Champaign. He is the author of *The Shock of the Real: Romanticism and Visual Culture, 1760–1860* (2001) and a historical novel, *Hosack's Folly* (2005). His current book is a study of literary Romanticism and music culture in the period 1770–1840.

Michael Wood is Professor of English and Comparative Literature at Princeton University. His most recent book is *Literature and the Taste of Knowledge* (2005). His other books include *The Magician's Doubts: Nabokov and the Risks of Fiction* (1994) and *Children of Silence: on Contemporary Fiction* (1998).

List of Abbreviations

E: *Emma, The Novels of Jane Austen*, ed. R. W. Chapman (Oxford University Press, 1932–4), revised by Mary Lascelles (Oxford University Press, 1965–6).

MP: *Mansfield Park*, ed. Chapman, rev. Lascelles.

NA: *Northanger Abbey*, ed. Chapman, rev. Lascelles.

P: *Persuasion*, ed. Chapman, rev. Lascelles.

PP: *Pride and Prejudice*, ed. Chapman, rev. Lascelles.

SS: *Sense and Sensibility*, ed. Chapman, rev. Lascelles.

MW: *Minor Works, The Works of Jane Austen*, ed. R. W. Chapman. Oxford: Oxford University Press, 1954, revised by B. C. Southam. Oxford University Press, 1969.

Letters: *Jane Austen's Letters*, ed. Deirdre Le Faye. Oxford University Press, 1995.

A Note to the Reader

Nowadays, the status of Jane Austen texts, once a quiescent issue in Austen criticism, is a lively subject. A very fine range of editions is available not only for scholarly and classroom use but also for – lacking a better term – ordinary readers, a vast public, who read Austen's novels (often every year!) for pleasure: Chapman's landmark edition of the 1920s; the related and distinguished set from Oxford World Classics; the revised edition from Penguin, based on challenging new editorial principles; volumes published variously by Broadview Press and W.W. Norton, and Longman, among others; and, most ambitiously and impressively of all, the monumental new Cambridge Edition of the Novels of Jane Austen. The multiplicity of differently authoritative editions of Austen's novels raises fascinating questions. To some extent, of course, Austen's novels are a marketing opportunity, but more critical questions are at stake than the bottom lines of publishers. What is it that makes an Austenian text authoritative? Who gets to say so? Is it necessary to establish a single definitive edition when so many important, carefully prepared and annotated editions are available? Is there really such a thing as a definitive text?

On one hand, the plurality of editions seems to us an extremely healthy sign, testifying to the liveliness of Austen studies and to the healthy diffusion of scholarly authority, resistance, and debate. On the other hand, this very plurality makes settling on a standard set in this volume a difficult and vexing task. For the purposes of internal cross-referencing, it seemed important to regularize quotations using a single edition rather than oblige readers to fetch citations from different volumes of different editions; but every time we advanced a qualitative argument in favor of one set, an equally convincing qualitative argument on behalf of another emerged. Acutely aware that there is no single, fully satisfactory solution to this problem, we eventually decided in favor of the long-standard Chapman edition on purely practical grounds: it is mostly widely available to students in libraries and having been for better or worse the standard edition since the 1920s, it is the set almost invariably employed in the literary criticism alluded to throughout this volume and collected in the bibliography.

Acknowledgments

Claudia L. Johnson would like to thank Princeton University for the research support that made some of the work on this volume possible. Clara Tuite would like to thank the University of Melbourne, for the period of leave that enabled her to complete the bulk of the editing and writing of the Introduction. She would also like to thank the Australian Research Council for a grant that supported work on the volume and the editorial assistance of Michelle Smith in the crucial final stages.

To Michelle herself, we are enormously grateful for her generous assistance and her meticulous attention to detail.

Our editors at Blackwell Publishing have been encouraging and patient and discerning throughout. We would especially like to thank Al Bertrand, for his guidance in the early stages of the project, and Hannah Morrell and Emma Bennett, for seeing the volume through production. We were also particularly fortunate to be able to rely on Jenny Roberts as our copy-editor, and we thank her for her keen eye and unfailing good judgment. We are likewise grateful to David Luljak for his skill and judiciousness as our indexer and to Marcia Glass for her zealous attention as our proofreader.

Our greatest debts are to our contributors, for the intelligence and flair with which they collaborated in the project of showing the vitality, variety, and excitement of current Austen studies. We appreciate equally their patience and their sense of adventure.

in his essay "Describing What Never Happened: Jane Austen and the History of Missed Opportunities," *ELH* 73 (2006).

Mitchell Library, State Library of New South Wales, for Figure 5.1, *Mansfield Park* (London: Richard Bentley, 1833), frontispiece and engraved title page, by William Greatbatch after Pickering.

Matheson Library, Monash University, for Figure 5.2, *Northanger Abbey and Persuasion* (London: Chapman & Hall, 1872), front and back boards.

University of New South Wales Library, for Figure 5.3, *Mansfield Park* (London: Groombridge, 1875), illustration by A. F. Lydon.

Dover Publications, Inc., for Figure 5.5, *Pride & Prejudice* (London: George Allen, 1895), headpiece and ornamental capital letter on p. 89, by Hugh Thomson.

Lewis Walpole Library, Yale University, for Figure 22.1, James Gillray, *Fatigues of the Campaign in Flanders*.

The Trustees of the British Museum, for Figure 25.1, *Am I Not a Man and a Brother?*, by Josiah Wedgwood.

Wilberforce House Museum, Hull City Council, UK, for Figure 25.2, *Am I Not a Woman and a Sister?*

The British Museum, for Figure 25.3, Isaac Cruikshank, *The Abolition of the Slave Trade* and Figure 25.4, *The Rabbits*.

Every effort has been made to trace copyright holders and to obtain their permission for the use of copyright material. The publisher apologizes for any errors or omissions in the above list and would be grateful if notified of any corrections that should be incorporated in future reprints or editions of this book.

Introduction

Claudia L. Johnson and Clara Tuite

Writing at the outset of the twentieth century, Henry James famously complained that the public's enthusiasm for Jane Austen was being abetted by a "body of publishers, editors, [and] illustrators" who find "their 'dear,' our dear, everybody's dear, Jane so infinitely to their material purpose." To be sure, James acknowledged that Austen would not be so "saleable if we had not more or less . . . lost our hearts to her" in the first place, but he censured the "special bookselling spirit" which, with all its "eager, active interfering force" whips up a "stiff breeze" and drives the waters of reputation above their natural levels.[1] Writing at the outset of the twenty-first century, we can say with certainty that the waters of Austenian study, appreciation, and marketing have, far from subsiding, continued their steady rise, flooding beyond national and media boundaries. Shaped to some extent by the transformative energies of the global Austen surge of the mid 1990s – for we cannot really speak of *revival* in connection with a figure whose vitality has never abated – Austen study today is a diverse, expansive, excitable, critical life-form, with feelers that reach out and across disciplines. For popular audiences across the world, the plethora of cinematic adaptations and spin-offs of Austen's novels and life – and all the reviews and commentary they have in turn generated – have produced new modes of transmission and more diverse audiences. But Austen criticism has been fuelled by the momentum of that surge. This *Companion* seeks not only to describe the present state of Austen studies but also to explore how it both informs and is informed by changes and innovations within the broader field of literary and cultural studies.

We might characterize the fascination with Austen today as a form of reenchantment, a rediscovery of particular Austenian pleasures and of what Sonia Hofkosh, in her essay on *Northanger Abbey* and Austen's work more generally, refers to as Austen's "uses of enchantment." This reenchantment has occurred at least to some extent as an effect of the cinematic enchantment with Austen, the delivery of Austen in the form of a new repertoire of captivating visual effects. But it is not beholden to it. For despite truisms that abound about Austen having been rescued from print and delivered to new audiences through the screen – truisms that naturalize cinematic adaptation as the final destiny of print (as though cinematic reinvention is the only form of reinvention) – intriguingly, while Austen has been delivered to mass audiences in the mode of visual rhetorics, Austen readers have been inspired to return to the specificities of print and reading. Cinematic and televised versions of Austen, inevitably saturated with a sensuous visual detail notably lacking in the novels themselves, have encouraged a renewed attention to the specificities of print and reading, as other specific forms of cultural pleasure and forms of enchantment.

A particular area of recent scholarly intensity has been textual criticism and history of the book. As with interpretation, so with textual production and textual criticism, and there is now a new attention to the variability and changeability of the text. When R. W. Chapman's edition of Jane Austen's novels appeared in 1923 – touting its scholarly textual principles on its title pages – the status of Austen's texts (and Chapman's representation of them) was not a particularly lively or contested issue, but over the past decade the textual study of Austen has become intensely important, implicating as it does our most basic apprehension of the words and punctuation on the page and our concomitant sense of Austen as a writer with a certain style, and several new editions now vie with Chapman's. A number of essays in this volume engage with questions of textual production and the changeability of textual status, particularly in Part I, "The Life and the Texts." The essays in Part I introduce the reader to Jane Austen's life, produced by texts and their absences, biographies and letters; to her edited texts; and to the cultural and material contexts of production of the early published volumes and modern editions, as text, or as image, or as a combination of both. We start with Jane Austen's letters, "the key to everything," as Kathryn Sutherland suggests, "the contested place where the ordinary becomes extraordinary," and "the raw data for the . . . untransformed banalities which, magically transmuted, become the precious trivia of the novels." Here, then, the materials of a supposedly unexceptional life become the stuff of enchantment.

Was there ever a moment of disenchantment? Modern Austen criticism, which arguably begins with Reginald Farrer's 1917 tribute, seems at first to celebrate an entirely escapist, enchanted Austen, who passes over the "tyrannies and empires" that "erupt and collapse" here below, and for turning instead towards a "new kingdom of refuge from the toils and frets of life," a kingdom of "Art" existing "outside and beyond daily life" (Farrer 1987: 249). But Farrer's essay, shaped by his experiences on the Western Front during World War I, in other ways epitomizes a therapeutically disenchanted and disenchanting Austen, one who is to be revered for her remorseless iconoclasm and stylistic control, and thus in many ways Farrer's tribute prefigures D. W. Harding's classic 1939 celebration of an astringent Austen who hates precisely those people who adore her as quaint and civilized.[2] Though Harding's emphasis on irony and his insistence on Austen's fundamental orientation as a social critic profoundly influenced later generations of readers and critics, this disenchantment fostered its own sort of counter-enchantment with an author now cast as manly, acerbic, and clear-sighted, and as such it actually complemented rather than foiled the more popular mid-century evocations of Austen as the last exemplar of a blessedly clear world where judgments could be pronounced with wondrous ease.

From the 1970s until the 1990s, Jane Austen was the focus of a revisionist criticism, what we might call a compelling form of fascinated disenchantment. As Nicholas Dames suggests in his essay on "Nostalgia," Austen studies developed "a disenchanted critical practice" that sought to counter a nostalgic tendency in Austen criticism that sentimentalized Austen by associating her work with a world safely past and always already known. One way of explaining this disenchantment then would be to say that the object of analysis and disenchantment was a particular version, or versions, of Austen: canonical Austens identified with particular allegiances of class, race, gender, and sexuality, and a totem of an aesthetic greatness taken for granted and as a given. Powerful revisionist works of Marxist, feminist, new historicist, and postcolonial criticism sought to challenge established modes of reading, and to question the cultural and institutional alliances that had been forged in Austen's name. They illuminated ways in which assumptions of class, gender, and empire underwrote Austen's canonical status. This was part of a broader move in literary studies to illuminate the functions of the literary institution, and to problematize the category of the aesthetic which was often detached from social function. In particular, the historicist reading pioneered in Marilyn Butler's groundbreaking *Jane Austen and the War of Ideas* (1975, rev. edn 1987), which influenced much subsequent feminist and historicist criticism of Austen, was instrumental in transforming Jane Austen's oeuvre into something demanding serious historical analysis rather than a fetish invoked as a habit of ritualistic praise. Indeed, a mark of Butler's determination to demystify Austen studies is her readiness to question our knee-jerk assumptions about Austen's greatness: "are we right to call her a great novelist at all?" (Butler 1975: 298).

Subsequent studies that followed this path of compelling disenchantment illuminated the ways in which Austen's supposed absence of history was linked to the forgetting of history that marks a certain function of the canon in general, and it is not surprising that a good deal of scholarship from this period turned its sights on the novels of Austen's predecessors and contemporaries that hadn't attained canonical status (or in the case of once esteemed writers like Burney and Edgeworth, hadn't *retained* it). As early as 1924, E. M. Forster parodied a certain kind of Austen reading as a mode of uncritical praise: "I read and re-read, the mouth open and the mind closed. Shut up in measureless content, I greet her by the name of most kind hostess, while criticism slumbers."[3] Some revisionist criticism and scholarship enlisted Austen on the side of progressive, protofeminist social criticism, and some showed how Austen as well as the world of her novels were alike blinkered by ideology, but all of it disrupted Janeite slumber, and some of it was attacked in the press for violating her pristine aura, whether by discussing sexuality or simply by using big words.

More recently, however, Jane Austen studies in particular, and the discipline of literary studies more generally, has returned to forms of analysis that had to some extent been problematized or bracketed by such revisionist work – note how Butler herself had, for example, disparaged literary criticism as it was then practiced as disengaged with history. This renewed attention to literary form registers at once both a move away from many of the historicist readings that so compelled in the 1970s–1990s in their strenuous critique of the canonical Jane Austen, as well as a recalibration or refinement of the relationship between form and context. In this sense, much recent criticism has consolidated the insights of Marxist, feminist, and historicist criticism and gone on to develop analysis within the context of a more focused engagement with the specificity of the cultural objects and practices. Many of the essays in this volume, particularly in Part III, "Literary Genres and Genealogies," mark a return to questions of form, and demonstrate a reenchantment with Austen, with her particular modes of linguistic invention and rhetoricity (see, in particular, Margaret Anne Doody's essay, and the essays by Harry Shaw and Michael Wood). This reenchantment celebrates a sense of magic that is arguably intensified through rediscovery and that comes from a heightened appreciation of the ways in which Austen's linguistic spells are social acts, but spells nonetheless.

Many of these essays thus engage in what we might call the study of the historicity of form, and of form, style, and genre as modes of social practice. This means a new attention to the aesthetic features of the Austen text, as a form of practice and even as a "system," as Mary Poovey has suggested, in her essay "From Politics to Silence: Jane Austen's Nonreferential Aesthetic." Our volume registers this new interest in formal, stylistic, and generic concerns marking recent Austen criticism as part of that recalibration of the relationship between questions of context and form occurring within the development in literary studies that has been referred to, for better or worse, as the "new formalism" (see Levinson 2007), as distinct from older formalisms that were less routinely engaged with social contexts. We see this engagement with form as part of the much larger movement in literary studies toward what Ellen Rooney has referred to as "the revision and reanimation of form in the age of interdisciplinarity" (Rooney 2000: 25).

Another way of characterizing these long-term critical developments would be to say that the criticism of the early to mid twentieth century that was involved in the production of Austen as a canonical oeuvre, conceived of Austen as a supremely commanding and ironic writer who dealt confidently and knowingly in fixed meanings that were largely predetermined. Like most canonical literary criticism of the time, this work rarely considered the profoundly mediated nature of the canonical Austen text because, in large part, it naturalized authorial greatness in general. However, "disenchanted critical practice" demonstrated that there is no natural object. We might say that the result of this revisionist criticism has been not to controvert Austen's canonicity (as though this canonicity were some kind of conspiracy or delusion). Rather, it has demonstrated the ways in which the seemingly natural object of aesthetic beauty can never be separated from its prior readings, and that it is always experienced through them. In this sense, then, Austen's canonicity has everything to do with the intensely mediated nature of Austen as a cultural object of study and experience of textual pleasure. Austen criticism has been transformed over the last 10 years by the ways in which this insight has been incorporated as a kind of working practice.

The awareness of our own historically conditioned and contingent disciplinarity has imparted a new subtlety to the ways in which critics now negotiate their relation to prior readings, and it has also imparted a new urgency to the ways in which critics and audiences comprehend and conjure with the traces of past readings, past lives, and textual afterlives of Austen. Much Austenian appreciation and criticism is thus animated by a fascinating sense of rereading, reviewing and reencountering the known but in powerful new ways. It's about encountering that enchantment not once and for all, but ever and again. Something of the subtle affective intensity of the rediscovery of a familiar pleasure is what marks Austen current criticism. This sense of rereading has been to some extent an effect of the cinematic culture of adaptation, dissemination, and transformation of Austen. What the cinematic revival of Austen has achieved in particularly spectacular terms has been to draw attention to the transformative mediation which occurs with any act of reading, particularly with an author who is the subject of such profoundly intense and diverse reading cultures as Austen. Cinematic "versions" make manifest the multiplicity of textual versions, and thereby challenge the authority of any one version of the work, and of the author's intention, editor's version, or interpretive version of the work, or the autobiographical versions of the self and others that Austen produces. In this way, they foster an awareness of the variability of the text and its interpretations.

The most interesting forms of critical engagement demonstrate a mobility and a familiarity with these traditions of reception and interpretation. Current Austen criticism is marked by a deftness in reanimating past readings, and in understanding Austen as a product of these readings. Many essays in this *Companion* are keenly engaged in the negotiation of layers of readings, and in the negotiation of the Austen text as a historical object, one that projects the historicity of its own moment of production and original reception, but also those of later moments. This is the nature of the literary text as a historical witness and agent: the literary text projects history, a past, but that projection is always the product of interpretation. And in that sense it is always directed to the future moment of reception and interpretation and reinvention. A simpler way of putting this might be to say that contemporary criticism is about rereading rather than simply reading. It always acknowledges that the object of analysis and the analysis itself is always the product of a prior reading or a prior constitution of the text. This practice of rereading animates Part II, "Reading the Texts," where, in particular, the essays by Susan J. Wolfson and Linda Bree take it as their central theme.

Many of the essays in this volume also register Austen's own pleasure in writing, and in writing as a form of rereading and rewriting, as experimentation and pastiche. In the work of Jane Austen, as Emilio Cecchi, quoted in Anthony Mandal's essay, points out, "a curious stylistic joy is never absent." Much of that stylistic joy is linked to experiments in form and genre. Austen was for so long regarded as the enforcer of correct style, ridiculing lower and more popular literary and cultural forms, and carrying out this enforcement by nothing other than her atypical genius, her perfect style unself-consciously – and indeed often unconsciously – playing out its blind, relentless destiny toward the perfection of the realist novel. However, as the essays in this volume demonstrate, Austen worked *with* rather than against popular literary genres and diverse cultural forms. Part III, "Literary Genres and Genealogies," illuminates the intertextual indebtedness of Austen's fiction to genres such as gothic (Nancy Armstrong), sentimental fiction (Miranda Burgess), and history writing and historical fiction (Devoney Looser), and to contemporary practitioners of fiction such as Frances Burney, Maria Edgeworth, and Ann Radcliffe (Jane Spencer).

By the same token, essays in Part IV, "Political, Social, and Cultural Worlds," also produce encounters of tension and critique between Austen and contemporaries, where previously there had been untroubled concurrence. Mary Spongberg presents an analysis of Austen and Burke, in relation to Burke's account of England's transition from Catholic past to Protestant present, and Deirdre Coleman discusses Austen's relation to the uneasy alliance between feminists and abolitionists such as Hannah More. A number of essays in Part IV demonstrate rich and unexpected connections between Austen's fiction and wider cultural worlds: of war and mass media (Gillian Russell), masculinity (E. J. Clery), consumption (Barbara Benedict and Diego Saglia), music (Gillen D'Arcy Wood), and theatre (Daniel O'Quinn). Gillen D'Arcy Wood relates the piano practice of Jane Austen the biographical subject to her development of novelistic interiority, and her complex exploration of feminine "accomplishment," social display, and the famous reserve of Jane Fairfax in *Emma*. Similarly, where critics once assumed a censorious asceticism on Austen's part in relation to material things and commodities, Diego Saglia suggests how Austen was "deeply versed in the rituals of conspicuous consumption," and how these rituals pervade her fiction. These serious considerations of Austen's relation to material and to extraliterary culture thus recall and relegitimate the back matter of R. W. Chapman's editions of Austen's novels, with their pictures of carriages, dress, ballrooms and the like, except that while those seemed to testify to the antique charm of Regency England, these are used as instruments of sustained analysis.

Austen has been recast and reconfigured in many ways, and some of the essays here demonstrate the rich multitude of generic uses to which Austen's later readers put her writing, such as Edward Copeland on silver fork reworkings and Katie Trumpener on Austenian New Woman novels. Part V, "Reception and Reinvention," also devotes attention to another feature of contemporary Austen studies, no doubt an effect of the recent Austen surge: the opening up of dialogues between academic and popular modes of Austen reception. Although early twentieth-century Janeites were eminent authors and scholars – think of Forster, Kipling, Caroline Spurgeon, and Chapman himself – the subsequent professionalization of literary study created a largely impassable chasm between popular readers and readings and "legitimate" academic ones, and thus critics rarely discussed the movies, plays, radio broadcasts, and fiction inspired by Austen well before the boom of the 1990s. Many of the essays here celebrate the interplay between the scholarly and the popular, and display keen interest in fan culture and in affective forms of critical practice. No longer does criticism disavow affective allegiance or the supposedly anachronistic acts of reception informed by sexual identification. Rather than bracketing affect, many of our essays engage with, practice, and cultivate different forms of what Deidre Lynch refers to, in her essay on "Jane Austen and Genius," as "Austen-love." There is a new respect for the intriguing affective ecologies that attach themselves to Austen, in all their effusive glory (see especially the essays by Fiona Brideoake, Mary Ann O'Farrell, and Judy Simons). Ten years or so ago we might have asked, with Pierre Bourdieu, and as a rhetorical question, "Is it legitimate to invoke the experience of the lover, to make of love, as an astonished abandon to the work grasped in its singularity, the only form of understanding which accords with the work of art?" (Bourdieu 1996: xvii). Today, though, we are far less concerned about the "legitimacy" of love than we are inspired to think about its uses, and about how love crosses intellectual and corporeal domains, high and low. Our *Companion* reflects and licenses this wider move away from the bracketing of evaluation and affect associated with much materialist and new historicist criticism and canon critique, and toward emphasizing cultures of affect and appreciation as productive cultural formations, and working to reconstruct a range of cultures of reading and reception and reinvention.

Practices of affect and history converge as memory. One way that contemporary critical theory and practice has opened up has been in relation to new understandings of history as a practice of cultural memory. Many of the essays in this volume are concerned with the ways in which history is about the moment of original production and reception but also about later interpretations. Cultural objects are changed by these acts of reception. They speak of both the earlier and later moments. In particular, Daniel O'Quinn's essay engages the relationship between historical reading and theatrical and social performance as acts of memory.

This brings us to another site of intense scholarly interest: Austen and history. The question of how historical Austen is continues to intrigue and fascinate. A number of essays in our volume analyze the diversity of Austen's modes of historical representation (Spongberg, Jones, Looser, Coleman). Mary Poovey's essay, for example, examines "the narrative system" Austen developed in order to "carefully manage the historical traces her novels contain." Gillian Russell, in her essay "The Army, the Navy, and the Napoleonic Wars," argues for a particular kind of mark of the historical in Austen's fiction, claiming that Austen's fiction can be thought of as "a kind of military library," where the "hum of wartime, if not the blast or cry of battle, pervades her fiction." As Devoney Looser suggests, the question of Austen, history and historicity needs to address how history has usually been understood. It is also about recognizing, as Devoney Looser does, that the practice of history can mean an engagement with wars or with the most minute details of current everyday life and social history. History is not always about proper context; it is often about complex affective states and journeys and reflections and speculations. In a similar way, a number of essays engage the question of time, and the complex relations between past, present, and future that inform Austen's fiction (see Mary Favret's essay on "Jane Austen's Periods," and the essays by Daniel O'Quinn and Michael Wood). These essays engage the multiple temporalities that disturb and complicate Austen's seemingly smooth and unruffled realistic textual surface.

As the essays in the *Companion* demonstrate, discussions about history and historicity in relation to Austen often involve the materialism of sociohistorical analysis in relation to broad social and historical contexts; and they can also involve an engagement with the materialism of a signifier in a particular discursive field, and a sense of the text itself, in all its minute detail, as a projection of history. The text as a projection of history implies a sense of temporal dislocation – inevitably anachronistic but productively so too – in its capacity to inhabit multiple historical moments. For, as a projection of history, the text is a revelatory relic and record of the past that exists in the present and is projected toward the future. It never occupies one single moment, but speaks with the voice of the past as activated in the present of reading, moving toward the future, and back again. The Marxist cultural historian, Raymond Williams, in *The English Novel: From Dickens to Lawrence* (1970), brought the term "worldliness" to the debate about Austen and history, where it is a byword for mercenary impulses and for something opposed to passion. (Williams formulates this as part of a recasting of the familiar Austen/Brontë opposition.) He writes "A certain worldliness, readily understandable in earlier periods (though never, I think, as persuasive as it is made out), made for the qualification of love; found its value as social exchange and respect, as most coolly in Jane Austen" (p. 61). Our *Companion* celebrates this worldliness, as the stuff of history and social details and life and complexity and love. This worldliness is the stuff certainly of "social exchange," but of social exchange conceived of as a complex and layered world and multiplicity of engagement. We would say, pace Williams, that a certain worldliness makes for the intensification of love, and that it does so most warmly in Jane Austen. Part IV, "Political, Social, and Cultural Worlds," in particular, presents the worldliness of Austen's worlds and of their multiplicity.

Something of this worldliness informs Humphry Repton's conception of the "Modern Living Room" in his *Fragments of the Theory and Practice of Landscape Gardening* (1816), featured on our cover. Landscape gardener, professional improver, and protagonist in debates about the picturesque, Repton was fond of advertising his handiwork with before-and-after illustrations designed to show the improving effects of his miracles of modernization. Thus the lively, crowded afterstory of the "Modern Living Room" is contrasted to the gloomy *before* of the "Ancient Cedar Parlour," inhabited only by a circle of clunky empty chairs that mutely regard each other in overupholstered discomfort. Such brisk and insouciant refashionings of the complicated relations between past and present help explain the generous sprinkling of ironic and parodic allusions to Repton that Austen features as homage throughout *Mansfield Park*. The ambivalent nature of such homage notwithstanding, the "Modern Living Room" features a scene of a certain companionability, warmth, and sociability that we think Austen would have readily recognized and understood. Here are people in animated conversation, a woman playing a harp, men and women of different ages conversing in chairs, strolling the room, and sitting on light elegant chairs reading: reading silently, alone; reading aloud communally at a table, and reading to and with a child, the little girl pointing out the words with her outstretched arm. Apart from these multiple scenes of reading, Repton's "Modern Living Room" also features books on shelves – *a lot* of books on shelves, with gaps on the shelves to indicate where books have been taken down for the purposes of reading for the occasion. Books, in short, are central protagonists in this vision and experience of "modern living." This vision features, as do the novels of Jane Austen, in the words of Miranda Burgess, "print culture – reading – as inseparable from social life."

As we know, and as Austen's novels remind us ever and again, a book is not simply an object, but a practice and a sociable event and occasion, a bit like a party. And Austen appreciated both, as her letters to Cassandra from over a fortnight in London in April in 1811 amply suggest. Staying in Sloane Street, Austen wrote to Cassandra with news of a weekend of visiting the Liverpool Museum, the British Gallery, going shopping ("spending all my Money [and] spending yours too"), and staying in with a cold instead of going to a play, and then going out to see Molière's *Tartuffe*, but missing Mrs Siddons (*Letters*: 179–80, 184). She also writes of trying to acquire a copy of Mary Brunton's *Self-Control*, "but in vain" (*Letters*: 186), and in reply to Cassandra's news about an acquaintance who had just read *Sense and Sensibility*: "No indeed, I am never too busy to think of S&S. I can no more forget it, than a mother can forget her suckling child" (*Letters*: 182). Even so, she did look forward to a party: "The day of the Party is settled, and drawing near; above 80 people are invited . . . & there is to be some very good Music. One of the Hirelings, is a Capital on the Harp, from which I expect great pleasure" (*Letters*: 179–80). So do we, and we hope the reader finds this volume to be an occasion of pleasure.

NOTES

1   James's remarks, originally appearing in "The lesson of Balzac" (1905) and reprinted in *The House of Fiction*, are included in B. C. Southam's invaluable *Jane Austen: The Critical Heritage, 1870–1940*, vol. 2. London and New York: Routledge & Kegan Paul, 1987, p. 230.

2   D. W. Harding (1980). Regulated hatred: An aspect of the work of Jane Austen. In Monica Lawlor (Ed.). *Regulated Hatred and Other Essays on Jane Austen* (pp. 5–26). London: Athlone Press. Harding's essay was first delivered as a lecture in 1939 and first published in *Scrutiny* 8 (1940), pp. 346–62.

3   From a review of Chapman's edition of Austen's novels originally published in *Nation and Athaenaeum*, January 5, 1924, and reprinted in E. M. Forster's *Abinger Harvest* (pp. 145–8). London: Edward Arnold, 1936.

Part I
The Life and the Texts

1

Jane Austen's Life and Letters

Kathryn Sutherland

Jane Austen's life, as a recoverable narrative, is almost exclusively a matter of family construction, with authority drawn either from the teller having known her or, more tenuously, claiming family relationship to her. Such a narrowly deduced documentary basis for any life is inevitably problematic regardless of how rich the surviving evidence might be; and in Jane Austen's case the evidence is also scarce. She was surrounded by family, at every waking and almost every sleeping moment, yet apparently they saw so little. Family makes, inherits, and transmits what we know as her life; it is only familial. Refracted through the prism of family, her life is also their lives: her relationships, variously perceived, to them; and their relationships, variously perceived, to each other. Through her they live; through them what we imagine as her life is shaped and circumscribed, even as it is revealed. The trickle of nonfamily biographies, which became a torrent in the final years of the twentieth century, derives, as it must, from these early accounts. Here's the problem: how is it possible to recognize in their carefully fashioned portrait of a conformable family member the writer of such startlingly original novels: novels, moreover, that point up the difficulties and constrictions of family identity? Looked at from the other end, no one would now be interested in the life of Jane Austen if it were not for what she wrote. Though we know we must not, under pain of the crassest naïveté, read the novels into the life/the life out of the novels, nonetheless we seek to connect them: the fiction must have a plausible psychogenesis. It does not; and not only does it fail in this respect, it is disconcerting to discover how little in the early family accounts sought to make the connection.

In the absence of diaries, which were either destroyed or never existed, the letters are the only evidence we have of a personal Jane Austen speaking/writing in her own voice, unmediated by fictional form. But they, too, are almost exclusively predicated on family communication and survive through family management. Her sister Cassandra can claim a unique role in channeling our thoughts about Jane Austen along certain lines. What we recover from the letters, as details of a life lived, what we conjecture as imagined possibility, are both derivable from the evidence preserved and the gaps created in the correspondence as Cassandra stewarded and selectively transmitted it. In this sense Cassandra is Jane Austen's primary biographer, her relationship to the early sources that of an editor. Editing is choice, and until fairly recently, it tended in its critical methodology to submit the allowable variability of its materials to the service of a single "correct" text. Jane Austen, by Cassandra's critical editorial act, is unsurprisingly unheterogeneous – a sister, a daughter, only a family member.

There is the suggestive comment made by Caroline Austen, Jane Austen's niece, who spent extended periods of time with the elderly Cassandra, that Cassandra wanted the younger generation of Austens to remember Aunt Jane, but made sure none of them individually remembered or could reassemble too much: "it must be a difficult task to dig up the *materials*, so carefully have they been buried out of our sight by the past generat[ion]" (Austen-Leigh 2002: 186–7). It is Caroline who describes how some time in the 1840s Aunt Cassandra "looked over and burnt" the bulk of her correspondence from her sister. "She left, or *gave* some as legacies to the Nieces – but of those that *I* have seen, several had portions cut out" (Austen-Leigh 2002: 174). Cassandra's intervention – whether of destruction or dissemination – fragmented the textual record at the same time as it safeguarded and preserved her sister's memory for the next generation of Austens. But the inevitable consequence of her actions was to fuel speculation. By an inexorable logic, as Caroline's words concede, once we know something has been destroyed ("buried out of our sight") it becomes far more significant than any available knowledge. Cassandra's culling and distribution of family mementos may have been no more than an old woman's final act of housekeeping, but it has been viewed suspiciously ever after, within and beyond the family, as an act of censorship and suppression. Whatever her motives, she created a record with deliberate holes in it.

There are at the latest count 160 letters (161 when Austen's will is included) extant from an original correspondence calculated by Deirdre Le Faye, using patterns established in the more prolific periods of communication, at around 3,000. The letters from Jane to Cassandra, by general consent the focus of the correspondence, are represented by 94 surviving specimens. Of those she may have written to her six brothers, Francis (Frank) is represented by eight, and Charles by only one. No letters survive from Jane to her eldest brother James, nor to Edward, adopted in 1783 by his father's distant cousin, Thomas Knight of Godmersham, Kent; nor to Henry, purportedly her favorite brother. Of George, her handicapped second brother, there is no mention, and he is only rarely glimpsed in the family record. The family friend and fellow inmate of the cottage at Chawton, Martha Lloyd, later Frank's second wife, has four letters; Jane's cousin Philadelphia Walter has one. In the next generation, James's daughters Anna and Caroline have 16 and 10 letters each; his son, James Edward, has three. Fanny Knight, Edward's eldest daughter, has six, and Charles's daughter Cassandra (Cassy) has one. The extended private world of friends and acquaintances is represented by only six letters: one to her old friend Alethea Bigg; one to Charles Haden, Henry Austen's sociable doctor; a formal note to Lady Morley, to whom an early copy of *Emma* was sent; a letter to Catherine Prowting, a Chawton neighbor; another to Ann Sharp, former governess to Edward's children at Godmersham; and one to Frances Tilson, wife of Henry's banking partner. The public world is represented by six letters to the publisher John Murray, each one no more than a brief note; by one famously indignant letter to Richard Crosby, who bought and failed to publish the manuscript of "Susan" (*Northanger Abbey*); and by a short correspondence of three letters to James Stanier Clarke, pompous librarian to the Prince Regent.

The proportions, which are undoubtedly skewed by accidents of survival unconnected to Cassandra's editorial decision, weigh heavily in favor of a predominantly female domestic correspondence, extended in later years to the elder of Austen's nieces and nephews. Its chief function is to maintain family connections and to share news, where news can be as trivial as the cost of a hair cut or as momentous as birth, death, or a brother's promotion. Where the addressee is Cassandra, the letters invoke a reader whose sympathy, on almost any topic, can be taken for granted. Theirs is an implicit intimacy which is difficult to decode because it is inevitably understated, by design "unyielding" (Favret 1993: 133) to other eyes, and drawing upon a deep reserve of shared (that is, known to each other though not necessarily identical) feelings and responses to books, to family members, and neighbors, and to the world in general. "[T]o strangers," Caroline Austen wrote, the letters "could be *no* transcript of her mind – they would not feel that they knew her any the better for having read them" (Austen-Leigh 2002: 174). Which leaves hanging the question of what the letters might reveal to those who did know Jane Austen.

As the daughters of the house, Cassandra and Jane would by convention be delegated to write letters whose contents would then circulate within a further family group or among friends and neighbors: "Your letter gave pleasure to all of us, we had all the reading of it of course, I *three times* – as I undertook . . . to read it to Sackree, & afterwards to Louisa" (*Letters*: 233). These letters are records of social events and are themselves social events whose reach and interpretation the writer soon loses power to calculate or control, as Austen observes writing from Lyme Regis, on Friday September 14, 1804, to Cassandra in Hampshire:

> My Mother is at this moment reading a letter from my Aunt. Yours to Miss Irvine, of which she had had the perusal – (which by the bye, in your place I should not like) has thrown them into a quandary about Charles & his prospects. The case is, that my Mother had previously told my Aunt, without restriction, that a sloop (which my Aunt calls a Frigate) was reserved in the East for Charles; whereas you had replied to Miss Irvine's enquiries on the subject with less explicitness & more caution. – Never mind – let them puzzle on together. (*Letters*: 93)

Austen summarizes with cool amusement the little drama of miscommunication that the multiple reading of Cassandra's letter raises among its female audience, teasing out its capacity to reinflect the same news as represented in other letters. Instructions for reading, in the form of explicit advice on how to edit their contents for wider consumption or for reading aloud, are a feature of her own letters: share this, suppress that, and keep this to yourself (e.g., *Letters*: 126). And in a late letter to her niece Fanny, whose tangled love life is submitted to her aunt's advice: "I shall be most glad to hear from you again my dearest Fanny . . . and write *something* that may do to be read or told" (*Letters*: 287). Where "the true art of letter-writing . . . is to express on paper exactly what one would say to the same person by word of mouth" (*Letters*: 68), the potential for misunderstanding in the wrong hands (or eyes) is considerable. This is only one of the ways in which the open family letter, filled with a mix of news, gossip, and opinion, addressed to the taste and capacities of one reader but shared by many, can without great violence be recast into the material of fiction. It is easy too to imagine that, read aloud, the staccato revelations of the letters would act as prompts to conversational development and misinterpretation among a knowing circle, as they do in the subtle epistolary subplot of *Emma*. (Volume 2, chapter 1 offers an extreme example.)

After Cassandra's death in 1845, the bulk of her own preserved letters went by bequest to Fanny Knight (Lady Knatchbull), presumably because so many were written either to or from Fanny's childhood home of Godmersham, Kent, during the extended, usually separate, visits each sister made there. This fact makes Godmersham (like Cassandra) a steady though not constant frame of representation for the news, events, and revelations the letters provide. How will their communications be received in the grander Godmersham circle? How might the reality or idea of Godmersham impress itself upon the writer's style? Though the sisters wrote personally to each other, they also wrote as denizens of the households they happened to inhabit, keeping in view, however discreetly, the importance of family networking and mutual assistance. As Austen put it to Cassandra from Godmersham on June 30, 1808, ". . . it is pleasant to be among people who know one's connections & care about them" (*Letters*: 137–8). After 1805, the financial assistance of the prosperous, landowning Edward Austen (he took the name of Knight officially in 1812) became indispensable to the domestic well-being of the Austen women. When in 1884 Lord Brabourne, Fanny's son and Jane Austen's great-nephew, published his mother's collection of letters, he did not fail to make the case that they offered a counterimage to that provided by James Edward Austen-Leigh in his *Memoir of Jane Austen* (1870), the first proper biography. Austen-Leigh was the son of Jane's eldest brother, he had grown up in her childhood home Steventon parsonage, enjoyed his aunt's conversation and encouragement as a young writer, and attended her coffin to its grave in Winchester Cathedral. In a particular sense, repeated elsewhere in the tightly knit Austen family, his own early life replicated aspects of her life. But the account of Jane Austen that Austen-Leigh pieced together in the late 1860s is marked at every turn by half knowledge and the accidents of survival – broken memories, scraps of letters, yawning gaps in the evidence; and by a further defense – middle-class propriety. By contrast, Brabourne exploited the potential offered by Godmersham and its material luxuries, as glimpsed in his mother's large share of the letters, to fill in some of the gaps and to upstage Austen-Leigh's confected portrait by one of his own. Where Austen-Leigh worries that the letters may reveal anything at all, Brabourne makes wildly exaggerated claims for their contents.

Austen-Leigh took his cue from his sister Caroline in begging the reader "not to expect too much from" Jane Austen's letters (Austen-Leigh 2002: 50). Caroline had written a short memoir of her own, in March 1867, to assist her brother, and she states firmly there that ". . . there is nothing in those letters which *I* have seen that would be acceptable to the public . . . they detailed chiefly home and family events: and she seldom committed herself *even* to an *opinion*" (Austen-Leigh 2002: 173). Though the revised second edition of the *Memoir* (1871) reconsidered this dismissal in making use of letters that the nieces and nephew had each received from Aunt Jane, Austen-Leigh guessed correctly that there were further letters which would change the record in unimagined ways, if only he could lay his hands on them. "I have no letters of my aunt, nor any other record of her, during her four years' residence at Southampton," he admitted; "and though I now began to know, and, what was the same thing, to love her myself, yet my observations were only those of a young boy, and were not capable of penetrating her character, or estimating her powers" (Austen-Leigh 2002: 65–6). From May 1801, when Steventon ceased to be her home, until July 1809, when she settled at Chawton, Jane Austen's life was, outwardly at least, rootless and impressionable: a series of temporary homes and lodgings in Bath and Southampton; holidays at Lyme Regis and other seaside resorts; extended visits to family in Gloucestershire, Hampshire, and Kent; shifting friendships and acquaintances. For that whole period of change, turmoil, and excitement, Austen-Leigh provides only four letters. Lacking precise information, even his estimate of a "four years' residence at Southampton" is wrong by about 18 months. Letters for this period, among the sharpest and, in their way, most revealing Austen wrote (nos 49–67 in Le Faye's edition), were all out of reach at Godmersham. Although this crucial gap was filled somewhat in the next generation, when William and R. A. Austen-Leigh's enlarged biography, *Jane Austen: Her Life and Letters. A Family Record* (1913), absorbed Brabourne's major collection, it has retained its symbolic force into the present in the familiar narrative of Jane Austen's life as two broken but curiously symmetrical parts. Thanks to an uncritical reliance on James Edward Austen-Leigh's avowedly partial knowledge, the "two-distinct-but-matching-creative-periods" theory has become a biographical truism among Austen scholars: Steventon and Chawton, separated by an eight-year blank during which she was miserable and depressed (that is, not in the Hampshire countryside), and in a sense nonexistent.

The *Memoir* records letters to children, a few to the adult family circle, and a few to public figures. But this is nothing compared to the 96 letters (all but two Austen's) made public by Brabourne 13 years later. A generation younger, with no personal memories or perceived loyalties to muddy his contract with the reader, Brabourne simply saw his mother's cache of letters as an "opportunity": ". . . no one now living can, I think, have any possible just cause of annoyance at their publication, whilst, if I judge rightly, the public never took a deeper or more lively interest in all that concerns Jane Austen than at the present moment" (Brabourne 1884: 1, xi–xii). Of course,

Austen-Leigh was not disinterested: at the very least there was the prestige that would accrue to him in his declared relationship to Jane Austen. His study delights in tracing her eminent admirers and his own connections to them. And as the comparison he invites the reader to make with Elizabeth Gaskell's recent successful *Life of Charlotte Bronte* (1857) suggests, Austen-Leigh too was not blind to the market value of memorializing an unassuming yet remarkable female talent, another modest spinster daughter of a country parson. His memoir, published to coincide with the reissue of Austen's novels in Bentley's "Favourite Novels" series, prompted the assiduous convergence of family and commercial interests that would mark the upturn in Austen's popularity in the last decades of the nineteenth century. But there are nonetheless telling differences in the appeals he and Brabourne made to the public. By contrast, Brabourne's Jane Austen is only a property to be marketed, not a beloved aunt to be protected. Every aspect of his book points the contrast; but above all the visual distance between its frontispiece portrait of a fashionably posed pubescent girl and the demure piece of domestic goodness chosen by Austen-Leigh for the original *Memoir* of 1870. The engraving, from a portrait that Austen-Leigh commissioned, is a startling distortion into conformity of Cassandra's satiric cartoon, its original. By contrast, the Rice portrait, as it is now known, of a teenage girl came to light fortuitously as Brabourne prepared his portrait-in-letters of a Kentish Jane Austen. Both are highly coded images, both are problematic in their partiality, though issues of likeness have in recent years been overshadowed by questions of authenticity in the case of the Rice portrait. More pertinently, when viewed in historical perspective, these two Victorian-issued images illustrate the contrasting uses to which the primary biographical data is regularly put. If Austen-Leigh's official portrait is uncommunicative by design, the symbolism of a "teen Jane" promotes letters which, in Brabourne's estimation, are "the confidential outpourings of Jane Austen's soul to her beloved sister, interspersed with many family details which, doubtless, she would have told to no other human being" (Brabourne 1884: 1, xii). Though the particular circumstances – in family rivalry and social status – for this willful misreading of the letters have long disappeared, their legacy endures in the competing biographical conventions which either hide Austen in respectable and productive provincial obscurity or set her ambitions on a wider and more glamorous stage.

I

Jane Austen's letters are the key to everything. We may accuse one branch of her family of exaggerated reserve and another of blatant opportunism, but their opposition traces the fault line in her writings; the contested place where the ordinary becomes extraordinary. The puzzle of the letters stimulates us to articulate just what it is that makes Jane Austen's fiction so special. The letters are the raw data for the life and the untransformed banalities which, magically transmuted, become the precious trivia of the novels. More intriguingly they are the key to what has always been the most important and the most baffling issue, what D. A. Miller refers to in his recent gripping study as "The Secret of Style" (Miller 2003). In the eulogy written only a few months after her death and first published as "A Biographical Notice of the Author," a preface to Murray's 1818 edition of *Northanger Abbey and Persuasion*, Austen's brother Henry stated that "Every thing came finished from her pen; for on all subjects she had ideas as clear as her expressions were well chosen." It is a claim which has proved remarkably resilient over the centuries. In Henry Austen's case, brotherly pride and the conventions of obituary writing are sufficient excuse for such extravagant endorsement, but what is most interesting about his remark is that it roots his sister's talent as a novelist in her aptitude for "familiar correspondence." What he wrote was this:

> The style of her familiar correspondence was in all respects the same as that of her novels. Every thing came finished from her pen; for on all subjects she had ideas as clear as her expressions were well chosen. It is not hazarding too much to say that she never dispatched a note or letter unworthy of publication. (Austen-Leigh 2002: 141)

We may observe with some amusement his immediate retraction in the shape of carefully edited (modified, paraphrased, and censored) extracts from two of his sister's "finished" letters. We are also right to suspect his intention: he is clearly uncomfortable with the taint of commercialism or impropriety attaching to the idea that Jane Austen labored over her novels. But we must not therefore dismiss his point: there is no difference of style. Other male members of the Austen family were equally anxious to delimit the sphere of a specifically feminine writing practice. In the next generation, Austen-Leigh used the physical evidence of the letters – "her clear strong handwriting," her "art in folding and sealing" – to deflect enquiry from anything as potentially countersocial and selfishly absorbing as creative writing: "Some people's letters always looked loose and untidy; but her paper was sure to take the right folds, and her sealing-wax to drop into the right place" (Austen-Leigh 2002: 77). This is an absurd substitution for genius. But we are not therefore right to dismiss what it is used to illustrate: the originality of her achievement. I take this originality, this perfection of style, to be her accomplished minimalism: what Miller calls her "curious self-fashioning into the selfless medium of Style" (Miller 2003: 106). For the early family biographers the style and look of the letters provided a code that legitimated as it moderated, and allowed them to feel comfortable with, Austen's literary genius. In the family, the letters functioned as a cover, literally, for novel writing (Austen-Leigh 2002: 173).

  With few exceptions, Jane Austen's letters are confidential family publications, much as the juvenilia were the confidential family publications of an earlier stage in her development. The earliest extant letters, from January 1796, when she was just 20, contain traces of the same arch motivation and expression, the same performative exuberance as the teenage fiction (Jones 2004: xxxi). Their revelations of her courtship by Tom Lefroy, for example, are tuned to the liberationist ethic that supports the rampant egotism of her juvenile adventurers; details are sketched using the same repertoire of absurd phrase and distorting perspective: "Imagine to yourself everything most profligate and shocking in the way of dancing and sitting down together"; "Mr. Tom Lefroy . . . has but *one* fault . . . it is that his morning coat is a great deal too light"; "I am very much flattered by your commendation of my last Letter, for I write only for Fame, and without any view to pecuniary Emolument" (*Letters*: 1–3). This is a kind of writing in which details of personal experience – of sensation and action – are entrusted to a form of language that designedly betrays them, leaving the extent of what is revealed highly problematic and personal investment troublingly hijacked – unless one has the key to decipher them. Though the style of later letters is more muted, they retain a commitment to discomposure; what Carol Houlihan Flynn describes in an incisive essay as "jarring catalogues of 'little matters' that unsettle a reader looking for coherence." Austen herself captures wonderfully the continuing wayward importance of "little matters" to her epistolary art when she confides to Cassandra, in September 1813, that "I am still a Cat if I see a Mouse" (*Letters*: 225). And Flynn sums up the search for a subject, which characterizes so many of the letters, as Austen's exploration of "the limits of a stream of consciousness located somewhere between Sterne and Samuel Beckett" (Flynn 1997: 101–2).

The potential for disorientation in a form, the personal letter, whose cluttered impersonality and bizarre conjunctions of topic and tone confound our expectations, is pointed up in the opposed reactions first of family, and later of critics. To the embarrassment of the cautious Austen-Leigh, Henry Austen had publicly defended admittedly highly selected extracts as "more truly descriptive of her temper, taste, feelings, and principles than any thing which the pen of a biographer can produce" (Austen-Leigh 2002: 142). In the early twentieth century, H. W. Garrod, Keats's editor, found in Austen a less artful correspondent, describing her letters as "a desert of trivialities punctuated by occasional oases of clever malice" (Garrod 1928: 25). More recently, and in contrast to the traditional critical valuation of Austen's elegantly ordered novels, a direct consequence of the feminist reestimation of women's autobiographical writing has been the recuperation of the cultural suppleness and multi-vocality of the letters. At stake here is the generic difference between letters and novels, by which letters can evade and even invert the merely imaginary (and largely conservative) solutions that fiction offers to the problem of female dependency and marginality. Letters come into their own when we acknowledge them as expressions of women's dual allegiances: at the service of general society and a distinct female perspective (Kaplan 1988). This late recognition of the relevance of what disturbs in the letters – the difficulty of reading their private idiolect – accords with a revisionist scrutiny of the unpredictable reach of voices in the novels (Tandon 2003: 112–30). Here is the basis for a reappraisal that equips the twenty-first-century reader to transform Henry Austen's observation of affinity into a wholly new appreciation of the "familiar correspondence" between letters and novels.

An agreement between the epistolary voice and the fiction is never lost because Austen's letters almost always imply an audience of more than one. They may be confidential, but they are not exclusive. There is an art in letter writing, and Austen is not above gesturing to it (*Letters* 121: 156). Here's the challenge: how do we, the uninitiated, learn to read the letters? Where the biographical archive is so sparse, it is tempting to use the letters to fill silences. They are almost all we have from the profoundest silence of all, that between the completion of the juvenilia (1793) and the publication of *Sense and Sensibility* (1811). But unlike the self-conscious truncations of the juvenilia (guessing games played with a knowing audience), the letters are genuinely incomplete. Only ever half a conversation, we rarely have even that half continued without interruption for more than a few letters at a time. Where the subject matter of the famous six novels turns the knowingness of the juvenilia on its head by examining the limits of communication – its intended and unintended deceptions and our partial knowledge of one another even under conditions of the most intense social surveillance – the formal limits of the letter point to a different kind of truncation or fragility.

In a literal sense letters are spaces to be filled. Austen has a keen sense of the identity of the text of a letter with its material form: how words alone do not convey her meaning, but are supported or betrayed by their disposition on paper, by her handwriting, even by the paper itself. Cassandra's hand, she regularly notes, is by contrast far neater and tighter than hers, fills the page more satisfactorily, and in doing so signals her greater willingness to undertake the social responsibility of sending news: "I am quite angry with myself for not writing closer; why is my alphabet so much more sprawly than Yours?" (*Letters*: 17; and see 76, 151); "I cannot write any closer" (*Letters*: 79); "You are very amiable & very clever to write such long Letters; every page of yours has more lines than this, & every line more words than the average of mine. I am quite ashamed – but you have certainly more little events than we have" (*Letters*: 131); "I *will* leave off, or I shall not have room to add a word tomorrow" (*Letters*: 18). Typically, the sisters sent two letters each per week when apart, each letter filling a single sheet folded to form four pages and written over two or three days, the next one begun within hours of the latest sent rather than in response to the direct prompting of the postal service; a continuous if unsynchronized conversation: "Your letter is come; it came indeed twelve lines ago, but I could not stop to acknowledge it before" (*Letters*: 52). Letters 52 to 55, written by Jane to Cassandra between June 15 and July 1, 1808, represent one half of such a sequence. And since these letters are bound by conventions of space and duration, news must fit its vehicle: it cannot assume more space than there is left of the single sheet; on the other hand, the sheet must be filled. Of the spaces Austen filled – and we tend to know her life as a sequence of spaces filled rather than of actions (Steventon, Bath, Southampton, Chawton, Winchester; the mahogany writing desk, a makeshift sofa, a donkey cart) – the spaces of the letters, like the material fragments of manuscript fiction, carry a special significance. But unlike even the fragmentary fiction there is an essential bond between the writing materials of the letter and its contents, which marks the letter as incomplete in a further sense without its original carrier:

In another week I shall be at home – & then, my having been at Godmersham will seem
like a Dream, as my visit at Brompton seems already. The Orange Wine will want our
Care soon. – But in the meantime for Elegance & Ease & Luxury – ; the Hattons' &
Milles' dine here today – & I shall eat Ice & drink French wine, & be above Vulgar
Economy. [continued below address panel] Luckily the pleasures of Friendship, of unre-
served Conversation, of similarity of Taste & Opinions, will make good amends for
Orange Wine. – (*Letters*: 139)

The sentiments are explicit enough, but the editorial information inserted in square
brackets, telling the modern reader that Austen squeezes in the final messages of her
letter below the address panel, provides a ready example of her constitutionally "vulgar
economy," and of the dependence of epistolary meaning on more than an ability to
read its text – in this case, on the evidence of its documentary carrier. Perhaps a clue
to the importance of the letters lies not in their inwardness (which the uninitiated
cannot penetrate) but in their outwardness – what they display to our eyes. Hence
the great value of Jo Modert's (1990) *Manuscript Letters in Facsimile*.

In particular, the letters to Cassandra perform a surrogate function in recording an
intimacy we know existed between the sisters but which has left few other traces. We
hear it in their elliptical familiarity which gestures to the vital complicity between
writer and recipient: "I must get a softer pen. – This is harder. I am in agonies"
(*Letters*: 218); and in the antiphonal responses to now silent questions or in the piling
of contextless scraps of news:

> I am to meet Harriot at dinner tomorrow . . . On Tuesday there is to be a family meet-
> ing at Mrs C. Milles's . . . Louisa goes home on friday . . . These are our engagements;
> make the most of them. – Mr Waller is dead, I see . . . Edward began cutting Stfoin
> on saturday . . . There has been a cold & sorethroat prevailing very much in this
> House lately . . . I want to hear of your gathering Strawberries, we have had them three
> times here . . . (*Letters*: 130–1)

We hear it in the way these letters create a picture of the writer which is intended to
overcome distance and in which her body, her situation as she writes and reads,
is essential to the effect: "I am in the Yellow room – very literally – for I am
writing in it at this moment" (*Letters*: 125); "it is now half past twelve, & having
heard Lizzy read, I am moved down into the Library for the sake of a fire which
agreeably surprised us when we assembled at Ten, & here in warm & happy solitude
proceed to acknowledge this day's Letter" (*Letters*: 137). To read the full range of
Austen's letters is to discover the difference in tone which marks those to Cassandra
from her other correspondents. The letters addressed to Cassandra can now seem the
most complexly coded of all, paradoxically because they were the least guarded,
the most reliant upon a shared idiolect with its private mechanisms for recalibration;
on occasion called to offer compensation and expansion, at other times laughter or
forgiveness:

You used me scandalously by not mentioning Ed. Cooper's Sermons; – I tell you everything, & it is unknown the Mysteries you conceal from me. – And to add to the rest you persevere in giving a final e to Invalid – thereby putting it out of one's power to suppose Mrs E. Leigh even for a moment, a veteran Soldier. (*Letters:* 169)

I looked at Sir Thomas Champneys & thought of poor Rosalie; I looked at his daughter & thought her a queer animal with a white neck. – Mrs Warren, I was constrained to think a very fine young woman, which I much regret. She has got rid of some part of her child, & danced away with great activity, looking by no means very large. (*Letters:* 61)

And "Tho' Sunday, my Mother begins it without any ailment" (*Letters:* 141); "My Mother is not ill" (*Letters:* 149). As Austen reminds her sister, in the flesh she and Cassandra are "the formidables" (*Letters:* 249).

It is only recently that critics have found a way to connect the letters to the novels, in part as a result of a new appreciation for what is by design disorderly and experimental in Austen's mature narrative method (Sutherland 2005: 306). On occasion the letters can read like jottings for fiction, offering clues to the kinds of risks she took as a novelist. This goes beyond, though it includes, what is visible from their characteristic graphic compression whereby topics are tumbled together, separated, or inappropriately yoked by dashes, an unparagraphed pileup of subjects and opinions, a paratactic rush of impressions unsorted by subordination. In the look of the letters we see reflected the look of the surviving working drafts of *The Watsons* and *Sanditon*. If we do not see it, we hear the same compositional compression in the interplay and encroachment of voice upon voice and topic on topic in the mature narrative style – though now as an artfully orchestrated fusion:

Former provocations re-appeared. The aunt was as tiresome as ever; more tiresome, because anxiety for her health was now added to admiration of her powers; and they had to listen to the description of exactly how little bread and butter she ate for breakfast, and how small a slice of mutton for dinner, as well as to see exhibitions of new caps and new work-bags for her mother and herself; and Jane's offences rose again. They had music; Emma was obliged to play; and the thanks and praise which necessarily followed appeared to her an affectation of candour, an air of greatness, meaning only to shew off in higher style her own very superior performance. She was, besides, which was the worst of all, so cold, so cautious! (*E:* 168–9)

In the letters, as in the speech and presentation of more eccentric fictional figures (in the passage quoted above, Emma, in conspiracy with the narrator, parodies the flights of fancy of Miss Bates, that "great talker upon little matters" [*E:* 21]), slices of mutton, work-bags, and piano playing retain a vital unaccountability. In extreme form this is what, from the evidence of the working manuscript of *Sanditon*, Tony Tanner described as "asyndeton," making the homonymic joke that "Sanditon is built on – and by – careless and eroding grammar" (Tanner 1986: 260). On the experimental page of the letters this telegraphic style, which in the novels stands in for both sociable and mental spaces, dissolves into a freewheeling creativity.

The letters written to Cassandra between January 1801 and January 1809 have a particular claim to be considered as the equivalent of an author's notebook. Contrary to the artistic narcolepsy that the family wished to impose on the record of Austen's life throughout this time, these years should be reconsidered as the crucible for her talent, a second and certainly more painful novelist's apprenticeship, during which she set aside the literary models of epistolary fiction and tested the potential of her own epistolary voice. The collision of life and fiction that stalled *The Watsons* some time in 1805 is traceable in the bleak letters of this period and was a necessary stage in Austen's development from a precocious literary parodist into a writer able to record and transform mundane reality. Ironic, self-critical, and often misanthropic, their vistas cramped by the equally cramped accommodation and forced sociability of small-town life, these letters are also full of experimental observations, each one a narrative node, a small punctuation of detail more luminous for its detachment from any extended teleology of plot or characterization:

> Our grand walk to Weston was again fixed for Yesterday, & was accomplished in a very striking manner; Every one of the party declined it under some pretence or other except our two selves, & we had therefore a tete a tete; but *that* we should equally have had after the first two yards, had half the Inhabitants of Bath set off with us. – It would have amused you to see our progress; – we went up by Sion Hill, & returned across the fields; – in climbing a hill Mrs Chamberlayne is very capital; I could with difficulty keep pace with her – yet would not flinch for the World. – on plain ground I was quite her equal – and so we posted away under a fine hot sun, *She* without any parasol or any shade to her hat, stopping for nothing, & crossing the Church Yard at Weston with as much expedition as if we were afraid of being buried alive. (*Letters*: 87)

> Mrs Day has now got the Carpet in hand, & Monday I hope will be the last day of her employment here. A fortnight afterwards she is to be called again from the shades of her red-check'd bed in an alley near the end of the High Street to clean the new House & air the Bedding. (*Letters*: 123)

> We found our friend as comfortable, as she can ever allow herself to be in cold weather; – there is a very neat parlour behind the Shop for her to sit in, not very light indeed, being a la Southampton, the middle of Three deep – but very lively from the frequent sound of the pestle & mortar. (*Letters*: 167)

We might describe these vagaries of a fiction-making mind, a feature of the letters from this unsettled period, as both practice and release; like *The Watsons*, for whose growth out of and into the events of her own life we can find particular evidence. Are these the first minisketches for novels never written and never really intended? In such moments Austen's letters do seem like the decompositions we expect a novelist's letters to be. Reading Austen's letters from Bath, Lyme Regis, and Southampton is to recover what the official biography continues to deny: the creative challenge and stimulus of alien surroundings.

II

Biographies are built from interpretations rather more than from facts. In Jane Austen's case there are so few facts that almost all we can know are the narrative consequences of different kinds of interpretation. In the Victorian period, this is evident in the contradictory family views on the letters. More recently, the challenge for the modern trade biographers has been to recover a personal Jane Austen and a plausible emotional and psychological hinterland for a writer, freed from family defensiveness. It is difficult to disregard the interpretative stranglehold of a family who have so effectively determined the content, even the tone and emphasis, of the biographical tradition. The Austens were clever down the generations without being intellectual or anything more than broadly sympathetic to the mainstream in the arts; professional, comfortable, culturally conservative – and stalwartly middle-England. Their official stance, unlike our interpretations of the novels, has shifted little since the early twentieth century. It is extraordinary to consider how late Jane Austen's biography has retained the imprint of a family property; as late as 2004 and the publication of the second edition of Deirdre Le Faye's *Family Record*, with its self-conscious incorporation of the narrative shape and the authority of the Austen-Leighs' *Life and Letters*, itself an enlargement of the 1871 *Memoir* and Brabourne's collection of letters. Le Faye was engaged in the 1980s to revise the family biography by Mrs Joan Impey, wife of Lawrence Impey, whose mother was Kathleen Austen-Leigh, granddaughter of the author of the *Memoir* and Jane Austen's great-great niece. Le Faye is always respectful and unspeculative, even where the evidence cries out for comment or evaluation. For example, there are plenty of skeletons in the Austen family cupboard: in the marriage of aunt Philadelphia to the East India surgeon-trader Tysoe Saul Hancock and their domestic and business dealings with Warren Hastings; in the incarceration of another aunt, Jane Leigh-Perrot, on a charge of shoplifting; in the personal history of the so-called Comte de Feuillide, first husband of Jane's cousin Eliza Hancock; in Henry Austen's business dealings; in Frank Austen's association with the East India Company. Le Faye is reticent, and her family-derived "Record" has assumed the status of factual biography (an impossible concept) among a teeming industry of interpretative lives of Jane Austen.

Jane Austen was born in the village of Steventon in rural Hampshire, in the south of England, on December 16, 1775. She was the seventh of eight children (six sons and two daughters), and her father was the local Anglican clergyman. Her mother's family, the Leighs, had connections with Oxford academia and more distant aristocratic pretensions. Her father supplemented his income and the needs of his growing family by taking as boarders in Steventon rectory private paying pupils from good families. Jane's earliest years would have been spent in a bustling house filled with brothers and schoolboys; she may have picked up some learning herself in this environment. The overcrowding at Steventon may also explain why Cassandra, three years her senior, and Jane were sent away to school – briefly in 1783 and again in 1785–6 to Mrs La Tournelle's Ladies Boarding School, Reading (afterwards known as the Abbey School). Jane may have begun writing the short, parodic works we know as the juvenilia within months of leaving school. School apart, Jane lived at Steventon, with occasional trips to stay with family and friends in other parts of the south of England, until May 1801, when her father retired and moved his now reduced household (Mrs Austen, Cassandra, and Jane) to live in Bath. Jane was 25 years old. She had to her credit three manuscript volumes of juvenile writings; she may also have written by now the epistolary novella *Lady Susan*; and we know she had three full-length novels in draft, all to be published much later, and with unknown amounts of revision, as *Sense and Sensibility*, *Pride and Prejudice*, and *Northanger Abbey*. Mr Austen died suddenly in Bath in January 1805. After some uncertainty, various temporary lodgings, and extended visits elsewhere, the three Austen women, now joined by their friend Martha Lloyd, moved in March 1807 to Southampton, where they shared a house with Jane's brother Frank and his young wife. Jane probably wrote the aborted novel *The Watsons* in Bath. They remained in Southampton until July 1809 when the three Austen women and Martha Lloyd took possession of the cottage in the village of Chawton, Hampshire, the gift of Jane's brother Edward. Chawton, only 17 miles from Steventon, was Jane Austen's home for the rest of her life. She prepared for publication or wrote all six novels here, traveling the 50 miles to London for extended visits to stay with her brother Henry to see them through the press. She began to feel the symptoms of her final illness in spring 1816 but completed her sixth novel, *Persuasion*, and began a new novel, *Sanditon*, which she abandoned on March 18, 1817. She made her will on 27 April and was taken to Winchester for medical treatment on 24 May. Cassandra was her companion and nurse, lodging with her at No. 8 College Street, in view of the cathedral. Jane Austen died there in the early hours of July 18, 1817 and was buried in Winchester Cathedral on July 24.

Letters survive from 21 years of Austen's life; fiction from much longer. It is worth remembering that we have more fiction than life because it helps put into perspective just what is recoverable and what is conjecture. It also reminds us that what we are interested in is the life of the novelist: how she wrote; where her ideas may have come from; what her working methods may have been; how she prepared her manuscripts for the press. Frustratingly, these vital details are almost pure conjecture. Our knowledge of Jane Austen's life can only ever be fragmentary. In the early family biographies the fragment was a weapon against narrative, serving well the evasiveness of Austen-Leigh's procedure in the *Memoir*. Fragments may be spurs to our desire to know more, but they are also information dead ends, and Austen-Leigh's meandering style is loaded with fragmentary ruses: local Hampshire customs and anecdotes, lists, family genealogies, recondite allusions. The annotation now necessary to elucidate such ramified prose takes the reader even farther from its ostensible subject. Who owns Jane Austen? One interesting feature of the tenacious family hold on her life has been the emphasis on her brothers' talents, professions, and opportunities as contexts (or substitutes?) for hers. Jane Austen had six brothers, five of whom lived actively in society; she had only one sister. Yet the evidence of her letters, as of the novels, argues the overwhelming importance of female society as her laboratory, the ambit and testing ground of her fiction. But until very recently women have lived such hidden lives that it has always been easier to uncover the actions and opinions of their male counterparts, however insignificant. Her nephew, James Edward Austen-Leigh, was the first to suggest that Austen circumscribed her art to her brothers' talents, each brother taking a significant role in shaping her abilities. Accordingly, he writes that James had "a large share in directing her reading and forming her taste," while Henry, living in London, "was useful in transacting his sister's business with her publishers." Frank and Charles were naval officers, a fact which is embellished to explain why she "never touched upon politics, law, or medicine . . . But with ships and sailors she felt herself at home, or at least could always trust to a brotherly critic to keep her right" (Austen-Leigh 2002: 16–18). How else might Austen have known, not only about ships, but also and more generally about matters requiring literary judgment if it were not for her brothers? James Austen was no more than an occasional and mediocre poet; by contrast, six years after her publication debut Jane Austen was recognized by Walter Scott, the leading fiction writer of the age, as an important new voice. Henry may have acted as an unofficial literary agent, but he also failed in business and he seems to have been kept in the dark about her writings until the latest possible moment (*Letters*: 255, 335). The evidence afforded by Austen's increasingly confident independent literary negotiations – for example, with John Murray and the Prince Regent's librarian – has so far carried little weight; as has the possible assistance of her sister-in-law, Eliza Austen, in the publication of her first novel (*Letters*: 182).

From the beginning the public voice of the Austen family record relied on a private and largely unseen female account. Caroline Austen and Anna Lefroy, James Edward Austen-Leigh's sister and half-sister, are sources for the most intimate personal details that the biography records. Anna's memories reached back to the time when Aunt Jane was barely 20, and they are touchingly quirky. Jane Austen found a second self or mirror image in Jane Anna Elizabeth Austen, whose life intersects and annotates her aunt's in surprising ways. Brought to live at Steventon rectory in 1795, aged two, on her mother's sudden death, Anna remained there, mothered by Cassandra and Jane, until her father's second marriage in 1797. As a result, she maintained an intense attachment to the female household at Steventon and then at Chawton, often returning for long periods during later childhood and adolescence. The early bond was strengthened by a precocious talent for writing which Aunt Jane fostered. By a further coincidence, at the age of 20 Anna became engaged to and soon married Ben Lefroy, a cousin of that Tom Lefroy to whom Austen was attracted at 20 and who forms the subject of her earliest letters. In later life Anna was fiercely protective of Austen's reputation; she assembled notes for a family history, which has remained unpublished, though details from it have leaked into the public record, partly through the use made in later generations of another manuscript family history, written around 1880 by

Anna's daughter, Fanny Caroline Lefroy, who drew on her mother's memories and writings. Fanny Caroline's unpublished account of the Austens offered something new in speculating on the origins in romance or sexual love of Jane Austen's genius. She also handed down some of the few suggestions we have that Austen family life was not completely harmonious: for instance, she repeats Anna Lefroy's distrust of Henry Austen's easy charm and her belief that his bankruptcy in 1816 hastened Jane Austen's final illness. Fanny Caroline's manuscript, either directly or indirectly, has provided much of the romantic speculation in the twentieth-century biographical record.

Anna's half-sister Caroline, 12 years younger, remembered the daily routine at Chawton: Aunt Jane's early morning piano playing and the stories she invented about fairyland to entertain her little nieces. Caroline inherited pocket books, in which over several years her mother Mary, James Austen's second wife, kept a brief diary of events as they occurred. Mary was witness to two of the most important events in the slim record we have of Jane Austen's life. The first was her evident distress on being told (some time in early December 1800) that her parents were to leave Steventon and live in Bath; the second was her death, Mary having traveled to Winchester to help nurse her. Mary Austen is also a source (though not this time an eye-witness) for the circumstances surrounding Austen's acceptance and subsequent refusal of Harris Bigg-Wither's marriage proposal, which can be dated precisely to December 2–3, 1802. Characteristic of all three key events is that we come closest to Austen in moments of loss or negation; which is to say: we know her best (we have most authoritative documentary information) for the moments when she vanishes from view or for the things she did not do. She may have fainted (lost consciousness) on being told she must leave Steventon; she did not marry; she died.

What the submerged female biographical tradition suggests is that there were always other Jane Austens to be recovered; other, that is, than those described in the official account. For example, we know from Fanny Caroline's account that she disliked her sister-in-law Mary Austen, for her peevish ill-temper and neglect of her step-daughter. Under Mary's influence James too had become petty and self-regarding (*Letters*: 121); but the public record continues to overestimate his puny literary talent and its likely influence on his sister's work (Knox-Shaw 2004: 24–46). By contrast, it seems impossible to doubt the intensity of the bond with Cassandra. Yet it is equally impossible to consider their relationship in terms other than those of interdependence or conjoined polarity; a fusion which creates a sense of their complementarity or mutual completion rather than bringing into focus their individual aspects. Again, it is a highly defensive biographical strategy. Austen-Leigh established the terms for all subsequent investigation when he presented the sisters thus:

> They were not exactly alike. Cassandra's was the colder and calmer disposition; she was always prudent and well judging, but with less outward demonstration of feeling and less sunniness of temper than Jane possessed. It was remarked in her family that "Cassandra had the *merit* of having her temper always under command, but that Jane

had the *happiness* of a temper that never required to be commanded." (Austen-Leigh 2002: 19)

Claire Tomalin's recent reinterpretation of the materials elicits the verdict that Cassandra was "the moon and shadow to Jane's brightness" (Tomalin 1997: 195). There is perhaps an allusion here to the Gothic *coloring* of some late twentieth-century revisionist readings of the relationship: Cassandra as the repressive force compelling Jane into premature social retreat, through their ridiculously early rejection of romantic love and their compact of emotional withdrawal. The evidence for such a reading is the death of Cassandra's fiancé, Tom Fowle, when she was in her early twenties, and Austen-Leigh's remark that the sisters "were generally thought to have taken to the garb of middle age earlier than their years or their looks required" (Austen-Leigh 2002: 70). In some respects, the Cassandra–Jane relationship is a biographeme, or model, for the bipolar readings of the limited evidence for Austen's life, which are a persistent characteristic of all the biographies. Such readings, and they are a feature both of the official family sourcebooks and of popular trade biographies, go like this: Cassandra was Jane's dearest companion/Cassandra hampered Jane's emotional fulfillment; Jane relished the high life at Godmersham and enjoyed her brother Edward's good fortune/Jane resented Godmersham and did not think Edward shared his wealth sufficiently with his mother and sisters; Jane hated life in exile in Bath/Jane's horizons were expanded by life in Bath; Jane only felt at home in the Hampshire countryside/ Jane loved the social round of London.

A challenge for the future biographer will be to reveal the potential in Jane Austen's environment as convincingly as the family have persuaded us of its limitations. Opinions on family duty and proper female domesticity structure the early record in such a way as to provide a determining logic of limitation to explain her strengths as a novelist. Only recently have other models come into biographical contention. Austen's older cousin Eliza Hancock, later Eliza de Feuillide, and later still, after her marriage to Henry, Eliza Austen, born in India and brought up in England and France, is beginning to be seen as her adventurous, cosmopolitan, and "outlandish" other. Eliza was an inspiration for the anarchic creativity of the juvenilia. Later it was from her London home that Jane saw *Sense and Sensibility* and perhaps *Pride and Prejudice* through the press. Moving in smart London circles, she provided rich social and cultural opportunities. Like Anne Lefroy, a near neighbor in Steventon, who probably encouraged Jane Austen's intellectual aspirations in her childhood, Eliza may have offered a window on a different world. Both were intelligent, cultured women who may have helped release the creative potential in Jane Austen without offering or demanding in return a restricting emotional support. In addition, now that a significant barrier has been overcome, in the transference of Jane Austen's life onto screen, it may be that film's visual rhetoric will find in the relationships it explores (the love affairs which may have been or the communities of women within which she lived the greater part of her life) a persuasive and more satisfying interpretation of the puzzle which is Jane Austen.

Further Reading

Fergus, Jan (1991). *Jane Austen: A Literary Life*. Basingstoke and London: Macmillan.

Le Faye, Deirdre (2004). *Jane Austen. A Family Record* (2nd edn). Cambridge, UK: Cambridge University Press.

Modert, Jo (Ed.) (1990). *Jane Austen's Manuscript Letters in Facsimile*. Carbondale and Edwardsville: Southern Illinois University Press.

Nokes, David (1997). *Jane Austen: A Life*. London: Fourth Estate.

Spence, Jon (2003). *Becoming Jane Austen*. London and New York: Hambledon.

Sutherland, Kathryn (2005). *Jane Austen's Textual Lives: from Aeschylus to Bollywood*. Oxford: Oxford University Press.

2

The Austen Family Writing: Gossip, Parody, and Corporate Personality

Robert L. Mack

Few readers of Austen's novels are likely to forget their introduction to Sir Walter Elliot, of Kellynch Hall in Somersetshire. When we first meet him in the opening paragraphs of *Persuasion*, the status-obsessed baronet is engaged in his favorite "amusement" – poring over the pages of his well-thumbed copy of Debrett's *Baronetage of England* (P: 3). Like many characters in Austen's novels, Sir Walter is – in his own way – a reader, introduced to us in relation to books, or, rather, to *one* particular book. His relationship with the printed word is instantly recognizable as comically naïve. His vanity compels him to devote his time exclusively (and with an idiosyncratic mixture of pride and dyspeptic, dynastic anxiety) to those passages in Debrett's that detail the history of his own "ancient and respectable family" (P: 3–4).

Sir Walter is also a writer. Not, it must be admitted, a very ambitious writer, but a writer nonetheless. Much as his overwhelming sense of his importance limits his reading to the "two handsome duodecimo pages" (P: 4) of the *Baronetage* that can always transform the domestic distress of others into pseudo-Aristotelian feelings of "pity and contempt" (P: 3), that same self-importance compels him to restrict his marginal or interlinear "hand-writing" to the necessarily limited task of "improving" his "favourite work" (P: 3, 14). Thus does Sir Walter not only make the error of treating books as if they were objects – he goes so far as to mistake them for mirrors. His own "writing" might accurately be described as cosmetic. Or perhaps his peculiar relationship with Debrett's – the "book of books" (p. 7), as his daughter Elizabeth has been bullied into thinking of it – bears more resemblance to the traditional attitude in which the subject is said to stand in relation to the portraitist; Sir Walter's own painstaking brand of artistry resembles the miniature interference of a narrowly focused dilettante. And if a portrait is perceived to be inaccurate or unflattering, he seems to feel, one should have no qualms about touching it up. Many readers have recognized in the domestic tragedy of Sir Walter's monstrous vanity the psychological portrait of a peculiar kind of patriarch – the tyranny of a father who egomaniacally regards his own children as extensions of himself – one who, however much he prides himself on being a "good" parent, nevertheless remains incapable of imagining the inner lives even of those he supposedly holds dear.

Habitually supplementing the information in his treasured genealogy, Sir Walter has been reduced in the opening pages of *Persuasion* to using his own copy of Debrett's as a form of apotropaic talisman. "When he now took up the Baronetage," we are told, "it was to drive the heavy bills of tradespeople, and the unwelcome hints of Mr. Shepherd, his agent, from his thoughts" (p. 9). Sir Walter has managed to pass this attitude with regards to books and writing on to the eldest of his three daughters, Elizabeth, though for her the volume is not consolatory. The 29-year-old (unmarried) Elizabeth regards her family history with discomfort: "Always to be presented with the date of her own birth, and see no marriage follow but that of a younger sister, made the book an evil; and more than once when her father had left it open on the table near her, had she closed it, with averted eyes, and pushed it away" (p. 7). Family history has no charms for her, and nor (in a different way) does it for Anne Elliot.

It goes without saying that it is due only to her untimely death in 1817 that the last novel Austen completed opens with a scene that meditates on the relationships formed among members of a single family and their books; that it considers how acts of reading, writing, and interpretation can impinge upon or determine how individuals perceive themselves; that it shows how members of a family might strive to present a coherent (and more often than not self-consciously dignified) image of itself to the outside world. Austen's family did the same thing.

There is, after all, nothing absurd or silly about writing in the margins of a book. However narrow Sir Walter's interests, almost all good readers "talk back" to their books. The extent to which the volumes in any personal library have been scribbled in, dog-eared, or studded with the often impromptu page markers or notes to authors or characters remains no mean standard by which we can gauge the depth and extent of their owner's relationship to them. Real readers tend to grapple with their books. Austen herself, although well aware throughout her life of the simple and frequently prohibitive value of books, had never been above this activity of "writing back" and responding even to some of her favorite authors. The margins of the Austen family copy of Oliver Goldsmith's *History of England* are famously enlivened by no fewer than 30 comments from the hand of the young Austen. Her 1791 burlesque "The History of England," completed just one month before her 16th birthday and further supplemented by her sister Cassandra's delicately humorous watercolor medallions of British monarchs, is similarly best understood as a piece of extended paratextual commentary – a complementary manuscript evoked by much the same spirit of "call and response" that produced her marginal ripostes to Goldsmith. (It is of a piece with the pervasive spirit of the Austens that subsequent, unidentified members of the family would not hesitate further to add to the marginal commentary with their own, penciled remarks to Jane Austen's earlier judgments; "Bravo Aunt Jane" reads one well-known interpellation, "just my opinion of the case" – the result transforms Goldsmith's original into a palimpsest of both male and female voices.) In much the same manner, although several of her family descendants would testify to the novelist's life-long admiration for Richardson's *Sir Charles Grandison*, the burlesque of her own children's play on the same subject is likewise written in the affectionate spirit of a literal parody or "paratext" – one that is meant to be understood as existing within the contexts of an extended and playful conversation with its original.

The parodic impulse that so clearly defines the young Austen's response to literature is largely the product of this same decidedly *writerly* stance towards books and writing of all kinds – an impulse that prompted her to look upon any and all texts as in some way (to anticipate the critical vocabulary of Roland Barthes) *scriptable* or "writable." Less frequently noticed has been the extent to which the Austen family as a whole possessed a tendency to rewrite texts as they read them – the ways in which they were inclined to mimic in their own idiosyncratic manner the processes by which any given text came to be conceived or written in the first place. In his draft of a lecture originally written in the early 1930s, the Oxford philosopher R. G. Collingwood made two observations regarding Austen's achievement that are relevant to our purpose here. The first was to emphasize the degree to which the young Jane Austen's primal instinct for parody was truly remarkable. "[T]he odd thing about Jane Austen's nursery output," Collingwood pointed out, "is that instead of imitating she parodies. Her heroines languish and faint not because she imagines real ladies do so, but she regards the languishing and fainting heroine of the romantic novel as a delightfully funny figure, a figure to be treated ironically" (Collingwood 2005: 39). The second of Collingwood's germane observations went on to root the impulses underlying even the earliest of Austen's seemingly instinctive parodic expressions in the more immediate context of her family environment. "Genius," he paused to note, "is not produced *in vacuo*; on the contrary, it never arises except in social surroundings so exquisitely fitted to produce it that its voice seems almost the impersonal voice of these surroundings themselves." Austen benefited immeasurably from growing up as a member of a large and active middle class family "with plenty to read, plenty to do, and a sufficiency of people to talk to." "A family of intelligent children in a remote country place," he further commented, acquire "a kind of corporate personality which gives each of its members the sense of expressing something wider than himself. Jane Austen's novels are largely made up of gossip: but its peculiarity is that it is gossip seen from a point of view which raises it to the level of drama: and this faculty of seeing gossip as drama was developed . . . in the nursery of Steventon Vicarage" (Collingwood 2005: 36–8).

"Gossip" of this sort must be understood even *before* its supposedly alchemical transformation in the hands of the prodigal Jane to have constituted something more than groundless rumor concerning others, something more than the ostensibly trifling chatter of women. The word "gossip" (from the late Old English *godsibb*) denotes the spiritual affinity that connects any baptized individual to his or her sponsors. Gossip participates at its root level of meaning in an ethical vision that confers a kind of mystical sanctity on the connection between the present to both past and future generations. It is in this rather weighty sense of the term that the magisterium of the traditions of the Austen family "gossip" might best be understood. "Gossip" was the means by which Austen achieved herself as a novelist, and by which she would herself in time come to be the object of communal discourse.

On both sides of her family Jane Austen benefited from the long-established traditions of the minor English gentry. The inheritance on her mother's side (i.e., of the Leighs of Cheshire and Warwickshire) was distinctly more illustrious than that on her father's, and boasted some truly impressive academic achievements. But still, the ancestors of Jane Austen's father, from Hormonsden and Chevening in Kent were members of a substantial landowning family that worked to find its sons secure places in the church, in the law, and in military service. The novelist's paternal great-grandmother, Elizabeth Austen (née Weller, d. 1721), was well remembered by her Hampshire descendants for having made the bold decision to move from Horsmonden to Sevenoaks, where her younger sons could profit by the education afforded at what was then one of the finest grammar schools in the country. "The considerations of having my boys in the house with a good Master," she would later record in her own autobiographical account of the move, ". . . were the inducement that brought me to Sevenoaks, for it seemed to me, as if I could not do a better thing for my children's good, their education being my great care. . . ." "I always thought if they had learning," the redoubtable Elizabeth later paused to observe of her struggle to provide the novelist's grandfather – William Austen (1707–37) – and his brothers with the best possible background in life, "they might better shift in the world" (Lane 1984: 28). Elizabeth Austen lived to see her surviving sons secured as apprentices in respectable professions. She was herself, as her own descendants were quick to acknowledge, an ancestress who deserved special commemoration. The Austens not only valued her ingenuity and resolve, but took care to preserve her written account of her struggle single-handedly to maintain her large family in the face of adversity. Precisely how such accounts and letters survive in the first place, as Jane Austen was herself to observe toward the end of *Persuasion*, "one can hardly imagine" (*P*: 203). Claire Tomalin is no doubt correct in suspecting that this lengthy document – preserved in the form of a "rough draft" written "in a retired hour" under the heading "Memorandums for mine and my Children's reading, being my own tho'ts on our affairs 1706, 1707" – was intended to "encourage her children in the belief that intelligence and articulation could count for more than an inherited fortune" (Tomalin 1997: 14). Once recognized for what they actually contained, however, such documents were to be valued at their proper rate. Only by means of such first-hand records that sometimes survive within extended and "antient families" can a coherent narrative emerge testifying to past experiences and events. Jane Austen the novelist was to benefit from and participate in the family's peculiar kind of writerly "corporateness," as it were – although she was also to distinguish herself in so singular a manner as to expose the gaps and separations within that same sense of "corporation" as well.

This idiosyncratic gift for transmuting the inherently transient stuff of family "gossip" and tradition – the otherwise private and personal histories that constitute the material of all dynastic narratives – into material that might provide some form of verifiable (or at least reliable) textual *witness* to domestic and social history is a trait that a great many members of the Austen family have possessed. When combined with the family's tendency similarly to maintain a close and frequent correspondence when it came to passing on information to one another on important occasions, or keeping in touch about the more mundane routines of their daily lives, the information casually contained within the "archives" of domestic gossip formed the basis of a formidable – if sometimes carefully selective or retrospectively groomed – family record. Together, the Austens cumulatively wrote the volumes of their own family history *as* it happened and very much (to use Samuel Richardson's memorable phrase) "to the moment."

In fact, the early account of Elizabeth Austen stands at the beginning of an extensive body of Austen family writing that was preserved in diaries, in journals, and in the many strands of correspondence that for decades helped to connect an ever-increasing web of parents, children, uncles, aunts, and cousins that from the early decades of the eighteenth century connected the Hampshire-born Austens to the Austens of Kent, and that stretched throughout the southern counties of England. The letters of Jane Austen's father, the Rev. George Austen (1731–1805) provide clear evidence of his background as a cultivated Fellow of his Oxford college; yet they also afford insights into the routines of a hard-working country parson – into the daily rhythms of life at Steventon rectory. Not surprisingly, George Austen's most frequently quoted letter is the one that he wrote to his wife's closest relations on December 17, 1775, and in which he announced the birth of his daughter, Jane:

> You have doubtless been for some time in expectation of hearing from Hampshire, and perhaps wondered a little we were in our old age grown such bad reckoners but so it was, for Cassy [Cassandra Austen] certainly expected to have been brought to bed a month ago; however last night the time came, and without a great deal of warning, everything was soon happily over. We have now another girl, a present plaything for her sister Cassy [Cassandra, Jane Austen's elder sister] and a future companion. She is to be Jenny, and seems to be as she would be as like Henry, as Cassy is to Neddy. Your sister thank God is pure well after it, and sends her love to you and my brother, not forgetting James and Philly. (Lane 1984: 63)

One finds much what one would expect to find here – an attention to the concerns that would naturally have been expressed for the well-being of mother and child, a slightly apologetic protestation that the rush of events and the couple's comically poor "reckoning" had hindered an earlier attempt at correspondence. Yet one detects something more as well. George Austen's instinct is to install the newest member of the Austen family physically and physiognomically (she *looks* like her brother Henry, and so mimics by analogy the already established resemblance between Cassandra and Edward) as well as domestically (she will soon be a companion – a "plaything" – for her older sister). Moreover, the duplication of names (the two Cassandras mentioned in the letter itself, the recollection in the way of inherited, familial names of one "James" already a member of the immediate circle, and the gesture to another mentioned in the letter) and the collective emphasis ("*we* have now another girl") and the further situation of correspondents by means of their closest relationships (*your sister . . . you and my brother*) – all these reveal the extent to which George Austen thought of his family as a corporate entity – as being embodied or even united *within* a single body.

The letters of Jane Austen's mother, Cassandra Leigh Austen (1739–1827), evince much the same characteristics as those of her husband – indeed, they stress the inter-connectedness of the ever-growing clan even more emphatically. Cassandra Austen habitually composed charades and light verse for the entertainment of the entire family (see Lane 1984: 56); her facility for this sort of composition was passed on to her children, who came in time to compose with practiced ease such things as invitations, epistles, or prologues and epilogues for the seasonal family theatricals. When one of the school boarders at Steventon rectory was late in returning from the Christmas holidays, it was typical of Cassandra not to address a chastening letter to his parents, but more personally to entice him back with a series of verses reminding him of the good companionship of his fellows. Urging him to return to the Hampshire "Mansion of Learning," she concluded her lines:

> We send you this letter
> In hopes you'll think better,
> And reflect upon what is here said:
> And to make us amends
> Pray return to your friends,
> Fowle, Stewart, Deane, Henry, and Ned.
>
> (quoted in Tomalin 1997: 25)

Cassandra Austen's inclusivity and her tendency towards the comforting gestures of familiarity are reflected in the liberally bestowed and affectionate nicknames here (the general effect of which is to break down the barriers that would otherwise separate her own children from their schoolfellows) in her composition's final line; the naming of names again forges a perceived community. It is not so much the "ties that bind" as it is those more tender ties that connect which are most often stressed in Cassandra's regularly solicitous correspondence as well. In June 1773, some two-and-a-half years before Jane Austen's birth, Cassandra offered a typical summary of the activities of her own immediate family in a letter to her sister-in-law, Philadelphia Hancock:

> We will not give up the hopes of seeing you both (and as many of your young people as you can conveniently bring) at Steventon before the summer is over; Mr Austen wants to show his brother his lands and his cattle and many other matters; and I want to shew you my Henry and my Cassy, who are both reckoned fine children. . . . My sister Cooper has made us a visit this spring, she seems well in health, but is grown vastly thin – her boy and girl are well, the youngest almost two years old, and she has not been breeding since, so perhaps she has done. We expect my brother and sister Perrot to-morrow for a fortnight, we have not seen them near a twelvemonth. I have got a nice dairy fitted

up, and am now worth a bull and six cows, and you would laugh to see them; for they are not much bigger than Jack-asses – and here I have got jackies and ducks and chicken for Phylly's amusement. In short you must come, and, like Hezekiah, I will shew you all my riches. (Lane 1984: 62)

Cassandra's glancing reference to the narrative of Hezekiah (II Kings 20: 12–19) in her final line would appear on one level to be an open invitation to disaster; Hezekiah's ostentatious display of his treasures to the son of Baladin, the king of Babylon, was a proverbially foolish act of vanity – one that purchased present peace at the expense of future calamity. The potentially darker echoes of any such parodic allusion are in this instance laughed away, however, overwhelmed by a sense of the abundance to be shared amongst this family of fortune's favorites.

Jane Austen was to profit not only from her familiarity with the epistolary styles and traditions of her parents, elders, and forebears, but from the writings of her several siblings and cousins, as well. Foremost among the latter, naturally, was her half-cousin, "Eliza" (née Hancock, 1761–1813) who was subsequently to marry both the Comte de Feuillide and, following the latter's death in 1794, Jane Austen's own brother, Henry. Eliza's 20-year correspondence with another half-cousin, Philadelphia Walter, reveals just how extraordinarily rich the epistolary substrands of the extended Austen family correspondence can be. Eliza's early letters from France – written when she was still a young woman – sparkle with their author's vivacious intelligence, and gain from the manner in which she explains the court at Versailles ("It will perhaps amuse you to have an account of a new manner of dressing hair which is lately all the taste," Lane 1984: 73) are jumbled together in any given letter with a solicitude for the rather more circumscribed affairs of the various Austens, Hancocks, and Walters to be found in Tonbridge or Steventon.

Apart from the correspondence that has survived between Jane and her lifelong intimate – her sister Cassandra – the combined influence of Jane Austen's older brothers James (who was almost 11 years old at the time she was born) and Henry (four years her senior) has been most thoroughly documented within the traditions of Austen scholarship. James and Henry had in 1789–90 together undertaken – with the assistance of a small number of friends and acquaintances at St John's College, Oxford – to publish and edit a series of weekly periodical essays under the title of *The Loiterer*. The Austen's Oxford periodical ran to a total of 60 numbers in the course of just over one year. The subject matter of the individual numbers of *The Loiterer* varied according to the personalities and dispositions of its authors. Those essays written by James (then a Fellow of St John's, he wrote almost half of the entire periodical, contributing 29 essays) first concentrated on the popular undergraduate pastimes of the day, while later numbers moved away from scenes of college life, attempting to signal their own awareness of the larger traditions of the periodical essay, and experimenting with various forms of narrative and story-telling. It has long been thought that the 13-year-old Jane Austen contributed to the periodical in the guise of "Sophia Sentiment," whose epistolary demand for more variety in the ninth number of *The*

Loiterer (March 28, 1789) rings out with the same satiric voice one encounters in the juvenilia dating from as early as 1787.

The Loiterer was written and published by James and Henry at the same time the young Jane Austen was beginning to engage as a writer with the literary and stylistic trends of sensibility and Gothic. With this in mind, many critics and biographers have attempted to draw precise parallels between the work of James and Henry in *The Loiterer* and Jane Austen's own achievements as a novelist. There is good reason to do so. The final number of *The Loiterer* (for March 20, 1790) was to appear less than three months before the 14-year-old Jane would herself complete the manuscript of "Love and Freindship" (13 June 1790), and the juvenilia contained within the notebook later labeled *Volume the First* was written by Austen even within those months that *The Loiterer* was being published. I have written elsewhere (Mack 2006) on the possible relationship between *The Loiterer* and Austen's novels, but I would only emphasize here that it is not implausible to picture James, Henry, and Jane Austen working together on their several projects within the comfort of the Steventon rectory; some of the essays published in *The Loiterer* would almost certainly have been written during vacations when James and Henry were with their family in Hampshire. I might almost commit myself to the assertion that the novelist *must* have been encouraged in the pursuit of her own early activities as a writer by the comparative success and local renown granted to her brothers by their Oxford papers. Those looking to find in the periodical direct connections between James and Henry's periodical and the work of their younger sister may yet remain disappointed, but *The Loiterer* nevertheless stands as a genuine record of "the ideas and opinions that prevailed in Jane Austen's early environment"; there are, as Walt Litz observed many years ago, a great many obvious points of connection between *The Loiterer* and Jane Austen's early fiction. A return over and again to such subject as the manner in which style is related to morality (to the connections, in other words, between ethics and aesthetics), a general admiration for (if not emulation of) the periodic style of Samuel Johnson's *Idler* and his *Rambler*, specific allusions to the works of authors including Madame de Genlis and Rousseau, narratives that focus on the dangerous consequences of indulging an "excessive" sensibility, the epistolary style of specific narratives, and the internal development within *The Loiterer* itself of "a more complex merging of narrative structure with ironic methods" (Litz 1961: 253–4): these are merely a few of the more general characteristics that connect *The Loiterer* to Jane Austen's juvenilia and to novels such as *Northanger Abbey*.

The Austen brothers whose influence on their sister's writing has perhaps been overshadowed by that of James and Henry were Francis (or "Frank") Austen and Charles, the youngest child in the family, both of whom were dedicated to naval careers from about the age of 12. Frank Austen eventually rose to become First Admiral of the Fleet. The letters that he wrote home whilst serving under Nelson in the war against France were treasured by the family, and were crucial in shaping his sister's allegiances and loyalties throughout that campaign; it was by means of Frank's eye-witness accounts that Jane Austen learned to view such struggles, and it was from his point of view that she learned to appreciate the more practical consequences of such action. In a letter written from his ship, then off the coast of Africa, on October 27, 1805 and just days after the battle of Trafalgar, Frank informed the family:

> The fleets have met, and, after a very severe contest, a most decisive victory has been gained by the English twenty-seven over the enemy's thirty-three. Seventeen of the ships are taken and one is burnt, but I am truly sorry to add that this splendid affair has cost us many lives, and amongst them the most invaluable one to the nation, that of our gallant and ever-to-be-regretted, Commander-in-Chief, Lord Nelson, who was mortally wounded by a musket shot, and only lived long enough to know his fleet successful. In a public point of view, I consider his loss as the greatest which could have occurred; nor do I hesitate to say there is not an Admiral on the list so eminently calculated for the command of a fleet as he was. . . . As a national benefit I cannot but rejoice that our arms have been once again successful, but at the same time I cannot help feeling how very unfortunate we have been to be away at such a moment, and, by a fatal combination of unfortunate though unavoidable events, to lose all share in the glory of a day which surpasses all which ever went before, is what I cannot think of with any degree of patience; but, as I cannot write upon that subject without complaining, I will drop it for the present, till time and reflection reconcile me a little more to what I know is now inevitable. (Lane 1984: 140–1)

The Austens were nothing if not practical; Frank was a loyal mariner and he loved his country, but that did not prevent him from also being very much alive to his own career advancement; all his letters home helped further to connect the remaining members of the family to the affairs of the greater world beyond Hampshire. The correspondence between Jane and her "own particular little brother" Charles was typically no less informed by worldly affairs, although the degree of personal intimacy that existed between the two was – judging from the evidence that survives – somewhat greater. On occasion, the correspondence between the various brothers themselves – and Henry's account of their father George Austen's funeral, written to Frank, at sea, in January 1805 would be an excellent example here – could also be deeply dignified and personal at the same time.

Ultimately, however, if the Austen family heritage was shaped by an unusual degree of self-awareness and by a concern for the preservation of the family writing in the interests of fashioning a worthy and coherent narrative of domestic identity, so too was it shaped by an awareness of those occasions when it would be in the family's interest *not* to preserve – when it was wiser, perhaps, to destroy. Jane Austen's own diaries (if she kept any) have not survived; her sister Cassandra and at least one of her nieces burned by far the better part of the letters that remained in their possession. Paradoxically, the more widely circulated family writings and published memoirs that began to emerge in the early and mid-nineteenth century – from the pen of her brother Henry, from her nephew James Edward Austen Leigh, from her nieces Anna Lefroy and Caroline Austen – upon which we have since been compelled to rely for much of our official information about "Aunt Jane" were motivated by a concern for a carefully constructed self-representation that was to some extent merely a logical result of the importance with which they had always been taught to regard the traditions of family writing. It has often been lamented that the body of journals, letters, and memoirs of the Austens has been so sorely pruned and depleted in the interests of maintaining a certain degree of privacy. What is less often commented upon – and what remains so fascinating and so potentially useful to readers of Jane Austen's novels – is just how much survives and remains to be explored.

FURTHER READING

Collingwood, R. G. (2005). Jane Austen (?1934). In David Boucher, Wendy James, and Philip Smallwood (Eds). *The Philosophy of Enchantment: Studies in Folktale, Cultural Criticism, and Anthropology* (pp. 34–48). Oxford: Clarendon Press.

Lane, Maggie (1984). *Jane Austen's Family: Through Five Generations*. London: Robert Hale.

Litz, A. Walton (1961). *The Loiterer*: A reflection of Jane Austen's early environment. *Review of English Studies*, 12, 251–61.

Mack, Robert L. (2006). Introduction. *The Loiterer: A Periodical Work in Two Volumes Published at Oxford in the Years 1789 and 1790 by the Austen Family* (pp. xv–xx, xxxv–xlvi). Lampeter, UK: The Edwin Mellen Press Ltd.

Tomalin, Claire (1997). *Jane Austen: A Life*. New York: Alfred A. Knopf.

3

The Literary Marketplace

Jan Fergus

Jane Austen's lifetime, 1775–1817, coincides with some extraordinary shifts within the literary marketplace, that is, within the systems in place for producing and profiting from books, and for distributing them to booksellers and circulating libraries – and thus eventually to readers. Numbers and proportions of women novelists increased greatly over this period. So did prices of new novels, which tripled and even quadrupled, thanks primarily to inflation caused by the Napoleonic Wars, which led to higher costs for paper, printing, and advertising. Partly as a result, book clubs and circulating libraries proliferated, for they made expensive books available to members at relatively low prices. Periodicals too grew in number, and in them, during Austen's life, reviewers treated novels with increasing seriousness as literature, not simply as entertainments that were at best improving or harmless. Such developments, carefully studied now by scholars in the new field of book history, affected the ways in which all novels were printed and reviewed, bought and read, marketed, consumed, and interpreted. Austen's profits as a novelist, and indeed her success in publishing her novels, depended upon this market, which was in some ways more open than our own but also much more limited.

Overview of the Marketplace

To understand how the literary marketplace during Austen's lifetime affected her work, we need first to register some important differences between that market and our own. First, it was far narrower. In 2001 in the United States, 17,349 titles of fiction were published; in the United Kingdom in 2002, 11,810 adult fiction titles appeared. By contrast, when *Sense and Sensibility* was first published in 1811, it was one of just 80 titles of novels for adults produced in the British Isles in that year and, as will be evident, certainly not the most popular. And it was not cheap. Selling at 15 shillings (three-quarters of one pound), *Sense and Sensibility* cost at least $75, using the common method of calculating values, that is, multiplying pounds by one hundred to produce a result in today's dollars. By another calculation based on the buying power of British workers' average wages, those 15 shillings would come to about £400 today. Even the smaller sum would make a novel still too expensive for most buyers.

In Austen's time, even though readers could obtain such expensive luxuries through book clubs and circulating libraries, as Austen's family did, membership in them was also relatively expensive. No institutions circulated novels for free, as public libraries do now. Thus even the most successful novelist of the 1810s, Walter Scott, was no blockbuster by modern standards, though his novels did reach a larger public than did those of his contemporaries. His first editions grew from 1,000 printed of *Waverley* in 1814 to 10,000 of *Rob Roy* in 1817 (distributed as the first, second, and third editions – a huge growth, but still not to be compared with modern bestsellers).

William St Clair (2004) compiles figures for editions of Scott and other writers during and a little after Austen's lifetime, arguing that costs of such editions were kept artificially high by publishers so long as they enjoyed lengthy copyright protection. Novels, including all of Austen's, were composed and printed by hand in multi-volume formats even though cheaper printing by stereotype had been invented. Publishers produced perhaps 750 or 500 copies of unknown authors from 1750 and even well into the mid-nineteenth century. In our time, scholarly books are issued in precisely such limited editions, for even more limited audiences, and at prohibitive prices that make libraries their principal buyers. Until recently, however, novels could be profitably produced in comparably limited editions, that is, until multinational companies took over publishing and decided to focus almost solely on huge sellers. Before Patrick O'Brian's historical novels, influenced by Austen's, became a publishing phenomenon in the 1990s, their publisher Collins issued them in Great Britain in quite small editions, just 4,500 copies priced at £9.95, for instance, for the seventh in the Aubrey-Maturin series, *The Ionian Mission* (1981).

One advantage, then, of a literary marketplace that makes small editions possible and profitable is wider access to print. It was actually somewhat easier for an unknown novelist to get published in Austen's lifetime than now. When Austen encouraged her young niece Anna Austen Lefroy and nephew James Austen when they were trying to write novels in 1814 and 1816, she implied that publication was sure; few now would so encourage young aspiring novelists. In Austen's time, all writers, known or unknown, who wished to obtain payment for a novel, had four options for publishing: (1) by subscription, (2) by profit-sharing, (3) by selling copyright, and (4) on "commission," a system whereby the author was responsible for paying all the expenses of publication while the publisher distributed the copies and took a commission on all sold. Austen most frequently employed this last method. Until recently, its closest equivalent has been to employ a "vanity press" – that is, to pay for printing one's own works. Now, however, the internet allows self-publishing that bypasses reviewers and "bricks and mortar" establishments; Chris Anderson (2006) has even argued that online virtual inventories will actually allow publishers to make available works that appeal to very few readers – and still make profits. As yet, however, publishing on the internet or by a vanity press is not fully respectable, and books so produced are neither reviewed by the public press nor, if printed, sold in shops; authors frequently distribute them free of charge. By contrast, in Austen's lifetime a book published on commission was perfectly respectable, as likely as any other book to be reviewed and sold.

Austen never employed the first two publishing options available to her, subscription and profit-sharing. Publication by subscription was seldom elected by 1811. An author solicited subscribers for a proposed book, collected money, and kept records so that a list could be printed in the book as a kind of advertisement for its virtues: "Miss J. Austen, Steventon" appears as a subscriber in the first volume of Frances Burney's *Camilla* (1796). This option could be quite profitable if an author's reputation was superb, as was Burney's: she made at least one thousand pounds by subscriptions to *Camilla*, and a further thousand by selling copyright. But most writers made very little, sometimes not enough to cover costs of publication. Burney herself felt somewhat demeaned by the need to solicit subscribers, which many considered comparable to asking for charity. Paradoxically, then, though publication by subscription depended on an author's prestige, it was unprestigious.

In profit-sharing, an option frequently exercised by the novelist Amelia Opie, publishers paid for printing and advertising, repaid themselves as the books were sold, and shared any profit realized over and above the costs. If the sale did not cover expenses, the firm absorbed the loss. By contrast, an author who published for herself, as Austen did, took all the profits, not just half, but in practice this meant only about 50 percent more money. And an author who sold copyright received a fixed, clear profit, generally payable within a year of publication, however poorly – or however well – the work sold. Selling copyright thus removed the author from the ups and downs of the market, lamentably for Austen when *Pride and Prejudice* (1813), whose copyright she had sold for £110, went into three editions by 1817.

Somewhat easier access to print in the literary marketplace of Austen's lifetime helped the number of women writers to increase dramatically, rising from the 1760s by about 50 percent each decade through the end of the eighteenth century. Nonetheless, until the 1790s, men published far more novels than women did. Austen herself first tried to publish a novel in this decade: *First Impressions*, the version of *Pride and Prejudice* that she drafted between October 1796 and August 1797. As far as we know, her father offered the manuscript in 1797 to only one firm, that of Thomas Cadell and William Davies, wishing the work to appear first "under a respectable name" (Tucker 1983: 34). Cadell and Davies, publishers in 1797 of Ann Radcliffe's very successful *The Italian*, refused to consider *First Impressions*. Had George Austen tried one of the firms that offered profit-sharing, like Thomas Longman or the partnership of Thomas Hookham and James Carpenter, we might have had many more Austen novels to enjoy than we do. By 1803, however, Austen was comfortable enough with the market to sell *Susan*, later titled *Northanger Abbey*, to Benjamin Crosby, a less reputable publisher. He never issued the novel. Eventually Austen reclaimed her manuscript for the £10 she had been paid for it – close to the standard fee for hack novelists published by the Minerva Press (see chapter 41 for an account of this publishing house). When Austen's novels finally appeared in the 1810s, women were publishing nearly twice as many novels as men.

This surge of women writers occurred despite persistent conventional sanctions against publication as a violation of both modesty and caste, sanctions that account in some degree for the number of women who, like Austen, published anonymously. Accordingly, Henry Austen in his brief "Biographical Notice" of his sister's life argued that "Neither fame nor profit" figured among her motives for writing (*NA*: 6). Austen's letters firmly contradict Henry. She wrote to her brother Frank, "You will be glad to hear that every Copy of S. & S. [*Sense and Sensibility*] is sold & that it has brought me £140 – besides the Copyright, if that sh^d ever be of any value. – I have now therefore written myself into £250. – which only makes me long for more" (*Letters*: 217). Austen wanted to make money; so did other women who wrote. Publishing was after all one of the few means by which a woman of the middling or upper classes could receive payment for her labor. But with few exceptions, as Edward Copeland's (1995) research has shown, women could not live solely on their earnings from publishing novels; these funds had to supplement other sources of income. Even when women made significant yearly sums from novels, as did Mary Robinson and Amelia Opie, active in the late 1790s and early 1800s respectively and making about £150 a year from their writing, they were still strapped for cash.

Austen did not need to make money to support herself even though she exemplified her own pronouncement that "Single Women have a dreadful propensity for being poor" (*Letters*: 332). After her father died, Austen, her mother, and her sister Cassandra, lived together on a limited income, but they were assisted by contributions from the Austen brothers. This assistance continued, though reduced, after major financial reverses in 1816, when Austen's brother Henry's bank failed. Interestingly, despite this economic catastrophe in the family, Austen did not draw upon her literary earnings. She had invested them about a year earlier in £600 worth of stock (discounted, so costing less than £600) in the "Navy Fives," and she did not liquidate this investment nor withdraw the interest before she died in 1817. In other words, she was a savvy investor who guaranteed herself a financial reserve to draw on in emergency – an income of £30 a year.

Editions and Costs

Austen's power to invest her earnings indicates a fortunate independence of the market, for her earnings were not impressive compared to those of a number of her contemporaries – primarily because demand for her novels was not as high. Mary Brunton's novel *Self-Control*, for example, issued in 1811, went through four editions before *Sense and Sensibility*, also issued in 1811, came out in a second edition in 1813. Austen had ridiculed Brunton's novel as "an excellently-meant, elegantly-written

Work, without anything of Nature or Probability in it. I declare I do not know whether Laura's passage down the American River, is not the most natural, possible, every-day thing she ever does" (*Letters*: 234), but its overt moralizing and extravagant incidents evidently appealed to audiences. Sydney Owenson, Lady Morgan's *The Missionary; An Indian Tale*, issued in the same year, went through four editions in 1811 alone. And these more successful novels were both considerably more expensive than Austen's. Brunton's two-volume novel and Morgan's three-volume work each cost 21 shillings compared to Austen's 15 shillings in "boards" (cardboard covers).

We don't know the number of copies produced in these multiple editions of Brunton's and Morgan's work, but we do know sizes of all editions of Austen's novels printed for herself by John Murray, her publisher from 1815. His surviving ledgers show that these were not large – and none of his editions sold out. Murray printed 750 copies of a second edition of *Mansfield Park* in 1816; it sold only 252 copies before being remaindered in 1821. That is, remaining copies were sold at a great discount, but it is not clear to whom. Austen lost money by this edition. *Emma*, issued at the end of 1815 sold only 1,248 of 2,000 copies printed in nine months; it was also remaindered in 1821 when 1,437 copies had been sold. *Northanger Abbey* and *Persuasion*, produced posthumously in an edition of 1,750, sold 1,409 in a year and just 59 more before being remaindered three years later. These sales, while respectable, do not signal great success. Although it cost £1.8.0 in 1814, Maria Edgeworth's *Patronage* reportedly sold out the 8,000 copies of its first edition on the day of publication, and six editions of Walter Scott's three-volume *Waverley* (1814), for a total of 7,500 copies retailed at £1.1.0, were exhausted before a seventh was issued in 1817. Furthermore, Edgeworth received £2,100 for the copyright of her novel and Scott was offered £700 by the publisher Constable. In a lower tier, Morgan's 1814 *O'Donnel: A National Tale* was issued in three volumes, 2,000 copies, and sold out immediately at a price of 21 shillings; its several editions brought her £550 altogether.

By contrast, the first edition of Austen's *Mansfield Park*, produced in the same year by Thomas Egerton on commission, took six months to clear what were almost certainly 1,250 copies, based on the profit we know that she realized by publishing it for herself (at least £310 and as much as £347) and on the cost of printing other novels at that time. Similarly, because we also know Austen made £140 on the first edition of *Sense and Sensibility*, brought out too by Egerton, we can determine that 750 copies were issued. Austen was, according to her brother Henry's "Biographical Notice," "so persuaded . . . that its sale would not repay the expense of publication, that she actually made a reserve from her very moderate income to meet the expected loss" (*NA*: 6). In 1811, the expenses of publishing 750 copies of *Sense and Sensibility* would come to about £155, and advertisements would ordinarily take another £24 or so. The novel retailed at 15 shillings, but the books were accounted for to the author at the trade price of nine shillings and sixpence. If every copy were sold, receipts at the trade price would be over £356, leaving a maximum profit of about £140 after deducting expenses of £179 and Egerton's 10 percent commission on the sales (about £36). Austen was risking, then, about £180 on the chance of earning £140. In fact, however, her risk was substantially less. The buyer's market for novels was small, but sales to circulating libraries were fairly certain. A novel normally would have to sell between one half to two thirds of an edition to become profitable. For example, within five months of being issued in February, 1810, Maria Benson's *The Wife. A Novel* had sold 275 of the 500 copies printed, and in two more years another 49, realizing £7.6.4 to split with Longman, who had agreed to share profits with the author. If only 275 copies of *Sense and Sensibility* had sold, Austen would have had £130, less Egerton's 10 percent, to offset her expenses of £179; that is, she would have owed about £62. If the other 475 copies had been remaindered at the same price that Benson's novel was in 1813 (one shilling and sixpence each), Austen would have received another £32 or so. At worst, then, her loss was unlikely to be more than £30. Although she probably was unable to "reserve" such a sum from her own "moderate income" (her dress allowance had been £21 a year), she could perhaps set aside about half. And every additional copy of her novel that was sold at the full trade price of nine shillings and sixpence would reduce this possible debt. She would break even once 419 copies were bought, even allowing for Egerton's commission. Had Austen known earlier that even at worst her losses were likely to be manageable, she might have published sooner – perhaps when she inherited £50 in 1807.

Austen's unfortunate decision to part with the copyright of *Pride and Prejudice* for £110 was made in 1812, before she could predict that the first edition of *Sense and Sensibility* would sell out and bring her £140. By May 1813, *Pride and Prejudice* had become the "fashionable novel," according to Anne Isabella Milbanke, who was to marry Lord Byron. It is difficult to estimate the size of Egerton's first two editions of *Pride and Prejudice* since we cannot know how profitable they were. But based on his usual caution, Egerton probably issued a first edition of 1,000 copies in early 1813 and, in the following October, a second edition of perhaps 750. Had Austen published such editions for herself, she would have made about £475, allowing for Egerton's commission of approximately £100, when they sold out – if Egerton had brought them out as economically for her as he did for himself. After paying copyright, he made more than £450 on just these two editions by my calculations; a third edition was issued in a two-volume format with smaller print, so its possible costs and profits are even harder to infer. Certainly he produced the first two editions of *Pride and Prejudice* more cheaply than he had *Sense and Sensibility*, using cheaper paper and less of it though the novel was slightly longer. And furthermore, he seems to have been guilty of overcharging for *Pride and Prejudice*, priced at 18 shillings, three shillings more than *Sense and Sensibility*. The latter had in fact been slightly underpriced: Longman charged 16 shillings and sixpence for a shorter three-volume novel like Benson's *The Wife* early in 1810, and retained that price for *She Thinks For Herself*, which appeared almost exactly when *Pride and Prejudice* did and was of comparable length. Austen seems to have been professionally alert to Egerton's maneuverings, for she wrote shrewdly to Cassandra on January 29, 1813: "The Advertisement is in our paper to day for the first time; – *18ˢ* – He shall ask £1–1- for my two next, & £1–8- for my stupidest of all" (*Letters*: 201). For Austen, "shall" in the second or third person is always emphatic: it commands or threatens, to use an eighteenth-century grammarian's formula. By naming sums in excess of one pound – not yet appropriate for a three-volume novel – she jokingly suggests that she will imitate Egerton's sharp business practices. More seriously, she implies that she will not permit him to undercharge again when her own profit is at stake – and she did not. *Mansfield Park*'s first edition, brought out by Egerton on commission, retailed at 18 shillings. Austen had learned that in the market, her publisher's interests differed from hers, and this edition brought her more money than any other published during her lifetime.

Earnings

Overall, Austen received during her lifetime something over £631, perhaps as much as £668, as her literary earnings. After her death, her sister Cassandra had Murray produce *Northanger Abbey* and *Persuasion* on commission using cheaper paper than he had for *Emma* and *Mansfield Park*. This publication earned £518.6.5, more than any earlier Austen novel, even though the last 283 copies had to be remaindered at three shillings and a penny each – a far cry from the £1.4.0 retail price. Overall, Cassandra collected £784.11.0 from Murray on this edition and on the final sales of *Emma* and *Mansfield Park*. The sale of the five remaining copyrights to Richard Bentley in 1832 for £210 brought Austen's overall literary earnings to at least £1,625, most of which was received after her death. This sum was not insubstantial. Invested along with the £1,000 she had inherited from her fiancé, it would give Cassandra some security though not financial independence. Nonetheless, Austen's combination of publishing for herself and selling copyright was to be less profitable for her than the lifetime earnings achieved by sale of copyright by contemporaries like Edgeworth (£11,062.8.10) or Burney (£4,280) – or even Morgan, who indicated in 1824 that she had deposited more than £2,000 in the past two years from her literary earnings. Possibly if Austen had been willing to write otherwise, she too would have made more money, but as she wrote to James Stanier Clarke, "I must keep to my own style & go on in my own Way" (*Letters*: 312) – a powerful statement of authorial independence.

Austen could have earned a bit more, nonetheless, if she had made some different professional decisions – but not much more. For instance, in October 1814, John Murray offered the sum of £450 altogether for the copyrights of *Emma*, *Mansfield Park*, and *Sense and Sensibility*. Despite illness, her brother Henry dictated early in November an exasperated reply to Murray: "The terms you offer are so very inferior to what we had expected, that I am apprehensive of having made some great error in my arithmetical calculation" (Austen-Leigh and Austen-Leigh 1965: 310). He went on to point out that his sister had made more than £450 by one small edition of *Sense and Sensibility* and a moderate one of *Mansfield Park*. Henry's illness worsened, and Austen conducted most of the remaining negotiations, deciding to publish *Emma* and a second edition of *Mansfield Park* for herself. She would have done better, however, to have accepted Murray's offer. In that case, she would have received the full £450 within a year – bringing her earnings above £1,000 during her lifetime. Instead, because losses on the second edition of *Mansfield Park* were set against the profits of *Emma*, Austen received only £38.18.0 profit on her greatest work before her death. Ultimately, her heirs received a total of about £385 more from the sole edition of *Emma*, from the second of *Mansfield Park*, and from the sale in 1832 of the copyrights of the three novels for £42 each. In short, Murray's estimate in 1815 of the market value of her copyrights was if anything exaggerated, but not generous. Austen's refusal to accept Murray's £450 suggests how highly she valued *Emma* and how willing she was to risk a different valuation from the public.

Reviews and Readership

But who was that public? To answer that question is always the most difficult task for book historians as well as critics. Circulation of novels is not the same as editions or sales. After all, an edition of a thousand copies could reach many more readers through book clubs and commercial circulating libraries, and through practices of reading aloud at home and lending books among friends. And even if we can estimate numbers of readers, we can seldom know how they read – neither their reading practices nor their responses. Almost as if she could predict such difficulties, or the way that modern studies would focus on her different readerships over time and their varying interpretations, Austen herself recorded contemporaries' views of two of her novels, *Mansfield Park* and *Emma* – thus becoming something of a book historian herself. *Sense and Sensibility* had been reviewed briefly in two publications, *Pride and Prejudice* in three. (Later, *Emma* would receive 10 reviews, eight in English – the lengthiest by Walter Scott in the *Edinburgh Review*, produced at Murray's urging.) The "Opinions" or informal reviews were begun sometime in 1814 – I believe when Austen realized that *Mansfield Park* would not be professionally reviewed. These "Opinions" by family, friends, and friends of friends register widely varying responses to plots, characters, and even language in both novels, as well as readers' preferences for specific novels and characters. Austen has even twice documented how readers came by copies of her works – by loan from a relative to Mrs Charles Cage and by gift to Austen's brother Charles, who read it three times. The "Opinions" highlight amusing contradictions among readers' comments. Austen, for instance, copies her friend Martha Lloyd's comment that she was "Delighted with Fanny. Hated Mrs Norris," and immediately afterward her mother's opposite response: "Thought Fanny insipid. – Enjoyed Mrs Norris."

Such strong emotional responses to characters are typical of Austen's audience – and of some other readers whose comments have been preserved. For instance, Mary Russell Mitford wrote to a friend in December 1814 deploring "the entire want of taste which could produce so pert, so worldly a heroine as the beloved of such a man as Darcy" (L'Estrange 1870: 300). Less typical in the "Opinions" are assessments of plausibility or consistency in characters and incidents, reminding us of Austen's own censure of Brunton's *Self-Control* as having nothing of "Nature or Probability." Mrs James Austen, a sister-in-law, "Thought Henry Crawford's going off with Mrs Rushworth, very natural" (*MW*: 432) whereas her nephew Edward Knight, aged 20, considered "Henry C.'s going off with Mrs R. – at such a time, when so much in love with Fanny, . . . unnatural." His brother George, a year younger, was "interested by nobody but Mary Crawford" (*MW*: 431). Although we might assume that these young men read *Mansfield Park* only because their aunt wrote it, boys of similar age and younger at Rugby School and the Daventry Dissenting Academy in the second half of the eighteenth century read many novels that were written by women and focused on women. Schoolboys seemed to have had no trouble crossing gender lines in their reading – nor did many men, as Austen herself implies in *Northanger Abbey* when she allows Henry Tilney to declare that men read "nearly as many" novels as women.

Austen's "Opinions" also document a primarily female audience for fiction at this time. My own research into eighteenth-century provincial audiences for fiction has revealed that men were the primary consumers there through the eighteenth century, but also that when women chose to buy or borrow fiction, they preferred female authors; similarly, male customers preferred novels by men. These preferences predict that the rise in numbers of novels by women from the 1790s that bibliographers have actually revealed would accompany an increased female readership, just as reductions in male-authored novels would be associated with fewer male readers. Austen's "Opinions" bear out this prediction. She cites the responses of 14 men and 26 women to *Mansfield Park*, 13 men and 29 women to *Emma*. Obviously, her list is selective, not comprehensive, even in her own family: she does not record her brother Edward Austen Knight's opinion of *Emma*, but he is known to have complained that she made an apple orchard blossom in June in that novel. By the 1810s, when women are in fact publishing the majority of novels, they may also at this point actually constitute the majority of readers – as they have been supposed to do much earlier.

Austen's own attitudes toward and behavior within the literary marketplace are, then, highly conventional in most respects. She shows an eagerness to profit from it as well as appreciation of its offerings, especially in fiction. Austen alludes in her letters to at least nine male novelists and 21 female; judging from those allusions she resembles eighteenth-century provincial customers in preferring works by her own sex. She shows a certain wariness of the public side of the marketplace: she preserved her anonymity in her title pages, and she declined to meet Madame de Stael in London.

Nonetheless, she was a professional writer, for whom writing was of paramount importance. Her juvenilia reveal that from her childhood she was determined to see her works in print. Though she could have made more money from her novels, her choices in the marketplace were increasingly shrewd and professional. She learned how to increase her profits from Egerton, and she attempted to increase them further by employing Murray. And at the end of her life, she remained committed to publication. Although Austen noted in February 1817 her very disappointing first profits on *Emma*, she had begun a new novel, *Sanditon*, on January 27, 1817, and she had completed 11 chapters by the time she ceased writing on March 18. Five days earlier, she had written to her niece Fanny Knight that "I have a something ready for Publication, which may perhaps appear about a twelvemonth hence" (*Letters*: 333). Austen possibly hoped that the next year's profits would permit the publication of *Persuasion*, completed during the previous August. Her dividends on the money invested in the "Navy Fives" had accumulated for 18 months, amounting to £45 by the time she died. She may have planned to draw upon these also, if necessary, to publish *Persuasion* and perhaps *Northanger Abbey* as well. For in the same letter, she wrote to Fanny that "Miss Catherine is put upon the Shelve for the present, and I do not know that she will ever come out" (*Letters*: 333). The phrase "upon the shelf" is appropriately mercantile, whether applied to an unsuccessful debutante unable to come out into the market or to an unsaleable commodity like a book. Austen's mind and language seem to have been particularly attuned to marketing after the disappointing failure to earn money from *Emma* – yet in her continued work on *Sanditon* despite increasing ill health we can see evidence of her determination to make the most of her talent in the literary marketplace.

Further Reading

Copeland, Edward (1995). *Women Writing about Money: Women's Fiction in England 1790–1820*. Cambridge, UK: Cambridge University Press.

Fergus, Jan (1991). *Jane Austen: A Literary Life.* London: Macmillan, and New York: St Martin's Press.

St Clair, William (2004). *The Reading Nation in the Romantic Period*. Cambridge, UK: Cambridge University Press.

4
Texts and Editions

Brian Southam

For the worst of reasons, the history of Austen's texts is relatively uncomplicated. No manuscript of the six novels has survived save for the two chapters originally planned as the ending to *Persuasion*. So apart from this fragment, there are no manuscript readings of the six novels to put alongside the published texts either to amplify or challenge them. There is a similar absence of revision. Only three of the six novels – *Sense and Sensibility*, *Pride and Prejudice*, and *Mansfield Park* – went into second editions during Austen's lifetime, and the only revisions certainly attributable to the author relate to the incomes in *Sense and Sensibility* and an area of naval detail in *Mansfield Park*. Nonetheless, despite this textual paucity, from the 1890s onwards Austen's texts have attracted a large body of conjecture and emendation. This activity began as a Janeite hobby for Victorian and Edwardian classical scholars, as delighted to exercise their skills in emendation upon Austen as on Aeschylus. But the wheel has turned full circle. Editors and textual scholars of the present generation favor a conservative approach, no longer seeking to correct Austen's English and keeping emendation to a minimum; and whilst appreciating the vagaries and carelessness of Austen's original printers, accepting the wording and punctuation of the early editions at face value. And there is the presence of a long-standing phenomenon. Beginning in the 1830s and 40s, flowering in the 1890s, and continuing into the present day, is the figure of Austen both as a cultural icon and a literary-classic-cum-popular-author promoted worldwide in a variety of texts – printed, visual, and aural.

The Earliest Editions, Britain and America, 1811–33

Austen's arrival on the literary scene was modest and anonymous. The three volumes of *Sense and Sensibility*, "By a Lady" and "Printed for the Author," were published by Thomas Egerton at the end of October 1811 at Austen's expense. Sometimes called publishing "on commission," this was an arrangement widely used: the author paid for the cost of paper, printing, and advertising, while the publisher saw the book through the press, kept the accounts, and distributed the copies to the booksellers, charging the author a commission of 10 percent on copies sold. Austen was successful from the start, as the print run of about 500 or 750 copies priced at 15 shillings for the three-volume set (the standard format for novels at this time), was sold out by July 1813, making her a profit of £140. Egerton, a well-known publisher of fiction, advised a second edition, of about the same number, which appeared at the end of October that year, again at her expense. Someone, either Egerton or Austen herself, took the opportunity to make corrections and three significant changes, two referring to property and money, and omitting a joke about "a natural daughter," probably in response to the stiffening propriety of the day.

The title page announced this second edition as being "By the Author of 'Pride and Prejudice'," since that novel had already been published, at the end of January 1813, priced at 18 shillings. *Pride and Prejudice* came out at Egerton's expense as he had purchased the copyright from Jane Austen for £110, a profitable deal for him since the book sold briskly and went into a second edition as early as October 1813 and into a third edition sometime in 1817, now 12 shillings for two volumes, the chapters renumbered accordingly. There is no record that Austen had any involvement with these later editions.

Egerton also published Austen's third novel, *Mansfield Park*. This appeared, at the author's expense, in May 1814, announced as "By the Author of" the previous two novels. In an edition of about 1,000 copies, the three volumes were priced at 18 shillings. Although the edition sold out within six months, for some reason Egerton declined to reprint. Having already submitted the manuscript of *Emma* to John Murray, a far more prestigious publisher, Austen took the opportunity to offer him the new edition of *Mansfield Park*, an offer which he accepted, publishing the novel on commission in February 1816, with a print run of 750 copies, the three volumes at 18 shillings. Probably at the suggestion of her brother Francis, a serving naval officer, Austen corrected mistakes in her use of naval language; and throughout the novel the punctuation was changed, how much by Austen and how much by the new printers – a different one was employed for each volume – is uncertain.

Emma was published by Murray at the author's expense at the end of December 1815 – the title page dated 1816 – with a print run of around 2,000 copies, at £1 1 s. for the three volumes. The title page read "By the Author of 'Pride and Prejudice,' &c. &c." Finally, *Northanger Abbey* and *Persuasion* were published together by Murray as a four-volume set in December 1817, with a single title page, dated 1818. Priced at 24 shillings, 1,750 copies of the set were printed at the Austen family's expense. While Austen's name was not on the title page, the first volume was headed by an unsigned "Biographical Notice of the Author" by Henry Austen, naming his sister as the author of these works and declaring that "She could scarcely believe what she termed her great good fortune when "Sense and Sensibility" produced a clear profit of about £150. Few so gifted were so truly unpretending" (*NA*: 6).

But neither Henry's praise nor Walter Scott's glowing review of *Emma* in the *Quarterly Review* for October 1815 could save the novels: the second edition of *Sense & Sensibility* failed to sell out; the third edition of *Pride and Prejudice* was remaindered and some copies were probably wasted; in 1820, Murray remaindered 498 copies of *Mansfield Park* at two shillings and sixpence a set and 535 copies of *Emma* at two shillings; and in 1821, the remaindering continued with 282 copies of *Northanger Abbey* and *Persuasion* at three shillings and a penny. Ten years later, however, Murray must have seen some future in Austen, and he offered to buy the copyrights for five of the novels, *Pride and Prejudice* being owned by Egerton. Although nothing came of this, in 1832 Richard Bentley purchased the five copyrights for £210 – at this time, the duration of copyright for the three earlier novels was 28 years from their first publication, for the later three, 42 years. This purchase ended the Austen family's financial interest in the novels. Including Austen's lifetime earnings of approximately £631, they brought in a total of £1,625.

Copies of the early London editions were also sold by booksellers in North America and this was probably how Austen came to the notice of the bookseller-publisher Matthew Carey of Philadelphia, a man prominent in civic life and political circles, as well as a leading member of his own trade. *Emma* seemed a likely success following Scott's review and in 1816 Carey published a two-volume edition, priced at $2.50. Although there is no evidence that Carey contacted John Murray, the English publisher, strictly speaking Carey's was not a pirated edition, since at this time there was no reciprocal copyright agreement between the two countries. In the 1820s, Carey's son Henry went into partnership with his brother-in-law and Carey and Lea became America's leading publisher of fiction, enjoying great success with James Fenimore Cooper, Scott, and other British authors. Within the space of 11 months, between August 1832 and July 1833, they published all six Austen titles, each novel selling at a uniform price of $2 for a two-volume set. First came *Elizabeth Bennet; or, Pride and Prejudice: A Novel*. Following the style of the London edition, it was announced anonymously on the title page as "By the Author of 'Sense And Sensibility,' &c." and below this, "First American From The Third London Edition." "Miss Austen" appeared on the title page of *Persuasion*, the next to be published. The venture was a success and the initial print run of 750 for *Pride and Prejudice* was raised to 1,250 for the remaining books. In 1838, Carey relaunched the Austen titles as a collected edition with a print run of 1,500: each two-volume novel was now bound up as a single volume, the type set in double columns. And in 1845, Carey reissued the novels separately (*Pride and Prejudice* still titled *Elizabeth Bennet*), again printed in double columns but now in single volumes. Carey and Lea (later Carey and Hart) were intelligent in their marketing. They understood that the casual invocations and profanities of Austen's Regency social talk would not be well received by the revivalist crusading circles of Philadelphia and the East Coast. So the texts were given a precautionary cleansing. Devout expressions of gratitude or concern went out together with the imprecations: "Oh God!", "Good God," "Thank God," "for God's sake," "Lord!" "Good Lord!" "Lord bless me!" "Lord help you!" "Good heavens!" "For Heaven's sake!" and so on. Even

instances of Tom Bertram's "By Jove!" were lost to *Mansfield Park*, along with Mr
Price's seemingly innocuous exclamations of "By G——." With this dedeified text of
Elizabeth Bennet, the *National Gazette and Literary Register* of Philadelphia was able to
reassure its readers: "If the American world will read novels, let us have those of which
the moral is good, the text pure, and the instructiveness practical and domestic;
entertaining and ingenious, but free from all poison" (September 8, 1832).

The Bentley Years, 1832–93

Having purchased the Austen copyrights, Bentley put all six works into his "Standard
Novels" series. Advertised as "cheap" editions, these were published as single volumes
designed for the private purchaser as against the three-volume sets which sold mainly
to the circulating libraries. The "Standard Novels," priced at six shillings, were handy,
attractive little books, 6½ × 4 in. (16½ × 10 cm), with a pictorial frontispiece and a
smaller pictorial vignette on the title page itself, with a protective tissue between
them. For *Sense and Sensibility*, the first to be published, at the end of December 1832,
with 1833 on the title-page, Bentley asked Henry Austen to enlarge his "Biographical
Notice of the Author," now renamed "Memoir of Miss Austen," and all six titles –
Northanger Abbey and *Persuasion* together in a single volume – were published by the
end of July 1833. Anticipating a largish market – his print runs were 2,500/3,000 –
under his own imprint on the title page Bentley also listed bookseller-publishers in
Edinburgh, Dublin, and Paris. In October 1833, Bentley published all six volumes
together as a set, a "cheap and complete edition" priced at 30 shillings and "neatly
bound for the library." Regularly reprinted down the years, the Bentley volumes
remained the standard edition. As the sales increased, the binding decoration became
more varied and lavish, and the price per volume went steadily down: to five shillings,
three shillings and sixpence, and by 1846, two shillings and sixpence. Textually, the
reprints were reasonably sound. For *Sense and Sensibility* and *Mansfield Park*, the second
editions were used and overall the reprints retained the volume divisions and chapter
numbering of the original editions, although *Pride and Prejudice* copied the two-
volume third edition of 1817, and the dedication to the Prince Regent was dropped
from *Emma*. Moreover, the textual corrections were sensible, some of them anticipating Chapman's in his Oxford edition of 1923.

The volumes in the "Standard Novels" series continued to sell steadily, with
reprints every two or three years. The growth in the market was signified on the title
page of the final reprint, of 1869: among the copublishers named there were George
Robertson of Melbourne and Little & Brown of Boston. As the stereotypes were by
now badly worn, in 1870 the texts were reset for a "Popular Edition" in Bentley's
"Favourite Novels" series. This was in a larger format, 7¼ × 5 in. (18 × 30 cm), and
priced at six shillings a volume. Henry Austen's brief "Memoir" was now omitted in
view of the *Memoir of Jane Austen* by James Edward Austen-Leigh, also published by
Bentley in 1870. In 1871, the second edition of the *Memoir* was extended to include

the three most important manuscript works, *Lady Susan* and *The Watsons*, with *Sanditon* in a truncated form. The 1871 *Memoir* was produced to match the novels in size and style of binding and was regularly reprinted with them. The last complete edition of Austen to be published by Bentley, and the first in which the novels were numbered in the order of their original publication, was the elaborately designed "Steventon Edition" (including the 1871 *Memoir*), advertised as being "a superior edition" of 375 sets of six volumes at 63 shillings. It was produced with all the elegance that Victorian taste of 1882 could muster – with chocolate-brown ink on creamy hand-made paper, each page decoratively framed with border rules and small corner-pieces that differed from volume to volume, and with a dust jacket of primrose paper printed in blue and brown.

The Growing Market 1840–1923

Although the Bentley editions dominated the nineteenth-century market in Britain and overseas, with the expiry of copyrights in 1844, other publishers began to latch on to Austen's growing reputation. The novels featured in popular series: in 1846, *Mansfield Park* appeared in the Parlour Novelist Series, in 1851 in the Parlour Library Series, and from 1849 Austen titles were included in the Routledge Railway Library, the so-called yellowbacks, cheap reprints with garish pictorial front covers. By the 1870s illustrated editions began to appear and as the publishers were marketing the novels as more-or-less contemporary stories of romantic interest the ladies and gentlemen were depicted in Victorian dress – favorite subjects being the hero and heroine deep in conversation in a woodland setting or the heroine alone and engrossed in a letter.

By the 1880s, both ends of the market were catered for. Routledge, ever-enterprising, was willing to trade its Sixpenny Novels edition of *Sense and Sensibility* (1884) for soap wrappers, while bibliophiles were spoilt for choice. They could savor the elaboration and exclusiveness of Bentley's limited Steventon Edition of 1882; or the 12-volume set published in 1892 by Roberts Brothers of Boston, with top edges gilt, inserted frontispieces with protective tissues, highly elaborate typography with rules, blackletter, woodcut headpieces and so on, in a special edition of 250 copies on large paper, a second color and the frontispieces on japan paper; or the 10-volume set published by Dent in 1892 and edited by R. Brimley Johnson, with a limited edition – 100 copies for England and 50 for America – on larger, handmade paper, all edges uncut and superior impressions of the plates. The illustrations by W. C. Cooke, three to each volume, are significant as the first to try for a Regency flavor in the clothing of the characters and their setting. This opened the way for a succession of heavily illustrated editions: most popular of all, with the illustrations in use over a hundred years later, Hugh Thomson's *Pride and Prejudice* of 1894 with 160 line drawings and a multitude of added decoration, including a drawn title page and dedication; Charles E. Brock's *Pride and Prejudice* of 1895 with a drawn frontispiece and 39 line drawings;

then Hugh Thomson again, with lavishly illustrated editions of *Sense and Sensibility* and *Emma*, both in 1896, and a *Mansfield Park* in 1897, all these published by Macmillan. In 1898 Dent reissued their 1892 Brimley Johnson 10-volume edition, replacing the Cooke illustrations with watercolors by the brothers Charles and Henry Brock. Then there was an *Emma* in 1898 and a *Sense and Sensibility* in 1899, both published by George Allen and illustrated by Christiana Hammond, the finest artist of this period; her decisive and strongly characterized pen-and-ink drawings are neither whimsical nor overdecorative.

Over the next 60 or 70 years, the illustrations by these artists were used again and again in later editions and reprints – the watercolors by the Brock brothers, for example, reappeared in the Old Manor House Edition, 1906, from Holby of New York. The serious effect of these illustrations, especially those by Hugh Thomson (E. M. Forster was to call him, with a derisive misspelling, "the lamentable Hugh Thompson"), was in occupying the public imagination and in some part shaping a picturesque and sentimental image of the novels and the novelist – handing Henry James the opportunity to mock "the body of publishers, editors, illustrators, producers of the pleasant twaddle of magazines; who have found their 'dear,' our dear, everybody's dear, Jane so infinitely to their material purpose" ("The Lesson of Balzac", 1905, in Southam 1987: 270), a "material purpose" sustained into the twenty-first century in the Regency costumery and "heritage" values perpetuated in the texts of television and film.

R. W. Chapman and the Oxford Edition, 1923

The turning point in the textual and editorial history of Austen came with Chapman's Oxford University Press edition of 1923. This was the first scholarly edition of any English novelist and the first complete text of the novels to be "based," as it was announced on the title page, "on Collation of the early editions." Up to this point, only two editors had shown any such concern. Reginald Brimley Johnson, editor of the Dent set published in 1892, provided each novel with a bibliographical note and recorded that his texts "followed the last revised by the author." Far more important was Katharine Metcalfe, an Oxford tutor, whose edition of *Pride and Prejudice*, published by the Clarendon Press in 1912, was the first edition of any Austen novel to return accurately and with evident editorial judgment to the three editions published in Jane Austen's lifetime. In Metcalfe's edition, there was also an attempt at historical authenticity in the book's appearance, with facsimiles of the title pages of the original three volumes; the retention of the three-volume chapter numbering; and a Regency typeface, together with a matching layout of the page, including catchwords. This elaborate period reconstruction – some would call it mannered antiquarianism – was accompanied by a twentieth-century scholarly apparatus of equal elaboration, including a considerable Appendix entitled "Jane Austen and Her Time," with sections on

Traveling and Post, Deportment, Accomplishment and Manners, and so on. In short, the volume anticipates in virtually every detail the design and appearance of Chapman's 1923 edition. This was no coincidence. Katharine Metcalfe became Mrs Chapman in 1913 and the Clarendon edition was planned as a joint project. Employed at the Clarendon Press since 1906 and, after his military service in the First World War, appointed Secretary to the Delegates of the Press (in effect, its Publisher), R. W. Chapman was in a position to take his wife's volume as the prototype for his own edition, and indeed the setting of her 1912 text was used for his *Pride and Prejudice* volume of 1923. Metcalfe also published an edition of *Northanger Abbey* with Oxford in 1923, and that text too was used in Chapman's edition. But the notion of a joint project silently disappeared. Chapman acknowledged the help of others in the preparation of his edition and thanked his various correspondents for their textual and other suggestions but the name of Katharine Metcalfe/Chapman goes unrecorded here or anywhere else in Chapman's published writings.

Even 80 or 90 years on, much remains of permanent value in Chapman's edition: for example, the extensive notes on Vocabulary, Grammar, Punctuation, Reading and Writing, and Modes of Address; the Regency prints of places, fashions, and carriages; and the Indexes of Literary Allusions and Real Places are convenient listings. On the other hand, the focus of the detailed notes on the text is almost wholly on literary sources and on textual emendations and variant readings between the original editions (somewhat confusingly, the annotation and the textual matters are combined in a single sequence); while political issues, such as the Bertrams' trip to Antigua and the position of women, pass unremarked. Given the masculine-imperial culture of Chapman's generation, perhaps this was to be expected. Nonetheless, his elaborate apparatus of Notes, Appendices, and Indices carried a serious consequence. They bestowed a blanket air of finality upon this formidable edition, already monumental in its page size and style of presentation and its limit of 1,000 copies. It is as if there was no more to say, that the textual issues were laid to rest and that whatever Dr Chapman pronounced upon was the last word. That, at all events, is what many reviewers remarked. George Sampson wrote in the *Bookman*: "Mr. Chapman has left simply nothing for any succeeding editor to do" (January 1924). And it was to be many years before Chapman's sometimes overcorrective textual readings were reexamined.

Once his major task, the Oxford edition of the novels, was completed, Chapman turned to the manuscript works. These included *Lady Susan*, *The Watsons*, and *Sanditon*, and other smaller items, a total of five volumes published by Oxford between 1925 and 1927. Together with the two juvenilia notebooks Chapman edited in 1933 and 1951, these miscellaneous items were brought together in 1954 to form a substantial collected edition of the *Minor Works*, now added as a final volume 6 to his existing edition of the novels. Beyond this were Chapman's first and second editions of *Jane Austen's Letters* (1932 and 1952), *Jane Austen: Facts and Problems* (1948), and *Jane Austen: A Critical Bibliography* (1953 and 1955), all these published by the Oxford

University Press and together consolidating Chapman's position as the authoritative and authentic voice of Austen scholarship.

The Rise of the Student Edition

Chapman's edition remained essentially unchanged and in print for many years. From 1933 onwards, it was being marketed as "The Oxford Illustrated Jane Austen," with a final reprint manufactured in the United States in 1988 and sold from Oxford's branch in New York; and it continued to be regarded as the standard scholarly text. The revisions Chapman himself made to the second and third editions of 1926 and 1933, and Mary Lascelles to the reprints of 1965–6, left the texts unchanged and were confined to corrections and tidyings-up. Its one direct offshoot was the series of Austen titles included in the Oxford English Novel series between 1970 and 1971, reissued in a paperback edition in 1975. James Kinsley, the series editor, noted that the text was "substantially" Chapman's, that Chapman's textual apparatus had been "revised and his emendations reconsidered." The volumes also included a critical Introduction, a Select Bibliography, A Chronology of Jane Austen, very skeletal Textual Notes and Explanatory Notes only slightly improved on Chapman's.

The immediate effect of the postwar expansion in higher education in the 1950s and 60s was to create the market for student paperback editions introduced by leading critics of the time. Almost invariably, Chapman's text was used. Notable among these were Houghton Mifflin's long-established Riverside Editions, with *Pride and Prejudice* (1956) introduced by Martin Schorer, and *Emma* (1957) and *Mansfield Park* (1965) introduced by Lionel Trilling. These editions exemplified the minimalist practice of New Criticism: the texts are note-free and little more was provided. Trilling furnished his Introduction to *Emma* with four explanatory footnotes and added a two-page Biographical Sketch; Schorer's Introduction was note-free and followed by a Biblio-graphical Note listing his recommended reading and explaining his use of Chapman's text throughout. But at this time, styles of criticism and teaching were on the move. The scope of literary study was extending through historical and cultural fields, vastly increasing the pressure on library resources already stretched by larger student numbers; and together these forces created the need for a new kind of edition – compendious paperbacks (some approaching 650 pages) that included key passages from the critical literature plus a selection of background material, with well-known critics to edit the volumes and provide substantial introductions. In effect, these were texts equipped with their own essential reading. Among the pioneers were the Harbrace Sourcebooks, with Bradford Booth's *Pride and Prejudice* in 1963; the Norton Critical Editions, with Donald J. Gray's *Pride and Prejudice* and Stephen Parrish's *Emma*, both 1966; and the Bantam Critical Editions, with Robert Donald Spector's *Emma* in 1969. Over the years, some early series disappeared. But the most successful have evolved. For example, the notes and documentation in the third edition of the Norton *Pride and Prejudice*, 2001, have advanced in line with new interests and approaches, with sections on Film and

Class and Money, and an updated range of critical excerpts. The text is no longer credited to Chapman's Oxford edition; Gray has established his own and he explains its basis and his principles of emendation. Other significant student editions published in North America include Alistair M. Duckworth's *Emma* (St Martin's, 2002), Beth Lau's *Sense and Sensibility* (Houghton Mifflin, 2002) and, originating in Canada, the Broadview Editions from 1998 to 2004.

Unlike the American texts, the major British series – those published by Penguin and Oxford – carried no documentation. Nonetheless, over time they became oriented more specifically to student use. Oxford's first step, in 1980, was to include in their World's Classics series, as paperbacks, the Austen texts they had first published hardbound in the Oxford English Novels (1970–1), but without the Notes listing the textual variants. In 1990–5, these World's Classics paperback volumes were reissued with new critical introductions, and in 1998 they were reissued yet again, in a slightly larger format and with a change of title, as Oxford World Classics, with the Textual Notes restored. Finally, in 2003–4, the 1998 edition was thoroughly updated under the General Editorship of Vivien Jones, with new Introductions, extensive explanatory notes and other editorial material, including Appendices on Rank and Social Status and Dancing, and detailed textual notes.

The Penguin editions were also updated, along similar lines. The Austen titles in the Penguin English Library, published between 1965 and 1972, carried critical introductions, several pages of explanatory notes, and a Note on the Text in which the volume editors explained their use of Chapman's edition and their departures from it. Between 1995 and 1998, these Austen titles were replaced by a new set within the Penguin Classics series. Significantly, a textual adviser, Claire Lamont, was appointed, and each volume carried a considerable statement explaining the important decision to return to the first edition texts, now "edited afresh." The Notes took full account of the tradition of Austen scholarship and also drew attention to points of textual controversy. This was particularly important for *Sense and Sensibility* and *Mansfield Park*, with their revised second editions. The Note on the Text by Kathryn Sutherland, arguing the authority of the first edition text of *Mansfield Park*, 1814, and the equivalent section of Claudia Johnson's Introduction to the Norton edition (1998), in which she discusses the authority of the second edition text, together provide a case study in the methods, considerations, and scope of textual scholarship, particularly fascinating as the two editors arrive at different choices of copytext. Similarly, Johnson's edition of the Norton *Sense and Sensibility* (2002) argues the case for preferring the second edition text to Penguin's first edition text (edited by Ros Ballaster, 1995). (It is worth noting that the Norton volume editors were free to make their own choice of copytext.) A few years later, the Penguin Classics series as a whole was relaunched and the Austen titles came out as a group in 2003. The volume editors had the opportunity to update their introductions, notes, and further reading lists, and chronologies were added. One further change to the *Sense and Sensibility*, *Pride and Prejudice*, and *Mansfield Park* volumes was the addition of the Introductions that Tony Tanner had written over 30 years earlier for these volumes in the Penguin English

Library. The Penguin house editor judged that these Introductions were classics of criticism and as the Austen titles stand high among Penguin's best-selling titles, this considerable addition was thought to be commercially justified as well.

The Cambridge Edition

The new century opened with an edition appropriately up to date. Issuing from the Cambridge University Press, the Cambridge Edition takes full account of modern literary and textual scholarship and currently, in the absence of any rival, gives promise of fulfilling the publisher's ambition of being recognized as "the definitive edition for the twenty-first century." Among its leading features are explanatory notes longer and more detailed than in any existing edition, extensive introductions, and an accompanying *Jane Austen in Context* volume, 40 topical essays providing a broad biographical, critical, historical, and cultural background. The copytexts – to quote the General Editor's Preface – are "the latest edition to which [Austen] might plausibly have made some contribution"; specifically, the changes between the first and second editions of *Sense and Sensibility* and *Mansfield Park* are shown on the page, reflecting the view that rather than aiming at an ideal, perfected text, the edition should exhibit the text in its various stages and versions. The volume editors have added specialized appendices appropriate to each text and provided a list of the corrections and emendations they have made to the copytext. All in all, the Cambridge edition is visibly exact and comprehensive in its treatment of the *Juvenilia* (published in 2006) and the six novels (2005–6), and it only awaits the publication of the *Later Manuscripts* volume (announced for 2008) for a final judgment to be made. So far the reviews have been glowing. But textual and literary historians will want to consult the long and searching notice of the first two volumes – *Mansfield Park* and *Emma* – by Kathryn Sutherland (Professor of Bibliography and Textual Criticism at Oxford) in the *Review of English Studies* (2006), reminding us of the enduring scholarship and authority of Chapman's edition and its lasting contribution to Austen studies, including the Cambridge edition itself. There was also a notable exchange in the *Times Literary Supplement* between Professor Sutherland and Professor Janet Todd, the General Editor of the Cambridge edition, Sutherland's counter-claim being that Chapman's Oxford edition "remains the authoritative standard."

NOTE

For advice and information given to me in the preparation of this chapter, I would like to thank Brian Baker (Norton), Bruce Cantley (Houghton Mifflin), Alistair Duckworth, Sarah Emsley, Les Fairfield, Patti Houghton, Claire Lamont (Textual Adviser for the Penguin Classics edition), Judith Luna (Oxford University Press), Martin Maw (Archivist, Oxford University Press), Peter Sabor, editor of the *Juvenilia* volume in the Cambridge edition – and last, but not least, the editors of this volume.

FURTHER READING

Fergus, Jan (1991). *Jane Austen: A Literary Life.* Basingstoke, UK: Macmillan.

Gilson, David (2005). Later publishing history, with illustrations. In Janet Todd (Ed.). *Jane Austen in Context* (pp. 121–59). Cambridge, UK: Cambridge University Press.

Mandal, Anthony, and Brian Southam (Eds). (2007). *The Reception of Jane Austen in Europe.* London and New York: Continuum.

Southam, Brian (2007). *Jane Austen: A Students' Guide to the Later Manuscript Works.* London: Concord Books.

St Clair, William (2004). *The Reading Nation in the Romantic Period.* Cambridge, UK: Cambridge University Press.

Sutherland, Kathryn (2005). *Jane Austen's Textual Lives: from Aeschylus to Bollywood.* Oxford: Oxford University Press.

5

Jane Austen, Illustrated

Laura Carroll and John Wiltshire

From their first republication as items in Bentley's Standard Novels series in 1833 to their contemporary incarnations, Austen's novels have been presented, in one form or another, with illustrations. And not merely with illustrations: with decorative title-pages, inset motifs, ornamental headpieces, illuminated capital letters, decorative endpapers, garlands around the text and the illustrations, colored type and colored plates, cameos, Wedgwood urns, harps, gilt, and Regency stripes, to say nothing of contemporary dust jackets and paper covers bearing paintings of elegant females or photographs of costumed movie stars. So that illustration, in the usual sense – as pictorial elucidation of a text – is not quite what editions of Jane Austen represent. Even the captioned pictures which we naturally think of as faithfully serving the text have their own independent logic.

In his 1985 Panizzi Lecture *Bibliography and the Sociology of Texts*, D. F. McKenzie speaks of "the book as an expressive form," and suggests that "the material forms of books, the non-verbal elements of the typographic notations within them, the very disposition of space itself have an expressive function in conveying meaning" (1986: 1, 8). Though virtually initiating the contemporary focus on the book as a material object which encodes a variety of cultural significances, McKenzie had nothing to say about the illustrated volume. But the discipline he initiated, we suggest, could find no more fruitful object of attention than the publication history of Jane Austen's novels. A book exists "not just as aesthetic object but also as a commercial commodity" (Behrendt 1997: 35). Commercial value and aesthetic properties are each inextricably embedded in the physical form of the book and so in readers' experiences of the texts thus presented. In fact, we would argue, the cultural history of Austen cannot be understood without attention to the decorative packaging in which readers have long encountered her novels.

Illustration, however, is a term that itself needs to be unpacked. The artist commissioned to illustrate a volume is not guided by pure attention to the text (were there such a thing). While Austen's novels rarely specify appearances, they often supply, obliquely, detailed (and significant) information about the spatial relations among groups of people: the material the text provides for an illustrator to realize pictorially is thus at once both open to interpretation and heavily determined. Technical and industrial constraints come into play: neither publishers nor readers want illustrations clumped together, as Joan Hassall put it, "like an ill-mixed cake with all the fruit in one place" (1986: 215). They must be spaced at intervals, so the artist must find something in the text at intervals, to strike off from. The processes of reproduction – steel engraving, woodcut, lithography, photogravure – will also play a part. So will the directions of the publisher and the market that is aimed for. The artist may consult previous illustrations of the text. With all this taken into account, though, artists will bring to the illustrations their particular style or gift and the wish to demonstrate it. In short, there is no such thing as innocent or objective illustration.

Three kinds of decorated editions of Austen's novels proliferated in the nineteenth century and beyond. Each kind corresponds with significant phases or currents in the history of Austen's reception. First, issues of "standardized" volumes uniform with a publisher's series securely consolidate Austen's position among contemporary novelists. Then follows a phase of dissemination when cheap, plentiful, and relatively disposable editions present Austen's novels as entertaining and accessible reading matter. Finally, the appearance of the novels in collected sets of attractively bound and generously illustrated keepsake or gift books presents Austen as a "classic" author with a stable identity which is therefore available for repackaging. With each successive phase illustration and associated decorative matter assume greater prominence, covering the outside of the book as well as punctuating its pages of print.

Between 1831 and 1854 Richard Bentley, a "serious-minded craftsman-booklover" and enterprising Victorian publisher, brought out reprints of 126 novels by English, American, and continental authors in uniform one-volume editions inexpensively priced at six shillings each (Patten 2004). This was Bentley's Standard Novels series: neat, compact octavo books serviceably bound in plain dark cloth, each volume illustrated with formulaic front matter, sold at a price that made them accessible to a broad middle class and in a manner that encouraged the collecting of uniform sets as personal libraries. In size, manufacture, layout, and overall appearance, Bentley's Standard Novels resemble the set, such as Scott's Waverley Novels, which Cadell and other publishers issued through the 1820s and 1830s. But while Bentley produced the first English reprints of Austen's novels, issued in five volumes (*Northanger Abbey* and *Persuasion* together) they were not at first explicitly marketed as a freestanding series. Austen is placed firmly within a canon of writers appealing to mainstream contemporary taste, but her novels are not yet singled out as forming a consistent and distinctive oeuvre.

In Bentley's volumes the illustrative front matter comprises a captioned frontispiece, engraved upon a steel plate and depicting an incident from the novel, and a title page presenting the name of the novel and its author in elegantly spaced, hand-cut lettering at the top of the page, with the name and address of the publisher's firm

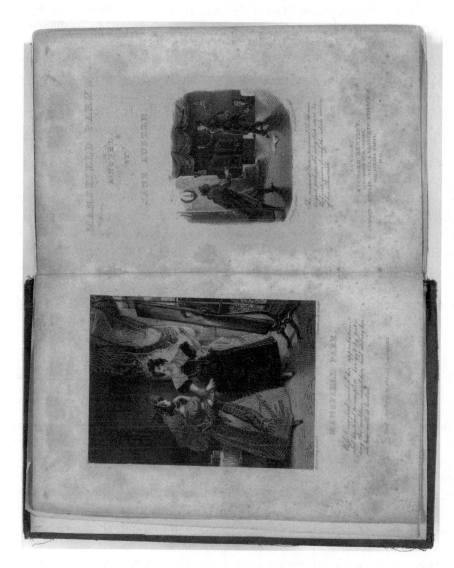

Figure 5.1   Mansfield Park (London: Richard Bentley, 1833), frontispiece and engraved title page, by William Greatbatch after Pickering. Mitchell Library, State Library of New South Wales.

at the bottom. Between the engraved text blocks is a small soft-edged vignette showing a second scene from the novel, also captioned. The captions are truncated sentences drawn from the text. The plates in Bentley's editions, engraved by William Greatbatch after drawings by George Pickering, are artistically conservative, with strong generic affinities to commercial art such as fashion plates, or depictions of scenes from the stage, rather than to the lively Hogarthian tradition of caricature and pictorial narrative flourishing in the work of contemporary illustrators such as George Cruikshank and "Phiz" (Hablot Knight Browne). To the twenty-first century eye these rather dark pictures seem, at first, unsuitably ponderous illustrations for Austen's supple and flexible novels. With their shadowed modeling and solid lines, their dark rooms, thick foliage, and heavy draperies, the engravings seem overly mannered. Theatricalized poses are given to the figures. Costume is of the 1830s, not the era of the story, but the classically arranged drapery is characteristic of late eighteenth-century pictorial fashion. Criticism of the illustrations for not conforming to the authentic dress and manner of the period began early, but it might also be argued that representing the characters in the costume of the date of the edition avoids casting the novels as documentaries of past times or as distant museum pieces.

A frontispiece and vignette prefacing the text presents less of a challenge to the smooth integrity of the fiction and the concentration of the reader than does fully fledged illustration interspersed throughout the pages. Since the incidents are chosen from the whole text of the novel, the frontispiece and title page have the power to signal a reading which the fully illustrated edition does not. The Bentley illustrations, in fact, initiate pictorial traditions taken up by many successive illustrators. *Mansfield Park*'s frontispiece (Figure 5.1) presents Fanny and Mary Crawford standing before a full-length mirror in Mary's room while Fanny tries on a gold necklace (vol. 2, ch. 8); Fanny gazes at her reflection in pleased wonder while Mary grasps her hand and gestures benignly toward the glass. Opposite, the vignette shows the moment of Sir Thomas Bertram's entrance upon a dramatically lit proscenium stage dressed with festooned curtains and framing a ranting Mr Yates; Tom Bertram observes happily from a darkened corner (vol. 2, ch 1). An interpretation of the novel is proffered in which Fanny is the metamorphic heroine of a kind of *Bildungsroman* of femininity, sexual maturation, and self-recognition, whilst the lesser comic pleasures of the theatrical episode (class, drama) are anticipated on the facing page. Mary and Fanny before the mirror reappear in Macmillan's deluxe edition of 1897; Edmund's presentation of a plain gold chain to Fanny appears in Groombridge's 1875 edition, Routledge's cheap edition of 1883, and J. M. Dent's 1908 edition; and Fanny putting on the chain and cross before the ball appears in an American edition put out by Little, Brown in 1898. Sir Thomas's confrontation with Yates appears in Dent's 1892 edition, Macmillan's 1897 edition, Dent's 1908 edition, and Chatto & Windus's edition of 1908.[1] Not all the plates in Bentley's editions are equally intriguing: the frontispiece to *Sense and Sensibility* is a dull picture of Elinor Dashwood walking with Lucy Steele, arranged in a style which seems calculated mainly to display the details of their improbably rich costumes. *Emma*'s frontispiece, though, effectively reproduces

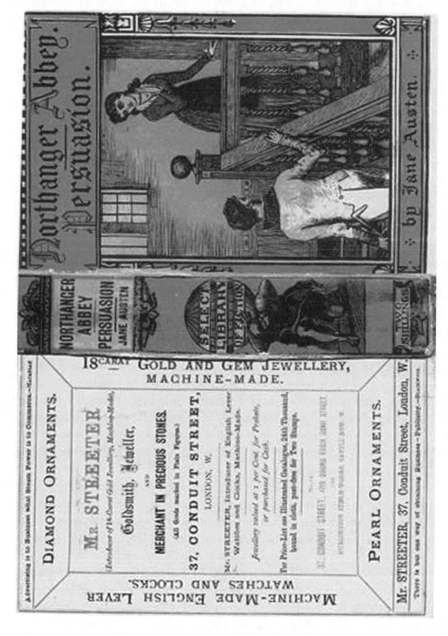

Figure 5.2 Northanger Abbey and Persuasion (London: Chapman and Hall, 1872), front and back boards. Matheson Library, Monash University.

the sly double-voicedness of that novel's narrative. It shows Mr Elton gazing ardently at Harriet Smith whilst delicately placing his hand upon Emma's incomplete sketch of her. The caption reads "There was no being displeased with such an encourager, for his admiration made him discover a likeness before it was possible" – a phrase which is representative of one aspect of *Emma*'s style inasmuch as a second reading points in a quite different direction than a first. Elton's pictured gestures likewise allow for a degree of (initial) readerly indecision about which woman is the real object of his attentions.

Bentley, who had purchased the copyright of *Pride and Prejudice* from Egerton, and the other copyrights from Henry and Cassandra Austen, progressively lost them between 1839 and 1860. A phase of miscellaneous publication followed. Single novels were issued by various firms, such as the cheap editions of Routledge's "Railway Library." These were crudely manufactured books, clad in glazed yellow paper over-printed with two or three flat colors, the back given over to advertising, meant for mass consumption and immediate amusement. The cover of *Northanger Abbey and Persuasion* reproduced here (Figure 5.2), is a simplified version of the Bentley frontis-piece to the same novels. Fine, sharp gradations of line are not available in woodcut prints and so the graphic emphasis is on simple forms, flat colors, heavy outlines, and broad drama. A knowing reader might identify the figures as Henry Tilney and Catherine Morland meeting unexpectedly on the stairs at Northanger, but to anyone else they can only be a generic young couple, perhaps about to engage in some sort of confrontation. The Gothic lettering is in keeping with the atmosphere of uncertainty and sensation.

Illustration soon began to colonize the interior of the book as publishers issued volumes with more than frontispieces. The most interesting of these is the Groom-bridge edition of *Mansfield Park* (1875), a curiosity or anomaly, since the firm issued no other Austen novels, and because the seven lithographic illustrations, in which external views – Mansfield as a Jacobean mansion, Fanny Price looking over the lawn towards Mary on horseback (Figure 5.3) – feature strongly, in darkened tones which seem, repeatedly, to emphasize the heroine's isolation. These somber, mute plates have no captions and are more directed toward establishing pervasive mood than represent-ing dramatic moments. They suggest an investment in the novel at odds with what was to become the received idea of "Jane Austen," a road not taken in the later history of Austen illustration.

It is during this period that the reputation of Austen's novels gains ground, helped along by the publication of James Edward Austen-Leigh's *Memoir* of his aunt in 1870, and by the advocacy of, among others, George Henry Lewes, who had read them aloud repeatedly with his partner, George Eliot. In 1859 he published an article in the widely read *Blackwood's Edinburgh Magazine* declaring her an unacknowledged and underappreciated "artist of the highest rank" (Southam 1968: 148). In the course of his appreciation, Lewes made some comments which have remained pertinent. Austen was a "dramatic," not a "descriptive" genius, he insists. "It is not stated whether she was shortsighted, but the absence of all sense of outward world – either scenery or

Figure 5.3 Mansfield Park (London: Groombridge, 1875), illustration by A. F. Lydon. University of New South Wales Library.

personal appearance – is more remarkable in her than in any writer we remember" (Southam 1968: 159). Other writers since have commented on the scarcity of physical detail in the novels. It might conceivably be said then that this novelist offers the illustrator an unparalleled opportunity. On the other hand, it might be said that the illustrator's art (however skilled) is radically at odds with the novels' own, "grafting," in Henry James' words in his Preface to *The Golden Bowl*, "a picture by another hand" on the author's own imaginative achievement, "this being always . . . a lawless incident" (James, 1909: ix).

  Phase three of this history begins in the high Victorian period, with the issue of sets of the novels lavishly illustrated throughout. J. M. Dent brought out the first deluxe set of the novels of Jane Austen in 1892, with illustrations by William Cubitt Cooke. Christiana Hammond produced sympathetic drawings for three of the novels during the 1890s. In 1895 George Allen published an edition of *Pride and Prejudice* featuring no less than 160 ornamental line drawings by Hugh Thomson. This was prefaced by an essay in which the then well-known critic George Saintsbury coined, not coincidentally, the term (in his spelling) "Janites." In 1898 Dent issued a new set, with color plates by Charles Brock and his brother Henry, to be followed by still another Brock-illustrated set in 1907. Both sets of illustrations, along with those made by Hugh Thomson, were widely reprinted during the first part of the twentieth century (Figure 5.4). From the middle of the 1890s onwards the editions Thomson

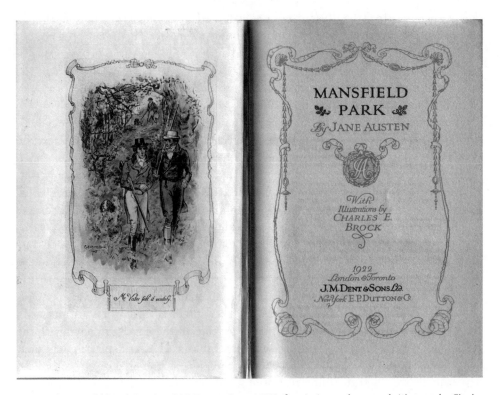

Figure 5.4   Mansfield Park (London: J.M. Dent & Sons, 1922), frontispiece and engraved title page, by Charles E. Brock.

and the Brocks produced for rival publishers were not only more copiously illustrated than any previous issues, but offered more consistently an interpretation of the texts. This was to influence not only other readers, but, perhaps more tellingly, the popular conception or image of "Jane Austen" – an Austen now seen through the visual presentation of her novels. The 1890s editions are "classic" novels, gift books handsomely presented, their gilt tooling and gilt page edges bespeaking state of the art modern technology as much as it does decoration, ornament, enjoyment of leisure. "Chocolate-box" is not necessarily an unfair description of their style; for one thing, like a box of chocolates, they have a visually distinct outside – typically a rich jewel color embossed in gilt with an Arts and Crafts inspired design – and inside, where delicate pen or brush drawings share the pages with neat regular blocks of text. A further performance of luxury and elegance is achieved in those volumes with colored plates. While the illustrations do direct and structure readerly engagement with the novel in ways discussed more fully below, the aesthetic presentation we find in these 1890s volumes is of a highly integrated and streamlined book object.

Thomson's vision of *Pride and Prejudice* is richly idiosyncratic, his edition a tour de force, and an important moment in the history of "Jane Austen." The spine bears the author's name but the front cover says "illustrated by Hugh Thomson." In a page of flowing handwriting, the illustrations are dedicated to a friend by Thomson, thus in effect claiming a kind of ownership of the volume. Moreover Thomson's presence can be seen to add value: his name designates an author-function comparable to that of the editor of a modern scholarly edition. The work is not solely Austen's but it has been punctuated and commented upon by a second person, with the authority of a consistent position and style.

Thomson's drawings for the novel were completed in the winter of 1893 and the spring of 1894. They consist of 60 illustrations with captions taken from the text, 40 drawings without captions, and, perhaps most remarkably, 61 exuberantly executed initial letters, done in the style of illuminated capitals from a medieval manuscript, with figures or incidents from the novel depicted within the letter. This hieroglyphic hybridization of picture and writing had been most famously deployed by Thackeray in his own illustrations for *Vanity Fair*, although there the puppet-like persons enclosed within the capitals are not, like Thomson's, ironized versions of the same figures who populate the novel and the larger illustrations. Throughout, even in the headnote to the Preface, Thomson's presence is felt. For the first time, the pictures were historicized: whereas previous illustrators show figures in more or less contemporary Victorian gear, Thomson's reproduce early nineteenth-century costumes and show characters amid appropriate "period" furniture. If the novels are now, with the aid of pictures, deemed to be universally accessible, they also depict figures from another era, the drawings, reduced by the printing process from much larger originals, appearing delicate and charming recreations of a vanished grace. The text is enclosed by figures of peacocks and cupids: at the opening in some form of contention, and at "The End" in harmony. But the nostalgic prettifying of the novel these decorations suggest is complicated by other elements. The witty allusions to allegorical bestiaries or morality plays in the form of the initial chapter headings contribute to this excess of visual meaning.

As the reader leafs through the book – and in this instance Thomson's *Pride and Prejudice* is typical of the work that was to follow in his wake – the illustrations immediately draw the eye and interrupt the reading. One turns the page, looks at the picture, then down to the caption, and back again at the picture, before resuming one's reading. Then, on reaching the line which supplied the caption, one looks back at the picture again before going on with the text. In this way the presence of illustrations regularly disrupts an immersive, absorbed, linear progression through the text and regularly propels the reader in mechanical looping movements (literally back and forth in the book and figuratively "in" and "out" of deep engagement with the novel). At the same time, the illustrations, many of them uncaptioned, and the capital chapter letters, perform the function of the frontispiece – predicting and guiding the reader's response.

One of the most playful and intriguing of Thomson's pictures is the head illustration to chapter 8 of the first volume. Its caption is "covering a screen." As with all of his captions, this is not a whole sentence but a fragment lifted from the chapter, in this case the one in which Elizabeth reaches Netherfield with her skirts dirty, looking "almost wild." And, like almost all of them, this illustration disregards the drama of the text and goes instead for a moment in its periphery. Here it foregrounds as a leading motif the very material that Darcy treats with ironic dismissal: the word "accomplishments," he pronounces, is applied "to many a woman who deserves it no otherwise than . . . covering a skreen." In effect the visual presentation reverses the emphasis of the text, and not only by giving graphic art priority over that "reading" that Darcy is later to recommend. Thomson comes firmly down on the side of young ladies who do what young ladies ought to do, never mind about skipping across fields. Perhaps he is merely presenting a gently humorous moment of bygone fashion, a time when young ladies did decorate screens with sketches of hunters and swains and other pastoral sights. But, unconsciously perhaps, this motif declares that the pursuit of his own art of adding pictures is, in effect, to screen the novel's own impact from view.

But if his illustrations, with their generically pretty young ladies, their impossibly tall Regency beaux, their drawing rooms dotted with portraits and sofas and writing desks – drawn with a light touch, though, in contrast to the Bentley or Groombridge illustrations – have generally been dismissed or found silly by later academic commentators, that is not the whole story. Of course *Pride and Prejudice* is not holy writ, and Thomson in his initial capitals and his uncaptioned chapter pictures was practicing another art, one more akin to his author's obliquely satiric genius. Chapter 13 in Volume I, for example, features a motif in which Mr Collins, hat in hand, holds an enormous olive branch spanning the top of the page whilst Mr Bennet, bemused, book in hand, stands on the other side. Chapter 14 shows the two gentlemen at opposite ends of a long table, with a young lady beneath in the initial capital D ("During dinner . . ."), apparently listening. Most remarkably of all, chapter 15 features a frieze-like presentation of the five Bennet sisters, bookended by their mother arranging at left and Mr Collins inspecting at right, Jane in the center with a "Not For Sale" sign over her head (Figure 5.5). The initial letter, just below (the M in "Mr Collins") shows him as what at first might be taken as a shuttlecock, but which is probably a hot air balloon. More ambitious decorative effects diversify the visual appearances of the pages: chapter 36 (II, ch. 13) in which Elizabeth assesses Darcy's letter, features a larger than usual head drawing: Elizabeth, letter in her left hand, her right arm holding a balance. Down the left side of the page into the initial letter runs a sword; and the letter itself features two monks. Is this saying "take this moment seriously"? Or sending it up? It is impossible to be sure.

What then of the cupids that appear a number of times in these fanciful ornamentations (never in the naturalistic illustrations) when the adjoining text features the word "love"? Chapter 20, which opens "Mr Collins was not left long to the silent contemplation of his successful love," features a tumbling cupid, arrow fallen out of his hand; chapter 24, in which Darcy succeeds in getting Bingley away from Jane, is headed with a tug-of-war, cupids on Bingley's side; Mrs Gardiner's warning Elizabeth "not to fall in love" shows a young lady admonishing a pestering cupid; the penultimate chapter, when Elizabeth asks Darcy to "account for his having ever fallen in love with her" shows a Darcy with a cupid pulling at his coat-tails; the drawing for "The

CHAPTER XV.

R. COLLINS was not a sensible man, and the deficiency of nature had been but little assisted by education or society; the greatest part of his life having been spent under the guidance of an illiterate and miserly father; and though he belonged to one of the universities, he had merely kept the necessary terms without forming at it any useful acquaintance. The subjection in which his father had brought him up had given him originally great humility of manner; but it was now a good deal counteracted by the self-conceit of a weak head, living in retirement, and the consequential feelings of early and unexpected prosperity. A fortunate chance had recommended him to Lady Catherine de Bourgh when the living of Hunsford was vacant; and the respect which he felt for her high rank, and his veneration for her as his patroness, mingling with a very good opinion of himself, of his authority as a clergyman, and his right as a rector, made him altogether a mixture of pride and obsequiousness, self-importance and humility.

Figure 5.5 *Pride & Prejudice* (London: George Allen, 1895), headpiece and ornamental capital letter on p. 89, by Hugh Thomson. Dover Publications, Inc. (Image reproduced from modern facsimile edition.)

End" shows a cupid and a peacock happily entwined. Even these cupids, so unpalatable to modern taste, are not just silly: the presentation of the text is offering a consistent, if probably tongue-in-cheek, reading. *Pride and Prejudice* is after all – among other things – a love story.

In all of the fully illustrated texts of Jane Austen except the Groombridge *Mansfield Park*, captioning plays an important role in mediating between the verbal fiction and the parallel world drawn in the illustrations. Almost all of Thomson's are drawn directly from the novels, but they are fragments of Austen's longer sentences. This partitioning-up of the text is exactly mirrored by the way the images depict scenes. Austen's sentence "Lady Bertram, sunk back in one corner of the sofa, the picture of health, wealth, ease, and tranquillity, was just falling into a gentle doze, while Fanny was getting through the few difficulties of her work for her" is rendered down, in caption form, to "Just falling into a gentle doze." And that is exactly what the illustration depicts: the ample Lady Bertram snoozing alone on the sofa, seen from across a room in which seven people are sitting, some animatedly discussing how the young Bertrams should behave while their father is away in Antigua, and while Fanny works. The comedy of the novel is cognizant of, and exploits, the modal dissonance between the domestic scene and the complex social geography in which it is embedded. The passing amusement of the illustration isolates the figure from this matrix, perhaps distracting the reader from the scene's implications. Earlier in the novel Mary Crawford's scathing reference to her Uncle's cronies is lifted from its context in her conversation to form a jolly "circle of admirals" (Figure 5.6), having stimulated the illustrator/reader's fancy in a way ironically at odds with contemporary critics' imaginative excursions from the same patch of text.

The Victorians and Edwardians felt that Thomson had "revived the gently humorous Jane" and the volume sold very well – by 1907, 25,000 copies (Spielmann and Jerrold 1931: 101, 91). Charles E. Brock's illustrations to *Pride and Prejudice* for a rival edition were commissioned by Macmillan and published in the same year. Thomson's *Pride and Prejudice* was succeeded by his illustrated editions of the other novels for Macmillan in 1896–7. Brock and his brother Henry each in their way continued the Thomson tradition. Henry Brock's watercolors of 1898 for *Pride and Prejudice* imitate the elegant flatness of Japanese woodcuts while Charles's scrollwork-framed vignettes of 1907 are closer in style to rococo porcelain painting.

Charles Brock's illustrations to *Pride and Prejudice* in 1895 do not take possession of the book in the way that Thomson's do. If Thomson had decorative head-letters, Brock has decorative garlands, which like Thomson's ornaments, but perhaps more emphatically, enclose the illustrations and title pages within a fluttering, girly context. But there are no other ornaments, and only one of the illustrations is inset within the text: the other 39 are formalized as illustrations of incidents in the novel, with captions in print (not, as in Thomson's, in his own hand). Oddly, more than half of them are on the page following the moment they depict, so that the reader would be invited to check their reading against the artist's interpretation. Another difference is that whilst Thomson's choice of incidents to illustrate is often (literally) eccentric, Brock's

A circle of admirals.

Figure 5.6   Mansfield Park (London: Macmillan and Co., 1897), p.54, illustration by Hugh Thomson.

regularly key into the major events of the narrative – the two proposals, Elizabeth before Darcy's portrait, Lady Catherine's confrontation with the heroine.

    Nevertheless, Brock chooses, or was commissioned, to illustrate several of the same moments as Thomson. At first glance a reader would conflate the two illustrators' styles – the gentlemen in top hats, the pretty ladies in bonnets, the same Regency props. But first impressions are misleading. Brock often achieves a telling interaction between his characters, where Thomson's are often, in comparison, listless. In their illustrations of the proposal scene, for example, the disposition of the figures is the same: Thomson's Darcy, leaning forward, on the left, has his hands clasped in front of him; his Elizabeth sits primly indifferent, on the right, her hands on the letter. But Brock's Darcy has both arms extended towards Lizzie in a gesture of appeal or supplication; she, grasping the arm of her chair, starts back in amazement or indignation. There is simply more going on. When Elizabeth deserts the party, saying "You are charmingly grouped" (I, 10), she is seen turning away, lifting her skirts in her eagerness, whilst the others turn back in consternation or surprise. Darcy stands by the piano as Elizabeth starts to play at Rosings, and Brock catches an attitude of polite confrontation as she twists towards him, with one arm braced, the attitude mimicking her defiant words (Figure 5.7). And in general, Brock makes much more use of body language, his figures have more eye contact with one another, his style has a theatrical and often comic dynamism Thomson's lacks.

Writing in 1905, in the wake of Thomson's, Brock's and Hammond's illustrated editions, Henry James made some pertinent comments on the rise of Jane Austen's reputation since the years in which Lewes had commented on her neglect. Responsible for Austen's currency, he remarked, "is the body of publishers, editors, illustrators . . . who have found . . . Jane so infinitely to their material purpose, so amenable to pretty reproduction in what is called tasteful, and in what seemingly proves to be saleable, form" (Southam 1987: 230). James's response to the increasing readership won by the illustrated editions is an early sign of the sometimes uneasy relationship between the "popular" Jane Austen and the values that, for some, reside within the novels themselves. His view of the prettification of the novels became orthodoxy. "The publishers are bitterly opposed to any imaginative illustrations," R. W. Chapman wrote of his 1923 edition (quoted in Gilson 1997: 296), though the "objective illustrations" chosen for those volumes continue the illustrative tradition by modifying it. With their plates of contemporary costumes, carriages, and locations, their conspicuously beautiful presentation, they blend the keepsake tradition into scholarship. With the rise in awareness of Austen's subversive irony, the earlier illustrated volumes came to seem increasingly dated, saccharine, and irrelevant (although freshly redecorated gift book sets and editions continued to be published). A new snobbery appeared, akin to Emma's survey of Mrs Elton's appearance at the wedding, "as elegant as lace and pearls could make her." Even historical picture books, such as Marghanita Laski's *Jane Austen and her World* (1969) or Lord David Cecil's *A Portrait of Jane Austen* (1978) have no truck with them.

The 1890s thus signal a turning-point in the history of Jane Austen's cultural reputation. At this moment her novels are marketed as consumer products to a broader readership through the power of the visual image. Thomson and his school laid their hands on "Jane Austen" in a way that was only to be superseded and rivaled by Chapman's 1923 edition, which was similarly to have a lasting impact on the reception of the author. In 1995, one hundred years after Thomson's *Pride and Prejudice*, another visual version of Jane Austen's novel was to give her work another audience, and initiate a new era of illustrated Austenization.[2]

"*You mean to frighten me, Mr. Darcy.*"

Figure 5.7   Pride and Prejudice (London: Macmillan & Co., 1895), p.161, illustration by Charles E. Brock.

NOTES

1   David Gilson's chapter in *Jane Austen in Context* (2005: 121–59) reproduces several of these illustrations.

2   With its dual emphasis on the spectacular "televisuality" of the English landscape and the body of Mr Darcy (in the person of the actor Colin Firth), the 1995 BBC miniseries of *Pride and Prejudice* introduced significant new dimensions into the iconography associated with Jane Austen. See Sarah Cardwell, *Adaptation Revisited: Television and the Classic Novel* (2002).

FURTHER READING

Miller, J. Hillis (1992). *Illustration*. Cambridge, MA: Harvard University Press.

Hunnisett, Basil (1979). *Steel-Engraved Book Illustration in England*. London: Scolar Press.

Sutherland, Kathryn (2005). *Jane Austen's Textual Lives: from Aeschylus to Bollywood*. Oxford: Oxford University Press.

Part II
Reading the Texts

6
Young Jane Austen: Author

Juliet McMaster

"Where Edward in the name of wonder," demands Edward's father, "did you pick up this unmeaning Gibberish? You have been studying Novels I suspect" ("Love and Freindship," *MW*: 81). So the 14-year-old author, in her own piece of fiction, highlights her critical awareness of the genre that she was to make her own. "The following Novel," she writes further, in her dedication to "Catharine, or the Bower," "... I humbly flatter myself, possesses Merit beyond any already published, or any that will ever in future appear, except such as may proceed from the pen of Your Most Grateful Humble Servt. / The Author" (*MW*: 192). Here already is a young writer acutely and delightedly aware of her power with the pen, equally ready to flaunt it, and (to adapt her own praise of novels) to parody by her "contemptuous censure the very performances, to the number of which [she is herself] adding" (*NA*: 37). It is this teenager's intense consciousness of medium that informs her youthful *jeux d'esprit*, and requires us to consider her as already not just a writer, but an "Author."

How should we relate these juvenile works to the six famous novels of Austen's maturity? The adjectives applicable to Austen's juvenilia might include: irreverent, rollicking, spontaneous, hyperbolic, violent, indecent, indecorous, outrageous; the very opposite of the familiar descriptors of the canonized work of the mature Jane Austen: balanced, measured, understated, disciplined, decorous, nuanced. However did this mature novelist grow out of that rambunctious child? Some readers shrug their shoulders at this mystery, and elect to neglect the juvenilia and concentrate on the novels. I would argue, however, that if you don't know the juvenilia, you don't know Austen. All that control, all that restraint in the service of exactness and the *mot juste*, all the fine moral imagination that can trace the delicate intricacies of an evolving relationship and summon full understanding through "the best chosen language" (*NA*: 38), are the more remarkable and the more valuable for growing out of the uninhibited gusto of youthful creativity. To the attentive reader of the juvenilia, Jane Austen's beautifully conscious art is charged with the energy of her youthful exuberance, and the brilliant control and precision are informed by the vitality and free-rein prancing dynamism that have been harnessed and channeled into finely articulated narrative.

Listen, and you can often hear that zestful teenage voice in the work of the seasoned novelist. The "parties of ladies" in *Northanger Abbey*, with their "important . . . business, whether in quest of pastry, millinery, or even (as in the present case) of young men" (*NA*: 44) are recognizably only one step on from the Beautifull Cassandra, who guzzles six ices at the pastry-cook's, and falls in love with a bonnet. When Elizabeth Bennet, after reading Darcy's letter, reproaches herself with being "blind, partial, prejudiced, absurd" (*PP*: 208), surely Austen is remembering her own cheerful claim in "The History of England . . . By a partial, prejudiced, and ignorant historian" (*MW*: 139). The child Catherine Morland at 10, who "loved nothing so well in the world as rolling down the green slope at the back of the house" (*NA*: 14), is kin to the exuberant child author, who rejoices in vigorous and dizzying motion: Laura of "Love and Freindship" rattles along in a coach between Edinburgh and Stirling; the sisters in "A Tour through Wales" hop in satin slippers alongside their galloping mother (*MW*: 176). I hear the zest and delight in enjoyment of the young author, too, in the joyful moments in the novels: in Elizabeth's "I am happier even than Jane; she only smiles, I laugh" (*PP*: 383); and in Anne's and Wentworth's "smiles reined in and spirits dancing in private rapture" (*P*: 240). The difference is that in the juvenilia the smiles are *not* reined in, but given vent in gusts of belly laughs.

Austen wrote the extant juvenilia, as her editors B. C. Southam and Peter Sabor have shown, between 1787 and 1793, at ages 11 to 17. Each was dedicated to a family member or friend, and presumably came in its own individual hand-made volume produced at the time of writing. But these first fine careless raptures being dispersed and lost, our source is the three manuscript volumes, *Volume the First* (now in the Bodleian Library in Oxford), *Volume the Second*, and *Volume the Third* (in the British Library's manuscript collection). Here the young Austen transcribed her fair copies, in a clear legible hand, often some years after the original composition. In this we can already glimpse the young professional at work. *She* knew the value of her early productions, and wanted them preserved. But for many years the Austen family kept them under wraps, reluctant to expose the juvenile *jeux d'esprit* to a Victorian readership that was inclined to canonize "their 'dear,' our dear, everybody's dear, Jane" (in Henry James's phrase).

In 1871, in the second edition of his *Memoir* of Jane Austen, James Edward Austen-Leigh hesitatingly included the playlet "The Mystery," probably chosen for its brevity, as an example of her "juvenile effusions": but he added, "The family have, rightly I think, declined to let these early works be published" (pp. 42, 46). It was not until the twentieth century that the juvenilia, incrementally and in clusters, reached the public. "Love and Freindship" and other works in *Volume the Second* were launched in 1922 by the clarion voice of G. K. Chesterton, who memorably announced that young Austen possessed "the inspiration of Gargantua and of Pickwick; it was the gigantic inspiration of laughter" (Chesterton 1922: xv), thus anchoring her early work in a great comic tradition. Fortunately Austen's juvenilia are now published in many editions, and are attracting some of the same searching and attentive study and commentary that the novels have long enjoyed.

The letters of dedication to each piece bear study in themselves, and I have argued elsewhere that they ought to be included in editions of Austen's letters (McMaster 2006). Here the author speaks *in propria persona* – as author. Of course she is burlesquing the often grandiloquent, often servile letters of dedication to eighteenth-century patrons. But she engagingly brings the business home: "My dear Martha," she begins "Frederic and Elfrida," "As a small testimony of the gratitude I feel for your late generosity to me in finishing my muslin Cloak, I beg leave to offer you this little production of your sincere Freind / The Author" (*MW*: 3). Here she feminizes and domesticates the official letter of dedication, which so often began, "My lord . . ." Or she may take off the solemn tone of the conduct book, as in writing to her little niece Anna, hoping she will derive from these "Miscellanious Morsels . . . very important Instructions, with regard to your Conduct in Life" (*MW*: 71). (Anna was seven weeks old at the time!)

Running through all her juvenilia is the young author's delight in her medium, her fascination with each genre and its conventions. How does a given genre *work*, she asks herself. What are its divisions and trajectory, its expected content and themes? A novel, now. It comes in chapters. Here we go, then: "The Beautifull Cassandra. A Novel in Twelve Chapters." And 12 chapters there are indeed, even though the whole work, chapter divisions and all, occupies only three pages of print. A play? Ah, it comes in acts and scenes. "The Visit: A Comedy in 2 Acts," complete with dedication, *Dramatis Personae*, "Act the First, Scene the first, a Parlour" (*MW*: 50). And yes, *characters* who have their exits and their entrances, their assigned speeches, their stage directions. An epistolary novel? Here we go. "Love and Freindship: a novel in a series of letters . . . Letter the First. From Isabel to Laura" (*MW*: 76). The orderliness that was to be part of the content of Austen's novels – the carefully incremental progress of each relationship, for instance – is here applied to the divisions and physical layout of the different genres she undertakes.

The parodic element that looms so large in the juvenilia is of course part of this intense consciousness of medium. Parody, we know, doesn't imply contempt. Austen is like her own Henry Tilney, who can parody Ann Radcliffe and still assert, "The person . . . who has not pleasure in a good novel, must be intolerably stupid. I have read all Mrs. Radcliffe's works, and most of them with great pleasure" (*NA*: 106). She and her family, she announced stoutly in a letter of December 18, 1798, "are great Novel-readers & not ashamed of being so" (*Letters*: 26). To parody a genre or a given work, you must know it very well, and observe its conventions very closely.

To examine "Love and Freindship" in relation to *Laura and Augustus* of 1784, the novel it chiefly parodies (which was probably by Eliza Nugent Bromley), is to recognize that young Austen, like Tilney, was a close and observant reader as well as a mocking one. Both works are subtitled "in a series of letters"; both have a heroine called Laura and a hero called Augustus; both feature (at least in the eyes of the protagonists) grossly tyrannical fathers and nobly resistant children; both have heroines who faint often and run mad at the climax. The difference is that *Laura and Augustus* is a three-volume tearjerker, "Love and Freindship" a hilarious burlesque of some 35 pages.

Austen's strategy in harvesting laughter from tragedy places hers among the best parodies in the language. I surmise that had it been published at the time, say by the young Byron of "English Bards and Scotch Reviewers" (1809), as it might well have been, it would have gathered an admiring readership and become firmly established in the canon.

Austen's technique in parodying a long and tragic novel is to double the heroines and distresses, and telescope the action. She provides the sensitive Laura with a bosom friend, Sophia, so that she can make the action risible by allowing her heroines to present it as a *pas de deux* – as in the famous case of their fainting "alternately on a sofa" (*MW*: 86). *Laura and Augustus* shows women of sensibility as the victims of a mercenary code enforced by tyrannical fathers. In "Love and Freindship" it is the heroines of sensibility who enforce a code, and it is every bit as exacting as the patriarchal one. A large section of the population, according to this code, has "no soul" (*MW*: 93), and may therefore be dismissed as "that Inferior order of Beings" (*MW*: 84). The category includes: anyone who has a steady income, or who thinks food and drink more nourishing than the "pleasing Pangs of Love" (*MW*: 83), or who does not admire *The Sorrows of Werther*, or who is named Bridget or Richard, or who is not above the middle size, or whose hair is not auburn. On the other hand, those who are like the heroines in the possession of "exalted Ideas, Delicate Feelings [and] refined Sensibilities" (*MW*: 100), belong to the body of the Elect, and have every right to plunder the sordid wretches who have money – money that may be "gracefully purloined" (*MW*: 88) or "majestically removed" (*MW*: 96) without any moral qualms.

Austen likewise reverses other expectations of the sentimental novel. *Her* heroines actually rejoice in their "distresses," and make the most of them. In *Laura and Augustus* we hear of harrowing griefs: "We lay eight days bereft of our senses," relates one narrator (1784, vol. I: 47); and on Augustus's death "for six hours [Laura] was in successive fits" (vol. II: 135). One can't but wonder at the specificity of this record of hours spent in unconsciousness; and Austen pounces on these statistics with considerable glee, suggesting an athletic competitiveness in her heroine. After witnessing her husband's fatal accident, Laura carefully records her spasms of unconsciousness: "I screamed and instantly ran mad . . . For an Hour and a Quarter did we continue in this unfortunate Situation – Sophia fainting every moment & I running mad as often" (*MW*: 99). In the eighteenth-century novel the almost clinical chronicling of sighs, tears, fainting and insanity, the physical manifestations of passion, often became the means of conveying the passion itself. Such novels of sensibility as *Laura and Augustus* could take the fashion too far, and so provide golden opportunity for Austen's parodic pen.

The epistolary convention also comes in for Austen's satire. Its great virtue was its immediacy – what Samuel Richardson called "writing to the moment." But in "Love and Freindship" Austen throws this advantage to the winds. Far from writing "to the moment," *her* Laura chronicles the events of her youth more than three *decades* after the event; she delivers her narrative in letters, yes, but it is simply chopped into arbitrary chunks, letter by letter. This is one way of poking fun at a convention that had become too fashionable.

In several other epistolary works, she develops her mastery through mockery. "Amelia Webster," which occupies hardly two pages in Chapman's edition, nevertheless accomplishes the courtship and marriages of three different couples. Parody is again to the fore. In Frances Brooke's long epistolary novel *Emily Montague*, the correspondents frequently end their long letters with the formula, "I have a thousand things to tell you, but . . ." – and then they sign off. It is the trope of *occupatio*, which takes time to say you haven't time; and Austen picks up on its absurdity. Here is the whole of one letter in "Amelia Webster": "Dear Maud / Believe me I'm happy to hear of your Brother's arrival. I have a thousand things to tell you, but my paper will only permit me to add that I am yr affect. Friend / Amelia Webster" (*MW*: 48). Amelia's "paper" must have been unusually minuscule. Similarly, Austen laughs at a convention that is so constantly concerned with the *process* of communication that communication itself languishes. Another correspondent in "Amelia Webster" seeks out as a mailbox "a very convenient old hollow oak . . . about a mile from my House & seven from yours" (*MW*: 48). One imagines the delicate Sally collapsing on the way to collect her mail. Young Austen's acute consciousness of medium provides her with an extra dimension for her humor.

A virtue of epistolary narration that she made full use of was the letter's potential for self-articulation, and the opportunity it provides for developing character and consciousness though voice. In "The Three Sisters" we find Mary Stanhope debating whether or not to accept the proposal of the odious Mr Watts, and in the process presenting the stalemate between her revulsion and her greed: "He has a large fortune & will make great Settlements on me; but then he is very healthy . . . I wont have him I declare. He said he should come again tomorrow & take my final answer, so I believe I must get him while I can" (*MW*: 58). Mary Stanhope is all before us, with her vanity and envy and acquisitiveness, and her inability to sort out the pros and cons of the decision before her.

The letters of "The Three Sisters" are sent to various off-stage correspondents who do not reply; but in "Lesley Castle" Austen has learned to take advantage of the potential for an *exchange* of letters within a community, and her sharply differentiated characters interact fully, and define themselves by their responses to one another. The stately Lesley sisters resent the intrusion of a new stepmother into their ancestral castle, and consider her, "in comparison with the elegant height of Matilda and Myself, an insignificant Dwarf" (*MW*: 123). Lady Lesley, on the other hand, writing to the same correspondent, denounces her new stepdaughters as "two great, tall, out of the way, over-grown, girls . . . Scotch giants" (*MW*: 124). Charlotte Lutterell, as the recipient of both these accounts, is "greatly entertained," and recognizes "you are both downright jealous of each others Beauty" (*MW*: 128).

The focus on the physical is typical of the juvenilia, where bodies loom large, desire is unfettered, and the decorum that pertains in the novels is mainly there to be shattered. Intimacy among the families in "Frederic and Elfrida," we hear, "grew to such a pitch, that they did not scruple to kick one another out of the window" (*MW*: 6). Lucy in "Jack and Alice" has her leg broken by "one of the steel traps so common in gentlemen's grounds," and screams "till the woods resounded again" (*MW*: 22). Eliza of "Henry and Eliza," after escaping with her infants from prison, "began to find herself rather hungry, & had reason to think, by their biting off two of her fingers, that her Children were in much the same situation" (*MW*: 37). Laura and Sophia's husbands, flung from their Phaeton, die "weltering in their blood" (*MW*: 99). There is more bodily violence in "Jack and Alice" alone than in all the six novels, where Louisa's fall from the Cobb is about as violent as it gets. But as in slapstick or in cartoon sequences, the physical collisions and disasters are comic, and one's sympathies are hardly harrowed. The characters take them in stride, and we do too.

The spirited little parody of the epistolary mode, "Amelia Webster," seems to have prompted Austen to further exploration of voice, and led to drama itself. The two minidramas "The Visit" and "The Mystery" immediately follow. And here and in the later "First Act of a Comedy" Austen is again audibly rejoicing in sending up a medium and its conventions. In "The Visit" the decorum of a formal dinner party is exploded as the guests arrive to take their places: "Bless me!" exclaims the hostess, "there ought to be 8 Chairs & there are but 6. However, if your Ladyship will but take Sir Arthur in your lap, & Sophy my Brother in hers, I beleive we shall do pretty well" (*MW*: 52). The conglomeration of bodies leads on to a dinner of "fried Cowheel & Onion," red herrings, and tripe. How unlike the decorum of our own dear Jane!

Alongside the dramas and the epistolary fictions, and from the first, Austen was also confident in taking the narrative into her own hands. She was already developing her own narrative voice, and often doing so by negative means, defining her own purposes through burlesquing those of previous writers. The earliest narratives (assuming that they were copied into *Volume the First* in approximately the same order in which she first composed them), "Frederic and Elfrida," "Henry and Eliza," and "The Beautifull Cassandra," are all third-person narratives. And in "The History of England" from *Volume the Second*, the young author is almost tyrannically authoritative. This time the audible authority is not confined to the letter of dedication. The teenage Austen takes on the dictatorial tone of the historian laying down the law, like her predecessors and butts Goldsmith, Hume, and "the nine-hundredth abridger of the History of England" (*NA*: 37; Fergus 1995: i), but without any pretensions to omniscience. Her admission that she is "a partial, prejudiced, & ignorant Historian" (*MW*: 139) certainly signals no crack in her authority, for this narrator assumes all the arbitrary power of the monarchs she chronicles. So of Henry VI she writes, "I suppose you know about the Wars between him & The Duke of York who was of the right side; if you do not, you had better read some other History, for I shall not be very diffuse in this" (*MW*: 140). The dignity of the formal historian is reduced to the capricious antics of a narrator like Tristram Shandy, who at the end of his first volume boasts to his reader "If I thought you was able to form the least judgment or probable conjecture to yourself, of what was to come in the next page, – I would tear it out of my book." Here, more than in the other third-person narratives, she is developing in exaggerated form the personal voice, arch and ironic, and the easy relation with her reader, that is so salient a feature of the finished novels. We are on the way to such friendly intimacies as "my readers . . . will see in the tell-tale compression of the pages before them, that we are all hastening together to perfect felicity" (*NA*: 250).

A recurring joke, especially in the third-person narratives, is the "life and adventures" interlude. Austen had read enough eighteenth-century novels to know that "interludes," or interpolated tales, were almost obligatory. So it is part of her parody of the genre that her characters call for these narratives at the most inopportune moments. Edward in "Love and Freindship," weltering in his blood, expires in the act of responding to his wife's demand that he tell her all that has befallen him (*MW*: 100). When Alice and Lady Williams find "a lovely young Woman lying apparently in great pain beneath a Citron-tree," their first request is "Will you favour us with your Life & adventures?" "Willingly, ladies," she obligingly responds, "if you will be so kind as to be seated." And "They took their places & she thus began" (*MW*: 20). So a little outdoor theatre is improvised, and the lady with the broken leg performs with aplomb, apparently unhampered by her injury, but helpfully winding up her narrative by accounting for it. The addicted young novelist cheerfully depicts the addiction to narrative in her characters too.

It is in "Catharine, or the Bower" that we find a work on the very threshold of becoming a full-fledged Austen novel, while at the same time, in the person of the heroine's flighty friend Camilla, still including the insanely self-interested characters of the juvenilia, who "inhabit a world of child-like ego, of greed without boundaries," as Margaret Doody characterizes them (Doody 2005: 112). In Catharine, for almost the first time in the juvenilia, we find a character with a developed subjectivity, a degree of self-awareness and self-judgment that sets her apart from the unreflecting takers and boasters of most of the juvenilia. The opening sentence sets a tone, of looking before and after, of an awakened awareness of the influence of circumstance, that sounds like the openings of *Sense and Sensibility* or *Mansfield Park*, in which the first sentence leads us far into the story and its dependence on social context.

> Catharine had the misfortune, as many heroines have had before her, of losing her Parents when she was very young, and of being brought up under the care of a Maiden Aunt, who while she tenderly loved her, watched over her conduct with so scrutinizing a severity, as to make it very doubtful to many people, and to Catharine amongst the rest, whether she loved her or not. (*MW*: 192)

This narrator, though still self-consciously occupied with genre (the nod to "many heroines" before hers), is also awake to the power of circumstance as a factor in character. Catharine is the way she is partly because of surrounding circumstances; and unlike the glorious guzzlers of the earlier juvenilia, she is morally aware. She lectures herself about the vanity of believing the handsome Edward is attracted to her (*MW*: 245). Nevertheless, on no better evidence than Camilla's passing assertion, she is swiftly convinced he is head over heels in love: "'Charming Young Man! How much must you have suffered . . .' Satisfied, beyond the power of Change, of this, She went in high spirits to her Aunt's apartment, without giving a Moment's recollection on the vanity of Young Women" (*MW*: 239). In that delightfully ironic "Satisfied, beyond the power of Change" we hear the voice of the Jane Austen that we know from the six novels, just as in Catharine's self-examination, however inaccurate, we recognize a potential protagonist of them.

In exploring the process by which young Austen finds and develops her own authorial voice in the juvenilia through her exuberantly developed consciousness of medium, I don't want to neglect her brilliance in inventing the voices of her characters, in their spoken as in their written language. These grossly greedy, narcissistic, self-aggrandizing personnel define themselves on the page largely by what they *say*: and from the first Austen was a master of dialogue. She rejoiced in individual speech habits, and she was inventive in concocting means of delivery as well as the style and content of speech. The dialogue is not limited to the dramas and third-person narratives, for the many letter writers also present developed scenes complete with oral exchanges.

In the early "Frederic and Elfrida" the circumstances of delivery are perhaps the best part of the joke. On a formal visit to a family newly arrived, Elfrida, Frederic, and a friend "with one accord jumped up and exclaimed":

> "Lovely & too charming Fair one, notwithstanding your forbidding Squint, your greasy tresses & your swelling Back, . . . I cannot refrain from expressing my raptures, at the engaging Qualities of your Mind, which so amply atone for the Horror, with which your first appearance must ever inspire the unwary visitor." (*MW*: 6)

The situation of the three visitors leaping to their feet during a formal visit and delivering, unrehearsed, such a speech, *in chorus*, is sufficiently absurd. But the formality of the diction, with its sycophantic apostrophe followed by outrageous insult elaborately couched as praise, adds to the joke. This degree of linguistic and dramatic inventiveness shows a verbal acrobat at work.

"Jack and Alice" provides an example of a technique in handling dialogue that we will see developed in the later novels: the privileging of the ridiculous over the merely sensible. Remember Lady Catherine and Darcy, as they discuss music: "'If I had ever learnt,' announces Lady Catherine, 'I should have been a great proficient . . . How does Georgiana get on, Darcy?' Mr. Darcy spoke with affectionate praise of his sister's proficiency" (*PP*: 173). Scintillating as *Pride and Prejudice* is intended to be, it is often the highly colored absurd characters, like Collins and Lady Catherine, whose speech is reported verbatim and at length; but for Darcy's ordinary comments summary will do. Similarly, in "Jack and Alice": the stunningly handsome Charles announces himself in a wonderful speech. In another reversal of the usual practice, Mr Johnson, father of the lovesick Alice, has come to invite Charles Adams to become his son-in-law. The young man responds:

> Sir, I may perhaps be expected to appeared [*sic*] pleased at & gratefull for the offer you have made me: but let me tell you that I consider it as an affront. I look upon myself to be Sir a perfect Beauty . . . My temper is even, my virtues innumerable, my self unparalelled. Since such Sir is my character, what do you mean by wishing me to marry your Daughter? Let me give you a short sketch of yourself & of her. I look upon you Sir to be a very good sort of Man in the main: a drunken old Dog to be sure, but that's nothing to me. Your daughter sir, is neither sufficiently beautifull, sufficiently amiable, sufficiently witty, nor sufficiently rich for me – . I expect nothing more in my wife than my wife will find in me – Perfection. (*MW*: 25–6)

What a monologue! And consider the analytical skills of the teenager who writes it, capturing the conventions of her day in order to send them up with such cheerfully devastating parody. Adams's opening observes the expected courtesies about social expectation: he knows he is "expected to appear pleased" at the proposal; and we meet again that concession about what is expected as opposed to what is actually delivered in Elizabeth's response to another proposal: "In such cases as this, it is, I believe, the established custom to express a sense of obligation for the sentiments avowed. . . . But I cannot" (*PP*: 190). It's the kind of intimation of things to come that we often come across in the juvenilia. We're familiar with the convention of the perfect heroine; here it is the male who has the "bewitching" qualities. Moreover, all those perfections of mind and body, though announced in the routine conventional terms, are totally negated when proclaimed by the perfect hero himself.

Austen's subtle use of register allows us to recognize this as literary prose of a high order. Charles Adams's vocabulary and syntax when he talks of himself are lifted from the conventional repertoire of novels. They abound with abstract nouns: perfect beauty, manners, address, elegance, peculiar sweetness, virtues innumerable, and so forth. But suddenly, in the middle of his speech, we are bumped down several notches in tonal register, to the colloquial and abusive. "Since such Sir is my character [and here comes the change] what do you mean by wishing me to marry your Daughter?" This is no longer novelese, but ordinary rough street speech. Mr Johnson is "a very good sort of Man in the main; a drunken old Dog to be sure, but that's nothing to me" (*MW*: 25). You wouldn't catch Charles Adams using a contraction like "that's" when he discourses on his own virtues.

What is Mr Johnson's response to this outrageous diatribe? "Mr Johnson was satisfied; & . . . took his leave" (*MW*: 26). His response is in reported speech, not verbatim direct speech like Charles Adams's. As with the exchange between Lady Catherine and Darcy, Austen knows when to leave well enough alone. In dialogue, as in her self-conscious play with narrative and dramatic modes, she is wildly overstated when it suits her, economic where it counts. The very brevity of many of the early works provides a concentration that is a salient part of their impact.

Jane Austen famously considered *Pride and Prejudice* "*too* light and bright and sparkling" (my italics; letter of February 4, 1813; *Letters*: 203). The lost earlier version, "First Impressions," seems to have been just as compulsively readable, for her friend Martha Lloyd had read it so often that Austen humorously suspected her of plotting "to publish it from Memory" (letter of June 11, 1799; *Letters*: 44). Earlier still, the young author felt no need to hide her sparkle under a bushel: and the juvenilia come with their own brilliant flashes of wicked wit – vividly illuminated through narrative, epistle, drama, and dialogue with their young author's gleeful delight in her medium.

Further Reading

Chesterton, G. K. (1922). Preface, Jane Austen, *Love and Freindship*. New York: Frederick Stokes.

Doody, Margaret Anne (2005). Jane Austen, that disconcerting "Child." In Christine Alexander and Juliet McMaster (Eds). *The Child Writer from Austen to Woolf* (pp. 101–21). Cambridge, UK: Cambridge University Press.

Fergus, Jan (Ed.) (1995). Introduction. Jane Austen, *The History of England*. Edmonton, AB: Juvenilia Press.

McMaster, Juliet (2006). Your sincere freind, the author. *Persuasions On-Line*, 27: 1. <http://www.jasna.org/persuasions/on-line/vol27no1/mcmaster.htm>.

Sabor, Peter (2006). Introduction. *Juvenilia*. The Cambridge Edition of Jane Austen: Cambridge, UK: Cambridge University Press.

7

Moving In and Out: The Property of Self in *Sense and Sensibility*

Susan C. Greenfield

Many readers have noticed that Elinor and Marianne Dashwood are as similar as they are different. Elinor sensibly interiorizes the sensibility that Marianne puts on display – and each sister prides herself on her particular distinction. But, as Tony Tanner put it long ago, "The fact that Marianne has plenty of sense and Elinor is by no means devoid of sensibility should alone convince us . . . that nothing comes unmixed" (Tanner 1969: 357). Feminist interpretations have since emphasized the sisters' painfully similar gendered constraints. At the novel's opening, both are disinherited and displaced from their beloved home at Norland, after which both fall in love with men who encourage and then effectively jilt them. Even Marianne recognizes a larger pattern when she snidely tells Elinor: "our situations . . . are alike. We have neither of us any thing to tell; you because you communicate, and I, because I conceal nothing" (*SS*: 170). At the novel's end, she repeats the point with more sincerity: "[Our situations] have borne more [resemblance] than our conduct" (*SS*: 345). Indeed, whether kept inside or let out, Elinor and Marianne Dashwood's suffering is much the same.

Sense and Sensibility was first published in 1811, but Austen began it many years before, perhaps first as an epistolary novel in 1795, and then as a third-person narrative in 1797; she may have revised the text around 1800, and "certainly [did so] between 1805 and 1810" (Johnson 2003: x). Though some early criticism is punctuated with negative references to the book's extended origins (A. Walton Litz calls *Sense and Sensibility* "a youthful work patched up at a later date," Litz 1965: 73), recent scholarship often – and rightly – stresses its historical range and complexity. In this spirit, I will argue that the novel's doubling heroines and plots represent a sustained critique of the ideology of individualism. The ideology, which privileges each person's "single distinguishable . . . existence over and above his place . . . in a rigid hierarchical society" (Williams 1983: 162–3), is commonly considered a hallmark of modernity. In 1957 Ian Watt made individualism central to the history of the "rise of the novel" by describing the genre as the "form of literature which most fully reflects" its values (Watt 1957: 13). Despite endless debates about the theory's validity, the problem of individualism continues to dominate novel studies. It is especially relevant for Austen, who is routinely credited with (or castigated for) being the first novelist to present the individual as a "fully consolidated and naturalized entity" (Armstrong 2005: 18).

But Austen's first published novel does not affirm what Watt calls the genre's "individualist . . . reorientation" (Watt 1957: 13) so much as test its limitations (Armstrong 2005: 16). For, if it exists at all in *Sense and Sensibility*, individualism is rarely available to those without property and thus rarely available to either Dashwood heroine. More specifically, the novel shows that a "central difficulty" with individualism inheres, as C. B. Macpherson puts it, in "its possessive quality" (Macpherson 1962: 3). Theoretically, individualism promises the right to self-possession; it promises that each individual has what John Locke (1963) in the *Second Treatise of Government* famously calls a *"Property* in his own *Person"* (§27). In fact, Macpherson notes, "the man without property in things loses that full proprietorship of his own person" (Macpherson 1962: 231). As Austen clearly recognizes, the situation is often worse for women. By doubling her heroines "without property in things," Austen emphasizes the gendered and economic exclusivity of self-possession. Both Elinor and Marianne Dashwood believe they have full property in their own persons. But such belief proves little more than a compensatory fantasy, for the sisters are as trespassed upon and commandeered as the homes they never own. The consequences are symbolically sexual, resulting for Elinor in a form of masochism and for Marianne in a metaphorical pregnancy and nearly fatal illness.

To begin clarifying, let me return to resemblance, which, though routinely countered by difference (like that between Elinor and Marianne), poses the greater challenge in the novel. Like fun house mirrors, *Sense and Sensibility* features three pairs of sisters – Elinor and Marianne, Nancy and Lucy Steele, and Lady Middleton and Mrs Palmer; three brothers who disinherit their siblings – Mr John Dashwood, Colonel Brandon's older brother, and Robert Ferrars (the last two steal their brothers' fiancées); two women who disinherit men – Mrs Smith and Mrs Ferrars; two insufferably indulgent young mothers – Mrs John Dashwood (Elinor and Marianne's sister-in-law) and Lady Middleton; and two flawed but sympathetic older mothers – Mrs Dashwood (Elinor and Marianne's mother) and Mrs Jennings, who becomes Mrs Dashwood's surrogate. There are countless specific references to resemblance as well, some of them comical: Sir John and Lady Middleton "strongly resembl[e] each other in [their] total want of talent and taste" (*SS*: 32), and Mrs Jennings is sure her grandson bears "the most striking resemblance" to "every one of his relations on both sides" (*SS*: 248).

Other resemblances are troublesome, especially those involving Marianne. Though she and Elinor are similar in many ways, only Marianne's openly excessive sensibility bears a "strikingly great" resemblance to their mother's (*SS*: 6). According to Colonel Brandon, Marianne also "greatly resemble[s]" the long dead woman he loved (*SS*: 57). Her name was Eliza, and she had an illegitimate child also named Eliza, whose own illegitimate child is fathered by Willoughby, who deserts her and then deserts

Marianne. Ironically, Marianne's unwanted resemblance to Eliza results from her deluded belief that she and Willoughby resemble each other positively. Marianne tells her mother she could never be "happy with a man whose taste did not in every point coincide with my own" (*SS*: 17), and she falls prey to Willoughby when too easily convinced that he meets these standards. After Willoughby becomes engaged to Miss Grey, Marianne continues to insist on their mutual love and expectations: "He *did* feel the same . . . for weeks and weeks he felt it. I know he did" (*SS*: 188). But had Willoughby's feelings actually resembled Marianne's, he would not have substituted her with a richer woman.

Indeed, part of the danger of resemblance is that it fosters such substitutions, making it possible for seemingly similar people to be exchanged. Willoughby knows that Marianne, the second Eliza, and Miss Grey differ in personality and desert, but their differences matter less than their resemblance as adoring women he can exploit. Colonel Brandon's hope to substitute Marianne for the late Eliza is more romantic but equally reductive. Worse still, when Marianne gets ill and nearly dies, Mrs Jennings and Mr John Dashwood expect Brandon simply to put Elinor in her sister's place (*SS*: 216, 227–8). After Marianne recovers, even Mrs Dashwood tells her eldest daughter how "desirable" it would be if Brandon married either "one of you" (*SS*: 336). At the novel's conclusion, Mrs Ferrars and Lucy Steele are comically abhorrent when, in different ways, each lets Robert Ferrars "entirely supplan[t] his brother" (*SS*: 376). But the situation merely exaggerates what could also happen to Elinor or Marianne. After all, this is a world in which "people may be substituted for one another . . . sons and lovers [are] interchangeable . . . and individuals seem neither integral nor unique" (Brownstein 1997: 47–8).

Given such a context, Marianne's sentimental "maxim, that no one can ever be in love more than once in their life" (*SS*: 93), becomes a sophisticated defense of individuality. When she is sure Edward will marry Lucy, Elinor tells her sister (and tries to convince herself) that after all "that can be said of one's happiness depending entirely on any particular person, it is not meant – it is not fit – it is not possible that it should be so." Marianne responds by denouncing the idea that "the loss of what is most valued is so easily to be made up by something else." It is the ready substitution of one "particular person" for another that appalls Marianne, and she grossly underestimates her sister in blaming her for the "resolution" and "self-command" that apparently enable her to accept this (*SS*: 263).

Invariably, the characters at greatest risk of such substitution are those whose lack of property limits their claims to individuality. *Sense and Sensibility* opens like all of Austen's major novels, with the exception of *Emma*, with the loss or threatened loss of home. Like Catherine Morland, Fanny Price, and Anne Elliot, the Dashwood sisters begin their story by leaving home, and like the Bennet sisters, they are disinherited by primogeniture. In displacing the Dashwood women from Norland, Mr and Mrs John Dashwood and their son also literally replace them. (Mr John Dashwood also dispossesses his neighbors by enclosing Norland Common and buying the adjoining farm, *SS*: 225.) Some women similarly victimize men, for Willoughby is "dismissed from [his aunt's] . . . house" when he refuses to marry as she directs (SS: 323), and Edward is "dismissed" from his mother's house when he does virtually the same thing (SS: 268).

But only the Dashwood women must rent a cramped – and significantly symmetrical (SS: 28) – cottage from their male cousin. Sir John Middleton is jovial, generous, and a vast improvement over Mr John Dashwood, but he is nevertheless their landlord and fond of enforcing his ownership. He routinely pops into the cottage without warning, and so often demands Elinor and Marianne's presence at his parties that the latter declares their "rent" is had "on very hard terms" (SS: 109). Willoughby and Mrs Palmer describe Barton Cottage as utopian and unique. Ironically, though, both also imagine having a cottage just like it for themselves (SS: 72, 107). (The loathsome Robert Ferrars also wants his own cottage, SS: 251.) Significantly, the sisters themselves spend relatively little time in the cottage. They move into it in early September, but, four months later, in early January, they leave for London with Mrs Jennings. Though they return again in late April, Elinor marries and moves to the Delaford Parsonage by early autumn; Marianne marries and moves out a year later (Moody 1999: 314, 320, 329, 332). Indeed, it is symptomatic of their lack of property that, over the course of the novel, the sisters change residences at least six times; they move to Norland, move to Barton, visit London, visit Cleveland, return to Barton, and then move to Delaford.

Each sister copes with her lack of personal property by imagining she has a Lockean property in her person. Each believes in her individuality, often, though not exclusively, figured as a particular quality of mind she herself has cultivated. In *An Essay Concerning Human Understanding*, Locke famously portrayed the mind as an empty space to be furnished; more than two centuries later, in 1929, Virginia Woolf described woman's enduring need for a literal and mental "room of her own," in *A Room of One's Own*. Treated like circulating objects, moved in and out of rooms by those who own them (including Mr John Dashwood, Sir John Middleton, and even Mrs Jennings), each sister needs to imagine her interior self as a kind of home.

This is especially clear with Elinor, the more inward and domestic sister. As the only character whose perspective is regularly rendered in free indirect discourse, Elinor seems to have the deepest and most protected thoughts – the ones only we can know. As a result, Elinor appears not to require actual privacy, for "Without shutting herself up from her family, or leaving the house in determined solitude to avoid them" she has "leisure enough to think." With "her mind . . . inevitably at liberty," Elinor has the illusion of mental space. This is crucial compensation, for instance, when Sir John Middleton sees Elinor in the window, skips the "ceremony of knocking . . . and oblig[es] her to open the casement to speak to him" (SS: 104–5). Sir John also has a habit of "collecting" young people, like objects, for display at his estate, a term later echoed by Robert Ferrars who looks forward to owning a cottage where he can always "collect a few friends" (SS: 32, 251). Elinor, in contrast, needs only "time enough to collect her thoughts" (SS: 260). Similarly, whereas women like Mrs Ferrars, Mrs

Smith, and Mrs Jennings get to be mistresses of their homes, Elinor's goal is to be "mistress of myself" (*SS*: 358). Her notorious reticence and reserve follow logically from such imagery. Domestic property is protected by doors, mental property by emotional concealment.

For all her claims to sensibility and its supposed inwardness, Marianne is the more external character – so much so that her perspective is rarely honored with free indirect discourse, as if there is no narrative need to probe the inner workings of her mind because she "conceal[s] nothing" (*SS*: 170). And yet, especially as the novel progresses and Marianne's sorrow deepens, she tries to create a sheltered and increasingly private space of self. Like her sister, Marianne is "able to collect her thoughts within herself" (*SS*: 221). On other occasions, she is "wrapt up in . . . her own thoughts" or "wrapt in her own meditations" (*SS*: 145, 160), as if blanketing the contours of her mind. There is also a telling scene much earlier, when, on the eve of the Dashwood women's departure from Norland, Marianne wanders "alone before the house" and offers a sentimental soliloquy:

> Oh! happy house, could you know what I suffer in now viewing you from this spot, from whence perhaps I may view you no more! – And you, ye well known trees! – but you will continue the same . . . you will continue the same; unconscious of the pleasure or the regret you occasion, and insensible of any change in those who walk under your shade! (*SS*: 27)

As she stands outside the "insensible" house, Marianne consoles herself with sensibility. She cannot possess the house, but she can possess a superior sense of suffering. She cannot claim the trees – which, by the way, may not "continue the same" since John Dashwood plans to cut some trees "down to make room" for a greenhouse (*SS*: 226) – but they are "unconscious" while she knows "pleasure" and "regret" (*SS*: 27). In the competition Marianne stages between the unfeeling property and her own feeling mind, the latter wins and moves on with her when she moves out.

The problem for both sisters is that economic and gender disadvantages limit their self-possession. For one thing, as Macpherson suggests, those without "property in things" lose "full proprietorship" of their own persons (Macpherson 1962: 231). For another, legally most women in Austen's period were the property of fathers or husbands. The Dashwood sisters are temporarily free of male owners, but they are, of course, destined to marry (and besides, only wealthy widows and maiden aunts like Mrs Ferrars, Mrs Jennings, and Mrs Smith have any self-sufficiency).

The sisters' status as property is perhaps best epitomized by their sexual vulnerability. Like countless novelists following Samuel Richardson, Austen figures each woman as a permeable space, vulnerable to male penetration and occupation. This is more obvious with Marianne whose relationship with Willoughby is unequivocally suggestive. Indeed, Austen hints at the possibility that Marianne and Willoughby may have had sex, even the possibility that Marianne – like the Elizas she so resembles – becomes pregnant. Such dangers reflect *Sense and Sensibility*'s late eighteenth-century origins, when the story of the fatally seduced and abandoned woman was wildly popular and highly conventionalized. Ultimately, Marianne is spared. At the novel's end, she seems certifiably virgin as she wonders where her own "most shamefully unguarded affection" might have led (*SS*: 345). Moreover, in marginalizing the ruined Elizas, Austen contrasts their clichéd finales with Marianne's narrow escape from the same, ever redoubling story. Nevertheless, a variety of other details suggest that Austen means for us to wonder about Marianne's erotic experience. She does so not to offer a "punishing . . . moral pedagogy" about the hazards of female sexuality, a reading Eve Kosofsky Sedgwick famously rejects in "Jane Austen and the Masturbating Girl" (Sedgwick 2003: 315). Rather, Austen evokes Marianne's possible sexual experience and obvious desire as the most trenchant examples of the failures of selfhood. Like Elinor, Marianne can possessively "collect" her own thoughts; she can imagine that her sensibility is worth more than a house she must vacate. But socially she remains an object of exchange, her value determined by whether and how a man claims her.

Willoughby's powers of ownership are evident from his introduction. In punning anticipation, Marianne falls while running in the rain and Willoughby takes "her up in his arms . . . and carrie[s] her down the hill. Then passing through the garden, the gate of which had been left open . . . he [bears] her directly into the house." Thus, their relationship begins with Willoughby's physical "intrusion" into Barton Cottage (*SS*: 42), which, within weeks "seemed to be considered and loved by him as his home" (*SS*: 71). When Mrs Dashwood speaks of improving the parlor, Willoughby reacts as if she were selling the room into prostitution: "And yet this house you would spoil, Mrs. Dashwood? . . . this dear parlour, in which our acquaintance first began . . . you would degrade to the condition of a common entrance, and every body would be eager to pass through" (*SS*: 73).

Willoughby seems perfectly familiar with common entrances and determined to keep Marianne's to himself. Exactly what he does there is ambiguous, but we know this much: in a scene that obviously echoes Alexander Pope's *The Rape of the Lock*, Willoughby takes up "Marianne's scissars [*sic*] and cut[s] off a long lock of her hair" (*SS*: 60). Because Marianne has little taste for Pope (*SS*: 47) and freely offers the hair that Pope's Belinda loses by force, she fails to see how the cut lock – like the unlocked gate through which Willoughby first bore her – marks her own vulnerability. The same chapter features a similarly charged literary reference when Willoughby tries to give Marianne his horse named Queen Mab. In *Romeo and Juliet*, Queen Mab is the "fairies' midwife," who, "when maids lie on their backs, / . . . presses them and learns them first to bear, / Making them women of good carriage" (1.4.54, 92–4), teaching women both to have sex and to carry their pregnancies well.

Significantly, in the very next chapter, at precisely the moment Brandon learns that the second Eliza is pregnant (with Willoughby's child), Willoughby whisks Marianne off in his carriage and the two of them drive "through the park very fast." They return much later, "delighted" and secretive until finally forced to admit that they spent the morning "going all over the house" at Allenham – the house that

Willoughby expects to inherit from his aunt and that Marianne thus presumes will be her "own" (*SS*: 67–9). We can only guess how far both erroneous presumptions influence Marianne's behavior. What is certain is that the evidence of their visit to Allenham House convinces many that they are officially engaged. After learning otherwise, Mrs Jennings is incredulous: "No positive engagement indeed! after taking her all over Allenham House, and fixing on the very rooms they were to live in hereafter!" (*SS*: 196). Marianne herself tells Elinor "I felt myself . . . to be as solemnly engaged to him, as if the strictest legal covenant had bound us to each other" (*SS*: 188).

Marianne learns of Willoughby's defection in January, when she and Elinor are staying in Mrs Jennings's London home. Shortly after, the papers announce that Charlotte Palmer "was safely delivered of a son and heir" (*SS*: 246). In April, the sisters, along with Mrs Jennings, Mr and Mrs Palmer, and the baby, go to the Palmer's estate at Cleveland. It is at Cleveland that Marianne becomes ill and, according to the apothecary, possibly infectious. And then something astonishing happens. Mrs Jennings urges Charlotte's "immediate removal with her infant," and, "within an hour," Charlotte and "her little boy" exit (*SS*: 307–8). At the novel's opening, Mrs John Dashwood arrives at Norland with the young male heir and forces the Dashwood women to move out, but in Cleveland, another mother and heir are pushed out of their house while the sisters (soon joined by their own mother) get to remain.

From a sexual perspective, the baby's departure suggests Marianne's literal and figurative escape from pregnancy. Having entered her home and her mind, Willoughby was well-positioned to complete his penetration. Instead, when Marianne gets ill and the baby is removed, her preoccupation with him is finally controlled. Thus, after recovering, she assures Elinor that her "remembrance" of Willoughby "shall be regulated" and "checked by religion, by reason, by constant employment" (*SS*: 347). Though critics have rightly emphasized the repressive and punitive force of such conversion, few have noted its simultaneous benefits. By reducing her thoughts about the man who arguably meant to possess and then discard her, Marianne may gain some proprietorship of mind. "My illness," she tells her sister, "has made me think – It has given me leisure and calmness for serious recollection. Long before I was enough recovered to talk, I was perfectly able to reflect" (*SS*: 345). Such *recollection* suggests that Marianne has moved beyond Willoughby's *collection* of disposable women. So too, her capacity for *reflection* indicates that instead of imagining that Willoughby's thoughts mirror her own, Marianne's mind will enjoy the power of "reflecting on its own operations"; for, as Locke puts it in *An Essay Concerning Human Understanding* (2.1.4), reflection is "that notice which the mind takes of its" self.

Ironically, by the novel's end, Elinor seems more trespassed upon than Marianne. There is no intimation of Elinor's specifically sexual vulnerability. But her mind is so "full of other people's feelings" (Lynch 1998: 238) – especially men's feelings – that she often bears the mental burden of *conception*. It is telling, for instance, that in the earlier scene where Sir John Middleton makes Elinor "open the casement to speak to him," he next ushers the (then still) pregnant Mrs Palmer into the cottage (*SS*: 105). The image prefigures Willoughby's intrusion at Cleveland when he "forc[es]" himself upon Elinor's "notice" (*SS*: 319) and shamelessly demands that she pity him for impregnating Eliza, deserting Marianne, and marrying a woman he despises. At Barton, when Marianne sprained her ankle, Willoughby carried her past the unlocked garden gate, "bore her directly into the house . . . and quitted not his hold till he had seated her in a chair" (*SS*: 42). At Cleveland, Elinor essentially takes her sister's place; she tries to leave the room, her hand "already on the lock," but Willoughby orders her to sit down and listen to his history (*SS*: 317). When he finishes and exits, Elinor famously feels for him against all reason. Rather than functioning like a private room, her "mind" is "oppressed by a croud [*sic*] of ideas," and it was "long, long before she could feel [Willoughby's] influence less" (*SS*: 333).

As this passage suggests, sensibility could itself be invasive. Adela Pinch has documented just how easily feelings move in eighteenth-century discourse, how "freely and fluidly" they spread irrespective of the "boundaries of individuals" (Pinch 1996: 1). David Hume, for one, describes "passions [as] so contagious, that they pass with the greatest facility from one person to another" (quoted in Pinch 1996: 1). Similarly, after losing Norland, Marianne and Mrs Dashwood "encourag[e] each other" in "affliction" (*SS*: 7). Elinor experiences "joint affliction" when Willoughby jilts her sister and she bursts into tears "scarcely less violent than Marianne's" (*SS*: 182). In scenes like these, sensibility is a symptom of women's resemblance to each other, another sign of their basic lack of individuality. But the problem only deepens when Elinor resembles Willoughby instead of Marianne and becomes so preoccupied with his suffering that she forgets "to think even of her sister" – or of the other women he damaged (*SS*: 333).

Her sympathy when Colonel Brandon describes the first Eliza is almost as disturbing. As Claudia Johnson notes, Brandon is disappointed that instead of dutifully dying upon being torn from him, Eliza first fell for other men (Johnson 1988: 66–7). Elinor is perfectly capable of recognizing irony when Lucy Steele demands pity for torturing her, and she easily satirizes Marianne's "passion for dead leaves" (*SS*: 88). But Brandon's self-serving sorrow about Eliza's poorly timed death leaves her only "full of compassion and esteem for him" (*SS*: 211). Later, when Marianne recovers and Brandon visits, Elinor "discover[s] in his melancholy eye . . . as he looked at her sister, the probable recurrence of many past scenes of misery to his mind, brought back by that resemblance between Marianne and Eliza" (*SS*: 340). Here, Elinor feels so obliged to make the "misery" in Brandon's "mind" her own that, despite Marianne's growing health, she sees her sister only as the substitute for his dead lover.

But nothing – neither her pity for Willoughby nor her identification with Brandon – compares with Elinor's masochistic compassion for Edward Ferrars. He is not charismatic or malicious enough to be a typical rake. Nevertheless, Edward courts Elinor's affection while engaged to another woman and leaves her as broken-hearted as Willoughby does Marianne. The novel's second volume opens with Elinor's reaction to the engagement, rendered in lengthy free indirect discourse. At first she is appropriately angry at "his ill-treatment of herself." But she quickly decides that he has "injured himself" more, and, after a "painful succession" of similar sympathies concludes by weeping "for him, more than for herself" (*SS*: 139–40). In choosing sensibility for Edward over indignation about his behavior, Elinor displaces herself as surely as she is displaced from Norland. The John Dashwoods occupy her home against her will, but Edward Ferrars occupies her mind because she privileges his experience – arguably even his life – to her own.

Before Elinor learns of the engagement, Marianne notices a "ring, with a plait of hair . . . on one of [Edward's] fingers." Marianne assumes the hair is her sister's. So does Elinor, despite the fact that she never gave Edward her hair, which would mean it "must have been procured by some theft or contrivance." In *The Rape of the Lock*, the Baron takes Belinda's hair by force, hence the poem's title. But whereas Pope satirizes Belinda for lacking "good-humour" about her loss (5.30), Elinor is "not in a humour . . . to regard [Edward's apparent theft] as an affront" (*SS*: 98). The allusion to rape is harrowing, not because Elinor faces a literal threat, but rather because she, unlike Pope's heroine, accepts the possibility of physical violation and seems untroubled, perhaps pleased, by her lack of consent. In fact, Edward is not the kind of man to rape a lock and the lost hair never even belonged to Elinor. Whereas the Baron steals with "Steel" scissors (3.171–8), Edward's lock proves to be a free gift from Lucy *Steele*. But why, one then wonders, does Elinor misidentify her own body part. Has she lost all sense of self?

If so, Edward's ironic advantage is that he shares some of the same capacity for such loss. For though he injures Elinor in ways she cannot possibly reciprocate, Edward remains comfortingly self-destructive. Thus, when he arrives at Barton Cottage after Lucy jilts him, Edward prepares to propose to Elinor by taking "up a pair of scissars [*sic*]" and "spoiling both them and their sheath by cutting the latter to pieces" (*SS*: 360). For Tony Tanner, the scene marks Edward's liberation – the moment his "feelings can break from the sheath" of social constrictions (Tanner 1969: 366). Given the scissors' phallic significance, however, one might just as easily view the cutting as castration.

Perhaps the scene paves the way for Elinor and Edward to have a more equitable marriage than courtship. For, by the time Edward proposes, he knows what it means to be dispossessed. As he tells Elinor, even before his mother disinherited him, she "did not make my home . . . comfortable" (*SS*: 362). Now he is indebted to Colonel Brandon for the "small and indifferent" parsonage at Delaford (*SS*: 284). The good news is that Elinor is "entirely mistress of the subject" of the parsonage (*SS*: 368), and, along with Edward, she plays a major role in its improvement. Together, they "superintend the progress . . . and direct everything as they liked"; together they choose "papers, project shrubberies, and invent a sweep" (*SS*: 374). In contrast, Marianne's entrance into Colonel Brandon's mansion appears sadly impoverished. Because she marries a man with real property, Marianne's position on it is fixed. For all the apparent benefits of becoming "the mistress of a family, and the patroness of a village," Marianne has, yet again, simply been "placed in a new home" (*SS*: 379).

Further Reading

Blackwell, Mark (2004). "The setting always casts a different shade on it": allusion and interpretation in *Sense and Sensibility*." *Eighteenth-Century Fiction*, 17, 111–24.

Edgecombe, Rodney S. (2001). Change and fixity in *Sense and Sensibility*. *Studies in English Literature, 1500–1900*, 41, 605–22.

Haggerty, George E. (1988). The sacrifice of privacy in *Sense and Sensibility*. *Tulsa Studies in Women's Literature*, 7, 221–37.

Kaufmann, David (1992). Law and propriety, *Sense and Sensibility*: Austen on the cusp of modernity. *ELH*, 59, 385–408.

McAllister, Marie E. (2004). "Only to sink deeper": venereal disease in *Sense and Sensibility*. *Eighteenth-Century Fiction*, 17, 87–110.

Roberts, Ruth (1975). *Sense and Sensibility*, or growing up dichotomous. *Nineteenth-Century Fiction*, 30, 351–65.

8

The Illusionist: *Northanger Abbey* and Austen's Uses Of Enchantment

Sonia Hofkosh

Illusions need not necessarily be false – that is to say unrealizable or in contradiction to reality. For instance, a middle-class girl may have the illusion that a prince will come and marry her. This is possible; and a few such cases have occurred. (Sigmund Freud, "The Future of an Illusion," 1927)

In clarifying his use of the word "illusion" (as distinct from "error" or "delusion") in his psychoanalysis of religious belief as wish-fulfillment, Sigmund Freud (1989: 39) is not referring to the courtship plot of *Northanger Abbey* or any of Austen's other novels which realize the marriage fantasies of middle-class girls. Nonetheless, we can take Freud's claim that illusions are not necessarily false or "in contradiction to reality" as an invitation to explore what I want to call Austen's modalities of enchantment. I am interested in some familiar issues in Austen criticism, especially pertaining to realism and its foundational strategies, irony and free indirect discourse. But I want to approach these issues by highlighting the unfamiliar – the experience of wonder, unexpected appearances and disappearances, the flights of fairies – evoked at the scene of Austen's writing, both within the courtship plot itself and in readers' responses to what has been cast as "the siren lure of her voice" (Miller 2003: 1). Such evocations of enchantment, like the uncanny, register the function of the strange within the familiar, the unexpected within what we accept or expect as the ordinary, the natural, or the real (Galperin 2003: 4–5).

Since Walter Scott's review of *Emma* in 1816, Austen's novels have been appreciated in terms of a nascent realism which, with its claims to verisimilitude, "draws the characters and incidents . . . immediately from the current of ordinary life": "the subjects are not often elegant, and certainly never grand, but they are finished up to nature, and with a precision that delights the reader" (Southam 1968: 59, 67). But insofar as realism, however commonplace or precisely mimetic, is, after all, a representation, and thus the illusion of reality, the realist may be considered as much a magician as a natural historian. "Realism is meant to be a riposte to magic and mystery," Terry Eagleton has observed, "but it may well be a prime example of them" (Eagleton 2003). Further, insofar as she executes this illusion with such dexterity, with what Scott admires as "peculiar tact," it is worth taking another look at Austen's "witchery by daytime," a phrase that refers to Samuel Taylor Coleridge's poem, "Christabel," but which I borrow to describe the kind of quotidian sorcery Austen performs in realizing the illusions of girls in her novels (H. Coleridge 1835: 114). If, as Scott asserts, Austen's realism signals the end of certain genres of romance – "The talisman and magic wand were broke, / Knights, dwarfs, and genii vanish'd into smoke" – it simultaneously introduces its own mode of enchantment, one especially marked by self-consciousness both in its performance and its effects. As at the moment in "Christabel" when the narrator directs our eyes to what he will not reveal in the motivation of his plot ("a sight to dream of, not to tell!") and thus to the occulted operations of narrative itself, Austen can rather flamboyantly call attention to the illusions that produce and sustain what appears to be immediately before us as ordinary life. When the narrator in *Northanger Abbey*, for example, "alert[s] us to her determination to work by concealment," obliging us thereby "to be aware of the claims and conventions of fiction as fiction" (Johnson 2003: xviii, xxi), she performs realism's "self-consciously illusory magic" (During 2002: 27).

My aim here is not to argue, *contra* Scott or those readers after him committed to Austen's realist priorities, that her work should be considered in the genre of the fantastic or the supernatural, like the Gothic romance of Radcliffe's *The Mysteries of Udolpho* (1794), which figures prominently in Austen's earliest finished novel, or the incipient science fiction of Mary Shelley's *Frankenstein* (1818), published in the same year as her last. Although both of these texts provide revealing comparisons for readers interested in elucidating Austen's fantasmatic edge (Wilt 1980, Levine 1981) – the line, as Nancy Armstrong has recently put it, that Austen insistently draws between mystery and reference, between, we could say, a girl's illusions and "what is actually before her eyes" (Armstrong 2005: 19). Rather, I want to consider the way that the realist paradigm that Austen is so often taken to initiate is itself apparitional, elabo-rated through a set of enchanted effects that rely on a dynamic of estrangement or displacement to achieve its normative status as ordinary, immediate, or natural.

In *Persuasion*'s observation that Anne Elliot "learned romance as she grew older – the natural sequel of an unnatural beginning" (*P*: 30), we might begin to apprehend enchantment's efficacy in how Austen finishes her novels "up to nature." However contingent the girl's desire (on the persuasion of others, for instance), however improb-able the fulfillment of her wishes, it is the illusionist's forte ("bewitching in the wit which often expressed it," *P*: 27) to make the most unlikely event look as much like "a common-place business" as the evening card-party that culminates "all the surprise and suspense" (*P*: 245) that Anne experiences on the morning of Wentworth's declara-tion and, indeed, throughout *Persuasion*. The novel's final chapter asks:

> Who can be in doubt of what followed? When any two young people take it into their
> heads to marry, they are pretty sure by perseverance to carry their point, be they ever

so poor, or ever so imprudent, or ever so little likely to be necessary to each other's ultimate comfort. This may be bad morality to conclude with, but I believe it to be truth. (*P*: 248)

Posited as inevitable ("who can be in doubt"), such an outcome explicitly contradicts the very premise of the novel, which is that eight years earlier two young people, not so very poor or imprudent, took it into their heads to marry and yet did not carry their point. Or is it a contradiction? That such an "unnatural beginning" ends up realizing the romance we have learned to expect, especially by this late novel, suggests that illusions are not so much in contradiction to reality as conducive to it, a factor in its very teleology.

When Coleridge "burst out into high encomiums of Miss Austen's novels as 'in their way, perfectly genuine and individual productions'" (Austen-Leigh 1870: 110), it may have been the natural finish Scott lauded that also delighted him. Or perhaps the author of the unfinished "Christabel" relishes not so much Austen's "fidelity to Nature" or the real as that quality he declares "the indispensable condition" of aesthetic pleasure, a quality which leads us to prefer a still life to a marble peach: the painting, like drama or, significantly, "a deeply interesting Novel," "is an *imitation* of reality, not a *Copy*" and so does not delude us into mistaking it for the real thing. He calls this pleasure "Illusion," a kind of waking dream, in which, "we *chuse* to be deceived" (Coleridge 1987: 264–6). In *Biographia Literaria*, he famously explains his effort to conjure in his early poems, including "Christabel," just such "willing illusion" – "a human interest and a semblance of truth sufficient to procure for these shadows of imagination that willing suspension of disbelief for the moment, which constitutes poetic faith" (Coleridge 1979, vol. II: 6).

Because "illusions need not necessarily be false," and may resemble truth or even become "in their way, perfectly genuine," to call Jane Austen an illusionist is not to say she is a great humbug, like the Wizard of Oz. To depict Austen as a practitioner of "witchery by daytime" is not to minimize the specific historical or political resonances of her novels nor to deny that her work is keenly attuned to the exigencies of social structures, material objects, or the body (Johnson 1988, Heydt-Stevenson 2005). To construe Austen's realism as an enchanted effect is not to diminish her achievement in perfecting a narrative technique so perspicacious in representing the inflections of individual subjectivity, nor is it to qualify the "moral intensity" motivating that realist project (Leavis 1973: 9). In fact, the modalities of enchantment I want to point to here are not "in contradiction to reality," not a falsification of or escape from the real world. Instead, "to be enchanted is to be struck and shaken by the extraordinary that lives amid the familiar and the everyday"; enchantment can be understood as "a mood of lively and intense engagement with the world," an opportunity for affective attachment, disturbing and deep but also potentially generative (Bennett 2001: 11, 4). Depicting occasions of such "lively and intense engagement," when a character in her novels or even a reader of them is struck and shaken into a sense of the real, a sense of self-consciousness, of being in the world, Austen shows that "the current of ordinary life" runs through unexpected channels. In deploying illusion as inseparable from the claims of the real, Austen puts into play something very close to Coleridge's "poetic faith," which entails a conscious choice, significantly more like making believe than believing, but nonetheless thereby intimating that as "imitation" or "semblance," illusion may be profoundly effective in creating real consequences, producing not only aesthetic pleasure, but also, like the wish of the middle-class girl fulfilled at the end of *Mansfield Park*, for example, "the whole delightful and astonishing truth."

". . . Her Chief Profit Was In Wonder"

Northanger Abbey is the novel most often regarded as Austen's explicit "riposte to magic and mystery," a counterthrust that does not so much wholly reject the charms of romance as transform and contain them into a mechanism of normativity (Litvak 1997). Although this novel's middle-class girl is introduced as an unlikely figure of romance – "No one who had ever seen Catherine Morland in her infancy, would have supposed her born to be a heroine" – her experience dramatizes the function of illusion within or as "ordinary life," the efficacy of enchantment in the realization of desire. Catherine's investment in illusion, her "willing suspension of disbelief," enables a "lively and intense engagement with the world" that generates a sense of subjective interiority as well as a prince "magically arrived" to marry her (Miller 2005: 252). In the scene in which she enters Mrs Tilney's "mysterious apartments" to search for "proofs of the General's cruelty" (either that he murdered his wife or imprisons her there still), Catherine experiences enchantment as the production of self-consciousness:

> it was some minutes before she could advance another step. She beheld what fixed her to the spot and agitated every feature. – She saw a large, well-proportioned apartment, an handsome dimity bed, arranged as unoccupied with a housemaid's care, a bright Bath stove, mahogany wardrobes and neatly-painted chairs, on which the warm beams of a western sun gaily poured through two sash windows! Catherine had expected to have her feelings worked, and worked they were. Astonishment and doubt first seized them; and a shortly succeeding ray of common sense added some bitter emotions of shame. (*NA*: 193)

Catherine is enchanted here, transfixed at the site of her own fantastic expectations. Yet the "astonishment and doubt" she feels derive from the very ordinariness of what she sees before her, from the very "common sense" that intensifies her response, both her agitation and her shame. The mahogany wardrobes and the neatly painted chairs strike her and shake her precisely in being at once so familiar and so strange, so unexpectedly just the thing one would expect. "Catherine had expected to have her feelings worked, and worked they were." Indeed, she has prepared her response, rehearsed it in her own room with the high chest and the Japan cabinet, probing their mysterious depths in "breathless wonder," cheeks flushed or pale, heart fluttering and knees atremble, to find, not "proofs of the General's cruelty," but "evidences of her folly," confirmation, that is, that her illusions produce the very stuff of the everyday, a counterpane or an inventory of linen. That she practices this "motionless wonder," that the repeated discovery of her illusions in and as ordinary objects is a "lively and intense" experience of *being* a self, suggests that enchantment has its uses in subject formation, especially in animating the very real sensations that are the basis for self-reflection. If for children enchantment therapeutically externalizes unconscious desire (Bettelheim 1976), Catherine's passion – for ancient edifices as well as for Henry Tilney – is enacted (and ultimately realized) as consciousness through the experience of wonder.

Catherine willingly, even eagerly, solicits such moods of enchantment – "Well, what then?" and "Well, go on," she urges Henry as he narrates the adventures awaiting her at Northanger Abbey. But it is not only Catherine's enchantment that is at issue in the telling of this tale. The reader has illusions too. When Catherine insists to Henry that "her attention had been fixed without the smallest apprehension of really meeting with what he related" (*NA*: 160), we likely disbelieve her. We consider Catherine one of Austen's most gullible characters, unable to distinguish fact from fiction, ordinary life from "visions of romance." Free indirect discourse, through which the narrative conveys subjectivity by rendering the character's internal voice, encourages this view of Catherine, but it may also be one of Austen's most proficient illusions, a kind of ventriloquism, articulating consciousness through dislocation. In the episode of the Japan cabinet, for example, the modulation from omniscient narration to Catherine's consciousness stages presence by destabilizing voice:

> Henry's words, his description of the ebony cabinet which was to escape her observation at first, immediately rushed across her; and although there could be nothing really in it, there was something whimsical, it was certainly a very remarkable coincidence! She took her candle and looked closely at the cabinet. It was not absolutely ebony and gold; but it was Japan, black and yellow Japan of the handsomest kind; and as she held her candle, the yellow had very much the effect of gold. The key was in the door, and she had a strange fancy to look into it; not however with the smallest expectation of finding any thing, but it was so very odd, after what Henry had said. (*NA*: 168)

If, seen in a certain light, yellow can have very much the effect of gold, and a coincidence, a mere whimsy, can have the immediate impact of a truth foretold, perhaps our sense that we are hearing Catherine's thoughts here bespeaks our own strange fancy. Aren't we as rapt as Catherine listening to Henry's story by the movements of the voice that appears to illuminate subjectivity? Even as we claim to know "there could be nothing really in it," isn't our attention fixed by such a performance of interiority? As in the ventriloquist's act, which must "sustain the illusion of the dummy's speech, while never letting us lose sight of the art by which this illusion is sustained," Austen's narrative technique has this enchanting effect (Aczel 2001).

Our belief in Catherine's gullibility (and our superior knowledge) becomes its own form of illusion. Though no Isabella, Catherine is neither as naïve nor as artless as she may appear. Well before her self-realization in Mrs Tilney's apartments and the encounter with Henry that follows, she clearly understands the efficacy of making believe. She is capable of dissembling, for instance, when her brother asks her how she likes John Thorpe – "instead of answering, as she probably would have done, had there been no friendship and no flattery in the case, 'I do not like him at all'; she directly replied, 'I like him very much; he seems very agreeable' " (*NA*: 50). When she wants to avoid dancing with him, "she fidgetted about if John Thorpe came towards her, hid herself as much as possible from his view, and when he spoke to her pretended not to hear him" (*NA*: 74) – "a cursed shabby trick" he comments, and he, like his sister, ought to know. Perhaps Catherine differs from Isabella only in making believe so convincingly, pretending with such sincerity; where Isabella's artifice is so "shallow" (*NA:* 218) that it eventually becomes transparent even to Catherine, Catherine's own is deep, a part of who she really is, or, at least, more effectively naturalized, like her love for hyacinths – a love she has just learned, she remarks, when, "unequal to an absolute falsehood" (*NA*: 174), she tries to deflect Henry's questions so she won't have to answer them. And this may be why, at the novel's conclusion, Isabella's "tricks have not answered" (*NA*: 218), while Catherine's have, for learning to love a hyacinth, like learning romance, implies that what appears to be quite natural in the end may well have had an unnatural beginning.

Catherine can be considered as almost perpetually enchanted because she is struck and shaken in "the current of ordinary life." The idea that John Thorpe may be in love with her is "a matter of lively astonishment" (*NA*: 148); a letter from James produces "sorrowing wonder" (*NA*: 202); her dismissal from Northanger Abbey renders her "breathless and speechless" (*NA*: 225). Yet Catherine is not the only middle-class girl in Austen's novels to experience such enchantment as the commonplace, the expected, the normative, within, that is, the parameters of the courtship plot itself. As Harriet Smith remarks when she ponders the possibility that she might marry Mr Knightley, "it seems as if such a thing even as this, may have occurred before" (*E*: 407). Indeed, such a thing has occurred in *Emma* in "the wonderful story of Jane Fairfax," which amazes Emma when she hears of it (she "even jumped with surprise . . . horror-struck." *E*: 395). In case after case, the desires of Austen's girls are realized as enchantment. "It is almost too wonderful for belief," Anne Elliot feels when she reads the news that Louisa Musgrove is to marry Captain Benwick, an event that makes the fulfillment of her own dream of marriage possible: "She had never in her life been more astonished" (*P*: 165). In *Sense and Sensibility*, Edward's announcement of Lucy's marriage to his brother is met at Barton Cottage with "the greatest astonishment and perplexity on a change in his situation, so wonderful and so sudden" (*SS*: 360). " 'This is an evening of wonders, indeed!'," Mr Bennet declares when Elizabeth finally convinces him that she really loves Darcy (*PP*: 377). Elizabeth's engagement to Darcy produces "astonishment" in Mr Bennet, "amazement" in her sister, and on her mother "its effect was most extraordinary; for on first hearing it, Mrs Bennet sat quite still, and unable to utter a syllable" (*PP*: 378).

Such enchanted effects are built into the courtship plot, a dynamic at stake for the reader as well. If we do not experience the wonder of the Bennets, that is partly because we have already suspended our disbelief in that plot as a truth universally acknowledged since the novel's opening sentence, an especially potent instance of Austenian irony which parodies the very expectations the novel will ultimately realize (Miller 1995, Neill 2003). Austen's "self-consciously illusory magic" works through such doubling, through the displacements implicit in irony as in free indirect discourse. Even when the ironic opening sentence is expressed as Mrs Bennet's wish, what reader of *Pride and Prejudice* is unmoved by its fulfillment, who doesn't willingly feel pleasure when Elizabeth's prince ("Ten thousand a year, and very likely more! 'Tis as good as a Lord!" *PP*: 378) comes to marry her? Further, if in *Northanger Abbey* Catherine consciously engages in the kind of make-believe that is associated with fiction (as when she notes that Henry's tale "is just like a book!" *NA*: 159), her everyday uses of enchantment cannot be separated from Austen's own authorship and the fictive plotting of the courtship narrative itself. In the final pages of the novel, where a Viscount unexpectedly appears to marry Eleanor and consequently also fulfills Catherine's desire to marry Henry, "Austen and her readers allow the rabbit, or the husband, to be pulled out of the hat." But this is no mere "gimmickry" (Levine 1981: 69–71): the realization of the girl's desire occurs with a wave of the authorial wand that embeds magic as a fundamental element of narrative design, including the reader in the "general satisfaction" its enchanted effects provide.

In *Northanger Abbey*, Austen may show us what she has up her authorial sleeve, preparing us from the opening chapter, as Catherine herself prepares, to expect the unexpected: "There was not one lord in the neighborhood; no, not even a baronet . . . [but] when a young lady is to be a heroine . . . [something] must and will happen to throw a hero in her way" (*NA*: 16–17). It should be emphasized, however, that such authorial legerdemain as is glimpsed here and in "the tell-tale compression of pages" at the end of *Northanger Abbey*, constitutes a regular feature of Austen's narrative design and an important correlative to her representation of the natural or the real. Consider the closing pages of *Mansfield Park*, where, in describing Edmund's dawning awareness that he loves Fanny after all, the narrator announces:

> I purposely abstain from dates on this occasion, that every one may be at liberty to fix their own, aware that the cure of unconquerable passions, and the transfer of unchanging attachments, must vary much as to time in different people. – I only intreat every body to believe that exactly at the time when it was quite natural that it should be so, and not a week earlier, Edmund did cease to care about Miss Crawford, and became as anxious to marry Fanny, as Fanny herself could desire. (*MP*: 470)

This is a moment of hyperrealism, in which the author appears to step out of the narrative to address us directly as teller of the tale. Such moments simultaneously expose the scaffolding of the fiction and invite the reader to inhabit its narrative structure. Openly admitting the contingency that fulfills Fanny's desire, that what is "quite natural" is a matter of what people are willing to believe, the passage enacts the illusionist's distractive art: it's only a trick, the author seems to say, and yet in appearing right here before you to perform it (I need a volunteer from the audience), I will create for you a sense of your own present, immediate reality. The author's appearance, in other words, as an "I" or as irony, sustains the illusion of self-consciousness, an illusion fundamental to the realist text, by displacing it onto the reader: we are self-conscious now, knowing we are reading when we hear the author's voice, or knowing we are only reading and thus hearing an "imitation" or "semblance" of the author's voice, thrown as if it were our own.

The Lady Vanishes

Seeking to explain what she calls "the miracle" of Jane Austen's authorship in the "astonishing" "Love and Freindship," penned ("incredible though it appears"), by a girl of 15, Virginia Woolf imagines that

> one of those fairies who perch upon cradles must have taken her a flight through the world directly she was born. When she was laid in the cradle again she knew not only what the world looked like, but had already chosen her kingdom. . . . Thus at fifteen she had few illusions about other people and none about herself. . . . When the writer, Jane Austen, wrote down in the most remarkable sketch in the book a little of Lady Greville's conversation, there is no trace of anger at the snub which the clergyman's daughter, Jane Austen, once received. (Woolf 1925: 146)

Disappearing from her cradle as a newborn baby, Austen returns with preternatural knowledge and insight beyond her merely mortal condition. The kingdom over which she presides is a world without illusions, a territory purged, we might say, of those "sudden and perplexing emotions" Emma associates with the "development of self." Flying with the fairy, "the writer, Jane Austen" transcends the local experience of the parsonage, the ordinary world within which "the clergyman's daughter, Jane Austen" would more narrowly and unremarkably reside. Her language ("the rhythm and shapeliness and severity of the sentences") contains no trace of the biographical speci-ficity that situates the clergyman's daughter within "the current of ordinary life," as an individual subject, embodied within a familiar field of social relations. Lady Greville may snub the clergyman's daughter, but the writer's representation of the conversation betrays no affective response. The lady vanishes so that the author can appear, wielding "the lash of a whip-like phrase" (Woolf 1925: 149).

In Woolf's account, Austen's achievement as an author consists in the evacuation of the illusions that conduce to subjectivity. Roland Barthes would later announce that "the author is dead: his civil status, his biographical person have disappeared" (Barthes 1975: 27). In Barthes' theory of authorship, "the prestige of the individual, or, as we say more nobly, of the 'human person'" is "pure superstition" (Barthes 1989: 49–50). And yet, as in Woolf's imagination of Austen's fairy flight, Barthes does not so much deny authorial "prestige" as relocate its magic in language, in reading, in "the staging of an appearance-as-disappearance" (Barthes 1975: 9–10). Such "pleasures of the text" may come closer to the aesthetic pleasure Coleridge names "Illusion" than the unsuperstitious Barthes might be willing to believe. Perhaps in conceiving of authorship as a disappearing act, Barthes might subscribe to Woolf's fantasy of Austen vanishing from her cradle, the author no mere human person but a "conjurer" who "makes us wonder" and whose "artful devices" "keep us on the tenterhooks of suspense" – "at once our senses quicken; we are possessed with the peculiar intensity which she alone can impart" (Woolf 1925: 147–50). Reincarnated as a property of language or as a function of reading, enchantment in Austen nonetheless performs its "witchery by daytime," creating a virtual reality, "a conscious logic, articulated with an extraordinary finesse" (or, as Scott put it, "peculiar tact").

Woolf's fantasy of the fairy perched on the infant Austen's cradle invokes a classic fairytale scenario (see chapter 35). I bring up the echoes of Woolf's fantasy in Barthes' formulation of the author's disappearance as "human person" to highlight the mechanism of displacement operative in the story of how the clergyman's daughter becomes the author of "the whip-like phrase," "a delineator of character" whose own character remains, as her nephew insisted, so completely "obscure" (Austen-Leigh 1870: 2) behind the curtain of her prose (Auerbach 2004: 289). The fairy story, at once so familiar and so strange, describes the unnatural beginning of Austen's realism, that kingdom of no illusions, where what Woolf calls "the ebb and flow of ordinary existence" appears as "nothing out of the way," if not also "natural" (Woolf 1925: 150–1). In his 1870 *Memoir*, James Edward Austen-Leigh recalls his "fascination" with the stories his aunt told him as a child, "the most delightful stories, chiefly of Fairyland" (Austen-Leigh 1870: 91). He also remembers a "curious" gift she gave to his mother: "a little rolled up housewife, furnished with minikin needles and fine thread . . . and in the pocket is enclosed a slip of paper, on which is written as with a crow quill" a verse inscription. This is "the kind of article that some benevolent fairy might be supposed to give as a reward to a diligent little girl" (Austen-Leigh 1870: 98–9). Even at home, in "the current of ordinary life" among her family, doing the domestic work of the nursery or the needle, Austen's effects are fascinating and "wonderful," as if with a wave of her fairy wand, a minikin needle, or a crow quill pen, her production rivets the attention of children or transforms a grown woman back into a little girl.

Austen-Leigh's Victorian appeal to the image of the fairy to describe his aunt's authorial gifts may be nothing in itself very remarkable, and Woolf, writing after *Peter Pan* (1904), may use the vocabulary of enchantment to convey the "elusive quality" of Austen's very "prosiness" (Woolf 1925: 149–50). But more recent criticism intimates that one need not believe in fairies to register the effects of enchantment in Austen's writing, to appreciate illusion as itself an opportunity for developing self-consciousness, not only in the characters in the novels, but in the readers of them as well. D. A. Miller, like Woolf, locates Austen's authority in her impersonality, a "thrillingly inhuman utterance," the "ghostly No One of enthralled imagination"

(Miller 2003: 2–3). As the disembodied voice of "Absolute Style," "the dazzling spectacle" of her "disappearing act" has transformative powers – it can turn a grown man back into a boy (or, maybe, into a girl) dreaming of "flashing the wondrous brand" that is Austen's language, that "swank Excalibur," enchanted sword of legend. That Miller avows this fantasy of mastery in Austen's linguistic kingdom *as* fantasy ("the creative eye of daydream") subtracts nothing from his own moving display of its powers. As the sorcerer's apprentice, Miller likely learned this technique from Austen, who, as we have seen, performs it through free indirect discourse and through irony and through her sudden appearances and disappearances as an author.[1]

So if Austen seems to have vanished, into her language or as language, as voice, such a disappearance can be seen as part of the apparatus of illusion that contributes to or even constitutes our sense of what feels real – what strikes and shakes us – in her writing. In this way, she may after all share some tricks with that great dissembler, the Wizard of Oz, both when he hides behind a screen, appearing in various forms and projecting his voice so that it seems as if someone else is speaking, and also when he is revealed in the end to be "just a common man," a ventriloquist, whose magic consists of "making believe" with paper and paint, needle and thread and bits of silk, but who still performs it quite to the satisfaction of his audience. Crucially, Baum's story doesn't dismiss Dorothy's adventure as a delusion induced by a bump on the head, a dream from which the girl must awaken to the real; instead, Dorothy's trip to Oz is explained by the science of air pressure and the behavior of cyclones, as if to throw the cloak of probability over the possibility that such a "strange thing" (Baum 1973: 94) could in fact occur. As a story about a girl's longing and the realization of her desire, engaging questions of (self-) knowledge, matters of the heart, and moral courage, *The Wonderful Wizard of Oz* reframes Austen's realist priorities as fairytale. Moreover, if Oz initially derives his power from deception, appearing in multiple guises and doing his wizardry in different voices, in the end he accomplishes his "magic art" (p. 273) with no wand but only ordinary materials – paper, paint, needle, and silk. All the more wonderful, then, that he gives the Scarecrow, the Tin Woodman, and the Lion "exactly what they thought they wanted" (p. 279). As for the girl, her wish to live in the current of ordinary life is finally realized as well, mobilized by the magic of her own desire.

NOTE

1   See also Christopher Miller, who finds in the dynamics of surprise that "by which Austen excites, in the best sense of the term, our wonder" (2005: 257); Jeff Nunokawa, who distinguishes the "spell of conversation" as "chief among the charms of Austen's world" (2005: 11, 2); and Claudia L. Johnson, "Jane Austen's Magic," plenary address, "Women's Writing in Britain, 1660–1830," University of Southampton and Chawton House Library, July 16, 2003.

FURTHER READING

Bennett, Jane (2001). *The Enchantment of Modern Life: Attachments, Crossings, and Ethics.* Princeton, NJ: Princeton University Press.

During, Simon (2002). *Modern Enchantments: The Cultural Power of Secular Magic.* Cambridge, MA: Harvard University Press.

Galperin, William H. (2003). *The Historical Austen.* Philadelphia: University of Pennsylvania Press.

Johnson, Claudia L. (2003). Introduction. *Northanger Abbey, Lady Susan, The Watsons, Sanditon.* Oxford: Oxford University Press.

Miller, D. A. (2003). *Jane Austen, or The Secret of Style.* Princeton and Oxford: Princeton University Press.

Nunokawa, Jeff (2005). Speechless in Austen. *differences: A Journal of Feminist Cultural Studies* 16: 2, 1–36.

9
Re: Reading *Pride and Prejudice*: "What think you of books?"

Susan J. Wolfson

Volume I. Reading the Markets

On her first visit to Netherfield Hall, Elizabeth Bennet declines to join at cards (lacking the stakes), and sits aside from its party of social snobs to "amuse herself . . . with a book" (*PP*: 37). Ever observant, Miss Bingley is quick to play a card of social capital:

> "What a delightful library you have at Pemberley, Mr. Darcy!"
>   "It ought to be good," he replied, "it has been the work of many generations."
>   "And then you have added so much to it yourself, you are always buying books."
>   "I cannot comprehend the neglect of a family library in such days as these."
> (*PP*: 38)

"Such days as these": in 1812, the year before *Pride and Prejudice* appeared, the *Edinburgh Review*'s editor, Francis Jeffrey guessed the "middling classes" and gentry included almost a quarter-million readers (20: 280). Professional authorship was not only possible but increasingly respectable. Even if the author of *Pride and Prejudice* would not (in female propriety) put her name to the title-page, she would capitalize on her reputation as "The Author of 'Sense and Sensibility'." When the firm of John Murray produced *Mansfield Park* and *Emma*, the title-pages were brand-named "By the Author of 'Pride and Prejudice'."

The four lifetime novels also carried a subtitle: *A Novel: In Three Volumes*. "Novel" was the new genre of the eighteenth century, in full bloom in the 1790s, when Austen drafted the manuscript that would become *Pride and Prejudice*. "In Three Volumes" is a reader-friendly form, enabling sequential purchasing or borrowing, and family sharing. Austen cannily shapes each volume along a dramatic arc. Volume I climaxes in crises: Elizabeth's refusal and Charlotte's acceptance of Mr Collins's proposal of marriage, Mrs Bennet's railing about the entailment of their estate to Mr Collins, and her husband's needling rejoinder: "I leave it to yourself to determine" (*PP*: 130) – precisely what women can't do legally, with a hint of Mr Bennet's complicity in the arrangement (see Irvine 2002: 17–18). Volume II ends in Elizabeth's angry rebuff of Mr Darcy's proposal, his long follow-up letter, then an impending tour with her unknowing aunt and uncle of Darcy's Pemberley, the "dreadful" prospect eased by assurance of his absence. The volume closes in a dramatic, one-sentence paragraph, vibrating with expectation: "To Pemberley, therefore, they were to go" (p. 241). Volume III works an elaborate denouement.

Austen's savvy in addressing, without catering to, the literary market reciprocates the signature market of her novels: the marriage market. Marked with "quickness of observation" (*PP*: 15) – that is, close attention, not haste – Elizabeth Bennet relays both markets. By careful reading, heroine Elizabeth will find "the man who, in disposition and talents, would most suit her" (p. 312); thus Austen means to find her readers. Not for nothing is *Pride and Prejudice* about reading, brimming with letters, the language of manners and behavior, conversations and chance remarks, reports and gossip, and a vast sign-system of family and connections, estates, homes, carriages, furnishings, and décor. All become objects of implied or provoked reading. A sympathy of readings proves telling, and so does openness to rereading. This is a novel in which the adage "first impressions are lasting impressions" proves a test rather than a truth: Austen's original title was *First Impressions*.

In 1797, at the marriageable age of 22, Austen tendered her venture in that popular eighteenth-century form, the epistolary novel, to publisher Thomas Cadell, who rejected it, unread, by return mail. If this seems a notorious blunder of first impressions, back then it was a rational decision for a market hot with sensation and Gothic thrills. Austen's novel had "no dark passages; no secret chambers; no wind-howlings in long galleries; no drops of blood upon a rusty dagger" – so John Murray's literary advisory reported 17 years on.[1] He was relieved about this, but in a decade when Lewis's *Monk* and Radcliffe's *Udolpho* were flying off the shelves, an unknown lady-novelist's wry, subtle etching of complications in the lives of local gentry was a non-starter. Books were costly to make, costly to buy. Byron's *Childe Harold's Pilgrimage*, an overnight success in 1812, was a luxury for most. At 30 shillings in paper wrapper, 50 bound, or in cheaper octavo, 12 and 25 respectively, a gentleman with an income of 100 shillings a week might purchase it, but not the skilled artisan earning 36 shillings a week. And the best-sellers in this day were Scott's historical romances and Byron's exotic poetic romances (in 1813 alone, his *Giaour* and *Bride of Abydos* each sold 12,500) – not Austen's mode. "I could no more write a Romance than an Epic Poem," she sighed to the Prince Regent's librarian (April 1, 1816; *Letters*: 312). It wouldn't be until the 1830s that her novels, in Bentley's Standards, would sell in the thousands.

The first hazard with *Pride and Prejudice* was taken by Thomas Egerton of the Military Library, Whitehall, a modest concern with an important address (principal royal residence well into the seventeenth century). He bought the copyright for £110. Though Austen hoped for £150, it was still a better deal than *Sense and Sensibility*, for which she paid all expenses. This was Egerton's first foray into novel-publishing, and a smart move. Issued January 1813 in economic duodecimo,[2] priced 18 shillings unbound and 25 shillings and sixpence bound, *Pride and Prejudice* sold well enough to command a new edition by June. (Yet it is telling that in 1817 a third edition proved too optimistic, was remaindered and probably pulped at the end of the decade.[3]) About half of the Regency print-runs of Austen's novels were purchased by the titled gentry, and upper-middle classes, the world she wrote about. The other half wound up in that institution satirized in *Pride and Prejudice*: circulating libraries, patronized by subscribers who, for a few pounds a year, could gorge on an ample inventory.

Novel-reader and library-patron as well as author, Austen contended not only with market forces but also with Enlightenment critiques of female education. Mary Wollstonecraft and Hannah More, though sharply at odds about the "rights of woman," agreed on novels as junk-reading. Heating sensation at the expense of reason, corrupting language, judgment, and social expectations, this was reading at its least educative. A gentleman could expect to be handed a university education and, if needed, a career. A girl's education tended to cease around the age of eight; her "finishing" was aimed at winning a hand in marriage with the advantage of "accomplishments, the only improvement they are excited, by their station in society, to acquire" remarked Wollstonecraft in exasperation (*A Vindication of the Rights of Woman*, 1792: 131). The curriculum was "a thorough knowledge of music, singing, drawing, dancing, and the modern languages" – so chirps Miss Bingley, with a dig at Elizabeth's legible deficiencies.

Elizabeth has no particular care for this business or for the attendant fashions, ribbons, and bonnets. She bounds three miles across dusty fields, springs over puddles and stiles, appalls Bingley's sisters with her muddy petticoat and ruddy complexion; her eyes are bright from exercise. She will freckle and tan from touring outdoors with the Gardiners, and a walk of several miles with Darcy will clinch their engagement. Austen collates this aberration from female "accomplishments" with Elizabeth's character as a reader. If Enlightenment rationalists worried about novels, novelist Austen redeems this pleasure as a rational pursuit in *Pride and Prejudice* (though she satirizes it elsewhere), saving her lash for "accomplished" ladies such as Miss Bingley, to whom a book is no more than a prop of self-promotion:

> Darcy took up a book; Miss Bingley did the same; . . . Miss Bingley's attention was quite as much engaged in watching Mr. Darcy's progress through *his* book, as in reading her own; and she was perpetually either making some inquiry, or looking at his page. She could not win him, however, to any conversation; he merely answered her question, and read on. At length, quite exhausted by the attempt to be amused with her own book, which she had only chosen because it was the second volume of his, she gave a great yawn and said, "How pleasant it is to spend an evening in this way! I declare after all there is no enjoyment like reading! How much sooner one tires of any thing than of a book! – When I have a house of my own, I shall be miserable if I have not an excellent library."

> No one made any reply. She then yawned again, threw aside her book, and cast her
> eyes round the room in quest of some amusement . . . (*PP*: 54–5)

Against this yawning calculator, Austen plots Elizabeth's happiness on an arc of
genuine reading, from first impressions and prejudices, to reflections and revisions,
to rereadings and surer comprehension, to union with a man of equal capacity.

It's an early cue that Darcy has a "more substantial" view of female merit
than social accomplishments: "the improvement of her mind by extensive reading"
(*PP*: 39). He and Elizabeth flirt in volleys about reading, whatever the text.
He grumbles that the "confined and unvarying society" of a country neighborhood
"can in general supply but few subjects for . . . study"; she retorts, "But people
themselves alter so much, that there is something new to be observed in them for
ever" (*PP*: 42–3). And then on to books, per se:

> "What think you of books?" said he, smiling.
>
> "Books – Oh! no. – I am sure we never read the same, or not with the same
> feelings."
>
> "I am sorry you think so; but if that be the case, there can at least be no want of
> subject. – We may compare our different opinions." (*PP*: 93)

Even so, Elizabeth registers Austen's double-bind about female bookishness. "I am
not a great reader," she rebuffs Miss Bingley's sarcasm (*PP*: 37). In Austen's book, no
woman is seen in formal schooling or mentored study; none aims to inhabit a library
(save Mary), let alone become a professional author.

For better or worse, the marriage-market is the prime investment for careful female
reading and self-improvement, with failure punishable by social death. The famous
single-paragraph first sentence of *Pride and Prejudice* sets the ethos in a spare 23-word
proverb: "It is a truth universally acknowledged, that a single man in possession of a
good fortune, must be in want of a wife" (*PP*: 3). If Austen's wit is that such a truth
is just pride of local prejudice, her darker social text is that for a single woman, the
hope declared *a truth* is all that matters. The syntactical rhyme of "in possession of"
and "in want of" is a social poetics, not metaphysical philosophy. Deftly tuning irony
with social realism, Austen's purchase on the suspect terrain of novel-reading is a
"marriage-plot" with a difference, worked out through comparisons of difference: love
at first sight; hate at first sight;[4] schemings and inertia, infatuation and anxiety.
Matches sad and happy, proposed and rejected, imagined and realized, become a moral
measure of character – *moral* not as orthodoxy but as existential trial amid passions,
impressions, interpretations, reviews, and not the least, prides and prejudices.

Volume II. Prejudice and First Impressions

Austen's title-words prove slippery in this trial of character. While *Pride* evokes the
prime deadly sin, in eighteenth-century social registers and philosophy, it might

denote a sense of rational self-worth, or (alternatively) smugness primed for "mortification." *Prejudice* might seem kin to dubious "first impressions"; but it might signify sound "latent wisdom" – the phrase Edmund Burke used with positive English pride in his conservative *Reflections on the Revolution in France*: "Prejudice renders a man's virtue his habit . . . part of his nature" (2nd edn, 1790: 130). No less a question is Austen's assignment of these attitudes: whose *pride?* whose *prejudice?* No character will have exclusive claim. Austen involves her readers in the question, using "free indirect discourse," a pulse of feelings, thoughts, and self-examination, to convey a voice of consciousness, at once personal and inflected by a shared social grammar.

That grammar extends to Austen's own world. Everyone knew that office-holders had to be members of the Church, that the power in Parliament was the hereditary House of Lords, that the districts for the elective House of Commons were controlled by conservative landowners like Mr Darcy, whose borough might amount to a few hundred souls: principal families, their employees, and tradespeople dependent on their patronage. Scarcely mentioned in this novel are the new manufacturing cities, teeming with miserably exploited workers, with no parliamentary representatives. In 1800, only 5 percent of Englishmen had the vote. Austen's social idiom was 2 percent of the population: "the little bit (two Inches wide) of Ivory on which I work with so fine a Brush" is "3 or 4 Families in a Country Village" (letters to her nephew, December 16, 1816; and niece, September 9, 1814; *Letters*: 323, 275). These families are serviced and defended by unnamed, or scarcely named, laborers – noncommissioned soldiers, tenant farmers, maids, cooks, housekeepers, servants, carriagemen – all reduced to agentless syntax: horses were brought, dinners were served, tables were cleared, girls were dressed. Ever-polite Elizabeth and Jane refer to their housekeeper only as "Hill" ("Mrs. Hill" is the singular courtesy of Austen's narrator).

The drama of *Pride and Prejudice* involves Misses with choices. Elizabeth forges her happiness in free refusals of Mr Collins and Mr Darcy, with leisure to amend prejudices and errors. Men are endowed with choice, especially elder sons who've survived their parents and the authority they might exert. Mr Collins, it is true, has to toady to his patroness, the formidable Lady Catherine de Bourgh; an earl's younger son, Colonel Fitzwilliam must seek a profession or a cushy marriage; steward's son and scoundrel Wickham, having blown his patronage, must fortune-hunt with his charm as bait. But men's social esteem is not birth-bound. Tradesman William Lucas gets knighted; amiable, "good looking," new-money Mr Bingley is "gentlemanlike"; for good sense and decency, tradesman Mr Gardiner earns this same compliment from Mr Darcy. Mr Bennet, with a modest £2,000 a year, is a "gentleman." To Lady Catherine's dismay at Darcy's proposal, Elizabeth replies: "He is a gentleman; I am a gentleman's daughter; so far we are equal" (*PP*: 356).

Such a daughter does best, however, with a handsome dowry or settlement, of which the Bennet girls are short. Austen has no traffic with the social decorum that keeps women innocent of financial reality. In *Pride and Prejudice* everyone keeps tabs: moral ledgers may be misread; financial ones are assiduously monitored. Women also bring assets of youth, beauty, and sweet temper. The debits correspond: foremost, age. Young Miss Gardiner was a beauty, an attorney's daughter with a fortune of

£4,000, the belle of the ball. As middle-aged Mrs Bennet, she's a joke, no match for Mr Bennet's library or bird-shooting with the more amiable Mr Wickham. As for his meagerly endowed, unmarried daughters, only his wife feels any urgency. Yet marriage is "the only honourable provision for well-educated young women of small fortune," as sober pragmatist Charlotte Lucas knows – "their pleasantest preservative from want" (*PP*: 122–3). Not to marry by age 28 (she's 27) is to resign to "spinster-hood," pitiful and dependent on male kin (if any).

Most women had no legal standing (a suitor seeks a father's permission). Wealthy widow Lady Catherine is the rare female property-owner. While Wickham's mother seems to have had a spendthrift license, and the Bingley heiresses enjoy some liberties, obedience to men (fathers, brothers, husbands) was the sanctioned norm. A rebellious girl (one who eloped, or refused her father's choice of husband) could be sent packing, even disinherited. Mr Collins's insistence that the Bennets shut their doors to truant Lydia is no singular meanness; he bears the social consensus and its discipline. Should Lydia ever tire of Wickham's deadbeat profligacy, she could not divorce him, only he her, with a claim to all her money and property, and any children (and their access to family providence).

Austen's uneasiness about this systemic male priority is coolly issued by the novel's least likeable (officious, rude, meddlesome, arrogant), most financially powerful, most self-possessed woman, Lady Catherine. "I see no occasion for entailing estates from the female line" (*PP*: 164), she declares to Elizabeth. Mr Bennet merely jests, "My cousin, Mr. Collins, . . . when I am dead, may turn you all out of this house as soon as he pleases" (*PP*: 61). If Elizabeth will accept no marriage of convenience with this "conceited, pompous, narrow-minded, silly" heir (*PP*: 135), her mother is the only woman to echo Lady Catherine; and like her, she is stigmatized:

> Jane and Elizabeth attempted to explain to her the nature of an entail. They had often attempted it before, but it was a subject on which Mrs. Bennet was beyond the reach of reason; and she continued to rail bitterly against the cruelty of settling an estate away from a family of five daughters, in favour of a man whom nobody cared anything about. (*PP*: 62)

Thus characters we have come to like immunize a perverse system as "reason," while censure is tainted as arrogance or foolish, hysterical, domestic prejudice: flawed character rather than flawed society. The tacit ideological grammar is Burke's master-trope national tradition: "an *entailed inheritance* derived to us from our forefathers, and to be transmitted to our posterity" – "the happy effect of following nature, which is wisdom without reflection," with any "spirit of innovation" the "result of a selfish temper, and confined views" (1790: 47).[5]

Yet the device of containing laudable critiques in illaudable characters is a common rhetorical maneuver – getting the argument said under cover of discredit. Milton's Satan conveys republican politics and proto-feminist language; in *Emma* it is silly Harriet Smith who wonders why a financially independent woman need marry. Even heroine Elizabeth is set between normative and aberrant measures. Austen may key

Darcy's first impression of her to Burkean aesthetics: she is a "beautiful creature" who seems "uncommonly intelligent" not by books but by looks, "the beautiful expression of her dark eyes"; he's the one with "a critical eye" (*PP*: 23). Yet it is Elizabeth's active, not beautifully expressive, intelligence that drives the romance plot, and does so in refusal of the Burkean ethos of *prejudice* – that "steady course" of "wisdom without reflection," with nothing "sceptical, puzzled, and unresolved" (1790: 130). Elizabeth's "liveliness of . . . mind" (*PP*: 208) is a temper for being skeptical, puzzled, and unre-solved, and it's the motor for her union with Darcy. On this lively measure even Lady Catherine seems Austen-invested. The author introduces her as "authoritative" (*PP*: 162) and gives her qualities akin to what we admire in Elizabeth: fearless, forthright self-possession, indifference to norms of male admiration, and ability to manage, even, without a husband.

Complementing these defections from "feminine accomplishment" is Austen's array of male characters with dubious claims to "masculine" character. Mr Collins and Mr Wickham verge on what Wollstonecraft describes as "the prevailing opinion" of the female character (Ch. II, *Rights of Woman*) – the one gaining an establishment by servile flattery; the other flirting for profit, living for pleasure, and unembarrassed about being bailed out by more capable men. So, too, "amiable" Mr Bingley: a creature of pleasure and few ideas, easily swayed, seldom questioning, always depending on Mr Darcy's judgment. Mr Bennet, though witty, confesses himself a poor patriarch, foolish in marriage and improvident of his children (Lydia's marriage looks like the second generation of his own – begun in heat, with no sound reading of character). Even Darcy can behave like one of the impassionata that Wollstonecraft satirizes. There is a world of meaning in Austen's having Elizabeth spurn his marriage-proposal not just from prejudice, but on the insulting plea of ardent love in defiance of reason, will, and responsible character.

Volume III. Romance and Reading

"Mortification" is Austen's keyword for the death of self-esteem and social credit, the agony of pride. "I could easily forgive *his* pride, if he had not mortified *mine*," Elizabeth glowers of her first impression of Darcy (*PP*: 20). He, meanwhile, feels the "mortify-ing" confusion of something "uncommonly intelligent" in her, a trouble to his habit of looking "only to criticise" (*PP*: 23). Elizabeth's supreme mortification is her reread-ing of the letter Darcy has thrust upon her after she has refused his proposal of mar-riage: "collecting herself as well as she could, she again began the mortifying perusal of all that related to Wickham, and commanded herself so far as to examine the meaning of every sentence":

> Of neither Darcy nor Wickham could she think, without feeling that she had been
> blind, partial, prejudiced, absurd . . . "I, who have prided myself on my discernment! –
> I, who have valued myself on my abilities . . . I have courted prepossession and

ignorance, and driven reason away, where either were concerned. Till this moment I never knew myself" (*PP*: 208)

Chastened rereading improves what she knows. "Widely different was the effect of a second perusal" upon another prepossession: the comments on her family were "mortifying, yet merited"; "Neither could she deny the justice of his description of Jane" (*PP*: 208). Closely read and reread, Darcy's letter pivots into the proxy of new courtship: "Mr. Darcy's letter, she was in a fair way of soon knowing by heart. She studied every sentence" (*PP*: 212). We do, too. Most of the previous chapter was the text of this letter (a vestige of the first epistolary novel), which we read, with Elizabeth, as an alternative narrative to the novel thus far, confronting our misprisions as she confronts hers. The moral work of this novel is focused on a call to "read, and re-read with the closest attention" (*PP*: 205). Austen stages a sequel to this chastening in an alluring scene of virtual reading, for both Elizabeth and us. This is Darcy's estate, "at the top of a considerable eminence":

> the eye was instantly caught by Pemberley House, situated on the opposite side of a valley, into which the road, with some abruptness, wound. It was a large, handsome, stone building, standing well on rising ground, and backed by a ridge of high woody hills; – and in front, a stream of some natural importance was swelled into greater, but without any artificial appearance. Its banks were neither formal, nor falsely adorned. Elizabeth was delighted. She had never seen a place for which nature had done more, or where natural beauty had been so little counteracted by an awkward taste. They were all of them warm in their admiration; and at that moment she felt that to be mistress of Pemberley might be something! (*PP*: 245)

Elizabeth's indirect discourse conveys more than real estate; she reads good government, even erotic attraction, out of this information. Everything about Pemberley is "handsomely fitted up," signifying its master, the "very handsome gentleman" Mr Darcy: "In what an amiable light does this place him!" Elizabeth thinks of the array, gilding the housekeeper's praises of "the best landlord, and the best master." By this point, the sign system verges on an exuberant parody of a readable text. "Yes," we say, the question of Darcy is settled. Just to be sure, Austen sets another sequel in his portrait, which Elizabeth reads and rereads, "returned to it again before they quitted the gallery." The motion is the reciprocal and revision of her first sensation about the place, when "apprehensions of meeting its owner returned." Now, as "Elizabeth turned back to look again" at the house, "the owner of it himself suddenly came forward."[6] Romance blooms in dramas of returns and rereading: "She read over her aunt's commendation of him again and again," Austen tells of a letter to her about Darcy's rescue of Lydia's reputation (*PP*: 327).

It is perfectly apt that, when Elizabeth and Darcy finally admit their love, his post-rebuff letter recalls a critical chapter in their history, on which they now reflect as partners in reading:

Darcy mentioned his letter. "Did it," said he, "did it soon make you think better of me? Did you, on reading it, give any credit to its contents?"

She explained what its effect on her had been, and how gradually all her former prejudices had been removed.

"I knew," said he, "that what I wrote must give you pain, but it was necessary. I hope you have destroyed the letter. There was one part especially, the opening of it, which I should dread your having the power of reading again. I can remember some expressions which might justly make you hate me."

"The letter shall certainly be burnt, if you believe it essential to the preservation of my regard; but, though we have both reason to think my opinions not entirely unalterable, they are not, I hope, quite so easily changed as that implies." (*PP*: 368)

The moment is charged for recursion: Austen provokes our return to II.12 to review that "opening." *Pride and Prejudice* is not only a romance of rereading but a laboratory for practice: "I must keep to my own style & go on in my own Way," said Austen to that Princely Librarian, unapologetically; "I am convinced that I should totally fail in any other" (*Letters*: 312).

Yet if the macro-text of Darcy's Pemberley is a set-piece of this style, a scene of pivotal reading, its project of undoing the prejudice of first impressions entails a seduction to Burkean prejudice. The well-managed estate is the iconic romance of patriarchy (country-house idealism since the Renaissance), in complete coincidence with the romance of Darcy. "Will you tell me how long you have loved him?" Jane queries Elizabeth, who replies, only half-jestingly, "from my first seeing the beautiful grounds at Pemberley" (*PP*: 373). Sir Walter Scott (no slouch on the cultural capital of a grand estate) marked this as the moment when the lady's "prudence had begun to subdue her prejudice" (*Quarterly Review* XIV: 194). Austen rewards her best re-reader with marriage to lavish wealth. Not the opposite of romantic success, it is the fantasy correlative. "Fortune" is both the glossy superstructure of romance and its material accomplishment.

At the same time (despite Austen's own sense that this novel "wants shade"), some demystifying shadows fall across the "rather too light & bright & sparkling" surface of *Pride and Prejudice* (so she sighed to her sister, February 4, 1814; *Letters*: 203). There is the socio-logic of Charlotte, casting for Mr Collins "solely from the pure and disinterested desire of an establishment"; he is "a most eligible match" not for love, or happiness, or even esteem, but for his "prospects," which, as Bennet heir, are "exceedingly fair" (*PP*: 122). For most women, romance is the luxury of novels like *Pride and Prejudice*; and Collins is still a better bet than Wickham (who in the 1995 BBC miniseries solaces a loveless match with drink and spousal abuse). If Austen's formal design sets Charlotte, Mrs Bennet, and Lydia as foils to Elizabeth's rational independence, the ledger of *Pride and Prejudice* gives a fuller account, of matches blind, pragmatic, calculating, acquisitive, in sum the probability for most of Austen's female readers, even in the gentry. Austen's romance-plot – the woman who marries up and happily

– is exactly Wollstonecraft's worry about novels, fictions that make female readers "restless and anxious," exciting an "overstretched sensibility" that "prevents intellect from attaining that sovereignty which it ought to attain to render a rational creature . . . content with its own station" (1792, IV: 83). The woman of rational contentment ("I am not romantic, you know," says Charlotte; *PP*: 125) is the antithesis of the bright and sparkling heroine around whom the romance of *Pride and Prejudice* builds, in promise without compromise.

What credits this romance is that its terms are not entirely utopian. Here is Elizabeth musing on the prospect of "connubial felicity" as Mr and Mrs Darcy: "It was an union that must have been to the advantage of both; by her ease and liveliness, his mind might have been softened, his manners improved, and from his judgment, information, and knowledge of the world, she must have received benefit of greater importance" (*PP*: 312). This is an opinion of sexual character – the man has judgment, information, and knowledge; the woman, a teasing, softening influence – so tuned to gender norms that Wollstonecraft could have taken it as a case in point. Mr Bennet puts a father's imprimatur on it all: "I know that you could be neither happy nor respectable, unless you truly esteemed your husband, unless you looked up to him as a superior." Although he means that someone of "lively talents" risks "the greatest danger in an unequal marriage" (*PP*: 376), the hierarchy is marked. Elizabeth may show how "a woman may take liberties with her husband" (*PP*: 388), but the grant is still his.

The heaviest shades fall on bookish, spinster-bound Mary, obtuse in social display, laughable in intellectual ambition, her learning good only for arid maxims, and stupid, even heartless moralisms – a bluestocking satire (of course Marsha Hunt wears glasses in the 1940 Robert Z. Leonard film). Yet Mary is more than a little Austenian, and what she's learned from books (say, Blair's *Lectures on Rhetoric and Belles Lettres*)[7] is on the same page as the moral business of *Pride and Prejudice*:

> By all that I have ever read, I am convinced that [pride] is very common indeed, that human nature is particularly prone to it, and that there are very few of us who do not cherish a feeling of self-complacency on the score of some quality or other, real or imaginary. Vanity and pride are different things, though the words are often used synonimously. A person may be proud without being vain. Pride relates more to our opinion of ourselves, vanity to what we would have others think of us. (*PP*: 20)

This could have been Austen's own conviction about *Pride and Prejudice*.

The project of reading *Pride and Prejudice* entails questions about what Austen is ultimately convinced of. Is the novel's romance core counter to the facts of most women's lives? Or do its penumbras and shades of social realism lend a verisimilitude of probability? The future Lady Byron wrote to her mother that her "interest" in the novel, "especially for Mr. Darcy," had to do with its effect as a "most probable fiction."[8] This is a novel, Claudia Johnson proposes, of "experiment with conservative myths," tuning these "to accommodate what could otherwise be seen as subversive impulses and values" into a vehicle of "incisive social criticism" (1998: 75). How to measure the lures and limits of fiction is a question not only about the probabilities of what happens in *Pride and Prejudice;* it is also a question for its readers. And it never seems settled.

"Also read again, and for the third time at least, Miss Austen's very finely written novel of *Pride and Prejudice*," wrote Scott in his journal, March 14, 1826 (1890, vol. 1: 155). For Austen's readers, too, impressions mean and matter because they are never final impressions. This is the deep pleasure not only in reading, but in rereading *Pride and Prejudice*.

NOTES

1 Smiles, 1891, vol. 1: 282; Murray had read *Pride and Prejudice,* and asked William Gifford (who edited Murray's *Quarterly Review*) for his views.

2 The sheets were printed with 12 pages (4 × 6.25 in. [10 × 16 cm]) on each side, then folded and stitched into a volume; each volume of *Pride and Prejudice* held about 300 pages.

3 I draw on St Clair's (2004) statistics. The success of the 1813 editions, realizing more than £450, propelled new sales of *Sense and Sensibility* (Fergus 1997: 21–3).

4 The wit is Marilyn Butler's (1975: 213), echoing Henry Crabb Robinson's diary (January 1819): "Elizabeth and the proud Darcy . . . at first hate" (Claudia Johnson and

Susan Wolfson (2003) eds. *Jane Austen's Pride and Prejudice. A Longman Cultural Edition.* New York: Longman/Pearson, p. 440).

5 Published in 1790, *Reflections on the Revolution in France* was still a best seller when *Pride and Prejudice* was published; England and France had been at war almost continuously for 20 years.

6 I am indebted to Deidre Lynch (1998: 131) for this supplement.

7 "Pride, makes us esteem ourselves; Vanity, makes us desire the esteem of others"; cited in Pat Rogers's Cambridge University Press 2006 edition of *Pride and Prejudice*, p. 470.

8 Letter, May 1, 1813; Johnson and Wolfson (2003: 430).

FURTHER READING

Johnson, Claudia (1988). *Jane Austen: Women, Politics, and the Novel.* Chicago: University of Chicago Press.

Jones, Darryl (2004). *Jane Austen: Critical Issues.* London: Palgrave.

Lynch, Deidre Shauna (1998). *The Economy of Character: Novels, Market Culture, and the Business of Inner Meaning.* Chicago: University of Chicago Press.

Todd, Janet (2006). *The Cambridge Introduction to Jane Austen.* Cambridge, UK: Cambridge University Press.

Waldron, Mary (1999). *Jane Austen and the Fiction of Her Time.* Cambridge, UK: Cambridge University Press, 1999.

Wiltshire, John (2006). *Jane Austen: Introductions and Interventions.* London: Palgrave Macmillan.

10

The Missed Opportunities of *Mansfield Park*

William Galperin

I

In a conversation with Fanny Price in *Mansfield Park*'s penultimate chapter, Edmund Bertram is worried that a particular "retrospect of what might have been – but what never can be now" may likely cause the novel's heroine "pain" rather than "pleasure" (*MP*: 455). To readers of the novel, however, not to mention Fanny herself, the referent of Edmund's "what" – the prospect of her marrying Henry Crawford – seems anything but a missed opportunity. And yet it is also typical of the various missed opportunities of *Mansfield Park*, beginning with the novel's divided and self-canceling allegiances, that its hero would appear to lament something whose loss both the narrative and, more particularly the narrator, are unambiguous in celebrating. As early, perhaps, as its neglect by the periodical press upon publication, *Mansfield Park* has remained the missed opportunity of the Austen canon: a novel that, although written at the height of its author's powers – and there is assuredly not a better or more sophisticated instance of free indirect discourse in any other Austen novel – chronically misfires in attempting to sway readers to a position and to a set of values that other aspects of the novel, notably the social world on which it dilates, stubbornly resist.

That *Mansfield Park* (1814) received *no* reviews despite its proximity to two works, *Sense and Sensibility* (1811) and *Pride and Prejudice* (1813) that had been published recently and generally well-received – and to which readers were alerted on the new novel's title page – is surely a missed opportunity for literary historians. But it speaks more immediately to a certain difficulty or opacity in the novel that Austen's contemporaries, including the family and friends whose "opinions" on the novel Austen gathered in 1814 and 1815, variously acknowledge. The more developed observations invariably come to an impasse for which the novel's striking verisimilitude or "natural[ness]" (as Austen's brother Frank put it) seems more a portmanteau description than an achievement whose virtues are entirely self-explanatory (Southam 1968: 48). There are, to be sure, members of the Austen circle who prefer *Mansfield Park* for its moral theme. But among those who admire it for "scenes" that, as Lady Gordon described them, are "so exactly descriptive, so perfectly natural," the reality onto which the novel opens seems relatively uncontained and continuous with life rather than a world bounded or circumscribed by narrative form. Or, quoting Lady Gordon once more, "there is scarcely an Incident or conversation, or a person that you are not inclined to imagine you have at one time or other in your Life been a witness, born a part in, & been acquainted with" (Southam 1968: 51).

That "life" essentially takes precedence over its representation is meant as a tribute to Austen's artistry. Nevertheless, such artistry remains ancillary, in the mind of many of Austen's contemporaries, to the world to which *Mansfield Park* continually gives access. Anne Romilly – writing to Maria Edgeworth – compared *Mansfield Park* favorably to Scott's *Waverley*, which she disliked for being too much a novel and too concerned with its hero rather than with "general manners." A good novel "must be true to life," she writes, "which [*Mansfield Park*] is, with a good story vein of principle running thro' the whole." But it is the latter virtue, leading to what Romilly terms an "elevation of virtue" or "something beyond nature," that Austen's novel curiously lacks. What it gives instead is "real natural every day life, and will amuse an idle hour very well in spite of its faults" (Romilly and Edgeworth 1936: 92).

It would not be very long, of course, before the "story vein of principle," which is missing for Romilly amid the novel's surplus of "every day life," would come to characterize Austen's achievement in *Mansfield Park* and elsewhere. In his influential assessment of Austen's career occasioned by the posthumous publication of *Northanger Abbey* and *Persuasion* shortly after her death, Bishop Richard Whately saw a far greater cooperation between the verisimilitude of Austen's representations and their ability to impart "moral lessons." In contrast to novels where the "purpose of inculcating a religious principle is made too palpably prominent," he writes:

> The moral lessons of [Austen's] novels, though clearly and impressively conveyed, are not offensively put forward, but spring incidentally from the circumstances of the story; they are not forced upon the reader, but he is left to collect them (though without any difficulty) for himself: hers is that unpretending kind of instruction which is furnished by real life; and certainly no author has ever conformed more closely to real life, as well as in the incidents, as in the characters and descriptions. (Southam 1968: 98, 95)

And it is *Mansfield Park*, not *Emma* or *Pride and Prejudice* nor the two recently published novels of which Whately's is ostensibly a review, that is singled out as containing "some of Miss Austin's [*sic*] best moral lessons, as well as her most humorous descriptions" (Southam 1968: 99).

Even granting that Austen's novel of "ordination" has its share of humorous instances and asides, Whately surely had many better examples of Austen's humor at his disposal, including at least one of the novels – *Northanger Abbey* – under review. His exaggerated claim, then, for *Mansfield Park*'s humor is more than just special pleading. It is consistent with his larger claim that the naturalness of *Mansfield Park* is really a contrivance – or a naturalizing apparatus – rather than a limit point (following Romilly and others) in which the "every day" is all that remains in the novel, for better or for worse.

Whately was hardly benighted in arguing for *Mansfield Park*'s artistry or for its commitment to moral principles. But his case for Austen overall is not very well served by the novel for which he reserves special praise. For what *Mansfield Park* lacks – thanks chiefly to a heroine who has seemingly learned everything she needs to learn and whose signature action is to say "no" over and over[1] – is a "story vein of principle" in which a character's desert is tied to some development or moral education. It is true that Fanny begins as the frightened ward of the Bertram household and ends triumphantly as both the wife of Edmund Bertram and the mainstay of the Bertram family. But it is the case too that, unlike Emma Woodhouse or Elizabeth Bennet, Fanny's material and temporal progress is disjoined from her moral development, which essentially precedes the narrative and from which "the circumstances of the story" are primarily a falling away. These "circumstances," to be sure, are readily assimilable to a "moral lesson" that the narrator means to inculcate and in which Fanny, whose perspective is frequently indistinguishable from the narrator's, abides as a paragon of virtue. But it is also the case that the circumstances of the novel's story, chiefly the practices of the novel's other characters and the details and circumstances by which their practices are shaped, operate not just as negative examples in the novel but as the only examples in effect – the only "real life" – that the novel truly considers.

Confronted, then, with a novel suspended between an "every day" represented with uncanny accuracy and a narrative or narrative perspective in which that same reality is found wanting, it is hardly any wonder that Austen's earliest readers routinely disarticulated the world viewed in *Mansfield Park* from the world judged. Although the novel is far from opaque in its attempts to distribute praise and blame, the only substance of *Mansfield Park*, the only reality, remains a world and a milieu where "principle" is largely an imposition – or, like Sir Thomas's sudden return from Antigua, an interruption – rather than an "unpretending" feature of the everyday. The invariable response of readers such as Mrs Pole, who, like Romilly and others, commends the novel's accuracy of representation,[2] is perhaps best seen as a subset of the silence with which the novel was met by professional readers upon publication. For the missed opportunity of *Mansfield Park* – in this case as a considerable achievement by one Jane Austen – is strangely homologous with all that the *narrative* knows on earth, where virtually everything, from the theatrical at Mansfield to Mrs Norris's parsimony to everyday sociability, goes largely unappreciated.

II

In effectively siding with *Mansfield Park*'s imitation of life over and against its apparent judgment of the "every day," Austen's earliest readers were actually following the novel's lead in its necessary dependence on a society and a world in which there are precious few alternatives to those who, like Henry Crawford, are at least bent on "doing something." But Austen's readers were also responding to something else in *Mansfield Park* that owes to the circumstances of its composition, particularly in relation to the two novels Austen had recently published and to which she had returned in the years and months preceding the writing of the new novel. Although the extent and nature of the revisions to *Sense and Sensibility* and, more immediately, *Pride and Prejudice* will always be a matter of speculation, the six years or so during which all six of Austen's novels were either written or revised (at least in part) for publication provided Austen with an aperture on her writing overall, and on the relationship of her achievement to the culture and milieu that she lived in and wrote about, that is fairly unique. Her well-known observation in a letter to her sister Cassandra, where *Mansfield Park* is described as representing a "complete change of subject – ordination" – from the just revised *Pride and Prejudice* (*Letters*: 202), is a comparative assessment that seems largely thematic in focus. Yet in light of the nearly two decades in which *Pride and Prejudice* was to one degree or other a work in progress, the comparison is perforce temporal and historical as well.

In all three early works, *Pride and Prejudice, Sense and Sensibility*, and *Northanger Abbey*, the rise of the novel as a regulatory and realistic instrument, in which the Austen heroine, as Walter Scott observed of her, is eventually "turned wise by precept, example, and experience" (Southam 1968: 64), is counterpoised to a past in which the heroine's early independence fashions a horizon of possibility that is foreclosed upon but scarcely forgotten. This memory persists thanks not only to the history *in* these novels, whose heroines are more expansive and more interesting early on, but also to the literary history that *Sense and Sensibility*, for example, helped write in its transformation from epistolary form – a form characterized in Austen's understanding by its constitutive indeterminacy – to the "[new] style of novel" (Scott in Southam 1968: 63) in its regulatory and probabilistic formation.

A central feature of the new style of novel – consistent with its turn from a world of possibility to one of "probabilit[y]" (Scott in Southam 1968: 63) – is its mode of narration in the form of third-person omniscience or free indirect discourse. While there is no disputing Austen's instrumentality in the novel's rise, or the gratification she took in her particular exercise of narrative authority, it is the case too that her works generally, but particularly *Mansfield Park*, seem bifurcated between an achievement that looks forward to the nineteenth-century novel, both in formal terms and as an instrument of regulation such as Whately describes, and a less wieldy fascination with the everyday and its minutiae that, as Whately also notes, is at cross-purposes with this regulatory function and the "unpretending kind of instruction . . . furnished by real life." The closer, apparently, that Austen conforms to real life (Whately's terms) the further she departs from the very project – the realistic project – that the "appearance of reality" ideally underwrites for Whately.[3] And that's because the peculiar "vividness of description" that *Mansfield Park*'s initial readers find so striking is not simply at variance with the moral lessons that both the narrator and the narrative continually inculcate; it is also redolent of a culture – a domestic culture – that is familiar despite being under siege or, as the narrative continually urges, decadent and increasingly moribund. That Mary Crawford's world, or even that of the Bertram sisters, remains a "retrospect of . . . what never can be now" was still news to Austen's largely female and privileged readership; and it is news, too, to many of the characters in *Mansfield Park*, whose actions, however derogated, stand in problematic juxtaposition to the relative inaction of the novel's heroine and the more modern – or, as a number of critics have described them, "Victorian" – standards by which the heroine, the narrator, and the novel's plot collectively bring the mostly female characters here to judgment.[4] Thus even as it works primarily to justify the rise and fall of emergent and residual cultural practices respectively, the division of form and content in *Mansfield Park* is no less a division *over time* that, in the spirit of Edmund's "retrospect" and its concern over "what might have been," looks backward simultaneously to a world where, among other things, women do more than simply say "no."

Dubbed "Mansfield Park" in an arguably ironic echo of Lord Chief Justice Mansfield's recourse to Elizabethan precedent in describing England as having "air too pure for slaves to breathe in,"[5] the world so vividly described in *Mansfield Park* is both a defection from what the narrative doggedly presents as an improved mode of social practice, as well as a stay against this new and improved mode that the titular irony very quickly picks up on. Although decadent and diminished on the arguments of both the narrator and new moralists such as Bishop Whately, the England or what amounts, again, to the primary content of *Mansfield Park* stands opposed in many ways to what, in Hayden White's phrase, remains "the content of form" here: namely, the England that is *becoming* "Mansfield Park." Mary Crawford's riposte supporting architectural changes wrought upon the chapel at Sotherton, along with newer, more relaxed, devotional practices – "every generation has its improvements" (*MP*: 86) – is more than just an exercise in unprincipled relativism. It attacks, in short, the developmental view of history to which the narrative – as opposed to the novel now – continually subscribes. Mary's statement explains too, then, why "Mansfield Park," both the site of slaveholders *sans* slaves and the work so titled, is no longer, strictly speaking, a site of competing ideologies or values. For in its necessary situation along an axis of development over time, "Mansfield Park" – the seemingly immaculate and domesticated counterweight to the imperial and military Britain that cannot go by any other name – is far from even-handed, especially in its teleology. Commensurate instead with Fanny or Susan or William Price's upward mobility, "Mansfield Park" properly names and masks a Britain very much in formation. It names a culture whose values and whose instruments of value, including the institution of the novel itself, are transparently self-serving rather than a reliable measure of a different – in this case residual – culture that may be derogated or expunged. But this is not all that the novel does. For every prospect of improvement along these lines, there remain, as Austen's contemporary readers quickly intuited, numerous "retrospects" in *Mansfield Park* where the "every day" is alternately mimetic and nostalgic. These retrospects make clear that "what might have been," to borrow Edmund's calculus once more, is a missed opportunity in several registers: a prospect whose prestige is linked not just to its foreclosure (as Edmund observes) or to its uncanny, if waning, persistence (as the novel effectively documents), but also to its confinement or (following Austen's early readers again) to its virtual quarantine now as an aspect of the "every day."

Two such opportunities occur in two nodal episodes – the visit to Sotherton and the private theatricals at Mansfield – that help shape and propel the narrative, especially in its initial stage. And they are remarkable in the way what is missed or "never . . . can be" in each instance is mobilized to justify what the narrative promotes in partnership with time.[6] The result in each case of Fanny's opportunistic reticence, the missed opportunity exposes two things in *Mansfield Park*: the winner-take-all logic that drives the narrative in the image of the imperium it serves; and the possibilities, both cultural and aesthetic, that the narrative and its heroine are impressed ultimately to defeat. The first such opportunity comes nicely in the form of a "prospect" that Fanny and her walking companions, Maria Bertram and Henry Crawford, are prevented from entering by a locked "iron gate" and an adjacent ha-ha that give Maria in particular "a feeling of restraint and hardship." Rather than waiting for their host, Mr Rushworth, to unlock the gate with a key, Maria accepts Henry's assistance in "pass[ing] round the edge of the gate," leaving Fanny to remonstrate by warning Maria that she will hurt herself. But Maria does not hurt herself. She negotiates the prohibitions with Henry's assistance and the two are quickly out of view, leaving Fanny "with no increase of pleasant feelings" which soon escalate to "disagreeable musings" (*MP*: 99, 100).[7]

The second opportunity that Fanny eschews involves her participation in the private production of the play *Lovers' Vows*. Like her rejection of the earlier prospect, a rejection (the novel suggests) with "literal" as well as "figural" implications, Fanny's ostentatious refusal to participate in the play ("No, indeed, I cannot act") is met again by a concomitant misery that, while ostensibly a function of jealousy over Edmund, operates "figuratively" once more in projecting or in retrojecting a smiling horizon of female agency and mobility: "Alas, it was all Miss Crawford's doing. She had seen her influence in every speech [of Edmund's] and was miserable" (*MP*: 145, 156).

III

The question of misery, especially as it impinges on both the heroine and the narrative perspective, in which Fanny's view is often simply echoed or appropriated, is a particularly vexing one. This is because the misery into which Fanny frequently shrinks, especially when she is compelled to say "no" to something, also puts an all-too-human face on a narrative whose dogged commitment to rewarding virtue and punishing vice finds issue in a plot that must resort either to clumsy inculpation – the elopements and dissipations that precipitate regime change at Mansfield – or in a perspective that must hold its nose, especially regarding those in whom value and virtue are supposedly vested. And so, when recounting the developments leading to Fanny's and

Edmund's eventual marriage, the narrative shifts temporarily to the first person and to a subject position that free and indirect discourse typically (or at least theoretically) transcends.

> I purposely abstain from dates on this occasion, that every one may be at liberty to fix their own, aware that the cure of unconquerable passions, and the transfer of unchanging attachments, must vary much as to time in different people. – I only intreat every body to believe that exactly at the time when it was quite natural that it should be so, and not a week earlier, Edmund did cease to care about Miss Crawford, and became as anxious to marry Fanny, as Fanny herself could desire. (*MP*: 470)

Even allowing for the resuscitation of something bordering on wit in *Mansfield Park*, the description is, comparatively speaking, a miserable one, both in its economy and in its nearly Aristotelian decorum, where the coming together of the hero and heroine is enough of a downer at this juncture to be kept from view.

This conflict, where the imperatives of form and ideology are presented as reluctant concessions, is worth exploring a little further. For the narrator's irruption into personhood at *Mansfield Park*'s close is more than simply a violation (however abbreviated) of decorum and form. It is a transgression that, in effectively yoking narrative deliberation to an affect of aversion, even misery, necessarily highlights both the pleasure as well as the "fate of pleasure" in all that has preceded it. To argue, of course, that only Fanny or Edmund or even Sir Thomas are the repositories of misery or dourness in *Mansfield Park* overlooks the fact that many, if not all of the characters, from the neurasthenic Lady Bertram, to the miserly Aunt Norris, to the gluttonous Doctor Grant, not to mention the remaining Bertram children, ultimately join with the novel's heroes and supposed winners in projecting a horizon of unhappiness and discontent. Thus even as there are – affectively speaking – no real winners in *Mansfield Park* save in the most monolithic register (e.g., William's success at cards and projectively as a naval officer), there remains a distinction in the novel, which gains traction at the level of style or attention, between a prospective view, aligned increasingly with things as they are becoming both at home and abroad, and a retrospective view, in which things at present – the "real natural every day life" that Austen's early readers were continually struck by – are infused with a sense of "what might have been."

It is the achievement of *Mansfield Park*, however fraught, that "what might have been" gains a material sanction at the level of representation or in everyday practice that is simultaneously forfeited at the level of story, whose miserable trajectory is a foreclosure on "real life," leading to a sense, again, that "what might have been" remains, unlike Keats's nightingale, born for death. Exactly "what might have been" may be a little hard to calculate at this stage or on the basis of what has transpired in the novel. That is because the representable world in this, the first novel of Austen's to be written at the time of its publication, appears to be a falling away, both temporally and ideologically, from what is not just the present (or the novel's moment of composition) but an impending and inferable future of which the events here, chiefly the rise and fall of specific characters, are both transitional and foundational.

But calculations can work by subtraction. And they do in the novel's largely negative way with a set of people, whose idleness and apparent decadence are a debit against certain imperatives, chiefly the "duties" (as Thomas Gisborne described them in his famous conduct manual that Austen was reading as she was conceiving *Mansfield Park*) of men and women respectively. It is frequently remarked that one of the primary features of Austen's early novels is that nobody in them works for a living, in contrast to the later novels, where the rising professional orders (in, for example, Edmund's clerical and William's naval vocations) are held in general esteem. The subtraction, then, of Henry and Mary Crawford and of Julia, Maria, and Tom Bertram from a projected sum of specifically defined duties, all pursuant to gender, runs in a different direction. It runs backwards in time, or better still *in place*, to a sum or plenitude, where feminization is neither a pejorative nor a codification but a reality; where what is close at hand is remarkably flexible and permeable rather than rigidly circumscribed. One aspect of this permeability is undoubtedly the prerogative of saying "yes" as well as "no," which leads the Bertram daughters, in particular, to actions that are also grist for both the narrator's and the narrative's program. Another aspect involves seemingly idle or effeminate men who have nothing better to do than to stage plays, to socialize, and to authorize certain architectural or landscape improvements. This feminized or domestic space is on the wane now, as evidenced by Sir Thomas and Lady Bertram who are, if nothing else, man and woman respectively. Yet even as they give a good sense, in their prototypically divided lives and separate spheres, of changes already afoot, the Bertrams make "doing something" – even if it's just a play or an outing (or in *Emma* a dance) – more *interesting* than just standing put or, in Lady Bertram's case, not moving.

For the basic division in *Mansfield Park* of story and event is a way of thinking finally in which "improvements" are both marked and countenanced – but only by dissociation from the grand narrative of progress and by relocation to the "every day." An example of this "every day," and of the pause or thinking to which it gives rise, is the frequently cited moment of Sir Thomas's encounter with Yates in what was Sir Thomas's closet prior to becoming the temporary stage for the performance of *Lovers' Vows*:

> He stept to the door, rejoicing at that moment in having the means of immediate communication, and opening it, found himself on the stage of a theatre, and opposed to a ranting young man, who appeared likely to knock him down backwards. At the very moment of Yates perceiving Sir Thomas, and giving perhaps the very best start he had ever given in the whole course of his rehearsals, Tom Bertram entered at the other end of the room; and never had he found greater difficulty in keeping his countenance. His father's looks of solemnity and amazement on his first appearance on any stage, and the gradual metamorphosis of the impassioned Baron Wildenhaim into the well-bred and easy Mr. Yates, making his bow and apology to Sir Thomas Bertram, was such an exhibition, such a piece of true acting as he would not have lost upon any account. It would

be the last – in all probability the last on that stage; but he was sure there could not be a finer. The house would close with the greatest eclat. (*MP*: 182–3)

I earlier noted that *Mansfield Park* provides the best and most sophisticated use of free indirect discourse in any of Austen's novels. Never is that more evident than in this passage, which morphs effortlessly, like Yates himself, from Sir Thomas's point of view to the narrator's before finally settling into Tom's, where most of the thinking transpires. Such thinking, like the pleasure it produces, is rightly inconclusive and overdetermined. But Tom's status as a reader proxy, disposed to reflect on what the novel makes available to the reader simultaneously, is consolidated in his notion of "true acting." For this bemused reflection speaks not just to the impetus, arguably, behind the private theatricals to begin with or, quoting Henry Crawford, to "what signifies a theatre" ultimately (*MP*: 123) – namely, the blurred boundaries of role-playing and true being that Yates enacts both here and in the role of the Baron, who discovers and endows his "natural son" Frederick with a new identity in Kotzebue's play. It speaks even more to the dynamic and necessarily unstable constitution of an "every day" that the narrative, in the image of Sir Thomas, works mightily to contain and to delimit. In the very way, then, that every generation has its improvements (or not), so the rising generation of *Mansfield Park* – represented primarily by Fanny – is able in one breath to renounce acting in the interests of transparency or morality, and equally capable of performance or duplicity whenever the occasion warrants, whether in appropriating sentiments and ideas in the passages that find Fanny in quotation, or in the headaches and somatic complaints by which she gains attention and, by turns, her way.

There is nothing wrong, or to the novel's detriment, in presenting a character, especially a heroine, who is as constitutively duplicitous as those on whom she chronically passes judgment, and who additionally serves notice that the masochist, in her unrivalled capacity to endure pain, will prevail in any given situation. It is consistent with the novel's invitation to thinking that it would necessarily seize upon such a character in defense of what the narrative promotes. But it is equally characteristic of *Mansfield Park* and of the missed opportunity that *is Mansfield Park* that this invitation is tendered only to be withdrawn. Such withdrawals are everywhere, from the many instances where Fanny's viewpoint and the narrator's are indistinguishable, to the elements of plot that succeed in disposing of all challenges to the emergent, more codified, world that the novel seemingly endorses in documenting Fanny's rise. And yet, as Austen's initial readers recognized, chiefly because it was so striking and unprecedented, the viewpoint of *Mansfield Park* is also frequently indistinguishable from Tom's perspective in Sir Thomas's closet. This is not necessarily because Tom is somehow the implied or surrogate narrator that Fanny remains in her invariable posture of silent observation and pity. It is because the novel's remarkable way with the everyday proceeds in the same slow motion, and with the same invitation to reflection and bemusement, as the scene onto which Tom accidentally happens. This bemusement is probably a good deal closer to Anne Romilly's sense of the novel's verisimilitude, which "will amuse an idle hour very well," than it is to the "humorous descriptions" that are inseparable, in Bishop Whately's view, from the novel's "moral lessons." But what is at stake finally, with Tom as a guide now, is less bemusement really than an appreciation or recognition of things that *Mansfield Park*'s inimitable way with "every day life" enables. Such a stance exposes – by continually exploiting – the representational opportunities that narratives, be they fictional or historical, routinely discard in their various subscriptions to probability and form (see White 1987, Phillips 2000, Zimmerman 1996). And it recalls and commemorates – and here Edmund's "retrospect" is key – the opportunities, the missed opportunities, that have been written out of history by time itself and by "the considerable changes in places, manners, books, and opinions."

NOTES

1 David Nokes describes Fanny as a "heroine [with] nothing to learn" (Nokes 1998: 413).

2 "Everything is natural, & the situations & incidents are told in a manner which clearly evinces the Writer to *belong* to the Society whose Manners she so ably delineates (Southam 1968: 51).

3 For an anatomy of the regulatory realism that Austen is often argued to have helped inaugurate, see especially Levine (1981). See also Miller (1989). I contest this view of Austen's achievement in *The Historical Austen* (Galperin 2003), taking my lead instead

from the responses of the novelist's earliest readers.

4 See Yeazell (1984) and Julia Prewitt Brown (1975: 80–100).

5 Quoted in Kirkham (1983). I am indebted to Kirkham for this connection.

6 See also my essay "Describing what never happened" (Galperin 2006), a small section of which is reproduced here.

7 "'Your prospects, however, are too fair to justify want of spirits. You have a very smiling scene before you.' 'Do you mean literally or figuratively?'" (*MP*: 99).

FURTHER READING

Duckworth, Alistair (1971). *The Improvement of The Estate*. Baltimore: Johns Hopkins University Press.

Galperin, William (1992). The theatre at Mansfield Park: from Classic to Romantic once more. *Eighteenth-Century Life*, 16, 247–71.

Galperin, William (2006). "Describing what never happened." Jane Austen and the history of missed opportunities. *ELH*, 73, 355–82.

Litvak, Joseph (1992). *Caught in the Act: Theatricality in the Nineteenth-Century English Novel*. Berkeley: University of California Press, pp. 1–26.

Said, Edward (1993). *Culture and Imperialism*. New York: Knopf, pp. 80–97.

Trilling, Lionel (1955). *Mansfield Park*. In *The Opposing Self* (pp. 206–30). New York: Viking.

11

Emma: Word Games and
Secret Histories

Linda Bree

In the autumn of 1814, Jane Austen's niece Anna was writing a novel, and sending chapters to her aunt for comment.[1] Austen was critical about many aspects of the draft, but enthusiastic about the general situation Anna had created: "You are now collecting your People delightfully, getting them exactly into such a spot as is the delight of my life; – 3 or 4 Families in a Country Village is the very thing to work on – and I hope you will . . . make full use of them while they are so very favourably arranged" (*Letters*: 275). This statement has often been regarded as a commentary by Austen on her work in general, but it is very precisely related to the novel she was herself working on that autumn: *Emma* was created between January 1814 and March 1815.[2] It is the only one of Austen's novels dealing with a small rural community in the way she recommends, with its concentration on the interlinking lives of the Woodhouses, the Knightleys, the Westons, the Eltons, and the Bateses, in and around Highbury, a "large and populous village almost amounting to a town." During the course of the novel Highbury itself comes to have a substantial presence: the "broad, though irregular main street" (vol. 1, ch. 10)[3] containing Ford's, "the principal woollen-draper, linen-draper, and haberdasher's shop united" (vol. 2, ch. 3), the Crown Inn, "an inconsiderable house, though the principal one of the sort" (vol. 2, ch. 1), and buildings such as the "brick house, sashed window below and casement above" (vol. 3, ch. 14), belonging to "people in business" (vol. 2, ch. 1) where gentlewomen of reduced means such as the Bateses can lodge; the large houses of Hartfield and Donwell Abbey situated on the outskirts in one direction, and the vicarage, "an old and not very good house" (vol. 1, ch. 10) up a dirt-track lane in another. Only one scene in the novel, the excursion to the nearby beauty spot of Box Hill, takes place away from this environment. London is 16 miles distant: the John Knightleys visit from their home in Brunswick Square and Mr Knightley, Harriet, and Robert Martin spend time with them there; Mr Elton goes to London to have a picture framed, and Frank Churchill to order a piano. All these events, however, are only talked of: London itself remains resolutely as offstage as Ireland, where the Campbells are visiting the newly settled Dixons ("Let the Portmans go to Ireland, but as you know nothing of the manners there, you had better not go with them. You will be in danger of false representations," Austen wrote to Anna, *Letters*: 269).

Austen herself was very familiar with village life, having spent her first 26 years, and later the five years leading up to the composition of *Emma*, living in the Hampshire villages of Steventon and Chawton respectively. She wrote with personal experience of evenings dominated by "the usual rate of conversation; a few clever things said, a few downright silly, but by much the larger proportion neither the one nor the other – nothing worse than every day remarks, dull repetitions, old news, and heavy jokes" (vol. 2, ch. 8). In Highbury, routine and repetition are the order of the day. The heroine, Emma Woodhouse, "handsome, clever and rich" as she is, has indeed "very little" – possibly too little – "to distress or vex her": her family has lived on the outskirts of the village for generations and she is now, since the marriages of her sister and (the event that prompts the action of the novel) her governess, permanently fixed at Hartfield taking care of her invalid father, and engaging in a narrow round of social and charitable activities. Accused by her London brother-in-law of having a newly flourishing social life, she points out that this has consisted of "Dining once with the Coles – and having a ball talked of, which never took place" (vol. 2, ch. 18). Even this level of activity is unusual: no one until now has made the most of the possibilities which do exist – there is a whist club for the men, but despite an available room no ball has previously been planned at the Crown, and though Box Hill is only seven miles from the village, it has remained unvisited. Emma, a wealthy inhabitant of the small island nation of Britain, has never seen the sea, which would be well within a day's travel in the family carriage.

Austen's enthusiasm for the depiction of the ordinary life of a country village community was not shared by many of those who read the novel on its publication in December 1815; and in fact despite the efforts of its publisher John Murray no second edition was called for in Austen's lifetime. Formal reviews were favorable, but reviewers clearly saw the novel as bland: it was "amusing, inoffensive and well principled"; "amusing . . . [with] no tendency to deteriorate the heart"; "the work will probably become a favourite with all those who seek for harmless amusement, rather than deep pathos or appalling horrors, in works of fiction" (Le Faye 2004: 232). Though the height of the Gothic vogue had passed, readers still looked for the excitement of larger-than-life incident in their fiction: at the climax of Mary Brunton's popular *Self-Control* (1811) the heroine was abducted to Canada by her obsessive suitor, and escaped by floating down the St Lawrence river tied within a canoe; Walter Scott's runaway hit, *Waverley* (1814), with its personalized account of the Jacobite rebellion of 1745, showed that fiction could address large questions of national identity and historical change. Even those readers of *Emma* themselves devoted to the creation of less dramatic forms of fiction were puzzled. Maria Edgeworth, the author of novels of domestic morality much admired by Austen and many others, complained of *Emma* that "There was no story in it" (Le Faye 2004: 231); Susan Ferrier, whose first novel, *Marriage*, would be a success in 1818, commented in very similar terms that "there is no story whatever." Unlike Edgeworth, however, Ferrier did not see this as a disadvantage: she found the novel "excellent . . . the characters all so true to life, and the style so piquant, that it does not require the adventitious aids of mystery and adventure" (Le Faye 2004: 231).

Austen's own earlier works had offered their melodramatic moments: the tale of seduction and desertion of two generations of women in *Sense and Sensibility*, Lydia's elopement and premarital cohabitation with Wickham in *Pride and Prejudice*, Maria Rushworth's adultery in *Mansfield Park*. In *Emma* the nearest the narrative gets to behavior of this kind is Emma's inaccurate speculation – always half-hearted, and later retracted – that Jane Fairfax might be harboring a guilty passion for the man who has just married her friend. Otherwise the most exciting events are a couple of timid schoolgirls being frightened by gypsies, and the theft – by report – of Mrs Weston's turkeys.

In such an environment people make their entertainments in unsophisticated ways. Word games, the early nineteenth-century equivalents of crosswords or Sudoku, were a common form of entertainment in Austen's own family, as is demonstrated by the survival of a book of family riddles and charades, and of a number of poems created by Austen herself depending on wordplay for their effect.[4] Harriet's collection of charades in *Emma* is entirely consistent with this, as are games of spelling from children's letters (though how long could it really have taken Harriet to puzzle over the five letters making up the word "Dixon"?). Mr Knightley's distinction between "amiable" and *aimable* in trying to put his finger on the deficiencies of Frank Churchill's personality (to Mr Knightley the French *aimable* signifies the surface virtues of having "very good manners" and being "very agreeable" while the English "amiable" looks deeper to "delicacy towards the feelings of other people," vol. 1, ch. 18) is related to this, but hints at extra dimensions of significance in plays on words. And the narrator of the novel has interests in wordplay at her own level too, for example in the variations rung on significant words such as "perfection" and "blunder." Simple forms of wordplay may hold innocent entertainment for Highbury's inhabitants, but they also open up larger questions of words and their meanings, and discrepancy between what is said and what is being conveyed.

The chief manipulator of words and their meanings in the novel is of course Emma herself. Emma is lively and intelligent, with a bright and sometimes brutal mind, and a vivid imagination – the narrator calls her an "imaginist" (vol. 3, ch. 3). However, surrounded by the respect of her social inferiors and the affection of her family, but with little mental stimulation outside herself, Emma has become intellectually lazy. Her good intentions as a girl were reflected in impressive "To do" lists rather than in carrying out the program of activities described; she has abilities in art and music, but has never practiced enough to fulfill her potential; she prefers to take as a friend Harriet Smith, whom she can patronize and manipulate, rather than Jane Fairfax, her intellectual equal; she has developed a quite conscious strategy of not thinking through her own ideas and actions if they promise to be uncomfortable ("Mr Knightley might quarrel with her but Emma could not quarrel with herself," vol. 1, ch. 9). Her way of arguing herself into a position she wishes to adopt, against her own reason and logic, is occasionally almost as brilliant as the John Dashwoods talking themselves out of giving Mrs Dashwood and her daughters any money at the beginning of *Sense and Sensibility*.

Like many bright people, Emma is particularly impatient of the intellectual shortcomings of others; but her position – something by which she holds great store – requires her constantly to impose restraint on the natural expression of strong feelings. Willingly patient and considerate with her valetudinarian father, she has to tolerate with at least outward politeness people who at best bore her and at worst are a constant irritant. Time and again Emma is described as biting back words she wishes to say: "she could not be complying, she dreaded being quarrelsome; her heroism reached only to silence" (vol. 1, ch. 13); more ominously "the forbearance of her outward submission left a heavy arrear due of secret severity in her reflections" (vol. 3, ch. 6).

It is perhaps inevitable that her pent-up frustrations eventually find an outlet in aggression, and that that aggression is directed towards Miss Bates. There is a curious and disturbing link between Emma and Miss Bates, who is first described as "neither young, handsome, rich nor married" (vol. 1, ch. 3), recalling by inversion the opening description of Emma as "handsome, clever and rich." The old maid Emma despises has no brilliance or wit, little intellectual capability beyond simple instinctive good nature, and – crucially – is "a great talker on little matters." Emma has long found Miss Bates difficult to tolerate (indeed, her dislike of Jane Fairfax – "Miss Bates's niece" – stems partly from having to listen to her aunt's constant chatter about her). During the dinner at the Coles's Emma mimics Miss Bates behind her back; Mrs Weston chides her "For shame, Emma! . . . You divert me against my conscience" (vol. 2, ch. 8). However, Emma's next comment at Miss Bates's expense, at the ball at the Crown, finds a more encouraging recipient in Frank Churchill. Frank's risk-taking nature, which influences Emma who yet never quite understands its meaning, sanctions an all too tempting loosening of the restraints of polite behavior in herself. And it is Frank's shameless flirting at Box Hill, stimulating Emma and making her uncomfortable at the same time, that finally prompts her to be rude to Miss Bates to her face. She does it by *not* biting back her words, and moreover she does it on the subject of word games. Miss Bates has been good-natured enough to accede to Frank's ridiculous suggestion that each of the party should – for Emma's benefit – say one very clever, two moderately clever, or three very dull things. "'Three things very dull indeed.' That will just do for me, you know. . . ." With sublime economy of language, "Emma could not resist. / 'Ah! ma'am, but there may be a difficulty. Pardon me – but you will be limited as to number – three at once'" (vol. 3, ch. 7).

It is worth remembering that the moment passes without much remark: Miss Bates is clearly hurt, but no one takes up her cause, the conversation meanders on, and in the general jadedness of what has been an unhappy day altogether, Emma's words seem to have been forgotten until Mr Knightley upbraids her, at which point "Emma recollected, blushed, was sorry, but tried to laugh it off" (vol. 3, ch. 7). Perhaps the reader, as well as Emma, only realizes the significance of this small act of cruelty once Mr Knightley points it out: the event has then to be reinterpreted.

This process of reinterpretation of events is central to the reader's experience of engagement with *Emma*, since it gradually becomes apparent that all the time the narrator is describing the routines of village life something quite other is going on beneath the surface. The narrative in fact proceeds in a variety of subtly differentiated ways: through Emma's consciousness (a complex network of rational and irrational observations, opinions, and conclusions), through what passes for an omniscient narrative voice, and through unexpected and destabilizing combinations of the two, where it is not at all clear what authority is to be gleaned from a particular observation or statement. Readers trying to be certain about the direction of the narrative are very inclined to find themselves, as in a maze, following a blind alley and having to retrace their steps. They need, early on, for example, to realize that Emma is not to be trusted – not because she is unreliable as a narrator in the traditional sense of trying to mislead the reader, but because she so often wittingly or unwittingly misleads herself.

She does this partly through overconfidence in her own intellectual abilities, and partly through unthinking assumptions about class and status. She is so keen that Mr Elton should want to marry Harriet, and it is so inconceivable to her that Mr Elton could consider her as a possible wife, that she willfully ignores any hint to the contrary, even when she is warned by John Knightley of intentions that are clearly visible to bystanders. The snobbery of which Emma is so often accused is in fact part of her intellectual laziness: reliance on traditional social structures absolves her from having to think through the strengths and weaknesses of each individual case, and yet, when it suits her, as with Harriet Smith, or with her eventual decision to accept the Coles's invitation to dinner, these values prove to be infinitely elastic as she simply reorders her principles to suit her wishes. To what extent is she justified in finding most of her neighbors beneath her, since she is more intelligent and lively than they are? And to what extent does the narrator – and behind the narrator her creator – agree with her views? The reader has to draw conclusions from the partial and fractured evidence available. Austen herself seems to have been prepared for her heroine to be condemned: she famously described Emma as "a heroine whom no-one but myself will much like" (Le Faye 2004: 119) – one of her more inaccurate opinions, as it turns out, since many readers have found Emma likeable, and some male critics have taken the issue even further: why does the reader "seem so ready to fall in love with Emma?" asked Tony Tanner, in the course of a persuasive account of the novel (1986: 177).

The formidability and fallibility of Emma's intellect is established very early on, and reaches a first climax with Mr Elton's proposal. Emma has been nurturing the romance between Harriet Smith and Mr Elton, in the face of Mr Knightley's assuring her that Mr Elton will not be interested in a girl of Harriet's obscure family situation. When Mr Elton finds himself alone in a carriage with Miss Woodhouse at the end of a dinner party, he takes the opportunity to propose. Even such a lively heroine as Elizabeth Bennet found herself temporarily nonplussed by a proposal from a self-deluding clergyman. Emma, having expressed her astonishment at what she sees as Mr Elton's opportunistic shift in affections from Harriet to herself – and his having had too much to drink – is withering: "I am exceedingly sorry: but it is well the mistake ends where it does . . . I have no thoughts of matrimony at present" (vol. 1, ch. 15); Mr Elton is dismissed.[5] Later, however, Emma seriously thinks through what has happened.

> Perhaps it was not fair to expect him to feel how very much he was her inferior in talent, and all the elegancies of mind . . . But he had fancied her in love with him; that evidently must have been his dependence; and after raving a little about the seeming incongruity of gentle manners and a conceited head, Emma was obliged in common honesty to stop and admit that her own behaviour to him had been so complaisant and obliging, so full of courtesy and attention as (supposing her real motive unperceived) might warrant a man of ordinary observation and delicacy, like Mr Elton, in fancying himself a very decided favourite. If *she* had so misinterpreted his feelings, she had little right to wonder that *he*, with self-interest to blind him, should have mistaken her's. (vol. 1, ch. 16)

In this wholly convincing passage, beautifully controlled rhythms of prose keep pace with the tracing of the thought processes of an intelligent mind trying to make sense of a very uncomfortable series of circumstances. It is wholly characteristic of Emma in combining a firm belief in her own superiority with a high degree of intellectual generosity, even a sense of humor strong enough to empathize with people she dislikes (remember the first visit to the married Mr Elton: "when she considered how peculiarly unlucky poor Mr Elton was in being in the same room at once with the woman he had just married, the woman he had wanted to marry, and the woman whom he had been expected to marry, she must allow him to have the right to look as little wise, and to be as much affectedly, and as little really easy as could be," vol. 2, ch. 14). Yet even here there is self-deception – because Emma, for all her honest reflections, will have learned very little from the episode, and will make very similar mistakes in face of the more complex deceptions of Frank Churchill and Jane Fairfax.

There is a celebrated incident in Henry Fielding's novel *Tom Jones* (1748), where most of the main characters, in a sequence of events far too convoluted to summarize here, converge at an inn in the village of Upton. They include Partridge and Mrs Waters, who under other guises at an earlier stage in their lives have been accused of being Tom Jones's parents, and who between them could solve the problem of his birth, and therefore resolve the plot (no lack of plot here!) several hundred pages before the novel actually reaches its triumphant conclusion. When, much later, the all-important matter of Tom's parentage is revealed, readers are bound to be puzzled as to why Partridge and Mrs Waters didn't sort everything out much earlier. Ah, says Fielding's narrator, glorying in his own art, if you look very carefully, you will see that at no time at Upton did Partridge and Mrs Waters actually see each other. A look back at the relevant scenes shows this to be the case.[6]

It was a technique Fielding brought with him from his experience in writing stage plays, where in comedy and farce matters of who heard what, when, and where were deployed to great effect. But it was entirely new to the novel; and it remained very rare until Austen combined it with the novelistic technique of unreliable narration to produce the extraordinary effect of *Emma*, sustained until a revelation enables the reader to discover, on revisiting earlier chapters, an entirely logical but quite different sequence of events from what appeared to have been taking place. Austen had tried the technique out, on a small scale, in *Sense and Sensibility*, where on a second reading Edward Ferrars' attitude to the Dashwoods, and his visits to Plymouth, are placed in a different perspective through the revelation of his relationship with Lucy Steele. But it becomes the driving force of *Emma*, in the comedy courtship triangle of Emma, Harriet, and Mr Elton, and then in the more complex and serious series of events centering on Emma, Jane, and Frank, and involving the whole of Highbury. One wonders whether the reviewers, or Edgeworth, or even Ferrier, had read the novel twice. For on rereading, as the layers of narrative begin to emerge, the reader begins to realize not only that he or she has, like Emma and her neighbors, been misled, but that the whole "story" of the novel has become something of a puzzle, requiring a solution from the hints and clues offered.

Unlike in the Elton/Harriet/Emma episode, the misleadings around Frank and Jane have not been accidental. "There are secrets in all families, you know," (vol. 1, ch. 14), says Mr Weston (a man constitutionally incapable of keeping any secret whatever). And while the hints as to what is going on are something of a game conducted by the narrator, the narrative which lies submerged through most of the novel is also hidden through deliberate intent on the part of Jane and Frank. Their "story" turns out to be one much more familiar in terms of the plots of the novels of the time. Jane is a typical fictional heroine through her elegance and accomplishments on the one hand, and her helplessness and vulnerability on the other. Threatened with having to earn her own bread as a governess, she has entered into a clandestine engagement with the wealthy but dependent Frank. Suffering from the conviction that her actions have been ethically wrong, she decides to break it off; but in the nick of time Frank's grandmother dies and the two are free to marry. Unlike Emma, Jane Fairfax has "seen the sea": indeed she nearly drowned in it, during the pleasure party at which she fell in love with Frank Churchill. For most of the novel their secret is kept. Once or twice it seems near to being revealed, but until Mrs Churchill's death frees Frank to marry Jane, Emma is duped, Highbury is duped, and so are all but the most perceptive readers. And yet on rereading in the light of knowledge of the engagement between Jane and Frank, the whole narrative shifts on its axis as the novel opens out into new possibilities of narrative, character, and action. It is as if every member of the Highbury community – while in some senses remaining as dull as ever – suddenly has a rounder and richer role to play. Even Miss Bates's garrulousness, no longer just a matter of tedium for Emma and her neighbors and high comedy for the reader, takes on a new significance through the hints she has offered, entirely unwittingly (and hardly attended to by her hearers), through her gossip.

A good example of this shift in narrative perspective is the long-awaited ball at the Crown (vol. 3, ch. 2). Even on a first reading there is plenty going on here, in terms of the dynamic between Emma and Frank, the hostility of the Eltons, Mr Elton's snubbing of Harriet, Mr Knightley's dancing with Harriet himself (commending her to the extent that "Emma was extremely gratified"), and then dancing with Emma for the first time. There is a general sense that something is not quite right: Mr Knightley tries in vain to find out why the Eltons are aiming to wound both Harriet and Emma, and Emma herself is having difficulty with Frank – she "could hardly understand him; he seemed in an odd humour" (vol. 3, ch. 2); though now she has determined they are not in love with each other, this merely confirms her view of him as slightly unstable. But in fact, the whole situation is far more complicated than Emma and the first-time reader, led by her, imagine: the unacknowledged lovers Frank and Jane are under increasing strain with each other, exacerbated by Frank's behavior towards Emma; Mr Knightley is trying to get to know Harriet as still a possible bride for Robert Martin; while Harriet herself, interpreting Mr Knightley's notice of her as encouragement of affection, is falling in love with him.

At the end of the novel the two main plots emerge in open parallel, as Frank and Jane are able to acknowledge their engagement, and Mr Knightley and Emma come to an understanding of their love for each other. Throughout the novel the narrator has commented – with varying levels of irony – on the importance of openness over secrets, and honesty over deceit, and inevitably this debate reaches a head as the secret engagement becomes a matter of public discussion. Emma is harsh on Frank when she finds out the truth about his relationship with Jane: "What right had he to come among us with affection and faith engaged, and with manners so *very* disengaged? . . . very wrong, very wrong indeed" (vol. 3, ch. 10). But when she goes on to criticize his lack of "that upright integrity, that strict adherence to truth and principle, that disdain of trick and littleness, which a man should display in every transaction of his life," there is a distinct sense of Emma overindulging again. And the narrator seems to agree: at the very moment of Emma's acceptance of Mr Knightley's love she reminds us that "Seldom, very seldom, does complete truth belong to any human disclosure" (vol. 3, ch. 13); and in fact the new openness which Mr Knightley claims between himself and Emma is immediately compromised by Emma's (surely correct) determination to keep from him the secret of Harriet's infatuation.

Critics have expressed differing views about Emma's prospects at the end of the novel that bears her name. She will see the sea, at last, on her honeymoon, but she will then return to the claustrophobia of Highbury life, with the Eltons and the Bateses as her neighbors, the Coles and the Perrys (since Mr Knightley has less sense of status than Emma) probably joining the group, and Mr and Mrs Robert Martin settling beneath the Knightleys' social notice. The two people who most disrupted the smooth running of the community through their secret romance, Frank Churchill and Jane Fairfax, will have left. The marriage between Mr Knightley and Emma speaks for continuity (a concept, like that of Englishness, associated with Mr Knightley throughout) rather than change. To emphasize this Austen shows the occasion on which they reach an understanding preceded by a conscious reprise of the very beginning of the novel, with Emma's concern, not this time about Miss Taylor's marriage, but about the imminent birth of Mrs Weston's first child and the changes that might occur as a result. In the first chapter of the novel Mr Knightley had walked into Hartfield to dissipate gloomy thoughts; on the day after this second reflection he walks again to Hartfield, this time to transform Emma's prospects by revealing his love for her. But even after this has happened life goes on for some time with no change at all, and when the marriage eventually does take place it chiefly means Mr Knightley comes to Hartfield permanently rather than walking over from Donwell each day. There is nothing here to compare with Elizabeth Bennet's transformation to the mistress of Pemberley, or Anne Elliot's glory in becoming a sailor's wife, or even Elinor Dashwood's or Catherine Morland's removal to rural rectories with the men they love; it has more in common perhaps with Fanny Price's eventual homecoming to Mansfield Park, in the novel which directly preceded *Emma* – but Fanny Price was an orphan niece, and becoming Edmund's wife was more than she had any right to expect. Austen ends her novel with an assurance of "the perfect happiness of the union" between Emma and Mr Knightley, and this time there is no suggestion of any lurking double meaning. It is a tribute to Austen's skill in creating such a lively, intelligent, self-misleading, self-searching woman as Emma Woodhouse – allied to the influence of twenty-first-century sensibilities about the nature of woman's lot in life – that we feel Emma may have deserved better than to dwindle into a Highbury wife: yet another twist in the complicated relationship between author and reader in this extraordinary novel.

Notes

1   The surviving letters, sent by Austen to Anna between July and November 1814, are reproduced in Deirdre Le Faye (ed.) *Letters*, and also in Jane Austen, *Later Manuscripts*, ed. Janet Todd and Linda Bree (2008).

2   See Cassandra Austen's note of the date of composition of Jane Austen's novels (*MW*, opposite p. 242).

3   By the author's request, citations from *Emma* are taken from the Cambridge Edition, ed. Richard Cronin and Dorothy Macmillan (Cambridge: Cambridge University Press, 2005), and will be indicated by volume and chapter numbers.

4   The album is owned by David Gilson; three charades, identified as by Jane Austen herself, are reproduced in Jane Austen, *Later Manuscripts*; authors of other charades in the volume include Austen's mother, her sister Cassandra, and her niece Anna.

5   The nearest precedent to Emma's highly unusual command of this episode is probably the scene in Sarah Fielding's *The Adventures of David Simple* (1744) in which the intellectually bright Cynthia, during the course of a coach journey, handles the unwelcome attentions of a drunken atheist with aplomb (Book 3, ch. 3); but Fielding was writing within a very different set of cultural parameters, before the cult of sensibility had led to a widespread belief, in fiction at least, that ideal women were vulnerable and helpless.

6   In a very similar way, "You will look back and see that I did not come till Miss Fairfax was in Highbury," Frank writes to Mrs Weston once the truth about his engagement to Jane is revealed (*E*: 437).

Further Reading

Barchas, Janine (2007). Very Austen: accounting for the language of *Emma*. *Nineteenth-Century Fiction*, 62:3, 303–38.

Gard, Roger (1991). *Emma and Persuasion*. Harmondsworth, UK: Penguin.

Johnson, Claudia (1988). *Emma*: "Woman, lovely woman reigns alone." In *Jane Austen: Women, Politics and the Novel* (pp 121–43). Chicago: University of Chicago Press.

Tanner, Tony (1986). The match-maker: *Emma*. In *Jane Austen* (pp. 176–207). London: Macmillan.

Todd, Janet (2006). *Emma*. In *The Cambridge Introduction to Jane Austen* (pp. 94–113). Cambridge, UK: Cambridge University Press.

Wiltshire, John (1992). *Emma*: The picture of health. In *Jane Austen and the Body* (pp. 110–54). Cambridge, UK: Cambridge University Press.

12
Persuasion: The Gradual Dawning

Fiona Stafford

In March 1817, a few months before she died, Jane Austen wrote to her favorite niece, Fanny Knight, offering advice on various matters, including marriage, spinsters, and motherhood. In the course of her affectionate letter, she admits to having abandoned her revision of *Northanger Abbey*, but adds that she has "a something ready for Publication, which may perhaps appear about a twelvemonth hence. It is short, about the length of Catherine. This is for yourself alone" (*Letters*: 333). Never inclined to write at length about her own novels, Austen was particularly reticent about *Persuasion*. A subsequent letter to Fanny informs her that "You will not like it, so you need not be impatient. You may *perhaps* like the Heroine, as she is almost too good for me" (*Letters*: 335), but Austen gives nothing more away. Fanny Knight, like everyone except Cassandra Austen, had to wait until the novel was published at the end of 1817, complete with a memorial to its author. Austen's last novel was indeed "short." Where *Emma* had filled three fat volumes, *Persuasion*, only running to two, was published together with *Northanger Abbey*. It would, however, be a mistake to assume that the author's rather off-hand tone is a reliable indication of the novel's interest or quality. There may be fewer pages than in earlier works, but within them, Austen included her most ambitious treatment of the passage of time and tackled the largest literary themes. Loss and suffering; memory and perception; the relationship between self and others; the tensions between competing systems of value; the choice, purpose, and very meaning of life; and the extraordinary power of human emotion, are all examined in Austen's last published novel; but its method is such that the full implications of its modest appearance are not immediately obvious. Reginald Farrer, the brilliant early twentieth-century admirer of Austen, observed of the novel's heroine: "Gradually, her greatness dawns" (Farrer 1917: 29). The same is true of *Persuasion* itself. That such a short book can allow for a gradual dawn is one of its many paradoxes.

Initial impressions may suggest that *Persuasion* is a light-hearted satire on the higher echelons of English society. The opening description of Sir Walter Elliot perusing his entry in the Baronetage and admiring his handsome physique takes us back to the world of Restoration comedy, where figures such as Lord Foppington were so fond of their own appearances. The heroine of the novel emerges slowly, seen first through the dismissive eyes of her father – "she was only Anne" (*P*: 5). Even at the first reference, however, the intrusion of the narrator's voice into Sir Walter's assessment makes clear that his views are as limited as they are firm, and that other perspectives are possible:

> His two other children were of very inferior value. Mary had acquired a little artificial importance, by becoming Mrs. Charles Musgrove; but Anne, with an elegance of mind and sweetness of character, which must have placed her high with any people of real understanding, was nobody with either her father or sister. (*P*: 5)

The skill with which Austen creates the Baronet's contemptuous tone, only to reveal its hollowness through the contrasting opinions of "any people of real understanding" (which of course includes both narrator and reader), is characteristic of her mature style. *Persuasion* is brilliantly satirical in places, but within its apparently unforgiving exterior lies a deep well of sympathy, admiration, and love.

Individual perspectives and their limitations afford numerous opportunities for comedy, but also reward more serious consideration. Sir Walter's vanity, for example, which is presented so directly in the first chapter, is also examined retrospectively, when Anne returns to Kellynch Hall to see the Crofts in residence. There is no detailed description of the Elliot family home, but in conversation, Admiral Croft mentions the very few practical alterations he has had to make. The one room in the house that he found intolerable was Sir Walter's dressing room – "Such a number of looking-glasses! oh Lord! There was no getting away from oneself" (*P*: 128). In a single surprised sentence, Sir Walter's personality and values are revealed in all their sorriness. Admiral Croft, whose rank has been acquired through his own ability and character, belongs to a profession despised by Sir Walter on the grounds that it raises "men to honours which their fathers and grandfathers never dreamt of," and (equally bad in his eyes) has the tendency to turn a young man into "the most deplorable looking personage you can imagine" (*P*: 19–20). For Sir Walter Elliot, the greatest blessings of existence are beauty and a baronetcy, and so the Navy, with its utter disregard for both, seems to represent something of a personal affront. Admiral Croft, on the other hand, whose scale of values could hardly be more different, is appalled by the extravagance of Sir Walter's full-length looking-glasses, and the idea of seeing only himself. As a practical man, his remark to Anne is a straightforward response to the physical experience of entering Sir Walter's room of mirrors, but his dismay at there being "no getting away from oneself" is magnified throughout the novel, refracted by different characters, images, and ideas.

The opposition between the values of the naval officer and the baronet are key to the narrative structure, informing the heroine's experience at every turn. Her own years of misery are a direct result of aristocratic disdain for professional men, manifest in Sir Walter and Lady Russell's view of her engagement to Wentworth as "a very degrading alliance" (*P*: 26). Wentworth, with neither title nor estate, has no entry in the Baronetage and must, therefore, be deemed a "nobody" (*P*: 23). His subsequent successes, which secure his place in the Navy Lists, however, allow Anne to trace his rising fortunes and to reflect at length on attitudes that remain immune to natural intelligence and energy. The painful eviction from Kellynch, too, arises from Sir Walter's refusal to curtail his disastrous extravagance for fear of appearing less splendid than his rank demands. The new residents, on the other hand, have increased their income through the Admiral's successful career and his wife's careful management.

In a novel that advocates the importance of revisiting, both literally and metaphorically ("these places must be visited, and visited again, to make the worth of Lyme understood," *P*: 96), the return to Kellynch is a symbolic moment. After the momentous accident at Lyme, the trip to Kellynch marks the opening of the second volume, and of a new phase in the life of the heroine. When Anne revisits her home, she is able to see her father's limitations more clearly, not merely through the continuing joke about his vanity, but also through recognizing that the outlook of the Crofts is diametrically opposed to Sir Walter's. Her realization that "Kellynch-Hall had passed into better hands than its owners" (*P*: 125) is crucial to her developing independence, as well as to the comic resolution of the plot. What had seemed a private catastrophe, forcing the sensitive young woman from her beloved home, subsequently appears to be an opportunity for far-reaching improvements. Anne's capacity for worthwhile reflection contrasts with her father's tendency to waste time gazing at himself. Her removal from Kellynch enables her to see the values she has inherited from birth from a new perspective, and to recognize that the "alterations" associated with the Crofts are beneficial not only to herself, but also the entire community. Those living on the estate benefit from the arrival of more responsible management, while Anne's realization of her own affinity with the Crofts helps her to reinterpret the past and strengthen her resolve in future. Mrs Croft, a figure of whom Mary Wollstonecraft would certainly have approved, shows just how content women can be when they are at ease with the world and confident of their own abilities as "rational creatures."[1]

Anne Elliot's personal history is in part a fable for contemporary society, through which Austen applauds the gradual shift in power from the old hierarchies of birth and inherited rank to the new meritocratic structures of the Navy. Her enthusiastic portraits of naval officers were an affectionate tribute to her own brothers, Francis and Charles, but also reflected the national gratitude to those who had risked their lives at sea in the struggle against Napoleon (Southam 2000: 265). Nor is admiration restricted to those whose careers have brought great wealth, as the idealized image of Captain Harville in his small, rented house in Lyme makes plain. His constant activity ("he drew, he varnished, he carpentered, he glued," *P*: 99) and devotion to his family are a further comment on the emptiness of Sir Walter Elliot's life, and show that in *Persuasion*, the Navy represents far more than an alternative route to power and influence. Intrinsic worth, personal responsibility, and the desire to contribute to the welfare of others are as evident in Captain Harville's confined living quarters as in the Crofts' residence. What Anne is especially struck by, however, is the "great happiness" she finds there. By the end of the novel, the idea of marriage to Wentworth constitut-ing a degradation seems ludicrous, and *Persuasion* concludes with unqualified praise for "that profession which is, if possible, more distinguished in its domestic virtues than in its national importance" (*P*: 252). The focus on home is a matter of public as well as private interest, just as the intense preoccupation with individual experience has meaning for the entire nation.

Anne's discovery, on returning to Kellynch, that change might be beneficial is con-trasted directly with Lady Russell's inability to accept the new arrangement. Her growing detachment from Lady Russell is nowhere more evident than the moment when she imagines her friend's discomposure on reentering the familiar scenes: "Anne had no power of saying to herself, 'These rooms ought to belong only to us. Oh how fallen in their destination! How unworthily occupied! An ancient family to be so driven away! Strangers filling their place!'" (*P*: 126). The language of lamentation shows Lady Russell turning into a caricature like Sir Walter, caught in the looking-glass world of her own preconceptions. Where Anne reluctantly sees the truth in Kellynch Hall, Lady Russell perceives only a threat to her assumptions about social order. Lady Russell's limitations are only condemned explicitly in the final chapter, but the Kellynch visit, like the scene in which her eyes are fixed on window-curtains because Lady Alicia has pronounced them the best in Bath, demonstrates the essential difference between Anne and her mentor. In the Crofts, Anne finds a refreshingly new approach to life, combin-ing "goodness of heart" (*P*: 127) with complete self-confidence (*P*: 48). If Lady Russell can only gaze at curtains ratified by aristocratic approval, Admiral Croft has no hesita-tion in looking through the windows of Bath and assessing what he finds according to his own judgment: "Here I am, you see, staring at a picture. I can never get by this shop without stopping. But what a thing here is, by way of a boat . . . I would not venture over a horsepond in it" (*P*: 169). While Admiral Croft's aesthetic assessments are left unexplored, his self-reliance and refusal to bend to others' opinions make a strong comment on the kinds of persuasion at work elsewhere in the novel.

"Getting away from oneself" is, paradoxically, the means to self-discovery. Sir Walter and Lady Russell fail to see the world through unbiased perspectives, and so cannot see themselves as others do. Confident, despite evidence to the contrary, that their social assumptions are unassailable, they are blind to the possibilities of finding the true worth of those around. Convinced of their social superiority, they remain unaware that even those closest often find them silly, dull, or self-satisfied. Elizabeth Elliot is similarly portrayed, while her youngest sister, Mary Musgrove, is too self-absorbed to attend to anyone, even her injured child. It is Anne who is most conscious of Mary's true situation in the world, because she is forced to listen to the successive complaints of Charles, Mrs Musgrove, and Louisa. The preoccupation with rank that gives Mary such an elevated sense of self is the very characteristic that lowers her in the eyes of all around and prevents her from seeing clearly.

The absence of concern with social hierarchy is also what distinguishes Anne from her sisters and makes her so much more appealing. Anne's response to impending financial ruin reveals her natural opposition to her family's values, in the preference for "honesty against importance," and "indifference for everything but justice and equity" (*P*: 12). From the opening chapters, different values are set in opposition, with Anne's essential morality being disregarded by her family and applauded by readers. The perpetual neglect of Anne's good sense is among the most painful ironies of the novel, but it makes her subsequent welcome by people who recognize her true qualities all the more satisfying.

It is not just Anne's sense of right, her natural gentleness, or her selfless attention to others irrespective of rank, that most distinguishes her from her family, however. Unlike Austen's earlier heroines, who learn about themselves gradually, Anne begins with a remarkable degree of self-knowledge. Her prehistory is entirely different from those of Elizabeth Bennet or Emma Woodhouse, and readers are alerted throughout to memories of painful experiences endured before the novel begins. Anne's unhappiness at the beginning is not caused by a neglectful father and elder sister, nor the enforced removal from her family home. We rapidly become aware that these unlucky circumstances are only part of a much longer history of misfortune, dating back to the death of her mother when she was 14, and a broken engagement at 19. In *Persuasion*, unlike any of her previous works, Austen is so specific about dates that readers can be in no doubt about the main emotional events of Anne's life and their precise relationship to the history of England. One of the most powerful oppositions of the novel is the contrast between the "short period of exquisite felicity" (*P*: 26) enjoyed by Anne with Wentworth during his time ashore in 1806 after the British triumph at Trafalgar, and the eight long years of solitude that have followed, prior to the novel's opening in 1814. If *Persuasion* is preoccupied with contrasts, the entire narrative is premised on the gap between then and now, and driven by a desire for reconciliation.

Nothing in the novel is straightforward, however. The double loss of Anne's mother and her fiancé have resulted in years of suffering and introspection which, though enormously damaging, have also left her with a special kind of wisdom, as well as residual sadness. Readers, privileged with insight into Anne's mind, recognize that her ability to offer comfort to the grief-stricken has been hard won and her recommended reading for those needing inner fortification, compiled from years of misery. Austen is, however, careful to avoid any easy equation between suffering and wisdom, or any complacency resulting from the years of purgation. Had she presented Anne reeling off titles of moral essays and sermons to Benwick, the difference between her heroine and the other, more self-satisfied, characters might have begun to disappear. A sense of moral superiority, as Austen demonstrates in the minor character of Mary Bennet in *Pride and Prejudice*, is hardly more attractive than the self-importance founded on wealth or position. Anne is rescued from any such danger by the paragraph revealing her amusement "at the idea of her coming to Lyme, to preach patience and resignation to a young man whom she had never seen before," and acknowledgement that "she had been eloquent on a point in which her own conduct would ill bear examination" (*P*: 101). If the Elliot family is renowned for its pride, the second daughter of the house is remarkable for her humility.

Anne's capacity to see the funny side of herself is, however, part of a gradual transformation that takes place over the course of the novel and becomes clearer on rereading. In the early chapters, her self-knowledge is often manifest in more melancholy
or irritable reflections, as she sees herself exploited, her own wishes routinely ignored.
Initially, demonstrations of Anne's clear-sightedness are hardly reassuring, revealing
both the flaws in her companions and an inclination to self-punishment. At Uppercross, for example, Mary's lack of interest in their departure from Kellynch is registered with painful clarity: "she must now submit to feel that another lesson, in the
art of knowing our own nothingness beyond our own circle, was become necessary for
her" (*P*: 42). Anne's insights into the human condition, which readers notice, even
though the characters do not, are far from consoling at this stage. The humble
acknowledgement of "our own nothingness beyond our own circle," though consistent
with some kinds of eighteenth-century Christian morality, almost seems to be turning
Sir Walter's world of mirrors into an image of life itself, where the abyss is masked
only by self-delusion. The rapid repetition of "our own" reflects the monotony of the
Elliots' life, while the alliterative "o"s are a visual reminder of their social circle and
its circularity. Anne's existence is circumscribed by her family, but if she perceives
her nothingness beyond, she is equally conscious of her invisibility within the perim-
eter. As *Persuasion* progresses, however, the heroine undergoes a remarkable transformation, evident not only in the observations of other characters, but also in her own
attitude towards the world.

Anne's ability to see comedy rather than tragedy in her companions increases
steadily. Driven home by the Crofts, she had gained "some amusement from their
style of driving" (*P*: 92), but listening to the younger Miss Musgrove in Lyme, "Anne
smiled more than once to herself" and is "amused by Henrietta's style of being grateful" (*P*: 103). Anne's amusement at Captain Harville's contrivances and curiosities
is very different in tone from the earlier observations on Mrs Clay's freckles or on
Mrs Musgrove, with her notoriously "large fat sighings" (*P*: 68) over her dead son.
Although these details have often been attributed to the narrator by those unwilling
to associate such unkindness to Anne, the distinction between narrator and heroine
is not always clearly defined. The depiction of Mrs Musgrove's grief is harsh, but not
necessarily inconsistent with the feelings of a woman entirely screened by her ample
hostess from the man whose loss she has mourned for the past eight years. Among
Austen's great achievements in *Persuasion* is the creation, through tiny details, of a
sense of growing happiness. The reaction of William Elliot, who makes his personal
entrance in the novel at Lyme, shows that Anne's lost "bloom" is recovering, while
the restrained disclosure of her emotional experiences finally bursts into "joy, senseless
joy!" (*P*: 168) More subtle, however, is the way in which all the characters and settings in the novel begin to appear differently as the heroine's outlook changes. "Alteration" is a loaded word in *Persuasion*, but by the end there is no "perhaps" about the
question of whether it implies improvement.

Anne's internal transformation changes the narrative style entirely, as the irritation
associated with the more satirical passages vanishes into general good will:

Glowing and lovely in sensibility and happiness, and more generally admired than she thought about or cared for, she had cheerful or forbearing feelings for every creature around her. Mr Elliot was there; she avoided, but she could pity him. The Wallises; she had amusement in understanding them. Lady Dalrymple and Miss Carteret; they would soon be innoxious cousins to her. She cared not for Mrs Clay, and had nothing to blush for in the public manners of her father and sister. With the Musgroves, there was the happy chat of perfect ease. (*P*: 245–6).

This remarkable paragraph, in which a new forgiving attitude embraces all the most annoying characters as well as Anne's friends, ends by reaffirming the source of her happiness: "the knowledge of his being there!"

While much pleasure is derived from the reunion between Anne and Wentworth, the deep satisfaction felt by many readers comes from the all-pervading happiness of the closing chapters, which contrast so powerfully with the novel's uncomfortable opening. By the end of the novel, Anne has attained independence from the Elliots, not merely through securing the husband for whom she has been yearning, but also through arriving at a completely antithetical perception of the world. Where her father remains caught in a prison of narcissism, Anne has escaped her own self-denying reclusiveness, and has emerged triumphant, to discover the best in everyone.

Austen's skill in evoking so many characters in a single paragraph is characteristic of her mature work. In *Emma*, she had developed a brilliant new form of monologue to convey the experience of just such a social gathering, when she presented Miss Bates at the ball. She had also perfected the free indirect style which enabled the narrator to slip almost imperceptibly into the consciousness of the heroine and allowing readers to see through the partial filter of Emma. *Persuasion* condenses these techniques, so that an entire roomful of people is conveyed through the eyes of the heroine, while new facets of her own character continue to be revealed. The recollection of so many minor characters at this late stage also frees the conclusion to concentrate on the major players. There is no need to prolong the ending with forecasting the future of the Crofts, Harvilles, and Musgroves, because they have all been adequately addressed by Anne at the party. And by this stage of her writing career, Austen knew very well that anything superfluous would dilute the power of her conclusion.

The rapid dispatch of Mr Elliot and Mrs Clay has often been identified as one of the flaws in the novel, and attributed to Austen's failing energy in the last months of her life (see, for example, Butler 1975: 279–91). But there can be few readers who feel much curiosity about them. In order to create the emotional intensity achieved in Anne, Austen has been careful to avoid investing too many other characters with psychological depth. Despite Mr Elliot's importance to the plot, he makes little lasting impact on Anne's emotional life, and so his interest is limited. Anne's physical attraction to Wentworth is so powerfully conveyed throughout that there is never any real sense of a serious rival, and once the declaration is made, Mr Elliot commands no further attention. Everything in the novel is pared down to essentials, anything surplus rejected. The economy of the narrative style is part of *Persuasion*'s rebuke to ostentation and unnecessary extravagance. No words are wasted and every detail has to earn its place. What matters most to Anne at the end of the novel, is the letter from Captain Wentworth, whose address could hardly be more succinct: "To Miss A. E. –." The directness of his prose – "I have loved none but you" – puts every conversation and every protracted sentence into the background, and leaves its recipient dazzled with joy (*P*: 237). After this, the last thing Anne or her readers require is the predictable flattery of Mr Elliot.

To suggest that *Persuasion* shows signs of diminishing energy or incomplete revision is to detract from its innovative power. The decision to restrain the potential narrative interest in Mr Elliot, Mrs Clay, Mrs Smith, Lady Russell, or Henrietta Musgrove is the corollary of the new intensity of focus on the feelings of the central character. Throughout the novel, Austen's dramatic skills are reined in, and permitted only at moments where Anne's response to the action and dialogue is central. The use of letters – so important a narrative device in the earlier novels – is similarly restrained in order to afford maximum impact to Captain Wentworth's declaration. Nor is there anything accidental about the climactic letter-writing scene, as the rejected manuscript chapters of *Persuasion* demonstrate.[2] In the draft conclusion, Austen had conceived an accidental meeting at the Crofts' house in Bath, in which Wentworth is tasked with testing the truth of reports that Anne wishes to resume residence at Kellynch after her marriage to Mr Elliot. Anne's robust denial of the rumor provokes Wentworth into confessing his unchanged feelings before a final chapter similar to that of the published novel. Although there is little difference in terms of the basic storyline, the effect of reading the discarded chapters, which are included in most modern editions, is to appreciate the care with which Austen crafted her novels. She finished her first version of *Persuasion* in July 1816, but was dissatisfied with the shift from Mrs Smith's house to the Crofts' and the ensuing love scene. As she revisited her work and saw that alteration would be an improvement, Austen set about writing an interim chapter bringing the Musgroves to Bath, and then composed the remarkable declaration scene, now transferred to the public space of the aptly named White Hart.

The gathering at the inn, which includes Anne, Mrs Musgrove, Mrs Croft, Captain Harville, and Captain Wentworth, is well chosen to encourage recollection and reconsideration. The conversations turn on engagements and the relative devotion of men and women; though ostensibly concerned with Louisa and Benwick, readers are only too aware of Anne's "nervous thrill" as she recognizes the "personal application" of so much of what is under discussion. Throughout the novel, Anne's inability to articulate her true feelings has been marked by politeness, silence, and a telling array of flushed cheeks, sighs, and tear-filled eyes, but nowhere is the body a more obvious index to the heart than here. The most powerful aspect of the scene, however, is Wentworth's silent presence. As he sits at the writing desk, he can hear Anne's opinions on female constancy, in a situation that evokes the distressing scene in the countryside, where Anne had overheard his views on the weakness of women. Her retort to Harville, "if you please, no reference to examples in books" (*P*: 234), also recalls earlier passages, where Anne had fallen "into quotation" (*P*: 85), or combated powerful emotion with reading. Now, she is speaking from first-hand experience, and her quiet resolution makes Wentworth drop his pen.

When the letter is opened, readers see at once that Anne's conversation is registered in his passionate sentences: "I can hardly write. I am every instant hearing something which overpowers me" (*P*: 237). Although this has sometimes been applauded as a sign of male domination vanquished by new female assertiveness ("Men have had every advantage of us in telling their own story . . . the pen has been in their hands," *P*: 234), the dynamic of the scene is such that Wentworth seems rather to be anticipating Anne's own reaction to the letter, when his feelings are perfectly echoed by her "overpowering happiness." The emotional triumph of this moment seems to obliterate all differences of gender, time, class, and character, and recollection of earlier difficulties only makes their ultimate resolution happier. Wentworth's letter contains the whole span of the novel, condensed into a matter of sentences. The eight and a half years of pain are acknowledged, but now recalled as evidence of proven devotion. The declaration of loving "none but you" is in part a reference to Wentworth's entanglement with the Musgrove girls, though memories of more recent encounters in Bath also contribute to the present, highly charged moment. The letter is Wentworth's concise version of *Persuasion*, and in offering it to Anne, he brings her own narrative to an end.

The contrast with the intense awkwardness of their initial reencounter is signaled by a careful echo of the scene where Wentworth silently removed the two-year-old boy from Anne's back: "She was ashamed of herself, quite ashamed of being so nervous, so overcome by such a trifle; but so it was; and it required a long application of solitude and reflection to recover her" (*P*: 81). Now, as she reads the letter, her agitation is even greater: "Half an hour of solitude and reflection might have tranquillized her; but the ten minutes only, which now passed before she was interrupted, with all the restraints of her situation, could do nothing towards tranquillity" (*P*: 238). At the end of the novel, Anne is denied "solitude and reflection," but what had been her habitual solace now seems less important than the opportunity to speak directly to the man she loves. She is at last free to leave her family in their looking-glass worlds, and embark on a more active life, experiencing things known hitherto only from books and hearsay. The novel's exploration of values ends by revealing the source of true happiness through the unlikely figure of Mrs Smith: "Her spring of felicity was in the glow of her spirits, as her friend Anne's was in the warmth of her heart" (*P*: 252). It is only in the closing paragraph that we realize Austen's characters have been on a philosophical journey like that of Johnson's *Rasselas*, where the Prince finally sees that happiness is an individual matter and returns to Abyssinia. Anne's final location is left unspecified, for by now it is clear that homes can be created anywhere, if happiness is within. At the end of the novel, Anne's true value is recognized and rewarded: "Anne was tenderness itself, and she had the full worth of it in Captain Wentworth's affection." "Worth," in the end, has less to do with money, rank, or family, than with inner feelings and mutual understanding.

NOTES

1 As Peter Knox-Shaw (2004: 237) points out, Mrs Croft's reference to "rational creatures" (*P*: 70) is an echo of Mary Wollstonecraft's arguments regarding feminine "want of firmness" in *A Vindication of the Rights of Woman* (1792).

2 The discarded manuscript chapters survive in the British Library. They were first published by James Edward Austen-Leigh in the second edition of *A Memoir of Jane Austen* (1871) and edited by R. W. Chapman in *Two Chapters of Persuasion* (Oxford: Oxford University Press, 1926). Southam (2001: 86–99).

FURTHER READING

Heydt-Stevenson, Jillian (2005). *Austen's Unbecoming Conjunctions*. Basingstoke, UK: Palgrave Macmillan.

Mudrick, Marvin (1952). *Jane Austen: Irony as Defense and Discovery*. Berkeley: University of California Press.

Tanner, Tony (1986). *Jane Austen*. Cambridge, MA: Harvard University Press.

Weissman, Cheryl Ann (1988). Doubleness and refrain in Jane Austen's *Persuasion*. *The Kenyon Review*, 10, 87–91.

Wiltshire, John (1992). *Jane Austen and the Body*. Cambridge, UK: Cambridge University Press.

13

Sanditon and the Book

George Justice

R. W. Chapman's title page for the first printed edition of *Sanditon* announces a "Fragment of a Novel written by Jane Austen, January–March 1817. Now first printed from the manuscript." The relations of part to whole and manuscript to print distilled on Chapman's title page have captured the imagination of readers and writers, who have written a number of continuations, beginning with Anna Lefroy's in the nineteenth century. Julia Barrett retitled her continuation *Charlotte*, but most have adopted the title *Sanditon*. None has called itself "The Brothers," by which the manuscript had been known in the family. Chapman's assumption of a whole work of art (a "novel") from which the unfinished manuscript pages have been somehow broken off was shared by early critics, including E. M. Forster, who wrote an influential, largely negative review of *Sanditon* after the publication of Chapman's edition. Chapman's view has some common sense to recommend it. Just as many readers want to know how Elizabeth and Darcy or Mr Knightley and Emma fare after the book pages end, it is natural to want to know what would happen to *Sanditon*'s Charlotte and Miss Lambe. And given the striking contrast between realism and exaggeration in *Sanditon*, it makes some sense to suppose that the manuscript represents an early draft that might ultimately have been finished to the level of polish in her already published works. But style and common sense notwithstanding, we don't know and cannot prove the author's aim in these manuscript pages, and the assumption that *Sanditon* is "unfinished" (in terms of narrative and polish) has damaged our ability to appreciate it for what it is. Considering the manuscript pages as they are, with a physical ending as conclusive as a book's final printed pages, can allow us better to understand it as a commentary upon the history of the book.

At Austen's death in July 1817, the novel we know as *Northanger Abbey* had still not appeared in print. Sold to the bookseller Benjamin Crosby with the title of *Susan* in 1803, the manuscript had remained unpublished so long that Austen had bought back the copyright in 1816 (through the agency of her brother, Henry). Therefore, at the time she was composing *Sanditon*, the earlier work was also a working manuscript rather than a completed novel. Focusing on literary history while adding a particular focus upon the physical media of print and manuscript, in *Sanditon* Austen revises portions of her earlier work as she rethinks, in darker terms, the pervasiveness of print in her culture. *Sanditon*, like *Northanger Abbey*, ridicules readers who write themselves into novelistic narration at the same time that it recovers and recreates novelistic art. As in Pope's *Dunciad*, the stuff of art and the detritus of culture are inextricable.

In this essay I would like to suggest that we see the manuscript of *Sanditon*, now held by King's College Cambridge, as a sort of pocket book, a handwritten commentary on the history of the novel. Its handwritten pages overwrite Richardson's *Clarissa* and Burney's *Camilla*, in particular, as well as Austen's own novels. What I am calling "overwriting" here refers physically to the way women and men in the nineteenth century wrote in the printed pocketbooks they bought in large quantities and carried with them as combinations of notebooks, travel guides, calculators, and diaries. But "overwriting" can also describe the finely written commentary Austen provides on some of the most influential of her eighteenth-century literary antecedents. Like marginalia, the commentary encapsulated in correspondence, and the "fan fiction" of devoted readers, *Sanditon,* itself a manuscript, engages familiarly with previous novels. In so doing, it demonstrates that printed books, the stuff of literary history, are entities with open spaces in the margins, waiting to be filled by a hand scratching out the effusions of the individual imagination.

In *Sanditon*, manuscript and print rely completely upon each other. We can see this throughout the novel from its opening, which plunges us into the world of advertising, a cultural craze about which Mr Parker is as nutty as his sisters and brother Arthur are regarding their physical health. Indeed, Regency culture's views of "physical health" and its relation to bathing spots are, as the novel's opening demonstrates, cultural constructions dependent on print.

A gentleman and a lady are overturned in their rented carriage – the narration provides us with little direct information about them (no names, and nothing more precise about their situation or the setting). The gentleman's sprained foot interrupts what were "his congratulations to his wife & himself" (*MW*: 364). It goes without saying that self-congratulation and pandering to others are the natural mode of advertising, and Mr Parker (as we learn to call him) is so wrapped up in this kind of rhetoric that he points erroneously to a cottage, situated "romantically" (more advertising-speak), as his cure.

In contrast to the narrator (here or anywhere else in Austen's work), Mr Parker himself speaks blandly:

> I wish we may get him to Sanditon. I should like to have you acquainted with him. – And it would be such a fine thing for the Place! – Such a young Man as Sidney, with his neat equipage & fashionable air, – You & I Mary, know what effect it might have: Many a respectable Family, many a careful Mother, many a pretty Daughter, might it secure us, to the prejudice of E. Bourne & Hastings. (*MW*: 382)

Mr Parker is genial rather than sinister, but in his own way he is more dangerous to those who hold Austen's worldview than *Sanditon's* hyperbolically menacing Sir Edward Denham.

Mr and Mrs Parker's having come upon the incorrect Willingden is itself the result of a printed advertisement, which he pulls out of his pocketbook to show to a bemused Mr Heywood. When he believes his newspaper cutting rather than the statements of Mr Heywood, Mr Parker demonstrates his association of the truth-bearing nature of the fixity of print with advertising.

> "Then, sir, I can bring proof of your having a Surgeon in the Parish, whether you may know it or not. Here, sir," – (taking out his Pocket book –) "if you will do me the favor of casting your eye over these advertisements, which I cut out myself from the Morning Post & the Kentish Gazette, only yesterday morng in London – I think you will be convinced that I am not speaking at random. You will find in it an advertisement of the dissolution of a Partnership in the Medical Line – in your own parish – extensive Business – undeniable Character – respectable references – wishing to form a separate Establishment. You will find it at full length, sir," offering him the two little oblong extracts. (*MW*: 366)

These "two little oblong extracts" remind us of how the Britain in which Mr Parker lives has increasingly become an "imagined community," to use the term made familiar by Benedict Anderson's study (1983). Mr Heywood accepts the ubiquity and power of printed information as he uses a fantastical agglomeration of news (from which Mr Parker has pulled his fragmentary "extracts") to justify his own skepticism: "if you were to shew me all the Newspapers that are printed in one week throughout the Kingdom, you wd not persuade me of there being a Surgeon in Willingden" (*MW*: 366). *The Oxford English Dictionary* cites the middle of the nineteenth century for earliest uses of "clipping" or "cutting" to refer to "a paragraph or short article cut out of a newspaper," but it is clear that the vocabulary as well as the practice is reflected in *Sanditon*.

The pocketbook in which Mr Parker places his clipping tells us even more about his culture's understanding of the interconnectedness of manuscript and print. "Pocketbook" referred to everything from a small-sized printed book to what we now call a wallet. The *OED* describes something in between those two things: "A book for memoranda, notes, etc., intended to be carried in a pocket; a notebook." Parker's pocketbook could have been entirely blank before his clippings and manuscript jottings, but more likely his pocketbook was bound with a combination of printed information and blank pages for the owner's notes, accounts of spending, and newspaper clippings. These books were improvements upon the blank books of the Middle Ages and Renaissance that were maintained by families and individuals and in many cases passed down through generations. Individual instances of these books can be extremely puzzling to modern readers. They often reflect a baffling lack of concern with providing information sequentially, even when supposedly organized by printed dates or categories. Margaret Ezell calls these bound manuscript pages "badly behaving books" (Ezell forthcoming) and their resistance to dominant modes of narrative and the structures of information we have inherited from the Enlightenment suggests a "preprint" orientation even when they are made from blank books preprinted with information.

For example, a copy of "Bell's Common Place Book for the Pocket Formed Generally upon the Principle Recommended and Practised by Mr. Locke" held by *Eighteenth-Century Collections Online* (ECCO) shows that even an overtly rational structure cannot contain or determine the uses to which these books were put. Although it "may be had of all the Booksellers in England by enquiring for *Bell's Library Common-place Book*," even the printed texts going by this name are not uniform. The advertisement for the volume provides prices for adding quires of paper, "and so in proportion for any quantity of paper the book may contain, deducting or adding two shillings for every quire that may be increased or decreased, and bound as above" (ECCO copy, ECCO 14). The preface to *Bell's Library Common-place Book* demonstrates "Locke's" method of indexing individual entries in the book for easy retrieval, basing entries upon the initial letter of the relevant work and the first succeeding vowel. However, the person who owned the copy reproduced in ECCO evidently eschewed those instructions and used it instead as an old-fashioned commonplace book, into which he copied extracts from poetry; hand copied items from newspapers, recipes, botanical illustrations; pasted cuttings, drawings, and whatever else apparently interested him at a given moment. There are a few "receipts for the bite of a mad dog" and other sets of instructions that seem to be included for other than practical reasons (and show up typically in commonplace books). The compiler(s) include pagination, but without a completed index it would be difficult to navigate the book. All of these features demonstrate a clear disjunction between the Lockean plan and the actual use.

Understanding the genre of the pocketbook helps us understand the genre of the eighteenth-century novel. In market terms, both the novel and the printed pocketbook represent transformations of earlier forms as well as an increasing presence in the market for books in their evolved forms. Both types of book, too, encourage writing: the pocketbook literally assumes that all of its consumers are writers, and, if the sneering commentary of reviewers and common readers alike signals elements of the culture, novels seem to produce novelists at the same time that they produce readers. Like the pocketbook, the novel contains disparate information on a wide range of matters both of individual interest to its keeper (and therefore personal and partial) and of broader social importance (and therefore "realistic"). Both pocketbooks and the common run of novels represent market dominance by a strategy of "variation upon a theme." The printed part of the pocketbook corresponds to the accurate description of the world aspired to by the realistic novel; the manuscript part of the pocketbook relates to the style, the point of view, and the partiality of the novel. The contents of Mr Parker's pocketbook are accurate and inaccurate at the same time: the advertisement he has pasted into it comes from a newspaper and presents accurately the fact of a surgeon in Willingden, but Parker's inaccuracy as a narrator – the personal part of what he's put in his book – results from his unavoidably partial point of view. Parker's pocketbook reverses the narrative method of *Sanditon* itself. Unlike Austen's fiction, with a "satiric realism" (Wiltshire 1992: 221) that penetrates into social reality, Parker's pocketbook relies upon a documentary realism that encourages wishful thinking. Mr Parker's pocketbook confirms that the realism of factual presentation can be as fanciful, as fictional, as the exaggeration of *Sanditon*'s characterizations. As a "Projector" (*MW*: 412) and the eldest brother in a "family of Imagination" (*MW*: 412), Mr Parker is skilled at producing plausible scenarios from the stuff of the quotidian, including clippings from a newspaper.

Mr Parker's hypochondriacal siblings produce fictional situations and relationships from that most grounded of realities: their bodies. But other characters in the novel produce books from the books they've read, or produce writing from spoken exchanges. Like a commonplace book, Sir Edward's conversation is itself a sort of transcription of his reading of printed matter:

> He began, in a tone of great Taste & Feeling, to talk of the Sea & the Sea shore – & ran with Energy through all the usual Phrases employed in praise of their Sublimity, & descriptive of the *undescribable* Emotions they excite in the Mind of Sensibility. – The terrific Grandeur of the Ocean in a Storm, its glassy surface in a calm, its' Gulls & its Samphire, & the deep fathoms of its' Abysses, its' quick vicissitudes, its' direful Deceptions, its' Mariners tempting it in Sunshine & overwhelmed by the sudden Tempest, All were eagerly & fluently touched; (*MW*: 396)

Not for nothing does Charlotte remark to herself "rather commonplace" after listening to his barrage of hackneyed phrases.

It is difficult to say whether Austen intended Sir Edward's narrative to resemble *Clarissa* or *The Female Quixote*, but it is clear Sir Edward not only reads but in a sense, writes or overwrites novels. Indeed, the characters in *Sanditon* are novelists-manqué – characters so engrossed in fiction that they might be said to novelize their own reality. Unlike Catherine Morland, the denizens of Sanditon are allowed, or compelled, to live with their delusions and hackneyed phrases. Charlotte Heywood, the manuscript's "heroine," would seem to be an exception to the rule, as she has a tempered imagination and a skill at reading properly. These qualities do not, from what we see, preclude her from taking an imaginative interest in Clara Brereton, who promises to become the heroine of a novelistic narrative Charlotte begins to imagine.

Once Charlotte arrives at the town of Sanditon, the mutual dependency of "the book" and "nature" becomes clear. Mrs Whitby's circulating library is a central landmark in the town. Sanditon, as a place, not only fictionalizes Brighton and other seaside resorts, but it also overwrites the town of Tunbridge as described by Frances Burney in *Camilla*. Readers at the time would have made the connection quickly, both from their own recollections of Burney's works and the direct references made in *Sanditon* to Burney's third novel. Sanditon is a place whose work depends on leisure, and the novel investigates this paradox throughout, as business – or busyness – bears small resemblance to productive labor. The circulating library in the town is firmly on the side of "leisure" as we see from Charlotte's first visit there: "Mrs Whitby at the Library was sitting in her inner room, reading one of her own Novels, for want of employment" (*MW*: 389). The consumption of novels fills a gap in work, and this gap between labor and leisure characterizes the resort community. There is no Mr Knightley here to represent the engaged management of the privileged; Charlotte's father has been left behind in the wrong Willingden as an anachronism.

As with the circulating library in the resort town in Burney's novel, Sanditon's library functions as a community center. "The Library of course, afforded every thing; all the useless things in the World that cd not be done without" (*MW*: 390); and the list of subscribers functions, as it does in *Camilla*, as a register of "who's who" in town for the season. F. G. Fisher's *Brighton New Guide* (in the edition of 1800, held by ECCO) describes the contents of that town's actual circulating libraries in ways that expand Austen's description of Mrs Whitby's library in the novel:

> These Libraries command delightful prospects, and are fitted up with great attention to the convenience of the subscribers; the catalogues to each are very extensive, and contain well-chosen collections of books on every subject of polite and useful literature; to which is constantly added all works of real merit as soon as published (or public approbation decided on their merits.) The daily Papers are regularly taken in, Morning and Evening, and laid on the reading tables, for the amusement of the subscribers, with Magazines, Reviews, &c. monthly; and what renders these rooms an agreeable lounge, is the certainty of meeting none but the most fashionable company.
>
> The terms of subscription are the same at all the Libraries, and are as follow: . . .
>
> Jewellery, Stationery, Perfumery, Tunbridge-Ware, Canes, Gloves, Toys, &c. &c. &c. sold on moderate terms; and grand and small Piano-Fortes let out, by the week, month, or year. (pp. 22–3)

Whereas Camilla is plunged into a bustling scene, and quickly into debt, Charlotte (or the narrator) realizes that here in Sanditon "the List of Subscribers was but commonplace" (*MW*: 389) and that despite Mr Parker's attempt to "encourage expenditure" she "began to feel that she must check herself" (*MW*: 390). (In its way, the list of subscribers in *Sanditon* is as perfect as the class list in Nabokov's *Lolita*: it provides a realism that is thoroughly saturated with a satirical poetics of the mundane.) To drive home the parallels between Camilla and Charlotte, the library at Tunbridge and the library at Sanditon, and the novels themselves, Charlotte "took up a book; it happened to be a vol: of *Camilla*" (*MW*: 390). At the same time, we are distanced from Charlotte: "She had not *Camilla*'s Youth, & had no intention of having her Distress" (*MW*: 390), and so Charlotte turns away having made only a few small purchases.

The links with *Camilla* and that novel's use of "subscription" go deeper. Burney had published *Camilla*, her third novel, "by subscription," and the list of subscribers prefixed to the novel's first edition in 1796 has received a great deal of attention. Indeed, as critics have noted, *Camilla*'s subscription list contains the first appearance in print of the name "Miss J. Austen, Steventon." Mr Parker, seemingly echoing the thoughts of the narrator/Charlotte, "could not but feel that the List was not only without Distinction, but less numerous than he had hoped" (*MW*: 389), in direct contrast with Burney's fat subscription list prefacing the printed volumes of *Camilla*.

The library stands in for its contents as Charlotte, "perhaps partly oweing to her having just issued from a Circulating Library," meets with Miss Brereton, from whom she "cd not separate the idea of a complete Heroine" (*MW*: 391). Miss Brereton seems poised to play a role in a completed *Sanditon* analogous to that of Mrs Berlinton in *Camilla*. Mrs Berlinton is an "elegant female" (III: 141), married to a hateful husband, and is in turn pursued by Alphonso Bellamy (né Nicholas Gwigg) in a manner similar to Sir Edward's Lovelacian pursuit. More evidence, then, of the intertextual overwriting that *Sanditon* produces in abundance. (A search for the phrase "elegant female" in ECCO produces 99 hits, most of which are from novels written after 1780, both obscure and well-known. In *Pride and Prejudice* Mr Collins persists in his attentions to Elizabeth Bennet and accuses her of acting "according to the usual practice of elegant females," *PP*: 180. Mr Collins, like Austen, seems to have taken that phrase, along with the concept, from fictions. The unrealism of the phrase is emphasized in the next line in *Pride and Prejudice* when Elizabeth sets up an opposition between "elegant female" and "rational creature.") Charlotte pulls back from her projection of the role of heroine upon Clara and allows her "subsequent observation" (*MW*: 392) to counterbalance the "spirit of Romance."

The library subscription list is not the only manuscript "underwriting" in *Sanditon*. In the eighteenth century, the word "subscription" was used conventionally with charitable undertakings. Some of these involved printed lists: for example, *An Account of the Rise, Progress and State of the London Hospital* (1748, held by ECCO) resembles a printed book subscription list. Near the end of the manuscript of *Sanditon*, Mr Parker raises the idea of a "subscription for the Poor Mullins's" (*MW*: 423). Mr Parker would seem to prefer the commercial subscription of Mrs Whitby's library to this charitable effort: "I am not fond of charitable subscriptions in a place of this kind – It is a sort of tax upon all that come – " (*MW*: 423). Despite this general rule, he asks his wife to speak to Lady Denham, suggesting that she put the case in narrative terms: "You have only to state the present afflicted situation of the family, their earnest application to me, & my being willing to promote a little subscription for their releif, provided it meet with her approbation" (*MW*: 423). The effort is withdrawn when his sister Miss Diana Parker adds a list of charities for Lady Denham's support that lack the geographic (and narrative) proximity of the Mullins's. "Subscription" implies an original manuscript signature (which may or may not be followed up with a printed reproduction). In the case of charitable efforts, subscription requires personal assent in handwriting to a realistic narrative that, like a novel, affects readers or auditors for financial gain. In Burney's *Camilla* there is a specific contrast between a frivolous library subscription and the possibility of using money for charitable purposes: Camilla puts in for a "subscription" at the circulating library in Tunbridge Wells for a cheap but flashy locket, but wishes she could withdraw it because she would prefer that the money squandered on the raffle go to a poor family whose cause was taken up by her beau, Edgar Mandlebert. Just as Burney condemns gambling, Austen ridicules Mr Parker's risky real estate speculation – itself dependent upon transforming land into print in a myriad of advertising and financial documents.

Austen's technique in *Sanditon* generally pushes the reader away from sympathy with any of the characters. Charlotte's character prevents reader identification, at least in what we have, because she is self-contained, rational, and happy. There are, so far as we know, no Emma-esque "evils" to her situation. The narration in *Sanditon* plunges us less into the consciousness of its main character than any of Austen's other post-*Northanger Abbey* novels. It is possible that Austen envisioned making Clara more central (thus giving a character like Jane Fairfax top billing), or perhaps focusing on Miss Lambe, the Creole schoolgirl who has inspired much recent interest.

We know very little of Austen's compositional technique, but it is possible that the intense interiority associated with her free indirect discourse would have been added at a later stage of revision. Once again, it is perhaps more useful to look at what is in front of us and try to figure out why *Sanditon* does the work of characterization through direct statements made by the narrator, physical descriptions and quotations of speech, and a thick overlay of literary references: all techniques that have much more in common with *Northanger Abbey* than with *Persuasion*. *Sanditon* contains more discussion of novel reading than the other novels written after *Northanger Abbey*. In that work, John Thorpe's ignorant approval of *Tom Jones* is pitted against the narrator's defense of the genre. Charlotte and Sir Edward are avid readers of novels, and therefore the genre itself is less in dispute than particular "taste" within the genre. Earlier, the narrator directly described Charlotte's experience with novels, saying that "she was a very sober-minded young Lady, sufficiently well-read in Novels to supply her Imagination with amusement, but not at all unreasonably influenced by them" (*MW*: 391–2).

Sanditon is immersed in the literary culture of the eighteenth century, with direct and latent reference to novels, poetry, and a culture in which reading books has created a distinct social milieu. Like the resort town of Sanditon, literature and the business that produces it depend on leisure and income. The invalids of the novel bear the relationship to physical health that a bad reader like Sir Edward Denham bears to a sensible reader like Charlotte Heywood. Sir Edward might be genuinely dangerous, despite the nearly risible exaggeration in his characterization (which is effected mostly through his own speech). Indeed, misreading in *Sanditon* is at least potentially dangerous to others whereas obsessive preoccupation with one's health provides amusement to each other (and the readers) in a leisure-oriented economy.

Though I have spent some time discussing *Sanditon*'s deep connections with *Camilla,* the other most obvious reference to another novel involves Richardson's *Clarissa*, with Sir Edward Denham's bungling self-conscious imitation of Lovelace's rakish seduction of women providing another sustained example of intertextual over-writing. Sir Edward is a character created almost completely through literary reference. He could almost be said to have "no character at all," at least no character not absorbed through (mis)reading. Sir Edward creates himself, much as Austen creates him, through literary reference:

> Sir Edward's great object in life was to be seductive. – With such personal advantages as he knew himself to possess, & such Talents as he did also give himself credit for, he regarded it as his Duty. – He felt that he was formed to be a dangerous Man – quite in the line of the Lovelaces. – The very name of Sir Edward he thought, carried some degree of fascination with it. – To be generally gallant & assiduous about the fair, to make fine speeches to every pretty Girl, was but the inferior part of the Character he had to play. (*MW*: 405)

Critics are divided on Sir Edward Denham. John Halperin (1983: 186) calls him one of Austen's most brilliant creations, but John Wiltshire (1992: 212–3) uses the word "preposterous," suggesting that he believes the character is an unsuccessful stock character from contemporary conservative novelists. C. J. Rawson pointed out in 1958 that there is an uncanny echo of Burney in Sir Edward, who is the most fantastical character in Austen's oeuvre since Lady Susan (Rawson: 1958: 253–4). Even if Sir Edward models "the Character he ha[s] to play" in eighteenth-century novels, he speaks in neologisms, with his comments on nature steadfastly resisting "the real language of men in a state of vivid sensation" as one of his favorite poets, Wordsworth, famously described it. Instead, Sir Edward seems to speak from books that have never yet existed. For example, at one particularly heated moment in a conversation with Charlotte, Sir Edward denounces critics of Burns who employ "Hyper-criticism [or] Pseudo-philosophy to expect from the soul of high toned Genius, the grovellings of a common mind" (*MW*: 398). The *OED* provides a citation from 1678 for "hyper-criticism," and Austen could have known the word from a burst of usage around 1780, including "Hyper-criticism on Miss Seward's Louisa" (1782), but she appears to have coined "pseudo-philosophy." Sir Edward uses this choice word twice, the second time suggesting that "pseudo-philosophy" lies at the heart of a reader's preference for Clarissa over her antagonist. Richardson's novel, in Sir Edward's reading, is about a "hero" (*MW*: 404) rather than a heroine, who is denigrated as an "opposing Character" (*MW*: 404).

Even though ridiculous, Sir Edward's exaltation of nature is perfectly appropriate for *Sanditon* and perfectly appropriate for this novel-produced character. His description of the sea, though "commonplace," defines him for Charlotte at first as "a man of feeling" – at least until he goes over the top. But still, the narrative of *Sanditon* – as distinct from the characters – does attempt to evoke nature, in terms common (although not commonplace) rather than original. The sea, so mangled by Sir Edward, infuses the narrative. Despite its chilly placement above the comfortable old town of Sanditon, Mr Parker's Trafalgar House provides a genuine view: "Charlotte having received possession of her apartment, found amusement enough in standing at her ample Venetian window, & looking over the miscellaneous foreground of unfinished Buildings, waving Linen, & tops of Houses, to the Sea, dancing & sparkling in

Sunshine & Freshness" (*MW*: 384). The word "freshness" carries both an atmospheric and literary burden, as the simplicity of the description of the water in the context of the human elements of "waving linen" and buildings makes nature and culture sing to each other. No matter that the conjunction of "dancing" and "sparkling" could have been suggested to Austen from *Samson Agonistes*, in a passage popular enough to have made it into *A poetical dictionary; or, the beauties of the English poets, alphabetically displayed* (Derrick 1761, vol. 4: 171). Austen's language, her narrative, and her characters appear fresh even when they are also overwritings of the literary tradition.

None of the published continuations of *Sanditon* does for Austen's work what Austen had done for *Clarissa, Camilla*, and her own *Northanger Abbey*: make its characters, situations, and stories dancing, and sparkling, while working within what has come before. With its focus on the exterior, dialogue, and strong characterization, *Sanditon* might provide the basis for an excellent motion picture. As immersed as it is in literary history and in the material object of the book, *Sanditon* has resisted, to this point, appropriation or, for that matter, successful publication.

FURTHER READING

Forster, E. M. (1998). "Sanditon." *Jane Austen: Critical Assessments*, 1925 (pp. 513–15). Ed. Ian Littlewood. Vol. 4. Mountfield: Helm Information.

Miller, D. A. (1990). The late Jane Austen. *Raritan: A Quarterly Review*, 10:1, 55–79.

Persuasions (1997). No. 19. [This edition of the journal of the Jane Austen Society of North America contains many interesting essays on *Sanditon*.]

Southam, B. C. (1994). *Jane Austen's Literary Manuscripts*. Oxford: Clarendon Press.

Tanner, Tony (1986). *Jane Austen*. Cambridge, MA: Harvard University Press.

Wiltshire, John (1992). Sanditon: The enjoyments of invalidism. In *Jane Austen and the Body* (pp. 197–221). Cambridge, UK: Cambridge University Press.

Part III
Literary Genres and Genealogies

14
Turns of Speech and
Figures of Mind

Margaret Anne Doody

A METAPHOR for Words Resemblance *brings.*
An ALLEGORY likens *Things to things.*
A METONYMY Name *for* Name *imposes,*
For Cause, Effect; *for* Subject, Adjunct *chuses.*
And vice versa.
SYNECDOCHE the Whole *with* Part *confounds.*
An IRONY dissembling *slily wounds.*
HYPERBOLE in Speech the Truth outflies.
A CATACHRESIS Words abus'd *applies.*

> (John Holmes, *The Art of Rhetoric made
> Easy: or, The Elements of Oratory. Briefly stated
> and fitted for the Practice of the Studious Youth
> of Great-Britain and Ireland*, 1739)

A number of excellent things have been said about Jane Austen's language, but no one has quite dealt with the choice, extent, and power of the figurative in Austen's style. I intend to pursue facets of Austen's style by putting in the foreground traditional rhetorical terms, especially noting the figures of speech much discussed in her own time. Which figures of speech made her figure in the carpet?

I am assuming that Austen possessed some formal knowledge of figures of speech and rhetorical tropes. She grew up with brothers who studied literature and rhetoric. Jane may have assisted brothers James and Henry in their Oxford periodical, *The Loiterer*. It can hardly be doubted that Rev. George Austen engaged with James and Henry in discussion – even casual or dinner-table discussion – of rhetorical and linguistic effects. And George Austen also instructed other boys who boarded in the house. At times the Austen family home must have generated an atmosphere of ink and chewed pens and dog-eared textbooks.

Among those textbooks, almost inevitably, must have been Anthony Blackwall's oft-republished *Introduction to the Classics* (1717), intended for "the Use and Instruction of younger Scholars," if also for "Gentlemen who have for some Years neglected the Advantages of their Education" (1725: A2R). *The Introduction to the Classics* is readable, even entertaining. Its declared object is to teach the student how to appreciate and read works of classical literature, and how to pick out and understand the effects of rhetorical figures. The second half of this relatively short book is "An Essay, on the Nature and Use Of those Emphatical and Beautiful Figures which give Strength and Ornament to Writing."

Blackwall's terminology is friendly to the reader without Latin. He intermixes figures and tropes from the Bible among his classical allusions. (His other famous work, equally suited to clerical libraries, was *Sacred Classics*, which impresses Richardson's Belford in *Clarissa*.) Blackwall includes references to modern English authors (Spenser, Milton, and Pope), providing an important model for Hugh Blair's spoken and published *Lectures on Rhetoric and Belles Lettres*. Blair's published *Sermons*, alluded to by Mary Crawford as preferable to what most clergy could compose for themselves, was in every vicarage or manse, but his three-volume *Lectures on Rhetoric* would also be found in the schoolroom bookcase and the clergyman's study. Blair's work is referred to by James Austen in *The Loiterer*, Number 59 (March 13, 1790), a satirical piece on style; Blair is so indispensable and so generally known that citing him will impress no one: "He will generally betray too much who mentions the Books which he has really read" (350).

Texts such as Blackwall's and Blair's are useful not only to the reader of literature, but also to the person who wants to write it. Blackwall emphasizes that the two basic requirements of good writing are clarity and variety.

> And indeed every *Author* that expects to please, must gratify his *Reader* with Variety. That is the universal Charm which takes with People of all Tasts [*sic*] and Complexions. 'Tis an Appetite planted in us by the *Author* of our *Being*; and is natural to an *human Soul*, whose immense Desires nothing but an infinite *Good* and unexhausted Pleasure can fully gratify. . . . The most musical and harmonious *Notes* too often and unseasonably struck, grate the Ear like the jarring of the most harsh and hateful *Discord*. (1725: 26)

The good writer, Blackwall emphasizes, must know how to vary effects, as Livy and Herodotus do, in length of sentence, rhythm, use of figures:

> The Reflections that are made by these noble Writers upon the Conduct and Humours of Mankind . . . are so curious and instructive, so true in their Substance, and so taking and lively in the manner of their Expression, that they satisfy the soundest Judgment, and please the most sprightly Imagination. (pp. 26–7)

From Blackwall, then, the young Jane Austen could have learned the gratifying news that qualities she liked were not only approved but could be achieved by a young writer who wished to be "taking and lively" and to please "the most sprightly Imagination." In the section on "Figures" Blackwall offers a clear definition of both Simile and Metaphor:

A Metaphor is a Simile or Comparison intended to enforce and illustrate the Thing we speak of, without the Signs or Form of Comparison. . . . So in short, a Metaphor is a stricter or closer Comparison; and a Comparison a looser and less compact Metaphor. (p. 161)

He praises the employment of metaphor:

This lively way of Expression is of extraordinary use in Description of a considerable length; it keeps the Mind pleas'd, and the Attention awake. So if an Author is oblig'd to give a large Account of Things plain and of common Observation, he must raise and ennoble them by strong and graceful *Metaphors*. (p. 163)

I am imagining the young Jane Austen, aged nine or ten perhaps, picking up Black-wall's book and enjoying its delineations of what language can do. Blackwall is not strictly necessary to my examination of Austen's figures; I wish only to point out that discourse about the resources of tropes and figures was not lacking in her world, and that in the eighteenth century a young woman not versed in the classics might yet have access to lucid discussions of rhetoric and clear expositions of the engaging resources of figurative language. I do not believe Austen used such figures uncon-sciously. Her texts offer some pointed references to knowledge of their resources, including comments on the difference between the literal and figurative, and the occasional use of a technical or classical term.

Northanger Abbey: Missing Similes

In *Northanger Abbey,* devices of language are consistently noted by the author, if visibly neglected by the heroine. Catherine Morland herself is strikingly devoid of informa-tion regarding figures of speech. She is puzzled by the inanities of boastful John Thorpe and his contradictory accounts of her brother James's gig; we are told this puzzlement is a result of ignorance of what language does:

Her own family were plain matter-of-fact people, who seldom aimed at wit of any kind; her father, at the utmost, being contented with a pun, and her mother with a proverb; they were not in the habit therefore of telling lies to increase their importance, or of asserting at one moment what they would contradict the next. She reflected on the affair for some time in much perplexity, and was more than once on the point of requesting from Mr. Thorpe a clearer insight into his real opinion on the subject; but she checked herself, because it appeared to her that he did not excel in giving those clearer insights, in making those things plain which he had before made ambiguous. (*NA*: 65–6)

Catherine cannot bear the ambiguous and has no method of combing out what is going on at a linguistic level. In her family, one parent deals in the pun – linguistic doubling, complexity without significant tenor; the other parent prefers the proverb – plain statement of folk wisdom, overtly significant tenor without complexity. The alliteration of "pun" and "proverb" indicates the comic problem.

Catherine Morland's chief trouble is her ignorance of figures of speech. Her reading in late childhood and adolescence includes works marked by metaphor and other devices, as seen in the first chapter's list of quotations "so serviceable" to heroines. The effect of this pileup of quotations on the page itself suffices to baffle and daunt readers wiser than Catherine – even the reader of *Northanger Abbey* (*NA*: 15–16). The snatches of poetry almost all include some form of comparison – Gray's flower "born to blush unseen" in the *Elegy* stands for the poor individual and his or her talents; James Thomson's "young idea" being taught "how to shoot" like a plant exhibits mental vigor under a teacher's care; Shakespeare's poor beetle and dying giant are equalizing comparisons, while the figure of "Patience on a monument" is a double transformation of personification and active metaphor. Poetic comparisons have made no dent on Catherine; they are merely lines she can repeat. Catherine is good at repetition. Much of her life is simple imitation, mimesis largely based on ignorance. Thus her initial mode of coping with Thorpe is to parrot him in his admiration of his horse and his driving: "she readily echoed whatever he chose to assert" (*NA*: 66).

Catherine's lack of analytic capacity is of a piece with her ignorance of the figurative, to which her parents have contributed. Puns and proverbs have long been held to be "low" uses of language. Blackwall wants to get rid of "Puns and Quibbles." Lord Chesterfield likes to think that the age of Charles II abolished them among polite society, though he spends time in his letters to his natural son deprecating proverbs:

> here is . . . an awkwardness of expression . . . most carefully to be avoided; such as false English, bad pronunciation, old sayings, and common proverbs; which are so many proofs of having kept bad and low company. For example; if, instead of saying that tastes are different . . . you should let off a proverb, and say, That what is one man's meat is another man's poison; or else, Everyone as they like, as the good man said when he kissed his cow; every body would be persuaded that you had never kept company with any above footmen and housemaids. (Stanhope 1774, vol. I: 180–91)

"Letting off" a proverb seems the equivalent of emitting bodily gas.

False English, bad pronunciation, reliance on "old sayings" – Austen uses all of these markers of rank and education to represent her characters. Sometimes the effect is clear, as in the portrait of Lucy Steele's "false English." More often, Austen's effects are ambiguous. We may hazard a guess that Catherine's mother came from a lower rank of life than that to which Catherine, in associating with the Tilneys, unconsciously aspires. We cannot, however, with certainty place Catherine's parents as more than slightly inferior in breeding, still less can they be considered inferior in morality. We can be surer of our ground in labeling them old-fashioned. Mrs Morland holds to the commonsense wisdom of the folk, while her husband has failed to realize that polite society since King Charles II's time has supposedly rid itself of wordplay. Though a clergyman he delights still in "childish Jingle."

Catherine's father is rare among Austen's characters as a punning male, and a punster neither malicious nor corrupt. Austen tends to put most puns into the mouths of women who are no better than they should be. Mary Crawford is the obvious example, but consider Miss Bingley and Mrs Hurst talking about Elizabeth and Jane:

> "I think I have heard you say, that their uncle is an attorney in Meryton."
> "Yes; and they have another, who lives somewhere near Cheapside."
> "That is capital," added her sister, and they both laughed heartily. (*PP*: 36–7)

The pun depends on the fusion of the semislang use of "capital" meaning "excellent" with London as both capital city and center of trade, and the economic meaning of "capital." Bingley's sisters rejoice at the low nature of Jane's mercantile uncle in the City, choosing to forget that their own wealth was derived from trade. The pun (here reflecting the Bingley's low birth, too) commonly pertains to an effervescence of mean exaltation or sourness in dubious female wits, such as Mary Crawford. Austen herself is above such strictures. Names of places and people often have a punning power – as in *Pride and Prejudice* itself: Long-bourne, Huns-ford. And what of Mery-ton, the little town so full of sex, high jinks, and shopping – a "merry town" indeed. Not to mention Mor-land, Nor-land, and the complex dishonest "Frank" Churchill.

Catherine cannot pun, nor can she compare. Her drawing, like her mind, is indiscriminate; her "houses and trees, hens and chickens" are "all very much like one another" (*NA*: 14). Active comparison is impossible when difference is invisible. Hugh Blair finely says that comparison, whether simile or metaphor, is "a figure of thought" (Blair 1783, vol. I: 351–2). Metaphor serves "to make intellectual ideas, in some sort, visible to the eye, by giving them colour, and substance, and sensible qualities" (p. 353). For Blair, metonymy and synecdoche remain "figures of speech," whereas simile and metaphor are primary "figures of thought." They provide means of taking our own reflections knowable to ourselves. They are thus really what I choose to call "figures of mind," tropes or turns by which the mind makes both connections and distinctions simultaneously. Through figures of mind the mind finds access to itself.

Catherine has little access to her own mind – a fact that attracts Henry's attention. Deriving enjoyment from following her thought processes better than she can, he engages in an elaborate simile that baffles Catherine:

> "I consider a country-dance as an emblem of marriage. Fidelity and complaisance are the principal duties of both; and those men who do not chuse to dance or marry themselves, have no business with the partners or wives of their neighbours."
> "But they are such very different things! – "
> " – That you think they cannot be compared together."
> "To be sure not. People that marry can never part, but must go and keep house together. People that dance, only stand opposite each other in a long room for half an hour." (*NA*: 76–7)

Comparison disturbs Catherine's mental geography. She is confounded by simile, a primary mode of intellectual inquiry from the Restoration through the eighteenth century. She rejects Henry's emblem and the hovering allegory that could take the emblematic simile (and the two of them) further in a direction flattering to her hopes. Likeness within difference confuses her, and this is both sign and cause of her troubles.

Catherine's deafness to simile renders her both vulnerable to victimization and inaccessible to a subtle reading of literature. Her love of Radcliffe's novels is not wrong. Indeed, Gothic novels are Catherine's first good source of information as to the evil in the world. This information alerts her emotional logic (more sound than her intellect) and leads her to suspect General Tilney of cruelty to his wife. So far, she is right. Catherine is certainly not meddling in matters that don't concern her – for if she is to marry into the family, she needs to know how the men treat their women. Catherine, however, is misled by her aversion to simile into belief that tenor and vehicle are inseparable, even fused, and thus she sets out on the absurd wild-goose chase of discovering General Tilney's murder of his wife. Though exhibiting imagination, she is impeded from further growth by her resistance of the figurative: General Tilney is not seen as *like* Radcliffe's villain, he must *be* "a Montoni."

This incapacity marks a gap between Catherine and her hero. Henry is not afflicted at home by puns and proverbs, but his life is made miserable by his father's iron-willed addiction to cliché. Henry's relief lies in rhetorical play, of which he is an addict rather than just a practitioner. Rhetorical play enables him to feel superior, to make fun of others, to parody their stupidity before their faces (as he mimics Mrs Allen). Catherine (an innocent mimic) is a happier person than Henry, and will never have recourse to rhetorical play as consolation. In Austen's novels, it is most generally the person who is unhappy who resorts to rhetorical play – Fanny Price, Maria Bertram, and Mary Crawford, as well as Anne Elliot. Rhetorically unengaged, Catherine will always misunderstand her husband. She will be a wife who, like Mrs Palmer or Mrs Bennet or Isabella Knightley, cannot understand her husband's irony. Husband and wife will remain unequally matched.

Sense and Sensibility: Broken Synecdoche

In Austen's saddest novel we leave the realm of simile for a more complex world of metonymy and synecdoche. John Holmes in *The Art of Rhetoric* (1739) defines "Metonymy" as the substituting of cause for effect or means for end (or *vice versa*), also of substitution of the adjunct for the noun, possessor for possessed. He cites as examples *"he has a good Heart, i.e. Courage"* or *"The Church, i.e. Religion,* forbids it." His Latin examples include, like Blair's, for the use of sign for the signifier the expression *Cedant Arma Togae,* or "Let Arms yield to the Toga" (war should give way to peaceful civil discussion) (Holmes 1739: 35–6). Synecdoche is found where "the *Whole* is taken for

Part," or where "a *Part* is taken for the *Whole*," for which Holmes cites "Give us this Day our daily *Bread*". Other (Latin) examples include "wings" ("*Ales*") for an eagle (*Aquila*) or "Quadruped" for a horse (Holmes 1739: 38).

Metonymy and synecdoche are easily confused with each other, even if metonymy refers customarily more to human categories and thought processes, while synecdoche pertains more often to a physical entity of which parts and wholes may be sundered. Both metonymy and synecdoche seem more literally and intimately related to what they apparently describe or point to than do metaphor and simile, where we have to make a conscious effort to recognize a gap and jump it. The delusion offered by metonymy and synecdoche is that there is no gap, that we know what is cause and what effect, who is possessor and what is possessed, or where to find the whole form whence this amputated part is taken.

The first line of *Sense and Sensibility* is "The family of Dashwood had been long settled in Sussex" (*SS*: 3). Here is a metonym concealing a sad paranomasia, a lost pun. The word "family" is the hidden substitution of the adjunct for a reality, a modified phrase referring only to male landowners in the line of successions. At any moment the "family" living in Norland consists of the rightful heir and his immediate kit of spouse and children. Owner follows owner, and what is outside this schema is not really "family." "Family" is redefined and cut down. Mrs John Dashwood considers half sisters as no sisters: "the Miss Dashwoods, . . . were related to him only by half blood, which she considered as no relationship at all" (*SS*: 8). Here a part is separated from a whole and nearly swept away.

Adjuncts or modifying phrases may spring up and metamorphose in meaning, while entities and their adjuncts (or modifiers) become irrationally separated from each other. The screens that Elinor had painted are produced in Fanny Dashwood's drawing room, ostensibly to be admired by family and friends. Once Mrs Ferrars hears who has made them, she sets them aside "without regarding them at all." Sour Mrs Ferrars then breaks into praise of the painted screens of Miss Morton, the woman she wishes her son to marry. The screens are a metonym for Elinor herself, as Marianne realizes when she bursts out in compensatory praise, trying to restore her sister Elinor, the whole person and personality, to the center of the group: "it is Elinor of whom *we* think and speak" (*SS*: 235). Mrs Ferrars angrily rebukes Marianne: "Mrs. Ferrars looked exceedingly angry, and drawing herself up more stiffly than ever, pronounced in retort this bitter phillippic [*sic*]: 'Miss Morton is Lord Morton's daughter'" (*SS*: 235–6). Here Jane Austen employs a technical or academic term from the tradition of oratory and rhetorical study: Demosthenes' orations urging the Athenians to stand up against the detested King Philip of Macedon are known as his "Philippics." The word is used comically by James Austen in *Loiterer* number 58 (March 6, 1790): "Having pronounced this bitter Philippic, he looked round with the triumphant air of a man, who does not think his arguments very readily answered" (p. 343). Jane would be familiar with the term through James; on the other hand (see chapter 2) it is possible that Austen supplied this sentence or part of it to *The Loiterer*, and picks up the "bitter phillippic" again in *Sense and Sensibility*.

In this bitterly comic scene, Mrs Ferrars endeavors by plain recital of the hierarchical fact of Miss Morton's paternity and consequent rank to establish an absolute definition sufficient to quell doubt or disrespect. Mrs Ferrars' assumption that her auditors revere blue blood actually reverses Demosthenes' democratic arguments against the threatening power of King Philip, as any reader of Hugh Blair would know. Blair praises Demosthenes for "energy of thought peculiar to himself" (1783, vol. II: 190). Demosthenes "warms the mind." "His actions and pronunciation are recorded to have been uncommonly vehement and ardent." The ardent simplicity, the fire, and defiance Blair admires, the "strain of magnanimity and high honour" (p. 191), describe Marianne – animated, impetuous, ardent; her "warmth" is twice mentioned by the narrator. Marianne would seem to have uttered the true protesting "phillippic," whereas powerful and authoritarian Mrs Ferrars is in the position of the King of Macedon. It is the style of the novel to transfer the important term to the wrong side.

In this novel important words have no set meaning. Abstract emotional words like "love," "approbation," and "esteem" (Mrs Dashwood cannot separate these) are open to debate, but even a noun substantive may be variously envisaged and interpreted. The word "cottage" has variant meanings. "Love in a cottage" may be a cliché in the eighteenth century and seems easy to define until Austen's novel shows we don't know what is meant by "love" or "cottage." Attributes may be forcefully and wrongly imposed, may grow hazy even in the concrete world of experience and phenomena. A man on a horse seems to Marianne a metonym of Willoughby – but the real entity she perceives proves to be Edward. The exchange of letters between a young man and young woman is a social metonym of engagement – but it is not in Marianne's case, although it is in Lucy's.

Objects carry an emotional significance here that is not mocked (as the projection of such significance is in the case of Harriet Smith's "treasures" in *Emma* later). But objects do mislead. Confronting her rival Elinor, Lucy Steele proves her relation to Edward by a set of well-arranged synecdoches as physical exhibits – she has his portrait, she has his letters, and her hair can be seen in his ring. The letters may be a social metonym of engagement, but they are also objects, sundered from their complete context, and are thus perfect if perverse examples of synecdoche.

Any instance of synecdoche demands that the reader perform a mental suture to restore the part to its larger whole. But a particular lost part might not belong to the whole we imagine for it. Marianne's letters to Willoughby are in her eyes absolute signals of a justified confidence; in another's eyes, they constitute imprudent self-revelation, if not sexual looseness. On the other hand, Willoughby's cruel letter putting an end to the relationship, and returning Marianne's lock of hair and former letters as detritus, is apparently a synecdoche: "a piece of his mind," as we say. But the letter, though his statement, is not his utterance, as we later find out, for a mind other than his own dictated it; the letter is not a piece of Willoughby's mind at all, but an infliction to which he submitted, the price of something else.

Marianne's lock of hair appears spurned by Willoughby, even though he begged for it before, but it turns out that it was not spurned by him and he would have preferred to have kept the souvenir – a part for whole. Elinor is also caught in the web of synecdoche. She supposes that the lock of hair in Edward's ring is hers. A lock of hair is the perfect synecdochic object, literally a part of a human being taken for the whole, to be loved the way the whole person is loved, and exhibited as a sign of union. But Elinor is misled, Edward wears not her lock of hair but (somewhat unwillingly) Lucy's. A part can be a part of another whole, bearing another significance altogether.

Elinor and Marianne, however different, are much alike, and equally different from Catherine Morland. Intelligent and well read, they understand simile, and they can appreciate the wilder reaches of comparison and relationship expressed in metonymy and synecdoche – but they still err. They can never be sufficiently warned. Colonel Brandon not only compares Marianne to the first Eliza, but makes a disconcerting connection between them, as if he were trying to stitch Marianne into a metaphor that makes her a replacement for the lost one, a metonymic change of one name for another. Even in marrying Marianne, Brandon may be marrying a metonym for his lost Eliza. She is his second choice, as he is hers.

The rending and distance involved in metonymy and synecdoche makes these the perfect figures of mind for unhappiness. Marianne's apostrophe to the trees of Norland is her passionate and self-consciously artistic goodbye. "And you ye well-known trees! – but you will remain the same. – No leaf will decay . . ." (*SS*: 27). But she underestimates Mr and Mrs John Dashwood's capacity for hacking. The apostrophized trees, which stand for the entire childhood home and for youth itself, are as fragile as autumn leaves, and doomed. Marianne's "passion for dead leaves" is an emotional activity finding a perfect synecdoche, something to which she can tie experience, a wildness which she can safely value because nobody else does. Dead leaves, dead locks of hair, parts that will never be whole.

Catherine Morland's deficiency in simile-making or simile-understanding makes us laugh, but the figurative problems at the center of *Sense and Sensibility* perplex intelligent minds. How to relate parts to wholes, or decide what is "part" and of which "whole"? Physical sense, "common sense," and sensibility alike may err. There is no relief in allegory. Willoughby called the horse he wishes to give Marianne "Queen Mab," after Mercutio's fairy queen, and animates the beast and their future with a kind of pun: "Queen Mab shall receive you." But Queen Mab belongs to the fairy world of ungraspable treasure and magic solutions. Insofar as the mare is an extension of Willoughby and a reflection of his love (and his playing at being wealthy), this meaning is lost in a mist, part of a world of illusion.

Abstraction and physical contacts: *Pride and Prejudice*

If the dominant trope of *Northanger Abbey* is the (missing) simile and the dominant trope of *Sense and Sensibility* is the broken synecdoche, *Pride and Prejudice* has a generous mixture of tropes, including metonymy and metaphor. But strong rhetorical functions link these tropes. We are told Catherine Morland's mother resorted to proverbs, but we never hear her do so. In our hearing, Elizabeth resorts to the proverbial: "There is a fine old saying, which everybody here is of course familiar with – 'keep your breath to cool your porridge'" (*PP*: 24). This is a strikingly "low" expression, an "old saying" (unutterably vulgar in itself according to Chesterfield, a breach of rhetorical manners according to Blair). Elizabeth deploys her "saying" as a deliberately vulgar challenge to Darcy. Will he take this ebullition as a proof that the speaker "has kept bad and low company"? The references to breath and base food can also remind Darcy of Elizabeth's physicality. In *Pride and Prejudice*, abstractions tend to collapse back into physical counterparts or causes, reminders of physical embodiment and body, organic or inorganic. We can see this if we compose a quick florilegium of memorable lines : "[Your nerves] are my old friends" (*PP*: 5); "what are men to rocks and mountains?" (*PP*: 154); "every savage can dance" (*PP*: 25). Dancing savages, rocks, plates of porridge – these things wait in the physical world for the breathing participant in life. Almost everything becomes physical and to a certain degree intimate. Elizabeth goes into Derbyshire to pick up "petrified spars," an unconsciously chosen image of what Darcy's love for her (so she fears) will have become. Feelings and experiences find embodiment in physical entities; practically everything is actually or potentially an active agent.

Anthony Blackwall admires the effect of giving human qualities to animals and animal qualities to inanimate objects: "Those are admirable and very beautiful *Metaphors* when the Properties of rational Creatures are apply'd to Animals, and those of Animals to Plants and trees: This way of treating a Subject gives Life and Beauty to the whole *Creation*" (Blackwall 1725: 164).

"Life and beauty" are qualities instinctively desired by Elizabeth Bennet and by some of those around this memorably "rational Creature," who has life enough to spare for those around her. The animation of abstract nouns, a particularly Austenian forte, is found here in the conversation of characters as well as in authorial narration. Yet in *Pride and Prejudice* Austen undertakes not only the animation of abstractions but a touch of true prosopopoeia, giving animation to nonhuman but not abstract subjects; we find a higher number of personifications of physical objects than in the other two early novels.

Mr Darcy early meditates "on the very great pleasure which a pair of fine eyes in the face of a pretty woman can bestow" – Elizabeth's eyes are energized and active, benevolently *bestowing* something (the antitype of Lady Catherine de Bourgh). Even in the view of an inimical rival Elizabeth's very clothes have an active power: a gown is "not doing its office" but a muddy petticoat also "escaped my notice" (*PP*: 36). A gown may not *do* its office, a petticoat may *escape*. This device lends a sense of physical immediacy and of activity to the whole, thus centering our reading, even when Elizabeth isn't there, on the animated and animating qualities of the heroine herself.

In Mr Bennet's plea to his daughter near the end of the novel we find a surprising mixture of what may be personification with cautious synecdoche. "I know your disposition, Lizzy. . . . Your lively talents would place you in the greatest danger in an unequal marriage" (*PP*: 376). What a surprising utterance! Mr Bennet thinks his favorite daughter would be capable of – in danger of – committing adultery, if her lively *talents*, unappreciated, looked outside the marriage for exercise and refreshment. The "talents" seem to be personified; they threaten to be cut off from Elizabeth as in synecdoche, yet they are most essentially related to her and thus rather a metonym than the amputated entity a synecdoche suggests. Mr Collins has absurdly imagined that Elizabeth's liveliness might be cut off, asphyxiated, while leaving her essentially the same – her father knows better. Elizabeth's "lively talents" are connected to her body and instincts, her sexuality. Surprisingly, Mr Bennet's insight brings into the end of the novel a reminder of Elizabeth's resemblance to Lydia – even though the plot has officially made the maximum effort to persuade us of their difference. Lydia too cannot be amputated from her family, Mr Bennet's initial conventional efforts notwithstanding.

The rhetoric of *Pride and Prejudice* characteristically searches for the universal, a turn introduced, parodied, and examined in the famous first sentence: "It is a truth universally acknowledged . . . ." Throughout the narrative, characters are given to large-scale generalizations; words such as "every," "none," "nobody," "always," "never," tumble out on all sides. "*Every* savage can dance" (*PP*: 15); "*Nothing* could be more delightful!"; "to her he was only the man who made himself agreeable *no where*"; "*Whatever* bears affinity to cunning is despicable" (*PP*: 40). The tendency to pronounce universal truths, inadvertently parodied by Mary Bennet and Mr Collins, is widespread. Such a colloquially philosophic tendency preempts the search for truth and fosters both pride and prejudice. Hasty and dismissive, universalizing is amusingly and subtly counteracted by the reiterated animation of the world found in the novel's tropes, and the constant suggestion of physical present and enjoyable reality.

The Hyperbolists: *Mansfield Park*

Mansfield Park develops the personification more modestly employed in *Pride and Prejudice*. It takes up to different effect the exaggerated absoluteness of the preceding novel's statements, with its "everybody" and "always," creating a more elaborate verbal game of exaggeration. *Mansfield Park* stands out as the Austen novel most fully employing personification, dealing with the heightened consciousness of things and our relation to things. The story begins, however, not with a personification but with a comic metonym that is halfway towards personification: "All Huntingdon exclaimed on the greatness of the match" (*MP*: 3). A whole county becomes a gasping excited gossip, and "the greatness" here prefigures the hyperbole that will become common in this novel. As Blair comments, "common conversation" and "common forms of compliment" abound in "extravagant Hyperboles" (Blair 1783: 376). It requires insight to notice that this statement is hyperbole, so conditioned are we to social exaggerations. "All Huntingdon exclaimed on the greatness of the match" passes in common conversation. It is seeing this sentence in company with other hyperboles that makes us aware of its shady magnification.

Miss Maria Ward with only seven thousand pounds of dowry is an investment which has profited more than could be expected: her own uncle "allowed her to be at least three thousand pounds short of any equitable claim" to a match with Sir Thomas Bertram. Maria Ward, an object exchanged for a high price, is thus a kind of personification of herself, a thing lacking "an equitable claim." "Good luck" seems to preclude talent or personal qualities. Here is a kind of reverse personification, in which rather than the object being made a person, the person is made an object. In Maria's "elevation" she seems (like Fanny later) a metonym of herself, a being whose identity is not knowable. When we come to know "Lady Bertram" under her new name (marriage entailing for women a literal metonymic change), we believe that this entity must always have been flaccid and inert. Only after a consideration of what her daughter Maria and her niece Fanny become under the pressure of experience might we begin to glimpse the possibility that this indolent stupid object, "Lady Bertram," need not always have been the manifestation of "Maria Ward." In the metonymy, she may have lost something.

Maria Bertram, resenting the future imprisonment she senses at Sotherton, turns her emotions into a poetics of multiple personification. She picks up the cue of personification from Henry Crawford's conventional classical assertion:

". . . You have a very smiling scene before you."

"Do you mean literally or figuratively? Literally, I conclude. Yes, certainly the sun shines and the park looks very cheerful. But unluckily that iron gate, that ha-ha, give me a feeling of restraint and hardship. I cannot get out, as the starling said." (*MP*: 99)

In this novel for the first time, we see characters' conscious knowledge of the literal and the figurative and the difference between them. But Maria's knowledge of literature and rhetoric brings no benefits. Indeed she may be likelier to fall because she can play with the tropes. Not wise to herself, Fanny Price more slowly picks up the difference between the literal and figurative. In her jealous vision of Edmund helping Mary to ride, she tries to explain away what she is seeing and to repress her sexual jealousy – or rather, the knowledge of it. She turns for relief to personification, making the "poor mare" the substitute for her emotionally overtasked and resentful self (*MP*: 67–8).

This swerve to evasive personification introduces a pattern of emblem-making. Objects not only have powers, they gain an abstracted significance and begin to participate in an allegory internal to the novel. This tendency to resort to emblems is shared among characters; to Maria, the iron gate and ha-ha are emblematic and she can read them in an allegorical and "literary" way. Rarely hitherto in Austen's novels does a character pick out an unconventional physical object as an objective correlative for a state of mind or relationship. But here that mental habit is fully developed and almost common. The amber cross received from William is an emblematic object to Fanny – and to Mary, a skillful reader of objects. Mary sees in Fanny's home-bred piety and affection a chance to link Fanny to her brother through the emblematic chain that she treacherously offers. In turn, Fanny feels that taking a chain which came from Henry is really chaining herself to him, and she is thankful when Edmund offers her the chain she really wants. All four characters are thus playing with an emblem of attachment. The desire for objects with emblematic value so dominant in the characters encourages the reader to accept tempting allegories teasingly offered here: amber, evergreens, a rose garden. We play with these as Maria Bertram does with the fence and the ha-ha at Sotherton. The reader may be happy to view Mary Crawford with her harp as emblematic of a siren. We notice that amber and the evergreen associated with Fanny are emblems of memory, and we are perhaps so satisfied that we overlook the fallibility of Fanny's memory, as when at Portsmouth she misremembers life at her uncle's home. If we are tempted to read the hot servitude in the rose garden as an emblem of slavery, we have Austen to thank, for Austen has seeded her novel with emblems and allegories, closely associated with a heroine who is attracted to this way of reading and interpreting. Fanny is so lonely that she supplies significance and emotional content in a bookish way. Though she at first seems unwilling to stand aside and note her own power of allegorizing, she relies upon it.

Things carry emotional weight, and they have the power to soothe, injure, or entrap. As a newcomer young Fanny is surrounded by a welter of things new and strange – sashes, French verbs, gold tissue paper, maps. As she progresses, things themselves acquire emotion and intellect, reflecting her ability to organize thought. Fanny glories in the heap of treasures in her cold little room. Of a detritus of odd or failed objects – considered not good enough for the official areas of residence – the lonely Fanny makes friends. Fanny is not alone in her love of things. Complaining about her inability to find a vehicle to transport her harp, Mary Crawford, in comic personification, speaks of offending "all the hay in the parish" (*MP*: 58). But that is really protesting the assertive cut grass that has dared to compete with her splendidly artificial harp. The laborers and farmers are somehow wrong in not setting her glorious harp and self above the humdrum hay.

Oddly connected with the pattern of personification is the employment of hyperbole – as in Mary Crawford's rhetorically witty complaint above. Blair observes that hyperbole is the natural vent of passion: "All passions, without exception, love, terror, amazement, indignation, anger, and even grief, throw the mind into confusion, aggravate their objects, and of course prompt a hyperbolical style" (Blair 1783: 378–9). "On innumerable occasions, it [hyperbolic personification] is the very Language of imagination and passion" (p. 385). We may suspect that, even in flip moments, hyperbole conceals or reveals a degree of even intense emotion. In *Mansfield Park* we are never far from passion, even if concealed passion, and characters' judgments find an outlet in excess. The tendency of persons in *Pride and Prejudice* to make judgments of others and of the world is here extended to almost wild exaggeration, as when Fanny's female cousins think her "prodigiously stupid" (*MP*: 18). Mrs Norris unpleasantly acts to the limit the charitable role: "could I bear to see her want, while I had a bit of bread to give her?" (*MP*: 7). "A Metaphor carry'd to a great degree of Boldness is an Hyperbole," as Blackwall says (1725: 181). Metaphor and allegory are thus quite closely allied. If an allegory is an extended metaphor, hyperbole is a bold one. Hyperbole, Blair interestingly comments, "consists in magnifying an object beyond its natural bounds. It may be considered sometimes as a trope, and sometimes as a figure of thought" (Blair 1783, vol. I: 376).

Mansfield Park, dealing with boundaries, parks, pales, borders, with geographical locations (including locations as images for bounded social gradations), reiterates figures that go "beyond natural bounds." Hyperbole combines with personification, not to ground observation in physical reality, but to draw physical reality into fantasy. Estates, dwellings grounds, and boundaries are remodeled to reflect fantastic notions of individual importance. Henry urges Edmund to remodel his parsonage into the false face of a gentleman's manor; his description is a bubble of peremptory desire. Hyperbole is a figure of mind, a reflection of emotion reacting on the speaking consciousness. Almost everyone employs it because almost all seem to wish to escape from themselves, and from something in their social or psychological (or even moral) "location." Hyperbole becomes fugue.

Emblem-making and hyperbole resist truth and truth-speaking throughout this novel. The ending of *Mansfield Park* is an unsettling instance. Poor Maria, offstage, is brought to book, disgraced by her divorce and rejected by Henry. She is to have "no second spring of hope or character" (*MP*: 464). She is certainly not helped by her father, who exiles her to a remote dwelling and refuses to recognize her as his daughter. At some level the reader must feel it ridiculous to imagine a beautiful, young, and healthy woman pining without hope of any kind. However officially "correct" Sir Thomas' judgment may be, his casting-off is another bitter example of hyperbole and self-gratification. Imagining Maria's "character" to be completely "destroyed" offers Sir Thomas the let-out he seeks. Hyperbole in *Mansfield Park* almost always sidles towards the liberating erasure of others – see Tom's prediction that Dr Grant will eat himself to death, a wish that comes true. The dreaded parsonage, now emptied of Mrs Norris and Dr Grant, becomes acceptable to Fanny, who takes it over in a hyperbolical personification that is yet another hyperbolical fugue: "the parsonage . . . soon grew as dear to her heart, and as thoroughly perfect in her eyes, as every thing else, within the view and patronage of Mansfield Park, had long been" (*MP*: 473).

Austen's own style at the end of this novel is equally troubling: "Let other pens dwell on guilt and misery. I quit such odious subjects as soon as I can, impatient to restore everybody, not greatly in fault themselves, to tolerable comfort, and to have done with all the rest." This dismissive impatience, almost an example of "novel slang," seeks to identify the author's feelings and the reader's, even in advance of complete narration. In *Loiterer* 59, James Austen commented satirically on the modes of modern writing most likely to please, by recommending what he really disdains, for example a Latinate vocabulary and "mythological allusions" (p. 349). But consider what follows, where James mocks authorial intervention:

When an author describes a scene which he wishes to be affecting, let him boldly pronounce it so himself. Nothing is so convenient to the reader as thus to be taught how he is to feel, nothing is more consistent, than to be at once the Painter and the Spectator of the Piece. . . . When he presents any image with which he wishes to depress his reader, he previously gives his cue by phrases similar to these: "It is melancholy to reflect:" . . . When on the contrary he wishes to elevate him; he begins, something in this manner – "We gaze with sensible delight on this bright and amiable picture;" "From this gloomy catalogue we turn with eagerness to a more pleasing retrospect." My readers will readily perceive what an appearance of amiable sensibility this practice diffuses over a Piece. (*Loiterer*, p. 349)

Jane Austen indulges precisely this practice in the ending of *Mansfield Park*. Much of this last chapter is spent in diffusing "an appearance of amiable sensibility" over an unpalatable ending. This soft diffusion, with sharp points coming through every now and then – at one moment Sir Thomas finds in the absence of Mrs Norris a consolation for his daughter's adultery – seems another form of hyperbole, an assumption of self-admiring sensibility in the authorial voice. May Austen be mocking herself, even as she writes this ending? Here – as nowhere else – she comes close to penning "From this gloomy catalogue we turn . . . to a more pleasing retrospect." In the last lines the imagined "perfection" of Mansfield and its parsonage must content us, even though we know we are being fobbed off with a lie.

Riddles and Refreshment: the Art of *Emma*

Emma's father "could not meet her in conversation, rational or playful" (*E*: 7), but the novel itself is full of playful rationality and irrational playfulness. The dominance of enigmas and word play surrounding Austen's most intelligent though not best-natured heroine, has been expertly dealt with by numerous critics, most notably in "*Emma*grammatology" (Holly 1989). *Emma* is notoriously the locus for the use of the riddle, a teasing play of metaphor or hidden pseudo-allegory.

Hugh Blair remarks:

Allegories were a favourite method of delivering instructions in ancient times . . . An AEnigma or riddle is also a species of Allegory; one thing represented or imaged by another; but purposely wrapt up under so many circumstances, as to be rendered obscure. Where a riddle is not intended, it is always a fault in Allegory to be too dark. The meaning should be easily seen though the figure employed to shadow it. (1783, vol. I: 375)

In *Emma*, the emblematizing and allegory so troubling in *Mansfield Park* are developed playfully into a riddling tension, an opposition version of the plot. The story deliberately runs the risk of being "too dark," since the reader will be deluded, as in a detective story. The heroine has a couple of strong antagonists who seek the shelter of obscurity, turning their riddle into a dark "allegory" before her unwitting eyes. They are living allegorically while Emma, merely reading interpretively, is deceived. The capacity to lie to oneself is profusely illustrated, though here presented as capable of amendment through the enlightened reason, as not in *Mansfield Park*, where lying to oneself remains a necessary cover to the very end. *Emma* is more extroverted; people know when they lie to others, sometimes even when they lie to themselves.

It is an aspect of the novel's ironic mode of story telling that the atmosphere seems bright while the true story is concealed in a conceited darkness. Irony abounds at every level of misinformation and misunderstanding, including the heroine's lack of understanding of herself. Consciousness of rhetorical devices is signaled at many turns. The term "Philippics" returns, in a most incongruous setting, the critiques of Isabella and her father upon bland gruel: "pretty severe Philippics upon the many houses where it was never to be met with tolerable" (*E*: 105). Spoken irony or sarcasm also abounds, and speakers display their own mastery of rhetorical tropes. Frank Churchill at Box Hill sourly remarks upon the retreating Eltons, "Happy couple! . . . How well they suit one another! – Very lucky – marrying as they did, upon an acquaintance formed only in a public place!" (*E*: 372). This apostrophe is not intended for the Eltons, who are out of earshot, but for Jane. What appears as gossipy satire on the absent is really a device for delivering a cruel stab to the person present. Frank chooses a veiled way of informing Jane (in a public place) that he considers their engagement a mistake. His utterance can be classified with allegory in the traditional definition: "Allegoria is a sentence which sheweth one thing in wordes, and another in sense" (Henry Peacham, *The Garden of Eloquence*, 1577). Allegory is constituted of multiple concealment, as Peacham defines it in relation to metaphor: "in a Metaphor there is a translation but of one word, but in Aligory of many" (D1R–D1V). The "translation" necessitated by Frank's bitter clever speech is the translation from Augusta Hawkins + Philip Elton to Jane Fairfax + Frank Churchill, and the "public place" is not the Eltons' Bath but must be translated by Jane as "Weymouth."

The novel shows the power of figures to hurt and to confuse, culminating in the excursion to Box Hill, a festival of bad behavior and awkward, even malicious, word games. Traditional rhetoric can even supply us with a name for Emma's insult to Miss Bates, when she tells the old maid that in a new game she will be limited to uttering only "three dull things" at once. This is an example of *Mycterismus,* "counterfyte scoffing, and manner of jesting, yet not so privy, but that it may be well perceyved," as Henry Peacham defines it. Emma is splenetic and scoffing at Box Hill and gives color to her spleen with a "frumping bolt" – almost rude enough for an Elizabethan – an uncivilized onslaught she soon regrets.

In this story, characters turn themselves or others into puzzles. False representation, omnipresent but hidden in *Mansfield Park*, comes into the open. Emma makes a portrait of Harriet that does not quite represent her. Mr Elton represents both himself and his pseudo-adored in a passable and heavily gallant "charade" or riddle. His verses misfire because the attempt is misrepresented in the interpretation, even though the technical constituent terms of the allegory are correctly divined. Harriet may be technically absurdly off the mark in coming up with "mermaids" and "sharks," but Emma fails to see herself as siren and Mr Elton as shark in courtship. In her endeavor to detect Jane's secret life, even clever Emma turns into a fool – essentially because her suspicions center on Jane's sexual life, and not on Frank's.

The novel's lurches towards representation – in painting, in engravings, in stories, in riddle books, in children's alphabets – demand a counteracting emphasis on the physical and immediate. Hence the comic mockery of Mrs Elton, who imagines coming on a donkey with a picturesque hat to the Donwell strawberry gathering, which she imagines as some painted pastoral festivity. The asinine bride has to be brought back with a jolt into the physical, as in Austen's wonderfully telegraphic monologue accorded to Mrs Elton in the strawberry picking, in which she descends from pretentiousness to frank admission of being too hot. The corrective to the mind's misrepresentation of the world lies in the senses' contact with the physical realm – as in *Pride and Prejudice*. But in *Emma* the consciousness of the heroine has the upper hand, and we are plugged into her mental world, in a brilliantly inventive exercise in *style indirect libre*. Physical entities that are not allegorical figure strongly, especially food – boiled eggs or mutton, baked apples, a leg of pork, arrowroot. Mr Woodhouse, sitting at the demanding center of Emma's life, is all reluctant physicality, even in his very attempts to keep the world of mortality at bay. He endeavors to keep the world safe from food and sex – and thus from death. He is notoriously incapable of appreciating conundrums or paradox. Admitting the existence of difficult connections and contrasts is a stress Emma's parent resists. He can be entertained like a child by collections of ornamental objects, and (unlike Frank) he can look at "views of Swisserland" and "some views of St. Mark's Place, Venice" without any thought of a real place, or any desire to go there (*E*: 363–4). For Mr Woodhouse, representations have practically ceased to function as representing anything else in any meaningful way. But that tendency of representations to resist firm interpretation also feeds Harriet's riddle book.

The Preface to a book of riddles, *A New Riddle-Book* (1778) tells us jocularly that "decyphering" riddles is

> a kind of Logic, . . . it consists in discovering truth under borrowed appearances . . . habituating the mind to separate all foreign ideas, and consequently preserving us from that grand source of error, the being deceived by false connections . . . In order to understand the world around us, we need the ability to decipher. Every Knave is an Aenigma that you must unriddle before you can safely deal with him, and every fool may be fathomed. What is making love but making riddles? . . . Even our gravestones can't tell the naked truth; tombs you see are sort [*sic*] of riddles! (vi–vii)

We may assume that Mrs Churchill's tombstone will be of the lying sort that requires further deciphering. Making love is "making riddles" in all cases in *Emma*. Emma's skill in deciphering riddles does not enable the confident heroine to escape that grand source of error, false connections. But the siphoning off of the delusory into riddles, and the introduction of notions of different truths under appearances, introduces and sustains within *Emma* an intellectual and moral culture which militates against the kinds of deception so rigorously practiced without being acknowledged in *Mansfield Park*. Allegory and emblem are not going to bear away the victory. In *Emma*, consciousness triumphs and logic wins.

The Mirror and the Nut: *Persuasion*

In *Persuasion*, Austen plays with different forms of representation, and the novel makes a new swerve towards metonymy. In some respects it is thus a retrieval of figures used in *Sense and Sensibility*. We begin with a man looking at a book. The "Baronetage" is a kind of magic mirror for Sir Walter Elliot, an abstraction of himself that gives him identity and consolation, even though the statements in the book themselves record the march of time and mortality – which he most dreads. In a strange figure of metonymy Austen gives us Sir Walter Elliot's life as he chooses to see it in the safe dry pages of the Baronetage. His "life," his entry, is for him his "life." He is all division, division into abstract parts.

Personification combines with metonymy to play a large role in *Persuasion*. Sometimes personifications involve a physical object ("these rooms had witnessed former meetings," *P*: 93). But the dominant personifications – in contrast to *Mansfield Park* – are reifications of abstractions, especially abstractions having to do with time. Anne's real waning physical body exists haplessly within this march of metonym and abstraction. Her desire for honesty is met with the insulting and insulating power of mental pretense, the sense of being governed by obscure and abstract rules (for preservation of appearance, making a figure in the world) rather than by contact with the real. Much of the time, verbs relating to Anne are in passive voice; the world affects her and – unlike active Frederick – she can do little to the world. This leads to interestingly odd constructions, in which passive voice and hinted personification meet to muffle a physical impact: "she found herself in the state of being released from him" (*P*: 80). Reflexive forms of verbs abound and multiply; near the end, Frederick proves redeemable and truly in love because the passive voice and reflexive style are applied to him ("He had no sooner begun to feel himself alive again, than he had begun to feel himself, though alive, not at liberty," *P*: 242). These grammatical figures show a Frederick, like his beloved, acted upon and affected, rather than taking the center of action.

Sir Walter's contempt for real bodies, his attention to flaws – red hair, freckles, suntan, wrinkles, a coarse complexion – make physical life a burden. Anne has imbibed some of her father's contempt of physical defectiveness. Her suppressed resentment when she meets Wentworth at the Musgraves' and he takes little notice of her is savagely expressed in her compensatory ruminations on the worthlessness of the Musgraves' dead son Richard and the unnecessary ludicrousness of Mrs Musgrave's "large fat sighings" (*P*: 68). In contrast to the story of Elizabeth Bennet, in this last novel the body is an irritation. Bodily weakness or imperfection is shared by a number of characters. Anne's father in a rage of synecdoche separates people into component parts, including the thick wrists and the freckles of his friend (and perhaps mistress) Mrs Clay, and the baldness or wrinkled faces of his male acquaintance. The body is by definition mortal, and Anne, unlike her father, cannot find a false abstract escape from facts of aging and death. No wonder that she personifies the years: "the years which had destroyed her youth and bloom had only given him [Frederick] a more glowing, manly, open look." Separated into her component parts, Anne, suffering "an early loss of bloom and spirits" (*P*: 28) is now seen (even by herself) as a poor thing. Yet she is not to be victim to the mournful sundering of synecdoche. Her little nephew injures himself, but the bone is only dislocated, not broken, and can be put back into its proper place. The dislocated can be relocated. Even Louisa Musgrave's damaged head can mend.

Frederick Wentworth, during his autumn walk with Louisa, picks up a tree fruit and a prosopopoeia and plays with them both, making a mock-allegory or fable: "Here is a nut . . . To exemplify, – a beautiful glossy nut, which, blessed with original strength, has outlived all the storms of autumn. Not a puncture, not a weak spot any where" (*P*: 88). While the speaker has a message, he does not quite believe in his example. Such a fully spelled-out playful parable has no power over us – nothing like the power of *Mansfield Park*'s gold chain and rose garden. Wentworth's allegory has its problems: the hazelnut is supposed to decay, cracking open so the new seed may take root. The nut Wentworth describes is more like Sir Walter (unprofitably impenetrable and fond of delusions) than like Louisa or Anne. Lasting a little longer than its fellows will be poor consolation for not following its destiny. We are reminded of the cycle of the year – Anne drearily enjoys "the sweets of poetical despondence" but the farmers are at work, "meaning to have spring again" (p. 85). Unlike Maria Rushworth (allegedly) Anne will know a "second spring." If Frederick doesn't quite believe in his own allegory, Austen creates a wider and gentler allegory of rebirth and transformation.

Anne saves herself by not giving herself over to poems, books, or pretty musings of constancy. Representations seduce but they fail human need. Benwick has a fine solitary taste for poetry while he is in mourning, but he is better off making love to the convalescent Louisa. Anne's love of the poetic is always balanced by her need for honesty – this is what she desires in retrenching to save Kellynch; the mere representation of honesty will not do. But Anne is never perfectly honest, just as she thinks Lady Russell is not perfectly honest, but lied in talking about having seen curtains instead of Frederick. Speech itself is not honest – in rewriting the novel's conclusion, Austen resorted to Frederick's letter, as if in Bath any open or true declaration and declaration of change would be impossible. The letter offers a certain combination of privacy and abstraction that somehow make it more true – even if what Frederick says is not entirely the case.

It may be said that Jane Austen believes that no human being ever was or can be completely honest. Even the very best persons may not wish to be. "But in such cases as these a good memory is unpardonable," Elizabeth Bennet declares firmly to Jane – she will refuse to remember any of Darcy's offenses, affectionately espousing dishonesty, wooing lack of clarity. Austen's portrayal of human dishonesty stems less from a Swiftian savage indignation, a desire to make strict satiric animadversions on human nature, than from a need almost tenderly rational, a desire to uphold the truth of the fallibility of both language and mind. We are fallible because the mind operates not in direct contact with reality but figuratively, through reflection, as Locke indicated. We require imagination, rhetoric, the figures of mind in order to arrive at any complex comprehension, and to communicate with each other. Yet the very qualities of these figures and the adroitness of our minds will lead us to a world of imperfection, in which we do not fully know ourselves or what surrounds us. Such a vision makes the writing of endings very difficult, as can be seen in the two compositions proposed for the end of *Persuasion*. I think the vision of the mind in ignorance rejoicing (with the help of delusion) in its unwitting participation in imperfection is mimicked so well in the ending of *Mansfield Park* that we cannot bear to see it.

FURTHER READING

Butler, Marilyn (1975). *Jane Austen and the War of Ideas*. Oxford: Oxford University Press; reprint 1988.

Collins, Irene (1994). *Jane Austen and the Clergy*. London: Hambledon Continuum, 1994; reprint 2002.

Doody, Margaret Anne (2005). Jane Austen, that disconcerting "child." In Christine Alexander and Juliet McMaster (Eds). *The Child Writer from Austen to Woolf* (pp. 101–21). Cambridge, UK: Cambridge University Press.

Johnson, Claudia (1988). *Women, Politics and the Novel*. Chicago: University of Chicago Press.

Knox-Shaw, Peter (2004). *Jane Austen and the Enlightenment*. Cambridge, UK: Cambridge University Press.

Mack, Robert (ed.) (2006). Introduction and notes to *The Loiterer: A Periodical Work in Two Volumes Published at Oxford in the Year 1789 and 1790 by the Austen Family*. Ceredigion, UK: Edwin Mellen Press Ltd.

15

Narrative Technique: Austen and Her Contemporaries

Jane Spencer

Austen's juvenilia contained joyful parodies of the excesses of fashionable sentimental fiction, and *Northanger Abbey*, with its delighted spoof of Radcliffean Gothic, continued her parodic vein into the full-length novel. Her later fiction, while moving away from parody as defining form, maintained a dialogue with her contemporaries. The Romantics, especially Scott and Byron, received some attention, and Austen increasingly responds to what Anne Elliot and Captain Benwick call "the richness of the present age" in poetry (*P*: 100, Deresiewicz 2004). She was interested in such contemporary developments as the science of the mind (Richardson 2001: 93–113). It is with the novelists, however, that she was most closely engaged.

In April 1811, writing of her so far unsuccessful attempt to get a copy of Mary Brunton's *Self-Control* (1810), she confided "I *should* like to know what her Estimate is – but am always half afraid of finding a clever novel *too clever* – & of finding my own story and my own people all forestalled" (*Letters*: 278). Her worry is understandable: at this point she was seeing *Sense and Sensibility* through the press, reworking *Pride and Prejudice*, and probably already beginning work on *Mansfield Park* (Sutherland 2005: 124, 226) – all of them, and especially the most imminent, novels in which self-control is at issue. There is relief in her report, a year and a half later, that:

> I am looking over Self Control again, & my opinion is confirmed of its being an excellently-meant, elegantly-written Work, without anything of Nature or Probability in it. I declare I do not know whether Laura's passage down the American River, is not the most natural, possible, everyday thing she ever does. (*Letters*: 344)

Relief, but also resentment: Austen, as she developed her own examinations of natural, possible, everyday behavior and psychology, had to contend with the greater immediate popularity of Brunton's more sensational work (Sutherland 2004: 256–8). In this letter she seizes on a late incident in the novel, the heroine's abduction across the

Atlantic to Canada and her subsequent escape by floating alone in a canoe down the St Lawrence river; but if all Laura's story had been so adventurous the novel would have felt less like a serious rival. Austen's more important point is that Laura is even less believable in the rest of the narrative, whose concerns are far closer to the domestic novels she was writing herself. Laura's life with her impoverished father, her need to steer a course between two suitors, one attractive profligate, one worthier but less exciting man, and her resistance to the morally suspect demands of people in authority over her, are not in themselves so far from the experiences Austen was exploring in her own fiction. What distinguishes her treatment of them is a psychological subtlety that is thrown into sharp relief by Brunton's didactic certainties. Despite its epigraph from the sixth book of Cowper's *The Task* (1785), about the necessary self-division of the good man, whose "warfare is within" (Cowper 1968: 540), Brunton's novel presents a heroine with self-control so complete that no internal struggle is necessary. When her aunt orders Laura to visit Mrs Bathurst's, where she will face Colonel Hargrave's advances, her resistance to wrongful authority is morally impeccable and effortlessly achieved. She responds with "resistless sweetness": the more Lady Pelham loses her temper, the more Laura responds with "saintlike meekness," and "serenity," "sympathetically avert[ing] her eyes" from the older woman's shameful display of anger. No wonder Lady Pelham hits her (Brunton 1986: 306). Against such impregnable perfection, Elinor Dashwood's irritable sarcasms and Fanny Price's peevishness stand out as studies in the complexity of attempts to do right.

Austen rewrote the domestic novel to do away with its naïve didacticism (Waldron 1999). She developed a narrative style to handle moral and emotional complexities, including the internal division that heroines like Brunton's lack. She found precedents in Fielding and Richardson (Harris 1989, Parker 1998), but a major influence on her was that of contemporary novelists, who, even as she dissected their shortcomings, showed her the way to her style. Burney, Edgeworth, Radcliffe, and Smith were especially influential. An important innovation they shared was free indirect discourse, a narrative technique crucial to the novel's inward turn. Accounts of this technique regularly name Austen its first extensive practitioner (e.g., Pascal 1977, Cohn 1983), but it was used significantly by Austen's immediate precursors and contemporaries, and enabled the development of "a style which could allow a woman writer to speak as one having authority" (Doody 1980: 268). In free indirect discourse, a text's dominant narrative style (typically third-person and past tense) incorporates, for brief snatches or longer passages, words emanating from a particular character, without such tags as "he said" or "she thought" to make their attribution explicit. Character and narrator momentarily merge and move apart again. A brief Austenian example indicates the style's deceptive simplicity. In *Pride and Prejudice*, when Elizabeth tells Darcy of Lydia's elopement with Wickham, she notices his distracted air as he paces the room. "Elizabeth soon observed, and instantly understood it. Her power was sinking; everything *must* sink under such a proof of family weakness" (*PP*: 278). Elizabeth's thoughts carry the narrative; they sound authoritative, but are not, and later chapters will reveal just what she has *not* understood at this point. Austen used free indirect discourse progressively more in her later novels, and some of its effects will be examined later, but first I want to note the importance of other techniques to the complex mixture that makes up Austenian narrative. She honed external, as well as internal, methods of presentation, drawing elements from a matrix of contemporary texts for the construction of her distinctive narrative style.

Dramatic dialogue is important to her. Richardson and Burney both used it extensively, Richardson's letter-writing characters often reproducing conversations that run like play scripts, complete with bracketed stage directions, Burney displaying a wide range of idiolects in comic dialogues. Austen learned from both, but for up-to-date, witty dialogue among educated people, she turned to Maria Edgeworth, the one novelist, she jokingly told her niece Anna Austen, that (apart from herself and Anna) she was prepared to like (*Letters*: 405). Edgeworth uses a high proportion of dialogue, to drive the plot as well as to illustrate character. In *Patronage* (1814) she opens the novel directly on a page of snappy dialogue among three of her main characters: apart from "he said"s and "she said"s, the single narrative phrase to interrupt the exchange is "Her brother Geoffrey smiled" (Edgeworth 1986: 3). More influential on Austen, because earlier, is *Belinda* (1801), where dialogue is also carefully employed. In this example it dramatizes the moment when Clarence Hervey discovers that his Rousseauistic project of rearing an unspoiled child of nature to become his wife is going wrong. Mrs Ormond reminds her impatient employer that he must wait for Virginia to be educated:

> "for, I suppose, you would be glad that your wife should, at least, know the common things that every body knows."
>
> "As to that," said Clarence, "I should be glad that my wife were ignorant of what *every body knows*. Nothing is so tiresome to a man of any taste and abilities, as *what every body knows*. I am rather desirous to have a wife who has an uncommon, than a common understanding."
>
> "But you would choose, would not you," said Mrs Ormond, hesitating, with an air of great deference, "that your wife should know how to write?"
>
> "To be sure," replied Clarence, colouring. "Does not Virginia know how to write?" (Edgeworth 1994: 373)

Clarence's self-congratulatory defiance of convention, his employee's hesitant common-sense, his own embarrassment as his ideals come up against disconcerting realities to which he is not, after all, superior, are deftly indicated through the externals of speech and expression: his blush speaks volumes. In the same novel, Lady Delacour's speech has the polish of a fashionable, witty woman. A dialogue between her and Belinda opens the second chapter:

> "Where were we when all this began?" cried Lady Delacour, forcing herself to resume an air of gayety. "O, masquerade was the order of the day — tragedy or comedy? which suits your genius best, my dear?"
>
> "Whichever suits your ladyship's taste least."

"Why, my woman, Marriott, says, I ought to be tragedy; and, upon the notion that people always succeed best when they take characters diametrically opposite to their own – Clarence Hervey's principle. Perhaps you don't think that he has any principles; but there you are wrong; I do assure you, he has sound principles – of taste."

"Of that," said Belinda, with a constrained smile, "he gives the most convincing proof, by his admiring your ladyship so much." (Edgeworth 1994: 19)

Lady Delacour's slippery wit contrasts with Belinda's quieter style, and the short exchange hints at larger thematic concerns: the two women's unacknowledged rivalry for Clarence Hervey's affections, and the question of whether Lady Delacour, who believes herself to be dying, is living a tragedy or a comedy. The comic ending is eventually ratified by Lady Delacour's own direction, as she organizes the final scene according to the dictates of sentimental comedy: "Captain Sunderland – kneeling with Virginia, if you please, sir, at her father's feet. [. . .] Clarence, you have a right to Belinda's hand, and may kiss it too. Nay, Miss Portman, it is the rule of the stage." She even directs her own family reunion: "Ha! here he comes. Enter lord Delacour, with little Helena in his hand. Very well! a good start of surprise, my lord" (p. 478). Like the sprightly, faulty yet warm-hearted women of Hannah Cowley's plays, Lady Delacour dominates comic dialogue and orchestrates comic action.

The influence of *Belinda* may be heard in the "light, and bright, and sparkling" tones of *Pride and Prejudice* (*Letters*: 299), a novel of brilliant dialogue; and in a more complex way in the troubled examination of theatricality in *Mansfield Park*. In omniscient narrative, too, Edgeworth's style anticipates Austen's. Her deft narrative summaries produce authoritative openings that swiftly establish character, subject, and moral tone without Burney's ponderous pronouncements. The first sentences of *Belinda* have a strong flavor of the decisive openings of *Mansfield Park* and *Emma*:

> Mrs Stanhope, a well-bred woman, accomplished in that brand of knowledge, which is called the art of rising in the world, had, with but a small fortune, contrived to live in the highest company. She prided herself upon having established half a dozen nieces most happily; that is to say, upon having married them to men of fortunes far superior to their own. One niece still remained unmarried – Belinda Portman, of whom she was determined to get rid with all convenient expedition. (Edgeworth 1994: 7)

The ironic narrative voice is established partly through a Fieldingesque air of worldly wisdom, and partly through a sparing use of free indirect discourse. In two short phrases: "most happily" (probably echoing the character's bland speech) and "to get rid" (suggestive of a coarser, unspoken thought), Mrs Stanhope's words invade the narrative and provide all that is needed to satirize her attitude.

Free indirect discourse can achieve a wide range of effects between the poles of satiric exposure and sympathetic involvement, depending on a number of variables: the size and nature of the gap between narrator's and character's expressions; the concentration on indirect speech, indicating an external perspective, or on indirect thought, indicating greater internalization; the emphasis in internal presentation on the character's reflection or on their sensation; and the degree to which the style is used to create a sustained focalization of the narrative through a particular character. The opening of *Belinda* clearly leans to the satiric pole, and this is in keeping with Edgeworth's narrative style generally. She shows little interest in sustained internal presentation. The reader is sometimes involved in Belinda's, and occasionally Clarence Hervey's, thoughts, but usually with a swift return to dialogue and action; while Lady Delacour, whose mysterious psychosomatic illness makes her the most interesting character, is uniformly revealed dramatically, through speech and gesture. The narrative is in fundamental agreement with her metaphor of life as a stage.

Much as she learned from Edgeworth about external presentation, Austen went to other sources for her internal styles. The influence on her of Samuel Richardson, her great eighteenth-century precursor in the representation of the inner life, has often been noticed, and it has recently been argued that even within his first-person style Richardson included early free indirect discourse (Bray 2003). Particularly influential was Frances Burney, who, in *Cecilia* (1782) and *Camilla* (1796) – the novels that were praised alongside *Belinda* in the famous defense of the novel in *Northanger Abbey* – developed ways of incorporating internal presentation into third-person narrative. *Cecilia* sometimes steers close to the heroine's thoughts, while *Camilla* investigates the mental processes of several characters. *Camilla*'s exploration of a courtship threatened by the heroine's propensity to get into social and financial scrapes, and her lover's tendency to suspect her of the worst motives, proceeds with close attention to shifts of mood and thought in both characters. Sometimes thought is given dramatic immediacy by being directly quoted. Here, Edgar Mandlebert resolves to treat Camilla more kindly: "She is still, he thought, the same; candid, open, flexible; still, therefore, let me follow her, with such counsel as I am able to give. She has accused me of unkindness; – She was right!" (Burney 1983: 422). At other times, thought is rendered in free indirect discourse, allowing for smoother transition and subtler modulation between narrator's and character's perspective. Camilla, persuaded by her spendthrift brother to borrow on his behalf, wonders what to do:

> To claim two hundred pounds of her uncle, in her own name, was out of the question. She could not, even a moment, dwell upon such a project; but how represent what she herself so little understood as the necessity of Lionel? Or how ask for so large a sum, and postpone, as he desired, all explanation? (Burney 1983: 501)

As well as free indirect discourse, Burney employs what Dorrit Cohn terms psycho-narration, an indirect technique in which the narrator describes the character's mental state (Cohn 1983). In one scene, Camilla's father tries to discover how her uneasy relationship with Edgar is progressing. While Camilla cries in a corner, the dramatic narrative pauses to allow for a summary of her father's thoughts:

> Her regard for Edgar he had already considered as undoubted, and her undisguised acknowledgement excited his tenderest sympathy: but to find she thought it without

return, and without hope, penetrated him with grief. [. . .] Camilla, nevertheless, excul-
pated Edgar from all blame; and, while touched by her artlessness, and honouring her
truth, he felt, at least, some consolation to find that Edgar, whom he loved as a son,
was untainted by deceit, unaccused of any evil. (Burney 1983: 344)

Cohn distinguishes psychonarration from narrated monologue (her term for what is
now more generally called free indirect discourse), which, as a rendition of the character's thoughts, can be translated into a direct representation of internal speech by
altering tense and pronoun. In psychonarration the narrator's superior awareness
compared to that of the characters allows for the development of an ironic perspective
on the mind, and also for the description of unconscious mental states (Cohn 1983:
11–14, 29). *Camilla* displays both later in this scene, when Mr Tyrold leaves the room
and the narrator turns to Camilla's mind. She is "soothed" and "invigorated" by her
father's kindness to her:

and her feelings received additional energy from the conscious generosity with which
she had represented Edgar as blameless. Blameless, however, in her own breast, she could
not deem him: his looks, his voice, his manner, . . . words that occasionally dropt from
him, and meanings yet more expressive which his eyes or his attentions had taken in
charge, all, from time to time, had told a flattering tale, which, though timidity and
anxious earnestness had obscured her from perfect comprehension, her hopes and her
sympathy had prevented from wholly escaping her. (Burney 1983: 345)

While phrases like "his looks, his voice," and the ellipsis that suggests thought trail-
ing off, approach Camilla's consciousness through free indirect discourse, the rest of
the sentence moves into a psychonarration that can describe the mixture of understanding and unconsciousness in her reaction to Edgar's behavior. At the same time
the narrator's movement from one character's mind to another's creates ironic discrepancy between their interpretations of events. Mr Tyrold is pleased to hear from his
daughter that Edgar is blameless, but the "truth" which he honors in Camilla is
revealed as less than complete when we see that "in her own breast" Edgar deserves
some blame. The feminine reticence Mr Tyrold has encouraged prevents full communication between father and daughter. With her ability to shift in and out of her
characters' minds like this, Burney reinvigorates the clichéd sentimental theme of
distress caused by misunderstandings. Her compound of sympathy and ironic perspective appealed to Austen, who drew on it to develop the far more complex and subtly
modulated presentation of inside views found in her own fiction.

Like *Camilla*, *Emma* is centrally concerned with questions of truth, deception, and
self-deception, and through her more sophisticated development of Burney's techniques Austen treats the theme on a deeper level. The focalization of much of the
narrative through Emma's consciousness offers a much greater concentration of inside
view than in Burney, and looks forward to Flaubert and James; but the narrator also
dips into other minds. When Mr Knightley suspects some understanding between

Frank Churchill and Jane Fairfax, the narrative sticks with him for several pages. Mr Knightley concludes that they are secretly communicating with each other: "but how it could all be, was beyond his comprehension. How the delicacy, the discretion of his favourite could have been so lain asleep! He feared there must be some decided involvement. Disingenuousness and double-dealing seemed to meet him at every turn" (*E*: 348). The passage dramatizes a typically Austenian moment, consciousness at the point of realizing an error: Jane Fairfax is not so perfect as Mr Knightley thought. The narrative's most consistent supporter of truth and openness rightly suspects that he is surrounded by double-dealing; but he is not able to be completely open with himself. In thinking of Jane as "his favourite" he is as self-deluded as is Emma in imagining herself in love with Frank.

Austen, like Burney, uses psychonarration, in her case coloring it vividly with phrases of free indirect discourse. Psychonarration expands the moment when Emma understands that Mr Knightley loves her:

> While he spoke, Emma's mind was most busy, and, with all the wonderful velocity of thought, had been able – and yet without losing a word – to catch and comprehend the exact truth of the whole; to see that Harriet's hopes had been entirely groundless, a mistake, a delusion, as complete a delusion as any of her own – that Harriet was nothing; that she was every thing herself; that what she had been saying relative to Harriet had been all taken as the language of her own feelings; and that her agitation, her doubts, her reluctance, her discouragement, had all been received as discouragement from herself. – And not only was there time for these convictions, with all the glow of attendant happiness; there was time also to rejoice that Harriet's secret had not escaped her, and to resolve that it need not and should not. (*E*: 431)

This is the moment of truth, occurring inwardly in Emma simultaneously with her outward listening to a truth-obsessed declaration of love: "You hear nothing but truth from me. [. . .] Bear with the truths I would tell you now" (*E*: 430). Yet the shift from Mr Knightley's declaration to Emma's consciousness reveals the disjunction between them even now, and her first resolve is to keep another secret from him. The deception, necessary to do right by Harriet (though it also lets Emma save face), occasions a general pronouncement on truth and openness, superbly balancing ironic awareness and sympathy: "Seldom, very seldom, does complete truth belong to any human disclosure; seldom can it happen that something is not a little disguised, or a little mistaken; but where, as in this case, though the conduct is mistaken, the feelings are not, it may not be very material" (*E*: 431). Emma's characteristic mental activity is reasoning: as she listens to Mr Knightley declare his love, the emotion of the moment, far from depriving her of reflection, makes her think and decide with all the more vigor. This representation of mental life as the activity of reason, typically centered on moral discrimination, is derived especially from Burney. In other places, however – most clearly in *Persuasion* – Austen gives more emphasis to the rendering of sensation, and here she is influenced by different models, especially Ann Radcliffe and Charlotte Smith.

Ann Radcliffe develops her female Gothic through incorporating the gloomy settings, evil counts, and supernatural terrors of early Gothic works like Walpole's *Castle of Otranto* (1765) into the Burneyan narrative of a young woman's experience. In *The Mysteries of Udolpho* (1794), Emily's exploration of the mysterious castle is presented through her perceptions: "she fancied, that she heard a low moaning at no great distance, and, having paused a moment, she heard it again and distinctly. Several doors appeared [. . .]. She advanced, and listened. When she came to the second, she heard a voice . . ." (Radcliffe 1998: 258). Catherine's discovery of the laundry list in *Northanger Abbey* not only parodies such writing, but takes it to greater sensational heights: "Darkness impenetrable and immoveable filled the room. A violent gust of wind, rising with sudden fury, added fresh horror to the moment. Catherine trembled from head to foot. In the pause which succeeded, a sound like receding footsteps and the closing of a distant door struck on her affrighted ear" (*NA*: 170).

Not all Austen's imitation of Radcliffe is mocking. Radcliffe is interested not just in evoking terror but in examining how it is produced in the mind. Famously, her apparently supernatural events have natural explanations, demonstrating the errors of those who jump to superstitious conclusions. Her heroines interrogate their sensations and search for rational explanations. Emily is surrounded by mystery, forced to interpret events on obscure evidence, critical of her own judgment but still liable to be misled by fear or hope. Radcliffe presents her inward debate when she hears in Udolpho a song last heard in Gascony, and thinks her lover, Valancourt, must be nearby: "these hopes were so new, so unexpected, so astonishing, that she did not dare to trust, though she could not resolve to discourage them. [. . .] Yes, it was possible, that Valancourt was near her, and she recollected circumstances, which induced her to believe it was his voice she had just heard. [. . .] who else, indeed, could it be?" (Radcliffe 1998: 387). Emily, it later transpires, is mistaken, but the narrative asks for sympathetic involvement in her thought processes rather than satirical detachment from them. We are alerted to the possibility of her error through her own self-doubt. Emily's awareness of the dangers of misreading makes her a positive model for heroines like Elinor Dashwood and Anne Elliot, who confront mysteries in a more realistic, everyday setting: the mystery of other people's behavior. Meeting Wentworth after eight years apart, Anne is hyperaware of the problems of interpretation: "Now, how were his sentiments to be read? Was this like wishing to avoid her? And the next minute she was hating herself for the folly which asked the question" (*P*: 60).

The Mysteries of Udolpho is Gothic for only a small proportion of its narrative (Castle 1998: ix), and Emily spends more time in tranquil meditation than in terror. The poetic descriptions of landscape for which Radcliffe is famous are often rendered through her sense-impressions, and give rise to experiences of sublime elevation or nostalgia and melancholy. Austen's novels are socially focused and very sparing of natural scenery – *Pride and Prejudice* does not allow the heroine to get as far as the Lake District, and the narrator refuses to describe the Peak District – but the emotional response to nature and place is nevertheless important in them. In *Sense and Sensibility*, Marianne's attachment to Norland Park and her rhapsodies about autumn get short shrift from her prosaic sister: "It is not every one," said Elinor, "who has your passion for dead leaves" (*SS*: 88). In *Mansfield Park*, Fanny Price's appreciation of trees and stars is an index of her sensitivity and isolation. In *Persuasion*, Anne's response to autumn, and the poetry of autumn, delineates her feelings after an eight years' parting from Wentworth. In her examination of the connections between landscape, poetry, and melancholy, Austen is responding not only to Radcliffe's novels but also, and more pointedly, to Charlotte Smith's. Smith made her name with her volumes of *Elegiac Sonnets* (the first published in 1784), in which a melancholy speaker muses on natural scenery and the emotions. Her many popular novels, beginning with *Emmeline* (1788), take the mood of her poems as a coloring for sentimental narrative. Motifs from many of Smith's novels appear extensively in Austen's work (Magee 1975). In particular, Smith's focus on the melancholy mind in *Celestina* (1791) provokes a response in *Sense and Sensibility* and a further consideration in *Persuasion*.

The eponymous heroine of *Celestina*, and Marianne in *Sense and Sensibility*, both love young men called Willoughby who behave mysteriously, each disappearing without proper explanation just when the heroine believed herself sure of his love. (Celestina's Willoughby, unlike Marianne's, turns out to have honorable reasons for his actions.) Both heroines are deeply attached to childhood places, Celestina sighing over having to leave Alvestone as Marianne does later over Norland. Marianne is not a poet herself, as Celestina – and, following her, Emily in *Udolpho* – are; but like Celestina she uses poetry to feed her emotions. Melancholy is Celestina's predominant feeling. She is frequently shown contemplating gloomy scenes with gloom. On the isle of Skye she broods on the unlikelihood of meeting Willoughby again:

> To indulge this increasing sadness, it was now her custom to walk out alone after dinner, and make for herself a species of gloomy enjoyment from the dreary and wild scenes around her. [. . .] she had been imagining how pleasant the most desolate of these barren islands might be rendered to her by the presence of her beloved Willoughby. She now rather sought images of horror. The sun, far distant from this northern region, was as faint and languid as the sick thoughts of Celestina – (Smith 2005: 216)

Seeking solitude and indulging sadness are Marianne's habits, too; but where Smith's psychonarration centers sympathetically on Celestina, Austen's tends to give us an inside view of Elinor rather than Marianne, and to sympathize with the character who (though herself affected by her lover's equivocal behavior) is putting up a resistance to melancholy.

In *Persuasion*, melancholy and landscape are revisited. Anne's sadness is given more narrative sympathy than Marianne's, but Smith's poetic melancholy is invoked to be transcended. During the walk to Uppercross, Anne gets pleasure from the twin beauties of autumn and poetry, but a moment of strong emotion, as she listens to Wentworth courting another woman, puts poetic recital out of her head: "Anne could not immediately fall into a quotation again. The sweet scenes of autumn were for a while put by – unless some tender sonnet, fraught with the apt analogy of the declining year, with declining happiness, and the images of youth, and hope, and spring, all gone together, blessed her memory" (*P*: 85). This teasing reference to a poem that Anne may or may not remember evokes Smith's sonnets, especially Sonnet 2, in which the year is already declining "At the Close of Spring," and in which human happiness can have "no second spring" (Fletcher 1998: 84–5). Smith's melancholy is countered not only by the farmer's labor, "counteracting the sweets of poetical despondence, and meaning to have spring again" (*P*: 85), but throughout the novel by the narrative movement towards the "second spring of youth and beauty" (p. 124) – and happiness – that Anne is starting to hope for by the beginning of the second volume. This movement is not the work of reason against the excesses of feeling, but that of reinvigorated hope against quiet despair: a natural rather than a moral regeneration. Austen does not refuse the pathetic fallacy used by Smith but redirects it from gloomy to hopeful natural signs, from autumn to spring. The novel's lyric feeling can be traced in its free indirect discourse, which – especially towards the climax of reunion – closely follows Anne's shifts of sensation, in a way that draws from Radcliffe's and Smith's work but moves beyond it. Where Radcliffe alternates the swift narrative of Gothic excitement with longer stretches of contemplative narrative in which the heroine's feelings and self-examination unfold, Austen's presentation of consciousness begins to combine excited speed with new layers of self-awareness. Anne "wanted to see if it rained. Why was she to suspect herself of another motive? Captain Wentworth must be out of sight. She left her seat, she would go, one half of her should not be always so much wiser than the other half, or always suspecting the other of being worse than it was" (*P*: 175). Inward discourse gains a new agitation here, a consciousness that encompasses both self-doubt and the struggle to move beyond it into action.

Burney, Edgeworth, Radcliffe and Smith provided narrative innovations that Austen incorporated into her mature style. Working through, with, and against the material they gave her, she developed an authoritative narrator sharper than Burney's, a dramatic dialogue pithier than Edgeworth's, and a flexible combination of psychonarration and free indirect discourse that transformed Burney's, Radcliffe's, and Smith's early attempts into a sustained and sympathetic inside view.

FURTHER READING

Bray, J. (2003). *The Epistolary Novel: Representations of Consciousness*. London and New York: Routledge.

Cohn, D. (1983). *Transparent Minds: Narrative Modes for Presenting Consciousness in Fiction*. Princeton, NJ: Princeton University Press.

Doody, M. A. (1980). George Eliot and the eighteenth-century novel. *Nineteenth-Century Fiction*, 35, 260–91.

Pascal, R. (1977). *The Dual Voice*. Manchester, UK: Manchester University Press.

Sutherland, Kathryn (2005). *Jane Austen's Textual Lives: From Aeschylus to Bollywood*. Oxford: Oxford University Press.

Waldron, M. (1999). *Jane Austen and the Fiction of Her Time*. Cambridge, UK: Cambridge University Press.

16
Time and Her Aunt

Michael Wood

I

Writing to thank Bishop Warburton for his preface to *Clarissa*, Samuel Richardson made a remark that now seems both edgy and very astute. At the time it no doubt seemed just edgy, and perhaps incoherent. Richardson found himself wishing that the bishop had not alluded to the fictional status of the letters that constitute the novel, although of course he himself had no desire to pass the letters off as authentic:

> Will you, good sir, allow me to mention, that I could wish that the Air of Genuineness had been kept up, tho' I want not the Letters to be *thought* genuine; only so far kept up, I mean, as that they should not prefatically be owned *not* to be genuine: and this for fear of weakening their Influence where any of them are aimed to be exemplary; as well as to avoid hurting that kind of Historical Faith which Fiction itself is generally read with, tho' we know it to be Fiction. (quoted in McKillop 1956: 44)

There does seem to be some prevarication here. The distinction between seeming genuine and being thought genuine is at first sight pretty tenuous, and Richardson's ostensible main argument, the one about influence and example, confirms any suspicions we may have. Simple readers, happy to believe documents are authentic as long as no one openly says they are not, are to benefit from being deceived, or at least from not asking questions.

But Richardson's overall argument is more delicate, less pious, and less manipulative. We may see the distinction between the air and the thought of genuineness, where the air is only an air and the thought, taken seriously, would be sheer delusion, as a first formulation of Richardson's second, apparently supplementary ("as well as") claim: that readers of fiction are not deceived, but commit themselves to a temporary, experimental belief. What we call illusion is the knowing acceptance of an illusion effect.

This proposition has been much discussed since Richardson, and indeed its contents now form one of the ordinary meanings of the word "fiction," providing precisely the grounds on which Frank Kermode, for example, distinguishes between "fiction" and "myth" ("Fictions can degenerate into myths whenever they are not consciously held to be fictive," Kermode 2000: 39). It is possible, perhaps even desirable, to read a lot of fiction without understanding much about how strange such a reading practice is, and the notion of the suspension of disbelief has played a large role in helping us to feel comfortable with the mystery – as if disbelief were our default position and we had only to let it go for a while. When he coined the phrase Samuel Taylor Coleridge was thinking of his own "supernatural, or at least romantic" contributions to the *Lyrical Ballads*, seeking to "procure for these shadows of imagination that willing suspension of disbelief for the moment, which constitutes poetic faith" (Coleridge 1993: 168–9). Disbelief is indeed often the probable or even expected reaction to the fantastic but the reverse is true of many modes of fiction, where we first have to learn to disbelieve, or to recognize the occasions where disbelief is the appropriate mode, and then pretend to believe again.

This is the situation Richardson was half trying to avoid and finally addressing with real clarity, and this is where his careful term, "that kind of Historical Faith," becomes so useful. It is also where his apparently prevaricating objection to Warburton's "prefatically" owning up to the fiction begins to seem downright modest. All Richardson is asking is that the preface should *not* say that the ensuing work is *not* genuine; most of his contemporaries among novelists were busy saying their stories were entirely genuine, and splashing the news across the title page. Think of Moll Flanders, for example, "Who was Born in Newgate, and during a Life of continu'd Variety for Threescore Years, besides her Childhood, was Twelve Year a Whore, five times a Wife (whereof once to her own Brother), Twelve Year a Thief, Eight Year a Transported Felon in Virginia, at last grew Rich, liv'd Honest, and dies a Penitent. Written from her own Memorandums . . ." (Defoe, *Moll Flanders*: title page). No hint of the nongenuine there, and every attempt at the documentary effect.

"Historical Faith," as distinct from Coleridge's "poetic faith," becomes a curious, criss-crossing affair. Faced with apparent history, we recognize an analogue to history, a world with its own Newgate and Virginia, or more intricately, we follow fictional fortunes through the historical world, imaginary toads in real plantations. And faced with manifest fictions, like Moll's penitence perhaps, we look for their historical home, deploying our skepticism and our belief, mentally conjuring up, for example, both the real penitent we think Moll is not and the admirably unapologetic woman we like to think she is.

The later developments of the novel as a genre have made it clear that Richardson's concern was seriously misplaced in one respect: his fear that historical faith could be "hurt" by an acknowledgement of fictionality. It can sometimes seem as if this faith is quite invulnerable, as if nothing will shake it: no amount of "dear reader" addresses, no degree of complication of narrative personae. The tricky author, from Fielding to Nabokov, can put on disguises, change names, shrink time, persistently foreground the act of writing and arrangement. Our historical faith survives it all, unblinking. Of course, reminders that a book is a book are not necessarily confessions of any kind of fictional status, and behaving like a famous fictional character may well be a perfect instance of realism. And if our author is doing everything to the story *except* make it up, we are likely to feel he or she is *not* making it up. Somewhere out there, independent of the narrative, prior to the narrative, is a young man called Tom Jones or something like it, and a young woman called Dolores (in Nabokov's *Lolita*) whose surname, we are told, merely rhymes with the one in the book. This person is the object of our unlikely but indispensable historical faith.

There is a strange breakage of this faith when Esther Summerson starts her narrative at the beginning of chapter 3 in *Bleak House*, since she seems to know she has some kind of writing contract. "I have a great deal of difficulty in beginning to write my portion of these pages . . ." (Dickens 1964: 30), she says. My portion? These pages? We don't have to conclude that Esther Summerson knows she is a character in a novel, but it is very hard otherwise to picture the narrative situation in which she is consciously writing half a book. "After all," as D. A. Miller says, "how would even the cleverest character divine that he or she is *being narrated?*" (Miller 2003: 71, Miller's italics). This same question is entirely cleared up in *Ulysses* when Molly Bloom addresses her creator – and the creator of her creator, perhaps, since the double subject is menstruation and virginity, for Molly a pair of annoying design faults in the female condition:

> its pouring out of me like the sea . . . damn it damn it and they always want to see a stain on the bed to know youre a virgin for them all thats troubling them theyre such fools too you could be a widow or divorced 40 times over a daub of red ink would do or blackberry juice no thats too purply O Jamesey let me up out of this pooh sweets of sin whoever suggested that business for women . . . (Joyce 1963: 914)

It's not clear how much Molly knows about the book she's in, but she knows the name of her author, and there is no article of historical faith that allows this. Any more than the narrator of *A la Recherche du temps perdu* should, by the protocols of fiction, be in a position to hint at Proust's own identity, as he does on two separate occasions. Albertine addresses the narrator by his Christian name, "which, if we give the narrator the same name as the author of this book, would produce 'My Marcel', or 'My darling Marcel'" (Proust 1988: 583, 2002: 64). The French is even odder, since it says "would have produced" ("*eût fait*"), a curiously speculative tense that might be unscrambled to mean something like "if I had allowed myself to mess around with the rules of fiction, as I am at this moment both doing and not doing, this would be the mind-bending result."

Still, as far as I can tell, no one's historical faith has been even slightly "hurt" by these moves and moves like them. We worry about the objective social conditions of Dickens's London, Molly Bloom is surely one of the most plausible characters known to fiction, and Proust scholars are still at work on all the "originals" of his many characters. Historical faith, we may feel, is if anything too healthy. Is there nothing that will stop its long triumph over whatever skepticism Richardson was worrying about?

II

There must be possibilities for such skepticism littered all over the history of the novel, but at the moment I am coming up with only two: Milan Kundera's fiction as contemplation;[1] and a certain form of irony in Jane Austen, closely related to what Miller calls "Absolute Style." "Austen," he says, "always writes like a real god, without anthropomorphism . . . Austen's narration . . . is at once utterly exempt from the social necessities that govern the narrated world, and intimately acquainted with them down to their most subtle psychic effects on character. It does not itself experience what it knows with all the authority of experience" (Miller 2003: 23, 32). To write like a real god is to seem to respect, of course, the "air of genuineness" Richardson called for. How could a god's work look like a fake? But a narration exempt from social necessities must also be a narration that reflects on possibilities, and its deep appeal will be to alternative history rather than to historical faith: to the illusions that cloud the human mind rather than to the necessity of illusion. It will rest on a sense that what might have happened can't quite be parted from what did happen, and of an irony devoted to the continuing expression of this perception.

One local sign of this sense and this irony, in *Pride and Prejudice*, is the beautiful zeugma involving time and Elizabeth Bennet's aunt. Walking with Darcy in the grounds of Pemberley, with her uncle and aunt "half a quarter of a mile behind," the talkative Elizabeth runs out of conversation. "At such a time," Austen writes, "much might have been said, and silence was very awkward. She wanted to talk, but there seemed to be an embargo on every subject" (*PP*: 257). Elizabeth tries to dilute the silence with a bit of tourist chatter: "At last she recollected that she had been travelling, and they talked of Matlock and Dove Dale with great perseverance. Yet time and her aunt moved slowly, and her patience and her ideas were nearly worn out before the tete-a-tete was over" (*PP*: 257). It is easy to imagine the eager banality of this discussion of scenery; easy also to miss the emotion that may be hiding in the flight from silence, just as it may have filled the silence itself.[2]

Time and an aunt are not the same kind of creature; even their forms of slow motion are different. But of course they are paired in Elizabeth's perception as they are in the trope. And the figure does more than mirror Elizabeth's impatience and concern. Austen is smiling at the conjunction of metaphysics and family that bothers her heroine. This is a perfect instance of style in Miller's sense, and it offers us a glimpse of Austen's ironic philosophy, or if you prefer, her irony about philosophy. It brings together, as if to mirror's life's confluences in a trick of grammar, two very different orders of contingency. There is the world of aunts, and everything they represent of family and society, kindness and curiosity. It's a world of aunts and not of uncles because it's a world of women. And there is the world of time, which is also the world of chance meetings (one day earlier and the visitors would have missed Darcy, one day later, knowing he was supposed to be there, they would not have visited), and the world of aging and healing. Time is the enemy of marriage for women in Austen, which is why its supposed healing powers are so often treated with skepticism. Aunts and time, together or separately, determine much of life – determine all of life, Austen's irony cryptically suggests – that we do not manage to take into our own hands. Henry Austen wrote that his sister didn't like to publish until "time and many perusals had satisfied her that the charm of recent composition was dissolved" (quoted in Miller 2003: 82). "Time and . . ." phrases occur in all six major novels, but with the exception of "time and the return of Harriet" (*Emma*) and "time and London" (*Sense and Sensibility*) they are all ready-made bits of philosophizing, and none of them has the edge and mischief of "time and her aunt." It's as if Austen had chosen this moment and this novel to freeze the frame on the cliché. There is no other "time and . . ." phrase in *Pride and Prejudice*.[3]

There are at least three possible Elizabeths detectable in this moment of slow motion. One is beginning to change her mind about her Darcy, and is willing to acknowledge that his generally haughty behavior has some justification in his real social standing. This Elizabeth is doubtless the same as the one who already thinks better of him for owning a property like Pemberley – it is a very good quality in a man, we might say, paraphrasing a character in *Middlemarch,* to own a large house in Derbyshire.[4] Elizabeth's own thought is "to be mistress at Pemberley might be something!" (*PP*: 245). And a moment later: "And of this place . . . I might have been mistress!" (*PP*: 246).

A second Elizabeth has always rather liked Darcy, in spite of his pride and rudeness, and all through her own professions of dislike. She refused him not because she didn't care for him but because his proposal was made in the form of an insult that no self-respecting person could accept. This second Elizabeth doesn't quite know what she feels as she waits for her uncle and aunt to catch up, and the language imputed to her ("It was gratifying to know that his resentment had not made him think really ill of her," *PP*: 256) reduces her complicated thoughts, her sheer uncertainty about how much she likes the man, to a safe and acceptable vocabulary.

A third Elizabeth intuitively understands that a moment of magic has occurred, that this half-accidental meeting with Darcy has solved every problem in an instant – the rest is just a working out of details. Of course her doubts will continue for many pages. But these doubts concern her chances of happiness, not her sense of what will make her happy. This is the Elizabeth who is so distressed by her father's amusement at the very idea that Darcy might want to marry her, and who later, insisting to her father that she is not making a marriage of convenience or snobbery, eloquently, although with some difficulty, says just what she means. Darcy is rich, proud, and unpleasant, her father says, but "this would be nothing if you really liked him" (*PP*: 376). In context – in the context of this conversation and the prevailing idea of marriage in the book – this must mean something along the lines of "if you no longer actively dislike him." This is why Elizabeth's response is so wonderful. "'I do, I do like him,' she replied, with tears in her eyes, 'I love him'" (*PP*: 376). Even then her father doesn't believe her, and his daughter has made her most fervent declaration of love to a man who isn't there. There is a sense in which the awkward silence created by the slowness of time and the aunt is never fully broken, and should not be. It is the silence of the real thing, beyond speech and convention, or inside speech and convention, haunting the spoken word in the way the truth in Flaubert haunts banality because it has no other home.

Historical faith is not hurt or even threatened by any of the narrative facts of the case, but the text, I suggest, does offer a challenging alternative. Here is a sequence in which the most important things are not said, or not said directly; and in which our central character appears to be three different persons. I can just about picture the first and second Elizabeths I described as coming together into a single complex portrait; but not easily, and the third Elizabeth is surely someone else. We can choose, of course, and then we shall not need an alternative to historical faith. My suggestion, though, is that our historical faith will be the richer for an acknowledgement of its speculative twin, something like the writing of possibility. The final focus there would not be a character, however complicated, but a brilliantly delineated set of character options, something like an Empsonian ambiguity at the level of human chances. William Empson evokes, for example, an irony that is "a generous scepticism which can believe at once that people are and are not guilty." People, often, cannot have done both of two things, but they must have been in some way prepared to have done either; whichever they did, they will still have lingering in their minds the way they would have preserved their self-respect if they had acted differently (Empson 1966: 44).

"Self-respect" is a little constricting but the point is clear. And in novels the different, unperformed action will, if we let it, do more than linger in our minds. It will become part of the texture of the work, an embodiment of the writer's and the reader's sense of what Henry James called "operative irony," which "implies and projects the possible other case" (James 1962: 222). It engages time and the aunt, we might say, and whatever alternatives there might be to both.

III

The great double subject of *Persuasion* is not time and her aunt but time and her godmother, or more precisely the intricate criss-crossing game they play in the heroine's mind and the ambiguity they create – perhaps an ambiguity of Empson's seventh kind, where "two systems of judgment are forced into open conflict before the reader" (Empson 1966: 226). D. A. Miller argues that *Persuasion* is "the great sentimental favorite in the Austen canon and, not coincidentally, the great false step of Austen Style" (Miller 2003: 68). I'm going to try to show that *Persuasion* at its richest doesn't abandon style in Miller's sense so much as convert it, a little erratically, into a kind of logical disturbance.

References to time are everywhere in *Persuasion*, but not – as is so often assumed – because of the lateness and autumnal quality of the work. Autumn is Anne's season when she is indulging her melancholy, and at one moment the narrator parts company with her subtly but completely on this subject. Anne, who loves "the influence so sweet and so sad of the autumnal months in the country," is once again taking pleasure "from the view of the last smiles of the year upon the tawny leaves and withered hedges, and from repeating to herself some few of the thousand poetical descriptions extant of autumn" when her thoughts are interrupted by Wentworth's making an admiring remark to someone else. "Anne could not immediately fall into a quotation again" (*P*: 84–5). "Some few of the thousand" and "fall into a quotation" are devastating but not unsympathetic. The same may be said of the mention of "the ploughs at work, and the fresh-made path" that "spoke the farmer, counteracting the sweets of poetical despondence, and meaning to have spring again" (*P*: 85). There is a witty mock-confusion of registers here. The farmer himself presumably doesn't have any temptation at all to poetical despondence, and actually even he can't have spring just because he "means" to. What he can do is work, and behave as if the return of spring were at least in part the result of his intentional labor.

Time in *Persuasion* is often presented as some sort of an agency – like an aunt, but a special kind of aunt, one to whom we delegate the chores we don't care about or don't believe in, one who will help us disguise our abdication. "Time makes many changes," we read (*P*: 225). "Time will explain" (*P*: 147). "We know what time does in every case of affliction" (*P*: 108), Anne says cozily in reference to someone else; but this is just what we don't know. Anne hopes "to be wise and reasonable in time," as if time had to do the job on its own (*P*: 178). We are told "she had been too dependent on time alone" in getting over her "little history of sorrowful interest" (*P*: 28).

All of these thoughts about time are banalities, but taken together they add up to an irony about "philosophy" in the sense of resignation or stoicism, as when the malicious neighbors in *Pride and Prejudice* are said to bear the family's good news "with decent philosophy" (*PP*: 309). It is perhaps significant that the word philosophy does not appear in *Persuasion* – or in *Emma* or in *Mansfield Park*.[5] Time as an instrument of this philosophy is the denial of luck; or it is chance converted into destiny. All you can do is wait it out.

The irony deepens when we realize that for Anne, especially, time is frozen at a moment of disavowed error, a mistake that for her cannot have been a mistake. This is where the aunt or godmother takes over, the whole world of pressures and observances that thrives on the passivity of the self. Wentworth is confident in his luck – rightly so, it turns out – and witty in his expression of his confidence. This is part of what attracts Anne to him, and very much part of what turns the godmother against him. Anne was "persuaded to believe the engagement a wrong thing – indiscreet, improper, hardly capable of success, and not deserving it" (*P*: 27). And here is the first hitch, the first shift into the territory of unacknowledged conflict. Anne can't have believed anything of the kind, and we know she didn't because she was forced to lie to herself from the start about her motives. "Had she not imagined herself consulting his good, even more than her own, she could hardly have given him up" (P: 28). We recognize the move; it is entirely plausible, deeply human and thoroughly in character. This is a person who is "glad to have any thing marked out as a duty" (P: 33). But did she really think anything like the thoughts presented here? The argument never comes up again, and is manifestly false anyway. How could marrying Anne be bad for Wentworth? Would she really, if this high altruism had not stood in her way, have defied Lady Russell and all her arguments about prudence and the rest? This is not quite the self-mortification that Miller shrewdly identifies, but it is just as painful. We are looking at one of those stories about self-respect that Empson evokes. Giving in to a persuasion she already half-believes is wrong, Anne pretends to be making an independent decision out of duty.

"She did not blame Lady Russell, she did not blame herself" (P: 29). But without being wrong, they have both, it seems, drastically failed to be right. If she were a godmother in a similar situation, she would have given very different advice, since she is "persuaded that under every disadvantage of disapprobation at home, and every anxiety attending [Wentworth's] profession, all their probable fears, delays and disappointments, she should yet have been a happier woman in maintaining the engagement, than she had been in the sacrifice of it" (P: 29). This is fastidiously worked out, and Anne scrupulously makes an allowance for hindsight and later luck, believing that even if Wentworth had been less successful than he turned out to be she would still have been right to marry him. All her wishes now are "on the side of early warm attachment, and cheerful confidence in futurity, against that over-anxious caution which seems to insult exertion and distrust Providence!" (P: 30). But how can a person not be to blame if they have got things wrong? Why, if she really endorses a cheerful trust in Providence, does Anne fall into such persistent, lovingly nurtured melancholy? And why can't Anne admit that she and Lady Russell were wrong, as everything in her own argument says they were?

First, "blame" may mean "accuse" or "complain of" rather "find responsible." But not seeking to place blame is still pretty close to wanting to find everyone blameless. Second, Anne now believes in providence for others, not for herself. What she believes – and this is an essential ingredient of her melancholy – is that she once had a chance of living in providence's good graces and has that chance no longer. And third, this lost chance is why she can't say, even to herself, that she was wrong, because then time (her youth) and her godmother would have had nothing to do with it, and she alone would have thrown away her happiness. This is surely Empsonian enough for an ambiguity of the seventh type, where "the total effect is to show a fundamental division in the writer's mind" (Empson 1966: 192).

In the character's mind, surely. In both the character's and the writer's mind, I want to suggest, although not quite in the same way or to the same degree. The division in both cases concerns the perils of imprudence, and in one sense the whole plot, with the extravagant vanity of Sir Walter Elliot, the group visit to Lyme Regis and Louisa's jump and fall, the shady career of William Elliot, is designed to make an argument by double negation. If imprudence is so brainless and so dangerous, and prudence so wickedly calculating, it can't be wrong to take extreme care and good advice in every important decision. This proposition is fine as far it goes, but of course no amount of care and advice can entirely secure us from error. Nothing can, precisely because caution too can cause harm. Both writer and character know this and wish they didn't.

The heart of the problem is the ambiguity lurking in the word "prudence" – well, not just in the word but in the whole realm of moral and affective action it engages – which can never be fully cleared of its negative charge, just as it is impossible to be careful without incurring the suspicion of being too careful. This is precisely the dilemma that writer and character are working out on the late pages of the novel; and a dilemma fully announced early in the book, where the logical opposite of prudence is not recklessness but romance: "She had been forced into prudence in her youth, she learned romance as she grew older – the natural sequel of an unnatural beginning" (*P*: 30).

The key words in what follows are "if" and "must," marvelous instruments for the negotiation of doubt. "If I was wrong in yielding to persuasion once," Anne says to Wentworth towards the end of the novel, "remember that it was persuasion exerted on the side of safety, not of risk. When I yielded, I thought it was to duty . . ." (*P*: 244). A double, and doubly deluded duty, as we have seen: notionally to Wentworth's own welfare and submissively to Lady Russell's authority. But at least Anne is not here saying she was right, only giving the reasons why she was wrong, if she was wrong. A page later she does something more extraordinary: exonerates herself, blames Lady Russell, and flatly contradicts her earlier, sounder persuasion that "she should yet have been a happier woman in maintaining the engagement, than she had been in the sacrifice of it." Now she says:

> I have been thinking over the past, and trying impartially to judge of the right and wrong, I mean with regard to myself; and I must believe that I was right, much as I suffered from it, that I was perfectly right in being guided by the friend whom you will love better than you do now. To me, she was in the place of a parent. Do not mistake me, however. I am not saying she did not err in her advice. It was, perhaps, one of those cases in which advice is good or bad only as the event decides; and for myself, I certainly never should, in any circumstance of tolerable similarity, give such advice. But I mean, that I was right in submitting to her, and that if I had done otherwise, I should have suffered more in continuing the engagement than I did even in giving it up, because I should have suffered in my conscience. (*P*: 246)

Wentworth promptly, gallantly takes the blame himself. He shouldn't have given Anne up, he should have renewed his proposal at a later moment. But he was "proud, too proud to ask again." Would Anne have accepted this new offer? "Would I!" is what she says (*P*: 247).

What attracts me here, and what reveals a deep pathos in Anne's mood, something the simple story of the second chance can't provide, however satisfactory it is as a fairy tale, is the perfect ambiguity of "I must believe I was right." In the obvious moral reading, "must" means that truth and impartiality point unmistakably in the direction of this belief; anyone would think the same. But don't we also hear, in "I must believe," the faint, almost desperate cry of the Englishwoman who can't accept happiness unless she banishes the very idea of recklessness from her world? It's not that Anne has to be right out of fastidiousness or moral hauteur, although she has plenty of both. It's that she has to hold together the pieces of her self in a story that will pass muster, if not entirely persuade. Remember this is the person who claimed to be all in favor of first impressions: "Her early impressions were incurable. She prized the frank, the open-hearted, the eager character beyond all others" (*P*: 161). And also the person who wishes she were not split in two, so that "one half of her should not always be so much wiser than the other half, or always suspecting the other of being worse than it was" (*P*: 175). In one sense these persons form a sequence: the young Anne who lost her bloom also lost her innocence and singleness of mind. In another sense the separate persons just *are* Anne, who she is and perhaps always was: a divided self divided from yet another self.

Time doesn't explain, it merely alters our requirements. But Anne needs her conflicting stories. Each one, as Empson might say, casts a correcting shadow on the other. The author understands this shifting need and also suggests something else, something that moves us, once again, beyond historical faith and into speculation: that all stories inhabit both real and virtual worlds and that the ghosts even of unperformed actions never go away.

Notes

1 Kundera bases his novels, he says, on "meditative interrogation" or "interrogative meditation," neither of which is quite as abstract as it sounds. For him a character is what he calls "an experimental self," although not necessarily or even usually his own. See *The Art of the Novel*, trans. Linda Asher. London: Faber, 1988, pp. 31, 34.

2 "Choosing language," Rachel Brownstein says, "is always Austen's subject" (Brownstein 1988: 61). It is part of this subject that one sometimes can't choose.

3 For the record, the other instances my computer found are "time and chance," "time and persuasion," "time and continual repetition" (*Emma*); "time and manner of devotion," "time and obligation," "time and attention," "time and the changes of the human mind," "time and absence," "time and habit,"

"time and variation of circumstances" (*Mansfield Park*); "time and attention," "time and distance" (*Northanger Abbey*); "time and strength, and spirits," "time and sickness and sorrow" (*Persuasion*); "time and chance," "time and address," "time and habit," time and judgment" (*Sense and Sensibility*).

4 "It is a very good quality in a man to have a trout-stream" (George Eliot, *Middlemarch*. Boston: Houghton Mifflin, 1956, p. 52).

5 There is a very funny instance in *Sense and Sensibility*, both defining and undoing the idea: "As it was impossible, however, now to prevent their coming, Lady Middleton resigned herself to the idea of it with all the philosophy of a well-bred woman, contenting herself with merely giving her husband a gentle reprimand on the subject five or six times every day" (p. 118).

Further Reading

Brownstein, Rachel (1998). Irony and authority. *Women's Studies*, 15, 57–70.

Deresiewicz, William (2004). *Jane Austen and the Romantic Poets*. New York: Columbia University Press.

Empson, William (1966). *Seven Types of Ambiguity*. New York: New Directions.

Miller, D. A. (2003). *Jane Austen, or the Secret of Style*. Princeton, NJ: Princeton University Press.

Southam, Brian (1964, 1966, 2001). *Jane Austen's Literary Manuscripts*. London: Athlone Press.

Tauchert, Ashley (2005). *Romancing Jane Austen: Narrative, Realism, and the Possibility of a Happy Ending*. London: Palgrave Macmillan.

17

Austen's Realist Play

Harry E. Shaw

I

Emma concludes when a final impediment between the heroine and hero is removed. That impediment, Mr Woodhouse's horror of change, appears insuperable. What breaks through the impasse it creates is not the process of internal enlightenment or learning that figures so prominently in much Austen criticism. Mr Woodhouse's dislike of a speedy marriage is removed, the narrator tells us, "not by any sudden illumination of Mr. Woodhouse's mind, or any wonderful change of his nervous system, but by the operation of the same system in another way" (*E*: 483).

The "system" of Austen's novels is a tight one – linguistically, formally, and ideologically. That may be all the more justification for asking if its operation might work, or be worked, "in another way." In a previous attempt to perform such work, I came up with the notion of reading, not with or against the grain of her novels (and those of other realist authors), but "through the grain." I tried to identify clearings, areas of freedom in the interstices of her works that promote play with the systems, aesthetic and social, that inform them. I sometimes found them in unlikely places – for instance, in the (very mild, very tentative) female impersonation of Henry Tilney. It seemed important to look for such possibilities, not least because of the role I was arguing that Austen plays in novelistic realism in nineteenth-century Britain. The sort of realism I was focusing on was what I called "historicist" realism: it placed human beings in their full social and historical setting. Following Lukács, I suggested that the nineteenth-century novel helped bring into European consciousness what history means and what it means to be in history. My argument was that authors such as Austen forwarded this project by inviting readers to engage in a set of mental activities that, if turned on the actual societies they inhabited, would reveal their social and historical dimensions. They did this by creating novels with an appropriate imaginative texture (Shaw 1999). But if this is true, then the nature and possibilities of the texture such authors as Austen create turn out to be crucial, and one question we need to consider is how much distance and perspective (play, if you like) working within that texture allows us. There are, to be sure, critical and theoretical voices that are less than hopeful about what happens as fiction trains us in modes of processing reality. When training becomes "disciplining," the possibility of productive, liberating play can evaporate.

This essay continues my earlier quest for play in realism, with a particular focus on *Emma*. My assumption is that in all respects, including the transmission of ideology, novels make their marks affectively, as they are performed in the imaginations of readers, and so I will explore how our minds play over the text of *Emma*. My aim will be to define certain aspects of the narrative experience of that novel, and also to provide some insight into what self-knowledge and self-deception mean in Austen, and what they do not. I will claim that self-deception and self-knowledge have an irreducibly social component, and that more is at stake in being deceived and undeceived than attaining a final, static clarity. Along the way, I will suggest that *Emma* is, on a fundamental level, the most elaborately "aesthetic" of Austen's novels. In her commentary on *Emma*, Claudia Johnson quips in passing that "we tend to read Austen's novels much as Mary Bennet would, as dramas of moral correction" (Johnson 1988: 127). One of my objects is to suggest an alternative to that unenviable readerly state.

Emma itself can invite, or seem to invite, such readings. When Emma believes that she has lost Knightley, for instance, she finds that

> the only source whence any thing like consolation or composure could be drawn, was in the resolution of her own better conduct, and the hope that, however inferior in spirit and gaiety might be the following and every future winter of her life to the past, it would yet find her more rational, more acquainted with herself, and leave her less to regret when it were gone. (*E*: 423)

Such thoughts can easily conjure up a familiar scenario, one in which the errant, too lively heroine learns, through the discipline of experience and suffering, to know herself and reality better.

In his classic essay on *Emma*, Lionel Trilling gave Emma's projected quest for greater self-knowledge rich contours and associations, suggesting that

> Jane Austen, conservative and even conventional as she was, perceived the nature of the deep psychological change which accompanied the establishment of democratic society – she was aware of the increase of the psychological burden of the individual, she understood the new necessity of conscious self-definition and self-criticism, the need to make private judgments of reality. And there is no reality about which the modern person is more uncertain and more anxious than the reality of himself. (Trilling 1965: 41)

Such existential exploration promises to redeem the conservative Jane Austen's significance for the liberal modern world. Despite the attractions of this view of what self-knowledge might signify in Austen, the idea that Emma's self-imagined growth in self-knowledge would involve the making of "private judgments of reality" raises doubts. Are we modernizing Austen unduly here? It's worth remembering that the last essay on which Trilling worked explores whether or not Jane Austen is indeed our contemporary, and comes to no firm conclusions (Trilling 1979).

Another mention of self-knowledge that occurs in the final pages of *Emma* is illuminating on this score. When Harriet Smith first meets Emma after having agreed to marry Robert Martin, she is "a little distressed – did look a little foolish at first; but having once owned that she had been presumptuous and silly, and self-deceived, before, her pain and confusion seemed to die away with the words . . ." (*E*: 481). Harriet was self-deceived, but now she knows better. What is the nature of the knowledge she has gained? Well, one could imagine a scenario in which her discovery was that, deep down, she had really loved Robert Martin all along. In fact, however, depth is just what is lacking here. Emma's mild assessment seems persuasive: "Harriet had always liked Robert Martin; and . . . his continuing to love her had been irresistible" (*E*: 481). However strongly Robert Martin might have felt, Harriet hadn't returned those feelings with fervor (and for that matter, she still may not). Her "love" for Mr Knightley seems even less substantial. Her self-deception, then, did not involve suppressing a passion for any of the men in her life. What did it involve? Harriet admits "that she had been presumptuous and silly, and self-deceived, before" (*E*: 481). I believe that all three adjectives sound in the same register; in different ways, they all suggest that Harriet's was a social mistake. She had no business to imagine that love would be appropriate (which is to say, possible) between a person in her social position and a person in Knightley's. It thus appears that, in this instance at least, self-deception and self-knowledge involve grasping your place in society.

We generally think of "self-deception" as a condition on the order of a pathology. Something deep and internal interferes with our normal powers of estimation. That something is often love, but other hard-to-unravel emotions can be involved. The example of Harriet's self-deception points in a different direction, toward a "self" that has less to do with passion than with the set of competencies that allow a person to make sense of the social world. When that set of competencies is out of order, the self can become self-deceived. Self-deception in Austen centrally involves a failure to put the pieces of the self together and into social perspective when judgment or action is required.

Austen's general use of the word "deceived" and other related words ("blind," "delusion," and "prepossession") bears this out. One of the standard dictionary meanings of "deceived" is "mistaken." When the word is used in this sense, it is normally used in the passive, which elides the presence of a willful deceiver and locates the problem in the person deceived, with the interesting result that all such deception becomes, in a significant sense, self-deception. Deception is in the eye (and I) of the beholder. This is the way in which Austen most often uses "deceived." What is involved is not that one character has been consciously duped by another, but instead that a character has made a mistake in judgment, has failed to size up a situation properly. The sizing up normally, though not always, involves a reading of social signs. When Knightley almost kisses Emma's hand but then draws back, she consoles herself with the thought that "They parted thorough friends, however; she could not be deceived as to the meaning of his countenance [that is, the look on his face], and his unfinished gallantry" (*E*: 386). Here, Emma is certain of her competence in reading the external signs that betoken mutual amity. (Her erroneous certainty about the meaning of Knightley's "unfinished gallantry" – which in fact stems from his wish to hide his love for her – does, however, stem from an internally induced self-deception.) Emma's earlier mistake about Mr Elton's intentions ("How she could have been so deceived!" *E*: 134) arises not from internal passion or the willful deception of others, but from her misreading of public signs available to any onlooker. When Emma turns her wit against Miss Bates on Box Hill, the latter, "deceived by the mock ceremony of her manner [not "by Emma"], did not immediately catch her meaning" (*E*: 371), another case of self-created deception involving a misreading of public signs.

Now of course there are situations in Austen in which deception results from individual passion. The most important of these is romantic love, but it is by no means the only one. When Edmund Bertram is "deceived" by the Crawfords ("Equally in brother and sister deceived!" *MP*: 459), though it is true that their social presentation enters into his deception, its mainspring is doubtless his growing love for Mary Crawford. Other passions and inclinations can also play a part. When he reads Frank Churchill's long letter of explanation and apology, Knightley describes him as "Always deceived in fact by his own wishes, and regardless of little besides his own convenience" (*E*: 445), and the assessment seems just. Knightley responds to the end of the letter, in which Frank describes himself as "Happier than I deserve," with the mordant comment, "Come, he knows himself there!" (*E*: 447). The figure self-knowledge cuts here is revealing. Is Knightley suggesting that love and good fortune have pushed Frank to the point of making a deep and lasting discovery about his own character? Or is he instead registering his ironic amusement at the way in which Frank's glib social adeptness has led him to a seemingly candid but actually manipulative and merely rhetorical description of himself that is truer than he realizes? In Knightley's words, we feel an ethically driven demand for a quality of self-knowledge that has transparency and depth. But even here, there is nothing of Trilling's modern achievement of a private take on reality.

A final use of "deceived" in Austen that is worth mentioning is typified by the narrator's description of Miss Bates as "the happily deceived aunt" (*E*: 157). Despite the insistence on the virtues of clarity that appears throughout *Emma* ("Oh! if you knew how much I love every thing that is decided and open!" Emma exclaims to Jane Fairfax, *E*: 460), there are times when a lack of clarity is valuable. A wonderful variant on this possibility occurs with a character in *Pride and Prejudice* whose innate goodness leads her to believe the best about others in the teeth of the evidence – Jane Bennet. In her misapprehension of the world, she is not typically described as being deceived; instead, she deliciously tries to excuse the faults of others by announcing that *they* must be "deceived," revealing in the process that she herself is deceived in her view of them. When Elizabeth tells Jane that she will soon find herself in an infinite regress of having to excuse the "interested people" who she suggests must have deceived Darcy and Wickham about each other, by finding a further set of deceivers who deceived the "interested people," she does so with amused exasperation at an innate goodness that refuses to draw the right conclusions (*PP*: 85). There thus turns out to be something, as Austen would say, "amiable" in the self-deception of certain characters. The quality of mind that Jane evinces here fascinated Austen. One need only think of the "elasticity of mind" of Mrs Smith in *Persuasion*, which Anne Eliot describes to herself as "the choicest gift of Heaven" (*P*: 154).

All of this bears on an attempt to imagine what Emma's self-knowledge would have looked like had she lost Knightley and been reduced to a series of winters of decreased gaiety, spent in getting to know herself better. There is little to suggest an existential dimension to the increased rationality Emma imagines herself as achieving, and much to suggest that a social dimension hovers in the wings. There is even, surprisingly, a hint that she might do well to think twice about a rigorous pursuit of her project, since under some circumstances being "happily deceived" is not an entirely bad thing. To sort out these complications, it will be useful to take a closer look at the state from which Emma would have been emerging, the state of self-deception.

II

Self-deception is a rich topic on which a great deal of work has been done. It has interested not only philosophers of various sorts, but also clinical psychologists, brain scientists, artificial intelligence experts, and psychiatrists. A traversal of this field produces encounters with an intriguing variety of viewpoints and opinions. Some philosophers worry about whether you can believe proposition "p" and proposition "not-p" simultaneously. A researcher from the cognitive sciences wing of the École Polytechnique adduces instead the example of "two beings who are at once united and separated by a terrible secret. Think of those couples [couples!] whose marriage has not been consummated after so many years because of the man's sexual impotence," and so on – clearly a case ripe for the growth of self-deceptions of compelling interest and juice (Dupuy 1997: 111). If we consider the first example and savor the second, we can see that the situations of mistaken knowledge we encounter in *Emma* don't quite fit their definition of what self-deception typically entails. The philosophers are interested in contradictory beliefs that seem well-formed, the cognitive scientist in a shameful objective fact that must be thrust from consciousness. For the self-deception in *Emma* to fall under such rubrics, Harriet would have to believe simultaneously that she is and is not in love with Robert Martin, or Emma herself would have to be in love with, say, Robert Martin, but too ashamed to admit it (though she would constantly make excuses to herself to visit Mill Farm). But for both Harriet and Emma, what appears to have taken place is that they have not solidified their feelings, or have failed to make sense of their social situations, or have made the wrong kind of sense of them.

The modern discourse on the subject of self-deception can nonetheless illuminate *Emma*. The work of the philosopher Herbert Fingarette is helpful in this regard. In his account of self-deception, Fingarette (2000) concentrates on a mental process he calls "spelling out." When you spell something out to yourself, you give yourself an explicit account of it. In Fingarette's view, self-deception occurs when someone purposefully omits to spell something out. He adds that there is nothing unusual in not spelling everything out. As a matter of fact, the intentional actions we engage in that we don't spell out to ourselves far outnumber those we do. We do all kinds of things intentionally and skillfully without being focally aware of just how we are accomplishing them. When we write using a pencil, we don't keep bringing to consciousness how we are forming the letters, how firmly we are holding the pencil, and how successfully we are keeping to the line. Yet in some way we must be intentionally aware of all of this, or our writing would sprawl. (One supposes that this is related to George Eliot's reminder in *Middlemarch* that an awareness of the squirrel's heartbeat would drive us mad, though I won't attempt to spell out how.) Self-deception builds on this basic and necessary aspect of our mental lives. Some have actually lauded our failure to engage in a rigorous and perpetual self-inspection that would demand that each new perception or assumption or belief be logically compatible with our existing set of perceptions and assumptions and beliefs. This failure can be a positive good, not just a necessary mental economy. It is socially adaptive in various ways; it also can pave the way for cognitive leaps, by allowing us to store initially discordant information until such time as we are in a position to use it.

It is helpful to recognize that possessing at least potentially discordant bits of perception and belief is the norm for human beings, not the exception, but we still have not quite reached the issue of self-*deception*, which is clearly a special instance existing in this general information situation. Fingarette's view is that self-deception occurs when we mobilize our normal lack of spelling out willfully, in a way that blinds us both to the facts we don't wish to face and also to our choice to avoid them. We tend to do this to escape what Fingarette calls "avowing" one or another of our connections with the larger world. We would rather not face what our engagements with the world reveal about who we are. One of the attractions of Fingarette's way of looking at issues of self-deception and avowal is that when one applies it to a situation or a text, narratives of various kinds tend to be the result. I believe that only narrative provides a mode of exploration robust and flexible enough to deal adequately with phenomena like self-deception.

Where does this leave us with the self-deception Harriet Smith admits to, and the increase of self-knowledge Emma imagines as consolation for the loss of Knightley and her other social comforts? Well, the example of Harriet seems reasonably straightforward. Harriet isn't self-deceived in the deep sense that most interests Fingarette, but his notions of "spelling out" and "avowal" can enrich our suspicion that what matters most about Harriet's self-deception is not a self-inflicted duplicity at the level of existential inwardness, but instead a misapprehension of the social self and its claims. Emma has taught Harriet to spell out her social reality incorrectly, to make the wrong connections with regard to the furniture of her existence. She has taught Harriet to "avow" the wrong relationship to her world as a whole, not just to Knightley. The situation with regard to Emma is more complex, particularly as it involves the way the reader spells out Austen's novel. On one level, it would seem absurd to suggest that Emma fails to spell out anything whatsoever. Her state in this regard would seem to be the reverse of Harriet's. In most contexts, Emma loves to pattern everything; Harriet's misfortune is that she gives credence to Emma's spellings and misspellings of reality. But to leave the matter there is to omit Emma's self-deceptive dealings with Knightley, not to mention the important subset of those dealings that involves the antipathy she feels for Jane Fairfax, something Emma herself is surprised that she cannot spell out.

I want to argue that there are parallels between how Emma spells out her world and how we as readers are led to spell out Emma. Emma needs to be reread. It is hard to imagine anyone sufficiently acute to take in all the ironies that accumulate around her, during a first traversal of the novel: the pieces are there, but they do not immediately light up in their full significance. In subsequent readings, things change. But I would maintain that there are two significantly different ways in which, on even a third or fourth reading, the pieces light up and fit into larger patterns. Some of the meanings remain dispersed, while others are punctually focused. The latter effect is exemplified when Emma, early in the novel, "playfully" remarks to Knightley that "Were you, yourself, ever to marry, [Harriet] is the very woman for you" (*E*: 64). These words light up with a precise double meaning when, upon rereading them, we realize that Emma is jokingly describing a situation that will in due course become, in her eyes, the reverse of a joke. The ironic double meaning here crystallizes as a purely formal effect, created for the joy of the reader. It is a grace note, not a causal part of the plot. Though later it may appear, at least to Emma, that her machinations have in very fact led Knightley to the brink of a marriage with Harriet, what reader imagines that this early comment could push him in such a direction? The speech exists instead as a skillfully contrived gift for the alert reader, ready to blossom into meaning. It is amusing because of its economical, proleptic encapsulation of what subsequently becomes Emma's worst fear, and because of the way in which Emma's dallying with images of marriage and Knightley ("Were you, yourself, ever to marry") reflects her own half-formed desires. It is a pointed index of Emma's lack of clarity about her own desires, and on a second reading, we enjoy it as such. We recall the future and snap the pieces together.

Not all the tropes on Emma's lack of clarity about her own desires assume such pointed form. Some are more dispersed in structure and effect; they remain sprinkled though a sequence that hurries us in another direction. Thus at the opening of the ball scene, Emma makes the passing judgment that Mr Weston's "open manners" are good in their way, but that "General benevolence, but not general friendship, made a man what he ought to be. – She could fancy such a man" (*E*: 320). Several pages later, having to give precedence to Mrs Elton is "almost enough to make [Emma] think of marrying" (*E*: 325). A few sentences later she describes her own relationship with Frank Churchill as "more like cheerful, easy friends, than lovers" – an intriguing and of course reversible set of categories (*E*: 326). We subsequently find Emma delighted with her friend Knightley's gallantry toward Harriet, and then dancing with Knightley himself and telling him that they "are not really so much brother and sister as to make it at all improper" (*E*: 331). All of these moments glance at Emma's unavowed (or is it incipient?) love for Knightley; some of them, in themselves, have the potential to produce the concentrated ironic force present in Emma's earlier speech about how Harriet would be a perfect wife for Knightley. But taken as part of the evolving experience of the scene, their effect is different. Even as we perform a second reading, we experience these dispersed moments as a pattern waiting to precipitate and solidify. Yet I don't think we feel impatient for their doing so. There is a pleasure in their latent possibility.

To enjoy the concentrated irony of Emma's comment about Harriet as the perfect wife for Knightley, we need to spell out its implications right on the spot (which, on a second reading, the compact ironic form it comes in more or less does for us already – we just need to "add water"). But there is a way in which we can enjoy the hints in the ball scene precisely by refusing to precipitate them into crystalline meaning. We simply notice, in passing, that they are there. We sense the pattern without pausing to spell it out. *Emma* can conclude only when a series of impediments is removed; these include Mr Woodhouse's aversion to marriage, but also Emma's lack of the knowledge that she loves Knightley. But while we are floating in its dispersed ironies, do we wish the novel to end? To be sure, the novel does end when Mr Woodhouse is worked on by his nervous system, in an unexpected way, to embrace a change that brings closure. But systems in Austen can work and be worked in many ways, by characters and readers – ways that are multifaceted enough to open up less final, more dispersed possibilities.

Emma can afford to wait. Here the social dimension of self-knowledge and self-deception again enters in. A lower-class heroine like Pamela in Samuel Richardson's novel entirely lacks the freedom to wait. Her self-deception about the attraction Mr B holds for her must be immediately and forcefully accompanied by a loud (and, pace Fielding, entirely sincere) avowal of her status as a woman of virtue. Otherwise, an actual, here-and-now spelling out (a conclusive narrative, if you like) of the fate worse than death Mr B plans for Pamela will overtake her. Emma has been described as a heroine with power (Johnson 1988). One mark of her power is that she has room to dally – and to wait. Even the brief panic she feels toward the end of the novel, when she imagines – against any reasonable estimation of the facts – that she has lost Knightley to Harriet, is itself an expression of her rank among the empowered. She has the leisure to create an inner drama that will propel her toward avowing her wish to marry Knightley.

Austen famously described Emma as a heroine no one but herself would much like. For those of us who find her easy to like, one of her attractions is precisely the ease that normally surrounds her, the way in which, in normal circumstances, she can dawdle and play with the elements of her social existence. We enjoy her freedom not to spell things out, which allows her to defer avowal and thereby to avoid being subsumed in a social role not entirely of her own choosing – or to achieve the same result by spelling things out in ways that are transparently faulty. We are invited to share this mode of being in the world partly through experiencing the dispersed ironies I have described, the moments when we feel in no hurry to precipitate dispersed irony into pointed, crystalline statement. (We are also, in the Box Hill episode, taught that a lack of clarity regarding what one is about can lead to malaise.)

What, then, would it have meant for Emma to become "more rational, more acquainted with herself" during the long, lonely days that would have resulted from losing Knightley? The evidence suggests that Emma would become better acquainted, not with the depths of her soul or its need to forge independent judgments of reality, but with herself and her feelings in relation to those around her. She would make fewer mistakes in spelling out such things, and grow ever more accurate in avowing her place in her social setting. She would gain the sort of knowledge of self (and of the various potential selves that coalesce in our actual self at any given moment) one gains at a party, not in a convent cell. Yet one supposes (and hopes) that she would achieve this with a certain amusement at the self that progressively came into focus, maintaining her privileged ease. One hopes that, unlike Mary Bennet, she would not be too quick to fit the pieces of reality that surround her into neat patterns, but would instead allow possibilities (and improbabilities) to play themselves out.

III

Raymond Williams credits Austen with "the development of an everyday, uncompromising morality which is in the end separable from its social basis and which, in other hands, can be turned against it." That morality is worked out as Austen "makes settlements, alone, against all the odds, like some supernatural lawyer, in terms of [an] exact proportion to moral worth" (Williams 1973: 116–17). The pattern this analysis falls into should by now be familiar. We are presented with, on the one hand, a semicompulsive, semicomic flurry of pattern-making (Austen arranges marriages "like some supernatural lawyer"), and on the other hand, a result that breaks free from the realities with which it has been so frenetically concerned (Austen's moral code is, in the end, separable from its social base). Williams might almost be describing Emma's own dealings with reality, or the two forms of irony, punctual and dispersed, that I have argued characterize her novel.

Williams might almost be describing Emma – almost, but not quite. To be sure, the delight he takes in Austen's matchmaking parallels a delight readers may choose to take in Emma herself. In "other" hands (such as those possessed by the reader), Emma's attempt to "make settlements" can be – and in the novel in fact are – separated from and turned against *her*. But there are other ways of delighting in her.

In his generous assessment of Austen's potential uses, Williams remains committed to the mode of putting the pieces together and spelling things out, counting on the moment when the morality Austen forges will indeed be turned against its social base. He is far from celebrating the impulse *not* to spell things out, for it is just that impulse which, to cite his own classic analysis, allows poets to ignore the productive labor of workers in the fields surrounding country houses and thereby to celebrate a high water mark of imagined civilization without taking into account the class exploitation on which it depends (Williams 1973: 26–34). It is doubtful that he would view with indulgence the class-based ease that I have suggested forms one part of the reader's experience of *Emma* and that supports the mentality of its heroine. Yet, when faced with a social network as dense and unyielding as the one Austen depicts in her novels, there may be some value even in "merely" formal ways of imagining an alternative to total immersion in, and control by, such networks. *Emma's* extensive use of the imaginative luxury of not putting the pieces together, not spelling things out, lacks the alert robustness of the practice of reading I have elsewhere described as "reading through the grain." Its ease and privilege are what make *Emma* the most purely aesthetic of Austen's novels, and that aesthetic quality is bound up with the privilege of Emma's own position. Still, this is a stance that readers, probably less privileged than Emma in their quotidian lives, may profit from sharing as they read and reread her. There is something to be said for a playful ease that allows alternatives to emerge for those who are not too quick to spell things out and thereby to avow a place in social reality as it currently exists.

FURTHER READING

Fingarette, Herbert (2000). *Self-Deception, with a New Chapter.* Berkeley: University of California Press. Original work published 1969.

Mele, Alfred R. (1997). "Real self-deception" [followed by "Open peer commentary"]. *Behavioral and Brain Sciences,* 20:1, 91–136.

Minma, Shinobu (2001). "Self-deception and superiority complex: derangement of hierarch in Jane Austen's *Emma*." *Eighteenth-Century Fiction,* 14:1, 49–65.

Shaw, Harry E. (1999). *Narrating Reality: Austen, Scott, Eliot.* Ithaca, NY: Cornell University Press.

Trilling, Lionel (1965). "Emma and the legend of Jane Austen." In *Beyond Culture* (pp. 28–49). New York: Harcourt Brace Jovanovich. Originally published 1957, in a slightly different form, as the Introduction to the Riverside edition of *Emma.*

Williams, Raymond (1973). *The Country and the City.* London: Chatto and Windus.

18

Dealing in Notions and Facts: Jane Austen and History Writing

Devoney Looser

Nowadays it may seem difficult to fathom, but Jane Austen was once branded an ahistorical writer. Little more than a generation ago, and for virtually all of the nineteenth century, critics tended to view her fiction – and her as an author – as quaint, sheltered, and detached. Her novels were said to demonstrate a lack of interest in history, whether of the distant past or of her own turbulent present. It was believed that she did not care about (or was ignorant of) history, because of her supposedly small-scale, circumscribed life. One need not go far to find critics making this argument. As an 1870 reviewer put it, Austen's "life was very quiet . . . The ways of the family were not much disturbed by public events, and it was only when her brothers were at sea, fighting their country's battles, that the troubles of the time awakened any strong interest in Jane Austen's mind" (quoted in Southam 1968: 227). Thank goodness for her sailor brothers, this reviewer seems to say, or Austen wouldn't have noticed there was a war going on.

Such cant was repeatedly put forward over the next century, whether in overt or subtle terms. The words "narrow," "little," and "provincial" were often used to describe Austen's work, whether as faint praise or insult (quoted in Southam 1987: 198). In the early twentieth century, Reginald Farrer called Austen's fiction "a new kingdom of refuge from the toils and frets of life," "hermetically sealed" – texts in which "all the vast anguish of her time is non-existent" (quoted in Southam 1987: 249). He praises Austen's universality, saying she "can never be out of date," because "she never was in any particular date" (quoted in Southam 1987: 250). Others agreed with this description of Austen's scope but differed in assessing its value. Arnold Bennett wrote that Jane Austen's fictional world "is a tiny world, and even of that tiny world she ignores . . . the fundamental factors" (quoted in Southam 1987: 288). Whether to praise it or run it down, Austen's fiction has repeatedly been characterized as small, remote, and not of her own era – beyond being interested in, or unwilling to appear saturated in, history. As Raymond Williams facetiously put it (before he argued to the contrary), "It is a truth universally acknowledged that Jane Austen chose to ignore the decisive historical events of her time" (1973: 113).

We ought now to say it *was* a truth universally acknowledged. Over the past 40 years, labeling Austen "ahistorical" has become a rare, rather than a dominant, critical act. She is routinely included where women's history, social history, and political history in her era are concerned. Austen was given her own entry in the *Companion to Women's Historical Writing*, the index of which shows dozens of references to her (Tuite 2005). She has become, as the title of William Galperin's important recent book put it, a *Historical Austen* (2003). That sea change in interpretation – from ahistorical to historical – reorients our approach to her work. It affords us the opportunity to understand her fiction as a record of the times it describes. It allows us to see her writings imbued in, rather than divorced from, history. It also gives us the chance to investigate how Austen's novels resemble, ruminate over, and enact features of history writing, as rendered in her own day.

After this shift in assumptions about Austen and history, much remains to be said. As Daniel Woolf has written, "Austen's opinion of history in its various shapes is not a new topic, though it has perhaps still not had the full attention it merits" (2004: 218). I cannot provide that full attention here, though I open up two long-standing truisms about Austen and history. I ask whether Austen and historical novelist Sir Walter Scott (1771–1832) ought to continue to be opposed in our accounts of the literature of the time. I then consider whether Austen should be seen as critical of history ("his-story") due to its supposed male bias, as some recent critics have argued. Before embarking on that work, I summarize the arguments that have led many in recent years to believe that Austen and history deserve to be linked.

Some of the most productive recent conversations on Austen and history discuss her fiction as it enacts features of history writing. As Deidre Lynch argues, "The old myth of Austen's detachment from history has made it difficult to acknowledge that her writing career coincides with a far reaching transformation in the protocols of historical representation" (Lynch 2003: 73). Recognizing that particular coincidence has proven fruitful to recent scholars (Armstrong 1990, Litvak 1996, Knox-Shaw 2004). We now have a growing body of scholarship that establishes how Austen's novels are in dialogue with eighteenth- and nineteenth-century historiography, in form and content.

Skeptics might ask whether a Regency era writer who never used the word "Napoleon" in her fiction could offer a historical orientation – a useful question. We might approach it by noting that the words "history" and "historian" appear 66 times in Austen's published works. By way of comparison, the word "present" is used 460 times, with most instances synonymous with "nowadays" (six uses), rather than in verb form or meaning a gift. "Past" appears 129 times, generally to indicate a distant moment in time, though occasionally to signify a time on the clock (i.e., "half past"). "Future" is used 111 times in Austen's writings (De Rose and McGuire 1982). Clearly, Austen's works demonstrate an interest in the movement of time. In terms of Austen's fiction, then, "history" should be understood quite broadly.

The word "history" is usually used in Austen's writings to mean a story, though not necessarily one of national import or of the distant past. *Pride and Prejudice* and

Northanger Abbey offer a "history of . . . acquaintance." Catherine Morland gives her history to Eleanor Tilney three times. Modest Fanny Price has a history, as does Jane Fairfax. Recent visits are often said to be worthy of "histories," and accounts of "history and character" abound. In almost all of these references, history is not political history (not an account of past great events), but something we might call novelized history or history-as-fiction – that is, history as the account of local or personal details. Such meanings of the word have largely dropped out of common use. History once signified "a relation of incidents (in early uses, either true or imaginary; later only those professedly true); a narrative, tale or story," according to the *Oxford English Dictionary*. Other definitions, most obsolete, implied "a story represented dramatically" or "a pictorial representation." History also signified a branch of knowledge recording past events, often in writing – for which *Northanger Abbey*'s "real solemn history" is itself used as an *OED* example (Looser 2000: 180). Obviously, "history" in Austen's day involved more than a reference to Napoleon or Henry VIII. But even if we investigate history in its narrower sense – in the "real, solemn" sense – it is inaccurate to say that Austen avoided history.

The most significant piece of evidence that Austen was deeply engaged with history is her early spoof of history writing. Titled "The History of England, from the reign of Henry the 4th to the death of Charles the 1st. By a partial, prejudiced and ignorant Historian," this short, funny piece from her juvenilia has received important scholarly treatment (Austen 1995b, Burton 1995, Kent 1981, 1989). As Christopher Kent has argued, Austen's "History of England" "was not escape from History. . . . It was rather revenge on history – on schoolroom history, a species of history-as-subject, still very much with us" (Kent 1989: 60). Evidence from her letters suggests her interest in history was not an early one later to be overthrown. Her private letters discuss war (*Letters*: 195–6, 272–4), reading newspapers (162–5), and educating herself about military and political history (198–201). Austen knew a great deal about and was keenly interested in the great events of her time and of past times.

Her novels, too, grapple with "real, solemn history." For instance, *Persuasion* ends with its heroine dreading "a future war [as] all that could dim her sunshine" (*P*: 252). Allusions to slavery and abolition are found in central passages in Austen's novels, particularly *Mansfield Park* and *Emma*. References to riots and spies have been discussed frequently in recent criticism of *Northanger Abbey*. Austen's characters also discuss reading history. In *Mansfield Park*, the privileged Bertram sisters ridicule their less educated cousin, Fanny Price, because she cannot recite historical facts. The Bertram girls exclaim to their Aunt Norris, "How long ago it is, aunt, since we used to repeat the chronological order of the kings of England, with the dates of their accession, and most of the principal events of their reigns!" as well as "the Roman emperors as low as Severus." This reported dialogue ostensibly proves Maria and Julia Bertram's education and Fanny's ignorance. To the savvy reader, however, this passage might lead to the opposite surmise. Ultimately, Fanny proves herself to be deeply thinking and reflective about the past, present, and future, while Maria and Julia, for all of their education, emerge as unwise and impulsive. This early conversation hints at their weaknesses, showing the sisters to be overly proud of their ability to regurgitate facts without much deliberation. (Severus ruled circa 200 CE, so an additional layer is that the sisters avoided memorizing many more names!)

Indeed, there is something in this passage about the recitation of regnal years that resembles mistaken ideas about Austen herself. Past critics assumed that because Austen's fiction did not recite facts and dates, she, like Fanny Price, was neither educated in nor reflective about history. But Fanny may be the most able historian of her fictional family, just as Austen may be the better historian of her time, when compared to what she mockingly calls the "nine-hundredth abridger of the History of England" (*NA*: 37). Today we have the opportunity to be more astute readers on the subject of Austen and history. A growing body of scholarship has emerged to demonstrate Austen's knowledge about both social history (customs, manners, and the like) and great political events (Roberts 1979, Woolf 2004). Regardless of whether we define it broadly or narrowly, historical material and its connection to Austen seems not only secure but profound.

The fallacy that Austen was either ignorant of or chose to avoid reference to history itself has a long history. We might trace it to the first short account of her life: her brother Henry Austen's posthumous "Biographical Notice of the Author," in the first edition of *Northanger Abbey and Persuasion* (1818). He claims that Jane Austen's life was happy, simple, and useful, though "not by any means a life of event" (1818: 3). In a postscript, he quotes a line from one of Jane's letters, in which she describes her fiction as "a little bit of ivory, two inches wide, on which I work with a brush so fine as to produce little effect after much labour" (1818: 8). Here, she likens herself to a painter of miniatures, the eighteenth-century precursor to a wallet-sized photo. (Of course, even if she meant to deprecate her own work with this description of its small scale, there is no necessary reason why smallness should imply ahistoricism.)

The biographical notice includes another sentence that has been much less frequently quoted. Henry describes his sister's voracious reading. He claims it was "very extensive in history and belles lettres; and her memory extremely tenacious" (1818: 7). Juxtaposing these two ideas – that she was well read and that she had a strong memory – he implies that history is something she had a good memory *for*. Jane Austen was intelligent, he seems to argue, and her reading (and recall) reflected it. From the first there was an opportunity to see her as *expertly* saturated in historical texts and facts. It was an opportunity most critics neglected to take up.

Instead, Austen's six novels were relentlessly contrasted to the voluminous (and "historical") productions of novelist, poet, and critic Sir Walter Scott. Although he eclipsed Austen for many years in both popularity and critical acclaim, Scott's star began to fall as Austen's began to rise, toward the end of the nineteenth century. As their letters and journals came into print, Austen and Scott's styles were opposed using their own words. What Scott called his "Big Bow-wow strain" (Southam 1968: 106) was contrasted to Austen's "little bit (two Inches wide) of Ivory." These self-contrasts seemed to present an open and shut case for critics. Scott was big, and Austen was little. Scott's fiction was magisterially historical and Austen's was charmingly beyond history. The amount of commentary reiterating that Austen was not of "the novelists of the type of Scott" (quoted in Southam 1968: 247) is simply staggering.

What happens when we question the idea that Austen and Scott ought to be opposed? Even if they may be said to differ in prose style (Scott did not traffic in the irony and humor now seen as Austen's signature) and in setting (Austen's in the present and Scott's most often in the distant past), the two authors ought to be scrutinized for resonances, not just divergences. The first and most obvious is their mutual respect. Scott wrote a positive review of Austen's *Emma*, and Austen imagined herself the critic of Scott (Southam 1968: 67; *Letters*: 203). Of course, mutual admiration need not suggest comparability. In private writings, both Austen and Scott expressed jealousy of each other's powers, which seems even more telling. In a letter to her niece, Austen wrote of Scott with her usual combination of jest and seriousness:

> Walter Scott has no business to write novels, especially good ones. – It is not fair. – He has Fame & Profit enough as a Poet, and should not be taking the bread out of other people's mouth. – I do not like him, & do not mean to like Waverley if I can help it – but I fear I must. (*Letters*: 277)

We know Austen held Scott's fiction in high esteem, but beneath the banter, there seems some concern. In private writings Scott expresses admiration for Austen's fiction in terms of his own lack of skill: "the exquisite touch which renders ordinary commonplace things and characters interesting from the truth of the description and the sentiment is denied to me" (Southam 1968: 106). Though each seems eager for differentiation, each also appears keenly aware of competing with the other. Austen apparently viewed Scott's fiction as having the ability to cut into her profits. Though she would later claim in a letter that she could not write a historical romance "under any other motive than to save my Life" (*Letters*: 312), her remark about Scott taking bread out of other people's mouths suggests she believed that they shared a readership. She must have thought they had more in common as novelists than they did as writers in what would later be understood as opposing subgenres: the "novel of manners" and the "historical novel."

We should not become so lost in Austen's and Scott's admiration or apparent anxieties to distinguish themselves – or in our own as critics to distinguish them from each other – that we underestimate their similarities. Both wished to remain anonymous novelists. (Austen was not revealed publicly as the author of her works until after she died, whereas Scott ultimately unveiled himself, after years of public speculation.) Both presented themselves as defenders of fiction, Austen with characteristic irony in her posthumously published *Northanger Abbey* (1818) and Scott with comparative defensiveness in his "General Preface" to *The Waverley Novels* (1829). They shared a publisher in John Murray. Both admired greatly Maria Edgeworth (1768–1849), author of celebrated historical *and* domestic novels. If Austen and Scott were so very different, would their careers share so many features?

I believe that, with further study, we will conclude that the two authors' writings are more substantively alike than we have given them credit for. The "historical novelist" does not steer clear of the themes of the so-called "novelist of manners" or vice versa. A look into Scott's *Saint Ronan's Well* (1824) provides an obvious starting point, set in a nineteenth-century English spa town, rather than in the distant European past of most of his novels. (Austen herself set her unfinished last novel, *Sanditon*, in a contemporary spa town.) *Saint Ronan's Well* contains some humor, satire, and much gossip, though it is not principally comic. It centers on the machinations of two half-brothers, one legitimate and one not, in their attempts to inherit the family estate. It also explores their competition over a long-suffering heroine, who is, for different reasons, pursued by each brother, one even going so far as to impersonate the other to win her. Ultimately, the heroine dies, and the novel ends in disaster for all of the principals. Scott concludes the book:

> The little watering-place has returned to its primitive obscurity; and lions and lionesses, with their several jackals, blue surtouts, and bluer stockings, fiddlers and dancers, painters and amateurs, authors and critics, dispersed like pigeons by the demolition of a dove-cot, have sought other scenes of amusement and rehearsal, and have deserted *Saint Ronan's Well*.

Saint Ronan's Well is set in 1812 – just at the time in which Austen's novels were first published. Though Scott's plot and diction may not seem Austenian, if we imagine Colonel Brandon's story of the ill-fated first Eliza in *Sense and Sensibility* as a full-length novel, the broad brushstrokes of the two narratives share signal features: two brothers in pursuit of one woman, one brother's death, the woman's death, and collective tragedy and heartbreak. In Austen, of course, there is redemption for the remaining players (excepting, perhaps, the second Eliza), rather than a culminating desertion of a central locale. We may not imagine *Sense and Sensibility* as a historical novel, but at least one critic has discussed it as such (Kroeber 1990). Still, no direct influence from Austen to Scott (or Scott to Austen) is required to prompt the realization that they have more in common than critical tradition has generally allowed.

Saint Ronan's Well was not successful, and is often called Scott's greatest fictional failure. His reviewers saw in it his foolish attempt to join the ranks of female fiction writers. *The New European Magazine*'s anonymous reviewer is particularly sporting and cruel. He pleads with the author, "We . . . most sincerely hope that our favourite will instantly, and for ever, break off his connexion with the housemaid; the nine maids of Pindus are the only females with whom he should be united for literary purposes" (p. 61). Scott, the reviewer implies, ought not to be connected to the material either of the housemaid or the lady author. Women (as characters? as readers? as models?) he should avoid, though he may consort with imaginary muses. *The Monthly Review* measures *Saint Ronan's Well* against its author's "numerous and powerful adversaries," indicating that he must yield "to Madame D'Arblay, to Miss Edgeworth, and to Miss Austin [*sic*]" (p. 62). The reviews suggest Scott trespassed onto female authors' territory, a criticism Scott later seemed to accept. In a journal entry from 1826, he claims that "The women do this better – Edgeworth, [Susan] Ferrier, Austen have all their portraits of real society, far superior to anything Man, vain Man, has produced of the like nature" (Southam 1968: 106). Such beliefs illuminate the ways in which the novel was being divided into masculine and feminine modes, a divide that would continue to be written and rewritten throughout the nineteenth century (Ferris 1991, Garside 1999). Reviewers and critics have long been quick to split up Austen and Scott on the basis of gender, an easy divide we would do well to question.

If the two authors deserve to be divided, it ought not to be over their supposed commitment to or interest in historical discourse. The time seems right to return to the question of whether and how Scott's first novel *Waverley* (1814) had an impact on the composition of *Emma* (1816), for instance. Patricia Meyer Spacks suggests, "young Waverley in some respects resembles a stereotypical eighteenth-century heroine" (2006: 283). What analogous features might we find in Scott's romance-reading feminized hero (Waverley) and Austen's supposedly masculine imaginist (Emma)? Many more such connections and linkages should be sought and reconsidered, given our now well-established sense of a historical Austen, as well as more nuanced ones of Scott's vast oeuvre.

Perhaps we have been prevented from seeking such linkages with the force they deserve because the history of the novel came to be told as a contest of Austen *versus* Scott, rather than Austen *and* Scott (alongside many others!). As the novel grew in stature, and as the question of who was the greatest English novelist – the so-called Shakespeare of the novel – arose, nineteenth-century critics argued over whether it was Austen or Scott who was the great playwright's true descendant. As G. H. Lewes put it in 1847, "In spite of the sense of incongruity which besets us in the words prose Shakespeare, we confess the greatness of Miss Austen, her marvelous dramatic power, seems more than any thing in Scott akin to the greatest quality in Shakespeare" (Southam 1968: 125). Lewes ranked Scott and Austen as the two contenders for the title but saw Austen as emerging triumphant – the more likely of the two to rise out of her own time. The comparisons of Austen and Scott to Shakespeare were not only about whose works would travel across history but also about which author best captured a kind of historical thinking.

Lest we think such exercises of measurement between the two authors are entirely a thing of the past, we need only look to Terry Eagleton's *The English Novel* (2005) to see a similar critical opposition (though a far different conclusion) in practice. Instead of using Shakespeare as his measuring stick, Eagleton uses Karl Marx. Austen, according to Eagleton, "Unlike Scott . . . does not think in historical terms" (2005: 114). Scott "was aware that historical forces were at work in society," knowledge that the supposedly "sequestered" Austen could not access (Eagleton 2005: 119). Eagleton would have us believe that Scott was a more advanced historical thinker than Austen, because she could not grasp the historical and political roots of social problems. Though the literary critical questions have changed, the mistaken notion that Austen is ahistorical where Scott is historical continues. Perhaps the best way to uncouple

Scott and Austen as authors deserving to be contrasted – and to free Austen from residual charges of ahistoricism – is to move beyond models that set up contests in terms of authorial dyads (Richardson vs. Fielding, Boswell vs. Piozzi, or even Words-worth/Coleridge vs. Shelley/Byron). Further work on this phenomenon is certainly needed.

As we have seen, a central binary for opposing Austen and Scott's fiction has been gender. In recent criticism, Austen has not always been cast as appropriately feminine nor Scott as the standard bearer for masculinity. Some critics have sought in Austen's fiction proof of her rejecting traditional feminine roles – a worthy project. At least one of those discoveries, however, deserves rethinking: her supposed denunciation of history writing, due to its male bias. The chief piece of evidence used to make this claim is from *Northanger Abbey*, where heroine Catherine Morland says:

> But history, real solemn history, I cannot be interested in . . . I read it a little as a duty, but it tells me nothing that does not either vex or weary me. The quarrels of popes and kings, with wars or pestilences, in every page, the men all so good for nothing, and hardly any women at all – it is very tiresome. (*NA*: 108)

This passage has been quoted so often that a widespread belief has arisen that Catherine serves here as Austen's mouthpiece, as her author, too, laments that history was "tiresome" because it had "hardly any women at all."

Attending to Catherine's side of the conversation alone (as some critics have done) is quite misleading. First, it is problematic to conflate the naïve Catherine – who later unthinkingly says she does not "speak well enough to be unintelligible" – with her knowing narrator or author. We ought not to ignore the response to Catherine's statement by her future sister-in-law, Eleanor Tilney. It may be that Eleanor better represents Austen's views (Kent 1989: 68). Eleanor gently chastises Catherine for finding history dull, exclaiming, "I am fond of history" (*NA*: 109). Catherine's reply is noteworthy:

> "You are fond of history! – and so are Mr. Allen and my father; and I have two brothers who do not dislike it. So many instances within my small circle of friends is remarkable! At this rate, I shall not pity the writers of history any longer. If people like to read their books, it is all very well, but to be at so much trouble filling great volumes, which, as I used to think, nobody would ever willingly look into, to be labouring only for the torment of little boys and girls, always struck me as a hard fate; and though I know it is all very right and necessary, I have often wondered at the person's courage that could sit down on purpose to do it." (*NA*: 109)

We might consider whether Catherine's reply – not her earlier exclamation about popes and pestilences – ought rather to be aligned with Austen. It seems possible to read this paragraph, in Catherine's trademark ingénue voice, as the wry stylings of an author who preferred to tell fictional stories, knowing that she was competing for book sales with better-respected ("very right and necessary") history writers. Perhaps Austen's voice is lurking in this section of her novel as commentary on the literary marketplace, rather than on the gender bias of history.

More compelling evidence may be gleaned from mature heroine Anne Elliot in *Persuasion*. In a climactic scene, Anne argues with her friend Captain Harville (in earshot of hero Captain Wentworth) about whether women or men show greater constancy in love. Anne argues that it is women who harbor strong romantic feelings longer because they are less often active in the public world. Harville says that it is men who are more constant in love and that "all histories are against you, all stories, prose and verse . . . But perhaps you will say, these were all written by men." Anne responds,

> Perhaps I shall. – Yes, yes, if you please, no reference to examples in books. Men have had every advantage of us in telling their own story. Education has been theirs in so much higher a degree; the pen has been in their hands. I will not allow books to prove any thing. (*P*: 234)

This line, like Catherine Morland's, has been pointed to by recent critics with a peremptory "Aha!" Here, it is argued, Austen is ventriloquizing her own sentiments by putting them in her heroine's mouth. Austen is against "all histories" – or at least all those written by men.

Once again we ought to look further. Later in the conversation, Anne and Harville declare they shall never settle their dispute, because each speaks from experience and, according to Anne, "begin probably with a little bias towards our own sex." After Harville describes the sailor's pain of going out to sea, leaving his wife and children on land, Anne exclaims, "I should deserve utter contempt if I dared to suppose that true attachment and constancy were known only by woman." Their exchange ends with his hand on her arm, and with hero Wentworth writing a renewed declaration of love to Anne as she has been speaking. Is it likely, given this more full context, that this "all histories against us" episode demonstrates Austen's devaluing of men, historiography, and books? It may well reveal a healthy skepticism toward men's ability to describe women and a disgruntlement about women's lack of access to education – and perhaps social and political power as well. But it also demonstrates the rational heroine's acknowledgement of *female* bias. This section of *Persuasion* offers witty exaggeration more than an exposé on the maleness of history. Of course, my readings are not the only possible ones of these rich scenes, but they ought to give us pause about repeating the claims that these oft-quoted sections reveal Austen railing against masculinist histories.

D. R. Woolf's recent call to treat Austen's attitudes toward history as "multi-stranded and open to modulation if not development" (2004: 232) is a crucial one. What counts as history in Austen scholarship is just as varied as what counts as history in her writings. "The history which gets exposed and restored to Austen's text varies enormously," as James Thompson has put it, because "what passes under the name of history ranges from explorations of class conflict on down to the more ordinary annotation to the obscure social details" (1986: 24). Perhaps we ought to be pleased with this variety, because where and how to locate history in Austen's texts *ought* to remain vigorously debated, as should most matters of great complexity and of literary and political consequence. Austen once cleverly remarked (paraphrasing Samuel Johnson) that one of her private letters dealt more in notions than in facts (February 8–9, 1807, *Letters*: 121). Where Austen's relationship to history and history writing is concerned, however, we would be wise to attend both to revisionary notions and to long-occluded facts.

FURTHER READING

Kent, C. (1986). Learning history with, and from, Jane Austen. In J. David Grey (Ed.). *Jane Austen's Beginnings: The Juvenilia and Lady Susan* (pp. 59–72). Ann Arbor, MI: UMI Research Press.

Looser, D. (2000). *British Women Writers and the Writing of History, 1670–1820*. Baltimore: Johns Hopkins University Press.

Spongberg, M. (2002). *Writing Women's History Since the Renaissance*. New York: Palgrave Macmillan.

Tuite, C. (2005). Austen, Jane 1775–1817. In Mary Spongberg, Ann Curthoys, and Barbara Caine (Eds). *Companion to Women's Historical Writing* (pp. 40–2). New York: Palgrave Macmillan.

Woolf, D. R. (2004). Jane Austen and history revisited: the past, gender, and memory from the Restoration to *Persuasion*. *Persuasions* 26, 217–36.

19

Sentiment and Sensibility: Austen, Feeling, and Print Culture

Miranda Burgess

My subject is the relationship between Jane Austen's novels and sensibility, that complex of emotional demonstrativeness and analysis, aesthetic taste, and empathic response that historians treat as a pervasive literary and social movement (or, as G. J. Barker-Benfield, 1992, would have it, a culture) in the second half of the eighteenth century. Reading Austen's novels with an eye to depictions of feeling no longer seems as counterintuitive or as predictable as it must once have done – to Charlotte Brontë, who found Austen incapable of "warmth or enthusiasm" and therefore unqualified to discuss "the Feelings," or Marvin Mudrick, who decreed that Austen's ironic style was a defense against "self-commitment and feeling" (Brontë 1995, vol. 2: 383, Mudrick 1952). Though such judgments continue to echo in criticism that types Austen as sensibility's decorous scold (e.g., Butler 1987, Rawson 1994), even there it is not always the case that Austen's approach to feeling is understood as a result of bodily deficiency or a (related) moral instinct. Her novels are now routinely included in discussions of emotion in eighteenth-century and Romantic literature, while readers who view them as antisentimental works are apt to see them as "a specific form within the genre of sentiment and sensibility" rather than as outside agents of generic and moral reform (Tuite 2002: 59). Though Austen's novels do not belong to the mainstream of novels of sensibility, they participate in the same conversation.

This chapter builds on the idea of sensibility as a conversation by suggesting, first, that Austen represented sensibility not merely as an emotional experience or a set of behavioral conventions but as the object of unresolved debate within her novels, and second, that Austen viewed conversation itself – and debate among her readers, for she defined conversation as "exchange of opinion" – as the goal of sentimental representation (*NA*: 36, 66). To make this argument is at once to underline the role of sensibility in contemporary thinking about the nature and significance of social activity, and to highlight the originality and force of Austen's contribution to it. It is also to point out that sensibility was a phenomenon intimately associated with print culture, and with novels in particular. Austen was not unique in representing print culture – reading – as inseparable from social life. This chapter will argue, however, that her novels were extraordinary both in their close and sustained attention to the relationship between print and sociability and in the questions of information transmission, reception, and social order they consistently explore.

Communicating Sensibility: The Social Effects of Print Culture

Eighteenth-century and Romantic-period writers tended to view print as what Marshall McLuhan called a "hot medium," a conduit for information and experience that acted forcefully on the senses of its users without requiring much participation or reflection (McLuhan 2003: 39–40, see also Keen 1999: 155–70). As such, as contemporaries imagined it, the print medium was uniquely fitted to interact with sensibility. It did so in a double sense, at once communicating raw material to a faculty represented as naturally responsive and educating this faculty in the variety and limits of appropriate response.

The roots of sensibility lay in the eighteenth-century medical and philosophical discourse of sensation: the science of the nerves, with its interest in immediacy of emotional reaction and its kinship to aesthetic and literary responsiveness (Todd 1986, Rousseau 2004). Cognitive scientists outlined a theory of nerves as the body's communicative devices, connecting "external Objects" to "the Brains, or the seat of Sensation" (Locke 1975: 136). Philosophers such as John Locke, David Hume, and Adam Smith, who turned their empirical gaze on these workings of "human nature," also examined the connection between cognition, emotion, and social order in essays on political philosophy. As their work circulated and was popularized in periodicals, pamphlets, and novels, sensibility as a natural, spontaneous emotional response came to be seen as a major source for moral character and, consequently, for social order as well (Eagleton 1990: 31–69, Johnson 1995a). This argument persisted from the late seventeenth century through the turn of the nineteenth: from Locke's *Two Treatises of Government* (1690), which founded all societies on the "natural" order of the conjugal household, requiring the discovery in women of an inherent capacity for submissive heterosexual love, to Edmund Burke's argument in *Reflections on the Revolution in France* (1790) that feeling for family and neighborhood provides a "natural" foundation for patriotic sensibility. Yet these and other philosophers of sensibility found themselves caught in a contradiction, at once describing what they decreed inherent in their subjects and schooling readers in what they implicitly acknowledged needed to be taught.

Historians of sensibility (e.g. Mullan 1988, Burgett 1998, Ellison 1999) have suggested that novelists sought to harness the "hot" quality of the print medium in order to communicate a uniformity of emotion to their readerships. By this means novels held out hope for a noncoercive source of social cohesion that would supplement or replace the forms of sentiment outlined in contemporary moral philosophy. It would have the added benefit of overcoming the impersonality inherent in print and its circulation to a widening anonymous audience, circumstances that increased the likelihood that readers' sentiments would deviate from the recommendations of novelists and philosophers while remaining dangerously unknowable. The letter that Sarah Fielding, herself a novelist of sensibility, wrote to Samuel Richardson about *Clarissa* (1748–9) is representative: "when I read of her, I am all sensation; my heart glows; I am overwhelmed; my only vent is tears; and unless tears could mark my thoughts as legibly as ink, I cannot speak half I feel" (Richardson 1804, vol. 2: 60–1). As evidence of communal sensibility, exchanges such as Fielding's with Richardson contributed to a growing sense that the moral character of readers, particularly women, could be assessed by reference to the degree of feeling – made visible in tears, blushes, and speechlessness – with which they responded to scenes of feeling in books (Spacks 2003: 55–86). The success of a lesson in feeling was measured by its dissolution into an appearance of natural cohesion even as reading remained its inescapable index.

In this way novelists of sensibility achieved the interlocking goals of inculcating uniformity of feeling among readers and overcoming the anonymity of print. But they did so at the cost of acknowledging the dependency of feeling on a sympathy communicated by reading. As a result the period retained an intense suspicion of print that was founded not only on its perceived contribution to emotional excess, the encouragement of feelings that might run away with their possessor, but also on its role in affective contagion, the passage of feelings from one unwitting individual to the next such that affect comes unmoored from its causes and a crowd of far-flung, imperfectly known subjects are brought to share in its effects. "No quality of human nature is more remarkable," wrote Hume in 1740, than "that propensity we have to sympathize with others, and to receive by communication their inclinations and sentiments, however different from, or even contrary to our own" (Hume 1978: 316). If audiences can be made to feel in spite of themselves, then what Paul Goring (2005) calls "the rhetoric of sensibility" – and print's ability to transmit it – becomes a powerful, even dangerous weapon of persuasion.

Recent scholarship has examined attempts to harness rhetorics of sensibility in support of philanthropic projects such as the abolition of the slave trade and the founding of shelters for prostitutes (Van Sant 1993, Ellis 1996). But contemporary writers also warned that the manipulation of print in the service of sympathetic feeling could foster corrupt forms of sentiment or mobilize unthinkingly reactive crowds. Writers of conduct books designed to school the manners and morals of young women invariably warned against novels, which, as Thomas Gisborne put it, "turn on the vicissitudes and effects of a passion the most powerful of all those which agitate the human heart," thereby "creat[ing] . . . a susceptibility of impression and a premature warmth of tender emotions" (Gisborne 1797: 217). As these remarks suggest, conduct writers were less worried about content than about what James Fordyce called the "tendency," or seductive effect, of novels, which was thought to be able to "work" readers "up into a storm" of feeling (Fordyce 1766, vol. 1: 119–20). Many such writers cautioned against printed sources of sensibility in more general terms. Some noted what Hester Chapone (1807) described as the potential for "sentiment and feeling" to create immorality "by degrees unless the avenues of the heart are guarded," which for Chapone means the careful selection of reading material (Chapone 1807: 73–4). Others focused on the broader social and political consequences of the spread of sensibility. Even as her poem "On Sensibility" proclaimed it the source of all charity and upheld its by now conventional connection with female virtue, Hannah More condemned its adherents for pursuing affective experience – "As if friend, parent, country were no more" – and lamented its displacement of other means and ends of human, particularly masculine, conduct:

> Yet, while I hail the Sympathy Divine,
> Which makes, O man! the wants of others thine!
> I mourn heroic JUSTICE, scarcely own'd,
> And PRINCIPLE for SENTIMENT dethron'd.
> While FEELING boasts her ever-tearful eye,
> Stern TRUTH, firm FAITH, and manly VIRTUE fly.
>
> (More 1782: 281–2, 284)

Nor were such fears limited to conservative writers, who were notoriously concerned about the circulation of excessive feeling. More moderate thinkers, too, worried about the political consequences of affective contagion, which they linked to the revolutionary movements galvanizing Ireland and France at the end of the eighteenth century. In the aftermath of the 1798 United Irishman rebellion, the editors of the liberal *Monthly Review* remarked that a newspaper "entitled 'THE PRESS,' conveying periodical exhortations to outrage and insubordination," was foremost among the "weapons" Irish revolutionaries had used to force the "dismemberment of the empire" and promote "the erection of an Irish republic under French auspices" (*Monthly Review* 1798: 207). The *Monthly* was not alone in its fears of the conjunction between print and revolutionary affect. When the viceroy ordered *The Press* shut down in early 1798, his agents were instructed not only to smash up the presses so as "not to leave a penny-worth standing," but also to carry away the fragments (Dowdall 1798: 2). The way in which sensibility focalized questions about the body and the will, the relations between subjects and appropriate public conduct, stood at the heart of contemporary anxieties about print culture, for which it remained both solution and focus.

Austen on Print and Sensibility: The Letters and The Novels

Always an acute observer of the literary scene, Austen addressed the connection between sensibility, volition, and print epigrammatically in her letters. The novels, as we will see, discussed it with equal sophistication, but more directly and at length. Her account of sensibility is marked by her characteristically ironic approach to matters of conventional wisdom. Writing to Cassandra Austen in 1809, Austen compares her current reading matter to her sister's:

To set against your new Novel, of which nobody ever heard before & perhaps never may again, We have got Ida of Athens by Miss Owenson; which must be very clever, because it was written as the Authoress says, in three months. – We have only read the Preface yet; but her Irish Girl does not make me expect much. – If the warmth of her Language could affect the Body, it might be worth reading in this weather. (*Letters*: 166)

As a leading example of the "national tale," Sydney Owenson's *Wild Irish Girl* (1806) is especially germane to Austen's discussion of literary affect. It belonged to a genre whose writers "mobilize[d] the affective resources available to fictional, as opposed to legal, language in order to generate sympathy for Ireland," much as the rhetoric of sensibility had been deployed on behalf of the slave trade or the sex trade (Ferris 2002: 3). In her observations, Austen at once confirms the anonymous, ephemeral quality that critics attributed to the contemporary novel and acknowledges the sensibility that was thought, for good or ill, to compose the genre's content and define its tendency. But Austen playfully resists the claim that print, even in the special case of the novel, is a medium able to "affect the Body" by provoking feeling in its readers, however receptive, even eager, they might be to surrender to its effects.

In *Sense and Sensibility* (1811), Austen extends this skeptical analysis to the emotional reactions of her heroine Marianne Dashwood, a self-conscious heroine of sensibility with a special relationship to books. Like Sarah Fielding responding to *Clarissa*, Marianne demonstrates her sensibility in her responses to literature: on meeting John Willoughby, she compares him to "what her fancy had ever drawn for the hero of a favourite story," and she describes William Cowper's poems – many of them wielding sentimental rhetoric for political ends – as "beautiful lines which have frequently almost driven me wild" (*SS*: 18, 43). Yet throughout the scenes that introduce Marianne and her capacity for feeling, Austen's narrator highlights the volitional quality of Marianne's sensibility and Willoughby's responses to it. In the two instances in the novel in which Marianne grieves, for her father's death and Willoughby's desertion, the narrator emphasizes the deliberateness as well as the violence of her feeling. "[T]he excess of her . . . sensibility" means that the "agony of grief" is "voluntarily renewed, . . . sought for, . . . created again and again" (*SS*: 7); she is "not merely giving way" to her feelings "but feeding and encouraging [them] as a duty" (*SS*: 77). Insofar as Marianne experiences a community of feeling mediated by print, it is only because she insists she can never "be happy with a man whose taste did not in every point coincide with my own. He must enter into all my feelings" (*SS*: 17). Thus when she discusses "her favourite authors" with Willoughby, it is

with so rapturous a delight, that any young man of five and twenty must have been insensible indeed, not to become an immediate convert to the excellence of such works, however disregarded before. Their taste was strikingly alike. The same books, the same passages were idolized by each – or if any difference appeared, any objection arose, it lasted no longer than till the force of her arguments and the brightness of her eyes could be displayed. (*SS*: 47)

"[M]y feelings are not often shared," says Marianne, "But *sometimes* they are" (*SS*: 88). But the narrator insists that it is only by act of will that Willoughby feels along with Marianne, even with the aid of books. If he has "caught all her enthusiasm," it is because it is his earnest and, initially, his self-interested wish to do so (*SS*: 47).

These passages demonstrate a pervasive skepticism about the affective power of print. Yet they also illustrate what is equally apparent throughout the novels: that to discuss feeling in Austen is inevitably to discuss mediation. Books and other printed objects are everywhere in Austen's works, and not only during discussions of sensibility and its cognate category, taste. In every one of the novels, they are chosen from piles on tables, collected in great houses, rented from circulating libraries, read in company or alone, made the object of lists, cited, debated, and quoted. From *Sense and Sensibility* to *Persuasion* (1818), characters treat books as indexes of sensibility. In *Emma* (1816), the parvenu Mrs Elton seeks simultaneously but unsuccessfully to demonstrate fine feeling for people and poetry by (mis)quoting a hackneyed phrase from Thomas Gray's "Elegy Wrote in a Country Church Yard" in sympathy with the impoverished Jane Fairfax: "Full many a flower is born to blush unseen/ And waste its fragrance on the desert air" (*E*: 282). In *Persuasion*, the fickle sensibility of Captain Benwick, a "young man of considerable taste in reading, though principally in poetry," gives "the appearance of feelings glad to burst their usual restraints" as he repeats "with . . . tremulous feeling, the various lines which imaged a broken heart, or a mind destroyed by wretchedness, and look[s] . . . entirely as if he meant to be understood" (*P*: 100). Conversely, to arrive at maturity, for more than one of Austen's characters, is to engage – or at least think of engaging – in active, thoughtful reading without arriving at any definitive position or conclusion. Fanny Price in *Mansfield Park* (1814) not only joins a circulating library and becomes "*in propria persona* . . . a renter, a chuser of books" but also becomes the instructor to her sister, to whom Fanny's "explanations and remarks" make "a most important addition to every essay, or every chapter of history" (*MP*: 398, 419). Marianne Dashwood's decision to abandon sensibility requires a year-long "course of serious study" (*SS*: 343). For Austen the print medium is not "hot" but "cool," requiring the active participation of its audiences in order to work its effects on their minds and hearts. Among these effects is sensibility, whether true or false, corrupt or pure, solipsistic or socially engaged. What matters is the reader's ways of reading.

Ways of Reading: Austen, Feeling and the Uses of Books

I turn now to one of the most famous, and controversial, passages in Austen's novels: the scene in *Northanger Abbey* (1818) in which Catherine Morland, staying at Northanger and operating under the influence of novels, is discovered investigating what she imagines to be the murder of her hosts' wife and mother. She is drawn up short by Henry Tilney, who will later become her husband:

"What have you been judging from? Remember the country and the age in which we live. Remember that we are English, that we are Christians. Consult your own under-standing, your own sense of the probable, your own observation of what is passing around you – Does our education prepare us for such atrocities? Do our laws connive at them? Could they be perpetrated without being known, in a country like this, where social and literary intercourse is on such a footing; where every man is surrounded by a neighbourhood of voluntary spies, and where roads and newspapers lay every thing open? Dearest Miss Morland, what ideas have you been admitting?" (*NA*: 197–8)

Traditionally read as a scene of education, in which a female Quixote seduced by lit-erature is chastened by the intervention of masculine rationality (e.g., Butler 1987: 175–9), this passage has in the last 20 years been discussed in different terms: as the narrator's, and Austen's, ironic nod to the quasi-Gothic perils of power relations in everyday English life (e.g., Johnson 1988: 43). It might prove especially fruitful to read the scene through the perspective of Wendy Motooka, who has argued that the universalizing philosophical projects of the period all harbored a tendency to degener-ate into quixotism – the inclination to view one's private beliefs as universally demon-strable and convincing – though some Quixotes were more powerful than others. For Motooka, as a result, representations of quixotism in literature serve as social critiques of contemporary moral philosophy, including the philosophy of communal sensibility (Motooka 1998). But the speech is also a matter-of-fact acknowledgement, not only of the role of will in a subject's being influenced by reading ("what ideas have you been admitting?") but also of the cooperation of "social and literary intercourse" and the universal penetration of print culture and its technologies of circulation.

Historians of the book have shown how the development of new trade routes, par-ticularly canals and turnpike roads, increased the distribution of printed texts through England after the late 1760s, making possible the expansion of reading institutions from provincial book clubs through small town circulating libraries (e.g., Raven 1992: 44–5). Austen's letters offer a snapshot of the book circulation enabled by such institutions and her own participation in it. One 1813 letter is especially saturated with the details of book borrowing, lending, and reading. It depicts a family, as Austen puts it, "quite run over with Books." Volumes are received from two different friends – at least one of which is borrowed from a circulating library and then lent to the Austens, who have in turn "dispos'd of [it] . . . Comp^{ts} & all, for the first fort-night" to other friends – as well as from the Chawton Book Society, whose rivalry with the "Steventon & Manydown Society" is detailed in this and other letters (*Letters*: 198–9). What is significant in Austen's account is the interpenetration of reading institutions, commercial, formal, and informal, with the intimate affairs of her family and, at the same time, with her experience of provincial sociability. The families of her community receive books from the same sources and read many of the same books. The books themselves – passed from hand to hand, read aloud or silently, alone or in groups, and discussed in person and in letters – become the common currency of social life.

In her book on interiority and literature, Deidre Lynch has shown how the circulation of print culture appears in Austen's novels as the background noise surrounding individual thought, feeling, and reading. She argues that the special office of novels, epitomized by Austen's works, is the "management of [the] opposition" between "the feeling-filled language of inside views" and the "impersonal discourses" of mass production that saturated the consciousness of readers and writers in the period (Lynch 1998: 212). In other words, the novels explore the experience of sensibility, and the possibility of individual feeling, in a world inundated by incessant conversation and for a mind continually pressed against by others' words. Reading *Sense and Sensibility* and *Persuasion*, Lynch concentrates on the permeability of the feeling mind to outer experiences, especially the experience of reading.

Yet, as Adela Pinch points out, there are many scenes in *Persuasion* that show the heroine Anne Elliot becoming equally impermeable to the noise of social life and print culture, so that the narrator repeatedly describes her as having "found herself" addressed by one or another of her friends or family (Pinch 1996: 152). In *Sense and Sensibility* Austen is still more explicit about the role of absorption in social imperviousness and thus in affective protection of the mind. In scene after scene, readers are told that "the abstraction" of Marianne Dashwood's "thoughts preserved her in ignorance of every thing that was passing before her" (*SS*: 193). By this means Marianne is continually "spared from . . . troublesome feelings . . . by remaining unconscious of it all; for she was as well able to collect her thoughts within herself, and be as ignorant of what was passing around her, in Mr. Gray's shop, as in her own bed-room" (*SS*: 221). Her calmer sister Elinor makes similar escapes: she continues to talk to Colonel Brandon while "the thoughts of both [are] engaged elsewhere," and the narrator describes her "mind" as "inevitably at liberty; her thoughts could not be chained" even as she sits surrounded by "her mother and sisters," by "the nature of [whose] . . . employments" – almost certainly reading aloud – "conversation was forbidden among them, and every effect of solitude . . . produced" (*SS*: 105, 162). In the piling up of such scenes, as in the scenes that demonstrate skepticism about the affective power of print, Austen emphasizes the mind's independence not just from the impact of texts but also from social life itself – even print-mediated social life, and even as she emphasizes that "placing around them their books and other possessions" is the way the Dashwoods "form themselves a home" (*SS*: 30).

The self-sufficient absorption of minds in *Sense and Sensibility* has led Eve Sedgwick and William Galperin to pinpoint Marianne Dashwood as the locus of eroticism in Austen's novels. Both argue that Austen's narrator, with what these scholars see as her promotion of Elinor's cooler ways of proceeding, punishes Marianne in ways that, for Sedgwick at least, participate in an implicit erotics of dominance (Sedgwick 1991, Galperin 2003: 109–20). While conceding that much Austen criticism, particularly analyses focused on sensibility, does engage in readings centered on "the spectacle of the Girl Being Taught a Lesson" (Sedgwick 1991: 833), I want to emphasize, instead, the ways, already listed, in which Austen allows for affective independence in characters and so in readers, illustrating, even in her most decorous heroines, the mind "at liberty" to feel and think. At the same time, I want to highlight the ways in which sensibility is externalized and explored in these novels in dialogue with the murmur of omnipresent print culture – not because mass culture or fashion makes sensibility a topic for idle chatter but because Austen's novels are self-conscious about their role in making sensibility an object of reflection and conversation for her characters and readers.

The novels model this kind of conversation. Elinor, Marianne, and Edward Ferrars argue sensibility three times in the opening volume of *Sense and Sensibility*, while the climax of *Persuasion* comprises a dispute about feeling that covers several pages, and the narrative heart of *Northanger Abbey* is a debate about reading and taste. These conversations evidence a tendency, marked by scholars of eighteenth-century sociability (e.g., Mullan 1988, Habermas 1989, Johnson 1995a, Ellis 1996), for sensibility to become an object of discussion, the focus of exchanges that are aimed at reforming or redefining contemporary society by means of the activity of conversation as much as the feelings that form its content. It is as a *topic*, not a contagious feeling, that sensibility is communicated, in novels circulated through transportation networks and advanced by reading institutions, to be considered and debated by Austen's readers.

The debate in *Persuasion* takes place as Anne Elliot and Captain Harville discuss the relative sensibility, in the form of emotional constancy, of women and men. The conversation climaxes in Harville's reference to books:

> "We shall never agree I suppose upon this point. No man and woman would, probably. But let me observe that all histories are against you, all stories, prose and verse. If I had such a memory as Benwick, I could bring you fifty quotations in a moment on my side the argument, and I do not think I ever opened a book in my life which had not something to say upon woman's inconstancy. . . . But perhaps you will say, these were all written by men."
>
> "Perhaps I shall. – Yes, yes, if you please, no reference to examples in books. Men have had every advantage of us in telling their own story. Education has been theirs in so much higher a degree; the pen has been in their hands. I will not allow books to prove any thing."
>
> "But how shall we prove any thing?"
>
> "We never shall. We never can expect to prove any thing upon such a point. It is a difference of opinion which does not admit of proof." (*P*: 234)

Two elements of this exchange are especially striking: its inconclusiveness ("We never can expect to prove any thing" – "never" and "any thing" repeated three times for emphasis) and its dependency on print. Harville's reference to "examples in books" also points self-reflexively to the printed origins of Austen's representation of the debate, which reproduces almost verbatim the conversation of Arietta with a "commonplace talker" in *Spectator* 11 (1711): "you men are writers, and can represent us women as unbecoming as you please in your works, while we are unable to return the injury." It is perhaps also worth recalling that the *Spectator* papers were presented as the collective produce of discussion in a reading and debating "club" (*Spectator* 1, 1711) and that they were designed to "furnish *tea-table talk*," especially "among reasonable women" (*Spectator* 4, 1711). The passage in *Persuasion* is offered to Austen's readers in a similarly sociable sense, emerging as the subject of conversation from the background "buzz of words" yet self-consciously enabled by it (*P*: 231). In leaving the reader without a resolution, Austen makes the scene a matter for debate outside the novel as well.

Persuasion was published posthumously together with *Northanger Abbey*, whose more explicit self-consciousness as a printed artifact allows the two novels to comment on each other. The discussion of sentiment and taste that lies at the heart of *Northanger Abbey* is thoroughly saturated not only with references to literature but also with the form of the printed book and its modes of circulation: like Austen's own, the Tilney family is overrun with books. Henry marks his taste for novels by forgoing "reading . . . aloud" to his sister in favor of "running away with the volume," which is "particularly her own," and so replaces a "hot" understanding of the print medium – conveying stored voices to a passive, receptive reader – with a "cool" one leading to analysis and conversation (*NA*: 107). In terms of sociability, the stakes of this transformation are high. Henry's speeches dramatize the power of the debate on sensibility to displace the spread of revolutionary sentiment: the "dreadful riot" his sister expects to come from London – "a mob of three thousand men assembling in St. George's Fields; the Bank attacked, the Tower threatened, the streets of London flowing with blood" – is forestalled by its revelation as "'a new publication . . . in three duodecimo volumes, two hundred and seventy-six pages in each, with a frontispiece to the first, of two tombstones and a lantern," to arrive from "a circulating library" (*NA*: 112–13). Austen's ironic answer to fears about affective contagion in *Northanger Abbey* is an explicit reminder of the coolness, inhering in the materiality and distribution, of the printed word.

Conclusion: Conversation and the Possibilities of Print

In assessing the worth of books, Henry Tilney remarks that it "must depend upon the binding" (*NA*: 107). There is more to the joke than Henry knows. For the self-reflexive conclusion of *Northanger Abbey* asserts that the "tendency" of the work itself becomes subject to debate "by whomsoever it may concern" precisely because its readers are holding a bound and printed volume – "the tell-tale compression" of whose "pages" relieves suspense about the ending – in their hands (*NA*: 250, 252). When it comes to determining the tendency of her novel, and the morality of feeling, Austen goes silent in deference to her readers while reminding them of their conversational power.

In such moments, William Galperin has argued, Austen forswears representation to gesture outward, beyond the boundaries of the text. In this way she signals the complexity of the social life through which her novels circulate, and gestures, by refusing to take a single, uniform position, to the multitude of trajectories this social life might take and the conclusions it might reach (Galperin 2003: 31). For Austen, conversation – the exchange of opinion, especially about books – is the real locus of sensibility: the medium of social life and the source of social order as well, perhaps, as the momentum of social change.

FURTHER READING

Barker-Benfield, G. J. (1992). *The Culture of Sensibility: Sex and Society in Eighteenth-Century Britain*. Chicago: University of Chicago Press.

Eagleton, Terry (1990). *The Ideology of the Aesthetic*. Oxford: Blackwell.

Ellis, Markman (1996). *The Politics of Sensibility: Race, Gender and Commerce in the Sentimental Novel*. Cambridge, UK: Cambridge University Press.

Johnson, Claudia L. (1995). *Equivocal Beings: Politics, Gender, and Sentimentality in the 1790s*. Chicago: University of Chicago Press.

Lynch, Deidre (1998). *The Economy of Character: Novels, Market Culture, and the Business of Inner Meaning*. Chicago: University of Chicago Press.

Mullan, John (1988). *Sentiment and Sociability: The Language of Feeling in the Eighteenth Century*. Oxford: Clarendon Press.

20

The Gothic Austen

Nancy Armstrong

Northanger Abbey was the first of Austen's major novels to be drafted (1794) and the last to appear in print (1818). Written and revised when Gothic fiction was the rage, the novel's willingness to poke fun at Ann Radcliffe's *The Mysteries of Udolpho* has encouraged scholars and critics to align Austen's novels with Augustan reason and wit in contempt of the irrationality of sentimental literature in general and the excesses of Gothic romance in particular. Picking up where the feminist reclamation of sentimental literature during the 1980s and 1990s left off, Claudia Johnson invites us to consider whether *Northanger Abbey* can be read as a defense rather than a satire of Radcliffe, posing the question I mean to address: "Is Austen possibly a Gothic novelist herself?" (Johnson 2003: ix). In opposition to the economy of wit character-izing the Austen style, Gothic romance tends, like sentimental literature, toward the prolix and extravagantly conventional in order to push human feeling and behavior beyond the limits of reason and decorum (Walpole: 10). In appearing to "sabotage" these devices, according to Johnson, *Northanger Abbey* actually translates them into ordinary speech and social interaction and so breathes affective energy into the novel of manners (Johnson 2003: ix). But if *Northanger Abbey* does ridicule Gothic, then what do we make of the satiric treatment of Radcliffe? Can we abstract a paradigm from this novel for reading the Austen novels appearing during the 25-year period between *Northanger*'s first draft and its final publication? This essay proposes a way of doing exactly that.

Historians tend to think that when John Locke formulated his theory of property in 1679–80 to counter Robert Filmer's argument that the power of monarchy was virtually unlimited on this earth, he had only landowning interests in mind (Macpherson 1964). If Austen has anything to say about the matter, Locke's theory of property retained explanatory power well after monarchy ceased to pose a threat to landowners, not only because he argues for the owner's sole right to possess his land, but also because he seems to insist on the subsidiary notion of property as that which each individual has "in his own person," elaborated in *Essay Concerning Human Understanding*. Whether or not Locke had landowning men in mind when he came up with this second form of property, by including it in his *Second Treatise of Government*, he extended citizenship in theory to all who had property in themselves. Gothic offered novelists a way of exposing a discrepancy between the two forms of property. When novels whisk a heroine off to a remote castle, monastery, or convent, she becomes – in fact, if not by law – the property of others, valued only for the material resources attached to her position and possessing no ability to use them to her own advantage. Because the ability to give or withhold consent depends on self-ownership, such standard Gothic plot devices as imprisonment, attempted rape, stifled speech, intercepted letters, and falsified historical accounts create conditions that neutralize even the minimal agency required to withhold consent. By yoking the notion of the property intrinsic in a person to the traditional notion of property as land, Locke made it possible for the difference between them to emerge as a contradiction: are you who you are because you belong to a "house," meaning both family and land, or are you who are you are by virtue of something you possess within yourself, the sense, sensibility, wit, accomplishments, or civility you bring to a household and by so doing make it yours? Gothic conventions put the two kinds of property on a collision course where each imperils the other.

Austen organized what would otherwise be a novel of manners around this contradiction – central to British literature in the decades following the French Revolution – and so formulated a language for imaginatively sustaining civility in a world undergoing violent social transformation. In her novels this incorporation works in two directions. It limits the forms of violence and cruelty that can be inflicted even on heroines like Fanny Price and Anne Elliot, endowed with one kind of property but not the other. At the same time, Austen uses Gothic conventions to turn each novel into a Gothic castle of sorts – a framework in which the traditional notion of property as vested in land deprives individuals of the basis for making rational decisions, the means of self expression, and even the power to withhold consent. Where in *Northanger Abbey* the irreverent wit and devastating logic of the Austen sentence appear opposed to the Gothic excesses it debunks, such sentences constitute a world that wit cannot illuminate nor logic master so long as the two forms of property composing that world seem poised to cancel each other out.

When is a House a Castle?

Austen's heroine enters Northanger Abbey with a head full of Gothic fiction, and uses its conventions to read the architecture, furniture, *pater familias*, and his dead wife as more of the same. She is upbraided by Henry Tilney, the second son of a landowning family, for eschewing empirical evidence and common sense, and the ethical weight of the novel seems to fall on his call for a rational response:

> "What have you been judging from? . . . Does our education prepare us for such atrocities? Do our laws connive at them? Could they be perpetrated without being known,

in a country like this, where social and literary intercourse is on such a footing; where every man is surrounded by a neighborhood of voluntary spies, and where roads and newspapers lay every thing open? Dearest Miss Morland, what ideas have you been admitting?" (*NA*: 197)

Henry is correct that it is ridiculous to believe that his father imprisoned and murdered his wife. Even Radcliffe's demonic Montoni never actually committed that crime. But it is equally ridiculous for Henry to assume that Catherine's education and experience can explain his father's alarming violations of civility and good taste, much less his mood swings: the Abbey is no more ruled by reason than by a secret history of crime and passion. The novel thus invites us to heed Henry's rhetorical questions and consider what *Northanger* might share with Gothic fiction.

While Austen uses Henry to punish Catherine for confusing his father's abbey with Montoni's castle, she also grants him little more freedom than the hero of a Gothic tale when it comes to marrying the woman of his choice. Families marry whom they choose, individuals don't. The inhabitants of the Abbey are subject to a force heedless of both reason and sentiment because heedless of the first requirement for the exercise of either, namely, the property each individual has in himself or herself. Individual family members are members of a single corporate body. When we clear away the confusion produced by both Radcliffe and common sense, we discover that Henry is subject to a family economy rooted in land: "Northanger Abbey having been a richly endowed convent at the time of the Reformation [and then falling] into the hands of an ancestor of the Tilneys on its dissolution" (*NA*: 142). Henry is a second son in need of an occupation, and the parsonage he plans to occupy is the General's domain and subject to his wishes: "It is a family living Miss Morland; and the property in the place being chiefly my own, you may believe I take care it shall not be a bad one" (p. 176).

Catherine has little property of the kind the General hopes to accrue by taking her into his family, but she is more than the nonentity that Mr Allen acquires through marriage to Mrs Allen, a woman who possesses only "the air of a gentlewoman, a great deal of quiet, inactive good temper, and a trifling turn of mind" (*NA*: 20). Austen never assures us that Henry Tilney values Catherine's educability over the adulation she bestows on him, but she does put her heroine through a series of trials that establish good manners as the grounding and guide for her expressions of sympathy. In a world where people deploy the outward signs of such virtue to their own advantage, genuine feeling, when properly expressed, appears intrinsic to Catherine – property that she has, so to speak, in her person.

She acquires this property as she abandons a Gothic reading of social relationships within the Abbey. Its architecture initially prompts her to read the Abbey as a fictional castle complete with winding passageways, forbidden chambers, and a mysterious chest of drawers. Although Catherine soon scolds herself for imagining that the chest of drawers in her bedroom contains evidence of some tale of persecution, the pall that General Tilney casts over his household sustains her conviction that he is a ruthless tyrant cut to Montoni's pattern: "What could more plainly speak the gloomy work-ings of a mind not wholly dead to every sense of humanity, in its fearful review of past scenes of guilt?" (*NA*: 187). Catherine misses the mark in assuming the cause of his gloom, but in pursuing his material interests, he does behave like a modern Montoni. Discovering Catherine's scant inheritance, he proceeds to devalue the bond between Henry and Catherine:

> Turned from the house, and in such a way! – Without any reason that could justify, any apology that could atone for the abruptness, the rudeness, nay, the insolence of it. Henry at a distance – not even able to bid him farewell. Every hope, every expectation from him suspended, at least, and who could say how long? – Who could say when they might meet again? – And all this by such a man as General Tilney, so polite, so well-bred, and heretofore so particularly fond of her! It was as incomprehensible as it was mortifying and grievous. (*NA*: 226)

The syntactical disruptions here, along with such nouns as "abruptness," "rudeness," and "insolence," put us in a world where behavior is not regulated by decorum. Adjec-tives such as "incomprehensible," "mortifying," and "grievous" indicate that the novel has indeed taken a Gothic turn where the exchange of women turns women into property and discounts affective bonds. Catherine thus appears not to have taken Radcliffe seriously enough, failing to detect the cause so transparent to the reader.

When the notion of property "in oneself" runs aground on the notion of property in a "house," the heroine so dispossessed undergoes an internal split, releasing – much like a genie from its bottle – the Gothic affect that accompanies the breakdown of that one-body-to-one-mind equation we call the modern individual (Armstrong 2005). The individual imprisoned in a Gothic castle is a mind imprisoned in a body not hers to command. The illusion of individual responsibility, individual account-ability, and thus individual value vanish with civility, and all those who harbor this illusion, as Catherine does, are subject to the paranoid conviction that something has gone very wrong. As the ethos of individualism gives way to an older and still more pervasive notion of the body as family property, reason, sympathy, the manners that reflect that notion of the body become mere performances rather than self-cultivated properties.

Catherine's expulsion from the Abbey uncovers the semiotics of Gothic architecture in a way that Radcliffe's romance, being romance, does not. By dissolving the indi-vidual body into a corporate body, Austen in no way locates the problem in the landowning classes or implies that it is self-destructive to marry into them. That is, after all, what the General disrupts and what Austen's archly comedic ending finally achieves. The novel reaches its nadir, not because Catherine has been taken into a "house," but because she has been tossed into the category of bodies that simply don't matter (Butler 1993: 10). That the possibility for happiness and the narrative endeavoring to realize it are consequently over implies there is no more life outside a "house" in Austen than in a Radcliffe novel. It is only there – and through some accommodation of family prerogatives to individual feelings – that one can sustain the illusion of self-possession.

No Joking Matter

D. A. Miller (2003) best explains how and at what cost Austen's style remains detached where her heroine is personally invested, and strikes us as most playful when it is recounting that heroine's moments of humiliation. I want to consider what makes these heroines susceptible to such debasement – especially in the novels following *Northanger Abbey* where the operation of Gothic conventions can't be read as satire. Let us assume that Austen understood why Gothic fiction was popular and wanted to use those conventions without becoming a Gothic novelist herself (Miles 2002: 42). Let us assume further that to do so she dropped the reference to Gothic architecture but still used Gothic conventions to expose the contradiction between the notion of property in one's person and the more traditional notion of property as land. To test these hypotheses, let us see how she puts these conventions to work in the novel of manners.

Who can forget Mr Woodhouse, selfish monster that he is? Yet he is only the most adorable of a sequence of irresponsible fathers harking back to Radcliffe's M. St Aubert. Mr Woodhouse differs from Mr Dashwood, Mr Bennet, and even Sir Thomas Bertram only in that the latter hand over the responsibility for marrying off their daughters to willful and selfish women, while Emma's father hands that responsibility over to Emma herself. The "bad mother" offers Austen's heroine to some lesser Montoni who wants her for something, whether imagined wealth and position or the simple thrill of possessing a woman clearly superior to himself, something other than the wit, reason, kindness, or integrity she has in herself. Austen's novels, like Gothic novels, adhere to the principle that it takes bad parents to create conditions where Gothic flourishes.

A father who abdicates his economic responsibilities, and a mother who aggressively pursues them, together put their daughters in much the same position as a Gothic heroine, vulnerable to poseurs and predators. Ensconced in Hartfield with her father, Emma seems an exception to the Gothic strategy of removal that pulls the foundation of traditional property out from under the heroine and throws her back on whatever property she has in herself: Marianne Dashwood on her sensibility and self-expression, Elinor on her good sense and self-restraint, Elizabeth Bennet on her wit and intelligence, and so forth. But even Emma finally recognizes what she shares with Fanny Price or Elizabeth Bennet, who each have a parent eager to hand her over to an inappropriate husband to bring in property. Austen's opening description of Emma's relation to her father reads like Gothic mismatch: "The evil of the actual disparity in their ages . . . was much increased by his constitution and habits, for having been valetudinarian all his life, without activity of mind or body, he was a much older man in ways than in years" (*E*: 7). In scoffing at the idea that Emma's governess should marry Mr Weston and "have a house of her own," Mr Woodhouse presages Emma's dismal future (*E*: 8). Though drained of the malevolent eroticism that infuses such relationships in Gothic fiction, she is as good as married to her father in that she never gets "a house of her own" in the end.

I am hardly the first to note how often Austen draws on the language of suffering – anxiety, torment, mortification, and despair – to express the heroine's reaction to the humiliation parental dereliction brings upon her. By rendering this suffering with Gothic hyperbole, Austen's wit amuses us at the heroine's expense. Anticipating a letter from Willoughby, Marianne Dashwood receives one from her mother instead, "and in the acuteness of the disappointment which followed such an extasy of more than hope, she felt as if, till that instant, she had never suffered" (*SS*: 202). "We may treat it as a joke," as Robert Ferrars explains on hearing that his brother forfeited his inheritance to honor his impecunious contract to Lucy Steele, "but upon my soul, it is a most serious business" (*SS*: 298). Though put in the mouth of an otherwise silly man, this statement serves as a coda for the whole novel. The threats tormenting Austen's protagonists would be no laughing matter if not represented with Gothic excess. Disappointed in love, the Dashwood sisters face a future no less bleak than the one Jane Fairfax anticipates in her remove to Ireland as a governess. Fanny Price's benefactor, Sir Thomas, pressures her into a loveless marriage by returning her to her parents' home in Portsmouth, where she finds herself in a home mismanaged by an indolent mother, terrorized by an alcoholic father, and filled to overflowing by unruly siblings. Against this background, Sir Thomas's reason for expelling Fanny from Mansfield Park seems more sinister precisely for being couched in understated terms:

> He certainly wished her to go willingly, but he as certainly wished her to be heartily sick of home before her visit ended; and that a little abstinence from the elegancies and luxuries of Mansfield Park, would bring her mind into a sober state, and incline her to a juster estimate of the value of that home of greater permanence, and equal comfort, of which she had the offer. (*MP*: 369)

The Gothic effect depends on putting the heroine through a form of self-annihilation such that she must conclude she is nothing in and of herself. The teeming house and harbor that await Fanny at Portsmouth are the most obvious instance in Austen's fiction of a heroine suddenly transformed into someone virtually indistinguishable from any other. But even in *Emma*, replacement rather than matchmaking becomes the name of the game, as Harriet Smith, the natural daughter of a man of unknown rank, appears to take Emma's place in Mr Knightley's affections. Likewise, the day after he is refused by Elizabeth Bennet, Mr Collins "scarcely ever spoke to her, and the assiduous attentions which he had been so sensible of himself, were transferred for the rest of the day to Miss Lucas" (*PP*: 115). Here the occasion for comedy, the transfer of interest from one woman to another, can be devastating. Convinced that Willoughby and Edward Ferrars intend to marry other women,

Marianne and Elinor are swept into a kind of death spiral that deprives them of their sensibility and sense, respectively, so that the sisters feel and behave as two halves of one individual. In no other novel does Austen so clearly rely on the device of doubled heroines to demonstrate that whatever their individual virtues, one woman, when detached from her "house," becomes much like another, but every Austen heroine endures a dark moment when she suddenly understands her self is not hers to govern and improve.

Nothing makes this point more effectively than the seduction plot. A staple of Gothic fiction – whose ruins are littered with the remains of women who entrusted their affections, and usually their bodies, property, and children as well, to self-serving men – the rake goes to work behind the scenes of each Austen novel, exposing the interchangeability of women. Lydia Bennet falls under the same spell as Darcy's sister who had nearly eloped with Wickham; Fanny Price rebuffs Henry Crawford who then entices Maria Bertram; just as Colonel Brandon's ward fell victim to temptation, so her illegitimate daughter succumbs to Willoughby, the man who breaks Marianne's heart, and Frank Churchill engages Emma in a flirtation that duplicates and deflects attention from his secret engagement to Jane Fairfax. These suppressed narratives surface during the novel, showing that the past never dies but repeats itself and so insists on the interchangeability of women.

Once we identify the Gothic with the narrative conventions that break apart the two kinds of property formulated by Locke and bring them into contradiction, we are left with the twofold question: why was it necessary to establish this contradiction in the first place, and how did it ensure the continuing popularity of Gothic fiction? We know how Austen did it – namely, by incorporating Gothic tropes within the novel of manners. But how she appealed to a nineteenth-century readership turned on what she rendered phobic by this move.

The Unthinkable

Turning to *Persuasion*, published with *Northanger Abbey* in 1818, we find a heroine threatened with self-annihilation because she *does* belong to a family of some distinction and property: "Anne, with an elegance of mind and sweetness of character, which must have placed her high with any people of real understanding, was nobody with either father or sister: her word had no weight; her convenience was always to give way; – she was only Anne" (*P*: 5). As if it were not enough to stifle her self-expression, first by thwarting her attempt to marry for love, then by encouraging her to marry to secure the family estate, the novel concludes by linking Anne's fate to her poor and debilitated girlhood friend, Mrs Smith. About to slide off the map of those individuals acknowledged for their intrinsic attributes, Mrs Smith is rescued by Captain Wentworth through her friendship with Anne, and she goes from a woman who can barely get by to one who can both enjoy and be appreciated for the property she has in herself, "for her cheerfulness and mental alacrity did not fail her; and while these prime supplies of good remained, she might have bid defiance ever to greater accessions of worldly prosperity" (P: 252). Lest this tribute make her intrinsic property outweigh the advantages of belonging to an established house, the novel gives each a share in the other's abundance. Mrs Smith gains property through Anne's intervention, and Anne gains some of Mrs Smith's cheerfulness through hers, chiastically linking the two kinds of property.

Captive to her family, Anne languishes and "her bloom had vanished early" (P: 6). But once the novel starts, she can afford the luxury of following her heart against the dictates of property because she is no longer attracted to a man who had "nothing but himself" to bring to marriage (P: 26), for Captain Wentworth has "distinguished himself" and "made a handsome fortune" (P: 29–30, Solinger 2006). The navy is exactly what Sir Walter, her father, criticizes it for being, "the means of bringing persons of obscure birth into undue distinction, and raising men to honours which their fathers and grandfathers never dreamt of" (P: 19). In this respect, the navy works counter to Gothic conventions that expose the powerlessness of the property one has in and of oneself once detached from property that descends through a family. However we look at it, some combination of land, wealth, and position is prerequisite to the exchange of personal property that makes for a companionate relationship: "Anne was tenderness itself, and she had the full worth of it in Captain Wentworth's affection" (P: 252). Coming after so many years of their "loving" each other even after "hope is gone" (P: 235), can such a conclusion really be the source of readers' gratification?

Until now, I have used the term "property" as if it were something one either does or does not possess, something solid in contrast with the ineffability of intrinsic attributes. But "property" is not so monolithic as I have implied. There is no such thing as inheritance pure and simple. Austen's novels revolve around conflicting property forms and claims: settlements on second sons, dowries, women who inherit property, purchased commissions in the military, hereditary entailments, widows and children left unprovided for, legal derailments of hereditary arrangements, British estates that depend on colonial plantations, wealth that originates in trade, and so forth. The result is a snarl of competing interests. When Admiral Croft leases Kellynch Hall because Sir Walter Elliot cannot pay his debts; when the heir to the baronetcy, Anne's cousin Walter, fears that Sir Walter will sire a son and deprive him of an inheritance; when this same Walter refuses to help Mrs Smith recover the money coming to her on her husband's death; how can we know what belongs to whom? Anne's life – including her initial rejection of Wentworth, her visit to Uppercross and then to Bath, as well as her cousin's offer of marriage – is choreographed by a need to maintain the family estate.

If contemporary readers fasten onto the concept of property in oneself as the more problematic strand of discourse in Austen's fiction, it is no doubt because we live in an age of embattled democracy, where the situation is the reverse of what it was in Austen's day. The notion of property in oneself, the very substance of the liberal individual, is both firmly established and clearly on the defense in our own century. Reading retrospectively, we enjoy Anne's achievement of a form of individual gratification that would not have been possible had she married a man of title. But Austen's original readership probably did not revel in the triumph of the "little guy," or what was then an emergent form of value, over and above distinctions based on rank. Self-ownership in the fiction during Austen's time serves much the same purpose Warren Montag attributes to that form of property in Locke: "it consolidates the alliance between the laboring classes and agrarian capitalists, by asserting that any attack on even the largest productive estate simultaneously calls into question the humblest laborer's ownership of his very person" (Montag 2005: 155). While Austen's readership did not encompass this social spectrum, the principle nevertheless applies. By showing the new form of property to be powerless unless backed up with land, Austen's novels provided her readership with a basis for identification. In the process, Gothic conventions rendered each of the two opposing forms of property relatively monolithic. We may smile at the patently artificial endings that reconcile the two forms of property at the conclusion of each Austen novel, but a smile hardly guarantees a novel's success. It is possible to enjoy such an ending because a complex and conflicted tangle of vested interests has been torn apart and consolidated into a binary opposition. Thus we must ask what Austen accomplished by creating this contradiction in the first place: what do the two kinds of property, as she represents them, allow her to exclude from consideration?

Austen's way of posing a contradiction among forms of property makes the world feel whole, as if virtually anyone can claim one form of property, if not another. Of all her novels, *Persuasion* makes it most obvious what cannot be thought, much less discussed, when all the world is property. In this novel, Austen reverses her own formula and fashions a heroine out of material she had previously dismissed as lacking intrinsic value, namely, all the faceless Miss Greys and Miss Mortons, women whom men pursue strictly for the property attached to them. It follows that Anne cannot receive acknowledgment for the property she has in herself by marrying into a "house," as she would were she to accept her cousin's proposal. Instead, she rejects a house in the country in favor of a ship in the Royal Navy.

Austen goes to some lengths to establish a warship as an ideal home. "Women may be as comfortable on board, as in the best house in England," Mrs Croft assures Mrs Musgrove early on in the novel (*P*: 69). Why should a novel take pains to transform a ship into a home, if not to turn the English home into a vehicle capable of extending the English definition of property throughout the world? As it insists that British domesticity can be established virtually anywhere, Captain Wentworth's floating household directs our attention to the very threat that it endeavors to keep at bay: "the dread of a future war [was] all that could dim [Anne's] sunshine" (*P*: 252). The timing of this reminder of war is notably bad, suggesting, against the background of turbulence, that the principle of property is up for grabs. But Austen's other novels also contain within them the traces of what they strive to render unthinkable.

Northanger Abbey intimates that the world of property is not all that stable. Overhearing Catherine repeat the rumor of "something very shocking" in London, something "more horrible than anything we have met with yet," Eleanor Tilney implores her "to satisfy me as to this dreadful riot." As if to render the idea of a riot impossible, Henry ridicules it by showing that Catherine was referring to "nothing more dreadful" than a new Gothic novel. But he also lends substance to the idea by explaining that his sister is imagining "a mob of three thousand men assembling in St. George's Fields; the Bank attacked, the Tower threatened, the streets of London flowing with blood, a detachment of the 12th Light Dragoons . . . to quell the insurgents" (*NA*: 113). Austen's other novels offer briefer glimpses of a wider world that puts property in question: Colonel Brandon "was with [his] regiment in the East Indies" while the woman he loved, having been forced into marriage with his older brother, ran off, became pregnant, and contracted consumption (*NA*: 206); Edward Said calls attention to Sir Thomas's property in Antigua and his involvement with slavery (1994: 25); and closer to home, within a half mile of Highbury to be exact, are the gypsies who appear out of nowhere to frighten Harriet Smith out of a shilling. Lacking respect for private property and insisting on their rights to travel freely, settle nowhere, and live off the excesses of the well-to-do, Austen's gypsies call up the specter of the migratory laborers who roamed the English countryside and set fire to farms that refused them work (Thompson 1971).

Pride and Prejudice alone seems to lack any trace that cannot be integrated into a world made all of property. If *Persuasion* can be called Austen's melancholic novel, *Pride and Prejudice* is the "too light & bright & sparkling" novel, the one that Austen felt "wants shade." But she came no closer to identifying that missing element than expressing a regret that she hadn't included something external to the plot or even to the novel itself, "an Essay on Writing, a critique on Walter Scott, or the history of Buonaparte – or anything that would form a contrast & bring the reader with increased delight to the playfulness and Epigrammatism of the general stile" (*Letters*: 203).

D. A. Miller rightly observed that had Austen found her fiction wanting, she could have worked such a topic into her plots (Miller 2003: 102). The missing element cannot be named. Property provides the conceptual ground on which her fiction, like Radcliffe's, is constructed, and from property, Austen builds a world over which her words sustain the illusion of complete command. Yet at arbitrary points in her other novels, phenomena that challenge the integrity and solidity of property, phenomena that do not belong in a world of property, emerge within it and are almost instantaneously dispersed (the gypsies), relegated to the margins (slavery), pushed into the past (the British presence in the East Indies), or into the future (war). At such moments the Gothic – which exposes the ephemerality of property – and realism, for which property is contrastingly intractable, become one and the same.

FURTHER READING

Armstrong, N. (2005). *How Novels Think: The Limits of Individualism from 1719–1900*. New York: Columbia University Press.

Macpherson, Sandra (2003). Rent to own; or, what's entailed in *Pride and Prejudice. Representations*, 82, 1–23.

Miles. R. (2002). The 1790s: the effulgence of Gothic. In J. E. Hogel (Ed.). *The Cambridge Companion to Gothic Fiction* (pp. 41–62). Cambridge, UK: Cambridge University Press.

Miller, D. A. (2003). *Jane Austen, or The Secret of Style*. Princeton, NJ: Princeton University Press.

Montag, W. (2005). On the function of the concept of origin: Althusser's reading of Locke. In S. H. Daniel (Ed.). *Current Continental Theory and Modern Philosophy* (pp. 148–61). Evanston, IL: Northwestern University Press.

O'Farrell, M. A. (1997). *Telling Complexions: The Nineteenth-Century English Novel and the Blush*. Durham, NC: Duke University Press.

Part IV
Political, Social, and Cultural Worlds

21

From Politics to Silence: Jane Austen's Nonreferential Aesthetic

Mary Poovey

. . . from politics, it was an easy step to silence. (Northanger Abbey)

During the 1780s, the implementation of the 1774 Booksellers' Act gradually eroded the publishing monopoly that had stifled the English book trade for much of the eighteenth century, and, by the middle of the next decade, the market had become receptive to aspiring authors to a hitherto unprecedented extent. Even during the war with France, the number of new works of fiction continued to increase annually. After a brief retreat during the most frightening years, from 1793 through 1795, the industry rebounded, issuing 91 new novels in 1796, then 79 and 75 in each of the next two years, respectively; a large number of these – 28 in 1798 – were Minerva Press Gothics (Garside, Raven, and Scholwerling 2000). At the same time that sensational fiction was dominating the book market, William Godwin declared that "literature" was the "engine" driving political change, and government officials began carefully monitoring all print for signs of seditious libel (Godwin in Keen 2004: 3). In this context of commercial possibility and heightened political sensitivities, an eager young writer would have had much reason to hope that her first venture would succeed and equal reason to worry that it might be taken the wrong way – as too topical, too political, or simply too escapist. In 1797, when Jane Austen tried to enter the print market with *First Impressions*, she was presumably aware of these matters, but she was not deterred. What did deter her was the lack of interest her prospective publisher, Cadell and Davies, showed in the manuscript when they returned it, unread, to the would-be author.

In this essay I argue that the social and political conditions under which Austen composed and revised her novels are almost impossible for modern readers to recover from the texts themselves, *even though* the published novels contain allusions to events with which we know Austen was familiar. In a moment I will speculate about *why* Austen so carefully managed the historical traces her novels contain, but my initial goal is to describe the narrative system she developed to do so. This system, which enabled Austen simultaneously to register and to deflect attention away from histori-cal realities, deemphasizes the capacity of language to refer to actual events, and stresses instead the medium of representation itself. Because the aesthetic that under-writes this system has profoundly influenced both subsequent novelistic practice and the institution of literary criticism within which so many of us now read her novels, it is important to understand how it works before we attempt to recover why it might have seemed so appealing at the beginning of the nineteenth century.

Pride and Prejudice – the name under which the revised *First Impressions* was finally published in 1813 – contains several linked sets of allusions to historical circum-stances that we know directly affected Jane Austen. Because these references do not all take the same form, reviewing them individually will help us see how the novel encourages the reader to subordinate a referential understanding of language to an engagement with the theme of representation. The first set consists of allusions to the militia, which appear primarily in volumes one and two. If we were to read them referentially, these passages would invoke the war with France, which most directly affected Austen through her brother Henry, who joined the Oxfordshire militia in 1793. While it is possible to use these passages to specify the novel's historical setting (1794 or 95), however, two features discourage us from treating these allusions as literal references. First, the name of the militia is blanked out, with the conventional eighteenth-century long dash formulation ("the ——shire," *PP*: 74). Second, and more importantly, nearly every mention of the militia downplays the protective function that real militias played in the 1790s. Instead of representing the soldiers defending England, these passages either place individual soldiers in or adjacent to commercial establishments (as when Colonel Forster and Captain Carter are depicted "standing in Clarke's [circulating] library," *PP*: 30) or specifically associate the soldiers with the "double danger" of inappropriate romantic attachments and the allure of expensive finery (as when Brighton is said to pose the "double danger [of] a watering place and a camp" or when Lydia reports socializing with the soldiers and purchasing "a new gown, or a new parasol," *PP*: 237, 238).

The way the text presents the militia, then, tends to discourage readers from refer-ring Austen's passages to real military men like Henry, much less to the war being waged beyond Britain's shore. The militia allusions thus minimize the effect that references to the actual war might have had both in the action of the novel and for its readers – especially those who, like Jane Austen, had relatives who might have come to harm. A second set of allusions, which picks up and elaborates the theme of dangerous commerce, is considerably more prominent in the novel and correspond-ingly more consequential. Such allusions invoke another situation we know to have been familiar to Jane Austen: insufficient finances. The Austen family had never been wealthy and, with Austen's father making less than £100 a year in 1797, Jane's letters reveal constant worries about money during the entire period in which she composed, revised, and published *Pride and Prejudice*. In 1797, Jane's personal savings totaled only £7; in 1801, when the family sold almost everything in preparation for the move to Bath, she watched her books and writing desk go with considerable sadness (*Letters*:

84, 85); and in 1805, when Jane's father's death further impoverished the family, Henry had to lend the family £50 to help it stay afloat.

In the first three quarters of *Pride and Prejudice*, money is mentioned only twice, both in incidental ways: in the first, Lydia borrows money from Jane and Elizabeth to "treat" her sisters to lunch at the Meryton inn (*PP*: 219); in the second, the Gardiners pay their bill at another inn when they are suddenly recalled to Longbourne (p. 281). As soon as the narrative reveals that Wickham has eloped with Lydia, however, the subject of money virtually explodes into the text, and references to it quickly amass the coherence of a full-fledged plot. Even after it makes its presence known, however, this money plot initially unfolds away from the narrative we read, for the events it includes all occur in places that Elizabeth, the novel's principle focalizer, does not occupy. Thus, because Lydia has been allowed to follow the militia to Brighton and Elizabeth is traveling with the Gardiners, Elizabeth first hears about her sister's elopement through a letter from Jane, who has stayed behind in London. This same letter also reveals that Colonel Forster fears that Wickham might have no intention of marrying Lydia (*PP*: 273). Finally, when Elizabeth's father and Mr Gardiner go to London, they discover (and then report) that Wickham is deep in debt and that he now demands money to marry Lydia. Thus the subject of money erupts into the domestic plot through a mode of narration that calls attention to its status as representation (the letters) but it does so because of a role it has long played in an unnarrated, but profoundly consequential, money plot: all the while that he was flirting with Elizabeth and Lydia, Wickham was incurring bills he could not pay.

What we are seeing here is a narrative that embeds its allusions to real situations in a complex system that simultaneously invokes these situations and manages their effects – both in the narrative and, as a consequence, for the reader. Thus far, we have seen two of the forms this management takes: the foreclosure of reference, which is clearest in the military allusions; and direction of the reader's attention, which is achieved by controlling access to various plots and the information they contain. This last dynamic foregrounds the mediation that representation performs, both as a theme in the novel and, through the embedded letters, as a distinctive mode of narration. In *Pride and Prejudice*, the reader can experience the real threat that war and family debt might have posed for a young woman like Elizabeth only by – and through the buffer of – an imaginative engagement with the novel's domestic romance. As my description suggests, this narrative management operates within the textual system at the same time that it polices its borders. Thus, for the first three quarters of the novel, the narrative's focus on the domestic plot blocks the reader's access to the money plot; as it does, it implicitly discourages a literal reading of the novel's events and actively modulates the reader's response to the danger an actual lack of money would have posed. Over the course of the narrative, Austen adds a third mode of management to the two I have just described: she gradually recasts or translates the money plot's primary terms into another set of terms that promise comfort instead of posing a threat. Thus Austen transforms the fiscal jeopardy the Bennet girls face into a romantic threat, which, while potentially emotionally painful, can be solved within the domestic plot. Bringing the money plot out from under the romantic plot inaugurates this transformation, for only after events that are initially kept in the background of the narrative system become the primary strand of narration can Austen begin to rework their terms.

This reworking begins when it becomes obvious that Lydia poses a financial threat to her family. Initially, the amount Wickham demands seems like a sum the Bennets can manage: a settlement of the girl's share of the 5,000 pounds she is to receive upon her parents' death and 100 pounds a year for her father's lifetime (*PP*: 302). But Mr Bennet immediately realizes that this cannot be correct, and, in a conversation between Mr Bennet and his oldest daughters, the magnitude of the danger suddenly becomes clear. "There are two things that I want very much to know," Mr Bennet tells Jane and Elizabeth in his characteristically laconic way: "one is, how much money your uncle has laid down, to bring it about; and the other, how I am ever to pay him" (*PP*: 304). His daughters' shock forces their father to be more explicit. "'Money! my uncle!' cried Jane, 'what do you mean, Sir?'" When Mr Bennet speculates that 10,000 pounds is probably Wickham's real asking price, one of the girls bursts out again: "Ten thousand pounds! Heaven forbid! How is half such a sum to be repaid?" (*PP*: 304). At this point, the narrative foregrounds the monetary issues that, within the narrative system, have always underwritten the domestic plot and also lays out the monetary arrangements that will dictate the future: the narrator informs us that Mr Bennet never saved any money; Mr Bennet says he will not advance money for Lydia's wedding clothes; Mr Gardiner uncovers exactly how much Wickham owes; and we find out that Wickham ran away with Lydia only because he was trying to evade his creditors.

The most important revelation about money, however, does not appear in these scenes, but in another letter, which begins to neutralize the twin threats of poverty and disgrace the money plot introduces. In this letter, Mrs Gardiner informs Elizabeth that Darcy, not her uncle, paid off Wickham's debts (*PP*: 321ff). Instead of wondering how much money Darcy paid, Elizabeth's first response is to imagine that he has done this for her. Only after she has indulged this fantasy does she realize that the obligation the Bennets have thus incurred can never be repaid in kind. Soon, Mr Bennet makes it clear that *if Mr Gardiner had paid Wickham*, the "obligation" would have been financial and the "return" would have had to be cash. Since Darcy has paid the money, however, this particular obligation has been dissolved:

> "And so, Darcy did every thing; made up the match, gave the money, paid the fellow's debts, and got him his commission! So much the better. It will save me a world of trouble and economy. Had it been your uncle's doing, I must and *would* have paid him; but these violent young lovers carry every thing their own way. I shall offer to pay him to-morrow; he will rant and storm about his love for you, and there will be an end of the matter." (*PP*: 377)

As this passage makes clear, Darcy's actions neutralize the threat that a monetary obligation would have posed to the Bennets by translating debt into a gift of love.

Even before Mr Bennet makes this explicit, in fact, Darcy has already alluded to this translation by rebuffing Elizabeth's attempt to thank him on behalf of her family. "Your *family* owe me nothing," he says to Elizabeth in the scene in which she expresses this gratitude. "Much as I respect them, I believe, I thought only of *you*" (*PP*: 366). Once Elizabeth says she will marry Darcy, he completes this translation by saying that he "owes" her for the rebuke she has given his pride (*PP*: 369). Thus, by marrying Darcy, Elizabeth is able to "repay" him – not in money, but in love. And by making the money plot first disrupt, then be absorbed by, the domestic plot, Austen translates a monetary debt into mutual love.

In the narrative system that is *Pride and Prejudice*, these translations – the transformation of a financial payment into the bestowal of a gift, then the conversion of the gift into love – address and symbolically resolve the threat that the money plot posed to its romance counterpart. This resolution culminates when the money plot is banished from the novel, as the romantic relationships the narrative has long followed conclude successfully in marriages. The event that initiates this resolution is actually not Darcy's decision to help Wickham but Elizabeth's change of heart about Darcy, for, as the passage I have just quoted reveals, he acts in order to respond to or communicate with her. Elizabeth begins to change her mind because of a series of portraits of Darcy: the letter Darcy writes to explain his relationship with Wickham, then two images of the gentleman that Elizabeth encounters at Pemberley. The letter inaugurates the change, but it is not until she arrives at his family estate, hears the admiring servant's praise of Darcy, and then sees the portrait that hangs in Pemberley's gallery that Elizabeth realizes she has been wrong. At this point, Elizabeth knows that she would now accept Darcy if he were to offer again, and, for the first time, she imagines the fantastic scenario to which the narrative is leading: marriage with Darcy and herself as mistress of Pemberley.

In this scene and in the events it precipitates, we see Austen foregrounding representation – moving it from a mode of narration (the letters) to a subject worthy of notice in and of itself. As a theme addressed in and as a component of *Pride and Prejudice*, representation first distorts, then reveals the true value that Darcy and his family estate embody. This has been obscured for much of the novel, for until Elizabeth reads Darcy's letter, the reader has had access to him only through the focalization of other characters – first Wickham, who has a reason to misrepresent Darcy's character, and then Elizabeth, whose mediation, unbeknownst to the reader and to her, is prejudicial because prejudiced. Until Elizabeth – and, with her, the reader – learns to see the mediation that representation always involves, she – and we – do not have access to the value Darcy incarnates because we cannot see him as he really is. This is the lesson Elizabeth gradually learns from Darcy's letter, the housekeeper's words, and the portrait at Pemberley: seeing these objects as mediations gradually teaches Elizabeth to look at how information is conveyed, who conveys it, and where it surfaces. Once Elizabeth learns this – once Darcy's true value is revealed and the two lovers reach their mutual understanding – the subject of representation goes the way of the money plot: it disappears from the novel. As a theme, the subject of representation is banished from the novel when Darcy clears the way for Bingley and Jane to marry by explaining to his friend that he – Darcy – had previously not disclosed Jane's presence in London because he had misinterpreted her interest in Bingley. With that misrepresentation and that misunderstanding out of the way, the path is clear to the double marriages in which the novel culminates.

I need to describe one additional aspect of this dynamic before I can begin to suggest why Austen might have developed such a complex, nonreferential narrative system. In the action of the novel, Elizabeth's change of heart about Darcy is not quite sufficient to initiate the actions that bring about the happy ending, for Elizabeth must find a way to convey this change to Darcy, who, as a man, is uniquely qualified to act. Austen narrates the sequence in which this happens in a manner that is extraordinarily complex, even for this complexly narrated novel. Elizabeth rehearses her revelation late in the novel, in the exchange in which she and Darcy playfully try to recover the "foundation" of their love (*PP*: 380). In this dialogue, Elizabeth associates her revelation that she had come to admire Darcy with what she describes as a "resolution" to thank him for finding Wickham and smoothing the way to Lydia's marriage. In retrospect, Elizabeth claims to consider this act a "breach" – not just of etiquette, but of some "promise": "My resolution of thanking you for your kindness to Lydia had certainly great effect," Elizabeth jokes. "Too *much*, I am afraid; for what becomes of the moral, if our comfort springs from a breach of promise, for I ought not to have mentioned the subject?" (*PP*: 381). This claim/disclaimer is interesting not simply because, syntactically, it takes the form of a declarative sentence that is also interrogatory, but also because it culminates a sequence of references that has no origin in the text itself. In volume III, chapter 18, Elizabeth remembers, and refers the reader to, an earlier scene depicted in the novel, but this scene (III: 16), which describes her "resolution," seems to refer to a still earlier moment, which is not narrated. In volume III, chapter 16, which details the "breach of promise" to which Elizabeth refers in chapter 18, the narrative describes and Elizabeth executes her "resolution": "I can no longer help thanking you for your unexampled kindness to my poor sister," Elizabeth blurts out. "Ever since I have known it, I have been most anxious to acknowledge to you how gratefully I feel it" (*PP*: 365). When we go back to the scene to which this refers, however, the scene that describes Elizabeth's discovery that Darcy found Wickham and paid his debts (III: 10), we find no description of Elizabeth reaching such a "resolution." Instead, the narrative presents Mrs Gardiner's letter, which conveys the information to Elizabeth, then devotes a paragraph to the "flutter of spirits" Elizabeth experiences, and then turns its attention to Wickham, who interrupts Elizabeth's reflections and the narrative's description of her response (*PP*: 326–7).

If there is no textual origin for the resolution Elizabeth claims to have made to thank Darcy, Austen does mention another "resolution" that Elizabeth also makes between the time she learns of Darcy's generosity (III: 10) and the moment she actually thanks him (III: 16). Elizabeth reaches this resolution in apparently unpremeditated response to another "resolution," Lady Catherine De Bourgh's "resolution to prevent [Darcy's and Elizabeth's] marriage" (*PP*: 360). When Lady Catherine demands that Elizabeth promise not to enter into an engagement with Darcy, Elizabeth retorts: "I am only resolved to act in that manner, which will, in my own opinion, constitute my happiness, without reference to *you*, or to any person so wholly unconnected with me" (*PP*: 358). While it is difficult to see how this resolution could be the same resolution to which Elizabeth refers, in volume III, chapter 18, as her "breach of promise," Austen does present it as the resolution that animates Darcy, for he says that it was Lady Catherine's reference to this outburst, and not Elizabeth's "eager desire of expressing [her] gratitude" that led him to renew his proposal. "My aunt's intelligence had given me hope, and I was determined at once to know every thing" (*PP*: 381).

I have so carefully detailed this sequence because its function is so central to the novel – this is the exchange in which the obfuscations of misrepresentation and misunderstood representation are dispelled – and because I can find no textual way to account for its peculiar structure, as a sequence of references that points either to an unnarrated event or to a narrated event that uses the same word but is clearly *not* the event to which Elizabeth refers. While the nonreferential aesthetic I have been describing makes it impossible to know for sure, I suggest that the peculiarity of this sequence contains a clue about why such an aesthetic might have seemed appealing to Jane Austen. For what this sequence enacts is the capacity of representation to block or waylay reference, and this subject – the problematic nature of the relationship between representation and that to which it supposedly refers – was rendered inescapable by the historical situation in which Austen composed and revised *Pride and Prejudice*. This situation rapidly developed during the spring of 1797, when Austen was presumably making *First Impressions* ready for its (unsuccessful) submission to Cadell and Davies. Like the breach of promise that Elizabeth associates with her resolution to thank Darcy, the event that brought this situation to a head – the passage, in May, of the Bank Restriction Act – also sanctioned a breach of promise: the act allowed the Bank of England to ignore the promise printed on the face of each of its notes to redeem paper notes with gold. By so doing, the Bank Restriction Act created a monetary and epistemological situation that resembles the narrative dynamic I have been describing. Just as Austen suspends or waylays the textual referent of Elizabeth's "resolution" in the pages of *Pride and Prejudice*, so the Bank Restriction Act, in relieving the Bank of England of its obligation to pay, disrupted what had previously seemed to be the referential nature of paper money: whereas the Bank notes had (presumably) once referred to the gold that backed them, after the Restriction, they referred, at best, to something else – the public's confidence that paper would function as money; at worst, as many people feared, the notes referred to nothing and thus had no value at all. By making the *merely* representational nature of paper money visible, then, the Bank Restriction Act inaugurated a situation that threatened to imperil the "comfort" of England. I suggest that it was, in part at least, to acknowledge this situation, but also to manage the anxieties it aroused, that Austen developed an aesthetic capable of alluding to, and symbolically reworking, the actual conditions in which she composed and revised this novel.

The formal homology between Austen's narrative treatment of Elizabeth's broken promise and the epistemological effect of the Restriction Act does not, by itself, *prove* that Austen had the Restriction Act in mind when she composed or revised *Pride and Prejudice*. I can – and will – adduce additional evidence to support this conjecture, but I want to insist that, given the nonreferential nature of her aesthetic, *no* evidence from inside or outside the text could conclusively prove such a claim. I have found no explicit reference to the Restriction Act in any of Austen's writing, and even her epistolary allusions to banks and high prices, which I cite in a moment, do not prove that she blamed the Restriction for the monetary volatility that persisted throughout the time in which she worked on *Pride and Prejudice*. Taken together, however, all of this circumstantial evidence seems to me to make a strong case for this conjecture, and seeing the broken promises authorized by the Restriction behind the fictional promises whose violation brings about the happy ending of *Pride and Prejudice* helps to explain why Austen used not one, but *three*, breaches of promise to initiate her happy ending. To support my case, let me elaborate why the Restriction Act was so important and potentially so disruptive.

The Bank Restriction Act was implemented to prevent a run on the Bank of England, which the Bank's directors had begun to fear early in 1797 when French warships were rumored to be anchored off England's coast preparing to invade. The directors convinced Parliament, and then the king, that if enough people responded to this threat by demanding gold, the Bank would break, since its gold reserve was not and had never been large enough to secure all of the circulating paper. Because the nation's creditworthiness was tied to the solvency of the Bank, such an event would have had disastrous consequences – not just for the Bank's shareholders and government officials, but for the economic and political security of Britain as well. Originally intended to last only six months, the Restriction Act remained in force until 1821 – in other words, for the remainder of Jane Austen's life.

Austen's contemporaries fiercely debated the question of whether it was the Bank Restriction Act that caused the volume of currency to increase so dramatically, but, whatever they decided about this, no one could escape the price volatility an inflated currency caused. Jane Austen repeatedly registered this in her letters, when she cited the prices of many of the things she bought. In the spring of 1797, two platoons of sailors mutinied, partly to protest the fluctuating value of the military's wages. These mutinies, at Spithead and Nore, might well have reminded Austen of another mutiny, which had occurred in 1795 and which involved Henry's military unit, the Oxford-shire militia, for this mutiny also protested inflated prices. In the wake of the Restriction Act, and partly because of these military protests, money became a controversial and intensely political matter at the turn of the nineteenth century. Money remained a political issue for the nearly quarter of a century that ensued, even though the Bank did not break, for the rise in prices and the fall in the value of Bank notes eroded public confidence in the Bank and in the government it supported. Since public confidence was the only remaining basis for Great Britain's public credit and its circulating currency, any erosion of public confidence threatened public credit, the likelihood that the Bank's notes would pass as money, and the ability of the government to fund the protection of the nation.

Even if we do not know what Austen thought about the Bank Restriction Act, we do know that she was familiar with banks and with the relatively new banking industry more generally. We know this both because Jane joked with Henry about a "fantasy bank" in an early letter (Nokes 1997: 134) and because Henry became a partner in an actual bank in 1805; this was the source of the £50 he gave his family that year. (The bank failed in 1816.) We can only infer that Austen was putting the finishing touches on *First Impressions* during the months in which legislators discussed relieving the Bank of its obligation to pay, but we know for a fact that she revised the manuscript during the Restriction Period, for she had to have begun the revisions some time after Cadell and Davies rejected the manuscript in November 1797. If B. C. Southam is correct in dating these revisions to 1809–12 (Southam 1964), then Austen reworked the manuscript during the height of the Restriction period, when it was clear that the Act's original term had expired and no one could have known when – or even if – England would restore the Bank's money to its customary basis in gold.

It is this social situation – a state of fiscal, political, and epistemological uncertainty provoked by the sudden visibility of the role that representation had always played in Britain's credit economy – that I think inspired Austen to develop the nonreferential aesthetic I have been describing. I am suggesting that Austen developed this aesthetic to manage the anxieties this social situation produced. The narrative system I have described manages these anxieties partly, as I have demonstrated, by foreclosing reference; but partly, as I have also argued, it manages them by raising the actual issues that provoked them in the safe, because fictional, world of the novel and by translating the form they actually took into other terms, which a complex narrative system could rework and dismiss. Finally, this narrative system provided a symbolic resolution to real anxieties by foregrounding the theme and effects of representation because the idea that representation is a *problem* was precisely what Austen's contemporaries had to learn to overlook.

Identifying the Restriction Act in the background of *Pride and Prejudice* also helps me explain the tone in which the novel's famously fantastic conclusion is cast. Like the novel's narrative system, its tone is complex and multilayered, but each of its resonances, like the dynamics of the narrative, can be referred to the Restriction. Most obviously, the novel's conclusion is gratifying and would have reassured the novel's readers: if three broken promises could bring about Elizabeth's marriage to Darcy (Lydia's promise not to disclose that Darcy attended her wedding, Mrs Gardiner's promise not to reveal Darcy's payment of Wickham's debts, and the "promise" Elizabeth breached in thanking Darcy), then surely the Bank's violation of its promise would bring no harm to the nation. Beneath this reassurance, however, the conclusion also sounds a second tone, the irony for which Austen is justifiably famous. As the signal of an author's awareness that a gap always separates words from the meanings they convey, irony is the signature of representation-made-visible – that is, of the very fact about representation that the Restriction made visible. And third, the nostalgia the conclusion conveys, as the tonal mark of lost possibilities, expresses what passage of the Restriction Act made clear and what must have grown more obvious as the Restriction period dragged on: the power associated with landed gentlemen like Darcy was beginning to wane in favor of the power exercised by the moneyed men who backed the Restriction. Whatever its other effects, after all, the Restriction Act and its prolongation made it clear that the Bank of England's directors were successfully equating the interests of the Bank – and not the landed gentry – with the welfare of the nation as a whole. Thus the gentle rebuke Elizabeth deals to herself – "what becomes of the moral, if our comfort springs from a breach of promise" – preserves what Darcy represents in a kind of historical aspic, memorializing the comfort he can confer in the novel as an appealing, but increasingly distant, possibility for Austen and her readers. The way in which Austen memorializes the possibility associated with Darcy is also deeply ironic, of course, for sanctioning the violation of Lydia's and Mrs Gardiner's and Elizabeth's promises can clear the way for Elizabeth to know, and for Darcy to act upon, their mutual love, but sanctioning the Bank's violation of its promise to pay, as this resolution implicitly does, acceded to the transformation of political power that was already beginning to marginalize Britain's actual landed gentry.

The anxieties that we know the Bank Restriction Act to have provoked in many of Jane Austen's contemporaries register in *Pride and Prejudice*, if they do at all, in a muted and indirect way – through the complex dynamics of a narrative that forecloses reference, the thematic and formal treatment of representation, and the ambiguous register of tone. But this makes sense, too, for, unlike her more radical peers, Austen did not want literary writing to be a political engine, nor did she want simply to provide escapist fantasies for her readers. The aesthetic she developed, which curtails reference by raising, then dismissing, the issue of representation, constituted an engagement with the social situation that her readers could experience, but not find distressing. That this engagement was complex as well as enjoyable should come as no surprise – given the complexity by which Austen made Elizabeth Bennet's engagement to Darcy so pleasurable for readers to share.

FURTHER READING

Garside, Peter, James Raven, Rainer Scholwerling (Eds) (2000). *The English Novel 1770–1829*. Oxford: Oxford University Press.

Keen, Paul (Ed.) (2004). *Revolutions in Romantic Literature: An Anthology of Print Culture, 1780–1832*. Ontario: Broadview Press.

Le Faye, Deirdre (1997). *Jane Austen's Letters: New Edition*. New York: Oxford University Press.

Nokes, David (1997). *Jane Austen. A Life*. Berkeley and Los Angeles: University of California Press.

Southam, B. C. (1964). *Jane Austen's Literary Manuscripts*. London: Oxford University Press.

22

The Army, the Navy, and the Napoleonic Wars

Gillian Russell

I

Jane Austen grew to maturity as a writer during one of the most significant conflicts in British history – the Revolutionary and Napoleonic Wars of 1793–1815. Apart from the Peace of Amiens of 1802–3 and the temporary "peace" of 1814, Britain was at war with France for an exhausting 22 years. The first truly "world" war, fought in many theatres on both land and sea, the struggle against France had profound effects on many levels of British society – political, cultural, and economic. By 1814 a quarter of a million men were serving in the regular army, while the navy grew tenfold between 1789 and 1812. However, as Linda Colley has shown in an influential argument, more than bodies were mobilized in defense of the nation (Colley 1992). The French Wars also entailed a struggle for hearts and minds and had an enduring effect on nation formation, as patriotic loyalty was encouraged in order to counter the French threat abroad and its domestic counterpart, radical disaffection, at home. What it meant to be a "true" Briton became an ideological battleground, as keenly disputed as the English Channel or the field of Waterloo. While no battles were fought on the British mainland during the Wars, the impact of the conflict was inescapable, particularly in the region which Austen knew best – the south-east of England. Between 1798 and 1803 when invasion by Napoleon's forces was felt to be imminent, the south coast was on full alert, the resources of the auxiliary home defense force, the militia, being augmented by volunteers, the first attempt at mass mobilization in British history. It is estimated that by 1804 around half a million men, consisting of regular soldiers, the militia, and the volunteers, were under arms in Britain.

Austen had a personal interest in the fortunes of war in the form of the career of her brother Henry, who joined the Oxfordshire Militia in 1793 and later became an army agent. Henry's military connections underpinned his later venture into banking and were also relevant, as I will suggest, to Austen's emergence as a published writer. Two other brothers, Francis (Frank) and Charles, had more conspicuous careers in the

Royal Navy, Frank rising ultimately to the rank of Admiral of the Fleet (in 1863) while Charles became a Rear Admiral and Commander-in-Chief of the East India and China Station (1850). Both men were on active service when Austen was writing her major novels. In spite of these contexts, Austen's fiction has traditionally been regarded as incurious about the subject of war, though that view has recently undergone serious revision (see Southam 2005, Fulford 2002, Favret 2005). Soldiers and sailors are as ubiquitous a presence in her novels and letters as they were in the streets, Downs, and coastal waters of southern England. The hum of wartime, if not the blast or cry of battle, pervades her fiction. This chapter will outline two major aspects of Austen's engagement with the wartime conditions of late Georgian Britain: how her fiction addresses the professionalization of the military and its implications for the gentry class to which she belonged; and associated with this, her exploration, particularly in *Persuasion*, of war as a media event. The French Wars are significant, not only for their global scale, but also because they coincided with a major expansion of the print trade and the consolidation of the Romantic reading public. Austen's fiction is remarkable, I will argue, for its representation of how print culture spread news about war, shaping and influencing public opinion; as products of print culture her novels are also part of that very process, with implications for how we interpret them and her achievement as a professional writer.

The army and the navy, in addition to the church, were the main professions open to gentlemen of Austen's class, particularly those without prospects of inheriting wealth and property who needed to make their fortunes. Becoming an officer in the regular army entailed the purchase of a commission and was thus more expensive than joining the militia, the officers of which were chosen by the Lord Lieutenant of the relevant county; as regular army service could involve service overseas it was also riskier than the home-based militia. Austen's militia officers are George Wickham in *Pride and Prejudice*, who seeks refuge in the service after he crosses his patrons in the Darcy family, and *Emma*'s Mr Weston, who comes from a family that is "respectable" and "rising" but of limited financial resources and ambitions (*E*: 15). For both men the militia offers opportunities for geographical and class mobility: it enables Weston to meet and marry the eminent Miss Churchill of Yorkshire, while for Wickham the army is a means to reinvent himself beyond the reach, he thinks, of his Derbyshire connections. Becoming a soldier takes Colonel Brandon in *Sense and Sensibility* even further afield, to the East Indies. Austen implies that as a younger son of a family whose estate is "much encumbered" Brandon had little option but to pursue a military career (*SS*: 205). By suggesting that Brandon's experience of the East would include knowledge of "nabobs, gold mohrs, and palanquins," that is, the trappings of oriental corruption, Willoughby implies that the Colonel's military service was motivated by self-aggrandizement (*SS*: 51). For the Colonel himself, however, soldiering is associated with estrangement and suffering. While he was overseas with his regiment, his first love, Eliza, married against her will to Brandon's brother, had fallen from virtue and it was "nearly three years" before he could return to England to discover her on her death bed (*SS*: 207). Another military officer who speaks "feelingly" about his

position as a younger son is Colonel Fitzwilliam in *Pride and Prejudice* who, in conversation with Elizabeth Bennet, contrasts his situation with that of Darcy: "A
younger son, you know, must be inured to self-denial and dependence" (*PP*: 183).
The very fact that Fitzwilliam is in the army is a sign of the constraints on him as a
gentleman though, as Elizabeth Bennet boldly points out, as a son of an earl he has
very little to complain about. Austen's representation of military service is therefore
an important aspect of her finely calibrated sense of interclass and intraclass, gender,
and familial hierarchies, enabling her to render the different experiences and competitiveness of men such as Willoughby and Brandon, or Fitzwilliam and Darcy, in the
ironic light of the more profound disadvantages of genteel women.

The status of the military as a profession is also raised by Edward Ferrars in *Sense
and Sensibility*. He preferred the church but "that was not smart enough for my family.
They recommended the army. That was a great deal too smart for me" (*SS*: 102). In
nominating the "army," by which Ferrars means an elite regiment in the regular army,
as "too smart," Austen was alluding to the military as a means of access to the "right"
social circles, with possible long-term consequences for a gentleman's career. For most
of the eighteenth century becoming an officer was regarded as a means to an end – the
enhancement of status – rather than as a vocation of intrinsic value to the nation.
Socializing was therefore not merely a distraction from the serious business of war,
but a means of gaining notice, as well as reinforcing the ties with civilian society that
affirmed one's gentlemanly identity. Thus Wickham confides in Elizabeth Bennet that
it was "the prospect of constant society, and good society" that attracted him to the
militia, rather than, implicitly, a burning desire to serve his country (*PP*: 79). *Pride
and Prejudice* as a whole explores the integration of the military into provincial polite
society, in the form of the redcoat presence at balls and assemblies, and the spectacle
of military encampments near places such as Brighton. The latter, part of the mobilization against Napoleon, were also opportunities for communal festivity and entertainment. As I have argued elsewhere, theatricality was crucial to military ideology
and practice in this period (Russell 1995). Display, parade, and ceremonial ritual,
including the ritual of punishment, reinforced the group identity, hierarchy, and
discipline that were essential to the effective conduct of war on the battlefield. The
sociable behavior of soldiers of all ranks – ranging from attendance at balls and play-
houses to drinking in taverns – was an extension of this theatricality, forming a zone
of interaction between military and civilian worlds that was important in maintaining
the bond between the people of Britain and their defenders.

This zone of interaction, as Austen's fiction reveals, had gendered and sexual meanings. The mobility that was intrinsic to military life not only facilitated access for
gentlemen officers into families and social situations that were closed to men whose
rank and background were more normatively fixed, but also endowed the officer with
an additional element of mystery and allure. Hence the appeal of Wickham for the
Bennet girls partly derives from his status as an exotic outsider in Meryton. Captain
Frederick Tilney in *Northanger Abbey* is another officer interloper, whose behavior both
intrigues and baffles Catherine Morland. Described as "a very fashionable-looking,

handsome young man," Tilney has no compunction in using Catherine as a foil in order to conduct a flirtation with Isabella Thorpe, who is engaged to Catherine's brother, in the very public context of the Bath pump rooms (*NA*: 131). Catherine is compelled to sit by in uncomfortable silence as he speaks, "low" and urgently, to Isabella (*NA*: 147). Henry Tilney later attempts to assuage Catherine's anxieties over his brother's interest in Isabella. "His leave of absence will soon expire, and he must return to his regiment," Henry advises. "And what will then be their acquaintance? – The mess-room will drink Isabella Thorpe for a fortnight, and she will laugh with your brother over poor Tilney's passion for a month" (*NA*: 152–3). It is clear that Captain Tilney's visit to Bath was an interlude in active service and therefore subject to the particular conditions and constraints associated with "R and R" – sexual irresponsibility, self-indulgence, even desperation. Henry Tilney's advice to Catherine is both reassurance and a coded warning, his reference to the male homosociality of the mess-room acknowledging the predatory behavior of his brother and the vulnerability of any young woman who flirts with an officer. As a socially responsible man of taste, who combines parish duties with pump room politesse, Henry Tilney is contrasted with his mercurial soldier brother and with his father, the calculating General Tilney who shows Catherine Morland the door of Northanger Abbey when he discovers that she is not an heiress. A soldier who could have seen service in the American War of Independence and who has gained his social position and wealth through marriage, General Tilney represents Austen's sharpest critique of the officer as a man on the make. As Carolyn D. Williams has shown, Austen's depiction of the General may have been influenced by the dubious career of another general, John Gunning (Williams 1998: 41–62). The latter was brother to the celebrity Irish beauties, the Gunning sisters, and owed his career to their influence with their aristocratic husbands. In the early 1790s he became notorious for a complex scandal involving his wife, the novelist Susannah Minifie Gunning, and their daughter Elizabeth Gunning, which culminated in Gunning expelling his wife and child from his household. Soon after, the General was sued for adultery with the wife of a supplier of military uniform. The barrister Thomas Erskine famously apostrophized Gunning as a "hoary lecher." While General Tilney's peccadilloes do not extend beyond the acquisition of the latest china or a Rumford stove, together with his son, the "gallant" Captain Frederick, he reflects the view of the officer class that had prevailed for most of the eighteenth century – as gentlemen who were both inside and outside their class, glamorous defenders of the nation who were also, potentially, its greatest threat.

Such a view conditions Austen's representation of the military in *Pride and Prejudice*. Lydia Bennet swoons at the prospective "glories of the camp" at Brighton: "its tents stretched forth in beauteous uniformity of lines, crowded with the young and the gay, and dazzling with scarlet; and to complete the view, she saw herself seated beneath a tent, tenderly flirting with at least six officers at once" (*PP*: 232). This prospect evokes a satirical print by James Gillray, "Fatigues of the Campaign in Flanders" (1793), depicting generals, including the Duke of York, consorting with female camp

Figure 22.1   James Gillray, *Fatigues of the Campaign in Flanders*, Lewis Walpole Library – 793.5.20.1+.

followers (Figure 22.1). The implicit argument of Gillray's print is that by engaging with "society," here identified with the sexual charms of women, Britain's defenders risked the security of their class, their masculinity and ultimately, their nation. *Pride and Prejudice*, written and published during the height of the Peninsular War, would seem to endorse this view, in its representation of the giddy Lydia "sighing for a soldier" and the superficiality of George Wickham. However, considered as a whole, Austen's fiction suggests a more complex position on changing attitudes towards the officer class in this period. Rather than martial virility being compromised by an engagement with female "society" or, conversely, female "innocence" being exposed to a predatory soldiery, the novels highlight the mutual investment of men and women in the sociable, affective, and erotic dimensions of wartime experience. A striking example of this is the only reference to a rank and file soldier in Austen's work. In *Pride and Prejudice* Elizabeth Bennet returns from her visit to Netherfield to learn from Kitty and Lydia that "several officers, had dined lately with their uncle, a private had been flogged, and it had actually been hinted that Colonel Forster was going to be married" (*PP*: 60). As Tim Fulford has noted, the flogging of soldiers and sailors was politically contentious, part of an antiwar critique by radicals such as William Cobbett (Fulford 2002: 165–8). The insouciance with which the younger Bennet girls refer to the flogging, making it less important than the prospect of Colonel Forster's marriage, suggests their callous immaturity. But the very fact that this "information," in Austen's terms, is conveyed within a network primarily of women also has relevance to the arguments about war in which the critique of flogging featured. A crucial issue for radicals such as Cobbett and John Thelwall was that the army should not be used as an instrument of tyranny against the people. The numerous barracks constructed across England after 1789 were regarded as problematic because they detached the affections and loyalties of the ordinary soldier from the mass of the people to whom he belonged: barracks could corrupt those inside as much as they were capable of oppressing those without. Underlying such critiques was the principle that the military was part of society as a whole, to which it owed obligations and duties. While Austen's fiction does not endorse a radical position on the role of the army, its emphasis on military sociability shares a concern with the place of the armed forces in civilized society. Elizabeth Bennet's curiosity about Colonel Fitzwilliam's career, the delight Lydia takes in a uniform and even gossip about a flogging all suggest that, far from being passive spectators of war, women were implicated too in both its pains and its pleasures.

II

Austen's fiction therefore reflects a profoundly ambivalent view of the military, which only began to change after the victories of the Peninsular War and the emergence of Wellington as a national hero. As a bastion of Britain's imperial and commercial power, the Royal Navy was regarded more positively, but not without some qualification. Admiral Crawford in *Mansfield Park*, who keeps a mistress and whose circle is the target of Mary Crawford's questionable joke about "Rears and Vices," indicates that the senior service could be as worldly as its counterparts in the army. As Brian Southam (2005) has shown, *Mansfield Park* is a study in the workings of patronage in the navy, of which Austen had direct knowledge in the form of the careers of her brothers. The promotion of Fanny Price's brother William is dependent upon the political influence of Sir Thomas Bertram and strings pulled by Admiral Crawford at the behest of his nephew Henry, who wants to ingratiate himself with Fanny. Henry Crawford, like Willoughby, Darcy, and Frank Churchill, is one of those gentlemen whose wealth and familial status mean that military service is optional. He experiences some envy of the fact that Fanny's brother has tested himself, both mentally and physically, in the heat of battle: "he wished he had been a William Price, distinguishing himself and working his way to fortune and consequence with so much self-respect and happy ardour," to which Austen adds crisply "The wish was rather eager than lasting" (*MP*: 236). Crawford's "war envy" is a sign of how the ideological security of the gentleman was beginning to be threatened by changes in the reputation of the military profession as a result of the French wars. The navy, as exemplified by the career of Horatio Nelson, demonstrated that active service in defense of one's country could confer a value and status on the individual surpassing that of rank, defining in the process too a different kind of masculinity, forged by what Crawford discerns in William as "the glory of heroism, of usefulness, of exertion, of endurance" (*MP*: 236).

Austen develops this theme more fully in *Persuasion*, published posthumously in 1818 but set during the peace of 1814 before the renewal of hostilities that culminated in the Battle of Waterloo. In the character of Captain Wentworth, a younger son without a fortune who rises by means of talent and good luck to the rank of captain and £25,000, Austen represents the officer class of the navy as an alternative to the degenerate landed gentry, exemplified by Sir Walter Elliot. Wentworth has the charm of other military characters in Austen's fiction – he is as adept in the concert or dining room as he is on the quarterdeck – but his ease in polite society is contextualized in terms of the more authentic sociability which he practices with his fellow officers, based on mutual respect, informality, steadfastness, and honesty. Anne Elliot encounters this naval brotherhood when she visits the Harvilles at Lyme: Austen's description of naval hospitality as "bewitching" (*P*: 98), a term also applied to the "wit" of Wentworth (*P*: 27), suggests that in their own way naval manners could be as seductive as those of a redcoat. "These would have been all my friends," Anne ponders wistfully (*P*: 98), and in general *Persuasion* commends the naval profession as a more inclusive social model in which women might find a place as "friends" rather than as primarily wives, daughters, or mothers. Austen's emphasis on the navy "at home" – as consumers, readers, and playgoers rather than as distant defenders of the nation – reflects the long-standing concern in her fiction with the familiarity of wartime experience. As Mary Favret has argued (2005), *Persuasion* is suffused with the sense of war as part of the everyday and in particular, with anxiety, loss, and wounding, of both the mind and the body. The pain of war is implicit elsewhere in Austen's fiction, for example in the reference to flogging in *Pride and Prejudice*, the sufferings of Colonel Brandon, or in the life of Jane Fairfax, a war orphan, but *Persuasion* represents her most sustained exploration of war as an affective experience.

The French wars had such an impact, *Persuasion* suggests, largely because of the role of print in mediating them to an eager reading public. The growth in the number of newspapers after 1750, combined with improvements in transport and postal services, meant that news of Britain's wars could be disseminated more quickly and widely than ever before. Families such as the Austens learnt about what was happening in the theatres of war by a combination of the press and private correspondence. Sometimes these media could overlap, as the newspapers relied on dispatches and letters from soldiers and sailors for their information about the wars: in 1800, for example, *The Times* published a letter from Frank Austen to his commander giving details about an action in which his ship, the Petterell, had been involved in the Mediterranean: "I have a lively pleasure," he declared, "that this service has been performed without a man hurt on our part" (Austen 1800). The time taken to convey news of major battles may seem slow in comparison with real-time news coverage of war today – it took 16 days for news of the battle of Trafalgar to reach the Admiralty in London – but once reports had arrived in the metropolis they could be conveyed comparatively quickly via newspapers which normally reached Steventon, for example, one or two days after publication in London. The simultaneity of reading about war in the newspapers helped to define it as a national experience, creating an "imagined community" in Benedict Anderson's terms (1983). Conversely, the anxiety of not knowing, of scanning the newspaper for information that was not there, was also experienced collectively through the medium of print.

The importance of the newspaper as a medium of information about the French Wars and the role of men as gatekeepers of that intelligence are apparent in *Mansfield Park* when Henry Crawford discovers news of William Price's ship by means of his uncle's newspaper, the Admiral "having for many years taken in the paper esteemed to have the earliest naval intelligence" (*MP*: 232). Crawford then uses this news of William to promote his interest with Fanny. Much of Austen's commentary about the Wars in her letters takes the form of the relaying of information about Frank and Charles gleaned from the newspapers: in 1805, for example, she reported to Cassandra that their mother had "seen in the papers that the Urania [Charles's ship] was waiting at Portsmouth for the Convoy for Halifax" (*Letters*: 101). The fact that the Austens could discover information of direct personal interest to them reflects how the Georgian newspaper could combine news of general national importance with specific quotidian detail about fleet movements, battles, promotions, or losses. The men named in this way (and implicitly the women reading about them) were therefore accorded a wider national significance and value: family news was war news and vice versa. Print culture in the form of the newspaper could enable men of Austen's class to achieve publicity and status in a way they never had before, to the envy of stay-at-home gentlemen such as Henry Crawford whose dubious claim to newspaper fame is a mention as "the captivating Mr. C" in the "matrimonial *fracas*" at Wimpole Street (*MP*: 440).

The status of the French Wars as partly a reading event, what Mary Favret has called the period's "war literacy," was a matter of concern to some commentators (Favret 1996: 181). Samuel Taylor Coleridge argued that the private opinions of combatants, some of which made it to the newspapers in the form of letters, were liable to misinterpretation: "The impression made by each Officer on his relatives and connections spreads in ever-widening circles; and from the nature of our imagination, a few particular facts attested by an eye-witness of our own acquaintance, will produce a livelier conviction for, or against, a whole cause, than the clearest general reasonings . . . communicated through the common channels of public information" (1978: 44). Seeking to assert the authority of his own opinion on the war, Coleridge implicitly genders the information flow to and from the battlefields of Spain, contrasting the uncontrollability of feminized "private" talk about war, prone to imaginative excess, with the clarity and rationality of public "information" regulated in the proper channels. It is precisely the circulation of war news in these "ever-widening circles" and the impact of war on the imagination that forms the subject of *Persuasion*. Austen's last completed novel needs to be seen in the context not only of newspaper publicity but also as part of a response to the French Wars by print culture as a whole – in other words, the emergence of a Romantic war literature. Some of this literature took the form of the kind of poetic meditation on war that has become familiar to us from World War I. But equally significant was the literature debating and theorizing war, such as Charles William Pasley's *Essay on the Military Policy and Institutions of the British Empire* (1810) which Austen read in 1813, as well as manuals and treatises giving practical advice to the aspiring soldier and sailor.[1] One notable promoter of the latter kind of text was Thomas Egerton, the publisher of *Sense and Sensibility*, *Pride and Prejudice*, and *Mansfield Park*. From the late 1790s Egerton was mainly known as a publisher and seller of books of military interest, promoting his "Military Library" at Whitehall. It is possible that Henry Austen's military connections, deriving from his period in the Oxfordshire Militia, were a factor in persuading Egerton to publish Jane Austen's novels, which stand out in the publisher's largely military output. This aspect of Egerton's profile has received comparatively little attention in Austen studies: it is relevant because it locates her fiction as a kind of "military library" in its own right, linking her endeavors as a literary professional with her brother Henry's circle and with an entrepreneur such as Egerton.

Another publishing enterprise relating to the French Wars that is directly relevant to Austen's fiction is the *Naval Chronicle*. Established in 1799, this journal claimed to be "open to all the gradations of the Navy": its aims were "to do good, and to give pain to no one," offering a source of "amusement and instruction" to sailors at sea and informing the public as a whole of the value of the naval profession, "by whose exertions Great Britain stands pre-eminent in the scale of political importance" (1799: iii). Its coverage included biographies of notable sailors, "naval poetry" (including prologues and epilogues from shipboard theatricals), a register of naval events, letters containing information about engagements and battles, weather reports from Plymouth and Portsmouth, illustrations by naval artists, accounts of births, deaths, and marriages, and a list of "ships lost, destroyed, captured, and recaptured." The 1799 Prospectus for the journal also stressed the importance of its "Literary Department" which relied on the "Communications of Naval Friends" (n.d.: 2). Austen was certainly familiar with the *Naval Chronicle* as Frank and Charles gave accounts of their exploits in its pages (Southam 2005: 54, 230). The project of the journal – its promotion of the moral utility of the naval profession, its rhetoric of inclusiveness, its intellectual curiosity and emphasis on plain-speaking, its very vocabulary of friendship, doing "good," "exertions" – all suggest that it was a major influence on Austen's fiction and on *Persuasion* in particular. Most importantly, the inclusiveness of the community implied by the *Naval Chronicle* also extended to women. The journal's reference to marriages and births acknowledged women as part of the larger naval "family": in 1814, for example, the birth was announced of Austen's niece Cassandra Eliza, daughter of "Captain Austin [*sic*], of HMS Elephant" (Southam 2005: 291). Some of the notices in the journal were more poignant. In 1799 the death by drowning of a Lieutenant Kinmeer was reported: his father, also serving in the navy, first learnt of his son's death "by seeing it in a newspaper accidentally." In commenting that "the shock can be conceived, but not described," the writers of the *Naval Chronicle* were acknowledging the suffering of war and the role of print in mediating it (1799, vol. II: 548). Austen does something similar in *Persuasion* when Wentworth gives an account of how he was nearly drowned with his sloop, the Asp: "I should only have been a gallant Captain Wentworth, in a small paragraph at one corner of the news-papers; and being lost in only a sloop, nobody would have thought about me." "Anne's shudderings were to herself, alone," Austen comments (*P*: 66). *Persuasion* as a whole is concerned with what it means to imagine and experience conflict in the "ever-widening circles" of those connected with soldiers and sailors in Britain's theatres of war, circles which were increasingly being made more visible by print culture and thereby accorded national political significance. Moreover, Austen suggests that the virtues of those who wait at home were as valuable as those who fought in their name: significantly, the qualities which Henry Crawford envies in William Price – "usefulness," "exertion," "endurance" – are identified with Anne Elliot, suggesting that she, and women in general, were capable of their own "glory of heroism." In its attentiveness to the role of print culture in defining the boundaries of the political nation – the meritocracy represented by the *Navy List* being contrasted with the otiose dynastic histories of the *Baronetage*, Sir Walter Elliot's favorite reading – *Persuasion* also makes implicit claims for the novel itself as a rational "channel of information" about war, and for novel writing itself as a profession of comparable "national importance" to the army and navy.

Austen's fictional representation of wartime was part of a broader phenomenon, a Romantic war literature that is only beginning to receive recognition. Real-life William Prices, and even the private soldier, the flogged nobody of *Pride and Prejudice*, would subsequently use print culture to achieve public names for themselves in the many military memoirs that appeared after 1815. In its deployment and exploration of the power of print and the rehabilitation of the military profession, Austen's fiction reflects the conditions that led to the emergence of these subaltern voices. The after-math of war also features in her novels in the form of the deceptive stability of High-bury in *Emma*, circumscribed by a world of change, or conversely, the mania for alteration in *Sanditon*, in which the England of Austen's early work seems no longer recognizable. *Sanditon* is also a novel about the forgetting of war, its becoming history, the entrepreneur Mr Parker regretting naming his housing venture Trafalgar House because "Waterloo is more the thing now" (*MW*: 380).

Finally, for a writer whose work has been traditionally regarded as oblivious to the world of war, it is remarkable how frequently Austen's iconic status has been mobi-lized at times of crisis such as World War I, the London Blitz, and even the Iraq War that began in 2003. In an essay on the Iraq War for the US PBS program *Newshour*, first broadcast in May 2003, Roger Rosenblatt asked the question: "Which was of greater importance, Jane Austen's novels or Napoleon's conquests and defeats . . . what matters most in a war . . . ? Sometimes one wonders what constitutes news at all." For Rosenblatt, Austen's novels represent war's antithesis, the enduring realities of domestic or private life, marriage, birth and death, but his comment is also an uncon-scious acknowledgement, and ultimately a product of, her own questioning of the affective experience of "news" and what "matters most in a war."

NOTES

I would like to acknowledge the research assistance of Neil Ramsey. I have also benefited considerably from discussions with Neil about military memoirs of this period.

1 For Austen's response to Pasley see Vivien Jones (2005). Reading for England: Austen, taste, and female patriotism. *European Romantic Review*, 16:2, 221–30.

FURTHER READING

Cohen, Monica (1996). Persuading the navy home: Austen and married women's professional property. *Novel*, 29:3, 346–7.

Fulford, Tim (1999). Romanticizing the Empire: the naval heroes of Southey, Coleridge, Austen, and Marryat. *MLQ: Modern Language Quarterly*, 60:2, 161–96.

Ragg, Laura M. (1940). Jane Austen and the war of her time. *The Contemporary Review*, 899, 544–9.

Sales, Roger (1994). *Jane Austen and Representations of Regency England*. London, Routledge.

23

Jane Austen, the 1790s, and the French Revolution

Mary Spongberg

Until recently, Jane Austen held a unique status in British literature, as the writer least affected by the French Revolution. Since the nineteenth century, readers and critics alike sought to distance "their" Jane from the tumultuous politics, polemical narratives, and improbable plotting that characterized the British novels of that Revolutionary decade, which grappled with the big issues of the day. Early reviewers of her novels celebrated Austen's focus on the minutiae of daily life in the English countryside, her ability to "give interest to the circle of a small village" (Southam 1968: 71), to "delineate with great accuracy the habits and manners of a middle class of gentry" (Southam 1968: 72). Contemporary readers of Austen were relieved by the absence of the Revolution in her work. Austen's writing served as an antidote to the "French disease" that had infected women's writings during this period. Her novels did not have readers doubled over in paroxysms of grief or confused with convoluted and overtly political narratives. She did not subject them to discursive footnotes, educative asides on mechanics or metaphysics, epistolary exchanges, glossaries of local dialect, or other forms of "solemn, specious nonsense" (Sutherland 2002: 84) that plagued novels of English life during this period. Nor did Austen preach sermons or engage in moral commentary. She resisted the confessional and the autobiographical in her works. The generic hybridity, adopted by writers of the 1790s who sought to "novelize" the great events of the day, is not to be found in the mature works of Jane Austen.

Avoidance of the tendencies described above endeared her to readers and critics alike and marked her as decidedly different from the "fanatical authoresses" (Southam 1968: 71) who had preceded her. Reviewers noted the absence of dark passages, secret chambers, and howling winds in her works, Gothic devices that framed both Jacobin and anti-Jacobin novels of the 1790s. Such excesses were to be left to "ladies' maids and sentimental washerwomen" (Southam 1968: 8), an unfortunate reminder of the newly "modern" novel's tainted French heritage as "Romance."

Sir Walter Scott believed that it was Austen's ability to produce a "correct and striking representation of that which is daily taking place" that marked her as a truly modern author (Southam 1968: 64). Underpinning such praise for Austen's modernity was a sense in which she had created a distinctly English novel, free from the romantic tendencies that had accompanied the form across the Channel. While Austen's works appeared on the Continent during this period, she was far less popular with French readers than Maria Edgeworth, Lady Morgan, and Amelia Opie. Scott compared Austen to Edgeworth in his review, claiming for her a "remarkable power of embodying and illustrating national character." Unlike Edgeworth, who used generic allusions to France in her tales of Ireland, effectively "provincializing" England, Austen resisted Francophilia, quietly celebrating the insularity of England's "Home" counties. Madame de Staël, who invented "the art of analysing the spirit of nations" (*Blackwood's Edinburgh Magazine* 1818, quoted in Isbell 1994: 1), dismissed Austen's novels as "*vulgaire*" (Southam 1968: 26). Scott however understood that she had captured with "originality and precision" (Southam 1968: 64) the essence of the English middle classes at that critical juncture when they were shaping national identity in their image.

Austen's novels also evinced a particular relationship to history that set her apart from other writers of the 1790s. The history of the French Revolution was written as events unfolded, and consequently new historical understandings of the Revolution evolved throughout the decade. Supporters of the Revolution believed it would wipe out the past and inaugurate a new epoch in history. Conservative critics feared as much was true. As Ronald Paulson has demonstrated, the publication of Edmund Burke's *Reflections on the Revolution in France* in 1790 saw the historical sense in which the term revolution was used, shifting meaning from its original sense as "a return to a point of origin," to its modern meaning as "an abrupt, broken and unpredictable sequence of events" (Paulson 1983: 51–2). Critical to Burke's sense of history in the *Reflections* was this new understanding of revolution. It allowed him to decry any sense in which the Glorious Revolution of 1688 might be understood as the progenitor to the French Revolution. Burke's *Reflections* offered a critical revision of English nationhood itself, as he read the violent upheavals of the past as signs of natural growth, effectively jettisoning any aspects of British history that did not reflect a culture of chivalric masculinity. Underpinning Burke's reinterpretation of history was a reassertion of the patriarchal authority of the English throne, a patriarchal authority that Burke had softened through his appeal to an ideal of sentimentalized manliness. Burke's model of history was distinctly gendered, historical progress guaranteed by paternal patriarchy, good government ensured by primogeniture. He recast the Revolution of 1688 as a "small and temporary deviation from the strict order of a regular hereditary succession" (Burke 1790/1989: 68), ignoring its repudiation of the divine right of the eldest to rule in the state, which decoupled the ideology of the state and the ideology of the family, undercutting the basis of primogeniture.

Many women writers who responded to Burke's *Reflections* reacted as much to his understanding of British history as to his vehement denunciation of the Revolution.

Mary Wollstonecraft explicitly rejected the patriarchal parameters that bound Burke's understanding of history, arguing that what history demonstrated was that "man had been changed into an artificial monster by the station in which he was born" (Wollstonecraft 1791/1993: 9). Helen Maria Williams plumbed the dark recesses of the *ancien régime* to uncover explanations for present calamities, while Charlotte Smith and Mary Robinson looked to contemporary events in France in order to offer alternate understandings of the past. The fate of persecuted or endangered women, such as Mary Stuart and Anne Boleyn, also animated women's writing in this period. Women's historical production during the Napoleonic Wars posed a significant site of political resistance to the historiographical tradition espoused by Burke, identifying the cause of female oppression with those institutions celebrated in the *Reflections* as guaranteeing the slow and dignified evolution of English liberty. While Burke had personified the fate of France in the reviled figure of Marie Antoinette, women writers drew on the historical annals of England and Scotland, using the lives of ill-fated queens to contest the historical claims made by Burke and to generate what Greg Kucich (2000) has called "sympathetic history," an alternate feminine history of the nation.

Austen's novels are, however, set emphatically in the England of the present. The rural hamlets featured in her works bear the traces of a nation at war, but the effects of the Revolution are felt from a distance. The shortage of men, the fear of rebellion, the crises caused by changes in the value of capital, are all embedded in her novels, as they are in the private writings of her contemporaries, between more prosaic descriptions of troublesome servants, turnips, and what was had for tea. Neither complaisant nor oblivious to the events in France, such writings document the localized effect of the Revolution as experienced by Britons, buffeted by time lags in news, the vagaries of the postal service, and a real sense of distance from the action on the Continent.

The apparent distance Austen felt from the Revolution has shaped the way historians have read her for almost two centuries and contributed to their failure to interrogate the silence surrounding the Revolution in her works. Early observers of Austen's fiction understood her to be deliberately eschewing the literary heritage of France. As a critical tradition evolved around her in the nineteenth century however, a myth of an "unconscious" Austen emerged. This "unconscious" Austen lived through one of the most dramatic periods in history, yet according to her biographers had "absolutely nothing" to say about the "great strifes of war and policy which so disquieted Europe" (Austen-Leigh 2002: 173). Until recently historians have done much to bolster this myth, using her novels to "prove" that the middle classes of Britain were unscathed by the revolutionary wars. While historians recognize Austen as a great source of social history, they have failed to see her works as offering politically perceptive insights on the social dislocation occasioned by the war, or to read her as engaging in the historiographical debate that emerged out of the Revolution.

In tracing the ways in which historians have colluded with this myth, this essay will argue that the failure to interrogate Austen's silence regarding the Revolution has functioned to depoliticize Austen's engagement with history. It will read Austen's

"History of England" (1791) and *Northanger Abbey* (1817) as responses to Edmund Burke. While her silence on the Revolution rendered her work "patriotic," in keeping with the anti-Jacobinism that became consensus during the Napoleonic Wars, her refusal to acknowledge the Revolution disguised the extent to which she was involved in satirizing Burke's celebration of England's history. This strategy allowed her to effectively undercut his arguments about the relationship between historical progress, property, and chivalry in a contemporary British context. Such a reading will complicate our understanding of Romantic feminism and Austen's participation in it.

It is true that Jane Austen did not experience the French Revolution as "event" in the same way as other writers of the 1790s. She did not entertain Marie Antoinette as Mary Robinson had in prerevolutionary Paris. She was not toasted at the British Club in Paris for her contributions to Liberty like Helen Maria Williams and Charlotte Smith. She did not conceive a "barrier child" with her Republican lover, as did Mary Wollstonecraft, nor did she spend years in exile, as was the fate of Fanny Burney. Yet like these women, Austen was a writer whose identity was formed by the cultural politics of the 1790s. The scandal of authorship generated by women's participation in the Revolution left few women writers unscathed, and shaped Austen's authorial identity and the efforts of her family to render her authorship respectable following her death.

The years when Austen first sought recognition as an author directly correspond with the period when women's literary production was represented as a sexualized and unpatriotic activity, threatening the moral fiber of the nation. As early as 1793 the conservative polemicist Laetitia Matilda Hawkins suggested in her *Letters on the Female Mind* that it was the patriotic duty of all Englishwomen to remain ignorant of the Revolution. Writing as Britain prepared for war with France, Hawkins articulated a comforting model of English womanhood, congratulating her countrywomen on their general ignorance of matters of state. The whole world might be at war, she wrote: "and yet not even the rumour of it reach the ear of an Englishwoman . . . " (Hawkins 1801, vol. 2: 194).

With the death of Mary Wollstonecraft and the scandal surrounding the publication of William Godwin's *Memoirs* (1797), women who had ignored Hawkins were found guilty of the violation of sexual morality and generic decorum, their loyalty to England rendered suspect. The *Memoirs* became the object through which women writers on all sides of the political spectrum were vilified. Even the most virtuous of female authors, Hannah More, felt the sting of this scandal, when labeled a Jacobin in the *Anti-Jacobin Review*. While more radical writers in the 1790s embraced authorship under their own name, Austen sought anonymity, suggesting that she was aware of the perils it posed for women. Whether or not Wollstonecraft's fate was discussed in the sitting room at Steventon, Austen's letters to her family suggest that an anxiety around authorship persisted throughout her career.

Following Austen's death, her family did much to defend her privacy. Sharing her concerns about the respectability of authorship, the earliest portrait, written by her brother Henry, was essentially a celebration of an eventless life. This "eventlessness" has characterized biographies written by later generations of Austens and marked her life in stark contrast with her contemporaries. James Edward Austen-Leigh's *Memoir of Jane Austen* (1870) retained an essentially hagiographic tone, while expanding for 11 chapters upon the notion that Aunt Jane's life was without "event." The publication of Lord Brabourne's *Letters of Jane Austen* (1884) consolidated the domestic image of Austen. Brabourne, Austen's great-nephew, grandson of Edward Austen Knight, was concerned to establish a different family view of Aunt Jane, that of his father's family in Kent. The move out of Hampshire reinforced the historical shift established by Austen-Leigh, who had imbued his aunt with the bourgeois values of Queen Victoria, to whom Brabourne's *Letters* were dedicated. Historians following Brabourne have read her novels in relation to England's victory at Waterloo rather than in the crucible of revolutionary war that shaped them. Instead of reflecting the exigencies of war forced on the lesser gentry, her novels represent a victorious England, richer and more powerful than before. With this shift too came a change in the perception of Austen's own class status, as she moved from an impoverished position as spinster in a landless gentry family, to a more aristocratic milieu.

What earlier readers had seen as daring, perceptive, and deliberate about Austen's art came in the wake of family biographies to be described dismissively as "maiden lady realism" (Southam 1987: 187). Her supposedly "eventless" life became conflated with the idea that she was completely detached from the politics of the revolutionary decade in which her literary career was forged. Richard Simpson (1870) led this charge shortly after the *Memoirs* were published. By claiming that Austen, "lived and wrote throughout the period of the French Revolution and European wars without referring to them once . . ." (Southam 1968: 242), Simpson was largely responsible for creating the myth of an unconscious Austen.

When literary histories of Britain during the Revolution began to appear, Austen was absent from such works. Although the *Memoir* indicated that *Pride and Prejudice, Northanger Abbey*, and *Sense and Sensibility* had been drafted in the 1790s, no mention is made of the novels in works such as Edward Dowden's *The French Revolution and English Literature* (1897) or Allene Gregory's *The French Revolution and the British Novel* (1914). The *Cambridge History of English Literature* published during World War I, does not feature Austen in the volume on the French Revolution. Instead she appears in the nineteenth-century volume; as a "disciple" of Burney in her last novel *The Wanderer*, it was possible to form a "picture of actual human life, without reference to the French Revolution" (Burney 2001: 6).

By the time Europe was again plunged into conflagration in 1914, so remote had Austen's oeuvre become from any suggestion of war or strife, that it served a palliative function. When diversion was needed from "sergeant majors and bayonet fighting . . . none was better at it than Jane Austen" observed W. B. Henderson, a soldier in the Royal Garrison Artillery (Gassert 2002:18). Reading Austen was recommended as nerve therapy for severely shell-shocked soldiers seeking solace in the little piece of England her novels provided. On the home front too, she was read as consolation.

A grieving Rudyard Kipling read Austen's novels aloud in the months following the loss of his son on the Western front, and later immortalized Austen's hold on the imagination of the fighting man in his story "The Janeites" (1924).

Following World War I, social historians used Austen's novels as proof that the middle classes of England were largely unscathed by the Napoleonic Wars. England's preeminent social historian of the interwar period, G. M. Trevelyan, frequently resorted to Austen's works when describing the middling orders in the early nineteenth century. In *History of England* Trevelyan observed "Never was country-house life more thriving or jovial, with its fox-hunting, shooting, leisure in spacious and well-stocked libraries. Never was sporting life more attractive" (Trevelyan 1926: 582–3). For Trevelyan "the mirror that Miss Austen held up to nature in the drawing-room" made it "hard to detect any trace of concern or trouble arising from the war." European historians offered a more caustic analysis of Austen's art. Echoing Madame de Staël's opinion of Austen, the French historian Elie Halévy observed in his *England in 1815* (1960: 514–5) that "the petty jealousies and hatreds, the littleness and meanness which characterized social relations in the country and provincial town, were portrayed by Austen with a merciless, if unembittered pencil."

By the 1960s, even the British Marxists, from whom we should expect a more nuanced approach to class and politics, were not immune to such opinions. Throughout the *Age of Revolution* (1962) Eric Hobsbawm allows the characters of Austen's novels to represent "most inhabitants of Europe" for whom the war meant "little more than the occasional direct interruption of the normal tenor of life" (p. 93).

Such views complemented the critical tradition that evolved around F. R. Leavis at Cambridge. Obsessed with the need for a culture uncontaminated by modern life, Leavis claimed that Austen's greatness lay in her lack of modernity, her ability to "let us forget our cares and moral tensions in the comedy of a pre-eminently civilised life" (1972: 15). As the road to Wigan Pier harkened, her novels were read as an idyllic reminder of England's past. The privileging of "style" as a category of analysis in Leavisite criticism, and its connection to timeless notions such as "moral significance," ensured a continuing sense of Austen as apolitical and ahistorical. The disavowal of Austen as an author forged in the 1790s was critical to her placement in the canon. Although a "subversive" school of Austen criticism emerged over the twentieth century, it did little to historicize Austen's writings or to suggest that she was engaged in the politics of the 1790s. While earlier reviewers represented Austen as the purveyor of "maiden lady realism" those of the "subversive" school saw her art more as maiden lady satire.

The publication of Warren Roberts's *Jane Austen and the French Revolution* in 1979 marked a significant shift in the way in which historians approached Austen. Roberts disabused historians of the notion that Austen was unconscious of the world around her, extensively documenting her engagement with politics, her understanding of the wars with Napoleon, and her relation to the nascent feminism of the period. Drawing on insights raised by Alistair Duckworth in *The Improvement of the Estate* (1971) and Marilyn Butler's *Jane Austen and the War of Ideas* (1975), Roberts understood Austen's politics to be "Tory" although unlike earlier commentators on this subject, he offered a more nuanced understanding of the meanings attached to that term during her lifetime. Roberts assumed that Austen's Toryism had a political dimension, and like Butler aligned her with Edmund Burke and other anti-Jacobin writers. Roberts depicted Austen as sympathetic to the French monarchy, owing to her relationship with Eliza de Feuillide, whose husband, a French aristocrat, went to the guillotine on February 22, 1794. Nonetheless, despite Roberts's account, historians following him have tended to view Austen as a repository of the social history of the period, while remaining largely uninterested in her politics.

In the same way that historians have rarely interrogated Austen's silence on the Revolution, they have seldom examined their assumption that Austen shared Burke's political perspective. While there is a consensus among scholars that Austen's writings were influenced by Burke, such consensus has been formed, as Claudia L Johnson (1988) has cogently argued, around the assumption "that because she was a member of a certain class she reflexively accorded with all its vales and interests" (p. xviii). The last section of this essay will interrogate the relation Austen might have had with Burke, suggesting that her "History of England" and *Northanger Abbey* were written partly as a response to his *Reflections*, not in the sense earlier scholars have suggested, but rather as a challenge to his masculinist vision of English history.

There is no mention of Edmund Burke in the extant correspondence of Jane Austen, or in that of her immediate family.[1] The silence around Burke is perplexing, as he was certainly known to the family, if not as the author of the *Reflections*, as the prosecutor of Warren Hastings, Governor General of Bengal and putative father of Austen's cousin, Eliza de Feuillide. Eliza attended Hastings's trial with her cousin Philadelphia Walter, who reported of Burke that his oration was "so hot and hasty" she could not understand what was being said. It is, however, very likely that the *Reflections* was the subject of conversation in literary households such as the Austens's. It was a bestseller in 1790, going through 11 editions within a year. Burke, who was isolated and unpopular over his prosecution of Hastings, found himself the subject of some celebrity. While radicals such as Mary Wollstonecraft and Catharine Sawbridge Macaulay wrote heated replies to Burke, bluestockings Fanny Burney and Elizabeth Montagu came to a new-found admiration after reading the *Reflections*.

There is no record of Jane Austen's reaction to the *Reflections*. She was at the time of its publication only 15 years of age. She had, however, begun to critique Whig historiography, having acquired a copy of Oliver Goldsmith's *History of England* in 1790, into which she made marginal commentary. In November 1791, exactly a year after the appearance of Burke's *Reflections*, Austen penned her "History of England," which turned on its head the very premises of Burke's vision of England's past. Critics have often observed that Austen's satire was aimed at particular versions of the English history put forward by Goldsmith, but it is possible that she was also employing her wild early wit against Burke.

Studies of the *History* have offered a personal rather than political context for Austen's Stuart partisanship: her subversion of the English past derived merely from loyalty to her ancestors the "Loyal" Leighs who were ennobled for their services to

Charles I. Thus while Christopher Kent (1989) has suggested "The Stuarts were her people, her claim to a place in History," he sees the *History* largely as a vehicle for her satirical skills. In a psychoanalytical reading of the *History*, Brigid Brophy (1968) has suggested that Austen's identification with the Stuarts must be understood as an adolescent defiance against a system that educated her for independence of mind, but assumed such independence would be curtailed upon marriage. For Brophy Austen's connection with the Stuarts was part of an elaborate fantasy world she created in response to her fear of dispossession as the youngest daughter of an impoverished clergyman. The *History* is a subversive text, in Brophy's analysis, only in its nonsense and illogic. Although Brophy suggested that Austen probably identified with the dispossession of Mary Queen of Scots because like her "she was also disposed of what she might have expected of her ancestry" she resists the possibility that such an identification might also be political (Brophy 1968: 35).

Yet this sense of dispossession was, of course, the result of the system of primogeniture Burke celebrated in the *Reflections,* a system that had hardened rather than declined in the wake of the Revolution of 1688, and that was played out in the politics of the Austen household. Austen's brothers had rejected their maternal ancestry as Stuart supporters, to become staunch and patriotic Hanoverians. In this context Austen's sympathy for the Stuarts renders the personal political and in keeping with the recovery of her maternal heritage in later works such as *Catharine, or the Bower* (Tuite 2002). In her *History*, Austen parodied the paradigms of Whig historiography which had been redefined by Burke in 1790 in terms that linked historical progress explicitly to paternal patriarchy and primogeniture. Austen's *History* is devoted to usurping the ordered and hierarchized network of relations that Burke imagined accounted for the history of the English state. Historical progress in Austen's text is guaranteed on opposite terms to those employed by Burke; she begins with the ascension of Henry the Fourth to the throne of England which he achieved by having "prevailed on his cousin and predecessor Richard the 2nd to resign it to him, & retire for the rest of his Life to Pomfret Castle, where he happened to be murdered" (MW: 139). Succession in Austen's *History* is usually the result of some vile deed. Paternity and heredity are frequently in question, if not rendered absurd, as in her description of Mary Tudor's accession to the throne: "They might have foreseen that as she died without Children, she would be succeeded by that disgrace to humanity, that pest of society, Elizabeth" (MW: 144). Mary Stuart's claim to succession and her brutal treatment at the hands of Elizabeth forms the dramatic centerpiece of Austen's narrative. Austen's rabid defense of Mary Stuart shares the hysterical hyperbole of Burke's description of the assault on Marie Antoinette in her bedroom at Versailles. Beginning the account of Mary Stuart's fate with a delightful summation of Henry VIII, "whose only merit was his not being *quite* so bad as his daughter Elizabeth" (MW: 142). Austen blithely subverts the conventions of masculinist historiography, privileging the significance of the daughter over the father and centering her "History of England" on the dynastic struggle between these two women.

Austen draws attention to what Burke's account of England's transition from Catholic past to Protestant present suppresses, that the violence of this transition was largely played out upon the bodies of women. The dynastic ambitions of Henry represent the complete antithesis of all that Burke ascribed to "ancient chivalry," as they were achieved through claims of incest, adultery, the displacement of faithful wives, the murder of others and the usurpation by a bastard of a legitimate heir. Burke's understanding of England's history is dependent on the erasure of women such as the wives of Henry VIII and Mary Stuart. Such erasure compounds the violence of their fate, ensuring the symbolic patriarchal order in death, as in life, by rendering them invisible to history. Thus while Burke predicted the disastrous fate of Marie Antoinette and sought to utilize the horror of her captivity to convince Protestant England to support Catholic France, Austen resists Burke's chivalric understanding of history, drawing attention to another ill-fated queen from France, anticipating the vindication of Mary Stuart, and other ill-fated queens, in the works of writers such as Mary Hays and Elizabeth Benger.

The erasure of women from history and the truth claims of history itself, are themes running through *Northanger Abbey*, a novel Austen began around 1798. Much criticism of this novel has focused on its parodying of the conventions of the Gothic novel, and has relied on a sense that Austen is also critical of the effect of such works on impressionable women readers. Such a reading is, however, considerably at odds with Austen's innovative defense of novels in the text, and her heroine's critique of the limitations of male-authored history. As Maria Jerinic (1995) has demonstrated, Catherine Morland is not manipulated by her experience of reading novels, she is validated by it. Furthermore, I would suggest, it is Henry Tilney, her suitor, whose reading of history renders his understanding faulty.

If, as Terry Robinson (2006) has recently suggested, Henry Tilney in *Northanger Abbey* might be read as Henry VIII and Catherine Morland as any one of the three Catherines who had the misfortune to be married to that king, Austen continued her critique of Burke's vision of English history in the years after the Terror. Henry VIII looms large over Northanger Abbey itself, once a site of female autonomy, a "richly-endowed convent" (*NA*: 142) confiscated by Tilney ancestors during the Reformation. The "awful memorials of an injured and ill-fated nun" (*NA*: 141) that Catherine imagines she might find there are emblematic of the Abbey's history of dispossession. Now owned by the bellicose General Tilney, the Abbey has become a site of female oppression, both real and imagined. When Catherine reveals to Henry her suspicions that the General had murdered his wife, he reproves her by lecturing her on the wild improbability of what she has conceived:

> "Remember the country and the age in which we live. Remember that we are English, that we are Christians. Consult your own understanding, your own sense of the probable, your own observation of what is passing around you – Does our education prepare us for such atrocities? Do our laws connive at them . . .?" (*NA*: 197)

These questions can be posed with such certainty because the "real solemn history" read by men such as Henry Tilney, pays scant attention to the women sacrificed to

Henry VIII's dynastic ambitions. Catherine Morland herself is almost relegated to such a fate, when she appeared to threaten the dynastic ambitions of General Tilney for his Henry. While it is often assumed that Henry Tilney's attempt to discipline the unruly and feminizing Gothic imagination here reflects the author's desire to do the same, such a suggestion is destabilized by Catherine's – and by extension Austen's – judgment on the General: that in suspecting him "of either murdering or shutting up his wife, she had scarcely sinned against his character, or magnified his cruelty."

The period following Wollstonecraft's death has frequently been depicted as the nadir of revolutionary feminism. It is better described as a time when women came to understand that the murderous treatment of women by the Jacobins in France and the posthumous vilification of Mary Wollstonecraft by anti-Jacobins in England were the product of the same misogynistic system of gender relations supported by men regardless of their politics. Such claims were made explicitly in works of radical women such as Mary Robinson and Mary Hays in the years following the death of Wollstonecraft. But they are also made in *Northanger Abbey*, where Austen domesticates the Gothic, depicting General Tilney as both the embodiment of Burkean ideals and the greatest threat to feminine virtue in the novel. Austen's sympathetic treatment of Mary Stuart in her *History* and her evocation of various Catherines in *Northanger Abbey* drew on long-standing discourses of Tory lament, but they also anticipate the reappearance of these women in the writings of Romantic women, who analogized their fate with the ill-fated women of the 1790s.

Notes

I would like to acknowledge the help and support of Helen Groth, Nicole Moore, and Clara Tuite in writing this article.

1 Deirdre Le Faye (2005) finds no mention of Burke in her exhaustive *A Chronology of Jane Austen and Her Family*.

Further Reading

Brophy, Brigid (1968). Jane Austen and the Stuarts. In B. C. Southam (Ed.). *Critical Essays on Jane Austen* (pp. 21–38). London: Routledge & Kegan Paul.

Burton, Antoinette (1995). "Invention is what delights me": Jane Austen's remaking of "English" history. In Devoney Looser (Ed.). *Jane Austen and the Discourses of Feminism* (pp. 35–50). New York: St. Martin's Press.

Gassert, Imogen (2002). In a foreign field: What soldiers in the trenches liked to read. *Times Literary Supplement*, May 10, pp. 17–19.

Jerinic, Maria (1995). In defense of the Gothic: Rereading *Northanger Abbey*. In Devoney Looser (Ed.). *Jane Austen and the Discourses of Feminism* (pp. 137–49). New York: St. Martin's Press.

Johnson, Claudia L. (1988). *Jane Austen: Women, Politics, and the Novel*. Chicago: University of Chicago Press.

Robinson, Terry F. (2006). "A mere skeleton of history": Reading relics in Jane Austen's *Northanger Abbey. European Romantic Review*, 17: 2, 215–27.

24

Feminisms

Vivien Jones

"Feminism" is not a term that Austen would have understood. She would have been perfectly familiar, however, with the concept of individual rights and, more specifically, "the rights of woman," as developed by women writers sympathetic to the ideals of the French Revolution and enshrined most famously in the title of Mary Wollstonecraft's *Vindication of the Rights of Woman* of 1792. Indeed, the language of rights is invoked in *Emma* – but only as a playful way of registering how seriously Highbury takes its arrangements for a ball: "A private dance, without sitting down to supper, was pronounced an infamous fraud upon the rights of men and women" (*E*: 254). As so often with Austen, the precise political implications of the irony here are difficult to gauge. Is this an attack on Highbury's parochialism, that it should invoke the language of rights in so trivial a context, or a collusive dismissal of such ideas in defense of conservative values – or neither of these things? This local difficulty of interpretation is symptomatic of long-standing critical debates about Austen's relationship to the kinds of contemporary ideas which in modern terms we would describe as "feminist": to the "wild wish," as Wollstonecraft puts it, "to see the distinction of sex confounded in society," and to see women treated as the rational equals of men (Wollstonecraft 1989: 126). Accepted by some commentators as unproblematically feminist because of its woman-centered concern with the politics of private life and sexual relationships, Austen's fiction has been seen by others as deeply traditional in its attitude to gender roles. In this essay, I want to revisit this still contentious issue: by locating Austen, in a properly historicist way, in the context of late eighteenth- and early nineteenth-century debates about the role and position of women; but also by invoking modern, necessarily anachronistic terminology to help illuminate her relationship with these debates. Austen, I shall be suggesting, is more postfeminist than feminist.

"Feminist" Austen

In making this suggestion, I don't want to play down those aspects of Austen's work which have led many commentators to identify her with a feminist agenda, the most obvious of which is the acute awareness of the financial and therefore social vulnerability of women of her class which is central to all her fiction. As the socialist and feminist Rebecca West put it in an introduction to *Northanger Abbey* in 1932, "it is surely not a coincidence that a country gentlewoman should sit down and put the institutions of society regarding women through the most gruelling criticism they have ever received." For West, "the feminism of Jane Austen . . . was very marked" and, she thought, "quite conscious" (Southam 1987: 295). Certainly, from the Dashwood sisters, excluded from their intended inheritance by their brother's "narrow-minded and selfish" wife in her first published novel, *Sense and Sensibility* (p. 5), to Anne Elliot, managing the effects of her father's irresponsible vanity in the posthumously published *Persuasion*, Austen's heroines demonstrate women's condition – in material terms, at least – to be one of precarious dependency. Like other critics since, West relates Austen's critique of women's social inequalities to Enlightenment ideas, to "the sceptical movement of the eighteenth century which came to a climax in the French Revolution" (Southam 1987: 295). In their different ways, Margaret Kirkham's *Jane Austen, Feminism and Fiction* (1983), Claudia Johnson's *Jane Austen: Women, Politics, and the Novel* (1988), and, more recently, Peter Knox-Shaw's *Jane Austen and the Enlightenment* (2004), take a similar view, identifying Austen with an essentially progressivist position. For Knox-Shaw and Johnson, the influence of Enlightenment skepticism on Austen's thinking produces liberal "centrist views," sympathetic to issues of gender inequality: in Johnson's phrase, Austen "defended and enlarged a progressive middle ground" (Knox-Shaw 2004: 5, Johnson 1988: 166). Kirkham goes further, claiming close kinship between Austen and Wollstonecraft as "feminist moralists of the same school," who shared "the common line of feminist concern and interest, stretching back to Mary Astell at the very end of the seventeenth century" (Kirkham 1983: xi).

Explicit evidence of that feminist "line" seems apparent when, at various key moments, Austen's novels echo the Enlightenment-inflected rhetoric of contemporary debates about gender politics and the position of women. In *Pride and Prejudice*, for example, desperately trying to convince Mr Collins that "no means no" after his unwelcome proposal, Elizabeth Bennet asserts her right to autonomous choice by describing herself in Wollstonecraftian terms: "Do not consider me now as an *elegant female* intending to plague you, but as a *rational creature* speaking the truth from her heart" (*PP*: 109, emphasis added). "Rational creature," as a definition of the human individual, can be found in countless eighteenth-century sermons, or in John Locke's much-reprinted *Some Thoughts Concerning Education* (1693), where the humanist principle "that Children are to be treated as rational Creatures" underpins his educational regime (Locke 1989: 115). But Elizabeth's opposition between rationality and elegance suggests a more specific immediate referent. In *Vindication of the Rights of Woman*, Wollstonecraft reappropriates Locke's phrase in defense of women's rationality: "My own sex, I hope, will excuse me, if I treat them like rational creatures, instead of flattering their *fascinating* graces"; and her stated aim is "to show that elegance is inferior to virtue, that the first object of laudable ambition is to obtain a character as a human being, regardless of the distinction of sex" (Wollstonecraft 1989: 75). Economically, Elizabeth is far from independent. As the closest male relative, under the law of entail, it is Mr Collins rather than herself or her sisters who is heir to her father's estate. But Elizabeth asserts her moral and intellectual independence, at least, and reaches for Wollstonecraftian rhetoric in order to do so.

In *Emma*, Austen invokes a different line of argument – this time articulating female oppression rather than asserting female autonomy. Jane Fairfax repeats a commonly drawn parallel between the condition of women and that of slaves when she describes employment agencies for governesses as: "Offices for the sale – not quite of human flesh – but of human intellect. . . . widely different certainly as to the guilt of those who carry it on; but as to the greater misery of the victims, I do not know where it lies" (*E*: 300). And later in the novel, when Jane is on the brink of taking up a governess post, Emma is struck by "The contrast between Mrs. Churchill's importance in the world, and Jane Fairfax's," and she muses on "the difference of woman's destiny" (*E*: 384). Comparisons between women and slaves were frequently drawn throughout the eighteenth century. In 1696, for example, in her *Essay in Defence of the Female Sex*, Judith Drake described the condition of European women as "not very much better" than slavery; Wollstonecraft makes use of the trope on several occasions; and in 1805, the Evangelical abolitionist, Hannah More, published a pamphlet entitled "Hints towards forming a Bill for the Abolition of the White Female Slave Trade," by which she meant the subjection of young women to the "arbitrary, universal tyrant," Fashion (Drake 1696: 22, More 1996: 36). Abolition (which Austen supported) was a respectable cause for middling-class women – indeed, it was already established in law by the time *Emma* was published – and, as Jon Mee argues, if such comparisons between women and slaves were subversive it was due to their feminism rather than their attitude to slavery. In *Emma*, and in the implicit comparisons which some critics have seen between Fanny Price's position at Mansfield Park and that of the slaves on Sir Thomas's Antiguan plantation, Mee suggests, Austen's "real concerns are . . . with the role of women within English society" (Mee 2000: 84).

And in *Persuasion*, as in the famous authorial defense of the novel in chapter five of *Northanger Abbey*, Austen briefly turns explicit attention to yet another feminist issue: the inequalities suffered by women writers – and, in the case of the novel, readers. Defending women's constancy in the climactic scene in which Captain Wentworth is finally convinced of her continuing affection, Anne Elliot reaches for what were by then familiar arguments about education and women's access to writing. Proof about the quality of women's affection is not to be found in books, Anne suggests, because: "Men have had every advantage of us in telling their own story. Education has been theirs in so much higher a degree; the pen has been in their hands" (*P*: 234). Once again, an Austen heroine articulates herself and her situation through familiar Enlightenment feminist arguments – here, about the inadequacies of female education and the consequent biases of male-authored history.

Such moments appear to endorse the "conscious" feminism which Rebecca West found in Austen's work. They certainly make Austen's familiarity with contemporary polemic about the status of women abundantly clear. But the precise status of such arguments in Austen's distinctly unpolemical fictions is rather less easy to discern. She remains, as Janet Todd put it in 1991, "an awkward subject for feminist criticism to cope with" (quoted in Looser 1995: 2) – or awkward if modern feminisms look for too direct a reflection of their own preoccupations. Austen's awareness of gender politics operates at the level of individual choice (or lack of it) rather than fueling any demand for structural social change.

For Austen's financially precarious heroines, marriage, with its promise of security, becomes "the grand feature of their lives," in Mary Wollstonecraft's phrase; and her wealthiest heroine, Emma, has to learn that marriage is what she, too, wants – in spite of her early protestations to the contrary. Wollstonecraft's words are of course meant negatively, and they point up one of the key differences not only between her version of Enlightenment feminism and Austen's position, but also between Austen and some of her twentieth-century critics – most notably Mary Poovey, in her influential Marxist-feminist study *The Proper Lady and the Woman Writer* (1984). Wollstonecraft is scathing about a gendered social system in which men are "prepared for professions," whilst women are offered no goals other than to "marry advantageously" (Wollstonecraft 1989: 129). Austen's moral realism is equally critical of individual women for whom marrying advantageously takes precedence over any other motive. But marriage nevertheless remains the grand feature of her novels, as it is of her heroines' lives. Her realism is tempered by romance: an essentially conservative form. Happy-ever-after endings, which conveniently combine material comfort with emotional satisfaction, are her heroines' reward for their moral integrity and for refusing to marry merely for mercenary convenience. Through their very form, therefore, Austen's novels make our pleasure as readers dependent on our acceptance of marriage as fulfillment or, as Poovey puts it, the promise of "an emotional intensity that ideally compensates for all the practical opportunities they are denied" (Poovey 1984: 237). Any critique of women's dependency is in constant tension with a perpetuation of the traditional social structures through which that dependency is maintained. Rather than suggesting that women's opportunities might be fundamentally different, Austen's principled heroines use their Enlightenment-inspired confidence to reform those structures from within. This coexistence of a "feminist" awareness with an essential conservatism, of an impulse for reform together with a readiness to work within traditional structures, is fundamental to Austen's fiction – uncomfortable though that has sometimes been for feminist commentators.

As this suggests, Austen's view of the role and status of women has to be understood in relation to her wider political context, and to the role played in that by women, and more particularly by the female domestic novel. Marilyn Butler's *Jane Austen and the War of Ideas* is still one of the founding texts of modern Austen criticism. It was Butler who first demonstrated the engagement of Austen's fiction with post-Revolutionary debates, arguing that her novels "belong decisively to one class of partisan novels, the conservative" and that "[i]ntellectually she is orthodox" (Butler 1975: 3). But as Devoney Looser has suggested, feminist and cultural critical approaches both to Austen's work and to her immediate context have permanently modified and complicated an older view of her as "a Tory proponent of the political and cultural status quo" (Looser 1995: 5). And in the second edition of her study, published in 1987, Butler refines her original account of Austen's politics in light of such critical developments, placing her within "a Tory women's tradition, which must also be thought of as proto-feminist" (Butler 1987: xxiii). Looser's valuable collection of essays was published in 1995 and since that time, as she predicted, feminist criticism's concern with "the gendered implications of Austen's writings" has focused particularly productively on the role of women "in creating and sustaining civil society" in the aftermath of the French Revolution and at a time of war (Looser 1995: 7, Kelly 1995: 32). What Johnson and others have identified as Austen's "progressivism" is perhaps more accurately understood in terms of a specifically female patriotism, the "Tory feminism" identified by Butler, serving the conservative reformist agenda of a govern-ing class made anxious and defensive by revolutionary radicalism. And it's in thinking about Austen's position in relation to this agenda of reform that "postfeminism" becomes a potentially useful concept.

Post-Revolutionary Gender Politics

Austen's first novels were drafted in the politically fraught 1790s when the war with Revolutionary France, which began in 1793, engendered an atmosphere of increas-ingly uncompromising patriotism. Traditional British liberties, based on "a sure principle of conservation" as the statesman Edmund Burke influentially put it in his *Reflections on the Revolution in France* (1790), were contrasted with the destructive "spirit of innovation" manifest, according to Burke, in the French ideal of *liberté* (Burke 1983: 119–20). Burkean conservatism explicitly combined "conservation" with "a principle of improvement." It spoke compellingly to a governing class anxious to maintain its position in the face not only of war, but of growing demands for social and political change. For Burke, as for other anti-Revolutionary writers, British liberties are enshrined in the established structures of church, state, and family. They are passed down through familial systems of inheritance, thus "binding up the constitution of our country with our dearest domestic ties" and "adopting our fundamental laws into the bosom of our family affections" (p. 120). Burke's powerful articulation of the intimate connection between family and state bolstered conventional ideas of the family and of women's role within it. At the same time, Burke's "principle of improve-ment" gave women a position of fundamental importance within the patriotic effort: as wives and mothers embodying and inculcating patriotic moral values at the heart of family and nation. For women, then, proper femininity became the sign of proper patriotism.

In this context, women writers came under particular scrutiny. Throughout the eighteenth century there had been a tendency to differentiate between those inspired by a "wanton" or by a "modest" muse (Duncombe 1981: ll. 139, 148): a judgment based as readily on women writers' lives as on their subject matter. In the 1790s, this took on a very specific resonance, as "patriotism bec[ame] more prominent than learning" (Guest 2000: 175). Those whose lives or writings were seen to transgress accepted norms of feminine behavior were identified as dangerously sympathetic to French radicalism and condemned, as the title of Richard Polwhele's virulently anti-Revolutionary poem of 1798 has it, as "unsex'd females."

For many conservative commentators, including Polwhele, this was a category epitomized by Mary Wollstonecraft. In spite of the emphasis on responsible motherhood in her *Vindication of the Rights of Woman*, the overtly polemical title of Wollstonecraft's text, with its claim to women's rational equality with men, meant that she became a byword, within the conservative press at least, for an inappropriately politicized form of femininity which "no decorum checks": a reputation compounded when the details of her unconventional private life were revealed to the public by her husband William Godwin in his 1798 posthumous memoir. Typically, Polwhele evaluates women writers according to their (gender) politics rather than their talent, and his poem contrasts the "Gallic mania" of the Wollstonecraftians, who have made the mistake of behaving as if they wished to "become a politician," with those writers who have maintained due feminine decorum (Polwhele 1798: 19 n; 18 n). Preeminent among the latter, and "esteemed, as a character, in all points diametrically opposed to Miss Wollstonecraft" (35 n), is the evangelical Hannah More, the embodiment, for Polwhele, of "modest Virtue." He depicts More as urging her followers, in a "voice seraphic," to "clai[m] a nation's praise" by using their moral influence to instill the traditional values which will secure national stability and cohesion (Polwhele 1798: 28, 30). And in 1799, More herself reinforced the contrast when she attacked Wollstonecraft in her hugely successful *Strictures on the Modern System of Female Education*.

This opposition between Wollstonecraft and More, in the context of a Burkean program of conservative reform, provides a helpful way of defining Austen's sexual politics, inseparable as they are from the context of a nation at war and, as the conflict dragged on, a growing crisis in the traditional institutions of authority. Though their very different political and religious assumptions often resulted in very different analyses of women's condition, More and Wollstonecraft were both acutely aware of addressing their female readers at a time of national and international crisis. Like other female polemicists of the period such as Catharine Macaulay, Mary Hays, Mary Robinson, and Priscilla Wakefield, they put questions of women's education, female equality, and the role of the family at the center of the ideological debates generated by the war. Wollstonecraft's desire to effect "a revolution in female manners" and her claims for female citizenship have been readily identified by modern commentators as "feminist" (or more accurately "protofeminist," since such claims were first described as "feminist" only at the end of the nineteenth century). Like Wollstonecraft, More argues strongly for educational improvement, but she makes it the basis of a distinctively female, essentially domestic, form of patriotism whereby women "act as the guardians of public taste as well as public virtue," occasionally moving beyond "their customary domesticity," perhaps, but "only in order to further the greater good" (More 1799, vol. I, 39, Colley 1992: 280). More's location of female duty at the heart of the national agenda has been celebrated by some recent critics as particularly enabling for women, but in her readiness to work with, rather than to overturn, the structural inequalities between the sexes, More fits far less readily than Wollstonecraft into the (proto)feminist category.

If we are to believe her great-niece, Austen was "a firm patriot and a strong believer in the superiority in the ways and merits of her native country over those of other lands" (Austen-Leigh 1920: 45). Certainly, the Austens were not just patriots, but Tories. They identified with the political grouping which defended the institutions that mattered to their family – the Church of England, the Navy, and a stable, essentially hierarchical social order. But as members of the professional class, or what David Spring refers to as the "pseudo-gentry" rather than the gentry proper (Spring 1983), the Austens were also strong defenders of merit, rather than mere birth, as the means to worldly success and personal happiness. Their particular form of meritocracy, with its belief in both intellectual and moral acumen, can be identified, in other words, as sympathetic to the movement for conservative reform in the face of national crisis, that "moral rearming of the gentry," as Marilyn Butler describes it, articulated at the time most powerfully by Burke and, more recently, by the historian Linda Colley (Butler 1986: 206, Colley 1992). For Austen, this broad political position is necessarily inflected by gender. As Deborah Kaplan has suggested, women like Austen existed within at least two cultures: the dominant culture of their social community, with its subtle hierarchies of rank and less subtle hierarchies of gender; and a "female culture" within which resistance to conventional expectations of how women should behave could be articulated, and which provided a "crucial bridge between modest, self-effacing femininity and . . . self-assertion" (Kaplan 1992: 13). What Linda Colley calls "womanpower," women's "own distinctive brand of patriotism," epitomized by Hannah More, is one of those opportunities for "self-assertion" (Colley 1992: 281); another is novel writing.

Unlike many other female novelists of the period from across the political spectrum, Austen chose not to write overtly polemical fiction. Her novels are not fictionalized case studies illustrating the wrongs of woman, like those of Wollstonecraft or Mary Hays; but nor do they contain the caricatures of 1790s feminists which are also a feature of the fiction of the period: Maria Edgeworth's Harriot Freke in *Belinda* (1801), Bridgetina Botherim in Elizabeth Hamilton's *Memoirs of Modern Philosophers* (1800), or Frances Burney's Elinor Joddrell in *The Wanderer* (1814). This does not, of course, mean that her novels are apolitical. Rather, they engage indirectly with the agenda of conservative reform through their focus on their heroines' moral rather than formal education, on the ethics of domestic life, and on the right to romantic fulfillment. In doing so, they inevitably engage with contemporary gender politics, putting the language and ideas of Enlightenment feminism to post-Revolutionary effect by representing them in essentially nonthreatening ways. And, as I shall be suggesting in more detail in the final section of this essay, it is this aspect of Austen's work, this sense that revolutionary feminism has been taken on board and superseded, which we might usefully think of as "postfeminist."

As we might expect, this is particularly evident in Austen's treatment of marriage: both in her heroines' courage in refusing marriage to men they cannot love; and in the social meanings of the marriages they accept. Having refused Mr Collins, Austen's "rational creature," Elizabeth Bennet, goes on to defeat the old order, in the form of his patron Lady Catherine de Bourgh. The effect of her spectacular marriage to Lady Catherine's nephew, however, is to invigorate and relegitimate, rather than to dismantle, the social power and authority represented by Pemberley, where Darcy is recognized as "the best landlord, and the best master" (*PP*: 249). In *Mansfield Park*, Fanny Price dares to refuse Henry Crawford, causing her uncle to echo Hannah More's lament that "not only sons but daughters have adopted that spirit of independence, and disdain of control, which characterise the times" (More 1799, vol. I: 144). Sir Thomas accuses Fanny of showing "that independence of spirit, which prevails so much in modern days, even in young women, and which in young women is offensive and disgusting beyond all common offence" (*MP*: 318). But, though Fanny, supported by the narrator, asserts her right to autonomous choice, it's the Crawfords, not Austen's heroine, who actually represent the dangerously unconstrained independence that More and Sir Thomas have in mind. He comes to acknowledge Fanny as "indeed the daughter that he wanted," and in marrying Edmund and taking up residence at Mansfield parsonage, she provides a chastened ruling class with new moral awareness (*MP*: 472). As we have seen, Emma acknowledges "the difference of woman's destiny," but the novel's comedic structure deflects the full political implications of her musings, killing off Mrs Churchill so that Jane Fairfax and Frank Churchill can marry. And in *Persuasion*, a modern, egalitarian ideal of marriage – as represented by the Harvilles, the Crofts, and subsequently, we assume, by Anne and Wentworth – is crucial to the new, postwar order epitomized by the Navy, the profession which is "if possible, more distinguished in its domestic virtues than in its national importance" (*P*: 252). Progressive ideas about gender are again used to patriotic effect: the Navy was also, of course, instrumental in Britain's defeat of post-Revolutionary and Napoleonic France.

Contemporary reviewers responded positively to what I have described as Austen's nonthreatening appropriation of the kind of Enlightenment feminist ideas brought to the fore by the Revolution controversies of the 1790s. First drafted in that decade, but not published until 1811 and 1813, when the war against Napoleon hung in the balance, *Sense and Sensibility* and *Pride and Prejudice* were praised in the pages of the *Critical Review* for offering "a great deal of good sense," for their "naturally drawn" characters and, in the case of Elizabeth Bennet, for a heroine whose "independence of character . . . is kept within the proper line of decorum" (Southam 1968: 35, 46). And the "good sense" of the still-anonymous Austen is an implicit point of comparison in reviews of Frances Burney's most polemical novel, *The Wanderer; or, Female Difficulties*. Published in 1814 but set in the 1790s, *The Wanderer* catalogues the vulnerabilities of a woman isolated from her family and trying to make an independent living. The reviewers objected that Burney's version of sexual politics was out of date. Their proud claim was that "an alteration insensibly progressive has effected considerable change in our idea of the gentleman and the lady"; and that the commonsensical women of the early nineteenth century know how to look after themselves:

> Nothing is so destructive to a certain species of high-wrought misery as common sense. . . . The evils which surround woman . . . are to be surmounted like all other evils, by prudence and firmness . . .: it is time now for the honour of one sex, that the other be brought to believe what is absolutely true . . . that . . . to betray unprotected youth and beauty, is not uniformly the first object of every man who happens to encounter them. (*Monthly Review* 1815, *Critical Review* 1814, cited Garside: 18, 5–6)

Gender relations are assumed to have moved on; the "evils which surround woman" require remedies no different from "all other evils"; and the clear implication is that the demands for equality made by 1790s feminists are no longer necessary. It's in this post-Revolutionary, "postfeminist" context that Austen is praised by Walter Scott in his 1816 review of *Emma* for her "knowledge of the world, and the peculiar tact with which she presents characters that the reader cannot fail to recognize" (Southam, 1968: 67), and begins to establish her critical reputation as the supreme writer of women's everyday experience.

Postfeminist Austen?

Since her early reception, Austen's contained, unpolemical rationalism has been appropriated at various historical moments – including our own – by those wanting to suggest that the "modern" gender relations of any given period render feminism's claims outmoded and unnecessary. In 1894, for example, just as "feminism" in its modern meaning was first coming into use, and radical ideas about gender equality were associated with the figure of the "New Woman," the critic George Saintsbury characterized Elizabeth Bennet as having "nothing offensive, nothing *viraginous*, nothing for the 'New Woman' about her." Instead, he suggests, Elizabeth has "by nature what the best modern (not 'new') women have by education and experience, a perfect freedom from the idea that all men may bully her if they choose, and that most men will run away with her if they can" (Southam 1987: 218). Eager to play down the claims of the New Woman, Saintsbury finds in Elizabeth a precursor "by nature" of what he calls "the best modern . . . women" – by which he means those who are assumed to have achieved, through education and experience, a state of "perfect freedom" from predatory masculinity. And in another 1890s review, Austen's "feminine gifts" are contrasted with Mrs Humphrey Ward's "didactic purpose" and "militant propagandism" (Southam 1987: 66).

The terms in which Saintsbury distinguishes between "modern" femininity and the New Woman echo those of *The Wanderer*'s and Austen's early reviewers. In our own "postfeminist" moment, they are reproduced in the distinction between acceptably independent femininity and what Bridget Jones, in Helen Fielding's chick-lit version of *Pride and Prejudice*, refers to as "strident feminism" (Fielding 1996: 20).

Ever since the publication of *Bridget Jones's Diary*, Austen has been enthusiastically adopted as the foremother of "chick lit," of popular fictions which sell themselves as reflecting and "respect[ing] readers and their ordinary lives" (Robinson 2003, Crusie 2005, Ferris and Young 2006). The typical chick-lit heroine is a professional woman who has achieved financial independence; but in its focus on individual lifestyle choices, rather than the social structures responsible for gender inequality, twenty-first-century chick lit identifies itself as postfeminist, knowingly distancing itself from the political demands of late twentieth-century feminism, and finding in the post-Revolutionary Austen, it would seem, a parallel structure of feeling.

"Postfeminist" is a contentious term. Always more than simply a chronological description, its suggestion that it comes after feminism inevitably also carries the political judgment that feminism's project is either realized or superseded (Modleski 1991, Negra 2004). In suggesting that it's a term that might help us understand Austen's political engagement with the gender issues of her time, I'm drawing particularly on what Angela McRobbie has recently defined as postfeminism's "taken into accountness": "post-feminism positively draws on and invokes feminism as that which can be taken into account, to suggest that equality is achieved"; "by means of the tropes of freedom and choice which are now inextricably connected with the category of 'young women', feminism is decisively aged and made to seem redundant" (McRobbie 2004: 256, 255). Austen's novels continue to escape attempts to label her as feminist or otherwise, and their complexity certainly defies chick lit's appropriation of her – even if popular marketing would have us believe otherwise. Her novels have recently been reissued with girly covers; the continuing box-office success of film and TV adaptations of her fiction has been further exploited with the release of *Becoming Jane* (Miramax 2007), an almost equally fictional "biopic" about Austen's flirtation with Tom Lefroy; and Austen fansites proliferate on the internet. But, reading back from the twenty-first to the early nineteenth century, Austen's postfeminist popular cultural success can nevertheless throw important light on the workings of sexual politics in her novels. In McRobbie's phrase, Austen takes 1790s feminist ideas into account, certainly, but she puts them at the service not simply of individualized fulfillment, but of a conservative agenda of reform, resolving her independent-minded heroines' difficulties through romance and marriage to suggest that a measure of equality, and certainly happiness, can be achieved.

FURTHER READING

Crusie, Jennifer (Ed.) (2005). *Flirting with Pride and Prejudice: Fresh Perspectives on the Original Chick-Lit Masterpiece*. Dallas, TX: Benbella Books.

Looser, Devoney (Ed.) (1995). *Jane Austen and Discourses of Feminism*. New York: St. Martin's Press.

McRobbie, Angela (2004). Post-feminism and popular culture. *Feminist Media Studies*, 4, 255–64.

Tasker, Yvonne and Diane Negra (Eds) (2007). *Interrogating Postfeminism: Gender and the Politics of Popular Culture*. Durham, NC: Duke University Press.

25
Imagining Sameness and Difference: Domestic and Colonial Sisters in *Mansfield Park*

Deirdre Coleman

Readings of *Mansfield Park* which link the novel to empire and to Britain's heavy investment in the slave trade have assumed center stage in recent decades, so much so that there is now a discernible backlash, with some critics exasperated at what they consider to be the tail wagging the dog. John Wiltshire, for instance, decries the way in which the postcolonial industry has "colonized" *Mansfield Park*, citing in support of his case some of the cruder arguments which have been canvassed – that Fanny Price is herself a slave, or that Mansfield Park is a mirror image of a West Indian slave estate. Wiltshire even goes so far as to dismiss the Antiguan connection as a "myth," nothing more than "varnish" which must be scraped away from the novel so that its true features can be clearly discerned once more (Wiltshire 2006: 69–86).

Wiltshire is right to argue that there is a problem with crudely identifying Fanny as a slave. But the problem arises, not because *Mansfield Park* does not register a connection between domesticity and colonialism, but because the narrative at every point canvasses "the distinction proper to be made" (*MP*: 10) on this as well as on all other subjects. For writers like Austen the most notable connection between domesticity and colonialism is the metaphor of slavery, mobilized polemically by her women contemporaries to critique their subjection within the wider culture. That Austen was interested in the rhetorical crossings of the slave trope, with its implied equivalence between white women and black slaves, is clear in the analogy drawn up in *Emma* between the "governess-trade" and the "slave-trade." It is important to note (because most critics, including Susan Fraiman, 2000, misread this scene) that it is not the admirable Jane Fairfax who draws out the analogy but the silly and vulgar Mrs Elton, who leaps on Jane's reference to "the sale – not quite of human flesh – but of human intellect" as a reference to the slave trade. Jane is quick to deny any such reference because of the enormous difference in guilt involved in the conduct of each trade ("I did not mean, I was not thinking of the slave-trade . . . governess-trade, I assure you, was all that I had in view") but her denial of any intended connection concludes with an equivocation which appears to readmit the analogy: "but as to the greater misery of the victims, I do not know where it lies" (*E*: 300). Not knowing where "the greater misery" lies, whether with white minds or with black bodies, suggests an incommensurability at work in the analogy – a lack of fit between spirit and matter scripted onto a misfit between white and black races. However we interpret Jane's agnosticism, the comment should make us wary of a too easy equivalence between African slaves and heroines like Jane Fairfax and Fanny Price. In this important scene, Austen does not, as Susan Fraiman argues, "exploit the symbolic value of slavery" so much as interrogate how the slave metaphor works (Fraiman 2000: 213).

In Austen's work the slave trade and abolitionism play an important role in the analysis of power relations, especially those arising out of gender-based oppression. The abolitionist movement's sentimental appeal to universal principles of liberty, equality, and fraternity engaged several key philosophical and political issues, such as the imagining of kinship, claims to personhood, and the vexed relations of equality and difference – relations which, galvanized by widespread agitation against slavery, touched not just on issues to do with class but with both sex and race, simultaneously. Such a confluence, whereby the sexual differences between men and women are linked to racial difference, can be seen in Hannah More's *Strictures on Female Education* (1799) in a passage where, in canvassing "the degree of difference between the masculine and feminine understanding," she concludes that the question must remain undecided, as undecided as the difference between "the understandings of blacks and whites; for until men and women, as well as Africans and Europeans, are put more nearly on a par in the cultivation of their minds, the shades of distinction . . . can never be fairly ascertained" (More 1799: 183). Several years later More's concern for a better and more rational education for women dovetailed with her abolitionist zeal to produce one of the period's most egregious deployments of the slave trade as a metaphor for woman's lot. Entitled "Hints towards forming a Bill for the Abolition of the White Female Slave Trade," this anonymous essay of 1805 exhibits the inherent asymmetry and competitiveness of the discourses of feminism and abolitionism; for despite her sign-off as "An Enemy to all Slavery," More suggests that white women's slavery to the male tyrant "Fashion" renders their condition "worse than that of their African brethren" laboring under the overseer's whip (More 1805: 37, rep. 1818).

Appeals to universal siblinghood ("African brethren") within the wider "rights of man" rhetoric of the 1790s were central to abolitionism's sentimentalist rhetoric, in particular its assertion of racial equality. The problem of such appeals can be seen in the movement's key emblem, the Wedgwood cameo of the kneeling and fettered slave who, with chained wrists raised in supplication, asks: "Am I Not a Man and a Brother?" (Figure 25.1). The politics of racial equality claimed here is deeply problematic, for while the slave's words invoke an egalitarian sameness, the image bespeaks subordination and difference. The slave's appeal to an abstract universal also represses sexual difference, a point made clearly by women abolitionists in the 1820s and 1830s who designed a matching cameo of a kneeling female slave who asks, "Am I Not a Woman and a Sister?" (see Midgley 1992) (Figure 25.2). Austen's fiction is peopled with numerous sets of sisters and brothers, creating that uncanny sense of doubling

Figure 25.1   Josiah Wedgwood anti-slavery medallion, *Am I Not a Man and a Brother?* The British Museum.

Figure 25.2   Am I Not a Woman and a Sister? Wilberforce House Museum, Hull City Council, UK.

and substitution which postcolonial critics see as figuratively reinscribing the colonial in the domestic (Plasa 2000: 35). That Austen was alert to the ideological contradictions rife in sentimental, abolitionist rhetoric can be seen in her deployment of siblinghood to anatomize notions of sameness and difference, equality and subordination. For instance the rhetorical question posed by Mrs Norris to clinch her case for adopting Fanny Price – "Is not she a sister's child?" – appears to satirize the Wedgwood medallion's motto, prompting us to see the emptiness of appeals to sameness and equality. For while it is true that in terms of the blood tie Fanny stands in the same relation to Aunt Norris as Lady Bertram's own children, this sameness counts for nothing, as evidenced by Fanny's subjection to "the pains of tyranny, of ridicule, and of neglect" (*MP*: 152). Furthermore, the emotional power of consanguinity invoked by Mrs Norris in the question, "Is not she a sister's child?", is completely annulled by her reassurance to Sir Thomas that, bred up together, Fanny will "never be more to either [brother] than a sister" (*MP*: 6–7). But being no more than a sister to Tom and Edmund does not mean that Fanny is a sister to them in the same way as her cousins Maria and Julia. Quite the contrary. Fanny is to be strictly schooled in the lesson "that she is not a *Miss Bertram*." Proper distinctions are to be made between the girls as they grow up because, in Sir Thomas's words, "they cannot be equals. Their rank, fortune, rights, and expectations, will always be different. It is a point of great delicacy" (*MP*: 11). For a matter of such "delicacy," the case is bluntly made: Fanny is inferior because of who she is. This inferiority, this insistence that Fanny must always be "the lowest and last" (*MP*: 221), is a point taken up with more zeal than delicacy by Aunt Norris who, from the start, reiterates the desirability that in all aspects of the girls' upbringing "there should be a difference" (*MP*: 19); a difference between light and dark, between the Bertram sisters' shining preeminence and Fanny's inferiority. In such an unequal family the social affections are inevitably stunted. Take, for instance, the rehearsals: Fanny and Julia both suffer from the pangs of jealousy but there is "no outward fellowship between them . . . They were two solitary sufferers, or connected only by Fanny's consciousness" (*MP*: 163).

Thus, despite the many sets of sisters, both literal and figurative, in *Mansfield Park* there is very little sisterly solidarity. The Ward sisters, all of whom have married very differently, are declared to be sisters in name only:

> So long divided, and so differently situated, the ties of blood were little more than nothing . . . a mere name . . . Three or four Prices might have been swept away . . . and Lady Bertram would have thought little about it; or perhaps might have caught from Mrs Norris's lips the cant of its being a very happy thing, and a great blessing to their poor dear sister Price to have them so well provided for. (*MP*: 428)

Ironically the meaninglessness of the blood tie is reinforced through the sisters' physical resemblance to each other: Lady Bertram and Mrs Price bear a great resemblance to each other but it is a sameness which only underscores difference. As readers we are invited to marvel that "where nature had made so little difference, circumstances should have made so much" (*MP*: 408). At the same time, however, and in contrast to the Ward sisters and the Miss Bertrams, there is the loving relationship between Fanny and Susan Price. In the end so great are Susan's claims that she causes the only wobble in Fanny's determination not to accept Henry Crawford's proposal. That sisters can be either everything or nothing to each other is also true of the relationship between brothers and sisters, the so-called "fraternal" tie which, for the narrator, represents a love higher even than the conjugal. William and Fanny Price, children "of the same family, the same blood, with the same first associations and habits," provide a perfect example of fraternal love "in all its prime and freshness." In the very midst of this celebration, however, the narrator reminds us that too often this love which is "sometimes almost everything, is at others worse than nothing" (*MP*: 235).

Austen works and reworks ideas of sameness and difference in *Mansfield Park* to an unusual degree. Even sunshine is "a totally different thing in a town and in the country," suggesting health and gaiety in a rural setting but in Portsmouth "only a glare, a stifling, sickly glare, serving but to bring forward stains and dirt that might otherwise have slept" (*MP*: 439). The dirt which is about to be illuminated at this point is the adulterous elopement of Henry Crawford and Maria Rushworth, news which makes Fanny Price experience a "shuddering of horror." As Ruth Bernard Yeazell notes, Fanny shudders at this juncture because of "people dangerously out of place, of accustomed categories blurred and confounded" (Yeazell 1984: 135). So shocked is our heroine that she cannot even name the guilty parties:

> A woman married only six months ago, a man professing himself devoted, even *engaged*, to another – that other her near relation – the whole family, both families connected as they were by tie upon tie, all friends, all intimate together! – it was too horrible a confusion of guilt, too gross a complication of evil, for human nature, not in a state of utter barbarism, to be capable of! (*MP*: 441)

Maria and Henry are simply a "woman" and a "man," and Fanny's own role in the drama is simply that of "another." The horror lies in the connection between the two families, the ties of intimacy which Edmund has pursued, claiming that the Crawfords "seem to belong to us – they seem to be part of ourselves" (*MP*: 196). This tie is repudiated by Fanny from the start, and it is her constant (albeit unvoiced) complaint to Edmund that "the families would never be connected if you did not connect them" (*MP*: 424). What is interesting about Fanny's shuddering reaction to the elopement is that, despite her consistent refusal to be connected with the Crawfords, she feels implicated in the adultery. Guilty complicity is of course a major theme of Thomas Clarkson's *History of the Abolition of the Slave Trade* (1808), a book which makes visible the complicated "mass" of wickedness and evil generated in England by colonialism and slavery. Even though the atrocities take place offshore, in a geographically remote part of the world, the evils of the slave trade form part of the texture of social, civilized life in the provincial ports of Bristol, London, and Liverpool. This is obvious every time Clarkson tries to harness to the abolitionist cause direct, eye-witness accounts of slavery. In the words of one former slave-trade surgeon he interviewed: "through that window you see a spacious house. It is occupied by a West Indian . . . If I give you my evidence I lose his patronage. At the house above him lives an East Indian. The two families are connected" (Clarkson 1808, vol. II: 25).

Body Trade

The scandal of the marriage market's trade in female flesh, so clumsily captured in More's 1805 essay, is a commonplace of eighteenth-century women's writing, as can be seen in one of Lady Mary Wortley Montagu's letters home from Turkey where she quips that women in the east are "bought and sold as publickly" as "in all our Christian great Citys" (April 10, 1718, Montagu 1965: vol. I: 402). The "coming out" trade in young marriageable girls crops up persistently in Austen's work, occasionally in quite brutal form, such as in John Dashwood's comment that Marianne's market price had plummeted so steeply as a result of her illness that she would be lucky to marry a man "worth more than five or six hundred a-year" (*SS*: 227). Or consider the first page of *Mansfield Park* in which Maria Ward's uncle calculates that, in marrying Sir Thomas Bertram, his niece was "at least three thousand pounds short of any equitable claim." For our purpose what is notable about the marriage market in Austen's work is that from the very start of her writing career in the early 1790s, this market is associated with colonialism. In *Catharine, or the Bower*, an unfinished novel which Austen started writing in 1792 when she was 17,[1] the destitute orphan Cecilia Wynne is shipped out to "Bengal or Barbadoes or wherever" (*MW*: 205) for a husband and a "maintenance," a fate (Catharine claims) "so opposite to all her ideas of Propriety, so contrary to her wishes, so repugnant to her feelings, that she would almost have preferred Servitude to it, had Choice been allowed her" (*MW*: 194). In invoking Bengal and Barbadoes, one destination representing oriental despotism, the other black slavery, Austen draws on two stereotypical comparisons deployed by British feminists in their claims for greater rights in the early 1790s,[2] a period also conspicuous for its marked overlap between feminist and abolitionist discourses. With the sugar boycott at its height, and scores of pamphlets targeting women consumers, women were enthusiastically taking up the cause, rousing their "sisters" into action with poems such as Mary Birkett's *A Poem on the African Slave Trade. Addressed to her own Sex* (1792, see Midgley 1992: 34).

In the same year that Austen was writing *Catharine*, a trial was taking place in London which featured the body of a young slave girl, allegedly flogged to death upside down on her passage from West Africa to the West Indies. With abolitionists and sugar boycotters keen to keep the atrocities of slavery at the center of public attention, the case of Captain Kimber received extensive coverage in the newspapers, including court transcripts of eye-witness testimony. In April 1792, ahead of the actual trial, the engraver Isaac Cruikshank circulated a print depicting the shipboard scene entitled "The Abolition of the Slave Trade" (Figure 25.3). Six months later another image began to circulate, an anonymous engraving of a London street scene entitled "The Rabbits" (Figure 25.4). Depicting a black rabbit-seller and a well-dressed young white woman, this engraving enters into a dialogue with Cruikshank's print. Indeed, in tying together the themes of commerce, household consumption, and the atrocities of slavery, it challenges the viewer to substitute the figure of the white consumer for that of Kimber's black victim. This is evident in the bawdy exchange in which, holding one of the dead rabbits by its hind leg and exclaiming "O la how it smells," the woman prompts the rabbit seller to protest: "Be gar Misse dat no fair. If Blacke Man take you by Leg so – you smell too." By pointing out the sameness that would be produced by the same upside-down circumstances, the rabbit

Figure 25.3 Isaac Cruikshank, *The Abolition of the Slave Trade*, published April 10, 1792 by S. W. Fores No 3 Picca. engraving BM 8079, The British Museum.

Figure 25.4 *The Rabbits*, published October 8, 1792 by Robt Sayer & Co, Fleet Street, London, engraving
BM 8217, The British Museum.

seller is in effect asking "Are you not a woman and a sister to that black female slave flogged to death on the middle passage?"

The figure of the rabbit seller, kneeling with left leg raised and right leg to the front, alludes to the popular Wedgwood medallion. To this extent "The Rabbits" mocks the kneeling slave, presenting us with a street hawker begging to be rid of his rabbits rather than his chains. But the true butt of the joke is the young white "Miss," challenged to face her shared humanity with Kimber's victim. The famous precedent for asserting the sameness and equality of a black girl and a white girl occurs in Laurence Sterne's *Tristram Shandy*, in a scene which, like "The Rabbits," links the sale of meat to flogging and misery. Here, in a sausage shop, we encounter a "poor negro girl" who has "suffered persecution" at the hands of a whip, the latter suggested by the girl's gentle flapping at flies "with a bunch of white feathers slightly tied to the end of a long cane." A listless figure of some pathos, this girl precipitates a conversation between Uncle Toby and Corporal Trim on the issue of whether or not black people have souls. The conclusion reached is "yes" for otherwise God would be setting one of his creatures "sadly over the head of another." And in Corporal Trim's memorable words, "Why is a black wench to be used worse than a white one?" The only reason must be that "she has no one to stand up for her," no one to afford her "protection" (Sterne 1760, vol. IX, ch. 6). A passing reference in one of Jane Austen's letters suggests that she had read *Tristram Shandy* (*Letters*: 93), but even if she had not she would have read about this scene in Clarkson's *History*, a book we know she admired (*Letters*: 198). Here, in a roll-call of honor to those who championed the cause of black people, Clarkson includes Sterne who "in his account of the Negro girl in his Life of Tristram Shandy, took decidedly the part of the oppressed Africans. The pathetic, witty and sentimental manner, in which he handled this subject, occasioned many to remember it, and procured a certain portion of feeling in their favour" (Clarkson 1808: 1, 60–61).

There is of course no sausage shop scene in *Mansfield Park* although a "little flogging" is deemed to be in order for the adulteress Maria Bertram. To quote the old seaman Mr Price: "by G– if she belonged to *me*, I'd give her the rope's end as long as I could stand over her" (*MP*: 440). A much more obvious and celebrated Sternean episode is the one involving the caged starling from *A Sentimental Journey* (1768). Imprisoned, the bird cries out for liberty in English words taught to it on the cliffs of Dover: "I can't get out, I can't get out" (Sterne 1768: 660–1). Maria Bertram, unhappily engaged to Mr Rushworth and in love with Henry Crawford, mimes Sterne's starling as she strolls with Crawford around the grounds of Sotherton, her future home with Rushworth. In a conversation which canvasses the literal and figurative meanings of the "smiling scene" which awaits her, Maria says of the iron gate and the ha-ha impeding their passage that they give her "a feeling of restraint and hardship. I cannot get out, as the starling said" (p. 71). Curiously, as critics of Sterne have noted, the starling episode is not so much metonymic of imprisonment as of African slavery. Struck by the starling's piteous cries and desperate fluttering against the sides of its cage, Yorick plunges from jaunty reflections on the prospect of imprisonment to a deeper meditation on slavery: "Disguise thyself as thou wilt, still, Slavery! . . . still thou art a bitter draught! And though thousands in all ages have been made to drink of thee, thou art no less bitter on that account" (Sterne 1768: 661).

Markman Ellis has written well of Sterne's use of confinement "to trope slavery in a metropolitan setting and sentimentalist scenario" (Ellis 1996: 72). The same might also be claimed of *Mansfield Park*, where the term "tyranny" is invoked – a word synonymous in revolutionary discourse with slavery and with men's illegitimate power over women. The iron fist in the velvet glove of English civility can be seen in the patriarchal Sir Thomas Bertram, who advises Fanny to go to bed after the ball. "'Advise' was his word, but it was the advice of absolute power" (*MP*: 280). This tyranny is seen again in the "unrepulsable" Henry Crawford who imprisons Fanny in the drawing room, oppressing her with his persistent and unwelcome attentions. Fanny grieves that Edmund, her chief protector, should leave her undefended during this siege, deliberately drawing himself off to read the newspaper so that Crawford might maximize a rare opportunity to press home his suit. Eventually, in a comic denouement, Fanny is saved by the ceremonious arrival of the tea-board. With Baddely the chief butler heading up a "solemn procession," the bustle of the urn and the cake-bearers deliver Fanny "from a grievous imprisonment of body and mind. She was at liberty, she was busy, she was protected" (*MP*: 344). As is the case with Sterne's "poor Negro girl," liberty for Fanny is "protection"; to use Corporal Trim's expression, having someone "to stand up for her."

After rejecting Henry Crawford's suit Fanny longs to flee from the sister as well. We read: "The promised visit from her 'friend,' as Edmund called Miss Crawford, was a formidable threat to Fanny, and she lived in continual terror of it" (*MP*: 356). Despite Edmund's insistent use of the benevolent, equalizing terms "friend" and "sister" to describe Mary, the language of unequal power relations – of dominance and submission, terror, and slavery – marks her interactions with Fanny, rupturing any such illusion of equality:

> Miss Crawford was not the slave of opportunity. She was determined to see Fanny alone, and therefore said to her tolerably soon, in a low voice, "I must speak to you for a few minutes somewhere;" words that Fanny felt all over her, in all her pulses, and all her nerves. Denial was impossible. Her habits of ready submission, on the contrary, made her almost instantly rise and lead the way out of the room. She did it with wretched feelings, but it was inevitable. (*MP*: 357)

Nina Auerbach, who thinks there is "something horrible" about Fanny, is captivated by Mary Crawford. She praises her pioneering feminist sensibility, her Wollstonecraftian "quest for sisters of gender rather than family, her uncomfortably outspoken championship of abused wives, her sexual initiative, and her unsettling habit of calling things by their names." Fanny's inability to "endure so universal an embrace" with Mary, her clutching instead at "the shreds of kinship," make her a disappointing heroine for Auerbach (Auerbach 1998: 447, 455). But for all Mary's protestations to Fanny – "Who says we shall not be sisters? I know we shall. I feel that we are born to be connected" (*MP*: 359) – she is, as far as Fanny is concerned, entirely deficient in proper feelings of sisterly solidarity. When Edmund relates Mary's anger and astonishment that her brother should have been refused, Fanny responds: "I *should* have thought that every woman must have felt the possibility of a man's not being approved, not being loved by someone of her sex, at least, let him be ever so generally agreeable." This betrayal, this essential unsisterliness of feeling towards other women stems, in Fanny's analysis, from Mary's uncritical devotion to her brother: "As a sister" she was "so partial and so angry, and so little scrupulous of what she said" (*MP*: 356). Earlier, in an incident involving choice between Edmund's chain and Henry's necklace, Fanny reflects: "Miss Crawford, complaisant as a sister, was careless as a woman and a friend" (*MP*: 260).

Notably, Fanny's achievement of a new, independent sense of identity occurs in her resolution of an unpleasant piece of sisterly rivalry in Portsmouth. This is the incident concerning the little silver knife, a dispute which canvasses two quite different versions of liberty. In restoring to Susan "full possession" of her knife, Fanny asserts the old-fashioned principle of liberty consisting in the right to undisturbed possession of one's own property. But a more modern understanding of liberty also emerges at this point, for Fanny's purchasing power enables her to lay claim to a new sense of personhood. The possession of independent means enables the formerly propertyless heroine to act for the first time *in propria persona* (*MP*: 397).

Conclusion

In 1790 Edmund Burke argued that England's political wisdom lay in granting to polity "the image of a relation in blood" (Burke 1790: 120). In a revolutionary era the imagining of kinship is a profoundly political act. On the one hand we see an essentially democratic appeal to a shared human nature, the rights of man leading on to the rights of women and to the rights of slaves. This opening out of the circles of reference in gendered and racial terms coexists with a movement inwards, a curtailing of the wider possibilities of kinship. The Crawfords, with their vitiated city morality, are cut away and the circle drawn tightly inwards. As Edmund exclaims towards the end of *Mansfield Park*, "My Fanny – my only sister – my only comfort now," a fraternal embrace which quickly shades off into the conjugal, the narrator briskly concluding: "Let other pens dwell on guilt and misery. I quit such odious subjects as soon as I can, impatient to restore every body, not greatly in fault themselves, to tolerable comfort, and to have done with all the rest" (*MP*: 461). But the comfort falls short of expectations, being only "tolerable," a disappointment connected, perhaps, to what Fanny herself described as her "reprobated and forbidden" love, one which "ought not to have touched on the confines of her imagination" (*MP*: 264–5). The incest taboo, explicitly invoked at the start of the novel, maintains its unsettling power throughout, leading Fanny to the brink of lying to her uncle, her lips "formed into a *no*, though the sound was inarticulate."

Sir Thomas, anxious about cousin marriage from the start, rushes in to articulate the word formed by Fanny's lips: "No, no, I know *that* is quite out of the question – quite impossible" (*MP*: 316). Just as the topic of incest gets articulated, only to be denied in its utterance, the slave trade is raised only to be greeted with "dead silence!" (*MP*: 198). Overt discussion is out of the question, either on account of boredom, or embarrassment or for some other reason. Austen's acute sense of just proportion, her attention to "the distinction proper to be made," led her to a sparing deployment of the metaphor of slavery in her fiction. She could never have blurred and confounded the categories of oppressed middle-class women and plantation slaves, as More does in her grotesque *jeu d'esprit*. At the same time, the shearing off of so many troubling family connections, the retreat to the "tolerable comfort" of an endogamous marriage, are Austen's way of keeping at bay the disturbing racial intimacies invoked by that appeal to a more universal siblinghood.

NOTES

1 For the textual history of this work see Peter Sabor's Introduction to *Juvenilia*, in *The Cambridge Edition of the Works of Jane Austen* (Cambridge University Press, 2006).

2 I am thinking here of Catharine Macaulay in her *Letters on Education* (1790) and Mary Wollstonecraft in her two *Vindication* tracts of 1790 and 1792. For more on this topic see Midgley (1998): 161–79.

FURTHER READING

Mee, Jon (2000). Austen's treacherous ivory: female patriotism, domestic ideology, and empire. In You-me Park and Rajeswari Sunder Rajan (Eds). *The Postcolonial Jane Austen* (pp. 74–92). London and New York: Routledge.

Roberts, Warren (2005). Nationalism and empire. In Janet Todd (Ed.). *Jane Austen in Context*. Cambridge, UK: Cambridge University Press.

Said, Edward (1994). *Culture and Imperialism*. London: Vintage.

Salih, Sara (2006). The silence of Miss Lambe: Sanditon and contextual fictions of "race" in the abolition era. *Eighteenth-Century Fiction*, 18:3, 329–53.

Tuite, Clara (2000). Domestic retrenchment and imperial expansion: the property plots of *Mansfield Park*. In You-me Park and Rajeswari Sunder Rajan (Eds). *The Postcolonial Jane Austen* (pp. 93–115). London and New York: Routledge.

Yeazell, R. B. (1984). The boundaries of *Mansfield Park*. *Representations*, 7, 133–52.

26
Jane Austen and the Nation

Claire Lamont

Jane Austen was born in 1775 in the village of Steventon, in the county of Hampshire, and was therefore a native of Great Britain. That entity had taken political form in stages: Wales was united with England in 1536; the crowns of England, Wales, and Scotland were united in 1603, and the parliaments in 1707. From then on the three countries on the island which the Romans had known as Britannia were to be considered a political unit. During Austen's life, in 1801, the Irish were brought into this polity, although since theirs was a different island, Hibernia, they were not *British*. In studying Austen one wonders whether it is remotely necessary to recall all this, since she, and the characters in her novels, almost always refer to themselves as *English*. That complicates the question of "Jane Austen and the Nation," and in this essay I shall start with the idea of Britain, and move towards that of England.

Jane Austen herself left England only once – to go on a short trip to Wales with her family in 1802 – and no scenes in her novels are set in Wales, Scotland, or Ireland. Her novels have no characters from these countries, although plays and novels of the late eighteenth century had frequently given satirical portraits of the clownish Welshman, the irascible Scot, and the fortune-hunting Irishman. She refers to lovers eloping to Scotland, although only Julia Bertram and Mr Yates appear actually to get there (*SS*: 206, *PP*: 273, *MP*: 442). In her *Juvenilia*, however, it is a different matter; in these lively and precocious sketches characters happily travel in both Wales and Scotland. Austen seems to have associated both countries with the settings of Gothic novels. Catherine Morland, reconsidering her belief in the realism of these novels, "dared not doubt beyond her own country, and even of that, if hard pressed, would have yielded the northern and western extremities" (*NA*: 200). The "extremities" are clearly Scotland and Wales. When she moves away from the Gothic Austen makes almost no use of the other countries within the union. As she warned her niece Anna, who was writing a novel, "you had better not leave England. Let the Portmans go to Ireland, but as you know nothing of the Manners there, you had better not go with them" (*Letters*: 269).

Political theorists are cautious in attributing national boundaries to the determination of geography (Renan 1882/1990: 18); but some allowance must be made for a smallish island off a major land mass, and especially during a continental war. Austen has the interest in the sea of someone whose early years were spent inland. While in *Emma* the heroine's father and sister discuss the sea in terms of health and the new fashion for sea-bathing, Emma's own wish to see it seems to be an expression of yearning for wider and more elemental horizons (*E*: 101), and anticipates the moving response to seeing the sea in *Persuasion*. In the two novels where scenes are set by the sea, at Portsmouth in *Mansfield Park* and at Lyme Regis in *Persuasion*, there is direct association with the navy. Britain's island status was of particular significance during Austen's adult life when the country was at war with Napoleonic France. Napoleon showed repeated intentions of invading Britain, which only the sea and the navy could prevent. This they did at the battle of Trafalgar (1805) at which Nelson destroyed the French and Spanish fleets. Napoleon was a soldier, not a sailor. After Trafalgar he decided on a course more suited to his military talents, which was the blockade of all continental trade with Britain (the "Continental System"). This changed the duties of the British navy, from set-piece battles like Trafalgar, to the support of merchant ships and harrying of enemy vessels. It is in this context that Frederick Wentworth in *Persuasion* makes his fortune in the capture of French ships.

To turn from a horizontal to a vertical view of Austen's nation we should ask how it was governed and how the ranks in society were ordered. Britain was, of course, a monarchy, but Austen's novels show almost no engagement with either the royal court or the nobility. The highest ranking among her significant characters is Lady Catherine de Bourgh, who comes from a "noble line" (*PP*: 356). Two other titled characters, Sir Thomas Bertram and Sir Walter Elliot, are baronets. Baronets are the highest rank of commoner, and Sir Thomas serves as a Member of Parliament in the House of Commons (*MP*: 20). Austen felt some ambivalence towards the monarchy. She upheld the institution – she had not been tempted by revolutionary republicanism – but found much to deplore in the behavior of the man who took over as Prince Regent in 1811. He was, however, a connoisseur of the arts, as his invitation to Austen to dedicate a novel to him shows. Her acceptance may have had an element of gratification in it; but is more likely to express her deference to the monarchy as the symbol of the nation, irrespective of the holder of the office whom she had earlier admitted to hating (*Letters*: 208). Austen's characters are for the most part below the level of an aristocracy. They are landowners large and small, clergy and other professional men and their families, plus tradesmen and servants. Most of these are described in rural settings where the chief source of value is in land and farming it. Exceptions are the naval characters, particularly William Price and Frederick Wentworth, who display the manly qualities necessary for the nation's defense. There is almost no mention of industry in Austen's novels, and almost certainly less than was warranted by Hampshire in the decades in which she lived there.

Benedict Anderson has famously described a nation as an "imagined community." A nation is too big for anyone living in it to know more than a few others; but its nationness is reinforced by our capacity to *imagine* our fellow inhabitants as people much like ourselves. In bringing this about Anderson awards particular significance to print, and especially to newspapers (Anderson 1991: 33–6). Newspapers are mentioned in Austen's novels, often with the implication that they are the occupation of idle men; Anne Elliot is the only woman described as reading them (*P*: 30). Austen is, however, always interested in the shaping of minds by shared reading, for instance Gothic novels, or the approved texts of sensibility. Reading in Austen undoubtedly fortifies an imagined community, but not only one. She frequently makes use of the parallel mindsets gained by differences in reading. The clash between a limited reading circle and what one might call public news occurs in *Northanger Abbey* when Catherine "in rather a solemn tone of voice, uttered these words, 'I have heard that something very shocking indeed, will soon come out in London'" (*NA*: 111–12). She is referring to a Gothic novel, but Eleanor Tilney supposes it to be news of an impending riot. The conduct book, which was supposed to set standards for the behavior of the nation's young women, is rejected by Lydia Bennet just before she embarks on a series of thoughtless and damaging life choices (*PP*: 68). Reading is symbolic of the nation in *Persuasion*. Sir Walter Elliot reads only the *Baronetage* (*P*: 3), which gratifies his sense of self-importance and maps out what is for him important about his country. His daughter reads the navy lists (*P*: 30), out of love and also through recognition of the importance of a different sort of person to the nation.

Linda Colley has suggested that what held Britain together in the eighteenth and early nineteenth centuries was Protestantism and seeing itself in relation to other countries overseas (Colley 2005: 5). Those overseas territories were both in Europe and in other continents where the British went on military or mercantile adventures. It is worth considering Austen's sense of her nation against these criteria. Writing in her own name, Austen is clearly conscious of the Catholicism of most of Europe. When her brother Francis is posted to the Baltic she expresses her respect for the Protestantism of Sweden (*Letters*: 215). When we turn to the novels, however, there is no sense of Protestantism as against Catholicism. One aspect of Austen's sense of her nation is the village Anglicanism which was a major part of both her life and her novels. That Anglicanism is not set against any alternative religion. Her villages have no Catholics, or Protestant dissenters, despite the fact that Catholic emancipation was an important political issue throughout her adult life. If Anglicanism is part of Austen's sense of her country, it is so in the novels without reference to any *other*. It is not argued for, or defended, it simply *is*.

Is the situation different when we turn to the other force which Colley mentions as holding Britain together, the overseas *other*? Austen's novels were all written when Britain was at war with either Revolutionary or Napoleonic France, and during decades of maritime and colonial expansion. Austen was 14 years old when the French Revolution broke out, and it is likely that her views on it were influenced by the story of her cousin, Eliza Hancock, who had married a royalist French officer who was guillotined in 1794. The novels are set later, for the most part during or just after the end of the Napoleonic Wars. During these wars her younger brothers Francis and Charles served in the navy, and three of her elder brothers in the militia, forces drawn up particularly to protect the country in case of invasion. Public events do not figure largely in her letters; but there are a few telling references. It appears that she withdrew from the celebrity culture engendered by the war. In 1813 she wrote to her sister Cassandra on the appearance of Robert Southey's *Life of Nelson*, "I am tired of Lives of Nelson, being that I never read any" (*Letters*: 235). In the same year she made her high-spirited comment that *Pride and Prejudice* "wants to be stretched out here & there with a long Chapter [. . .] about something unconnected with the story; an Essay on Writing, a critique on Walter Scott, or the history of Buonaparte" (*Letters*: 203). When she is seriously moved, as she was by the death of Sir John Moore at Corunna, she is brief and allusive, "This is greivous news from Spain" (*Letters*: 171). After Waterloo she was keen to hear accounts of the battle, and of Paris when it was once more possible for Britons to visit it (*Letters*: 297, 321).

When we turn to the novels such intimate and informed references to the war and to Europe are absent. The long wars must surely have meant that the country would be aware of threats of invasion and Britain's shifting alliances with European states in the hope of containing French expansion. Neither Lydia Bennet nor her mother, however, seem to have any understanding of what the militia is for, or why it might be strategically useful to have a camp at Brighton. Catherine Morland, whose Europe is that of Ann Radcliffe's novels, makes confident reference to "the South of France" (*NA*: 83, 106, 200). Otherwise France seems to make impact on Austen's characters mainly through the number of French émigrés who had arrived in England, many of them destitute since the French revolutionary government had in 1792 declared all émigrés traitors and their property liable to confiscation. *Sense and Sensibility* reflects the shifts they were driven to when Mrs John Dashwood gives each of the Steele girls "a needle book, made by some emigrant" (*SS*: 254). Even that level of sympathy is not shared by the xenophobic John Thorpe in *Northanger Abbey* who refers to Fanny Burney as "that woman they make such a fuss about, she who married the French emigrant" (*NA*: 49).

The response at home is little different if one follows British maritime expansion east and west. Austen had heard something of India through her aunt Philadelphia who had married in India and knew Warren Hastings. In the novels Austen does not use the term India; she writes of the East Indies, which at the time could refer to both the subcontinent and the islands of the Far East. Colonel Brandon in *Sense and Sensibility* had been to the East with his regiment. His conversation is dismissed as uninteresting by Marianne Dashwood who says mockingly to her sister, "he has told you that in the East Indies the climate is hot, and the mosquitoes are troublesome," to which Willoughby adds, "Perhaps [. . .] his observations may have extended to the existence of nabobs, gold mohrs, and palanquins" (*SS*: 51). These are of course the usual terms in which the unreflecting referred to India.

When it is suggested that young William Price might go to India his aunt Bertram's response is:

"William must not forget my shawl, if he goes to the East Indies; and I shall give him a commission for any thing else that is worth having. I wish he may go to the East Indies, that I may have my shawl. I think I will have two shawls, Fanny." (*MP*: 305)

Indian textiles were much coveted – here the famous cashmere shawls. What we notice about these responses to India is their sheer banality. They come at a time when drama, the novel, and even children's books were responding to the significant British presence in India. This banality cannot be attributed to ignorance on the part of the novelist. A family connection with Warren Hastings, however, was not needed for such remarks; what was needed was sharp observation of the society in which she lived.

If we turn to the West Indies, again Austen had access to particular knowledge through her family. Her father's friend and former pupil, James Nibbs, was heir to an estate in Antigua; her brother Charles held naval command in Bermuda. What do Austen's characters know about those islands which were important to Britain as sources of tropical goods and ports for the British navy? The most famous is Antigua in *Mansfield Park*. Antigua is one of the sugar islands and a modern reader cannot mention it without associating it with slavery. Nor could Fanny Price; on Sir Thomas Bertram's return it is she who gets up courage to "ask him about the slave trade." She does not get beyond that one question because her "cousins were sitting by without speaking a word, or seeming at all interested in the subject" (*MP*: 198). When Sir Thomas does tell his story, "in the most interesting moment of his passage to England, when the alarm of a French privateer was at the height, [Mrs Norris] burst through his recital with the proposal of soup" (*MP*: 180).

The well-traveled Mrs Croft tells Mrs Musgrove that she "never was in the West Indies. We do not call Bermuda or Bahama, you know, the West Indies." The narrator continues: "Mrs. Musgrove had not a word to say in dissent; she could not accuse herself of having ever called them any thing in the whole course of her life" (*P*: 70). The Bahamas, and especially Bermuda, are to the north of the Caribbean colonies and had economies based on the sea rather than on agriculture. The few people in Austen's novels who have been to the West Indies find on their return a society ignorant of geography and uninterested in their experiences. Only at the end of her career does Austen suggest that the West Indies might come to Britain. In *Sanditon* Miss Lambe, a wealthy "half Mulatto" from the West Indies, is brought to the resort for her health (*MW*: 387, 421).

These examples help us to assess the impact of countries overseas on Austen's characters. In each case there is a diminution from the knowledge and outlook of the novelist to that of the majority of her characters. There are a few exceptions: Fanny Price reads the journal of Lord Macartney's troubled embassy to China in 1792–4 (*MP*: 156); Anne Elliot translates an Italian song (*P*: 186). These heroines are untypical in their cultural awareness; if one asks what most people in Austen's novels think about the world elsewhere with which their country had such intimate and disturbing relations, the answer is, not much. Linda Colley's claim that the idea of Britain was fostered in its inhabitants by reference to an overseas *other* does not require that the process should be conscious. It is largely unconscious in Austen's novels. There rural life goes on, with its balls and card parties and all the small negotiations of rank and fashion, and anything taking place abroad is ignored or referred to in clichés. We notice, however, that those matters which Austen's characters retain only at the margins of awareness are particularly British. They concern the achievements of the *British* army and navy, or places subsumed into the *British* empire. Most of her characters are not interested in the areas of experience where Britishness came into play; they do not give much thought to what their country was doing on the world stage. As a consequence they very seldom uses the term "Britain" for their nation. If we don't notice this it may be because of Mr Bennet's famous reflection on the "satisfaction of prevailing on one of the most worthless young men in Great Britain to be [Lydia's] husband" (*PP*: 308). This is Bennet rhetoric; on the whole Austen's characters, like the narrator, use the terms England and English. It is time, therefore, to turn to Austen's Englishness.

Austen's Englishness takes some definition from its exclusion of the rest of Britain and the rest of the world. But why stop there? What about the north of England? That too is seldom mentioned in Austen's novels. *Pride and Prejudice* recognizes that the Lakes would be worth visiting; but the Bingleys have left the north of England where their family's fortune had been made in trade (*PP*: 15). As for the northern cities – well, Newcastle is a place to send Lydia and Wickham. Mrs Elton sums up Birmingham, the early industrial revolution city in the midlands, as "not a place to promise much [. . .]. One has not great hopes from Birmingham" (*E*: 310).

The counties of England in which most of the scenes in Austen's novels are set are Wiltshire, Somerset, and Gloucestershire (*Northanger Abbey*), Sussex, Devonshire, and Somerset (*Sense and Sensibility*), Hertfordshire, Kent, and Derbyshire (*Pride and Prejudice*), Northamptonshire and Hampshire (*Mansfield Park*), Surrey (*Emma*), and Somerset and Dorset (*Persuasion*). Franco Moretti points out that these are precisely the counties which are almost never used as settings in Gothic novels (1998: 16). Austen's novels frequently show women crossing the boundaries of these counties in order to marry (Moretti 1998: 14–15). Few things unite the country so convincingly as the expectation that a heroine may on marriage live happily in a county different from that of her birth. On the other hand Newcastle (in Northumberland) is at the outer limit of where an Austen woman can go on marriage, and happiness is not guaranteed there. For a novelist who is so precise in her reference to English counties, Maria Rushworth's banishment to somewhere unnamed is oblivion indeed (*MP*: 465).

Most of Austen's characters live in those parts of southern England which are an extended version of what we have come to call the "home counties." The *Oxford English Dictionary* dates the expression to 1898 and derives it from the "Home Circuit," the assize circuit which had London as its center. The exact counties included in that circuit kept changing, but never included counties as far north as Derbyshire, or as far to the south-west as Devonshire. What makes the term applicable to the geography of Austen's novels, however, is that all her counties are seen in some relation to London. Many of her characters divide their lives between the county of their main residence and London. Even the Dashwood sisters, living in reduced circumstances in Devonshire, manage to spend "the season" in London. Is Austen the first novelist to suggest that the real England is to be found in those counties which circle London but are clearly distant from it?

Another familiar phrase brought to mind by Austen's novels is "middle England." Although originally a geographical term it has in recent decades come to be used predominantly socially, to evoke what the *OED* defines as "middle class people in England [. . .] regarded as representative of traditional social values, non-metropolitan mores, or conservative political views." Austen's characters are good examples of "middle England," with this proviso, that many of them are insecure in wealth or social position. They are anxious, especially concerning those social transitions which are, particularly for women, marked by the death of the father and by marriage. While such people show nervous deference to those above them socially – witness Mrs Bennet's confusion in dealing with Mr Darcy and Lady Catherine de Bourgh – their behavior to those below them is more revealing. Within Austen's houses are servants, seldom named and allowed to speak only when their role absolutely requires it. Outside the house are the poor, whom Emma dutifully visits (*E*: 83). Maria Bertram, by contrast, shows no concern for the inhabitants of the cottages at Sotherton which she describes as "a disgrace" (*MP*: 82). These are examples of the social *other*, whose place in society "middle England" has difficulty in acknowledging. Beyond them are the racial *other*, the gypsies from whose presence in a country lane the instinctive response is flight (*E*: 333).

London was by far the largest city in Britain, and was the center of government, commerce, and the arts and a source of news and fashion; it was also, in comparison with the countryside, a center of materialism and vice. Austen's awareness of the city as a place of risk and opportunity is humorously conveyed in an early letter to Cassandra from London where she had gone with two of her brothers, "Here I am once more in this Scene of Dissipation & vice, and I begin already to find my Morals corrupted. [. . .] Edward & Frank are both gone out to seek their fortunes" (*Letters*: 5). In her novels London is a place of fashion, money, crowds, and behavior which has come loose from the structures and conventions still upheld in rural communities. London is where Marianne Dashwood is jilted, Lydia Bennet is lost, and where Maria Bertram compensates for a loveless marriage with a fashionable house. There are other cities in Austen's novels, in particular Bath and Portsmouth, but none approaches London for fascination and danger.

Austen's southern English counties are rural with agricultural landscapes. They lack the sublime of mountains but offer the beautiful in terms of well-tended agriculture. Her characters like to walk, although walks are threatened by rain and paths can be muddy. Where possible they enjoy a prospect, in which they admire those things which underpin society economically and socially – fertile and well-farmed land offering livelihood to the poor and acknowledging the guiding hand of the well-disposed landowner. After the description of such a view in *Emma* the narrator comments, "It was a sweet view — sweet to the eye and the mind. English verdure, English culture, English comfort, seen under a sun bright without being oppressive" (*E*: 360). We might note that Walter Scott's *Waverley* (2007), a novel which Austen knew, mentions *comfortable* as a word peculiarly English (p. 35). This passage is curiously rhapsodic in view of the moderation in what it offers: *comfort* as opposed to anything livelier, and a sun whose brightness is tempered to English taste.

Emma, meditating on Donwell Abbey, the home of Mr Knightley, reflects that "It was just what it ought to be, and it looked what it was [. . .] the residence of a family of such true gentility, untainted in blood and understanding" (*E*: 358). In a novel concerned with deceptive appearances she praises an ideal of integrity, associated with personal modesty and esteem for those values which are least susceptible to fashion. The shortcomings of Frank Churchill are revealed in his discontented remark, "I am sick of England — and would leave it to-morrow, if I could" (*E*: 365). *Emma* is the most consciously English of Austen's novels, and that quality, while it is given expression by the heroine, is represented in action by the significantly named Knightley brothers. They greet each other "in the true English style, burying under a calmness that seemed all but indifference, the real attachment which would have led either of them, if requisite, to do every thing for the good of the other" (*E*: 99–100). Mr Knightley, whose Christian name, George, is that of the country's patron saint, expresses himself, even in affairs of the heart, in "plain, unaffected, gentleman-like English" (*E*: 448).

A more ambivalent view of English values comes across in the reproof Henry Tilney delivers to Catherine Morland for imagining that his father, General Tilney, might have murdered his wife,

> "Remember the country and the age in which we live. Remember that we are English, that we are Christians. [. . .] Does our education prepare us for such atrocities? Do our laws connive at them? Could they be perpetrated without being known, in a country like this, where social and literary intercourse is on such a footing; where every man is surrounded by a neighbourhood of voluntary spies, and where roads and newspapers lay every thing open?" (*NA*: 197–8)

Austen's England may have derived its values from Christianity, and supported them with education and law; but what follows implies that the actual safeguard against murder is the fear of being found out, and the reference to "spies" is a reminder of the repressive legislation of the 1790s designed to curb expressions of pro-Revolutionary sentiment. Catherine's response sidesteps the assertion that in England it would be hard to commit murder and get away with it. Instead she acknowledges, in contrast to the lurid characterization of Gothic novels, that "among the English [. . .] in their hearts and habits, there was a general though unequal mixture of good and bad," implying that an Englishman would not be wicked *enough* to commit the murder she had attributed to the General (*NA*: 200). In *Northanger Abbey* the Gothic theme requires that England is contrasted with those parts of Europe which commonly featured in Gothic novels. In *Emma* the English countryside and English manners are not offered in contrast to those found anywhere else. English values in the novel are self-validating; indeed some sorts of behavior are too disingenuously undesirable even to be expressed in the English language. It is only in this situation that another language has to be brought in to help out a language limited by the blunt honesty of its speakers. Mr Knightley accuses Frank Churchill of being "amiable only in French, not in English" (*E*: 149), and Emma's behavior at Box Hill "had such an appearance as no English word but flirtation could very well describe" (*E*: 368), with the apparent implication that French would have supplied a more accepting term for it. Mary Crawford uses French for such a purpose in describing her brother's elopement with Maria Bertram as an "*etourderie*," a folly (*MP*: 437).

The nation state is usually seen as a modern reality whose origins are attributed variously to the sixteenth century (Balibar and Wallerstein 1991: 88, 105, n.2) or the eighteenth (Anderson 1991: 4). The countries of Western Europe, however, have been traced to a much earlier origin, the Germanic invasions after the collapse of the Roman Empire (Renan 1882/1990: 9–10). Following that distinction we can observe that Britain is a nation state to which dates can be given; but England? Austen's novels go in for almost no narrative history but there are indications that value attaches to things which have lasted a long time, especially if they have done so in an unshowy way. Mr Darcy is descended from an "ancient, though untitled" family (*PP*: 356); Uppercross village was until recently "completely in the old English style" (*P*: 36), and there are many instances of old trees. Age here is unspecified, but it implies that these things share with England itself an origin if not beyond then outside the calculations of time. This is not to suggest that Austen viewed English history as unstained in its long course. Modern readers have detected in *Mansfield Park* a profound horror at the country's engagement in the slave trade and slave ownership. Another less noticed expression of national shame is in Austen's references to the dissolution of the monasteries by Henry VIII. Her pain, explicitly expressed in her juvenile "History of England" (*MW*: 142–3), is echoed in allusions in *Northanger Abbey* and *Sense and Sensibility* and perhaps healed in *Emma*. Renan points out that nation-making involves a certain amount of forgetting (1882/1990: 11). Most of Austen's characters forget in advance by refusing to know anything much about times or places other than their own.

The idea of Britain has always needed to be negotiated and defended. A feature of Englishness is that it does not. The achievement of the English is to have created a culture which they regard as simply *normal*. The assumption of normality is largely unconscious; it expresses itself at best in self-sufficiency, at worst in complacency. Most of the characters in Austen's England know almost nothing about places outside their direct experience, whether those places endanger their lives like France, or support them like Antigua. And they don't need to. I mentioned above that religion in Austen's novels just *is*; her England also has that monumental quality of simply *being*.

Eighteenth-century rhetoric presented Britain as divinely favored: "When Britain first at heaven's command, / Arose from out the azure main" (quoted in Colley 2005: 11). By contrast there is a low-key quality to Austen's evocation of England. She would probably, had she known it, have agreed with Blake's muted evocation of "England's green and pleasant land." Her Englishness expresses itself as the standard of where and how one might live; and while one cannot justify this attitude one cannot deny its power of quiet seduction. Because of that it has survived to comfort troops in the trenches of World War I in Kipling's "The Janeites" (1924), and to assuage the stresses of urbanization and cultural dislocation in contemporary film adaptations.

FURTHER READING

Colley, L. (2005). *Britons: Forging the Nation 1707–1837*, 2nd edn. New Haven, CT and London: Yale University Press.

Jordan, E. (2000). Jane Austen goes to the seaside: *Sanditon*, English identity and the "West Indian" schoolgirl. In You-me Park and Rajeswari Sunder Rajan (Eds). *The Postcolonial Jane Austen* (pp. 29–35). London and New York: Routledge.

Moretti, F. (1998). *Atlas of the European Novel 1800–1900*. London and New York: Verso.

Sales, R. (1994). *Jane Austen and Representations of Regency England*. London and New York: Routledge.

Wiltshire, John (2004). Jane Austen's England, Jane Austen's world. In Beatrice Battaglia and Diego Saglia (Eds). *Re-Drawing Austen* (pp. 125–36). Naples: Liguori.

27
Religion

Roger E. Moore

Jane Austen knew a great deal about religion. For the first 25 years of her life, she lived in a country parsonage. Her father was the rector of Steventon parish, and her brothers James and Henry attended Oxford and took holy orders. In her formative years Austen would have witnessed much religious debate and discussion. Austen would have attended Morning and Evening Prayer services on Sundays and some form of daily devotion would most probably have been observed in the Austen household. Her "Prayers," which echo the *Book of Common Prayer*, reflect a deep familiarity with Anglican liturgy. Her youthful "History of England" betrays a lively interest in the Reformation and English history; her letters show awareness of and curiosity about contemporary preachers and religious movements. Archbishop Richard Whately observed that Austen is "not at all obtrusive" about religion in the novels, although this does not mean that she didn't feel deeply about religion or that her works don't in some ways disclose these feelings (Southam 1987: 95). The novels demonstrate a sustained, if subdued, interest in religion that suggests Austen's engagement with the ideas, controversies, and events of the eighteenth-century English church.

Although we often think of the eighteenth century as a spiritually somnolent time, in this period the Church of England was a battleground between a liberal faction urging change and a conservative faction desperate to defend tradition. Liberal, latitudinarian divines believed they were fulfilling the goals of the Reformation by removing the last forms of superstition and credalism from the Church; they disdained the subscription to religious formulae and creeds required in the Church of England and which seemed to them suggestive of the papal past (Young 1998). High Church Tories opposed this continuing spirit of reformation and sought to preserve the creeds, the church's ecclesiastical structure, and priestly authority. Later in the period, during Austen's lifetime, an evangelical party rejected both Tories and latitudinarians. Evangelicals exalted old-fashioned Calvinistic rigor, and they found little to admire in liberal theology or High Church devotion to tradition.

How might we position Austen with respect to these debates? Some critics have connected her with evangelicalism. Austen's letters do indeed seem to indicate that, as she grew older, she came to sympathize with the evangelicals. Whereas in 1809 she tells her sister Cassandra "I do not like the Evangelicals," in 1814 she remarks to her niece Fanny Knight, "I am by no means convinced that we ought not all to be Evangelicals, & am at least persuaded that they who are so from Reason and Feeling, must be happiest and safest" (*Letters*: 170, 280). Critics as diverse as Avrom Fleishman (1967) and Marilyn Butler (1986) have detected the influence of evangelicalism in *Mansfield Park*; the novel's addressing of clerical nonresidence and patronage, its consideration of the potentially corrupting effects of theatrical entertainments, and its presentation of quiet, rigoristic female piety have seemed to indicate Austen's subscription to the evangelical program.

As David Monaghan pointed out, however, just because Austen "shares some of the opinions expressed in the works of Hannah More and Thomas Gisborne" does not mean that the movement influenced her or that she saw her beliefs in an evangelical light (Monaghan 1978: 230). She derided authors like More who used the novel as a means to transmit a particular ideology (Waldron 1994). Austen blends the liberalism and conservatism of the period into her own unique form of belief, one that is more complicated and more subtle than the rigid evangelical agenda.

Austen's novels diverge from evangelicalism by giving virtually no rein to Calvinism. Her novels indicate a belief in the goodness of humankind and emphasize the possibility of improvement. Although many of the characters (e.g., Sir Walter Elliott in *Persuasion* or Mr Woodhouse in *Emma*) seem lost in their own vanity or myopia, characters like Emma Woodhouse and Elizabeth Bennet, who at least recognize their limitations and begin to change, imply Austen's confidence in human effort. This confidence suggests an allegiance to the latitudinarian theology popular in the late seventeenth and eighteenth centuries. Archbishop John Tillotson and John Locke, two of the most influential figures for eighteenth-century theology, were students of the seventeenth-century Cambridge Platonists and continued their emphasis on the simplicity and rationality of Christianity. In contrast to puritans, whose insistence on human depravity made the Christian life appear difficult and fraught, they believed a Christian life was relatively easy; they focused on the inherent goodness and freedom of the human will and proclaimed the ease with which people could cooperate with God in achieving salvation. According to Tillotson, God wants us to become divine creatures, and he "is most ready to afford his Grace and Assistance to us to this purpose, if we heartily beg it of him" (Tillotson 1702: 128). In *The Reasonableness of Christianity*, John Locke conceives of that Christian faith as a belief in Jesus as Messiah and "sincere Endeavour after Righteousness" (Locke 1999: 119). God honors the effort to live a good life by giving us "assistance": "If we do what we can, he will give us his Spirit to help us do what, and how we should" (Locke 1999: 163). Richard Allestree's *The Whole Duty of Man* (1658), often reprinted and widely read throughout the eighteenth century, takes a similarly benign view of God and humanity: God "commands nothing, which he will not enable us to perform, if we be not wanting in ourselves" (Allestree 1784: 27). Eighteenth-century preachers and writers of devotional manuals were especially fond of Titus 2:12: "The grace of God which brings Salvation unto all men hath appeared, teaching us that denying ungodliness and worldly lusts, we should live soberly, and righteously, and godly in this present world." This biblical verse neatly summarizes the century's emphasis on the universality of God's grace and the importance of moral duty in achieving salvation.

The optimism of eighteenth-century theology characterized all branches – High and Low – of the English church. Most Calvinists had been ejected from the church in 1662, and the remaining churchmen, regardless of party affiliation or worship style, followed in the tradition of Jacob Arminius (1559–1609), the Dutch theologian whose insistence on the necessity of free will in matters of salvation threatened Calvinist orthodoxy in the seventeenth century (Walsh and Taylor 1993: 42). Austen's novels have some affinity with the Arminianism of the age. Her characters are neither wholly good nor wholly bad (Ryle 1968). They suffer from pride, arrogance, selfishness, or vanity, but their faults owe more to unsatisfactory education than original sin. Austen rarely even invokes "sin" or "evil." Like John Locke, who referred to sins as "slips and falls," Austen refers to the "errors," "faults," and "slips" of her characters. At the end of *Mansfield Park*, Edmund Bertram finally abandons his feelings for Mary Crawford because she can give "no harsher name than folly" to the adulterous behavior of Henry and Maria, but generally "folly" is the way Austen describes the behavior of her characters (*MP*: 454). Although Emma pridefully attempts to control the affairs of all those around her, Austen merely classifies her behavior as "folly" that "might teach her humility and circumspection in future" (*E*: 475). Austen echoes many latitudinarian divines when her narrator describes Emma's hope, near the end of the novel, of becoming "more rational, more acquainted with herself" as a result of awakening from her foolish machinations (*E*: 423), but she also readily tolerates, even admires, her heroine's lapses without engaging in puritanical admonitions about backsliding.

Austen even refuses to treat more clearly dangerous characters, like Mary Crawford, as inherently bad or beyond redemption. Fanny Price comes close to regarding Mary as reprobate, and Fanny believes she might "be forgiven by older sages, for looking on the chance of Miss Crawford's future improvement as nearly desperate" (*MP*: 367). Edmund comes close to the same conclusion. His dismay at Mary's response to Henry and Maria's elopement leads him to consider a deep "evil" about Mary, but he refuses to ascribe this to anything other than a "corrupted, vitiated mind" that has suffered from its association with "the world" (*MP*: 456). Like the Bertram sisters, whom Sir Thomas discovers "had never been properly taught to govern their inclinations and tempers" and who had never been required to bring "into daily practice" what they had learned "theoretically" of religion, Mary behaves badly because she has been taught badly (*MP*: 463). If she could remove herself from the corruptions of the society in which she moves and let Mansfield "cure" her, she might well achieve some sort of redemption. Even Fanny's censorious estimation of Mary, as someone with a "mind led astray and bewildered . . . darkened, yet fancying itself light," suggests a common eighteenth-century hesitancy to exclude the possibility of interior change. Rather than being evil, Mary's mind is merely "led astray"; rather than being dark, it is merely "darkened" (*MP*: 367). Austen avoids regarding evil as an inherent or immutable category, and in the novels she implies the individual's ability to transform himself or herself by reconnecting with their truer, better nature.

Austen's confidence in human effort leads her at times to a distrust of clerical authority. The clergy in the novels are remarkable for their lack of spiritual vocation, and they pursue church careers largely out of necessity. Henry Tilney and Edmund Bertram are younger sons who need employment, while Edward Ferrars finally takes orders only after he is disinherited. Dr Grant cares only for pleasure and immediately abandons Mansfield parish when a long-coveted prebendal stall at Westminster becomes available. Edmund is by far the most sincere cleric in the novels but even he shows a surprising flexibility of principle. He participates in the performance of *Lovers' Vows* after he has protested vigorously against it and he pursues Mary, a woman who disrespects clerics as lazy and ridicules the trappings of formal religious worship (Waldron 1994). Mr Collins of *Pride and Prejudice* is merely risible.

Some of Austen's clerical portraits reveal a strain of old-fashioned Protestant satire. Drawing on medieval satiric models, early English Protestants like William Tyndale and John Bale developed the satire of the sensual priest into a fine art. Tyndale's *Obedience of a Christian* Man (1528) teems with references to priests who care more for their bellies than the souls of their parishioners, and his criticisms came to life in the works of Spenser, Bunyan, and Milton, among others. Austen's depictions often catch the flavor of the sixteenth- and seventeenth-century Protestant writers; Mary's indictment of Dr Grant's distress about the unpalatable "green goose" served at his table, for instance, recalls Milton's scathing indictment of prelates with "canary-sucking, swan-eating palats [*sic*]" (Milton 1931:19).

Austen's consideration of the problems of clerical nonresidence and pluralism also resonates with traditional Protestant skepticism about clerical hierarchy. She would undoubtedly have agreed with Sir Thomas Bertram's statement that a minister who "does not live among his parishioners and prove himself by constant attention their well-wisher and friend . . . does very little for their good or his own," but her novels seem to show little faith that ministers will do as he recommends (*MP*: 248). With the exception of Dr Shirley in *Persuasion,* a character few readers recollect, Austen's clerics do not exercise moral authority, and they inspire no one to improve their lives. The novels criticize authority figures of all kinds – parents and older friends as well as clergymen – and Austen manifests a Protestant focus on the individual's solitary, unmediated journey to grace, enlightenment, and understanding.

Austen's anticlerical humor and her occasional satire on nonresidence and pluralism may seem to mark her as evangelical. Unlike the evangelicals, however, she does not advocate change or criticize the church's practices or its traditional relationship to the state. In the eighteenth century, clerical positions were owned either by the Crown, the colleges of Cambridge and Oxford, or by private landowning gentry (Collins 1994: 19–34). They were hard to obtain, and an aspiring clergyman needed the help of well-placed family and friends to secure one. Securing an ecclesiastical living is a concern of many characters in Austen's novels. Edward Ferrars and Charles Hayter must seek out a living, while Henry Tilney and Edmund Bertram receive them from their fathers. Austen's novels never assail this patronage system, even though her novels dramatize the problems it can cause. When Mary Crawford impugns the sincerity of Edmund's vocation because his father reserves a parish for him, he responds with a spirited defense. He tells Mary and Fanny there is "no reason why a man should make a worse clergyman for knowing that he will have a competence early in life" (*MP*: 109). For Austen, whose brothers James and Henry used the patronage system to gain clerical positions, Edmund's statement would ring true. The clerical patronage system is accepted as a matter of course (Butler 1986).

Austen's evident acceptance of the church's institutional structure perhaps explains in part her suspicion of those characters who believe their private judgment or inner monitor is sufficient for leading a good life. She is not a theological radical and, like most members of the post-Restoration Church of England, would have been wary of religious enthusiasts' claim that private inspiration superseded Scripture or tradition in the attainment of salvation (Sykes 1959: 150). Austen preferred the sermons of Bishop Thomas Sherlock (1678–1761) "to almost any," she told her niece Anna Austen in a letter, and this information gives us some indication of her position on religious matters (*Letters*: 278). Sherlock was a Tory defender of orthodox dogmas and an antagonist of Bishop Benjamin Hoadly, who initiated the Bangorian Controversy when he questioned the validity of the church's authority over individual Christians. Austen might appear to sanction the inner light when she has Fanny Price tell Henry Crawford "We have all a better guide in ourselves, if we would attend to it, than any other person can be" (*MP*: 412), but Fanny most likely refers here to the importance of an inward moral compass, not to the private revelation typical of mystics or prophets.

Throughout the novels, Austen is wary of those who exalt their own inner light as the sole guide of their behavior. In *Sense and Sensibility*, for instance, Austen treats the cult of sensibility almost as a species of religious enthusiasm. Marianne Dashwood is certain of the goodness of her inward moral sense and refuses to question it. Upon telling Elinor about her visit to Allenham with Willoughby (a visit Elinor finds inappropriate), she assures her sister that "if there had been any real impropriety in what I did, I should have been sensible of it at the time, for we always know when we are acting wrong, and with such a conviction I could have had no pleasure" (*SS*: 68). But Marianne's reliance on the inward monitor causes her to ignore manners and protocols, and in the process to deprive herself of their very real protections. Although Marianne's instincts are often right, Austen points to the danger of equating one's inward feelings with the absolute certainty of conviction. Like Emma Woodhouse and Catherine Morland, both of whom discover the limitations of their private assumptions and judgments, Marianne's situation is an example of the dangers that can attend devotion to interior emotions and sensations.

Austen most clearly addresses the dangers of unaided human judgment in a conversation between Mary Crawford and Edmund Bertram at Sotherton chapel. Mary celebrates the abandonment of family worship at the Rushworth estate, arguing that individuals are best left "to their own devices" when it comes to worship: "Everybody likes to go their own way – to choose their own time and manner of devotion. The obligation of attendance, the formality, the restraint, the length of time – altogether it is a formidable thing, and what nobody likes" (*MP*: 87). Mary privileges the impulses of private will and judgment, and she regards the constraints of formal worship as irksome impediments to true devotion. Edmund counters Mary's claims by pointing out that one could not expect much from the "*private* devotions" of people who indulge in "wanderings" during a chapel service (*MP*: 87). Without religious guidance as well as strenuous mental discipline, Edmund implies, an individual's reflections, thoughts, and resolutions will always go astray, whether in the family chapel or in the privacy of one's room. This novel pervasively dramatizes the inability of virtually all the characters – Edmund included, ironically – to "fix their thoughts." This is especially true in the case of Mary, who cannot recognize compromising situations and underestimates the evil resulting from Henry and Maria's elopement. *Mansfield Park* demonstrates the dire consequences of a world without proper spiritual and moral discipline, and the clergy should be the ones exemplifying and inculcating such discipline, though they often fail to do so.

Some of Austen's characters appear drawn to the vestiges of England's religious past, before the Reformation disrupted the traditional fabric of religious life and authority, particularly to the still visible old chapels or the ruins of monasteries. Catherine Morland desires "to live in an abbey," and the novel chronicles her exploration of Northanger Abbey and her fascination with its monastic trappings, as mediated through Gothic novels. In *Mansfield Park*, Fanny Price worships in Portsmouth at the Garrison Chapel, a former medieval hospice, and her hopes of finding a grand space at Sotherton, like "the old chapels of castles and monasteries," are dashed when she visits its austere chapel fitted out in the modern style. When she recovers from the illness brought about by her disastrous affection for Willoughby, Marianne in *Sense and Sensibility* expresses a desire to "walk to Sir John's new plantations at Barton-Cross, and the Abbeyland" and hopes to go often "to the old ruins of the Priory, and try to trace its foundations as far as we are told they once reached" (*SS*: 343). Emma wants "a more exact understanding" of Mr Knightley's Donwell Abbey, like Northanger a dwelling built on the ruins of a religious house.

As Nikolaus Pevsner pointed out long ago, Austen is "without exception vague, when it comes to describing buildings," so when she actually engages in physical description and focuses on specific types of spaces, we should pay close attention (Pevsner 1968: 404). When these abandoned religious buildings have garnered any critical attention at all, they have been regarded as evidence of a conventional eighteenth-century interest in picturesque scenery. Certainly Austen had read William Gilpin's popular travel books, and she knew of the particular fascination with ruined monasteries among theorists of the picturesque. But Austen is never merely conventional. Even as – or rather, in fact, precisely as – sites of picturesque meditation, these old ecclesiastical spaces exert a powerful allure that requires examination, because it exposes the authority these superannuated institutions still exert, even in an attenuated, nostalgic form.

Austen's earliest writings consider the Reformation and its effects. In her "History of England," an uproarious parody of Tory histories such as Smollett's and Goldsmith's, Austen's narrator casts impartiality aside and says provocatively that she is "partial to the roman catholic religion," going on to sympathize with the Catholic Mary Stuart and her grandson, Charles I. She pillories Henry VIII and nullifies the significance of his separation from Rome by characterizing him as "a man . . . of no Religion" (*MW*: 143). Unlike eighteenth-century Protestant historians, she can imagine nothing objectionable about the monasteries and hilariously surmises that Henry's "principal motive" in suppressing them was to beautify the landscape with picturesque ruins. Clearly this is a parodic text, but Austen's parodies are never simple; they never merely negate their objects. Indeed – as in *Northanger Abbey* – they often circle back to reaffirm them. Her comments in the "History" resemble other, more straightforward pro-Stuart statements, as for example in her marginal annotations to a copy of Oliver Goldsmith's *History of England*. Austen's early writings demonstrate her willingness to question the Whig celebration of inevitable progress and to sympathize with individuals, ideas, and institutions that have been consigned to the dustheap (Kent 1989: 64). The place Austen seems to reserve for the remnants of England's monastic past may have its origin in her youthful musings on the Dissolution.

This interest might also owe something to contemporary debates over Catholic émigrés from revolutionary France and from stirrings in favor of Catholic Emancipation. From the 1770s onward, attempts to end the persecution of Catholics that had been in force since the reign of Elizabeth roiled England. Catholics slowly secured some freedoms, but the legal exclusion came to an end only in 1829. In 1780, when Austen was a small child, popular reaction against such measure produced the Gordon Riots, when mobs of Protestants chanting "No Popery" burned Catholic homes and chapels and attacked Newgate prison and the Bank (Hibbert 1959). Some of this anti-Catholic sentiment abated in the wake of the French Revolution, when members of the French clergy, and French Catholics in general, fled the murderously anticlerical projects of the Jacobins and took refuge in Protestant England, as amply dramatized in Frances Burney's novel *The Wanderer; or, Female Difficulties*, published in 1814 (Austen's name appears on the subscription list), but drafted during the 1790s. During the 1790s, Austen's slightly older contemporaries – Hannah More and Frances Burney herself – wrote pamphlets beseeching charity on behalf of indigent Catholic refugees, and in *Sense and Sensibility*, Mrs Fanny Dashwood gives each of the Steele sisters "a needle-book made by some emigrant," an indication that even this cold-hearted worldling participated in charity to relieve Catholics. Predictably, Austen does not engage in direct commentary on the treatment of Catholics in England, but in *Northanger Abbey*, when she shows the sublimely fatuous boor, John Thorpe, dismissing *Camilla* on the grounds that Burney married "an emigrant," we can infer pretty safely that Austen had little sympathy with religious intolerance and with the xenophobia that often came with it.

That Austen might have regarded the Reformation as an unfortunate event at first seems unlikely, but a close reading of *Northanger Abbey* suggests that the threat Catholicism once posed was now remote enough that some of the effects of the Reformation can be seriously lamented. Austen's descriptions of Catherine's exploration of the abbey in *Northanger Abbey* have an edge, and everywhere she calls attention to how Northanger has changed for the worse since the days of yore that Catherine reads about. The Tilneys seem uninterested in the historical circumstances that led to their attainment of the Abbey or the formerly sacred site upon which their house stands. Catherine finds it odd that the family "should seem so little elated by the possession of such a home"; she charitably assumes "the power of early habit only could account for it" (*NA*: 141). But Austen implies that the Tilneys sanitize their history. The family did not acquire the abbey through active means or greedily confiscate it (as records show so many gentry did); the house merely "fell" into the Tilneys' hands "on its dissolution."

The abbey's hidden history surfaces in the second half of the novel. "A village of hot-houses seemed to arise among [the walls of the Abbey garden], and a whole parish to be at work within the inclosure," Austen relates (*NA*: 178). Of course, the terms "village," "parish," and "inclosure" call to mind the abbey's former position as employer and guide for the organically interrelated people in its environs, a set of relations still cultivated and honored in modern, Protestantized versions by exemplary landowners such as Knightley or Darcy. But at Northanger Abbey a very different set of relations obtain. Whereas in the past the abbey contributed to the common good, under the present owners it has been "inclosed" and only serves the appetites of a capricious gentry landlord who adores pineapples and other luxuries. When describing the General's improvements to "the ancient kitchen of the convent," Austen points out the contrast between pre- and post-Reformation days: in the past, General Tilney's "endowments of this spot alone might have placed him high among the benefactors of the convent" (*NA*: 183), but now his wealth serves only his own glory as a nouveau-riche. Austen seems to call attention to the transformation secular modernization has brought. The "offices" that the General is so proud of are pantries, kitchen, and laundry, not religious services. And "the strictest punctuality to the family hours" at Northanger (*NA*: 162) refers not to prayers but to the regimented workings of a modern domestic establishment. Although Catherine's conflation of General Tilney with a full-blown Gothic villain suggests that the old and the modern abbeys could still have something in common – it is not for nothing that the now-dead Mrs Tilney is cast as the "injured and ill-fated nun" of Gothic romance – Austen seems ready to admit that the Abbey has not been improved since the Dissolution.

As opposed to Northanger, Donwell Abbey has not been badly improved and retains the "characteristic situation" of a medieval abbey; it is "low and sheltered," as monasteries often were, with "scarcely a sight" of the nearby stream, and its environs have not fallen prey to "fashion or extravagance" (*E*: 358). Unlike General Tilney, Mr Knightley seems to have preserved the Abbey's central place in the life of the community; he continues to foster the charity and moral example that the monasteries ideally offered. Clearly, part of Knightley's moral authority derives from the fact that, as the owner of a former abbey, he is a good steward of its resources and traditional social responsibilities. By firmly connecting him to the past, she suggests the enduring significance of the values associated with such ancient institutions and their presence on the land and in the ongoing history of England.

Although Fanny Price does not visit an old monastery, she mourns the loss of communal worship associated with monastic life. Fanny expects more than the "mere, spacious, oblong room, fitted up for the purpose of devotion" that she finds in the chapel at Sotherton (*MP*: 85). This suggests that, to her mind, true devotion is inseparable from the grand, highly decorated spaces of medieval churches and abbeys, and she takes no delight in the severe Protestant chapel she finds at the Rushworth estate. The plainness of the space is a sign to her of a lack of high-minded spirituality, and it would seem only natural that the devotions in such a place would eventually be "left off," as they were in the life of the late Mr Rushworth. We ought not to equate Fanny's views with Austen's, but they do show Austen's sensitivity to the allure of England's own past upon a young and romantic mind.

The references to the monastic past in Austen's novels may provide important clues to her sensibilities. In *Northanger Abbey* and *Mansfield Park*, which involve more extended discussions of religious spaces and which contain so many unspiritual characters, Austen expresses a kind of nostalgia for the religious institutions of the English past that implies some skepticism about progress and modernity. Austen herself moved about in the ruins of old monasteries – she attended school in the gatehouse of Reading Abbey and visited numerous homes, like her cousins' Stoneleigh Abbey, built on the remnants of religious houses – and she demonstrably had the legacy of the Reformation before her (Tomalin 1997: 44). Within 20 years of her death, the Tractarians had elevated monastic spirituality to the highest form of Christian living and John Henry Newman (no fan of Austen's!) had introduced monastic discipline at his establishment at Littlemore (Kollar 1983). Austen was certainly not a crypto-Catholic or proto-Tractarian, but we can say with confidence that her novels register an interest in the pull of tradition and in maintaining a connection with England's pre-Reformation past and in the sorts of community it created.

FURTHER READING

Butler, Marilyn (1986). History, politics, and religion. In J. David Grey, A. Walton Litz, and Brian Southam (Eds). *The Jane Austen Companion* (pp. 190–208). New York: Macmillan.

MacDonagh, Oliver (1991). *Jane Austen: Real and Imagined Worlds*. New Haven, CT: Yale University Press.

Waldron, Mary (1994). The frailties of Fanny: *Mansfield Park* and the evangelical movement. *Eighteenth-Century Fiction*, 6, 259–82.

Walsh, John and Stephen Taylor (1993). Introduction: the church and Anglicanism in the "long" eighteenth century. In John Walsh, Colin Haydon, and Stephen Taylor (Eds). *The Church of England c. 1689–1833: From Toleration to Tractarianism* (pp. 1–64). Cambridge, UK: Cambridge University Press.

Young, B. W. (1998). *Religion and Enlightenment in Eighteenth-Century England: Theological Debate from Locke to Burke*. Oxford: Clarendon Press.

28
Family Matters

Ruth Perry

Families shape the individuals born into them in large and small ways, consciously and unconsciously; but the kinship dynamics that structure power in families are perhaps the most invisible of these forces. I doubt that Jane Austen consciously mapped out the maternal and paternal lineage of her characters or calculated their social power within their families in these terms. But she was a creature of her society and well-attuned to gradations of material advantage and social power; and so the nuances of the families she imagined fully reflected the weighting of power that came from the kinship structures and inheritance practices of her day. In analyzing the kin arrangements she ascribes to her good characters and her thoughtless ones, their alliances and competitions, and the relative power of her heroines, one is struck again by how thorough and consistent her social arrangements were.

For example, the fact that her heroines are – famously – unmarried women, that is, daughters in a kinship system that was in the process of disinheriting female off-spring both psychologically and fiscally, means that these characters (until we come to *Emma*) are automatically drawn from the ranks of the dispossessed (Elinor Dash-wood), the displaced (Fanny Price), or the explicitly disinherited (Elizabeth Bennet). As I've explained at length elsewhere, the English kinship system in the late eighteenth century was changing to accommodate the new cultural drive to accumulate capital; marriage and inheritance increasingly played their roles in this process, allowing families to consolidate and focus wealth rather than distribute resources to their lateral branches (Perry 2004). What helped to collect and enlarge property in families – and ensure its transmission to the next generation – was the reduction of those family resources that went to maternal relatives or daughters so that wealth could build up for transfer in the paternal line. Although primogeniture had always been practiced in the aristocracy, it was beginning to be practiced at the turn of the seventeenth into the eighteenth centuries by gentry, merchants, and gentleman farmers. Middle and upper-class patriarchs wrote strict settlements into their children's marriage contracts in imitation of the aristocracy; and they limited dowries for their daughters to cash rather than land if there were male offspring.[1] These practices ensured a patrilineal system of inheritance, reinforcing the accumulation of property in the male line and undercutting distribution. Increasingly as the eighteenth century wore on, lineal configurations of kin were privileged legally over lateral configurations of kin and male offspring over female offspring in matters of inheritance As James Harlowe, Clarissa Harlowe's brother in Richardson's great novel of 1748–49, remarks "Daughters are chickens brought up for the tables of other men," pithily encapsulating what was then a relatively new cultural understanding of women's position in their natal families (1985: 77).[2]

Austen's novels give the latitude and longitude of her heroines' social vulnerability and relative poverty as women, even though they come from genteel families. As Austen remarked to her niece Fanny, "Single Women have a dreadful propensity to be poor – which is one very strong argument in favour of Matrimony . . ." (*Letters*: 332). In order to instantiate fully this "dreadful propensity to be poor," the heroines Austen imagines come from the disinherited branches of their families (again, until *Emma*), operating in largely maternal rather than paternal family networks. Although the traditional English kinship system had been bilateral and cognatic, tracing lineage back through fathers *and* mothers, and women had inherited both land and rank in earlier times, by Austen's day English inheritance practices had become largely patrilineal. The dreaded entail that gets so much attention in *Pride and Prejudice* was not even invented until the last decades of the seventeenth century – its function to consolidate rather than distribute property in extended families and thus to retain and enlarge estates rather than allow them to be subdivided. By Jane Austen's era, family property – whether inherited from mothers or fathers – tended to be funneled to male children or even collateral male relatives (e.g., Mr Collins) in the father's line (Perry 2004: 46–55, 214–18). So by way of expressing their vulnerability, Austen imagines her heroines as operating in the maternal branches of families where there was little or no material advantage to be had from their connections. Only the sickly Anne de Bourgh, an only child and the invalid daughter of arrogant Lady Catherine de Bourgh, stands to inherit a fortune from her mother – an embodiment, perhaps, of the wasting away of this earlier customary practice.

Thus in *Pride and Prejudice*, it is Mrs Bennet whose family of origin dominates the lives of the Bennet girls, disinherited as they are by the entail which will leave their father's estate away from them when he dies. Mr Collins, who will inherit Longbourn, is the son of Mr Bennet's cousin – with whom Mr Bennet apparently quarreled. But sycophantic Mr Collins only briefly touches the lives of the Bennet girls, a comic example of upward mobility for Mr Bennet to mock. It is Mrs Bennet's sister, Mrs Phillips, married to their fathers' law clerk who succeeded him as an attorney in Meryton, whom the younger sisters visit daily. And it is Mrs Bennet's brother, Mr Gardiner, in "respectable trade in London," with a good marriage and the ability to go into business to better his condition, who looks out for the two oldest Bennet girls. In traditional cultures, it is usually the mother's relatives who take responsibility for her daughters. This branch of Jane and Elizabeth's maternal kin, the Gardiners, are the relatives with whom Elizabeth and Darcy keep up after their marriage. Their paternal relative, on the other hand – Mr Collins – the relative with the initial material advantages to offer, is represented unsympathetically as ambitious, materialistic, morally obtuse, and self-serving.

Similarly, in *Sense and Sensibility*, it is their maternal relatives, Sir John Middleton and his mother-in-law Mrs Jennings, who befriend and help Mrs Dashwood and her daughters. However vulgar and whatever their shortcomings of tact or taste, both Sir John and Mrs Jennings are well-meaning, kind, and generous and look out for Elinor and Marianne. Their paternal relatives, on the other hand, true to Austen's usual pattern, are materialistic, selfish, and calculating. Mr John Dashwood, his wife Fanny and her brother Robert – as well as their mother Mrs Ferrars – have little family feeling but are governed instead by greed and competitive consumption. Robert's ostentatiously self-absorbed selection of an ornamented toothpick case is a priceless episode illustrating the triviality, insolence, and sense of entitlement of the type. Right at the beginning of the novel, we watch John Dashwood, Elinor and Marianne's half-brother through their father – whose young son Henry has just inherited Norwood, their home of many years – easily swayed by his wife's crude exaggerations against giving a fraction of their now-lavish wealth in a one-time gift to his disinherited half-sisters. Although John Dashwood promised his dying father to make his mother-in-law and sisters "comfortable," his wife complains that his generosity would "ruin himself, and their poor little Harry, by giving away all his money to his half sisters" (SS 8). She easily leads him into reducing his initial plan of giving his sisters £1,000 apiece to an occasional gift of game in season, the equivalent of nothing.

It seems unlikely that Austen toted up the relative advantages of maternal and paternal relatives in so many pounds and pence; but in working out the particulars of her families, and how their members were positioned vis-à-vis one another, she generally put those in patrilineal succession – those who were in line to inherit, who stood to gain materially because of the accident of their birth – several degrees lower in the moral scale. One obvious manifestation of this principle can be found in her portrayal of the thoughtlessness of eldest brothers. Protected against paternal displeasure or any other consequence of careless selfishness by mechanisms like the strict settlement which guaranteed their inheritance, these fast young men were out for their own pleasure, heedless of the good of their younger brothers and sisters. Like spoiled, rich children of any era, the characters of Tom Bertram (*Mansfield Park*) or Frederick Tilney (*Northanger Abbey*) showed that assured wealth without accountability could lead to moral bankruptcy. Uncontrolled and uncontrollable, older brothers can figure privileged positionality in Austen's kinship universe. Irresponsible about their obligations to their parents and their siblings – especially their vulnerable sisters – they were automatically handed wealth and consequence by virtue of their birth order without having to lift a finger.

Indeed, Austen holds *all* brothers accountable for how well they take care of their sisters. As in many another eighteenth-century novel, in Austen's books the way a brother treats his sister is a kind of moral litmus test. Because there were no legal provisions to enforce it, but only a time-honored ethical expectation, a brother's responsibility for his sister's welfare had come to feel supererogatory in this age of (male) individualism. We know that Henry Tilney is decent by his worries about abandoning his sister, Eleanor, when he goes to Woodston and by the intimacy of their affectionate teasing; and we know that John Thorpe cannot be trusted because he never seems to care about obliging any of his sisters (Perry 2004: 143–89). Darcy, on the other hand, an exceptional older brother, takes his obligations to Georgiana seriously; and Bingley provides an establishment and a home for *his* sisters, even including the married Mrs Hurst. These instances also illustrate the truism that women have more power where sibling solidarity is strong (the identification of brothers with their sisters). Darcy's sister and Bingley's sisters enjoy a secure and stable social position that even the brilliant Mary Crawford cannot command because she cannot "persuade her brother to settle with her at his own country-house" (*MP*: 41). Henry Crawford's aversion to "a permanence of abode, or a limitation of society," a selfish indulgence that he will not subdue even for Mary's sake, prevents him from making a home for his sister (*MP*: 41).

The Crawfords provide another interesting example of the energy and privilege of those whose power comes from paternal kin networks. They stand in direct contrast to Fanny Price in *Mansfield Park*, whose kinship claims come entirely through her mother's sister – as befits a small, pale, and insignificant heroine. The novel opens with the three Ward sisters – Lady Bertram, Mrs Norris, and Mrs Price – slotted into their different classes by three very different marriages, with Mrs Price sinking her pride to ask for assistance from her better-off sisters. It is a testimony to Sir Thomas Bertram's sober and family-minded character that he is so willing to help his wife's relatives. We know nothing of his family. Once again, the action involving the displaced heroine is played out among her maternal relatives. Even the Crawfords are invited to Mansfield Park by a daughter of their mother by a first marriage; Mrs Grant is their half-sister. But their money, their sophistication, their social brilliance – and their morals – come from their father's relatives. The Admiral with whom they lived until his wife died and he installed a mistress (thereby making it impossible for his unmarried niece, Mary, to continue under his roof) is their guardian and their father's brother. Their money must have come from that side of the family too, since Mrs Grant, offspring of their mother, never had more than £5,000. With a few notable exceptions, money tends to follow the men's side of the family in Austen's universe.

Not until we come to *Emma* does Austen offer us a heroine raised up with all the power of unalloyed paternal backing. "Handsome, clever, and rich," Emma is situated very differently from the disadvantaged protagonists of earlier novels. Her verve, energy, and, as Lionel Trilling put it, her "self-love," are unique among Austen's protagonists (and scarce in women characters more generally); they are key to why, according to Trilling, Emma "has a moral life as a man has a moral life" (1965: 154). He says, "We understand self-love to be part of the moral life of all men; in men of genius we expect it to appear in unusual intensity and we take it to be an essential element of their power." Emma, raised "with the power of having rather too much her own way, and a disposition to think a little too well of herself" (*E*: 5), has been favored and given freedoms that are rare for a woman in any period but may be more common in the upbringing of men. She has been raised to think as well of herself as men are taught to do, which is what Trilling meant when he referred to her extraordinary "self-love." In the terms of this essay, it is worth observing that with the exception of *Lady Susan*, which revolves around the patriarchally organized Vernon family, *Emma* is the first of Austen's novels in which the main characters operate almost exclusively in paternal kin networks rather than maternal kin networks. The Knightley brothers and their paternal birthplace, Donwell Abbey, make up one such node; Harriet Smith and Jane Fairfax also have their destinies determined by their fathers and their fathers' contacts. And Frank Churchill, that weak, unmanly, French-ified fellow whose amiability does not translate into English, has been appropriately enough swallowed up by his maternal relatives, the Churchills.[3]

It stands to reason that Emma, a woman with confidence and self-approval like a man, and an itch to influence others, a person slow to recognize her own egocentrism although generously disposed towards others, sure of her place in the world and quick to take umbrage at social slights (e.g., first upon the thought of receiving, and then of *not* receiving, the Coles's invitation) – such is the character whom Austen places in the protective circle of her paternal kin. Austen maximizes Emma's social strength by the way she configures her social world. Emma is a woman without brothers who stands in the direct line of her father's authority and material wealth; he thinks she can do no wrong and he does not want her to marry. Although she is a woman, she thus operates with the full power of her father's unconditional backing and she is the only one of Austen's heroines of whom this can be said.[4] Mr Bennet favors his "Lizzy" but does not set her apart materially from her sisters. Moreover, he can do nothing to insure a home for her once he dies. Anne Elliot in *Persuasion* operates within her father's orbit, but he ignores her advice and dismisses her importance since she has "lost her bloom." Anne, in turn, feels stifled by the world of her paternal kin – her favored sister Elizabeth, her cousins William Elliot, Lady Dalrymple, and Miss Carteret, and that hanger-on, Mrs Clay, who appears to be angling for her father. She escapes to the company of her mother's friend, Lady Russell, or her former school-fellow, Mrs Smith, whenever possible. And in the end, she decamps altogether with Captain Wentworth and leaves her father and his values behind. It is worth noting that her connection to Captain Wentworth this time around is through his sister, Mrs Croft, wife of her father's tenant.

Novel by novel, these explorations of the relative moral weighting of maternal and paternal kinship uncover another layer of power and privilege in the archeology of class and gender. Nowhere is this more apparent in Austen's novels, however, than in the way she handles marriages between cousins. Paternal first cousin marriages among the landed classes in the England of her day had a material advantage: they tended to consolidate property. Maternal first cousin marriages, on the other hand, had all the coziness and family feeling of endogamous marriage but without the additional benefit of keeping property in the family. Thus, in *Pride and Prejudice*, if one of the Bennet girls had married Mr Collins, their father's cousin, they would have kept Longbourn in the family. But Austen makes this paternal relative on Mr Bennet's side so repugnant that all material advantage pales in comparison to the dreadful alternative of actually being married to him. Similarly, the prospective marriage between Darcy and Anne de Bourgh discussed by Lady Catherine de Bourgh, although literally a maternal first cousin marriage, has the aura of a paternal first cousin marriage because Anne de Bourgh stands to inherit the way an eldest son would inherit. Imagined by their mothers, who were sisters, the match would have consolidated the property in these two branches of the family. But Austen never favors such marriages – probably because their material advantages call into question their spiritual and emotional bases – and so this marriage, while mentioned, never really has a chance.

The most promising paternal first cousin marriage in the Austen canon, the only one we believe possible, however briefly, is that in *Persuasion* between William Elliot, Sir Walter Elliot's heir apparent, and either Elizabeth or Anne Elliot. Lady Russell allows herself to imagine it when William seems to be taken with his pretty cousin, Anne: "I own that to be able to regard you as the future mistress of Kellynch, the future Lady Elliot – to look forward and see you occupying your dear mother's place . . . would give me more delight than is often felt at my time of life," she says to Anne (*P*: 159–60). Nor is Anne immune to the appeal of having Kellynch Hall restored to her as her home forever, even though she does not entirely like or trust Mr Elliot: "For a few moments her imagination and her heart were bewitched" (*P*: 160). William Elliot, a widower, has already been married to a woman of inferior birth with a large fortune but has latterly become more interested in his status as a future baronet; he now values "rank and connexion" (*P*: 148) more than he used to and so his cousin Anne's social status and cultivation are added attractions to his present choice. Like Sir Walter Elliot – and to Anne Elliot's disgust – he cares more than he ought for the family's connection (in the paternal line) to the aristocratic but otherwise awkward and uninteresting Dowager Viscountess Dalrymple and her daughter the Honorable Miss Carteret.

Paternal first cousin marriages – which, according to one historian, constituted 50 percent of the marriages among the British upper class (Trumbach 1978: 19) – must have carried with them a tinge of ambition and materialism in Austen's day for they never succeed in her novels. A marriage of true minds did not need the material advantage of consolidating two fortunes; one fortune was sufficient to content a couple in love. It was not the closeness of the family tie in cousin german or first cousin marriages that was at issue; such marriages were certainly legally and socially acceptable in Austen's day and as Glenda Hudson pointed out long ago, Austen had a warm spot in her heart for unions built on the foundation of habit and long familiarity (Hudson 1989: 125–31). As she exclaims in *Mansfield Park* when referring to William and Fanny Price's pleasure in each other's company, "Children of the same family, the same blood, with the same first associations and habits, have some means of enjoyment in their power, which no subsequent connections can supply" (*MP*: 235). Thus, marriages between adopted siblings, between in-laws, and between first cousins are not proscribed in Austen's texts but on the contrary, are imagined with disinterested love and reciprocity. Knightley and Emma act like brother and sister – in fact they *are* brother-in-law and sister-in-law, as are Elinor and Edward in *Sense and Sensibility*. Colonel Brandon and his beloved Eliza, as he tells the story, were brother and sister several times over. They were brought up as siblings; she was an orphaned cousin, a ward of Brandon's father, who was her uncle. Although she loved Brandon, she was forced to marry his older brother, in what seems to have been another disastrous paternal first cousin marriage. Her uncle guardian wanted her married to his heir to secure her fortune in the family; but the marriage was so miserable that Brandon tried to rescue her from it by eloping with her – in which attempt they were foiled.

But if paternal first cousin marriages are tainted in Austen's novels – the match in *Persuasion* between Anne and William Elliot has something unholy about it, the shade of some darker motivation behind it – maternal first cousin marriages are free from this corruption. The maternal first cousin marriages in *Mansfield Park* and *Persuasion* seem fitting, appropriate, and welcome. Indeed, they are longed for throughout, interrupted or postponed as they are by infatuations of the wrong sort.

There is, first of all, the attachment between Henrietta Musgrove and her maternal first cousin, Charles Hayter, who grew up together, living just a few miles apart. Their mothers were sisters whose marriages made a significant difference in their material fortunes. Carping Mary Musgrove, filled with her own family pride, does not think that Charles Hayter, "a country curate" (*P*: 76), is a suitable match for Miss Musgrove of Uppercross, even though, as a first-born son, he stands to inherit freehold property. Mary does not even like to acknowledge the family connection. And then Henrietta is, briefly, distracted by Captain Wentworth. But true love triumphs in the end, as the honest and right-thinking characters believe it should, and Henrietta's "old," and "established" regard for her cousin Charles asserts itself again; the minor obstacles in their path dissolve – Captain Wentworth seems to choose Louisa and Dr Shirley wants a curate – and we are assured of their future happiness.

The other significant maternal first cousin marriage sanctioned by Austen's plot structure is, of course, between Fanny Price and Edmund Bertram in *Mansfield Park*. Again, nothing material can be achieved by this match because neither stands to inherit within the family. The insignificance of Edmund's expectations, both in terms of income and status, is emphasized by Mary Crawford's scorn and her refusal to marry him if he sticks to his plan to be a clergyman. The point is accentuated when her interest in him revives when his older brother, Tom, lies ill, thus opening a possibility of Edmund's inheriting their father's baronetcy. "I never bribed a physician in my life" (*MP*: 434), writes Mary slyly to Fanny, suggesting that a future "Sir Edmund" would do very well with the Bertram property if he were to come into it. But of course, Tom does not die, Maria disgraces herself with Henry, and Edmund, in time, becomes "as anxious to marry Fanny, as Fanny herself could desire" (*MP*: 470). Austen's description of their coming together makes it clear how close to siblings they have been; this is another Austen marriage between close kin.

Loving, guiding, protecting her, as he had been doing ever since her being ten years old, her mind in so great a degree formed by his care, and her comfort depending on his kindness, an object to him of such close and peculiar interest, dearer by all his own importance with her than any one else at Mansfield, what was there now to add, but that he should learn to prefer soft light eyes to sparkling dark ones. (*MP*: 470)

Modern readers with a preference for exogamous romance, for otherness, may find the match tame, but in Austen's scheme, the pleasure of a first cousin marriage comes from a similarity of habits and mind and from long proximity. There will be no extraordinary wealth, no title in this marriage. Fanny will never overreach herself and Edmund will be content to be a clergyman and a second son. "Comfort" is the watchword of their marriage – the word is repeated five times on the first page of the last chapter. Comfort, not excitement, is what maternal first cousin marriages offer. But there is never a question about the probity of the match; its purity is guaranteed by the principals' status as *maternal* first cousins. Related through their mothers, they are protected from the effects of unearned privilege as Austen protects most of her good characters, by placing them carefully in the hierarchies of birth order and fortune. They have the advantage of kinship without the contamination of inherited power.

Thus does Austen imagine the kin arrangements of her characters as corroboration and guarantee of their fundamental qualities. Generosity and benevolence can generally be found among one's maternal relatives, although not usually accompanied by much cash. Paternal relatives, on the other hand, those who have been dealt wealth and power, are usually more withholding. Which comes first, however, the inherited privilege and wealth or attitudes of entitlement and selfishness, one cannot say. Nevertheless, one can see even in this brief survey that the uneven distribution of resources within families, naturalized by sex and birth order, when placed in tension with the more liberal imperatives of "family feeling," gave Austen a certain amount of material for her moral satire. Or, to put it another way, the new system of individualism and capital accumulation was often at odds with the older belief in reciprocity, loyalty, and the shared interests of extended families; and Austen was quick to see and satirize how this new economic basis for society affected family matters.

NOTES

1 The strict settlement was a provision, invented in the 1680s, which when written into a marriage contract, settled the lion's share of the property of the estate on the as yet unborn first son of the union-to-be and specified what portions he was to pay out to daughters and younger sons of that union when he came into the property.

2 James Harlowe also says on the same page, "daughters were but encumbrances and drawbacks upon a family."

3 For a brilliant statement of Frank's shortcomings as an Englishman, see Claudia L. Johnson (1995b), "Not at all what a man should be."

4 Miss Elliot, Anne's older sister in *Persuasion*, has a similarly reflected power from their father, Sir Walter Elliot, but she is not the only unmarried daughter that Sir Walter has and he is a less doting and more selfish father than Mr Woodhouse.

FURTHER READING

Hudson, Glenda (1992). *Sibling Love and Incest in Jane Austen*. New York: St. Martin's Press. Reprinted 1999.

Perry, Ruth (2004). *Novel Relations: The Transformation of Kinship in English Literature and Culture 1748–1818*. Cambridge, UK: Cambridge University Press.

Spring, Eileen (1993). *Law, Land and the Family: Aristocratic Inheritance in England 1300 to 1800*. Chapel Hill: University of North Carolina Press.

Staves, Susan (1996). Resentment or resignation? Dividing the spoils among daughters and younger sons. In John Brewer and Susan Staves (Eds). *Early Modern Conceptions of Property* (pp. 194–218). London and New York: Routledge.

Tadmor, Naomi (1992). Dimensions of inequality among siblings in eighteenth-century English novels: the cases of *Clarissa* and *The History of Miss Betsy Thoughtless*. *Continuity and Change*, 7:3, 303–33.

Wolfram, Sybil (1987). *In-Laws and Outlaws: Kinship and Marriage in England*. London and Sydney: Croom Helm.

29
Austen and Masculinity

E. J. Clery

Austen was the first to describe her work as narrowly "feminine." The famous image of "the little bit (two inches wide) of Ivory on which I work with so fine a Brush, as produces little effect after much labour" appears in her correspondence by way of contrast with the "strong, manly, spirited Sketches, full of Variety & Glow" written by her 18-year-old nephew (*Letters*: 323). When the Prince Regent's librarian, the Reverend James Stanier Clarke, an admirer of her writing, urged her to make a clergyman closely resembling himself the hero of her next novel, she refused on the grounds of female incapacity: "Such a Man's Conversation must at times be on subjects of Science & Philosophy of which I know nothing . . . And I think I may boast myself to be, with all possible Vanity, the most unlearned, & uninformed Female who ever dared to be an Authoress" (*Letters*: 306).

With her humorously self-deprecating excuses, Austen confirms the views of some of her detractors, and seems to subscribe to a strictly gendered division of labor in the literary sphere. And indeed, her practice of adhering in her fiction to what was "knowable" from the perspective of a gentlewoman was far more rigorously maintained than in the work of many other female writers of the time. Ever since Austen published her first novel, *Sense and Sensibility*, with the attribution (not uncommon at the time) "By a Lady," readers have responded to the apparently "feminine" limitation in the scope and style of her writing. The *British Critic* of May 1812 drew attention to the "intimate knowledge . . . of the female character" and recommended it to "our female friends" (Southam 1968: 40). This gendered view builds through the nineteenth century, giving rise to a plethora of patronizing compliments (Walter Scott, often seen as her earliest champion, is guilty in this respect) and cloying gallantries. Unsurprisingly, Charlotte Bronte and George Eliot, fearless explorers of the masculine realm themselves, rebelled against the model of female authorship she represented, emblematized by the "carefully fenced, highly cultivated garden" (Southam 1968: 126).

In the course of the twentieth century, this "sexed" Austen underwent further permutations. The perceived femininity that was once a basis for praise of a qualified kind, now became an occasion for abuse: a phenomenon which Lionel Trilling termed "the sexual objection" (Trilling 1955: 209). Mark Twain's notorious aversion to her work was explained by Trilling as viscerally gendered:

> The *animality* of [his] repugnance is probably to be taken as a male's revulsion from a society in which women seem to be at the center of interest and power, as a man's panic fear at a fictional world in which the masculine principle, although represented as admirable and necessary, is prescribed and controlled by a female mind. (Trilling 1955: 209)

H. W. Garrod's infamous lecture "Jane Austen: A Depreciation" (1928) protested at the marginalizing of men in her field of vision. In 1936 William Empson observed that it was a critical commonplace that "Jane Austen never shows men apart from women" (Southam 1987: 298). D. W. Harding and Marvin Mudrick connected her brilliant use of irony and satire with her own exclusion from a "normal" heterosexual destiny.[1] The masculinist reaction to Austen, that ultimately had the effect of presenting her as a far more complicated and oppositional figure than had previously been allowed, prepared the way for feminist reclamation. In much feminist criticism, Austen's identification with the woman's point of view is simply assumed: a new and more celebratory variation on the "sexed" Austen (e.g., Kirkham 1983, Sulloway 1989, Kaplan 1992).

And yet there is a neglected tradition in the early reception of Austen that challenges her identification with the feminine. The praise of Austen's very first reviewer (in the *Critical Review* in 1812) for her "knowledge of character" relates to the depiction of male characters in particular (Southam 1968: 35–6). The comparison with Shakespeare first appears in Richard Whately's review of Austen's posthumous works in the *Quarterly Review* in 1821:

> Slender and Shallow, and Aguecheek, as Shakspeare has painted them, though equally fools, resemble one another no more than Richard, and Macbeth, and Julius Caesar; and Miss Austin's [*sic*] Mrs. Bennet, Mr. Rushworth, and Miss Bates, are no more alike than her Darcy, Knightley, and Edmund Bertram. (Southam 1968: 98)

Scott had already drawn attention to Austen's minutely naturalistic "fools"; what is intriguing here is the high praise for the compelling and diverse characterization of the heroes: Knightly and Edmund Bertram on a par with Macbeth and Julius Caesar. Thomas Babington Macaulay likewise places her next to Shakespeare in the finely discriminated depiction of character, and for *his* examples he takes "four clergymen, none of whom we should be surprised to find in any parsonage in the kingdom, Mr Edward Ferrars, Mr Henry Tilney, Mr Edmund Bertram, and Mr Elton": "Who would not have expected them to be mere insipid likenesses of each other? No such thing"; they are differentiated by "touches so delicate, that they elude analysis" (Southam 1968: 123).

These appraisals represent an "unsexed Austen" and evoke a lost way of reading her, attuned to a quality of hyperrealism in her male characters, and especially the portrayal of young men beginning to make their way in the world. Writing to Clarke, Austen insisted that she was unqualified to depict the professional and intellectual world of men. But the evidence of her biography shows that this modesty was disingenuous. She had in fact a remarkably wide experience of men's lives and men's work. She grew up in a household centered on the formation of men. Her mother and father ran a small boarding school for boys, and these lodgers were treated as part of the family (Tomalin 2000: 24–33). She was the sister of six brothers, and remained closely involved in the lives and careers of five of them throughout adulthood, also taking an active interest in her older nephews.

Much remains to be done towards reconstructing the masculine life-world on which Austen's writing draws. The turn towards a historicist view of the novels from the 1970s onwards has inevitably done something to fill the gap, since history, as Catherine Morland observed, tends to foreground the doings of men. When critics investigate Austen's engagement with the ideas and events surrounding the French Revolution they restore some of the context of men's public activity that had previously been left out of the reckoning, even if this is not a stated aim (Butler 1975, Roberts 1979). Recent studies showing the relevance of Regency politics (Sales 1994) and wartime patriotism (Johnson 1995a, Southam 2000), also indicate Austen's subtle attention to masculine identities. We are gradually acquiring a fuller knowledge of the intellectual and professional affiliations of Austen's male relations (Collins 1994, Southam 2000, Knox-Shaw 2004).

In Austen's novels, men are faced with choices. The marriage plot is also a plot of vocation. Even if a young man has independent means, he must learn to fully embrace his responsibilities as a landowner, which includes a domestic establishment. If plot alone were taken into consideration any of the novels could be reconceived as fables of male self-realization. An heir to a large fortune is frustrated by his state of idleness, and longs to find a vocation. He eventually acquires a living as a country pastor and a penniless but loving wife (*Sense and Sensibility*). A young landowner is isolated by his wealth and rank, and only finds happiness when he recognizes his social responsibilities, begins to mix with a wider circle, and marries beneath him (*Pride and Prejudice*). A clergyman from a high-ranking family, a second son, rejects paternal pressure and marries for love (*Northanger Abbey*). A substantial landowner of middle age, absorbed in his work, becomes jealous when a younger man begins paying attention to the female neighbor he has known all his life, and is galvanized into making a proposal (*Emma*). A serious young man is torn between his desire to become a clergyman and his attraction to a lively fashionable woman who baulks at the idea of being a parson's wife. He eventually breaks with her and marries his sober cousin instead (*Mansfield Park*). An aspiring naval officer fails to marry the woman he loves, due to the snobbery of her family. Through bravery and good luck, he achieves wealth and status and wins her back (*Persuasion*).

These are the stories that are, and are not, told in Austen's six completed works. They are not subplots, but they function in counterpoint to the dominant strand of the narrative featuring the consciousness and feelings of the heroine. The exigencies of these male destinies drive forward the female plot, though in understated – perhaps one could better say *unstated* – ways. All the lacunae that distinguish the heroine's plot, the silences, the frustrations, the mysteries, the periods of waiting and hoping and agonizing, arise from the lack of knowledge about the development of the hero's plot, an ignorance shared by the heroine, the reader, and generally, it would seem, the narrator as well. It is a radical aspect of Austen's art that with few exceptions she denies direct access to the unspoken thoughts and views of her heroes. We are given their conversation, their externalized statements, but only rarely the privileges of their minds.

But let us temporarily set aside this asymmetry in the representation of heroines and heroes, and focus on the plot of vocation, vital both as a formal element and also in determining the social and moral coordinates of the novels. Austen has been called a "war novelist" (Pritchett 1970). The war with France manifests itself in her novels in the scarcity of men on the home front, the implicit proviso of every courtship; and for those male characters who remain at home, it gives added point and urgency to finding a worthwhile, meaningful occupation as an alternative to military service.[2] War polarizes gender roles and makes them more narrowly prescriptive: men's behavior, even more than women's, is placed under the spotlight. Every war through the eighteenth century and into the nineteenth century revives the civic humanist paradigm of masculinity, which elevates the military function above other more effeminate civilian occupations, and generates moral panic about the growth of selfish individualism in a refined commercial society. We find this gendered moral framework, which might be termed a "masculine ethic," in operation throughout Austen's work, and with increasing force in her later novels, composed after Britain had been at war almost continuously for more than 15 years, during the culminating stages of the campaign against Napoleon.

There has been considerable speculation about the contemporary resonances of the title *Mansfield Park* (for a summary see Wiltshire 2005). But if "Man's field" were nothing more than a pun on male vocation, it would be highly appropriate. Juxtaposed with "Park," it encapsulates the central tension in the novel between occupation and leisure. In *Sense and Sensibility* Austen had contrasted the delusory "manly beauty" of the selfish and dissolute Willoughby with the genuinely "manly unstudied simplicity" of Colonel Brandon, with his desire of being of service to others (*SS*: 43, 338). In *Mansfield Park*, the epithet "manly" is reserved for the naval characters, Fanny Price's brother and father. By this measure, the young privileged male civilians struggle to achieve anything that could creditably be called manhood, while the reader quickly learns that the established patriarch, Sir Thomas Bertram, has feet of clay. For at the start of the novel, as a consequence of his faulty management of the family, the fate of Mansfield Park hangs in the balance. Within a few pages we are told that Tom, the heir, "feels born only for expense and enjoyment" and has run into debts that require drastic economies (*MP*: 17). Our first glimpse of the Bertram girls finds them ominously absorbed in "the favourite holiday sport of the moment, making artificial flowers or wasting gold paper" (p. 14).

It is under this shadow, with the threat of internal corruption and collapse already apparent, that the significant events of the first volume take place: the arrival of the Crawfords, the visit to Sotherton Court, and the preparations for the performance of *Lovers' Vows*. For this reason, it would be wrong to see the Crawfords as the carriers of urban luxury into the pristine countryside. They are not serpents in paradise. Luxury is already there. But so is the factor that will lead to the eventual moral regeneration of Mansfield Park: the introduction of the child Fanny Price into the household, carrying with her a wartime ethos of self-sacrifice and fortitude through her family's association with the service in the navy.

In *Sketches in the History of Man*, Henry Home, Lord Kames, friend and associate of David Hume and Adam Smith, summed up the effeminizing threat of luxury:

> Luxury, a never-failing concomitant of wealth, is a slow poison, that debilitates men, and renders them incapable of any great effort: courage, magnanimity, heroism, come to be ranked among the miracles that are supposed never to have existed but in fable; and the fashionable properties of sensuality, avarice, cunning, and dissimulation, engross the mind. In a word, man, by constant prosperity and peace, degenerates into a mean, impotent, and selfish animal. (Kames 2007, vol. II: 408)

Tom Bertram, Mr Rushworth, and Mr Yates are all recognizably effeminate men according to this principle, in the sense that they are without vocation, unproductive members of society, who contribute nothing to the public weal, but only spend and consume. Yates is skewered by Sir Thomas as "trifling and confident, idle and expensive" (*MP*: 194). But Henry Crawford is the most effeminate of all, with the added danger of knowing the powers as well as the pleasures of effeminacy: his kinship with women enables him to attract and manipulate them successfully. Edmund, the second Bertram son, becomes ensnared in a more lengthy struggle between his attraction to Mary Crawford on the one hand, and his moral sense and vocation as a clergyman on the other.

Cinderella has long been seen as the mythic archetype underlying *Mansfield Park*, but an alternative candidate is "The Choice of Hercules," a seminal myth of public-spirited masculinity. The story has its source in the *Memorabilia* of the Greek Historian Xenophon, which became a recommended textbook for schoolboys in the eighteenth century. It was taken to illustrate the opposition between public virtue and private vice, most influentially by the Earl of Shaftesbury, who produced a visual plan of the story:

> HERCULES; who being young, and retir'd to a solitary place in order to deliberate on the Choice he was to make of the different ways of Life, was accosted (as our Historian

relates) by the two Goddesses, *Virtue* and *Pleasure*. 'Tis on the issue of the Controversy between these *two*, that the Character of HERCULES depends. (Shaftesbury 1713: 6)

The story and the iconography were popularized in Georgian Britain in the form of a cantata by Handel, a poem by Robert Lowth, and Joshua Reynolds's celebrated portrait *Garrick between Tragedy and Comedy* (Mannings 1984).[3] There are two elements in the tale that have particular relevance for *Mansfield Park*: first, that Hercules is genuinely ambivalent, as Shaftesbury put it, "torn by contrary Passions"; second, that Pleasure furthers her cause by disguise – in Lowth's poetic version of story she declares, "My name, fair youth, is Happiness . . . Tho' slander call me Sloth – Detraction vain!"

Edmund is at first readily taken in by Mary Crawford, although the warning signs are instantly noted by Fanny and the reader. But the true nature of the choice facing Edmund only becomes apparent when he stands, flanked by Mary and Fanny, in the old chapel at Sotherton and receives Mary's horrified reaction to the news that he is to be a clergyman. This scene gives rise to a dispute between Mary and Edmund (gently seconded by Fanny) on "manners" and the question of the public efficacy of the clerical profession: in effect, its "manliness." Mary states that "A clergyman is nothing," and disputes Edmund's claim that the clergy "has the charge of all that is of the first importance to mankind . . . guardianship of religion and morals, and consequently of the manners which result from their influence." She can see no connection between manners and church morality: "How can two sermons a week . . . govern the conduct and fashion the manners of a large congregation for the rest of the week?" (*MP*: 92–3). Clergymen are therefore redundant. Manners belong to the secular realm in polite society; her very dogmatism on the point suggests implicitly that women presume to reign in this sphere. Mary's evidence is taken from London, the metropolis, the measure of life in modern Britain.

But Edmund insists on wrenching the term "manners" away from the urban context, and from its secular and feminized meaning:

> with regard to their influencing public manners, Miss Crawford must not misunderstand me, or suppose I mean to call them the arbiters of good breeding, the regulators of refinement and courtesy, the masters of the ceremonies of life. The *manners* I speak of, might rather be called *conduct*, perhaps, the result of good principles; the effect, in short, of those doctrines which it is their duty to teach and recommend; and it will, I believe, be everywhere found, that as the clergy are, or are not what they ought to be, so are the rest of the nation. (*MP*: 93)

With this maxim, drawing on the rhetoric of patriotic nationalism, Edmund temporarily rests his case.

Mary has further resources, of course. When they retire to the wilderness in the garden at Sotherton, reminiscent of Hercules's "solitary place," she dazzles him with charming irrationalities and succeeds in leading him astray for an hour, leaving Fanny alone on a bench. Back at Mansfield Park, when the play-acting is proposed and he resists, she plays on his protective instinct and arouses his jealousy by consenting to another man taking the part of the clergyman Anhalt, her lover in the drama. In doing so she reinstates *her* version of manners, transforming his lack of gallantry and rude insistence on principle into civility and compliance under the force of her influence as a woman, enacting the process of feminization, and Circe-like, transforming him into an ineffectual mock-clergyman. Fanny, the voice of his conscience, is once again abandoned. In the final part of the novel, however, a gradual shift can be traced towards "manners" as moral conduct, outside the orbit of politeness and pleasure.

The device of the "Choice of Hercules" is most apparent in Edmund's predicament, but it is part of the extraordinary architectonic nature of the novel that it is replayed in a whole series of interlocking choices. Mary herself must choose between "domestic happiness" as represented by Edmund and a life of fashionable pleasure; Maria between public status with Rushworth and private gratification with Henry; Henry between selfish idleness and the moral purpose embodied by Fanny; Fanny must decide between her apparent duty to marry Henry and her personal sense of right, mingled with a hopeless and undutiful devotion to Edmund. The diffusion of the problem of self-determination then raises the question, What happens when a myth of masculine identity is applied to women as well? It brings to mind Trilling's remark that Emma "has a moral life as a man has a moral life" (1991: 124; see Johnson 1995b: 191–2). I will return at the conclusion of this discussion to elements in Austen that elide the difference between men and women.

Fanny's dilemma is resolved by the crisis in the choices of Maria and Henry. Their elopement absolves her of responsibility, and appears to render her period of exile in Portsmouth, her "solitary place," structurally redundant. But it serves a vital related function, in directly introducing the wartime setting for the drama of vocation. When we are ushered through the door of the Price's small house with the adult Fanny, we encounter with her a warrior society, its motions guided by male employment in the navy, the demands of service to the nation. It takes Fanny some time to recover from the initial shock of the domestic squalor and the marginal position of the women in the household, very different from the feminocentric world of Mansfield Park, revolving around Lady Bertram's sofa. But gradually she comes to appreciate the kindness underlying her mother's fretful manner, her sister Susan's natural acuity and capacity for improvement, and even Mr Price's merits suddenly strike her: he is "not polished" but "grateful, animated, manly; his expressions those of an attached father, and a sensible man" (*MP*: 402). Their spontaneity and openness of feeling, as well as their connection to the sphere of patriotic action, is in pointed contrast to the hopeless entropy of Lady Bertram and the crushing formality of Sir Thomas. It becomes possible to imagine the Price household as an environment that could produce William, the cynosure of manliness; after only a brief exposure Henry, who continues his courtship in Portsmouth, appears to Fanny distinctly improved.

When they were at Mansfield, Henry had experienced the electrifying effect of listening to William's stories of life at sea:

His heart was warmed, his fancy fired, and he felt the highest respect for a lad who, before he was twenty, had gone through such bodily hardships, and given such proofs of mind. The glory of heroism, of usefulness, of exertion, of endurance, made his own habits of selfish indulgence appear in shameful contrast; and he wished he had been a William Price, distinguishing himself and working his way to fortune and consequence with so much self-respect and happy ardour, instead of what he was! (*MP*: 236)

There is a perceptible echo of Lord Kames here again, when he remarks that "war is necessary for man, being a school for improving every manly virtue" (Kames 2007, vol. II: 414). In Henry's case the "wish was rather eager than lasting" and when the conversation turns to hunting he quickly recollects the advantages of being "a man of fortune at once with horses and grooms at his command" (*MP*: 237). But it is at the same moment, when he observes the "blunt fondness" and "genuine feeling" of William and Fanny together, that what Austen calls his "moral taste" is kindled, and he changes his plans from a quick flirtation with Fanny to honorable marriage. In this light, we need to adjust our ideas of what marriage with Fanny would mean. Uniting himself with the Prices would not be marrying beneath him. It would be a means of reconnecting with the manly virtues they alone seem capable of displaying.

In the end it is the Bertrams who receive the stimulating benefits of grafting the Prices onto their family tree. There have been complaints that the growth of mutual love between Edmund and Fanny is rather abruptly treated by Austen. But if we take the dynastic view the more important relationship is between Fanny and Sir Thomas, and this is resonantly affirmed by the narrator in the conclusion: "Fanny was indeed the daughter that he had wanted," manifesting along with the rest of the young Prices "the advantages of early hardship and discipline, and the consciousness of being born to struggle and endure" (*MP*: 473).

Looking at *Mansfield Park*, or indeed any of the other novels, we can establish that Austen had a great deal to say about masculinity, that she excelled at depicting male characters, even that she subscribed to a masculine ethic that underpinned her portrayal of social mores and historical change. But ultimately all of this must be weighed in the balance with her approach to form, and her gradual refining of a feminine aesthetic.

Austen is the founder of the modern romance narrative, as the first to recognize the extraordinary narrative power of keeping the hero's point of view in reserve. The suspense surrounding the hero's feelings and intentions drives the story forward in a way unequalled by shipwrecks, bandits, abductions, or eerie sounds. The precise method by which Austen develops the hero as enigma is a topic that has barely been broached. The ideological corollary of this technique – that, as Robert Miles nicely puts it, "Austen regards the feminine self as our 'default state'" – has been assumed more often than it has been investigated (Miles 2003: 120). At any time the reception of Austen by men must be a sensitive measure of anxieties about the boundaries of masculinity, and the degree to which the male reader can tolerate a feminocentric definition of humanity.

In her last completed work, *Persuasion*, Austen brought the technique to perfection: the voice of the narrator allied with that of the heroine; the reader perceiving not only through Anne's mind but also through her senses and a haze of emotion. Through this haze the hero is glimpsed, often indistinctly. His words and actions may be clearly recorded, but his motives remain more completely obscured than in any of the other novels. The narrative structure that creates this epistemological chasm between the main female and male protagonist naturally gives rise to the climactic dialogue on the different qualities of men and women.

The occasion for the conversation between Anne Elliot and Captain Harville, a naval officer and friend of the hero, is the problem of a currently fashionable mode of masculine emotional exhibitionism (Austen would satirize another version of it in the fragment *Sanditon*). Another friend, Captain Benwick, has immersed himself in the poetry of Walter Scott and Byron as a response to the death of his fiancée, the sister of Harville. But the posture of immoveable melancholy is quickly dropped when fate throws the convalescent Louisa Musgrove in his way. Now the transfer of a miniature portrait of Benwick represents the unreliability of his performance as man of feeling: once intended for Fanny Harville, it is now destined for Louisa.

Anne sympathizes with Harville's disillusionment: Fanny would not have forgotten Benwick so soon, "It would not be the nature of any woman who truly loved." This is to throw down the gauntlet, and "Captain Harville smiled, as much as to say, 'Do you claim that for your sex?'" (*P*: 232). Personal grief is momentarily forgotten as he and Anne ("smiling also") adopt the standard positions in the age-old *querelle des femmes*. First Anne invokes "outward circumstances": the difference between those of women "at home, quiet, confined" and those of men who have "always a profession, pursuits, business of some sort or another . . . and continual occupation and change soon weaken impressions." Harville objects that since the war ended, Benwick has himself been confined to home. Anne shifts the ground to "man's nature" but here Harville makes a preemptive strike, claiming the analogy between bodily and emotional strength. Anne reciprocally argues by analogy for the superior tenderness of women's feelings but, reverting to the idea of men's calling, proposes generously that they have the greater need for fortitude and forgetfulness.

Harville's next gambit is to remind Anne that "all histories are against you, all stories, prose and verse" – a move so hackneyed that he immediately anticipates its rejection. She complies with the observation: "Men have had every advantage of us in telling their own story. Education has been theirs in so much higher a degree; the pen has been in their hands. I will not allow books to prove any thing" (*P*: 234). This statement, which places in a more serious light Austen's protestations of ignorance in her letter to Clarke, has sometimes been taken as a feminist protest. But surely it is difficult not to sense a certain ironic undertow here, as Austen, bearing the pen herself, conscious of the brilliance of her own achievement in representing the female point of view while occluding and mediating the male perspective, causes the eavesdropping hero Wentworth to drop his pen.

The final move has the unpredictability of genius; clearly Austen even surprised herself, since this device for allowing hero and heroine to reach an understanding was a complete departure from the original fully worked version which survives in manuscript. After the hedging and maneuvering in the interests of sexual "bias," Harville "in a tone of strong feeling" attempts to bridge the difference by conveying his point of view as a sailor: "if I could but make you comprehend what a man suffers when he takes a last look at his wife and children, and watches the boat that he has sent them off in. . . ." Anne embraces this description, "I hope I do justice to all that is felt by you, and by those who resemble you. God forbid that I should undervalue the warm and faithful feelings of any of my fellow-creatures. I should deserve utter contempt if I dared to suppose that true attachment and constancy were known only by woman" and reciprocates with strong emotion in her turn, "All the privilege I claim for my own sex (it is not a very enviable one, you need not covet it) is that of loving longest, when existence or when hope is gone." The conversation concludes with a gesture: "'You are a good soul,' cried Captain Harville, putting his hand on her arm quite affectionately. 'There is no quarrelling with you . . .'" (*P*: 235–6).

In many respects the scene might be mistaken for a sentimental set piece by Sterne or Mackenzie or Burney: there is the rhetoric, the systematic emotional transaction, the physical gesture, even the Burneyesque name "Harville." But what sets it apart is the precision of the context and the language: after the debate to establish hierarchy, the powerfully egalitarian effort to establish a connection through empathy. The term "fellow-creatures" replaces men; Anne is a "good soul," not only an advocate for women: the latter term resonates with the watchword of enlightenment feminism, "no sex in souls." Distinctions of class as well as gender are swept away: the impoverished officer on half-pay breaks through etiquette and deference, and touches, in the spirit of comradeship and fellow-feeling, the lady, the daughter of a baronet.

This utopian moment, this mutual baring of souls, fulfills the pivotal purpose of reconciling Anne and Captain Wentworth. His letter is the continuation of the epiphany, incorporating Anne's gender-neutral terminology: "Too good, too excellent creature! You do us justice indeed. You do believe that there is true attachment and constancy among men." Austen's attention to the relationship of bodies and the direction of glances in the private apartment in the White Hart has the exactness of choreography. Anne had already approached the desk where Wentworth had been writing when he returns, places the letter before her, and hurriedly departs again; "sinking into the chair which he had occupied, succeeding to the very spot where he had leaned and written" she reads it (*P*: 237). It is as much this bodily merging of perspective as the content of the letter that offers a final healing vision to succeed the drama of sexual difference.

NOTES

1 On this interpretation and the "queer" tradition of Austen appreciation, see Johnson (1996 and 1997); cf. Miller (2003).

2 On the wartime "vocational crisis" as it affects the work of male poets, see Bainbridge (2003, esp. pp. 99–119).

3　Lowth's poem was included in many instructional miscellanies including *Elegant Extracts* (1789), cited in *Emma*; it was reprinted in Robert Dodsley's *Collection of Poems*, a set of which Austen owned until the move from Steventon (Austen 1995: 88).

FURTHER READING

Bainbridge, Simon (2003). *British Poetry and the Revolutionary and Napoleonic Wars: Visions of Conflict*. Oxford: Oxford University Press.

Barrell, John (1986). *The Political Theory of Painting from Reynolds to Hazlitt: The Body of the Public*. New Haven, CT and London: Yale University Press.

Kames, Henry Home, Lord (1778/2007). *Sketches of the History of Man*, 2 vols. Indianapolis: Liberty Fund.

Mannings, David (1984). Reynolds, Garrick, and the Choice of Hercules. *Eighteenth-Century Studies*, 17: 3, 259–83.

Pritchett, V. S. (1970). *George Meredith and English Comedy*. London and New York, Knopf.

Shaftesbury, Earl of (1713). *A Notion of the Historical Draught or Tablature of the Judgement of Hercules*. London.

30

The Trouble with Things:
Objects and the Commodification
of Sociability

Barbara M. Benedict

In all of her work, Jane Austen depicts the relations between women, between women and men, and between members of the same and different social classes. Her representation of social relations, however, requires also an examination of the relations between the subject and material culture, or, in other words, between people's sense of themselves and the things they desire, possess, and lose. Things had become plentiful, ubiquitous, and fascinatingly varied in the period from the Restoration in 1660 to the Regency: objects to find, buy, consume, and display – books, prints, cosmetics, decorative household goods, art objects – that had once been the envied possessions of the gentry were rapidly becoming widely available to the middling classes. And these things affected social relations. Even as they enriched people's minds and homes, they also, for many social observers including Austen, carried an ominous power to make everything seem an object for accumulation, consumption, and display, even intangible feelings, relationships, and people themselves. Things were becoming emissaries between people, and the spaces they occupied both in public and in the house inflected sociability, reorienting human interrelations from emotional and ideational, even idealistic, to thing-oriented. In particular, purchasable things become the means for the struggle between a cooperative and a competitive sociability. Austen dramatizes this overlap between the material and the moral, the collaborative and the rivalrous, through her characters' encounters in thing-cluttered spaces from shops to libraries, and through their attitudes toward the objects in their lives.

Shops

For everyone, there were more things to see and buy, and more public venues displaying them, including public museums, auctions, advertisements, prints and pictures, and, especially in cities, shops where, as the novelist and journalist Sophie von

La Roche (1731–1807) noted, there were "watchmakers, silversmiths, china-shops, confectioners without equal, and the goods . . . elegantly displayed behind . . . fine glass windows" (Williams 1933: 40). Shops, indeed, not only exhibited goods but advertised national progress:

> [At] Mr. Boydell's shop, London's most famous print dealer . . . I was struck by the excellent arrangement and system which the love of gain and the national good taste have combined in producing, particularly in the elegant dressing of inventions and ideas, not merely to ornament the streets and lure purchasers, but to make known the thousands of inventions and ideas, and spread good taste about, for the excellent pavements made for pedestrians enable crowds of people to stop and inspect the new exhibits. Many a genius is surely awakened in this way; many a labour improved by competition, which many people enjoy the pleasure of seeing something fresh – besides gaining an idea of the scope of human ability and industry. (La Roche 1933: 237)

With an enthusiasm that registers how new these displays were to eighteenth-century travelers, La Roche identifies some of the social concepts entailed by consumption that Austen both laughs at and lauds. La Roche praises a commercial enterprise that induces "crowds of people to stop and inspect" and to experience "the pleasure of seeing something fresh"; for her, this improvement liberates feelings of excitement and hope. However, the fusion she describes of "love of gain" with "good taste," and of "inventions" or things with "ideas," precisely expresses the ambiguous transition of values that Austen depicts, while the celebration of ornament and lure, and especially of "competition," novelty, and ambition exemplifies the refocusing of sociability from relational interaction to thing-centered rivalry and display. Shops and the things they stocked and sold became centers of the cultural shift that defined Regency sociability as triumphantly consumerist.

As venues for the exchange of goods, shops become stages for moral drama in Austen's novels. Although shopping could offer women cultural power as an activity through which they actively chose how to present themselves, this depended on their opportunities to shop, and the money they had to spend. Brief scenes throughout Austen's novels show how shopping reveals character: whereas the profligate Lydia Bennet purchases lavishly from a shop that happens to be near by while awaiting her sisters' arrival, *Sanditon*'s virtuous Charlotte Heywood resists the library's "Drawers of rings & Broches" she cannot afford (*MW*: 390).

The shop itself had become a place for recreation, replacing the drawing-room or mall and thus substituting commercial for social exhibition. Austen depicts this dynamic in her representation of shops as sites of a heartless commercial exchange that spreads from goods to information and people. In *Sense and Sensibility*, Colonel Brandon hears the shocking news of Willoughby's marriage to the rich Miss Grey in "a stationer's shop in Pall Mall": this is an apt venue for the relation of Willoughby's betrayal of love for lucre, especially in view of Willoughby's cruel letter to Marianne, itself overseen by Miss Grey (*SS*: 199). Earlier in the book, Elinor herself encounters in a shop the man whose narcissism will make him the prey of the mercenary Lucy Steele. As she and Marianne wait in "Mr. Gray's shop," the locus of the famous jeweler in Sackville Street, London, to "negotiate the exchange of a few old-fashioned jewels of her mother," they see the foppish Robert Ferrars giving "orders for a toothpick-case for himself," and "examining and debating" its "size, shape, and ornaments" with a deliberation both unchivalrous and unmasculine:

> At last the affair was decided. The ivory, the gold, and the pearls, all received their appointment, and the gentleman having named the last day on which his existence could be continued without the possession of the toothpick-case, drew on his gloves with lei-surely care, and bestowing another glance on the Miss Dashwoods, but such a one as seemed rather to demand than to express admiration, walked off with an happy air of real conceit and affected indifference. (*SS*: 221)

The contrast between the watching women and the self-displaying man dramatizes the transition between eighteenth-century and Regency culture. Robert's vanity and selfishness in keeping the young ladies waiting demonstrates the cultural power of the Regency male in a society stripped of men by the Napoleonic wars. The venue of the shop, however, also shows the centrality of consumption as a signifier of sexual availability.

The ubiquity and visibility of consumable goods in shops shapes the way consumers interact with the world about them, including other consumers. Visiting London, Sophie von La Roche marveled at the shops' clever display of goods, an aesthetic that enveloped people as well as things:

> Every article is made more attractive to the eye than in Paris or in any other town . . . We especially noticed a cunning device for showing women's materials. Whether they are silks, chintzes or muslins, they hang down in folds behind the fine high windows so that the effect of this or that material, as it would be in the ordinary folds of a woman's dress can be studied. Amongst the muslins all colours are on view, and so one can judge how the frock would look in company with its fellows. (La Roche 1933: 87)

La Roche identifies the plenitude of material goods on display with the exhibition of the female body: the fashionable muslin fabrics are arranged as if they were women, competitively ranking themselves against each other at a ball, just as Mrs Allen does at her first Assembly in Bath in *Northanger Abbey*: "There goes a strange-looking woman! What an odd gown she has got on! How old fashioned it is! Look at the back" (*NA*: 23). Like the shoppers La Roche praises, Mrs Allen marvels at the "new exhibit" before her, focusing on the consumable rather than the consumer. Indeed, the ability to rank commodities stamps the observer as an urban sophisticate. Mrs Allen, for example, comforts herself for her childlessness by noting that "the lace on Mrs. Thorpe's pelisse was not half so handsome as her own" – once again valuing things over relationships, the purchase over the person (*NA*: 32). In a parody of this dynamic, Henry Tilney inspects Catherine's muslin at the Bath Assembly with the keen eye of an expert: "'It is very pretty, madam,' said he, gravely examining it; 'but I do not think it will wash well; I am afraid it will fray'" (*NA*: 28). Henry's consumer knowledge is a testament to his feminized sociability even as his irony establishes his distance from superficial social discourse. By means of both shop and social display, moreover, the male gaze by which judgment is formed and to which, in theory, women submit themselves for such judgment is transferred instead to the shopping woman (Bermingham 1995: 491). Women as consumers become not only objects on display, but subjects locked in competitive evaluation.

Things

In literature, things have always reflected their owners. From the seventeenth century, writers had shown that the objects that characters acquired, accumulated, and displayed exhibited their personalities – either deliberately or involuntarily. By the Regency, however, English society was increasingly dedicated to what the sociologist Thorstein Veblen (1899) coined "conspicuous consumption": the acquisition and use of things for the purpose of displaying to others your wealth, power, and status. Austen's novels examine this behavior as a measure of the contemporary confusion of commercial and moral registers of value. Things, in Austen's world, can stand for – even substitute for – status, class, personal values, a sweep of feelings from nostalgia to envy, for, in fact, identity itself. Furthermore, they supply the stimulus for the consumption and commodification of value and meaning that Austen depicts as overtaking moral relations.

Austen's novels seem at first to include remarkably few descriptions of physical phenomena since the energy of the narrative rests in the emotional currents between characters, revealed through Austen's highly nuanced narrative and dialogue. Nonetheless, things – as collectibles, commodities, consumables, and concepts – abound in Austen's work: clothes, books, jewelry, carriages, foodstuffs, furniture, houses. Such objects simultaneously work as realistic details, the furnishings of characters' lives, and as symbols. However, because things are not only material themselves, but indicative of a materialistic mentality, they can also mislead characters. Moreover, because they embody class status and wealth, take time to acquire, and occupy space, they also become sites for the struggle between masculine and feminine, elite and middle-class values. Objects embody distinction, the fact of choice, and so they incarnate characters' decisions.

Objects thus become tangible – but, to Austen, inadequate or misleading – witnesses of experience. In *Emma*, Harriet Smith accumulates a collection of things that remind her of Mr Elton, whom she loved unrequitedly, including a sticky bandage and pencil stub nestled in a box of Tunbridge ware, objects that have intimately touched his body. Transformed by the associations she gives them into vessels of memory and feeling, yet preserved within a tourist trinket box, these pedestrian objects become relics for the inexperienced Harriet, as yet unable to differentiate between semiotic categories of objects, or to disentangle feeling from stuff. Emma, however, recognizes the ludicrous incongruity of investing used-up and discarded remnants of things with deep and romantic sentiment. The different responses of the two young women signal the difference in their emotional and intellectual capacities. Whereas Harriet fails to see the objects she has furtively collected within the wider context of their social meanings, Emma, albeit blind to her own folly throughout most of the novel, recognizes that things have an ontological purpose and existence beyond individual feelings about them.

Furthermore, Harriet's sentiment has been conditioned by commercial culture. Her Tunbridge ware box is an example of the souvenirs produced in the resort of Tunbridge Wells in Kent, small objects adorned with inlaid, colored hardwoods forming decorations or illustrations (Le Faye 2002: 63). It further symbolizes the inauthentic culture Harriet has absorbed: a culture manufactured by commercial interests and supplied with mass-produced goods, masquerading as emblems of personal meaning. In contrast, although the genuinely sentimental Fanny Price in *Mansfield Park* seems similarly to value objects for their personal – not fashionable – associations, she does so in a way that invests them with spiritual meaning. In the school room which serves as her parlor, she has a collection of

> possessions . . . Her plants, her books – of which she has been a collector, from the first hour of her commanding a shilling – her writing desk, and her works of charity and ingenuity were all within her reach . . . she could scarcely see an object in that room which had not an interesting remembrance connected with it. Everything was a friend, or bore thoughts to a friend . . . (*MP*: 151–2)

and serves as tangible evidence of pain remedied by affection. Things thus become symbols of experience – but of largely unhappy experience, for Fanny's collection emblematizes her neglect. At the same time, Fanny uses them as moral prompts to instruct her in self-denial and gratitude. This religious use of objects harkens to the Renaissance practice of including in a collection of art a *memento mori*, a picture or statue portraying death, to remind rich owners surveying their possessions of the transience of worldly pleasures.

The commodification of experience through collecting things extends beyond the literal accumulation of souvenirs to the mental accumulation of impressions, but both practices involve new ways of socializing. When in *Northanger Abbey*, Isabella Thorpe and the party to Clifton collect "spars" as souvenirs of their experience, their easy commodification of their holiday experience into tourist collectibles indicates not only their own shallowness, but the triviality of popular pleasures. They have accepted, without examining them, tourist values, which center on rapid consumption: "They had driven directly to the York Hotel, ate some soup, and bespoke an early dinner, walked down to the Pump-room, tasted the water, and laid out some shillings in purses and spars; thence adjoined to eat ice at a pastry-cook's, and hurrying back to the Hotel, swallowed their dinner in haste. . . ." This portrait shows tourist pleasure as the hasty gratification of trivial appetites, and depicts this enjoyment as group greed.

In contrast, Catherine is alone, excluded from the sociability of communal consumption. She, indeed, focuses on another kind of popular pleasure: that of imagining Gothic isolation, even confinement. When hearing of their journey, "Catherine listened with heartfelt satisfaction. It appeared that Blaize Castle had never been thought of . . ." (*NA*: 116). Indeed, Catherine wavers between waiting for the Tilneys in order to take her promised walk around Beechen Cliff above Bath and accompanying Isabella Thorpe, John, and her brother to Blaize Castle – not to enjoy their company so much as to dream of lost, lonely, and betrayed heroines, isolated and immured in the ruined edifice. In this substitution of fictional for social pleasure, she resembles Marianne Dashwood, who wishes to buy "every book that tells her how to admire an old twisted tree" (*SS*: 92): she is also mesmerized by a popular literary culture that makes aesthetic and moral effects substitute for social intercourse. Catherine's tendency to commodify experience as Gothic thrill is apparent when she eagerly queries John about Blaize Castle: "is it really a castle, an old castle? . . . like what one reads of? . . . are there towers and long galleries?" When Thorpe replies, "By dozens," as if quantity were quality, she declares, "Then I should like to see it" (*NA*: 85). The castle, as a reified Gothic experience, is a received delight, cheaply imitated and mass-produced like Isabella's horrid novels. Significantly, however, Catherine refuses to gratify that pleasure at the cost of the pleasure and duty of adhering to her promise to walk with the Tilneys.

If spars and ice creams physically represent the party's sociable consumption of commercial pleasures, literature also offers a means of sociability. Both Willoughby in *Sense and Sensibility* and Captain Benwick in *Persuasion* use Romantic verse as the passport to flirtation. When Isabella and Catherine "shut themself up, to read novels together," they again use fashionable objects as a means for intimacy (*NA*: 37). Of course, literature is not the only consumable that binds the two: their friendship proceeds through the "free discussion" of "dress, balls, flirtations, and quizzes," concepts equally shaped by current fads: the things surrounding the young women constitute the avenues for sociability (*NA*: 33). So powerful a grip has Gothic fiction on Catherine's mind, however, that it shapes her ideas of people and behavior. Austen's narrator notes this by a linguistic confusion that makes Henry himself seem a secretive place to be investigated: "[Catherine's] passion for ancient edifices was next in degree to her passion for Henry Tilney – and castles and abbies made usually the charm of those reveries which his image did not fill. To see and explore either the ramparts and keep of the one, or the cloisters of the other, had been for many weeks a darling wish . . ." (*NA*: 141). A prey to fashion, Catherine even goes so far as to believe her host General Tilney a Gothic villain. This unthinking habit of mind, which causes Catherine to accept fashionable values and make experiences into consumables, reflects the social culture of the Regency. Indeed, Bath itself exemplifies a commodified experience: its shops, assemblies, theatres, pump room, and concerts constitute packaged pleasures for tourists. As Henry Tilney observes, every visitor does and says the same thing, declaring Bath intolerable after six weeks, lengthening their stay, and leaving only when "they can afford to stay no longer" (*NA*: 78). The ostensible raison d'être of the place, its medicinal waters, symbolizes the true reason for visitors to come: unexamined consumption.

Jewelry

Whereas Austen's men most often reveal their characters through the consumption of food, women are often portrayed through the symbol of jewelry. Jewelry particularly carries an ambiguous charge because it simultaneously exemplifies a particularly feminine accouterment and symbolizes a vanity and wealth traditionally antagonistic to religious values. Whereas Elinor Tilney inherits "a very beautiful set of pearls" from her mother, symbolizing the purity expressed by her always wearing white and her mother's love for her, Mrs Elton in contrast gloats that "I see very few pearls in the room except mine," displaying her vulgar love of self-display (*NA*: 68, *E*: 324). Like her gown, her trimming, her hair, her shawl, Mrs Elton's jewels are worn to show off her wealth and taste – and do so far more exactly than she realizes. In another example, Isabella Thorpe's dreams of a rich marriage are symbolized by the accumulation of possessions, including rings: "She saw herself at the end of a few weeks, the gaze and admiration of every new acquaintance at Fullerton, the envy of every valued old friend in Putney, with a carriage at her command, a new name on her tickets, and a brilliant exhibition of hoop rings on her finger" (*NA*: 122). Rather than considering marriage a spiritual or affective union, Isabella perceives it as a triumph over rivals that will allow her uninhibited self-display. Nothing symbolizes this more succinctly than her "exhibition" of the fashionable bands of glittering stones, designed to be collected and worn in quantities, that replace the plain gold wedding ring of a love match.

Furthermore, jewelry exemplifies the shift of goods from traditional emblems of social relations to individually acquired symbols of self. When individually fashioned, it is highly personal, private property, worn on the body, and not subject to the crippling laws of primogeniture that stripped women of land and home, that will turn the Bennet women from Longbourn, and that impoverished the Dashwood sisters as they had Austen herself. At the same time, jewelry was becoming so fungible, since it could now be produced in factories in identical forms, that it evaded individual meanings. This became true even of rings like Isabella's, despite their deep, cultural significance. When Elinor Dashwood in *Sense and Sensibility* sees on Edward's finger a hair ring – that is, usually, a ring made of woven hair fastened with gold ends, but sometimes a gold ring set with woven hair in its central oval – she assumes that Edward surreptitiously obtained some of her own hair to make it; in fact, it is made of Lucy's hair, and symbolizes their engagement. Again, when she espies the gold ring symbolizing marriage that Lucy Steele ostentatiously displays specifically to distress her, Elinor incorrectly assumes that Lucy has married Edward Ferrars, whom she loves, rather than his brother Robert. In both cases, Elinor understands the general, social meaning of the rings, but mistakes the specific context: she misreads the objects as personal.

Chains also signify both metaphorical bonds and precious things. The gold chains that Edmund and Henry Crawford give Fanny Price in *Mansfield Park* exemplify the fusion of symbolic and literal meanings. Whereas the "prettily worked" chain of gold, offered by Mary Crawford yet the gift of Henry, is too large to hold her amber cross, the "plain gold chain perfectly simple and neat," emblematic of Edmund and the purity of the clergy, is just right (*MP*: 258, 262). Mary has "a collection" of such chains that she keeps in a trinket box, symbolizing the chaining in materialism of her own finer impulses (*MP*: 258). The amber cross from Sicily given to Fanny by her brother William, representing the suffering of Christ and piety, also operates as a memento of Fanny's past, and symbolizes her loyalty to her impoverished family. Moreover, since these ornaments mirror the gold chains and topaz crosses her brother Charles gave Austen and her sister Cassandra in 1801, they demonstrate how Austen's own life was inhabited by things that fused personal, social, and symbolic meanings.

Clothes

One of the most prevalent items of consumption in the Regency was dress. Like the desire to own jewelry, the passion for dress traditionally exemplified a frivolous preoccupation with appearances, indicative of vanity, improvidence, and feminine vice. When Lydia Bennet spends the money with which she planned to treat her sisters to a communal feast instead "at the shop out there," she buys a hat for herself so ugly that she must take it apart and remake it:

> Then, shewing her purchases: [Lydia said,] "Look here, I have bought this bonnet . . . I do not think it is very pretty; but I thought I might as well buy it as not. I shall pull it to pieces as soon as I get home, and see if I can make it up any better." When her sisters abused it as ugly, she added, with perfect unconcern, "Oh! but there were two or three much uglier in the shop; and when I have bought some prettier-coloured satin to trim it with fresh, I think it will be very tolerable . . . I am so glad I bought my bonnet, if it is only for the fun of having another bandbox!" (*PP*: 219)

Lydia here reveals more even than her usual heedless prodigality and selfish disregard for her family: she also reveals that what attracts her about the bonnet is merely purchasing it, merely accumulating more commodities. Still more profoundly, the incident also adumbrates her elopement with Wickham, a relationship similarly expensive and ugly, which to be tolerable to society must also be taken apart and dressed up by Darcy as a marriage.

Like many authors, Austen often uses clothes to symbolize character, and depicts characters who fuss over what they wear as vain or superficial, a traditional charge especially directed to women. Since what people could wear had been determined historically by governmental regulations, much of the criticism against women's clothes reflected a fear of social disguise, especially the pretense that women belonged to a class above their station. Austen, however, implicitly contrasts this old-fashioned discourse with the new fashion of madly enthusiastic sartorial consumption, the symbol of national progress, much of it indeed designed to display the wearer as culturally, and by extension socially, elite. Both Mrs Elton in *Emma* and Isabella Thorpe in *Northanger Abbey* enact their desire of social climbing through sartorial display. Whereas the older and more experienced Mrs Elton spices hers with aggressive competitiveness, however, Isabella's shop-till-you-drop mentality combines moral vacuity and an uncontrollable desire to flirt. When she remarks to Catherine, "Do you know, I saw the prettiest hat you can imagine, in a shop-window in Milsom-Street just now – very like yours. Only with coquelicot ribbons instead of green; I quite longed for it," she merely reflects fashionable taste; shortly thereafter, however, she uses the excuse of showing Catherine the hat to "set off immediately as fast as they could walk, in pursuit of the two young men" who admired her (*NA*: 39, 43).

In addition, Austen recognized that the injunctions to women to abjure finery generally stemmed from repressive male moral monitors, using either moral or economic rationales. Most criticism in the history of dress, indeed, was directed at women, despite its long history as a male preoccupation, partly because "their financial weakness . . . made them more dependent on their powers of sex attraction" than men (Ribeiro 1986: 16). Catherine Morland is an innocent victim of this social truth. Even before Bath, her growth into womanhood is signaled when "Her love of dirt gave way to an inclination for finery": an ironic juxtaposition of opposites that humorously equates dross and dress (*NA*: 15). When she learns that Henry and Eleanor plan to attend the cotillion ball and lies awake considering what to wear, the narrator takes the opportunity to burlesque the rationalistic moralism of conventional discourse:

> What gown and what head-dress [Catherine] should wear on the occasion became her chief concern. She cannot be justified in it. Dress is at all times a frivolous distinction, and excessive solicitude about it often destroys its own aim. Catherine knew this very well . . . and yet she lay awake ten minutes on Wednesday night debating between her spotted and her tamboured muslin, and nothing but the shortness of the time prevented her from buying a new one for the evening. This would have been an error of judgement, great though not uncommon, from which one of the other sex rather than her own, a brother rather than a great aunt might have warned her, for man only can be aware of the insensibility of man towards a new gown. It would be mortifying to the feelings of many ladies, could they be made to understand how little the heart of man is affected by what is costly or new in their attire . . . Woman is fine for her own satisfaction alone. No man will admire her more, no woman will like her the better for it. Neatness and fashion are enough for the former, and a something of shabbiness or impropriety will be most endearing to the latter. (*NA*: 73–4)

Like the feminist writer Mary Wollstonecraft, who deplored fashionable dress as "the badge of slavery" for women (Wollstonecraft 1792: 27), Austen reveals that it is, in fact, a part of female cultural competition. For her, however, clothes are designed less to make women attractive to men than to triumph over rival women: they are part of a female semiotic system. Catherine's vacuous chaperon at Bath aptly demonstrates this: "Dress was her passion. She had a most harmless delight in being fine" (*NA*: 20). Although her weakness for fashion merely serves as an occupation, not a moral threat, she nonetheless feels it as rivalry. In contrast, the spiritual Fanny finds clothes yet another symbol of her exclusion from enfranchised sociability. As the narrator explains, "young and inexperienced, with small means of choice and no confidence in her own taste – the 'how she should be dressed' was a point of painful solicitude" (*MP*: 254). Austen shows that clothes exemplify women's self-exhibition as a source of identity and of participation in a world of social and cultural relations – a world that the lonely and marginalized Fanny longs to join.

Food

The most evidently consumable of goods in Austen's work is food. Since food is a traditional aspect of communality, characters who eat too much or care too much about food clearly exhibit greed, but more importantly, they show one key way in which fleshly, or worldly, values encroach on spiritual ones. For the gourmet Mr Grant in *Mansfield Park*, for example, religious precepts fall a distant second to dinner, and although this vice pales beside that of the selfish and materialistic Crawfords or the competitive, undisciplined, and vain Bertram sisters, it sits on the same spectrum. General Tilney in *Northanger Abbey* reveals a similar passion for rich dining. His appetite for domination is exemplified by his command for "Dinner to be on the table *directly*!" irrespective of the convenience of his guests (*NA*: 165). The vast "village of hot-houses . . . unrivalled in the kingdom," he boasts, from which he produces exotic and out-of-season fruits in huge quantities – a hundred pineapples in one year – further symbolizes his ambition to outdo all competitors (*NA*: 178). Fascination with food often symbolizes selfish competitiveness.

However, both the occasion of eating and what actually is eaten can also designate social relations, or the failure of characters to act with good manners. More than any other of Austen's novels, *Emma* concentrates on food as a symbol of character. Mr Woodhouse's gentle megalomania, which Emma has in a degree inherited, appears in his incomprehension that his guests do not share his delicate stomach: "food," as Maggie Lane points out, "is a symbol of goodwill, and Emma must learn to be as generous with her heart as she is with her gifts of pork and arrowroot" (Lane 1995: 164). In *Sanditon*, too, food is a persistent theme signifying the failure of healthy social relations. Austen indicates the self-indulgence of the indolent Arthur Parker, "heavy in Eye as well as figure," in *Sanditon* through his obsession with his own food. Pretending to a self-disciplinary starvation, under the eye of his sisters "he scrupulously scraped off almost as much butter as he put on [his toast], & then [seized] an off moment for adding a great dab just before it went into his Mouth" (*MW*: 418). *How characters eat is thus as important as how much, or what,* for it not only dramatizes their manners but indicates their attitude toward consumption in general: as communal or competitive.

Conclusion

In scrutinizing Regency mores, Austen investigates the consumption of fashionable, commercial goods with an eye to three particular concerns. She explores consumption as the interplay between materialism and morality in which people's most cherished ways of valuing themselves and others rest not only on ideas, but on their uses and ideas of things. This interplay in turn entails a further cultural problematic: the understanding of people as socialized by things, or even the depiction of people as things themselves. This is a particularly gendered dynamic: the vain Captain Tilney treats Isabella as a disposable thing, as Willoughby does Eliza and Marianne, for example. However, women also make themselves commodities by fashioning themselves as marriageable and displaying their accomplishments of singing, sewing, painting, and playing instruments, like the Miss Beauforts in *Sanditon*. They thus become consumables to the gazing male, but consumables they have partly fashioned themselves (Bermingham 1995: 489–91). Finally, such a commodification of identity and feeling forces people into a constant competition mediated by consumable culture: women like Lucy Steele and Elinor Dashwood, or Mrs Thorpe and Mrs Allen, or Emma and Mrs Elton, and even brothers who must jockey for parental favors, like the Ferrars. Austen portrays this rivalrous commodification and consumption in a rich panoply of greedy, foolish, and self-deceived characters – from Isabella Thorpe and Catherine Morland to the enthusiast Mr Parker and his gluttonous brother Arthur – who dramatize the confusion of fleeting fashions, selfish appetites, and moral values. For Austen, the sympathy, humility, and duty that should regulate our behavior should also organize our consumption. Along with commodities and consumables, cooperation and sociability should be available in the shop.

FURTHER READING

Benedict, B. M. (2000). Jane Austen and the culture of circulating libraries: the construction of female literacy. In Paula R. Backscheider (Ed.). *Revising Women: Feminist Essays in Eighteenth-Century "Women's Fiction" and Social Engagement* (pp. 147–99). Baltimore and London: Johns Hopkins University Press.

Berg, M. and H. Clifford (1999). *Consumers and Luxury: Consumer Culture in Europe, 1650–1850.* Manchester, UK and New York: Manchester University Press.

Bourdieu, P. (1984). *Distinction: A Social Critique of the Judgment of Taste.* London: Routledge and Kegan Paul.

Campbell, C. (1987). *The Romantic Ethic and the Spirit of Modern Consumerism*. Oxford: Blackwell.

Kowaleski-Wallace, B. (1997). *Women, Shopping, and Business in Eighteenth-Century England*. New York: Columbia University Press.

McCracken, G. (1990). *Culture and Consumption: New Approaches to the Symbolic Character of Consumer Goods and Activities*. Bloomington and Indianapolis: Indiana University Press.

31
Luxury: Making Sense of Excess in Austen's Narratives

Diego Saglia

It is now generally accepted that Jane Austen was far from being self-denying. Her correspondence shows that, from her youth, she was deeply versed in the rituals of conspicuous consumption and self-display, particularly in such aspects as female fashions and ornaments, furniture, carriages, theatre-going, and dancing. And it is comparatively easy to find evidence in her letters in favor of the pleasures of consumption. Indeed, with a certain measure of irony, Austen declared she had little patience with the "poor & economical" people of Steventon, while she was much more impressed with her wealthy brother's lifestyle at Godmersham: "Kent is the only place for happiness. Everybody is rich there" (*Letters*: 28). Shopping, especially in London, was a favorite and irresistible activity. In April 1811 she wrote to Cassandra: "I am getting very extravagant & spending all my Money; & what is worse for *you*, I have been spending yours too" (*Letters*: 179). London, moreover, was the home of her brother Henry who, as a banker, led a life of luxurious consumption at several fashionable addresses before he went bankrupt in March 1816.

Critics have recently started to take seriously Austen's connections with material culture (Copeland 1986, 1995, Gay 2005, Selwyn 1999, 2005). Yet these connections cannot be reduced to mere lists of shops, muslins, and ribbons, for her accounts of the pleasures of consumption place objects and activities into a continuum that is inextricable from her everyday experience as woman and author. This emerges particularly during her stays in London, where she enjoyed cultural activities and the rituals of self-display as gratifying, privileged experiences. In May 1813 Austen wrote to Cassandra:

> I had great amusement among the Pictures [at the British Academy Exhibition]; & the Driving about, the Carriage been [*sic*] open, was very pleasant. – I liked my solitary elegance very much, & was ready to laugh all the time, at my being where I was. – I could not but feel that I had naturally small right to be parading about London in a Barouche. (*Letters*: 213–14)

Austen is well aware that she has just a "small right" to these pleasures and that, in view of her straitened circumstances, she has no claim to a life of luxurious expenditure and enjoyment. Even so, she does not reject but rather embraces and celebrates, with knowing amusement, the experience of luxury offered to her.

Underpinned by notions of privilege and distinction, Austen's involvement in the culture of consumption combines objects, actions, and signs that may be gathered under the collective heading of luxury. During the eighteenth century this concept had been gradually shedding its negative connotations to become a staple principle in assessments of economic and cultural modernity. On the basis of this progressive rehabilitation, luxury in the Romantic period was no longer simply the object of severe moral strictures, but rather a capacious concept signifying "politeness, respect-ability, and independence," as well as "modernity, refinement, and pleasure, not just among the elites, but among the middling classes" (Berg 2005: 15, 4). For Austen's rank, in particular, luxury was an instrument of socioeconomic distinction, a system of objects and actions keyed to the definition of intensely socialized masculine and feminine identities. In addition, luxury had a powerful impact on current notions of national identity.

In point of fact, early nineteenth-century commentators tended to see luxury, opulence, and refinement as distinctly ingrained in the socioeconomic fabric of the nation. Thus Mary Robinson assessed the system of luxury goods and entertainment in London, partly denouncing its negative effects, in her 1800 essay on the "Present State of the Manners and Society &c &c of the Metropolis" (quoted in Pascoe 1997: 138–9). Similarly, the fictitious Spanish author of Robert Southey's *Letters from England* (1807) repeatedly expresses his astonishment at the "domestic accommodations and luxuries," "the beautiful things in the shop windows" and "the opulence and splendour of the shops" in the capital (1951: 47, 50). An essay in *The Repository of Arts* for November 1809 observes: "It cannot be denied that, notwithstanding the hardness of the times [. . .] the meanest peasant now enjoys comforts superior to what our monarchs could command a few centuries ago, when humble straw composed the couch of majesty, and the rudest vehicle was a luxury unknown even to queens" (1809: 344). And, in 1816, the anonymous author of *Brief Remarks on English Manners* declares, with patriotic pride, that "our great encrease in wealth, has produced [. . .] an extensive system of luxurious competition in our mode of living" (Anon 1816: 11).

Statements such as these seek to make sense of the overwhelming presence of con-sumer goods, that "pullulation of objects" arising from the "ever-accelerating proces-sion of generations of products" that Jean Baudrillard indicates as an intrinsic aspect of modernity (1996: 1). In addition, they examine the link between things, activities (of production and consumption), and collective or individual identity. Their concep-tual background lies in the eighteenth-century debate on luxury and its various attempts at defining opulence, its ethical, economic, and cultural status, and the dis-crimination between "necessities" and "conveniences" or "decencies" and "luxuries" discussed by Adam Smith in *The Wealth of Nations* (vol. 2; Copeland 1986: 8–9). Drawing on this discourse, Romantic-period commentators recognized luxury as among the defining traits of contemporary Britain and repeatedly weighed its influence on codes of behavior and models of identity.

Luxury holds a relevant place in Austen's narrative universe. In *Mansfield Park* Henry Crawford is said to have been brought up "in a school of luxury and epicurism" (*MP*: 407). A few pages earlier, Fanny Price herself has been enjoying the newfound purchasing independence afforded by the £10 she has received from her uncle. Of Fanny the narrator remarks that "wealth is luxurious and daring" (*MP*: 398). In *Sense and Sensibility* Willoughby is "expensive" (*SS*: 210) and overtly associated with luxurious habits (*SS*: 331), and so is William Elliot in *Persuasion*. Yet, in the same novel, after her marriage to Frederick Wentworth, Anne finds herself "mistress of a very pretty landaulette" (*P*: 250) and therefore free to enjoy the pleasures Austen experienced in her brother's barouche in London in May 1813.

In fact, Austen "never endorses extravagance in her characters, and indeed unnecessary expenditure, especially on oneself, is a sign of moral weakness" (Selwyn 2005: 222). But luxury is no simple matter of a morally reprehensible excess. It is a nexus of pleasurable objects and activities, increasingly seen as separated from the processes of their production and, instead, prized for their symbolical value. As Arjun Appadurai explains, luxury objects are "goods whose principal use is *rhetorical* and *social*, goods that are simply *incarnated signs*" (1986: 38). Since Austen's luxuries are signs endowed with cultural and ideological implications, they take on a life of their own and act on the consuming subject in ways that, as will be shown, recall the concept of "commodity fetishism" developed by Marxist theory (Dant 1996). These incarnated signs also play a distinct role in the work of literary representation. Thus, in view of its contemporary relevance and sheer thematic weight in Austen's output, luxury cannot be reduced to the catalogues of "period objects" we may retrieve from her novels. Instead, it must be recovered as a significant component of the mechanisms of her narrative art.

At Gray's in Sackville Street: A Toothpick Case and a Negotiation

Although ubiquitous in Austen's canon, consumption is at its showiest in *Sense and Sensibility*, with its several instances of "consumer madness" (Copeland 1995: 96). Here, most of Austen's characters are obsessed with conspicuous consumption and emulation, or afflicted by the impossibility of consuming according to the mandates and expectations of their rank or inclination. In particular, luxury takes center stage when the Dashwood sisters go to Gray's, a fashionable jeweler's in the Piccadilly area of London. There, "Elinor was carrying on a negociation for the exchange of a few old-fashioned jewels of her mother" (*SS*: 220), that is, either trying to sell or pawn them, or possibly exchanging some old settings for more modern ones.

As is usual with Austen, this introductory remark implies more than is visible at first sight, for the use of "carrying on" and "negociation" is particularly revealing. The first expression indicates an action that had been going on for some time and therefore defines even the far from wealthy and ostentatious Elinor as a habitué rather than a newcomer in the world of luxury shops and "business." The second term, then, highlights her familiarity with the customer–seller relationship (indeed, one not exclusive to luxury shops) and the fact that she is an active player in this socioeconomic and cultural dimension.

Austen evokes a highly polished vignette set in an actual luxury goods establishment in the heart of London, where "luxury [. . .] fills every head with caprice [. . .] and shops are become exhibitions of fashion" (Southey 1951: 68–9). Yet, rather than reading this scene to recover what shopping was like in this period (fiction as documentary), we need to examine it as a complex intersection of signs that disclose how the novel works to produce certain meanings (fiction as aesthetic-ideological construct).

Since all the attendants at Gray's are busy, the sisters sit down and wait "at that end of the counter which seemed to promise the quickest succession" (*SS*: 220) because only one gentleman is being served there. As the narrator observes, "it is probable that Elinor was not without hopes of exciting his politeness to a quicker dispatch," thus highlighting her adeptness at playing with the social and emotional niceties of shopping. Moreover, the gentleman is an anonymous face, and the narrative invites us to focus on the object he is purchasing. As he is "giving orders for a toothpick-case for himself," the man ignores the two sisters apart from "three or four very broad stares" (*SS*: 220). He is busy determining "its size, shape, and ornaments [. . .] all of which, after examining and debating for a quarter of an hour over every toothpick-case in the shop, were finally arranged by his own inventive fancy" (*SS*: 220).

The toothpick case is the center of attention and the subject is completely absorbed by it: "At last the affair was decided. The ivory, the gold, and the pearls, all received their appointment, and the gentleman having named the last day on which his existence could be continued without the possession of the toothpick-case, drew on his gloves with leisurely care" (*SS*: 221). In evoking a subject totally dependent on a luxury object and its ornaments, Austen creates her own version of the fetishized commodity. As in the Marxist definition of this concept, the object is severed from its use or exchange value and acquires a symbolic meaning that makes it so essential to the purchaser's identity that it is no longer a manufactured good but rather a talisman on which all his desire centers and his existence depends. As Rachel Bowlby aptly observes, in such cases the consumer "is not so much possessor of as possessed by the commodities which one must have to be made or make oneself in the form objectively guaranteed as that of a social individual" (1985: 28).

The episode, however, must also be read in the context of a Romantic-period consumer culture in which this investment in a choice item of male jewelry was not so uncommon. At a time when all jewels were made to order, the range of men's ornaments had visibly shrunk in comparison with earlier eighteenth-century fashion. What remained to men were watches (to which a seal was usually attached), rings, the spyglass, and the snuffbox (Reade 1953: 244–5). Paralleling George "Beau"

Brummell's simplification of male costume and accessories, this contraction limited the range for definitions of masculine identity through the display of luxury ornaments. Thus such jewels as remained were highly personal objects made to fit individual requests and specifications and deeply expressive of the giver's and owner's identities. They were "things of selfhood" within a wider social economy of luxury objects and activities, things endowed with a subjective transcendence that effectively turned them into fetishes of identity. Given their importance and the fact that fewer items were available to men, the intense concentration of Austen's customer on his toothpick case is more than mere personal and selfish fancy.

Nonetheless Austen complicates the idea of self-making luxury, for, in her scene, the object is fuller and more "rounded" than its purchaser. All show and no substance, the precious case is still semantically richer than the man who, "adorned in the first style of fashion" and thus replicating the object's overworked surface, is ultimately "a person and face, of strong, natural, sterling insignificance" (*SS*: 220–1). Here, the use of "sterling" is particularly revealing. As its meaning is primarily related to precious metals or money, Austen employs this adjective in the semantically appropriate context. In this sense, it can mean "of standard quality," thus connoting the male character's aspirations to taste and elegance, as well as his desire of belonging to "the quality" (the elegant upper classes). Also, of an individual, it means "excellent," which he very obviously is not. Austen therefore uses "sterling" in its literal context to stress (through its metaphorical overtones) that the character conspicuously lacks the qualities of the precious object. The man has no significance or value, whereas the object is laden with value and, in addition, discloses what he has not or aspires to. The luxury ornament speaks of the subject – or, in poststructuralist terms, luxury speaks the subject – in the context of what Copeland perceptively terms "this novel's strangely inhuman world of things" (1986: 84).

The male purchaser at Gray's is a self enthralled by, or literally in thrall to, an object. Appropriately, it is only later that we discover he is Robert Ferrars, Edward Ferrars's younger brother, already defined as "silly and a great coxcomb" (*SS*: 148), who eventually displaces his brother's rights to primogeniture. Because of his fascination with luxury and money, he stands in clear contrast to Elinor and Marianne. The elder sister observes him carefully, then dispatches her own transaction in a sober and quick way: "Elinor lost no time in bringing her business forward, and was on the point of concluding it" when another irresponsible male consumer, her half-brother John Dashwood, enters the shop (*SS*: 221). While Elinor intervenes in this luxury dimension of objects and symbols, the dispirited Marianne ignores everything and "collect[s] her thoughts within herself" (*SS*: 193). In actual fact, earlier in the novel, after moving into Barton Cottage the impoverished sisters find comfort in their books, pianoforte, and drawings (*SS*: 30), and later Edward invites them to indulge in the "imaginary happiness" afforded by the pleasures of consumption as they conjure up the books, sheet music, and prints they would buy if they had "a large fortune apiece" (*SS*: 92). At the jeweler's, however, Elinor and Marianne variously control the lure of luxurious expenditure of which Robert Ferrars is such a willing victim.

In this resonant intersection of things and selves, luxury is a system of objects and gestures that double as signs and activate some of the central preoccupations in the narrative. It gives iconic status to money and class, affords a wry look at consumer practices in the capital, and clarifies Austen's definition of identity and social interaction through objects. Above all, it provides an insight into the disturbing possibility that things may take over the subject in the context of generalized luxury, commercial dynamism, and ubiquitous consumption that contemporary commentators saw as peculiar to Britain.

Pineapples in Gloucestershire

Although the term "exotic" does not feature in any of Austen's novels, exotic objects and luxuries appear in her narratives, often in seemingly marginal positions. One significant instance is that of General Tilney's pineapples in *Northanger Abbey*, where we read that

> Though careless in most matters of eating, he loved good fruit – or if he did not, his friends and children did. There were great vexations however attending such a garden as his. The utmost care could not always secure the most valuable fruits. The pinery had yielded only one hundred in the last year. (*NA*: 178)

An example of Austen's calculated use of free indirect speech, this passage, and especially the reference to the "one hundred" fruits, reveals the general as a self-displaying, boastful individual (Lane 1995: 95, Palter 2002: 368). His true meaning, moreover, lies concealed under a semblance of generosity and conviviality. Indeed, even though the pineapples are ostensibly aimed at his friends and family, in actual fact their production, display, and consumption belong in a cycle of power that begins with the general and ultimately returns to him. A "living status symbol" and a "symbol of hospitality" (Olsen 2005, vol. 1: 284), in Austen's novel this fruit acquires much more sinister overtones.

That it should fall to pineapples to qualify the general as a despot is not so outlandish as might at first appear. To begin with, this fruit, first brought to England in 1657 and probably grown and fruited there from the 1660s, has a long history in English literature well before Jane Austen (Palter 2002). In the early eighteenth century it replaced the orange as a chic novelty, and Alexander Pope was among the chief promoters of its cultivation. Additionally, the pineapple was fraught with ideological connotations from the outset. On August 14, 1668, John Evelyn recorded tasting his first ever pineapple, a morsel of "that rare fruite called the *King-Pine*" appropriately handed to him by the king himself: "His Majestie having cut it up, was pleased to give me a piece off his own plate to tast of" (1995: 3, 513). Later, in his *Essay upon Gardening* (1793), Richard Steele called the pineapple "This prince of vegetables" (1793: 16) and stated that a "pinery" was "what every gentleman of rank and fortune would wish to possess" (p. 113). The fruit was also called the "prince" and sometimes the "king" of fruits because of its green crown of leaves (Taylor 1769: vi), and among its varieties were (and still are) the "old queen" and the "king pine."

A "kingly" fruit symbolic of absolute power, in *Northanger Abbey* this edible luxury emblematizes monarchic and establishment authority at a time of potential revolution hinted at in the references to riots (*NA*: 113) and to Gothic fictional misrule as opposed to English stability (p. 200). When consumed by the general's "friends and children," it gives actual physical substance to conservative ideology: eating pineapples also means partaking of, and feeding off, conservative patriotism. If *Northanger Abbey* is about "the prerogatives of those who have [. . .] 'real power' and the constraints of those who do not" (Johnson 1988: 36), then the pineapple is power incarnated in, and acting through, luxury food. The fruit is the emblem of an ideological system which Austen examines further by alluding to the technology for its cultivation:

> The walls seemed countless in number, endless in length; a village of hot-houses seemed to arise among them, and a whole parish to be at work within the inclosure. The General was flattered by her looks of surprize, which told him almost as plainly, as he soon forced her to tell him in words, that she had never seen any gardens at all equal to them before. . . . (*NA*: 178)

To impress Catherine even more, the general adds that his hothouses are "unrivalled in the kingdom" (*NA*: 178), another boastful remark stressing his monarch-like control over men, women, and machinery. Thus Austen unveils the technological and labor structures underpinning the production of the pineapple. The large number of workers, in particular, is required by the complexity of this process as detailed in many contemporary publications (listed in Loudon 1822: iv–v). But Austen's vignette is also concerned with political and socioeconomic implications, since it focuses on a "village" and a "parish" employed to gratify the luxurious appetites of the Abbey; while the word "inclosure" hints at contemporary changes in the landscape and socioeconomic situation of the countryside. If countless Enclosure Acts were passed during the French war years, turning common into private land and driving poor villagers towards the cities (Clark and Dutton 2005: 188–91), here, by contrast, people are enclosed within the economy of the Abbey and its production and accumulation of luxuries for its ruler.

More than just a picture of technological progress, Austen's scene reveals the dystopian technological side of the general's Gothic villainy. And, in its encapsulation of the economy of luxury and its human costs, it recalls similar treatments in contemporary poetry by Anna Letitia Barbauld, Charlotte Smith, and Mary Robinson (Saglia 1999). At the pinnacle of this social, political, and economic structure stands the general, a man of luxury, a "consumer-mad" figure (Copeland 1995: 92). With its modern improvements the Abbey is a microcosm of the advances in technology and production typical of contemporary Britain. By the same token, the country house and its estate are a microcosm of absolutism and establishment conservatism embodied in the fruits consumed in the Abbey's luxurious apartments.

The Windows of Bath

In December 1797 Frances Burney wrote to her sister Susanna Phillips: "We know not yet what will be our taxes, &c – nor what our means of answering such calls [. . .] The new threefold assessment of taxes has terrified us rather seriously [. . .] We have, this very Morning, decided upon parting with 4 of our new windows. A great abatement of *agremens* to ourselves, & of ornament to our appearance" (1972–84, vol. 4: 49). Relating the effects of taxation on her recently inaugurated "Camilla Cottage," Burney makes plain the luxury value of windows as indicators of wealth and conspicuous consumption. The window tax, first introduced in 1696, was employed by successive administrations to fill the state coffers and, in the late eighteenth century, to finance the French wars.[1] Specifically, at the end of 1797, when Burney is writing, William Pitt "introduced a bill to treble the assessed taxes [. . .] on inhabited houses, windows, male servants, horses and carriages" (Emsley 1979: 70).

Austen's novels feature several references to windows which, as incarnated signs and "eloquent" luxuries, contribute to her socioeconomic discriminations. In *Pride and Prejudice* Mr Collins counts the windows on the façade of Rosings and details "what the glazing altogether had originally cost" (*PP*: 161), while in *Mansfield Park*, Sotherton has "many more rooms than could be supposed to be of any other use than to contribute to the window tax" (*MP*: 85). It is in *Persuasion*, however, that Austen heightens the luxury value of windows and turns them into active features in the sections in Bath, an urban setting where windows play a vital role.

Built for sumptuous display, Bath has always been a city of windows and shop windows. The beauty of its extraordinarily homogeneous Georgian architecture owes much to the elegant rows of windows ornamenting its façades. Indeed, Bath is the perfect place for the vain Sir Walter Elliot, one of whose favorite objects is the mirror.[2] And windows at the time were sites of luxurious display (both external and internal) composed by curtains and other decorations which, in contemporary fashionable magazines, received as much attention as other elements of interior design. In August 1816 *The Repository of Arts* informed readers that "Perhaps no furniture is more decorative and graceful than that of which draperies form a considerable part" (quoted in Agius and Jones 1984: 22). Regency windows were elaborate structures made up of blinds, muslin curtains, curtains proper, and draperies (looped, twined, or draped on top), cornices and valances, tassels, rosettes, wreaths, and fringes, all supported by curtain rods and poles, and decorated in the Greek, chinoiserie, or Gothic styles. And Bath itself boasted a nationally renowned upholsterer, John Stafford, one of "the most famous of the provincial interior designers of the Regency" (Reade 1953: 71), whose illustrated designs graced the pages of the *Repository* between August 1819 and July 1820.

Unlike *Mansfield Park* or *Pride and Prejudice*, *Persuasion* posits windows also in terms of ornaments that, as part of the luxury display of Bath, unveil some crucial meanings in the text. In particular, in book II, chapter 7, as Anne Elliot and Lady Russell are driving around Bath, the latter's gaze is focused on some beautiful window ornaments:

> "You will wonder," said she, "what has been fixing my eye so long; but I was looking after some window-curtains, which Lady Alicia and Mrs Falkland were telling me of last night. They described the drawing-room window-curtains of one of the houses on this side of the way, and this part of the street, as being the handsomest and best hung of any in Bath, but could not recollect the exact number, and I have been trying to find out which it could be; but I confess I can see no curtains hereabouts that answer their description." (*P*: 179)

This may be a lie, since Anne perceives that Lady Russell's eyes are in fact turned in the direction of Captain Wentworth. Yet whether Lady Russell is telling the truth or not is difficult to ascertain. As Austen filters the scene through the heroine's consciousness, we have no reliable evidence to help us decide whether she sees him or not. For our purposes, however, the interest here lies not so much in Anne's disappointment at her friend's probable clumsy manipulation of her own trust. Rather, it lies in the object Lady Russell chooses possibly to deflect attention from the actual target of her curiosity, an object that once more functions "as a metonymy for her fixation on material wealth" (Heydt-Stevenson 2005: 194). With a familiar move, luxury again takes center stage and becomes symbolic of Lady Russell's notion of her own class (and her original opposition to Wentworth) and her inability to see beyond it. Indeed, she is a remarkably blind character, already introduced in book I, chapter 2 as entertaining "prejudices on the side of ancestry" and "a value for rank and consequence, which blinded her a little to the faults of those who possessed them" (*P*: 11). Most importantly, she tends to be "unfairly influenced by appearances" (p. 249) and therefore cannot see the merits of Wentworth or the faults of William Elliot.

In this narrative snapshot, the curtains shift from their function of display to one of concealment, as they hide reality and modify or prevent our vision of it. Luxury acts as a screen, once again a socially and economically meaningful one. But Lady Russell's intentions backfire. If windows are both external and internal luxuries, she evidently miscalculates in using them as instruments to divert her gaze and hide her own thoughts. As a textual device controlled by the narrator, the luxury curtains actually give us further insight into this character's inability to see. Anne's refusal to believe the luxury decoy, by contrast, is another instance of her muted but steadfast resistance to authority and her questioning of the principle of filial submission (Johnson 1988: 146). As signs that express and reveal, windows and curtains enable us to see into the delicate balance between Anne and Lady Russell, and thus gauge the shifting levels of persuasion, conviction, and resolution between them. Instead of concealing, the luxury ornaments of Bath make plain the inability of the provincial gentry to see beyond the limited sphere of their cultural, class, and economic concerns.

The Work of Luxury in Austen's Novels

Critics have often remarked on the role of objects in Austen's fiction. Barbara Hardy has drawn attention to her use of "expressive things," "usually sunk below the surface, seldom loud or flaunted even when playing an important part as a personal or social symbol, or a dramatic property, useful tools in the craft of fiction" (1975: 181). Edward Copeland has discussed Austen's use of "positional goods" (1995: 11), and Jillian Heydt-Stevenson has commented on her recourse to "anamorphic objects" (2005: 17). Deidre Lynch, in addition, has argued convincingly that the development of character in Austen is inseparable from an "education in consumer capitalism" in the context of a "configuration of objects and practices" such as circulating libraries and window shopping (1998: 8).

This attention to objects naturally points in the direction of an examination of luxury and its aesthetic and ideological values. Because of its complex status as both thing and sign, luxury touches on the interrelated spheres of selfhood, the nation, politics, and the economy, not to mention the literary artifact itself. For, at the time, new books such as Austen's novels were "expensive luxuries which could be bought, if at all, only by the richest groups in society" (St Clair 2004: 196). Addressing the presence and effects of luxury and its consumption, Austen's fictions represent them through her typically ambivalent moral evaluation and attention to nuance. In her novels and letters, luxuries may be good or bad, but they are invariably relevant on the basis of the effect they have on the subject.

Through her uses of luxury Austen tells us something about self and society, the construction of self as a socialized entity, the mechanisms of modernity, as well as how her novels work by calibrating the relation between detail and context. In different ways, sumptuous objects and activities may take over the subject (as fetishes), allow us to see into the characters, and make plain the ideological conditions under which they exist. Luxury anchors Austen's fiction to contemporary practices of consumption, contributes to her ideological work on discrimination and distinction, and reinforces her characterization and carefully developed narrative actions.

If, to interpret Austen's uses of luxury, we must reevaluate its presence and role in her writings, we must also rediscover its connections with her life experience. Austen herself seems to authorize this focus on luxury in such epistolary passages as the following, when, writing to Cassandra from Kent between June 30 and July 1, 1808, she anticipates an impending period of hard work back in Hampshire and humorously consoles herself: "But in the meantime for Elegance & Ease & Luxury [. . .] I shall eat Ice & drink French wine, & be above Vulgar Economy" (*Letters*: 139). For Austen, luxury (good or bad, excessive or controlled) is an integral part of life and the work of writing. Thus recovering her uses of luxury and its effects on the self is a further step towards a fuller understanding of the author's inexhaustible tales of historically and culturally situated signs, selves, and social groups.

NOTES

1   The window tax was originally part of a series of assessed taxes to target signs of conspicuous wealth, and was initially aimed at houses with more than nine windows, the rate and amount of taxation increasing according to the number of windows. It was repealed in 1851. On taxes in Austen's times, see Olsen (2005, vol. 2: 651–3).

2   Commenting on Sir Walter's dressing-room at Kellynch, Admiral Croft observes "Such a number of looking-glasses! oh Lord! there was no getting away from oneself" (*P*: 128). Later, in Bath Sir Walter and his eldest daughter Elizabeth take pleasure in inviting their guests "to admire mirrors and china" in the "handsome drawing-rooms" of their new apartments (*P*: 219).

FURTHER READING

Berg, M. (2005). *Luxury and Pleasure in Eighteenth-Century Britain*. Oxford: Oxford University Press.

Berry, C. J. (1994). *The Idea of Luxury: A Conceptual and Historical Investigation*. Cambridge, UK: Cambridge University Press.

Copeland, E. (1995). *Women Writing about Money: Women's Fiction in England 1790–1820*. Cambridge, UK: Cambridge University Press.

Hardy, B. (1975). The objects in *Mansfield Park*. In J. Halperin (Ed.). *Jane Austen: Bicentenary Essays* (pp. 180–96). Cambridge, UK: Cambridge University Press.

Hardy, B. (1976). Properties and possessions in Jane Austen's novels. In J. McMaster (Ed.). *Jane Austen's Achievement* (pp. 75–105). London: Macmillan.

Selwyn, D. (1999). *Jane Austen and Leisure*. London: Hambledon Press.

32
Austen's Accomplishment: Music and the Modern Heroine

Gillen D'Arcy Wood

I

In 1775, the year of Jane Austen's birth, a family of Swiss inventors placed two "human" automata on show in Covent Garden. One lifelike doll wrote verse, while the other, an adolescent girl, played the harpsichord. The Jaquet-Droz automata defined virtuosity in both its historical senses – as a luxury exhibit, and a mechanical mode of performance – while capturing also, in their visual equation of writing, music making, and mechanics, the specter of virtuosity as it would come to haunt Romantic literary culture. Austen would later belong to a generation of Romantic writers whose accredited achievement lies in their production of original rhetorical techniques, including Austen's free indirect discourse, that advertised an individuated, fully psychologized human subjectivity, in truly "lifelike" characters. Viewed against a historical background occupied by the Jaquet-Droz automata, as emblems of a new toxic proximity between writing and mechanical virtuosity, the intensity of this movement in literary culture to which Austen belonged bears all the marks of cultural reaction.

This essay argues that both Austen's fiction and the avant-garde orchestral music of early nineteenth-century London can be described as romantic reactions against virtuosity and its mechanized image of culture. Austen's work thus offers a far more complex representation of feminine pianistic "accomplishment" than might appear on first reading. Indeed, this essay makes the case for the formative role played by contemporary musical culture in Austen's life and literary style. It casts Austen and her radical contemporary, Beethoven, as fellow technicians of the romantic-humanist subject. Beethoven fashioned, out of the conventions of Viennese sonata form, a compelling language of personal self-realization, while Austen, in her creation of the virtuosic Jane Fairfax in *Emma*, participated in the imagined professionalization of female accomplishment in the post-Waterloo period, and integrated music into the larger artistic project of the novel: the narrativization of Emma's "inner life" through free indirect discourse. Each developed, in their respective media, the raw materials of modern, bourgeois, "psychological" art.

Austen and Beethoven were both creatures of the 1790s who came to public notice in Britain in the 1810s. Growing up, Austen learned the fashionable Viennese piano music that was the young Beethoven's *lingua franca*. From the age of 12, she practiced the piano most mornings and, in the evenings, would often perform for her family, until her fatal sickness forced her to discontinue (see Austen-Leigh 1952: 6). She was still taking weekly lessons and learning new repertoire at the age of 20 – "I practise everyday as much as I can" – unusual even for accomplished women of her class (*Letters*: 7). Despite the limited income of the Austens after the death of her father, a good quality piano was hired for her at Southampton and later at Chawton (Piggott 1980: 6–9). Printed music was expensive, so Austen belonged, as did innumerable amateur musicians of her time, to an informal, woman-driven network of music copyists and borrowers. As such, domestic music culture ran in parallel with a literary culture of female sociability in which "the purchasing, lending, and borrowing of books were closely connected with other social networks" (Tadmor 1996: 167–8).

The music in Austen's possession at the time of her death, some half of it copied out meticulously in her own hand, amounts to nearly 1,500 pages. Her repertoire included drawing-room songs, opera transcriptions, and dances, but also a strong sampling of 1790s solo piano music imported from Vienna – Schobert, Pleyel, Hoffmeister, Steibelt – as well as the London "school" of Clementi, J. B. Cramer, and J. C. Bach. The collection suggests she was a fine amateur pianist. The most difficult of the sonatas in the Chawton books – if they were at Austen's command – would rank her among her own female characters, if not at the near-professional excellence of Jane Fairfax, then certainly higher than Emma Woodhouse. Marianne Dashwood and Anne Elliot perhaps best represent her own standard.

The piano music of the 1790s is not an idle footnote to Austen's world and fiction. The first questions put to Mr Elton about his bride in *Emma* require him "to tell her Christian name, and say whose music she principally played" (*E*: 181). Musical repertoire functioned as an indispensable shorthand of taste and character; music was, as Leo Plantinga puts it, "woven into the very fabric of social interaction: it was part of the system of signs by which people communicated with each other" (Plantinga 2004: 3). In *Sense and Sensibility*, Edward Ferrars speaks of books and music in the same breath, as do Elizabeth and Colonel Fitzwilliam in their conversation at Rosings Park in *Pride and Prejudice*. Austen's close involvement in the booming music culture of her day is expressed likewise in *her* letters, where she talks about music as much as she does about books. And yet, for all this, her musical life remains at the margins of Austen biography and academic criticism of her fiction.

One reason for the marginalization of music in Austen criticism is the ambivalent image of music given in the novels. Marianne Dashwood's pianism is antisocial, a symptom of her melodramatic self-absorption. Sir Thomas Bertram blames his daughters' dissipation on their education in accomplishments rather than morality. Mary Crawford plays the vixen at the harp, while Elizabeth Bennet's relaxed attitude toward piano practice contrasts appealingly both with Mary's sullen anxiety for "display" and Georgiana's sequestration following the failed elopement with Wickham, for which she punishes herself with scales. Willoughby and Frank Churchill employ their musical talents for seduction and deception; and, perhaps most notoriously of all, Jane Fairfax's flawless performances at the piano suggest a proportional emptiness of personality, one whose identity has been consumed by the imperatives of female accomplishment, of which she is the cold paragon.

Austen's ambivalent representation of musical accomplishment in her fiction appears to contradict her own personal commitment to music, but chimes with a popular discourse of the 1790s, namely, the debate over female education. Jane Fairfax was an object of more than just Emma's anxiety. She embodied a widely published concern about the inflationary effects of female accomplishment on young women's education. Hannah More decried the "frenzy for accomplishments," as did Maria Edgeworth, Erasmus Darwin, Clara Reeve, John Burton, and others. Mary Wollstone-craft expressly opposed female "accomplishments," as vehicles of virtuosic self-display, to the cultivation of intellectual and moral "virtues" (Wollstonecraft 1995: 262). In Austen's unfinished *Sanditon*, the Miss Beauforts delight in those "showy acquire-ments" More deplored, which were sought after by young women hoping only "to make their fortune by marriage" (More 1799, vol. 1: 62–3). According to this critique, accomplishment was a relic of court culture, where women were defined solely by their power to captivate through exhibition: Miss Beaufort looks for "praise & celeb-rity from all who walked within the sound of her Instrument" (*MW*: 421). The emerging professional middle-class ideology represented by the 1790 reformists, of all ideological stripes, demanded, in place of virtuosic identity, a nonperformative, inward, rational, essentially literary self. For women, argued Wollstonecraft, "the grand end of their exertions should be to unfold their own faculties and acquire the dignity of conscious virtue" (Wollstonecraft 1995: 95). Austen's novels, in their enforcement of antivirtuosic standards and innovations in psychological depth, stand as exemplary agents of this reformist agenda.

Most of the 1790s critique of accomplishment focused on the proper employment of private time. Defenders of accomplishment, such as Catharine Macaulay and Thomas Gisborne, perceived music's utility in "supply[ing] hours of leisure with innocent and amusing occupation" (Gisborne 1799: 84). Recent critics, however, have regarded accomplishment only in public, performative terms. For Gary Kelly, "singing and playing music displayed the young woman's body and bearing at social occasions to attract a suitor" (Kelly 2005: 257). Mary Poovey likewise nominates piano playing as one of the "only thinly disguised opportunities for the display of personal charms," which served as "an acceptable version of men's personal competitiveness" (Poovey 1984: 29). While such language is faithful to the viewpoints of More and Edgeworth, it deflates the controversy into settled fact, and is dubious in its sweeping generality. It might just as easily be argued that collaboration, not competitiveness, was the hallmark of Georgian women's music culture – as Jane Austen's borrowing of music and encouragement of her piano-playing nieces attest. It is even more certain that private practice, not public performance, formed the greater part of a Georgian woman's musical life. As to the actual *pleasures* of music – to which Colonel Brandon gives his attention during Marianne's performance in *Sense and Sensibility* – or musicianship as an expression of self and its autonomy, as with Anne Elliot, who "in music . . . had been always used to feel alone in the world" (*P*: 47), modern criticism is entirely deaf.

Obscured in the critique of accomplishment, past and present, are the dramatic class ramifications of music's wholesale entry into the domestic realm after 1790, to the point where even a tradesman's family might be expected to own a piano. Music catalogues that, in the 1760s, might have contained a hundred items, by 1790 had thousands, and by the 1820s could offer selections from tens of thousands of available musical scores (Loesser 1955: 252). With such a vast literature came a new language of repertoire, composers, singers, and music theory – an entire new discursive dimension of middle-class life – that is abundantly documented in Austen's novels. "Musical" Mrs Weston, of modest origins, enjoys command of an aesthetic vocabulary denied to women of her class only a generation before. She is thrilled by Jane's Broadwood, and grills her about it, "having so much to ask and to say as to tone, touch, and pedal" (*E*: 220). Music was no longer the preserve of the elite, no longer even a safe distinguisher between the gentry and mercantile classes. The middle-class amateur musicians, and the aristocrats they sought to emulate, played the same repertoire of German sonatas, Italian songs, and such "Irish melodies" as Frank Churchill includes in his anonymous gift to Jane Fairfax.

The drawing-room music Austen played *was* distinguishable, however, from the working-class popular fare of the music halls. As an international language representing the emerging aristocratic-bourgeois coalition of Europe, drawing-room songs could be multilingual but were without "all the distinguishing marks of working-class music: no dialects, no vulgarity, no low humour" (Temperley 1981: 118–19). Austen's own prose followed the same prescription, as a new form of standard "polite" English that made no distinctions between region and class and, in doing so, asserted a middle-class and distinctly female sovereignty over the practice of fiction. The latter-day critique of accomplishment fails to recognize the convergence of interests in middle-class literature and music of the Regency period. It thereby perpetuates an interdisciplinary blindness, a partisan literary-cultural representation of the Georgian music culture to which Austen and her fictional heroines belonged, viewed exclusively through the ancient negative paradigm of vanity and visual display, and updated with a veneer of gender politics that diminishes both women and music. The countermanding image to the antiaccomplishment critique – of the empowerment of middle-class women by the technological and commercial advances in music culture – is exemplified by Austen herself: a Georgian woman privately absorbed by the demands of an artistic discipline and whose musical life, like her heroine Anne Elliot's, lay entirely outside the more vulgar demands of accomplishment (Wells 2004: 103). More broadly, piano playing, and in particular the regimen of practice, positioned British women such as Austen at the vanguard of a new, disciplined approach to time management and mechanical efficiency that was the domestic analogue of their male counterparts' education in the professions. The rewards for that discipline were what one critic called, in Beethoven's contemporaneous symphonies, a drama of "psychological development" (Marx in Senner et al. 1999: 67), the privilege of romantic interiority that was the subject and matter of Austen's novels.

As the foregoing sketch suggests, the piano, and female pianism, should rightly be considered alongside women's writing at the vanguard of what Nancy Armstrong (1987) has described as the feminization of nineteenth-century culture. Since the early 1700s, women had enjoyed positions of cultural influence in English music. With the massive advance of the piano into the domestic sphere at the turn of the new century, where women could act as both patrons and performers, that power increased exponentially. In other words, Austen's pianism, like her fiction, belonged to what More called "this revolution of the manners of the middle class" (More 1799, vol. 1: 62). Austen herself, for all her satire of young "prodigies," takes the disciplines of accomplishment seriously enough to cite Emma's lack of "steadiness" in learning music and drawing as an adumbration of her larger character deficiencies (E: 39). Piano-playing was only partly about women as domestic ornament, as the 1790s critics themselves recognized: "we condemn only the *abuse* of these accomplishments," stipulated Maria Edgeworth (1798, vol. 2: 531, my emphasis). The fact that Mrs Elton claims to be "passionately fond" of music but refuses to play (as does that other recent bride, Lady Middleton) is a more telling character indictment than Marianne Dashwood's self-indulgence at the piano or Jane Fairfax's irritating perfection (E: 276). In Austen, failure to meet the minimum terms of accomplishment is worse than their abuse. With the new movement in serious music in the 1810s, embodied in Beethoven, began the gradual rehabilitation of domestic music making from the battering it had received at the hands of the education reformers of the 1790s. In Jane Austen's novels, the entry of her heroines into the "world" mirrored the admission of young Regency males into the professional ranks. The new Viennese repertoire, and the discourse of self-expression that surrounded it, was likewise a central means by which, as the century of the piano progressed, British women of the middle class participated in the broader professionalization of culture, and "could step forth as an object of knowledge" (Armstrong 1987: 134; see also Kelly 1993: 1–5).

II

In place of an inner life, Jane Fairfax offers only a collection of epithets. She is the "really accomplished young woman" – an ideal Elizabeth Bennet protests never to have met with – whose superior performance at the piano inspires Emma to practice for an hour and a half (a unit of time no serious musician would use to quantify their practice). But she is also a woman of "such coldness and reserve" (E: 166) that Emma, for all her good intentions, cannot properly befriend her. Nor is the reader, on first reading, given much latitude to disagree that "her composure was odious" (E: 263).

Virtuosity is pure exteriority, while Austen's novels are grounded in the virtues of interiority. That said, the tension between Jane and Emma is as much founded on their uncanny similarities – same age, same gentility, same accomplishments – as on their differences. As Knightley observes, Emma sees in Jane Fairfax a feminine ideal she herself fails to meet. The two women are different expressions upon the same principle.

In the terms provided by the antiaccomplishment discourse of the 1790s, a direct correlation exists between Jane's virtuosity at the piano and her "unbecoming indifference," her apparent lack of feeling (*E*: 263). Maria Edgeworth worried about young women becoming "mere machines" through improper modes of practice, while James Fordyce, who actually defended music education against what he acknowledged as the "prevailing opinion," expressed a consensus concern about the "vast expense of time" by which women "lose the labour of years, that might have been directed with lasting benefits into some other channel" (Edgeworth 1798, vol. 2: 537, Fordyce 1800, vol. 1: 200). Femininity itself appeared to be at stake, in the sense of how women's bodily movements appeared at the piano. "To be graceful," Burke had declared, "it is requisite that there be no appearance of difficulty" (Burke 1782: 226). If grace inspired admiration, virtuosity threatened the opposite: the empty "wonder" of mechanism, the defeminization of women, and the cultural obsolescence of beauty itself. In Burney's *Camilla* (1796), the doll-like Indiana Lynmere is called an "automaton," shorthand both for superficial beauty and a criminal deficiency in self-reflection (see Lynch 1998: 192–9). In *Emma*, the culprit isn't vanity, but too much practice. The demands of accomplishment have turned Jane Fairfax into a Jaquet-Droz doll: "Oh! The coldness of a Jane Fairfax!" (*E*: 269).

The relation between time, mechanization, and the larger enterprise of nineteenth-century industrialization is clearly evident in the music culture of the 1810s, and bears upon the antivirtuosic ideology of *Emma*. Johann Malzel, inventor and charlatan, patented the metronome the year *Emma* appeared, and Beethoven was the first composer to indicate metronome markings in his published music. Added to this was an explosion in pedagogical literature, designed to regulate young women's time spent at the piano. Mary Bennet would no doubt have owned one or more of the primers in piano technique that flooded the market from the early 1800s, beginning with Clementi's *Introduction to the Art of Playing on the Piano Forte* (1801). Clementi, a celebrated virtuoso who renounced the concert platform in order to build a musical empire embracing all aspects of the industry, from piano manufacture to publishing to pedagogy, was intent upon building a permanently expanding market for music, starting with texts for children.

By the 1810s, the domestication of virtuosity, as the critics of the 1790s had feared, was complete. With the great proliferation of instruments and performers, and the professionalization of pedagogy, skill levels rose exponentially. The social effects of this are felt at Mrs John Dashwood's "small musical party" in *Sense and Sensibility*, where "the performers themselves were, as usual, in their own estimation, and that of their immediate friends, the first private performers in England" (*SS*: 218). The competitive tension evoked here concerns the ambiguous place of musical performance and criticism between the domestic sphere of "immediate friends" and the greater public approbation of "England," which the unnamed performers anxiously claim. With public concerts in abeyance during the Napoleonic Wars, elite music culture continued under the semiprivate auspices of society hostesses, where professionals and highly skilled amateurs increasingly crossed paths. Emma's anxiety over Jane Fairfax's "superior playing" belongs to this historical moment of music's incipient profession-alization, when amateur musicians of the old order "tended more and more to become listeners" (Shera 1939: 26).

Reading Jane Fairfax's pianistic accomplishment in this light, her training appears closer to Michel Foucault's description of the modern technologized self than to a Regency governess. The bodily discipline represented by pianistic accomplishment, and its temporally exacting ratio of practice to performance, points to a professional, disciplinary understanding of time, to "the principle of a theoretically ever-growing use of time: exhaustion rather than use; it is a question of extracting, from time, ever more available moments and, from each moment, ever more useful forces" (Foucault 1979: 154). As the proleptic image of the new female professional, Jane Fairfax is the most modern character in all Austen, until the end, when she lapses into a more archaic pose: like that other ill-starred Austen pianist before her, Marianne Dashwood, she wanders the meadows alone, and wills herself ill. The consummation of this reverse is achieved in the theatrical disclosure of her secret engagement: her inner life, rather than nonexistent, turns out to be the hidden mechanism of the plot itself, with an unwritten richness Emma can only meditate on in wonder. The virtuoso foil of *Emma* turns belated heroine in a tale of virtue besieged.

Only in our second reading of the novel, when we know in advance of Jane's engagement, do we pay attention to signs of her psychological complexity, the most unequivocal of which is a series of musical clues, heretofore unremarked, that contra-dict her reputation for soulless virtuosity. In their discussion of the recent dinner party at the Coles', Harriet and Emma touch upon the exhibitions of Emma and Jane at the piano. The narrator specifies that they were the only two performers, and Harriet's relation of the event situates the episode firmly within the historical opposition of virtue and virtuosity, here called "taste" and "execution." Says Harriet: "Mr. Cole said how much taste you had; and Mr. Frank Churchill talked a great deal about your taste, and that he valued taste much more than execution" (*E*: 232). The discursive imperative to place these terms in opposition, and to embody them in a "contest" between two representative performers, represents a foundational trope of music criti-cism across the centuries. In Austen's lifetime, the most famous piano "duel" took place between Mozart and Clementi at the palace of Emperor Joseph II in Vienna in 1781, "won," of course, by Mozart, who derided Clementi as "a mere *mechanicus*" (Mozart 1985: 793). In 1791, a German newspaper employed the identical principle in elevating Beethoven's "weight of idea" and "expression" over the "astonishing exe-cution" of his rival Vogler (Sonneck 1926: 13). According to the impromptu court of musical opinion at the Coles' party, an opinion crafted by Frank Churchill, Emma plays Mozart to Jane Fairfax's Clementi. In Fordyce's terms, Jane's "execution" is inseparable from "affectation" (Fordyce 1800, vol. 1: 202). Emma's lack of technical proficiency at the piano, like Elizabeth's in *Pride and Prejudice*, is actually a virtue, a testimony of taste and time better spent (as Darcy says), while Jane's virtuosity is necessarily at the expense of taste, because in acquiring it she has mechanized herself beyond the reach of natural feeling. Mary Wollstonecraft declared, as an almost theological truism, her preference for "expression to execution," and that "a person must have sense, taste, and sensibility, to render their music interesting. The nimble dance of the fingers may raise wonder, but not delight" (Wollstonecraft 1787: 43–4). The opposition between virtue and virtuosity served as a kind of discursive compulsion, a rhetorical twitch that disfigured aesthetic discourse throughout the eighteenth century and beyond. It was a definitive Georgian formulation beyond Wollstonecraft's, or Austen's, powers to resist: Jane's superior pianism is inseparable from a moral deficiency, from her "disgusting . . . reserve" (*E*: 169). Such is the Highbury opinion, at least, but Emma, to her great credit, will not allow it to stand. When Harriet attempts to commend her taste above Jane's execution, Emma replies, "Ah! But Jane Fairfax has them both." The correctness of this judgment is born out by Jane's redemption at the conclusion of the book: she is heart-stricken, not heartless. With the help of a musical-historical lens, however, we need not simply believe Emma, but can extrapolate her aesthetic judgment (as she does not) into more generous expectations of Jane Fairfax's character.

At the very middle point of the novel, Jane receives the mysterious gift of the Broadwood piano. In the history of the piano industry, Broadwood was the first industrial giant, selling pianos at eight times the volume of the largest Viennese company. In the brief period in which Austen published her novels, the Broadwood company almost doubled in value, to about £140,000, and was one of the largest consumers of wood in London. The "large square" piano Frank buys for Jane was the Broadwood staple. While the quality of Viennese pianos was uneven, and individual pianos themselves uneven in tone, Broadwood focused its design innovations on creating homogeneity and "depth" of tone, and broadening the piano's expressive capability: "what they desired above all was the richest possible aural presence" (Cole 1998: 309). The symbolic exchange integral to bourgeois commodity value – where a standardized, mass-produced item bears the utopian promise of individual expression – is embodied both in the Broadwood piano and in Beethoven, Broadwood's most famous client.

The Beethoven Broadwood is the stuff of legend, and is associated with his so-called "late style" music – some of the most dense, enigmatic repertoire in the European canon – which abstracted the Viennese tradition of the late eighteenth century into the syntactic units of musical convention, mixing archaic elements with an avant-garde sensibility. The *Diabelli Variations,* a consummate example of late style Beethoven, rings an extraordinary set of changes upon a banal popular waltz tune. The work offers an ironic critique of the language of drawing-room music and, by extension, of amateur accomplishment itself. It marks a historical rupture between the amateur pianism of the salon and the professional concert repertoire of the future, but in the form of a parodic homage to the pre-Napoleonic era (Kinderman 1987: 114–15).

Irony, in Austen and late Beethoven, is thus directed toward the same historical object, the parlor room culture of the 1790s. In terms of literary language, Austen likewise manufactures a middle Georgian idiom – her own "late style" – for the purpose of educating the reader in the powerful conventions of the new middle-class politeness, with its subtexts of self-interest and ignorance, suggesting that we resist our own uncritical incorporation in that discursive regime. The construction of Jane Fairfax's repelling "reserve" in *Emma* as an item of received wisdom is a subtle example of how the conventions of polite discourse – in this case antivirtuosic critique – shape perceptions with such fluid immediacy that only an authorial intervention has the power to expose the "truth."

Until her romantic recuperation, Jane Fairfax *is* late style in *Emma,* a disintegrating parlor room subject who presents, like Beethoven's late "Broadwood" piano music, only the "rigid, inexpressive face of convention" (Subotnik 1991: 29). Before we know the reason for Jane's artifice, she is artifice incarnate, an abstraction of politeness:

> The like reserve prevailed on other topics. She and Mr. Frank Churchill had been at Weymouth at the same time. It was known that they were a little acquainted, but not a syllable of real information could Emma procure as to what he truly was. "Was he handsome?" – "She believed he was reckoned a very fine young man." "Was he agreeable?" – "He was generally thought so." "Did he appear a sensible young man; a young man of information?" – "At a watering-place, or in a common London acquaintance, it was difficult to decide on such points. . . ." (E: 169)

Jane embodies forms of politeness disengaged from social meaning. She is "indiffer[ent] whether she pleased or not," a phantasmic character whose unsociable "reserve" precedes her as a form of negation, an empty subject into which Emma pours her own inchoate and objectless anxieties. Her robotic conversation, in its sheer, affectless banality, threatens to expose the rhetoricity of Emma's own talk, the discursive limits of her much-valued "openness." No wonder "Emma could not forgive her."

Jane's mystery Broadwood is accompanied by sheet music by J. B. Cramer, probably his famous *84 Etudes* (1810), whose fusion of romantic lyricism and advanced technical demands inspired Beethoven himself, and pointed toward a progressive synthesis of musical virtue and virtuosity. Cramer's *Etudes* were a staple of early nineteenth-century concert repertoire, especially among professional women performers. The new imperative of bourgeois professionalism – musically embodied in Cramer and Beethoven – required both advanced technical specialization and an ethos of subjective expression and individual depth. Playing Cramer's *Etudes* on a Broadwood piano, therefore, Jane Fairfax should not be mistaken for a musical automaton. That said, the residents of Highbury, in codifying her by these terms, are not "wrong." Jane, alone among the women of Austen's fiction, faces a life of work rather than marriage. The text limits her vocational prospects to governess, but the subtext expands them in the direction of the modern female professional, of Jane Fairfax as working concert pianist. Among other things, antivirtuosic critique expressed anxiety over the professionalization of culture, of which Jane Fairfax is the "odious" female proto-image. Jane as soulless paragon, as working Jaquet-Droz doll, is the abjected other that the romantic subject, Emma, creates both to assure herself of her own uniqueness and to certify her own leisured status. According to the internal logic of *Emma* – on its *first* reading – one may have the rich inner life of a genteel woman *or* be merely accomplished. On second reading, these choices for Austen's women appear more as a form of exchange: Jane and Emma are transformed from opposites into doppelgängers, a composite figure of the new bourgeois woman of the professional class for whom the romantic promise of a rich inner life serves as recompense for a disciplined relation to time and "accomplishment."

III

Virtuosity is a codeword for triviality, and has been the grounds for neglect of Austen's participation in Regency music culture, a culture apparently so at odds with the literary virtues she was in the process of establishing through her fiction. But Austen's rich musical life, and especially her lifelong absorption of Viennese sonata form, was entirely consistent with, not opposed to, the romantic project of interiority she advanced in her novels. Beethoven's music, to its contemporary audiences, offered a unique, temporal sensation of subjective freedom – the "development" of the theme – that attained its sublime limit, its objective shape, in the final recapitulation of that theme. The *Eroica* symphony, whose first movement represents perhaps the most famous example of this effect, debuted in London the year Austen published *Mansfield Park*. Through the hidden figure of Beethoven in the text of *Emma*, the novel can be understood to dramatize the same social contract as Beethovenian sonata form, both at the structural level of the romance plot – the heroine's development finds its objective limit in marriage – and at the rhetorical level of free indirect discourse, which marries, dialectically, the subjective and objective viewpoints of character and narrator.

As an example of the latter, the opening of *Emma* is remarkable for its introduction of a consciousness in place of plot, and for its radical subjectivization of time. The family governess has married, a reception has taken place at Hartfield and, with her father nodding off to sleep, the heroine is left in the company of her thoughts:

> The event had every promise of happiness for her friend. Mr. Weston was a man of unexceptionable character, easy fortune, suitable age and pleasant manners; and there was some satisfaction in considering with what self-denying, generous friendship she had always wished and promoted the match; but it was a black morning's work for her. (E: 6)

Thus the subtle work of free indirect discourse in *Emma* begins, with its occasional marking of mental agency ("considering"), interwoven with unmarked shifts between the stale language of conventional wisdom ("Mr. Weston was a man of unexceptionable character"), Emma's personal rationalizations ("self-denying, generous friendship"), and judgments we must attribute to the diffuse presence of the narrator, such as when Mr Woodhouse is described on the next page as "a valetudinarian all his life, without activity of mind or body." The effect is not a settled integration of subjective and objective viewpoints, but a constant, sometimes imperceptible dialectic, a sonata-style "development."

From her earliest years at the piano, Austen was exposed to the new musical language of sonata form and its social possibilities, just as she enacted, in her conscientious, lifelong practice regimen, a ritual of paraprofessional discipline that was the hallmark of her class and gender, and integral to British middle-class women's destiny of cultural leadership in the nineteenth century. These features of Austen's musical life, language, and sensibility appear in her novels in literary translation, as in her creation of Jane Fairfax and her experiments in free indirect discourse.

We would be wrong, therefore, to accept Austen's critique of musical accomplishment in her novels at face value, especially in *Emma*. As a paragon of style living on the margins of polite culture, with only her accomplishments to recommend her, Jane Fairfax is the closest figure we have for Austen herself – a proto-professional woman living by her talent. Both possess the modern professional's armor, a shell of reserve, an "indifference whether she pleased or not" (see Miller 2003: 67). Charlotte Brontë, adapting Emma's view of Jane Fairfax, complained of a lack of "warmth or enthusiasm" in Austen's prose (Southam 1968: 127). But Jane Fairfax's secret is also Austen's. Neither are mere virtuosi, bereft of an inner life. Both possess execution *and* taste. Jane Fairfax, as rehabilitated virtuoso, mirrors Austen's own phantasmic narrative presence as a figure of pure style – the accomplishment ideal – that is both empty and replete. The narrative dictates that Jane Fairfax must be each of these things in turn, but the unique satisfaction of reading Austen's prose is to experience both at once, to wonder how it is that while so little appears to be said, nothing seems left unaccomplished.

FURTHER READING

Leppert, Richard (1993). *The Sight of Sound: Music, Representation, and the History of the Body.* Berkeley: University of California Press.

McVeigh, Simon and Susan Wollonberg (Eds) (2004). *Concert Life in Eighteenth-Century England.* Aldershot, UK: Ashgate.

Parakilas, James et al. (1999). *Piano Roles: Three Hundred Years of Life with the Piano.* New Haven, CT: Yale University Press.

Piggott, Patrick (1979). *The Innocent Diversion: A Study of Music in the Life and Writings of Jane Austen.* London: Clover Hill.

Steinberg, Michael P. (2004). *Listening to Reason: Culture, Subjectivity and Nineteenth-Century Music.* Princeton, NJ: Princeton University Press.

Wallace, Robert K. (1983). *Jane Austen and Mozart.* Athens: University of Georgia Press.

33

Jane Austen and Performance: Theatre, Memory, and Enculturation

Daniel O'Quinn

With the exception of a few tantalizing fragments of the *Juvenilia*, Jane Austen, unlike Fanny Burney, did not write plays. However, in recent years, two full-length studies have demonstrated Austen's deep and abiding interest in theatrical representation and theatrical sociability (Byrne 2002, Gay 2002). Numerous critics have felt that the novels share certain representational strategies with the theatre and with varying degrees of success have metaphorically deployed the theatre as an analytical tool for understanding narrative dynamics (see Litvak 1992). But this metaphorization of the theatre comes at a cost. The shift from theatre as a lived social and material praxis which takes place in a specific time and place to notions of theatricality strips theatre of the very elements which define its operation in the cultural field. For that reason, this essay moves in a fundamentally different direction: it asks not what the theatre can tell us about Jane Austen's novels, but rather what Jane Austen's novels can tell us about the theatre. The analysis will focus on *Mansfield Park*, not only because it is so explicitly concerned with the theatre, but also because so much of the criticism which addresses Austen's theatricality lives and dies on its ability to offer insight into what is at stake in that novel's complex frustration of our readerly desires. *Mansfield Park* is a problem text in the best senses of that term and I will argue that much of the difficulty it poses is integrally related to complex transformations in the lived practice of the theatre that ultimately impinge on the question of cultural reception.

Aside from broadening our understanding of cultural production and reproduction, especially among women, recent scholarship on Romantic theatre has revolved around three key propositions. First, the social practice of going to the theatre underwent a radical change in the early nineteenth century. With the emergence of illegitimate venues, the spatial and social dynamics of playgoing were diversified (see Moody 2000). Second, as a result of the drastic expansion of venues and the diversification of audiences, theatrical practice itself went through a period of extraordinary innovation and experimentation. Whether it be in the realm of set design, acting style, playwrighting, or even management, audiences were confronted with new and often competing representational modes. And finally, despite, or perhaps because of, all this change, theatre remained the central popular medium of the era: it constituted the primary locus where representation and sociability came together on a nightly basis. As it had for much of the eighteenth century, the theatre operated in the realm of culture much like movies and television do now. It was the only cultural practice which was dealt with on a daily basis in the newspapers. And it provided social and cultural fodder for that all-important Austenian communicative act: conversation. Yet even with a sense of the centrality of theatre to Georgian society, it is difficult to write the preceding sentence without immediate qualification, because the question which remains unaddressed, and perhaps unanswerable, for various methodological reasons pertaining to the transience of theatrical and conversational performance, is precisely what theatre does to its audience and by extension to a society.

If analysis is confined to London theatres, one can argue that the entire theatrical enterprise is involved in a complex form of autoethnography. Even in productions which appear to have little or nothing to do with everyday life, the audience is summoned into a set of relationships both among themselves and in relation to the play which allow for a continual evaluation and valuation of their lived experience in the metropolis. If we grant that the social experience of theatregoing opens onto a sense of being in a space together at a particular moment in time, then this autoethnographic imperative has the potential to take on a totalizing force when metropolitan culture is exported to the provinces and the colonies. There is ample evidence of such a potential subsumption of local culture in the newspapers. Papers as far away as Bengal regularly reprint reviews of London plays. Since readers in Bengal will not be attending these productions, what is elicited in these reviews is a stance towards representation itself that attempts to replicate the sociability of the metropolitan audience. In short, model forms of sociability which cohere around acts of representation are here put into motion, much like the stagecoach in volume three of *Mansfield Park*, and the resulting permeation of provincial and colonial society plays a crucial role in the formation of national character.

Within the British Isles, this permeation is extremely powerful, but it is important to recognize that this dissemination of cultural materials generated moments not only of ideological alignment, but also of varying levels of resistance (see Kruger 2003, Moody 2007). We know from Austen's biography that she not only saw plays at both legitimate and illegitimate venues in London, but also regularly attended plays in Bath which either repeated, with a difference, successful productions from London, or had a critical relation to this flow of cultural capital (see also Byrne 2002: 29–67). We also know that play texts, reviews, and paratheatrical texts such as theatrical biographies and reminiscences flowed through the proliferating avenues of commercial print culture. Paula Byrne has demonstrated that Austen was an enthusiastic participant in private theatricals (2002: 3–28). In this context, private theatricals constitute an important locus for enquiry not only because one can track this cultural permeation among elites which themselves flowed between town and country, but also because the emergence of commercial patent theatres in provincial centers forces one to reevaluate the relationship between theatrical production and the "audience" in ways that open onto questions of cultural reproduction (see Russell 2007, Rosenfeld 1978).

The Immortality of a Twelvemonth

The most famous engagement with questions of theatrical production in Austen radically limits the question of reception as a social experience. Edmund and Fanny are terrified by how the Bertram's production of Elizabeth Inchbald's *Lovers' Vows* might be received by the neighbors, but the production is famously interrupted before the first full rehearsal. In doing so, the novel both raises the question of how the private theatrical might play in front of an audience and offers an analysis of the experience of being a performer. However, the former question is put aside in favor of a different one, which fragments and isolates reception itself: how does Fanny feel when she watches/participates in the rehearsal of Edmund and Mary's scene? Austen's analysis of Fanny's multiple erotic affiliations in the passage is extraordinary, but the field of meaning is narrow. Fanny's experience as a participant observer is not shared with anyone other than the players (see Nachumi 2001). However rich her emotional and aesthetic relation to the performance might be, it remains distinct from the complex experience of watching the same scene in the presence of another. And the distinction is precisely that which separates an individual reader's exploration of interiority through the novel and an audience's social exploration of sociability itself on any given evening at the theatre. One can easily imagine Austen representing the social scene of performance reception in novelistic discourse – the complex interaction between Anne and Wentworth during the musical performance at Bath's New Assembly Rooms in *Persuasion* is a perfect example – but she chooses to focus on rehearsal. By frustrating the public performance and focalizing our understanding of the rehearsed scenes through Fanny, the reader's attention is drawn away momentarily from the problem of social relations in order to focus on the relationship between performance, performativity, and memory.

Mansfield Park, in its attempt to theorize theatre's social operation on and among its audience, narrows the field of enquiry by focusing on Fanny's, and the closely aligned narrator's, reception of fragments of *Lovers' Vows*, which are referred to but never cited in the narrative. It is first and foremost an analytical decision in the strict sense of the term, in that it looks at one element of a larger social problematic. The problem is broken down into manageable parts which will be synthesized at a later point. The reason this is necessary is that the very question of reception is so complex. Austen is remarkably explicit about how this potential performance comes to Mansfield Park. Mr Yates's arrival at the outset of chapter 13 instantiates a compensatory desire for theatre:

> He came on the wings of disappointment, and with his head full of acting, for it had been a theatrical party; and the play, in which he had borne a part, was within two days of representation, when the sudden death of one of the nearest connections of the family had destroyed the scheme and dispersed the performers. To be so near happiness, so near fame, so near the long paragraph in praise of the private theatricals at Ecclesford . . . which would have immortalized the party for at least a twelvemonth! And being so near, to lose it all, was an injury to be keenly felt, and Mr. Yates could talk of nothing else. Ecclesford and its theatre, with its arrangements and dresses, rehearsals and jokes, was his never-failing subject, and to boast of the past his only consolation. (*MP*: 121)

Mr Yates's theatrical aspirations amount to a desire for momentary fame, specifically in the society columns of the newspaper and in the conversations of "the TON": he seeks the immortality of a twelvemonth which is ostensibly guaranteed by theatre's place within the social. On the one hand this marks his shallowness, but on the other it also indicates precisely why theatre as a social experience was so important. The members of the Bertram household are receptive to his endless stories about failed performance, because they allow for a rehearsal of the social relations which surround theatrical performance. Yates's reminiscences activate a desire among the Bertrams to relate to representation and each other in what amounts to a ritualized performance of sameness, which rehearses the past but nonetheless opens onto an experience of the future – that is, the relationship between Maria and Henry, which tellingly repeats itself in more consequential form late in the novel. By taking up Mr Yates's desire, the members of the household at Mansfield Park imitate the past social practice of the inhabitants of Ecclesford who themselves had imitated key social rituals first experienced many years earlier in London around the first performance of *Lovers' Vows*. Even Edmund's resistance to the play amounts to a replication of past resistances to Kotzebue's original work. This repetition of past social practices amounts to a form of social and cultural dissemination, which relies not only on the repeatability or citationality of the play itself, but also on the citationality of social performance. What the novel recognizes is that this citationality conditions both the past and the future, and thus the *Lovers' Vows* section of the novel becomes not only a site for meditations on memory, but also the proleptic trigger which structures the future of many of the novel's characters.

It is here that the search for an appropriate play is so resonant (see Byrne 2002: 187–200). As the interested parties cast their eyes across the archive of past performances to repeat at Mansfield Park, Austen emphasizes the inextricable relationship between the iterative qualities of social performance and the act of reading. As Tom Bertram or Mr Yates read plays in search of an appropriate fit, one is forced to ask what kind of fit they have in mind. At one level, Tom's decisions are those of any theatrical manager: what script suits the particular strength and size of my company? What performance can I stage in the theatrical space at hand, and, most importantly, what will my audience want to see? The last question proves to be quite strange because it remains completely unclear who is the intended audience of the play. Mrs

Bertram and Mrs Norris certainly; neighbors perhaps, but most importantly, near relations including Henry and Mary Crawford, should they choose not to perform in the play. When Tom decides upon *Lovers' Vows*, the very play whose failure at Ecclesford instantiated the desire for plays at Mansfield Park, it becomes clear that repetition is the name of the game and that the audience for this play is composed precisely of those people who are destined to be in it. Thus Austen takes the autoethnographic imperative of Romantic theatre to its logical and ideal conclusion. The manager here chooses a play perfectly suited to his players and his audience because they are one and the same.

Many commentators have noted how the characters in *Mansfield Park* both repeat and modify the roles they take up in the failed production of *Lovers' Vows*.[1] In this light it is important to remember that theatrical success is measured by repetition. It is through repetition that the theatrical experience not only generates capital, but also permeates the social. Could we not argue that one of the key problems for Austen in *Mansfield Park* is that social success – that is, the reproduction of social status, familial wealth, and local power – however transitory, is measured in a similar fashion? This would suggest that Austen's concern with the theatre and the social has less to do with the internal dynamics of any particular performance, than with the way these performances repeat and thus consolidate suspect forms of autoethnography. It is important to recognize that these repeated acts of self-consolidation are aligned quite explicitly with all the characters who enthusiastically take up Mr Yates's self-aggrandizing desires. Austen's exploration of this social phenomenon operates on the level of critique, but it is a critique aimed at carving out a different relation to the culture, which always already lays out the terms in which performances will be understood and valued. In other words, could we not argue, as William Galperin does, that Austen is attempting to explore how one has to act on the past in order to generate a different future, but here locate the argument in the repetitive dynamics of performance itself (Galperin 2003: 154–79)?

This would help to explain why so much of the representation of the Bertram's private theatricals revolves around problems of memory, precisely the faculty that, as Mieke Bal states, "concerns the past and happens in the present. Thus it can stand for the complex relationship between cultural analysis and history. The elements of present and past in memory are what specifically distinguish performance and performativity" (Bal 2002: 183). Before exploring the theoretical implications of this assertion, let's think about how pervasive the question of memory is to the production of *Lovers' Vows*. Mr Rushworth, the ridiculous manifestation of mindless Tory tradition, is overwhelmed by the task of remembering his "two and forty speeches" (*MP*: 139). No matter how hard he rehearses he cannot get his lines and this is not simply because he cannot retain them, but rather because he cannot let go of who he is. In order to remember his part he has to forget who he is, and thus momentarily replace one version of the past – his life – with another – his experience of reading and rereading a script – in order to perform in the present. Now Rushworth may not know who he is to begin with, but his inability to remember is intimately tied to Maria's remarkable ability to forget her engagement and her predilection to forget again and again every time she rehearses with Henry Crawford. Paradoxically, the excessive repetition of forgetting, which characterizes the almost constant rehearsal of Maria and Henry, not only drives their relationship, but also ensures that Mr Rushworth will never get his lines. He has too much to lose in this memory game.

Every performance in the novel generates identities that have iterative elements. For example, playing Anhalt inscribes Edmund in a history that he may not realize is his own, *and* his performance in the role instantiates a futurity in which he is already located. Both Austen and Mary Crawford recognize that casting Edmund in the role of Anhalt is not a distortion of his character, but a revelation that Edmund and Fanny cannot bear. The theatre puts Edmund's relation to his past into question and thus his inconstant response to it is perfectly apposite, because his relation to tradition is itself vexed. He both resists and succumbs to performance, because his job, both within the story as the second-born son destined for the clergy, and within the narrative as the mediator between generations, is essentially that of the historian who legitimates the hollow narratives which consolidate the power of landed figures as different as Rushworth and his father. His job is to forget through endless repetition all of the possibilities set in motion not only by Mary and Henry Crawford, but also by the aborted play. And yet it is precisely these possibilities – desire, adultery, fashionable sociability – that are memorialized by the novel. Austen's most trenchant critique turns on the fact that it is Edmund, not Tom, who oversees the permeation of the dynamics of the play throughout the rest of the plot. He is the one who, because of his interlaced heterosexual and homosocial desires, keeps the Crawfords in play and thus stage-manages, in spite of himself, the denouement he will be called upon to officially forget. Mr Rushworth can't perform his lines because he has to constantly be reminded of who he is; Edmund can't but perform his lines because his narrative function requires that he constantly forget himself and where he came from. This is why they both need Fanny.

They both come to Fanny to rehearse because of her strange relationship to the story of landed power. Her biological family, having been ejected from the realm of elite sociability because her mother did not replicate its social and sexual script, exists adjacent to the world of Mansfield Park as its constitutive outside. Their explicit ties to the navy specify precisely what maintains the material conditions necessary for the social replication described above. If we understand theatre as a particularly visible locus for this kind of social reproduction, then it makes sense that Fanny remains outside the play as an audience member and yet is continually called upon to assist with the act of memory required for the performance to unfold in the present. She is called upon to secure both ends of the process of social replication: she is folded, against her wishes, into both the origin and end point of the play. In spite of the fact that she consents to read the part in rehearsal, she refuses the call to act, and this gives us a very clear sense of Fanny's future in the novel. She is ultimately unable to help Rushworth or Edmund or Mary forget sufficiently to remember their lines, *and* she remembers the unperformed play too well to forget for a second how all the characters unconsciously repeat their roles throughout the story.

As an analyst of how theatre permeates society, Fanny understands that the issue is ultimately tied to the complex problem of memory and its precarious relation to subjectivity. As she states to Mary Crawford during their first meeting after Sir Thomas shuts down the play and burns every copy of Inchbald's script,

> There seems something more speakingly incomprehensible in the powers, the failures, the inequalities of memory, than in any of our intelligences. The memory is sometimes so retentive, so serviceable, so obedient: at others, so bewildered and so weak; and at others again, so tyrannic, so beyond controul! We are, to be sure, a miracle every way – but our powers of recollecting and of forgetting, do seem peculiarly past finding out. (*MP*: 209)

Austen's representation of Mary Crawford's response is telling: "Miss Crawford, untouched and inattentive, had nothing to say; and Fanny, perceiving it, brought back her own mind to what she thought must interest" (*MP*: 209). Fanny goes on to praise Mrs Grant's gardening, until finally Mary Crawford states what the reader and Fanny already know: "To say the truth . . . I am something like the Doge at the court of Lewis XIV; and may declare that I see no wonder in this shrubbery equal to seeing myself in it" (*MP*: 209–10). Fanny's attention to how memory operates in the social praxis of putting on *Lovers' Vows* uncovers a theoretical problematic at the heart of social and cultural reproduction that is inextricably tied to memory. Mary Crawford does not accept the premise, or rather, it does not interest her, because it is precisely what most threatens her narcissism. When she states that her pleasure at Mansfield Park lies, like the Venetian magistrate at Versailles in Voltaire's *Louis XIV*, in "seeing herself there," she indicates that what most interests her about social performance is that it can operate like a mirror and endlessly present herself back to herself. In the face of the precariousness and volatility of memory, Mary attempts to close the auto-ethnographic loop which defines theatrical practice such that the audience and the players are all conjoined in a phantasmatic sameness. And hence she is not interested in the implicit heterogeneity of reception, or those around her, except as they can be reconstituted as mirrors for her self.

The Constancy of Siddons

The second part of Austen's analysis of theatre's permeation of social relations comes later in the third volume of the novel, and in this case she focuses on the question of reception in a much more expanded temporal field. I am referring to Henry Crawford's reading of sections of *King Henry VIII* and Austen's careful rendering of the effect of his performance on Fanny and Edmund. Significantly, the choice of plays is Fanny's, but her reading of Cardinal Wolsey's speech in Act III, scene ii is interrupted by the sudden appearance of Edmund and Henry. The speech comes after the discovery of Wolsey's deception and gives expression not only to his fall from power, but also to his pride. Like the congruence of roles between novelistic characters and dramatis personae in *Lovers' Vows*, there is a certain aptness to Henry's mastery of this speech: he is, in effect, performing in a mirror. But the situation is far more complex. Fanny, one could argue, is conducting an analysis of Henry's duplicity before he arrives in the room. The Shakespearean text is a site for thought. More importantly, Henry proves himself a master of all the roles in the play:

> The King, the Queen, Buckingham, Wolsey, Cromwell, all were given in turn; for with the happiest knack, the happiest power of jumping and guessing, he could always light, at will, on the best scene, or the best speeches of each; and whether it were dignity or pride, or tenderness or remorse, or whatever it were to be expressed, he could do it all with equal beauty. – It was truly dramatic – His acting had first taught Fanny what pleasure a play might give, and his reading brought all his acting before her again; nay, perhaps with greater enjoyment, for it came unexpectedly, and with no such drawback as she had been used to suffer in seeing him on the stage with Miss Bertram. (*MP*: 337)

Henry's virtuosity has historical effects: it reminds her of his earlier rehearsals of *Lovers' Vows*, only it is repetition with a difference, because it does not replicate the social relations which so overdetermined her reception of Inchbald's play. In the context of what has previously been stated about memory as mediation, how do we understand the "unexpected" quality of Fanny's pleasure? It would appear that somehow in this scene of reading the transmission of culture ruptures the temporal continuum and speaks in a way distinct from its initial historical context.

I think the answer lies in the choice of theatrical text. Samuel Johnson, arguably Austen's favorite author, argued that "pomp is not the only merit of this play. The meek sorrows and virtuous distresses of Catherine have furnished some scenes which may be justly remembered among the greatest efforts of tragedy. But the genius of Shakespeare comes in and goes out with Catherine" (Johnson 1959: 152). It was with the backing of this opinion that Sarah Siddons took up the role of Katherine in 1788 and fundamentally altered the production history of the play. Prior to Siddons's performance in the role, the productions paid little attention to the suffering Queen and focused instead on spectacle and the homosocial rivalry among the male characters. Siddons's powerful performance of the Queen's marital resignation reoriented the play such that it became, henceforward, an exploration of the perils of normative femininity.

Summarizing much of the contemporary response to Siddons's performance in the role, Hugh Richmond demonstrates that her understated performance of noble suffering amounted to a kind of protonaturalism. As he states:

Siddons was not noted for a sophisticated histrionic technique, but for a compelling authenticity of personality which can only be called "sincere" in the same subjective spirit as the modern Method. There was no way that other performers could avoid attuning their acting to the intensity of her interpretations. (Richmond 1994: 51)

In other words, Siddons's performance of sincerity demanded similar styles of performance from the other players, thus her intervention in the role reoriented the entire representational paradigm. Significantly, contemporaries recognized that the effect of sincerity blurred the line between player and role; here is Thomas Campbell: "there is a strong resemblance between the historical heroine and her illustrious representative. They were both benevolent, great, simple, and straightforward in their integrity; strong and pure, but not prompt in intellect; both religiously humble, yet punctiliously proud" (cited in Richmond 1994: 148).

Siddons's proto-naturalism is both an example of the power of a player to significantly intervene in the cultural and social field, and a historical mystification of the notion of "sincerity" itself, which has been central to much of the criticism of *Mansfield Park* (see especially Trilling 1965: 206–30). After all, the equation of player and role implies that the social is traversed by representational effects whose impact is not only tangible, but also mobile.

The transportability of something as seemingly rooted as "sincerity" is crucial for Austen, because it goes right to the heart of the process of enculturation and social reproduction that animates much of *Mansfield Park*. In the scene of reading, Austen carefully records Fanny and Edmund's affective relation to Henry's remarkable ability to become the roles he is representing. When asked to account for his facility in the roles, Henry attributes his acting skill to the fact that he

once saw Henry the 8th acted. – Or I have heard of it from someone who did – I am not certain which. But Shakespeare one gets acquainted with without knowing how. It is part of an Englishman's constitution. His thoughts and beauties are so spread abroad that one touches them every where, one is intimate with him by instinct. – No man of any brain can open at a good part of one of his plays, without falling into the flow of his meaning immediately. (*MP*: 338)

The uncertainty as to whether he saw the play or not is significant, because it suggests that the cultural transmission of Siddons's reorientation of the play is not simply a matter of private experience but rather of cultural memory. But Henry is mistaken about how one comes to know Shakespeare. Despite his initial recognition of the way performance history impinges on identity, Henry tries to argue that there is something in the Shakespearean text which effectively reads itself. The shift in production history instantiated by Siddons's reinterpretation of Katherine is ample evidence contrary to this position. It was through Siddons's agency that new meaning was generated, and Henry's suggestion that this is somehow attributable to a spectral Shakespeare amounts not only to an erasure of Siddons's cultural labor, but also to a mystification of theatrical reception. And that combination of erasure and mystification, here tellingly figured as an act of forgetting, has the notable effect of canceling Siddons's cultural agency. This perfectly captures Henry's misogyny, but more importantly demonstrates how a cultural event elicits – and has elicited – ongoing acts of resistance.

The Theatrical Reader

Henry appears to have forgotten about Siddons, but his performance, like that of her coperformers, is attuned to the intensity of her past performance. Fanny did not see Siddons, but the model of femininity propagated by her performances is so much a part of cultural memory that Fanny aspires to its combination of constancy, sincerity, and subjection. In other words, Austen plays out the effect of Siddons's performative intervention by showing the enactment of its cultural and social reproduction. Her key recognition is that her readers share this cultural memory and thus have the potential to be hailed, in the act of reading, into a critique of the entire process. Austen's silent invocation of Siddons's enactment of sincere femininity, like other silences in the novel, has the curious effect of demanding that the reader actively reconstitute that which is forgotten and in so doing replicate the very intervention encoded in Siddons's earlier performance.[2] And with that reenactment, the reader can observe the dynamics of enculturation and social reproduction.

It is around this act of readerly observation that I believe Austen synthesizes her analysis of theatre's permeation of social relations. With the expectation that readers will bring their cultural memory to bear on the scene of reading, Austen calls for a historical reader. The fact that she calls for a memory of the cultural medium that is, by its very nature, transient is important because she wants to highlight not only how representation inheres in and propagates through social relations, but also how understanding this process requires a relation to memory that is fundamentally more self-reflective and complex than that presented by Fanny. Fanny's relation to history—whether it be the history of the slave trade or of the theatre – is largely mediated through books and she generally fails to elicit knowledge from conventional ethnographic informants – those who have seen slavery or the theatre such as Sir Thomas, Tom, or Henry – or Edmund for that matter. As we have already seen, these men have too much of a stake in forgetting to be of much use.

So Austen, by her very reticence, activates the cultural memory of her readers throughout her treatment of *Lovers' Vows* and *King Henry VIII*. The choice of materials is crucial, for she puts into play two productions connected to two of the most notable women of the theatre in the years immediately prior to the composition of the novel. At the very least, *Mansfield Park* requires that the reader remember who Inchbald and Siddons were and recollect their relationship to the reproduction of social and cultural value. This is particularly important when we consider that both Inchbald's adaptation of Kotzebue and Siddons's performance as Katherine are explicitly connected to the hypostatization of "sincerity" as a fundamental trait of British national character. William Galperin has shown this to be the case in his analysis of Inchbald's treatment of Englishness in *Lovers' Vows* (Galperin 2003: 170–3). And even Siddons's contemporaries – James Boaden and Thomas Campbell foremost amongst them – recognized that her performance not only constituted a subtle reading of *King Henry VIII*, but also ensured that it would be mobilized as a prescriptive formula for nineteenth-century notions of femininity (see Richmond 1994: 36–54). Galperin and Siddons do what I believe is required to understand Austen's intervention: they read the act of reading as a process that acts on both the past and the future simultaneously. In other words, they remember in the terms suggested by Bal above.

But this relationship to memory is different than that presented in the novel. As Bal's insight pertains to the theatre, it involves the evaluation and reconstitution of moments in theatrical culture as part of a self-reflective analysis of social reproduction. This historical objective ruptures the autoethnographic imperative of Romantic theatre, or at least opens the loop so that autoethnography can become a productive rather than a reproductive practice. That this requires a shift out of the realm of the theatre into the representational practice of the novel may be an indication of the power of performance to replicate what Arjun Appadurai refers to as the ethnoscape, but it may also suggest why Austen left playwrighting for the juvenilia (Appadurai 1996: 33–4). I think there is ample evidence in *Mansfield Park* that she recognized the potential for theatrical culture to manufacture tradition and regulate social relations, but one can also argue that theatre in that novel is a perilous place for women, not only in the way that Lord Kenyon might suggest, but also in the way that Henry Crawford's erasure of Siddons's art and Sir Thomas's destruction of every copy of Inchbald's play demonstrates. Despite its integral place in the historical and cultural fabric of the nation, women's agency – whether they are players, writers, or readers – is easily forgotten by the homosocial dynamics of national culture. Perhaps the transience of agency necessitates the materiality of print no less than the desire for Austen's novels to reconstitute the effect of feminine autonomy. At the very least, this would help to explain why *Mansfield Park* is less satisfying, but, in my opinion, more valuable than say *Pride and Prejudice*. The later novel underscores the power of forgetting and fully demands that the reader remember that which they may not have known – that is, the ideological forces that reproduce the means of social and cultural production.

NOTES

1 Byrne's reading of *Lovers' Vows* (2002: 149–76) is the most detailed analysis of both the play and the casting.

2 See Pascoe (1997: 12–32), for a bracing discussion of Siddons's place in the cultural memory of Romanticism.

FURTHER READING

Byrne, Paula (2002). *Jane Austen and the Theatre.* London: Hambledon and London.

Galperin, William H. (2003). *The Historical Austen.* Philadelphia: University of Pennsylvania Press.

Gay, Penelope (2002). *Jane Austen and the Theatre.* Cambridge, UK: Cambridge University Press.

Kruger, Loren (2003). History plays (in) Britain: dramas, nations, and inventing the present. In W. B. Worthen and Peter Holland (Eds). *Theorizing Practice: Redefining Theatre History* (pp. 151–76). New York: Palgrave.

Moody, Jane (2000). *Illegitimate theatre in London, 1770–1840.* Cambridge, UK: Cambridge University Press.

Pascoe, Judith (1997). *Romantic Theatricality: Gender, Poetry, and Spectatorship.* Ithaca, NY: Cornell University Press.

Part V
Reception and Reinvention

34

Jane Austen and Genius

Deidre Lynch

Men like Coleridge . . . had gone through the furnaces of culture where even less creative people might have been inflamed to creation. Jane Austen was not inflamed or inspired or even moved to be a genius; she simply was a genius. (Chesterton 1922: xiii)

Introducing into her novels a series of enraptured readers – *Sense and Sensibility*'s Marianne Dashwood and John Willoughby, for instance, who "idolize" the same passages in the same books by William Cowper and Sir Walter Scott (*SS*: 47); *Persuasion*'s Captain Benwick, whose favorite topics of conversation are "poetry [and] the richness of the present age" (*P*: 100) – Austen reveals herself to be a shrewd observer of a watershed moment in the history of literary reception. "More writers became objects of a fantastic admiration in the first half of the nineteenth century than in all previous centuries combined," Jonah Siegel observes, reprising what Benwick says and what Austen's contemporary John Keats had declared in the 1818 sonnet "Great spirits now on Earth are sojourning." But this shift occurred, Siegel adds, not "because of any dramatic increase in the quality of English writing but because of a notable increase in the need to admire" (Siegel 2000: 96). Austen's references to this new culture of literary appreciation vividly bring to view the social frameworks enabling aspirants to taste to claim admiration themselves for their individual ways of admiring. Hence in *Sense and Sensibility* Marianne's belief in her superiority to Edward Ferrars: he can safely be condescended to, although a man of wealth, because he is, she finds, incapable of being "animated by" Cowper (*SS*: 18).

Marianne's own animation by the dead poet she loves testifies to another noteworthy feature of this culture of literary appreciation: as Siegel puts it, "it was in authorship that English culture found its particular call to admiration" (2000: 96). When Austen was not quite four years old, Samuel Johnson began publishing his *Lives of the Poets* (1779–81). Shortly after her death came the prefaces eventually known as *Lives of the Novelists* (1821–24), Walter Scott's counterpart to Johnson's group biography. Johnson's and Scott's enterprises indicate the priority the Romantic era's protocols for literary appreciation assigned to the enterprise of understanding the personalities of authors and, through that study, understanding the nature of genius, that term that was at this moment beginning to designate a kind of heaven-sent creative power and the special individual distinguished by it. This developing usage – and the difficulties it posed as well as the opportunities it created for Austen's own devotees in the nine-teenth and early twentieth centuries – are the subjects of this essay.

Increasingly during Austen's lifetime literary experience began to be centered on the endeavor to discover between the lines the traces of a living spirit that could only partially be revealed in the dead letter. Whereas Johnson had abridged character analysis in the *Lives* and insisted that "my business is with his poems," a nineteenth-century successor like Isaac D'Israeli – author of the oft reissued *The Literary Character, Illustrated by The History of Men of Genius* (1795, 3rd edn 1822) – pointedly revised those priorities. D'Israeli's "business" lay, that booster of genius worship stated, with authors' "poetical feelings" (quoted in Cafarelli 1990: 94). Biographical reading is what "the ideology of genius seems to demand" (Elfenbein 1999: 125): Edward Dowden, late-Victorian founder of academic English studies, believed the writings of "every great writer" to be "fragments of a great confession" (quoted in Lootens 1996: 23). Such new ways of doing things with texts made reading, more emphatically than before, a scene of human connection, the site of a common emotional culture linking impassioned author and sympathetic reader.

Austen's acquaintance with these codes of literary consumption is evident in the deftness she displays when parodying them. Take, for instance, the November 1813 letter in which Austen, gleeful over the publication of *Pride and Prejudice*, begins spinning a story that sees her riding her success all the way to a marriage with Frances Burney's son, the teenaged Alexandre D'Arblay, and so parlaying authorial triumph into an ostensibly greater prize – achievement of the fan's dream of a close, quasi-familial connection with a favorite writer. Consider, too, another letter, written a month earlier, where Austen imagines herself, similarly, as the second wife of the poet George Crabbe (*Letters*: 243). These letters are joking, of course. For one thing, the role of the author who solicits the tribute not just of a reading but also of his readers' erotic love was in 1813 monopolized by glamorous Lord Byron, as Austen well knew; Reverend Crabbe by comparison was improbable idol material (see Cronin 2005: 292). (Austen's often quizzical relationship to the Byromania of the nineteenth century is a topic to which I shall return.[1]) Still, when she facetiously imagined herself Crabbe's soul mate, Austen predicted a significant element of her own posthumous reception history. When, after some delay, Austen joined the roll call of great authors, she did so as, notoriously, the object of readers' most zealous affections. Hence, Henry James's admission that more than one "amoroso" has lost his heart to her (1905: 62).

Even as jokes, then, these Austen letters underline something crucial about the protocols of literary reception her Romantic contemporaries bequeathed to succeeding generations: how, in making the author rather than the work the spur to admiration, they mandated that connoisseurship should be mingled with something more personal – something like conjugal love, for instance. Yet geniuses – then an increasingly discussed population – at once invite *and* forestall such intimate identifications. Their surplus of personality as much as their excellence makes them larger than life, their hyperindividualism positions them (according to D'Israeli's account of "the literary character") in "eternal conflict with the most monotonous and imitative habits of society" (1822, vol. 1: 133), and the sources of their sublime powers are veiled in mystery. And, for these reasons, the discussion that unfolded in the nineteenth century increasingly identified geniuses as a species constitutionally *apart* from their readership – inhuman, even, and so figures of threat as well as transcendence. The imaginative territory assigned the genius became, ambiguously, a space both of abnormal pathology (as for the Byronic artist figure who is mad, bad, and dangerous to know) and of that kind of other-worldliness that Keats captured with his reference to "great spirits" and which Scott registers in *Lives of the Novelists* when he lauds select writers as "holy men" who in life are martyrs and whom, after death, we "canonize" (quoted in Siegel 2000: 101).

Scott's borrowings here from the idiom of religious faith predict how subsequent devotees of the English cult of literature would do their utmost to venerate genius as "an authorized, mediated means of focusing on the divine," and yet, as Tricia Lootens notes, nineteenth-century canonizing texts consistently found it tricky to balance between the "generic sanctity of religious divinity" and "the distinctive glory" of the mavericks whom they liked to enshrine (1996: 28). Where women writers were concerned, such trickiness was exacerbated. As my essay's citations from the script of Austen-love will suggest, there was considerable friction between the lofty ambition and nonconformity celebrated by many nineteenth-century genius worshippers, the Byromaniacs especially, and the discretion and modesty expected of proper ladies. And Austen was (and is) often deemed to have worked on too small a scale to be a true genius (again, modesty plays a role here, as in the ambiguously laudatory references made by devotees from Scott to Virginia Woolf as to how the novelist "knew her limits," e.g., Woolf 1937: 171–2).

But while considering how the idiom of Austen-love has been pressured by the ideology of genius, this essay will engage an additional possibility. Austen's jokiness about readerly adulation is perhaps one sign that she did not just deviate but also actively *dissented* from her era's codes of literary greatness. It is as if she already knew how inadequate that framework would be as a measure of her creative achievement. In 1870 the critic Richard Simpson underscored that anomalousness as he ascribed to Austen an "ethical dread of the poetic rapture" – contributing to a strain of commentary that invoked Austen, as we shall see, in part to bring genius worship down to earth. Tellingly, however, the remark occurs in an essay in which Simpson also calls Austen a "prose Shakespeare" (quoted in Southam 1968: 244, 243). The writer who benefits so regularly from *that* name-dropping – and "prose Shakespeare" was a commonplace of nineteenth-century Austenian commentary – is assured a place among the celestials. And indeed, as this essay's conclusion will suggest, admirers have never had trouble discussing Austen as a divinity: "she always writes like a real god," D. A. Miller asserts (2003: 32).

The semantic transformation the term "genius" underwent during Austen's lifetime is worth sketching at this point, since it precipitated many of these complexities within the English cult of literature – the tension between Miller's veneration for Austen's godlike impersonality and Katherine Mansfield-style aspirations to personal intimacy included. Originating in Latin as a term for the tutelary spirit/angel that classical mythology allotted to every human individual, "genius" began the eighteenth century as, for the most part, a synonym for aptitude or ability. But a developing usage made genius stand for a small group of sublimely gifted *people*, as treatises instructing the public in good taste began insisting on the gulf that separated genius from talent ("true genius," one commentator insisted, is rare precisely because it encompasses so much more than "a little judgement, a tolerable memory, considerable industry," Gerard 1774: 8). Increasingly, "genius" labeled "those who are esteemed greatest in any department of art, speculation, or practice" (*OED*, 2nd edn).

The nineteenth century linked it to a distinctive personality profile. "A man of genius is . . . dropt among the people" D'Israeli asserted in 1822 (vol. 1: 52): the line envisions the artist as a changeling child, untouched by acculturation, the better to emphasize that geniuses are born, not made. "Learning is borrowed knowlege [*sic*]; genius is knowlege innate and quite our own," Edward Young had written in 1759 in the essay launching the Romantic practice of genius worship (p. 36). This emergent usage cast genius as a vehicle for individualism, as well as for heterodoxy. The concept thus at its origins appealed powerfully, as Andrew Elfenbein argues, to figures who felt oppressed by traditional hierarchies, since this emergent emphasis in aesthetics on nature and originality and this downplaying of education (Young's "borrowed knowledge") were auspicious for groups "traditionally . . . kept out of literary production" (Elfenbein 1999: 35). New, unlettered aspirants to the genius role – peasant poets like Robert Burns, for instance, or women writers – recognized how qualities such as "enthusiasm," "warmth of imagination," "rapture," and "sensibility of heart" had become part of the arsenal of greatness and how, in this scheme, demonstration of a range of emotional experience surpassing that of ordinary people could entitle one to authorship.

To some extent the Romantic era's cult of Shakespeare confirmed that realization. That the Bard – of obscure origins, relatively uneducated – epitomized the *natural* genius was a truism of popular aesthetics. Regardless of his circumstances, it was declared, Shakespeare would still have warbled "his native wood notes wild" (as Milton put it in an oft-quoted line). (Henry James revived that tag-phrase of Bardolatry in an odd ornithological account of Austen's light touch – which, he wrote, leaves the reader "hardly more curious of her process, or of the experience in her that fed it, than the brown thrush, who tells his story from the garden bough," 1905: 60; the terms G. K. Chesterton uses in my epigraph likewise place Austen in this tradition.) And Bardolaters liked to conclude from Shakespeare's disregard for the rules of the drama, as from anecdotes about his youthful deer poaching, that it was genius's nature to run wild. Genius "delights to range at liberty"; its "lawless excursions," comparable, William Duff explains, to "the course of a comet . . . blazing, though irregular," were expected to burst bounds (1767: 283, 167–8). Genius was superior to mere conventions, whether those involved poetical correctness or moral propriety.

A predictable conclusion follows on the heels of that last premise: "Genius in society is . . . in a state of suffering," D'Israeli declares in *The Literary Character*. The book's 1822 edition invokes the voice of experience to support this argument about artists' maladjustment, as D'Israeli transcribes a marginal note that Byron himself – exiled from England by rumors of domestic cruelty and sexual perversion – had made in his copy of the edition D'Israeli published four years before (vol. 1: 133–4). The torment added, of course, to the mystique of genius, and might sponsor reverence of the sort a worshiper might accord to a martyr, but these were not its only effects. To make genius a distinctive personality type was to open up the possibility of understanding it as a category to be *diagnosed*, this according to arrangements that coupled mental superiority with bodily debility or offset the authority that intellectual superiority conferred with allegations of psychological instability (Felluga 2005: 13, Cafarelli 1990: 139–43). From Boswell's *Life of Johnson* on, in fact, the hagiographic element in stories of the author's exceptionality was shadowed closely by the medical idiom of the case history (see Deutsch 2005: 82–103). A century after Boswell, in 1891, the criminologist Cesare Lombroso cast Byron as an example of the hereditary degeneration of the genius, attending more to the poet's club foot than his poems (Wilson 1999: 2). Such preoccupation with pathology could pose problems for the logic of incarnation that underpinned genius worship, challenging the tacit contract the faithful made to demote mortal bodies in favor of the immortal art that bodies house.

Misery in the evocative but vague style of Lord Byron's Giaour was one thing. A detailed, symptom-enumerating account of "the irritability of genius" or of the "perpetual fever among authors and artists" (chapter titles in *The Literary Character*) was quite another. The latter mode seemed to remodel the pantheon as a hospital – registering the linkages that in contemporary psychological theory connected imaginative powers, refined sensibilities, and fragile nerves. The most explicit engagement with the new meanings of genius that Austen undertakes in her fiction takes shape in response to just those linkages and occurs, tellingly enough, in *Sanditon* – the novel, left unfinished at Austen's death, set in a seaside resort whose economy depends on illness and on overheated imaginations' capacity to engender illness in otherwise sound bodies. Entrapping the heroine, Charlotte Heywood, in bookish conversation, Sir Edward Denham, *Sanditon*'s vaguely Byronic rake, defends in general the "Aberrations" of "Genius" and in particular the dissolute personal life of the poet Burns, a "Man," Sir Edward declares, "who *felt*": "It were Hyper-criticism, it were Pseudophilosophy to expect from the soul of high toned Genius, the grovellings of a common mind – The Coruscations of Talent, elicited by impassioned feeling in the breast of Man, are perhaps incompatible with some of the prosaic Decencies of Life" (*MW*: 398). Sir Edward is convinced that the promptings of a genius's feelings, vehicles of a higher truth and morality, will not brook denial. He grants great poets *carte blanche*. (He grants it to himself too, on the grounds that, a great original, he is about to blaze a new path in the annals of seduction, p. 359.) That belief closely connects his ideology of genius to the modus operandi of the fiction's "family of [self-styled] Hopeless Invalides." (One family member reports, for example, that "my feelings tell me too plainly that . . . the Sea air would probably be the death of me," p. 387.) Genius poets and hypochondriacs alike are granted "exemption from the wages of socialization" (Miller 1990: 65). Seasoned readers of Austen's fiction, alerted to the omnipresence of bullying in social intercourse, will worry about the attentions such figures demand from others who have not been so exempted.

The fact is, neither Byronic gloom nor "perpetual fever" stood up well under the scrutiny of that "fine strain of feminine cynicism" that readers like the Victorian novelist Margaret Oliphant discovered in Austen's pages (Southam 1968: 217). That episode in *Sanditon* involving Sir Edward's self-important rhapsodizing is infused with Austen's characteristic preference for the ironic over the histrionic. The episode suggests, by extension, the difficulties which that preference created when it became time to usher Austen into the pantheon in her turn. In fact, in 1932 scenes resembling this one from *Sanditon* appeared in Stella Gibbons' *Cold Comfort Farm*, a novel that revived Austen herself in the person of its heroine, recently orphaned Flora Poste who aims to write "a novel as good as *Persuasion*" when she is "fifty-three or so," but who in the meantime is tidying up her rural relatives and marrying them off (1938: 21). Over the course of the narrative, little perturbs Flora, the exception being her encounters with a member of the tribe of "geniuses and intellectuals" (p. 80). This is Mr Mybug, who divides his time between ineffectual attempts to seduce Flora and the book he is writing on Branwell Brontë – "a tremendous genius, a sort of second Chatterton" (p. 108) – and, according to Mybug, the true author of *Wuthering Heights*.

In 1774 Alexander Gerard in his *Essay on Genius* had lauded the transgressiveness of the original genius with the declaration that "we would scarce wish even the redundancies of his natural force and spirit to be lopt off by culture" (p. 13). Flora's triumphs at Cold Comfort Farm involve promoting rational cultivation within a community previously resigned to letting Nature take its course (hence her contraception advice to her cousins' fecund hired girl and deft management of their oversexed bull). Confronting the "fertile" imagination celebrated in late-eighteenth-century aesthetics, one that "loses itself in a wilderness of its own creation" (Gerard 1774: 45), Flora as a matter of policy would begin lopping. Apparently, Gibbons believes this to be Austen's policy too.

One might find Gibbons's burlesque inadequate to the earlier novelist's moral seriousness, but at least Flora is a figure of formidable will power; Gibbons uses her unflappable heroine to quarrel with the gentle Janeism that accompanied Austen's nineteenth-century canonization. And indeed her contemporary, W. H. Auden, granted Austen a similar toughness. In the 1937 poem "Letter to Lord Byron," Auden briefly entertains the idea that the libertine poet might have scandalized the lady novelist, but then, remembering her clear-eyed candor about finances, reconsiders: "You could not shock her more than she shocks me."

The Victorians, by contrast, had talked up Austen as safe and even salutary – an author one might admit into the family circle without worrying about geniuses' proclivities for violent passions. Hence in 1855 the man of letters Thomas Macaulay prescribed for his 12-year-old niece "a steady course, wholesome as fresh air and plain food, of Jane Austen" (1982: 256; cf Southam 1987: 8–11). The standing of a writer so valued seems an uncertain thing, the risk being that the medicinal value comes at the expense of the mystique. In multiple respects – for example, her death at the height of her powers, her anomalous relationship to marriage culture – Austen's life appears to fit the storylines of authorial exceptionality established in her lifetime. (As intimated above, the cult of Shakespeare long empowered her admirers by lending them its language of the born genius.) But the terms of Austen's canonization were impacted through the nineteenth century by her admirers' half-heartedness in deploying these discourses. When in 1870 her nephew, J. E. Austen-Leigh, wrote her biography, he felt compelled to qualify every statement made there about this author's genius with assertions about her modesty, amateurism, and preoccupation with home duties. The sentence about "dear aunt Jane" opening the *Memoir* set the tone: "Her talents did not . . . in any degree pierce through the obscurity of her domestic retirement" (2002: 9). Austen-Leigh identifies Nature as the "cradle" of his aunt's "genius," bestowing on Austen the childhood that poetry like William Wordsworth's had made requisite. During her youthful "strolls along those wood-walks, thick-coming fancies" must have risen in her mind, but, Austen-Leigh adds, scrupulously, "she brought them all into subjection to the piety which ruled her in life, and supported her in death" (24–6).

The *Memoir* is delicately balanced between canonizing Austen as an author and – reflecting a contemporary "cult" of womanhood and the resurgent Mariolatry of Victorian England – canonizing her as a saint. The sanctity so bestowed can be drearily generic. Profiles of Austen authored by Victorians often do as their period's biographical collections of "Good Women" do: they "impale" her with "domestic morals" (Booth 2004: 57). (In one such volume Charlotte Brontë figures under the heading "The Good Daughter.") Tricia Lootens observes that, at a time when the glory of the masculine canon was "believed to arise from purely individual genius," reverence for the "relics" of canonized women was reverence for the glory of "the sex" (1996: 10).

Still, the nineteenth-century creation of "The Legend of St. Jane"[2] could have granted Austenian readers a route back to genius in the archaic sense of the term and back to the guardian spirits of Roman mythology. When he recounts the rise in late antiquity of the cult of the saints, the historian Peter Brown describes how, in providing the early Christians with protection and "invisible companionship," the saints took over – and made more intimate – a role previously assigned to the nonhuman figures of gods and "geniuses." Early Christians ceased to pursue involvement with "the shimmering presence of a bodiless power" and sought instead "the face of a fellow human being among the dead," thereby establishing a cult that was, Brown emphasizes, in some respects cozy compared to the tradition it had replaced. At origin saints were adamantly local heroes, even the fellow citizens of the faithful (Brown 1981: 55, 51). For the sequel to this history, we might look to the reading group who, in the novel *The Jane Austen Book Club*, devise a bibliomantic divination toy called "Ask Austen" (Fowler 2004; cf Raff forthcoming). When they make the novelist their guru, intercessor, personal prophet, and (a variation on these roles) matchmaker, the book club members can be seen as reassigning the tasks – the work of mediating between heaven and earth especially – that Brown's early Christians removed from geniuses and assigned to saints.

These readerly investments in situating admired authors in a celestial sphere where they see all eternity and see into our hearts inform a persisting undercurrent in the history of Austen's reception, in ways my conclusion will engage shortly. It is worth underlining first, however, the tensions between this determination to look *up to* the author and the intimacy expectations that post-Romantic readers formed as they learned to read biographically, and also the tensions between this determination and that account of Austen we glimpsed in Flora Poste's confrontation with Mr Mybug. As Stella Gibbons showed us, there is a strain of Austenian commentary that, presuming on Austen's firm location in the mundane, enlists her as a foil to the genius, sometimes precisely so as to *ground* the enthusiastic flights such figures both enacted and inspired in their admirers. In this context, Austen's sense is touted as a corrective to the genius's sensibility and unruly subjectivity – often, however (though not always) in a manner that intimates doubts about whether she is capable of a comparable visionary power.

Nineteenth-century readers working along these lines tended to segregate the kind of woman's writing that Austen modeled from its competition in the sanctification stakes – from compositions by lyric poets of passion like L. E. L. (Letitia Landon), for example, or by novelists working in the ardent tradition of Mme de Staël's *Corinne*.[3] Hence this declaration in an 1822 survey of "Female Literature of the Present Age": "we turn from the dazzling brilliancy of Lady Morgan's works to repose on the soft green of Miss Austen's sweet and unambitious creations" (quoted in Ferris 1991: 48). The language here, lifted from Edmund Burke's aesthetic treatise on the sublime and the beautiful, domesticates Austen as it allies her firmly with Burke's latter category; this, however, at a moment acknowledging the sublime to be "the proper sphere of a great Genius" (Duff 1767: 53). Sixty years later, Margaret Oliphant in her *Autobiography* drew to different effect on the example of the domestic novelist who renounced sublime originality for restful familiarity. Recycling Austen-Leigh's famous description of the Austenian scene of writing – the *Memoir*'s story of the novelist so unassuming that she wrote in the common sitting-room – gave Oliphant a way both to depict her own relation to authorship and to question her contemporary George Eliot's way of occupying the role of great writer (Oliphant 1990: 30). Isolated from domestic disturbances, "kept . . . in a mental greenhouse," Eliot, Oliphant asserts, "took herself with tremendous seriousness" (pp. 15, 17). Oliphant's identification is with the novelist who, she believes, would anticipate her in gauging the worldly advantages of Eliot's unworldliness.

An 1821 "Letter to Lord Byron" by "John Bull" (in fact, J. G. Lockhart, Walter Scott's son-in-law) likewise uses Austen to call genius on the carpet, as it wields Austen's example, or, more precisely, that of her characters, against the poet, prompted by exasperation with Byron's program of self-dramatization, his way of selling not simply poetry but himself. In a passage in which Lockhart describes that marketing of the Byronic hero, the voice of the critic suddenly falls silent and readers find themselves eavesdropping on a conversation among the characters of *Emma*:

> You thought it would be a fine, interesting thing for a handsome young Lord to depict himself as a dark-souled, melancholy, morbid being, and you have done so, it must be admitted, with exceeding cleverness. . . . every boarding-school in the empire still contains many devout believers in [your] amazing misery . . . How melancholy you look in the prints! . . . Now, tell me, Mrs. Goddard, now tell me, . . . dear Harriet Smith, and dear, dear Mrs. Elton, do tell me, is not this just the very look that one would have fancied for Childe Harold? (Lockhart 1947: 80–1)

Moving directly from this ventriloquist act to discussion of *Don Juan*, evidence that Byron can get beyond histrionic melancholy and produce a work of *true* genius, Lockhart never gets around to mentioning Austen by name. He is obviously dependent on her satiric insight – but the omission suggests a gendered logic that might trouble us, one aligning the female novelist with the literary consumption Lockhart ascribes to her characters and distancing her, correspondingly, from the literary production that created them. Such alignments recur in the history of Austen's reception. Thus in the essay on Austen in which he recycles language lauding Shakespeare's natural genius, Henry James interjects a disparaging note into the kudos for wood notes wild: if initially in his discussion it is Austenian readers who are obtuse (because her light felicity leaves them "hardly more curious . . . than the brown thrush"), that obliviousness ultimately encompasses the author as well, as James turns to picturing Austen as a figure who sometimes "lapse[s]" into "wool-gathering" (1905: 63, cf O'Farrell 2006: 2). Neither author nor audience knows what she is doing, James insinuates. They have that in common.

Austen was "normal, central, and sane to the point of genius": so declares Kathryn Sutherland, taking the critic F. R. Leavis's verdict on D. H. Lawrence, the end point of Leavis's *Great Tradition*, and transferring it to Austen, Leavis's starting point (Sutherland 2005: 53). In the context created by post-Romantic exaltations of the genius, an ascription of "normality" positions Austen in the mundane world where her readers are – eliminating the distance between loved author and loving fan and facilitating their intimacy.

But Sutherland, I sense, wants us to note the paradox inscribed in the concept of a writer who is a genius at normality. For to read the phrase straight is to overlook the role that descriptions of Austen's detachment and of the enigmatic qualities of her irony have played in reception history. Thanks in part to the example of Shakespeare (the author veiled in an obscurity so deep that it baffles biographers looking for confessions), Austen's readers have had to hand models of greatness that are centered not on the force of personality, but on the force of impersonality. And since the nineteenth century many of those readers have concluded from the perfection of the Austen novel that the creator of such perfection perforce remains inscrutable. She, oracle-like, can see into *their* hearts, but that intimacy remains unreciprocated and they can know her only through her effects, as audiences know the "myriad-minded" Bard who loses himself in his dramatis personae, or, for that matter, as the faithful know the Creator. Such descriptions of Austen's genius – Miller's paean to Austenian impersonality; Virginia Woolf's insistence in 1928 that "Austen we needs must adore; but she does not want it; she wants nothing" (1986, vol. 2: 463); Reginald Farrer's 1917 description of how, "aloof," this creator "disappears" into her creation (quoted in Southam 1987: 247–8) – echo the credo that modernism reworked from Victorian codes of literary reverence: a faith, as James Joyce put it, in the godlike artist who "remains within or behind or beyond or above his handiwork, invisible, refined out of existence, indifferent, paring his fingernails."

Woolf also declared Jane Austen, "of all great writers" to be "the most difficult to catch in the act of greatness" (1986, vol. 4: 155). If, on the one hand, this recalls Victorian defenses of the lady novelist's modesty, read otherwise, it evokes the powers of a miracle-working divinity.[4] This description places Austen at a supernatural distance from the reader's world – as from the world of personalities and individualities, normalities and abnormalities, brought into being by Romantic discussion of the genius.[5]

NOTES

1   In 1812, recording the frenzy generated by Byron's *Childe Harold's Pilgrimage*, Annabella Milbanke coined the term "Byromania" in a satiric poem on the disorder.

2   An actual title, used by the Janeite Earl of Icclesleigh in 1902 (Southam 1987: 57).

3   Keeping Austen off the ambitious heights might, however, have worked to her advantage: with nowhere to fall, she was spared the doom that nineteenth-century culture made almost de rigueur for its women of genius, one that would have seen her repeating the Sapphic leap to oblivion. See Prins (1999), for the importance of Sappho's suicide for nineteenth-

century histories of female authorship, especially her observation that "women poets turn to Sappho as a trope for performing the infinitely repeatable loss of the 'Poetess'" (p. 175). Masochistically, de Staël had used Corinne's story to demonstrate that sorrow was the inescapable fate of the woman of talents.

4   "A *Genius* differs from a *good Understanding* as a Magician from a good Architect," Young wrote: "*That* raises his structure by means invisible, *This* by the skilful use of common tools" (1759: 16).

5   I would like to thank Mary Favret and Heather Jackson for helpful readings of this essay.

Further Reading

Austen-Leigh, J. E. (2002). *A Memoir of Jane Austen*, Ed. K. Sutherland. 1870. Rev. edn 1871. Repr. Oxford: Oxford University Press.

D'Israeli, I. (1822). *The Literary Character, Illustrated by The History of Men of Genius*, 3rd edn, 2 vols. London: John Murray.

Elfenbein, A. (1999). *Romantic Genius: The Prehistory of a Homosexual Role*. New York: Columbia University Press.

Lootens, T. (1996). *Lost Saints: Silence, Gender, and Victorian Literary Canonization*. Charlottesville: University Press of Virginia.

35
Jane Austen's Periods

Mary A. Favret

Did Jane Austen have a period? Did she have periods? How would we know if she did?

Putting the question in the past tense – *did she* rather than *does she* – highlights some of the trickier problems of literary periodization, of assigning a period to a writer, especially a woman writer. To say Austen *has* a period or *belongs* to a period, regardless of the exact period attributed to her, is to mark the act of periodizing as a function of the present. Periodization aims to set its objects in the halo of a singular, illuminating present or what has come to be called "context." A writer by this scheme is understood best and everlastingly as a creature of her contemporaneous moment, a given "now" that filters out more complex relationships to time and history.

But to ask if Austen *had* a period is to venture differently into the past, and with less assurance (or fear) of once-and-for-all-ness. She may never have had a period. She may have had a period, and then stopped having it. She may have missed some periods, but not others. She may simply have had a regular series of periods. Making the period a question of the past and not the present opens it to another angle on temporality: not periodization, but periodicity. Whereas periodization "sets aside time and so constitutes it retroactively" from the vantage of the present, periodicity "interferes" with and actively structures the experience of time (Aravamudan 2001: 332). In entertaining the periodicity of periods – that they come and go and come again – a reader might begin to wonder about their explanatory power, or their ability to situate Austen in a single moment. Alongside an interpretive tradition that places Austen within a defining period, and alongside the ensuing arguments over what period best defines her, there is another tradition that links her with the rhythms and spells of periodicity. In this other tradition she is the author of the everyday, the village round, the barely noticed comings and goings of domestic routine. Such periodicity invites a kind of reading not easily rendered in the linear logic of historical chronology. "All six, every year," was the famous response of philosopher Gilbert Ryle when asked if he read novels; and his Janeite manifesto of periodicity has been followed – now and then, here and there – by countless Austen readers.

For Jane Austen, the question of period has proven elusive, sliding off into repetitions and lapses that trouble chronological assignment. The difficulty may have something to do, like the mythical phases of the moon, with a desire to comprehend the phenomena of girlhood, womanhood, and spinsterhood. Deidre Lynch has noticed that "at recurring intervals, Austen has caused trouble for literary history." What Lynch calls "her problematic femaleness . . . compounded by spinsterhood and childlessness" has prompted Austen's periodic period troubles (Lynch 2000: 9). The difficulty is complicated, no doubt, by a lapse of nearly 10 years in Austen's writing, a hiatus between the early fiction composed in Steventon parsonage, before moving with her parents and sister to Bath; and the work of revision, new writing, and publication which followed her settling at age 33 in Chawton. A historically minded critic such as Roger Sales (1994) restricts his consideration of Austen's period to these later years, the brief decade of the novels' publication, thus cutting off the influences of girlhood and adolescence. Virginia Woolf, on the other hand, insists on the continuity between girl and mature writer: "The child who formed her sentences so finely when she was fifteen never ceased to form them" (Woolf 1984: 142). A sentence, of course, is also a type of period: for Woolf, those teenage periods recurred for the rest of Austen's life. Unpublished girl and/or published spinster, Austen has been over the decades since her death awkwardly inserted into the history of English literature, a history usually constructed, as Lynch puts it, through "narratives about the legitimate transmission of a patrimony" (Lynch 2000: 9). Without the culturally visible markers of marriage and motherhood, the unattached female's relationship to her period remains unmarked, its dating open to question: is she the daughter of Samuel Johnson and his age; the mother of Henry James, E. M. Forster and the modernist novel; or always the maiden aunt, surveying the family legacy from a loving but detached perspective? If it doesn't indicate the capacity for cultural reproduction and transmission, what purpose does a woman writer's period serve? In Austen's case in particular, the period of writing appears to come and go and come again, moved from one decade to another, one century to the next.

Sleeping Beauty

Virginia Woolf's response was to cut Austen loose from the patrilinear so as to spin an extraordinary fantasy about Austen's relationship to the temporal turnings of the globe. "One of those fairies who perch upon cradles must have taken her a flight through the world directly she was born," Woolf muses. As a result, ". . . at fifteen she had few illusions about other people and none about herself. Whatever she writes is finished and turned, set in its relation, not to the parsonage, but to the universe" (Woolf 1984: 136) – its own planet, with its own period of revolution (note Woolf's shift in tense). Woolf's eldritch vision shifts the question from the linear sequence of historical period to periodicity – finished turnings – of a nearly astrophysical bearing. Her vision also unwinds the romance underpinning the periodizing impulse. Written over in Woolf's other-worldly tale is the opening scene of Sleeping Beauty, where the fairies assemble around the cradle to confer their gifts on the newborn princess. In the ensuing struggle between kind and disgruntled fairies, the princess is told she will reach maturity, prick her finger on a spindle, bleed and perish: the end of girlhood. Then she is told no: that when she reaches maturity she will be pricked and bleed, but fall asleep and awaken again when kissed by her true love: her girlhood will be magically suspended through the years. In the fairy tale version, the maiden Sleeping Beauty awakens at the age of roughly 115 to the kiss of the prince who has discovered and fallen in love with her. The story Woolf revises is not just this allegory of problematic femaleness caught somewhere between girlhood and womanhood; it is also an allegory of periodization. Unlike Rip Van Winkle, the fictional contemporary of Anne Elliot, Sleeping Beauty experiences little disorientation when roused from her slumbers.[1] Though creatures of different centuries, Sleeping Beauty and the Prince seem unruffled by the historical gulf gaping at the center of their mutual attraction. No one seems concerned about the difficulties anachronism might pose to their union. And when the entire kingdom, put to sleep for one hundred years, happily reawakens to hail the marvelous marriage, no one worries about the consequences of reviving this long-lost society. But, of course, this is the heterosexual romance of fairy tales, not literary history. Or is it?

Woolf's revisionary fantasy helps to diagnose the deep cultural desires that aim to fit the woman writer within the frame of this romance. From the point of view of Woolf's contemporaries, Jane Austen, having barely reached maturity as a writer, died (or did she?) and her reputation slumbered through much of the nineteenth century. There were whispers and rumors; a group of kin and cognoscenti knew where she could be found. But for the most part she remained out of sight, undiscovered. In the late nineteenth century (in her case only a half century was required) she was awakened from this cultural sleep and embraced by a group of loving princes (notably George Lewes, William Dean Howells, and her own nephew, James Edward Austen-Leigh). A half century after that, she was awakened again, in the 1920s and 30s, now truly awakened to an adoring kingdom.[2] Another half century passed, she was roused yet again, this time by feminist scholars, half-hoping, half-fearing to find in Austen a suitable companion. The cycles of her reawakening have accelerated ever since: there was a revival in the mid-1990s, and again in 2005, the romance recycling rapidly in the kingdoms of film, video, and popular culture. The sheer pace of this temporal revolving begs for a resolutely unromantic, more genuinely *historical* Austen to flutter open her eyes at our twenty-first-century kisses. And so, in an ironic return Austen herself might appreciate, the newly, unromantically, historical Austen has been assigned to the Romantic period.[3]

The distance of 200 years is part of her attraction now. In fact, having been Victorian and Augustan and Modern and Feminist and Antifeminist makes her more fascinating to her new readers. In *Romantic Austen: Sexual Politics and the Literary Canon*, one of the more sophisticated recent considerations of Austen's relationship to literary periodization, Clara Tuite probes versions of Jane Austen that result from the "high-Janeite period of the 1930s," the "long high-Janeite period" from the 1920s to the 1960s, "the high period of feminist literary canon formation, . . . the 1980s"; and "the most important period with regard to the canonical production of Austen," the later nineteenth and early twentieth centuries (Tuite 2002: 4, 3, 9, 12). Tuite thus insists on dating the vagaries of Austen's periods, even as those periods shrink, expand, and overlap with one another. The back-dating that produces, for instance, an Augustan Austen – a designation which arose in the 1930s and points back to the patrician world of early eighteenth-century literary culture, which in turns points back to first-century Rome – is subsumed into a larger play of periodizing. Tuite associates this play with a sort of historical shell game that again recalls Sleeping Beauty. A "hyper-canonical" Austen, she argues, is forever helping to "rejuvenate," "revive," and "recon-struct" an otherwise lost kingdom of British culture (usually rural, propertied, and elite) (Tuite 2002: 13). In this reading, Austen's canonical role has never been to mark the period of her lived present but rather the reawakening of some desired, anterior period. For Tuite, the fairy-tale gesture (gift or curse) that removes Austen from the contingencies of her own contemporaneity into the "ahistory and . . . inescapable transhistoricity" of the canon ought to be traced to a particular historical moment she calls Romantic (Tuite 2002: 2). "Only by considering the specific social, political, cultural and economic transformations of the Romantic period, and the ways in which Austen's fictions engage such transformations, . . . [can we] begin to account for Austen's centrality within the British Literary canon" (Tuite 2002: 1). This trans-historical Sleeping Beauty, with her annoyingly recurrent periods, could only be the historical product of one period, the Romantic.

Tuite sends Austen back into the Romantic period, the source of those cultural energies that, with remarkable centrifugal force, propel Austen back out into a literary canon unmoored from any present, where she is condemned to reviving fairy-tale versions of the past. The Romantic period, for all its social and political specificity, thus serves Tuite as a sort of antiperiod, rejecting any grounding "now." Compare this Romanticism with that recently offered by James Chandler, in *England in 1819*, where these same years in the late eighteenth and early nineteenth century – the years of Austen's life and career – provide the breeding ground for historicism, the very methodology wielded by Tuite against the fairy forces of ahistory and transhistoricity. With detailed readings of historiography, historical theory, and Romantic-era texts, Chandler demonstrates that historicism, the interpretive method that seeks to under-stand objects by placing them within a delimited and contingent temporal frame (year, decade or period) itself emerged in the Romantic period. "[O]ur undertheorized concept of the 'historical situation,'" Chandler argues, "can be situated in the history of Romanticism," alongside "a new and urgent sense of contemporaneity" (Chandler 1998: xiv–xv). Chandler's Romantic period is thus the Period of Periods, the work of its writers providing the conceptual matrix which allows Tuite (and us) to differenti-ate along a historical continuum the various "high periods" of Austen reception or to measure Austen's (or any other writer's) reception against the "the specific social, political, cultural and economic transformations" of her contemporary context.

Romanticizing Austen's period leads to the antiperiod of nonpresence that concerns Tuite; it leads as well to the birth of periodization and its validation of the contemporaneous that Chandler documents. But it also leads to an encounter with periodicity, to the turnings and returnings that appeal so strongly to Woolf and trouble historicism's investment in a series of marked, dateable, and thereby differentiable periods.

Attentive to the rich context of the novelist's life, Galperin nevertheless, in his account of *The Historical Austen*, tends like Woolf to turn Austen away from the familiar outlines of a delineated historical period. He considers her novels in light of the undernoticed routines and minutiae that escape or distract from the "ordinary business" of historicism. For him, Austen is "historical" not simply by virtue of framing and dating devices. Rather, because of her attention to the periodic rather than the momentous, Austen writes a "history of the present" that questions the value, and perhaps the possibility of presentness. One step beyond Tuite's view that her period has made her ahistorical, Galperin's Austen presents a world of unwritten histories and elusive temporalities. If her fiction, as Scott suggests, poses "a form of forgetting," it also transfigures Austen's experience of her contemporary world through a slippage of tenses. A "pervasive anteriority" of could- and might-have-beens dwells in the uncanny, inordinate detail of her novels (Galperin 2003: 5). Galperin turns to *Emma*, that hymn to the turnings of the everyday, and finds in the desire to have a dance an "anterior wish for a version of the future on which the present (or erstwhile future) has subsequently foreclosed" (p. 206). One might say Galperin attends to the beauty sleeping, not yet awakened and matched up. Holding on to romance more for its unrealizeability, for the way it slips or fades from the realm of the probable (and the marriageable), Galperin makes Austen Romantic, and makes Romanticism less a literary-historical period (a delimited "now") than an always possible (if unrealized) future (Galperin 2003: 86–8).

Thus Romanticism, Austen's current period, is a period that alternately erases, sustains, and evades the periodizing impulse. What Chandler locates as a "new and urgent sense of contemporaneity" in the Romantic period, the period of *periodization*, nevertheless opens onto a romance of belatedness, recursiveness, and possibility: temporal complications of the "now." If the period of periodization sets aside time, constituting *that* present retroactively from the vantage of *this* present, it also effectively puts time to sleep as a passive rather than an active principle of experience, to be reawakened or reactivated only by the present kiss of historicism. I want to follow the lead of Galperin and Woolf by turning instead to periods of *periodicity* in Austen's work which, as suggested at the opening of this essay, actively structure one's ongoing experience of time. By periodicity I mean to invoke, along with the turnings and returnings already mentioned, the periods that constitute Austen's prose: her sentences. Nowhere is the temporally interfering and structuring potential of periodicity more evident than in Austen's own use of periods, those sentences which she finished and turned years ago when she was writing, not sleeping. Her fiction did not simply document a period but, as Chandler puts it in reference to the writers he considers, it effectively "worked on" history, "critically constructing or reconstructing the given in history" (Chandler 1998: xv). Even as she wrote about romance, Jane Austen wrote about periods.

Periods upon Periods

"We might meet . . . anywhere indeed, could we but be in the same place together. We have only to hope that such a period may arrive." (*MW*: 112)

. . . the felicity of being with him for the present bounded her views; the present was now comprised in another three weeks, and her happiness being certain for that period, the rest of her life was at such a distance as to excite but little interest. (*NA*: 138)

"It is a period, indeed! Eight years and a half is a period!" (*P*: 225)

A quick glance at these excerpts from Austen's fiction suggests that for the characters here, "period" serves primarily as an index of human contact: it is a marker of meeting, of being in the company of another, or the time between one moment of communion and another. It is more than anything a period of feeling, waxing and waning for instance with one character's "happiness," another's "hope." The freighted sense of rendezvous evoked by these selected "periods" contrasts sharply with the historicizing impulse that uses periods to divide or exclude.[4] Resistant to the charms of any sleeping beauty, the "periodization strategy," as Russell Berman puts it rather polemically, is "designed to separate the readers of th[is] present from the claimants of the past" – that is, from a present identified as different and over (Berman 2001: 325). In Austen's *Emma*, Mr John Knightley puts the matter more gently, but also reveals his own privileged relationship to periods. Concerned about Jane Fairfax's attachment to her daily routine of going to the post office, even in the rain, he invokes the distancing power of periodizing: "The post-office has a great claim at one period of our lives," he acknowledges, and his universalizing statement employs the present tense only to divide it into his past and her future. "When you have lived to my age, you will begin to think that letters are never worth going through the rain for" (*E*: 293). "Being altered by time, by the progress of years" – positioning oneself beyond this designated "one period of our lives," as John Knightley does – allows him to put the claimants of the past behind him, and he extends a similar prospect to this young woman. "Time will generally lessen the interest of every attachment not within the daily circle," he promises, as he imagines Jane Fairfax entering a progressive narrative of marriage and reproduction. From Jane's perspective, the advice is kindly given and "far from giving offence"; yet it elicits "a blush, a quivering lip, a tear in the eye" (*E*: 294). Unmarried and, by the laws of social economy, unmarriageable, Jane is in no position to step outside this "one period" of her life. Nor is she ready to accept a daily circle which does not include precious communication from other times and places. With no sure prospects and many, various claimants on her affections (she turns from her interlocutor because "her attention was now claimed by Mr Woodhouse"), the single woman, caught between girlhood and spinsterhood, remains in an undifferentiated now. She both resists and cannot access John Knightley's disaffected and self-confirming "period strategy."

The conversation between Jane Fairfax and John Knightley demonstrates just one instance of Austen's own complex consideration of how the experience of "period" carries differential values and possibilities, especially along the lines of gender. John Knightley moves smoothly from one period to another in his life, shedding the pressing claims made by one "now" upon another. Jane Fairfax, on the other hand, committed to her "daily errand," embraces the complex temporality of the mail (reading in the present what was written in the past; writing now what will not be read until later and elsewhere). In the novel she figures a vexed and unsettled temporal position: Emma speculates about her past; John Knightley, Mrs Weston, and Mrs Elton imagine different projects for her future; and nearly everyone – reader and perhaps narrator included – overlooks the full truth of her present (see Galperin 2003: 180–4). Her shadowy presence in the novel indicates the difficulty of determining the precise outlines of her period. In a rare moment of free indirect discourse with the elusive Jane Fairfax, the narrator shares her sense that for a woman in her situation, unmarried and without a dowry, periodizing can be costly:

> [S]he had now reached the age which her own judgment had fixed on for beginning [to seek employment as a governess]. She had long resolved that one-and-twenty should be the period. With the fortitude of a devoted novitiate, she had resolved at one-and-twenty to complete the sacrifice, and retire from all the pleasures of life, of rational intercourse, equal society, peace and hope, to penance and mortification forever. (*E*: 165)

The work of the novel, in part, is to rescue Jane from a self-periodization that can only be self-sacrificing.

Jane Fairfax's counterpart in the novel, Emma Woodhouse, had by contrast "lived nearly twenty-one years with very little to distress or vex her" (*E*: 5). Given securities and prospects Jane has not, Emma nevertheless resists the impulse to wield the period as an instrument of detachment. Before the exchange between Jane Fairfax and John Knightley, a conversation about periods takes place between Emma and his brother. In it Austen demonstrates Emma's more creative manner of structuring and restructuring the experience of time – and her relationship to others. Meeting for the first time after having argued, Emma decides "it is time to appear to forget" that she and her brother-in-law "had ever quarreled." On a number of levels, Knightley resists this easing of differences, reminding her, "I was sixteen years old when you were born." Emma is unfazed: "'A material difference then,' she replied – 'and no doubt you were much my superior in judgment at that period of our lives; but does not the lapse of one-and-twenty years bring our understandings a good deal nearer?'" (*E*: 99).

In her own version of uneven development, Emma wants the movement of time to bring not distance but equity, a nearer understanding that might produce a collapse of – or "a seeming to forget" – differences. Knightley's insistence on dated periods will return to plague him later in the novel, when he reckons he is, in fact, both too old and too late to engage Emma's heart, "He *had* despaired at one period," but Austen generously dismantles the temporal obstacle of years in the course of 30 minutes: "Within half an hour he had passed from a thoroughly distressed state of mind to something so like perfect happiness, that it could bear no other name" (*E*: 431–2). Emma, for her part, spends much of that same half-hour (when she had proposed "taking another turn" with Knightley in the shrubbery) mentally scrolling through the events of the novel, taking license again to restructure her sense of what had passed. The narrator displays Emma's "wonderful velocity of thought," as she recollects and revises her past, recalibrating her previous relationships even as she listens in the present to Knightley's confession of love. "And not only was there time for these [new] convictions . . . there was time also to rejoice" (*E*: 430–1). In this scene, Austen's sentences open up the registers of time available to romance: past, present, and future are all palpable in this revisionary moment. There was time, and there still is time and time is not singular (one period; 16 years) but variable, malleable.

This ample revolving of time, the possibility of taking another turn, seems denied to Anne Elliott and Captain Wentworth throughout most of *Persuasion*. In her last finished novel, Austen performs her most ambitious work on temporality, but she does so with what seems greater urgency, against greater odds. At the heart of the novel lies the question of the period, whether it will open to the temporal bleed of past, present, and future, or remain fixed and closed. "It is a period indeed! Eight and a half years is a period!" cries Captain Wentworth, yet his outburst has none of the Knightley brothers' self-assertion: it is a wail of despair (*P*: 225). Those eight and half years remain outside the narrative: we are given a brief account of the events preceding it and most of the book recounts what followed it, but it remains a history unwritten. Initially Wentworth understands the period as a mark of difference, and therefore of emotional detachment, so that he can see his former lover and declare she was "so altered he should not have known [her] again" (*P*: 60). Anne similarly clings to the desensitizing force of years, but her periodizing recalls Jane Fairfax's self-immolation:

> . . . she began to reason with herself, and try to be feeling less. Eight years, almost eight years had passed, since all had been given up. How absurd to be resuming an agitation which such an interval had banished into distance and indistinctness! What might not eight years do? Events of every description, changes, alienations, removals – all, all must be comprised in it; and oblivion of the past – how natural, how certain too! (*P*: 60)

This "periodization strategy" pushes itself upon Anne, the would-be spinster, both as survival strategy and as inevitability: "how natural, how certain too!" The fullness invested in those years, "events of every description," will help empty out her heart. Yet the question at the center of her historicizing deliberations – what might not eight years, or any other period of time, do? – remains open.

The question of this one period – everything or nothing, alienation or reunion – filters into the temporal texture of the novel, so that you can open any chapter and encounter sentences awash in layers of retrospection, doubt, and conjecture; in shocks and lapses, alarms and forgettings. In this regard, the scene of Wentworth's outburst, near the finale, is characteristic of this novel more generally. Here Wentworth is testing how much time it takes to make a meaningful – and irrevocable – difference.

> "You have *not been long enough* in Bath," said he, "to enjoy the evening parties of the place."
>
> "Oh! No. *The usual* character of them *has nothing for me.* I am no card-player."
>
> "You were *not formerly*, I know. You *did not use to* like cards; but *time brings many changes.*"
>
> "I am *not yet so much changed*," cried Anne, and stopped, fearing she hardly knew what misconstruction.

A chasm yawns at the end of every sentence.

> After *waiting a few moments*, he said – and as if it were the result of *immediate feeling* – "It is *a period, indeed! Eight years and a half is a period!*"
>
> Whether he would have proceeded farther was left to Anne's imagination to ponder over *in a calmer hour*; for *while still* hearing the sounds he uttered, she was startled to other subjects by Henrietta, *eager to make use of the present* leisure for getting out, and calling on her companions *to lose no time*, lest somebody else should come in.
>
> They were obliged to move. Anne talked of being *perfectly ready*, and tried to look it.
> (*P*: 225, emphasis added)

Austen sets the temporal registers in wrenching competition, with the result that there is no time, almost no tense, for communion between the two principles (unlike Emma's generous "there was time . . . there was also time"). Wentworth and Anne are delicately probing for a chance to return to the past, to overcome the daunting "period" of their separation, transforming it into something generative. Simultaneously, however, other forces are pressing them onward and apart, demanding their "readiness" and responsiveness to an on-rushing present, determined to "lose no time" in such retrospective activity. Rarely in Austen's fiction does the force of History as a lived experience – not of the past but of a headlong present – press so strongly and feel so threatening. Even though the lovers marry at novel's end, yet Anne has to learn to "pay the tax of quick alarm": her husband may be called to war any minute.

Few authors are as renowned as Jane Austen for the poise, wit, and self-sufficiency of their sentences: in this general, grammatical and aesthetic sense, Austen can be said to own not a period but rather *the* period. Or many periods. Austen's prose makes us believe and participate in the meaningfulness and aesthetic satisfactions of a well-rounded period. And yet, as I have tried to show, when Austen writes periods upon periods, she calls into question the costs of fixing a period, especially for women. Not surprisingly, the sentences of her fiction find ways to turn periods into less definite, more heterogeneous temporal situations, where the claims of past, present, and future tangle, compete, and sometimes collapse into one another. These are not the periods of a simple historicism, with its impulse to restrict temporality to the single moment of a work's production – and its end. They display, rather, what Russell Berman calls literature's "anamnestic mission": in their periodical turns and returns, they "maintain a distinct relationship to time, in its ability to remember – a phenomenon that occurs in every act of reading – and in its imaginative capacity to project" (Berman 2001: 326, 329). The raw material for such literary periods might be found in the overflow of *Emma*'s Miss Bates, those barely conscious, unending turnings of detail, interjection, sudden recollection or tedious habit. Yet in these novels Austen is not a talker but a writer, mastering (through revision, through returning) the periods with which Miss Bates still wrestles. Perhaps the best way to start thinking about Austen's periods, then, is to understand them as neither fairy tales nor forms of knowledge, but as measures – and not the only measures – of thought; and to acknowledge that our thinking is not always as finished and well-turned as we would like.

NOTES

1   Washington Irving published "Rip Van Winkle" in *The Sketchbook of Geoffrey Crayon* in 1819. Irving has his hero fall asleep before the American Revolution and awaken 20 years later.

2   Oxford University Press first published the complete novels of Jane Austen in 1923. For Austen's reception in these years, see also Lynch, "At Home With Jane Austen" (1996), as well as the essays by Tuite, Trumpener, and Johnson in Lynch's *Janeites*.

3   In *The Romantic Ideology* (1983), Jerome McGann pointedly excluded Jane Austen from

the ranks of the Romantic. Recent critics have responded by reformulating what Romanticism and the Romantic period signify. See for example Clifford Siskin, *The Historicity of Romantic Discourse* (1988) and *The Work of Writing* (1999); Lynch's chapter on Austen in *The Economy of Character* (1998); Tuite, *Romantic Austen* (2002); and Galperin, *The Historical Jane Austen* (2003).

4   Marshall Brown understands the period as a sort of negative knowledge, naming "not what things are, but what they are not" (2001: 309, 316).

Further Reading

Chandler, James (1998). *England in 1819: The Politics of literary Culture and the Case of Romantic Historicism*. Chicago: University of Chicago Press.

Galperin, William H. (2003). *The Historical Austen*. Philadelphia: University of Pennsylvania Press.

Lynch, Deidre (1996). At home with Jane Austen. In Deidre Lynch and William B. Warner (Eds). *Cultural Institutions of the Novel* (pp. 159–92). Durham, NC: Duke University Press.

Lynch, Deidre (Ed. and Intro.) (2000). *Janeites: Austen's Disciples and Devotees*. Princeton, NJ: Princeton University Press.

Sales, Roger (1994). *Jane Austen and Representations of Regency England*. London and New York: Routledge.

Tuite, Clara (2002). *Romantic Austen: Sexual Politics and the Literary Canon*. Cambridge, UK and New York: Cambridge University Press.

36
Nostalgia

Nicholas Dames

Did Jane Austen faint upon learning that her family was relocating from Steventon, her childhood home in Hampshire, to Bath, 70 miles and a lifetime away? The apocryphal story of her unhappy swoon was dismissed as soon as it was first mentioned, in William Austen-Leigh and Richard Arthur Austen-Leigh's 1913 *Life and Letters*. The authors concede, however, that the telling absence of any letters from Austen to her sister Cassandra in the following weeks, from late November 1800 to early January 1801, suggests that these presumably destroyed documents contained unusually strong expressions of private regret. The mystery surrounding Austen's reaction to this sudden alteration of her living arrangement – her first real moment of leaving home, perhaps – has tended for Austen's biographers to function as a riddle, the answer to which might illuminate her character. Was she, as the *Life and Letters* has it, "determined to face a new life in a new place with cheerfulness" (Austen-Leigh 2006: 123)? Or was she, as J. E. Austen-Leigh put it in his 1870 *Memoir* of his aunt, "exceedingly unhappy" at the move, since "the loss of their first home is generally a great grief to young persons of strong feeling and lively imagination" (1870: 59)? Did her love of home triumph even over filial duty? Or did regret rapidly yield to the anticipation of new horizons? Austen's own comments on the matter are tantalizingly sibylline. "I get more and more reconciled to the idea of our removal," she writes to Cassandra in the first extant letter after the move was announced. "For a time we shall now possess many of the advantages which I have often thought of with Envy in the wives of Sailors or Soldiers" (*Letters*: 68). The last line could indeed be read as straightforward praise of mobility's joys – freshness of scene, expanded knowledge, freedom from the usual constraints on female movement – or as a bitterly ironic jibe at the forced migration she was resigned to undergo. The question about Austen's sentiments at this crucial juncture of her youth linger, and can be restated in multiple ways: was she forward-looking or backward-turned? Or: was she a nostalgic, and if so, in what way?

The question is as important to Austen's fiction as it is largely unanswerable as a biographical conundrum. It is crucial in relation to the themes of Austen's novels, where heroines such as Marianne and Elinor Dashwood, Fanny Price, or Anne Elliot (herself eventually placed among "the wives of Sailors") are forced to leave stable homes for strange new places, and must reconcile themselves to their fractured lives. It is even more crucial in relation to a history of Austen's readers, for whom the nexus of issues that haunt "nostalgia" – the separation of past and present; sentimental regret versus a hardheaded realism; the past remembered accurately versus the past remembered fondly – have been continually rehearsed and reshuffled. What we can't know about how Austen left her childhood home behind is exactly what Austen's readers have most relentlessly sought to know about themselves and their fellows: do we read Austen to recapture a vanished past we would like restored in all its detail, or do we read Austen to teach us the falsity of that idealized past?

The terms of the debate are evident as early as the first major reissue of Austen's novels, in 1833, as part of Richard Bentley's *Standard Novels* anthology series. Scarcely two decades after the beginning of Austen's publishing career, reviewers greeted the reprinted novels as carrying news from a disappeared world. The notice in the *Literary Gazette* on March 30, 1833 advised members of the "rising generation" to acquaint themselves with a fictional milieu that, rather than remaining contemporary, was with "every hour . . . becoming absolute historical pictures." Already a major element of both the educative value and readerly pleasure promised by Austen's novels was felt to be their historicity, their appeal to communal memories of "a country dance, or the delights of a tea-table," even (or especially) if those communal memories of quasi-rural gentility and quiescence were more imaginary than real. Behind the *Gazette's* recommendation of Austen lies a suspicion that the reader who comes to Austen through Bentley's reprint is likely to know Austen's world only through Austen herself – what quickly vanishes in the memories of parents and grandparents is still safely available in her narratives. Austen, that is, is important for her detailed, realistic portrayal of a bygone world, and the pleasure her novels give is a nostalgic one: imaginatively inhabiting a world as pleasant as it is vanished.

The nexus of pleasure and obsolescence described by the *Gazette's* anonymous reviewer would become foundational for later Austen readers and critics, who tended to either supplement that pleasure, or contest that obsolescence, while not fundamentally disagreeing with the assumption that, for most readers of Austen, the primary pleasure is that of temporarily living in a historical world utterly disconnected from the present. One of the most notable nineteenth-century assessments of Austen to attempt to add to the pleasure her novels supposedly provide was James Austen-Leigh's 1870 *Memoir*. Austen-Leigh addresses himself to readers who, steeped in Austen's fiction, have formed the desire to know everything about the places she lived – particularly the forsaken village of Steventon – as well as all the forgotten details about her time. Thus the *Memoir* devotes pages of description and analysis to the minute details of late eighteenth and early nineteenth-century provincial life: the kinds of meals eaten; the table-settings upon which they were served, and the times of day at which they were consumed; the austere furnishings of genteel rooms; the stately dances; the more self-sufficient gentlefolk, who relied less on servants for menial tasks; the rutted and muddy roads; the earthier and more colorful language used, even by squires and clergymen. "They may be little things," Austen-Leigh writes, "but time gives a certain importance even to trifles, as it imparts a peculiar flavour to wine" (1870: 8). The logic here is particularly important for a reception history of Austen: as her world recedes, the smallest things gain importance for our attempt to imaginatively inhabit it; and – most crucially – Austen's novels seem not to provide enough of these details, given Austen-Leigh's desire to supply them in abundance. Notably laconic about the gustatory habits or decorative tendencies of her time, Austen seems to call for supplement, as if the nostalgic desire her novels create (oh to live then, and with those characters!) cannot be fully whetted without further help, help particularly with historical "trifles." Thus the elaborately footnoted editions in which Austen now appears, from the scholarly Cambridge Edition of her novels to the appearance in 2003 of *The Annotated Pride and Prejudice*. The most lasting legacy of Austen-Leigh's desire to supply the details Austen withholds, however, and the spiritual ancestor of contemporary annotated editions, is R. W. Chapman's 1923 collected edition of Austen's works, which provided nineteenth-century illustrations of such material indices of Austen's culture as walking-dresses, curricle gigs, and concert rooms.

If the *Gazette* reviewer describes Austenian nostalgia as both educative and pleasurable, and Austen-Leigh as more a desire inspired and yet only partially satisfied by the novels, their shared assumption is that what Austen's readers want – and what Austen can provide them – is access to a past preferable to the present: more genteel, more entertaining, less abrasive, more settled. Austen "belongs," as G. K. Chesterton wrote in 1913, "to a vanished world before the great progressive age of which I write" (p. 105). The keynote of Austen criticism from the late nineteenth century onward is, however, a persistent doubt that that past is genuine. Where the *Gazette* reviewer and Austen-Leigh take for granted the essential reality of the past Austen gives us, after Henry James it is more common to imagine an Austen who inveigles readers into believing in a past that never existed. Lumping Austen with her conventional opposites, the Brontës, James gently criticized a fashion for "their 'dear,' our dear, everybody's dear, Jane," a cultural appetite that is "so amenable to pretty reproduction in every variety of what is called tasteful, and in what seemingly proves to be saleable, form" – and that can be described as "a beguiled infatuation, a sentimentalized vision" (James 1984: 118). The inauthenticity of Austenian nostalgia is connected to Austen's continued commercial success: what Austen and her popularizers are selling, in James's view, is a prettified image, not access to reality. It is worth noting here that James's Austen, by virtue of what he calls "the extraordinary grace of her facility," is at least partially responsible for the commercialized sentimentality of her editors, illustrators, and publishers; they have, for James, merely made "saleable" the nostalgic pleasures that Austen already has supplied.

This "sentimentalized vision" is virtually equivalent to a definition of the term "nostalgia" in the twentieth century, and when later twentieth-century critics return to James's analysis of Austenian nostalgia as a false desire, they do so primarily in order to separate themselves from it, to carve out a space for a nonnostalgic version of Austen. A crucial move, for instance, in late-twentieth-century feminist reconsiderations of Austen is to disown the nostalgia that clings to her image. As Sandra Gilbert and Susan Gubar complain in their seminal 1979 book *The Madwoman in the Attic*, Austen has been turned into "a nostalgic symbol of order, culture, England, in an apocalyptic world where all the old gods have failed or disappeared" (Gilbert and Gubar 1979: 111). The problem is that nostalgic inauthenticity – the desire for Austen's time and milieu, to live with her novels and in them, a desire that is by its nature unfulfillable – fails to accurately *see* the past it thinks it wants. Claudia Johnson has put this memorably: "It is no accident, of course, that as modern readers find themselves more nostalgic for the stateliness and stability Austen's world is said to apotheosize, Austen's class gets higher and higher, and she herself is claimed to be more and more conservative" (Johnson 1988: 167). The corrective to a pervasive nostalgia is, as these critics and numerous others have implicitly claimed, a disenchanted critical practice that would be more accurately historical, and would show us a more insecure, anxious, and socially incisive Austen, one who – far from celebrating the social world she wrote about – instead invites us to see its fissures and failures.

That so much brilliant and convincing critical work has come out of the antinostalgic drive of twentieth-century Austen critics – who, as I would argue, can ultimately trace their lineage to Henry James's analysis of her public's "sentimentalized vision" – is certainly one very strong argument for remaining suspicious of the nostalgic appeal Austen can hold. Such suspicion has opened up countless new avenues of approach to Austen, and has added fascinating complexities to our understanding of her relation to gender norms, the imperial geopolitics of her time, and even the act of novel writing. Yet as critics such as Claudia Johnson have recently argued, one important side effect of such work is to widen the gap between the historicist paradigms professional academic critics employ and the persistently nostalgic appeal that Austen holds for a remarkably wide popular audience. Academic critics whose work is devoted to erasing the nostalgic encrustations upon Austen's image have had the (either amusing or disheartening) experience of watching a concomitant boom in what James called the "pretty reproductions" of Austen, particularly in the spate of recent film versions of the novels, most of which seem to have learned little or nothing from the denostalgizing energies of academic critics, and which have been just as viably "saleable" as James noted in 1905. The public that reads (or views) Austen, that is, continues most often to come to her to have a nostalgic craving satisfied, despite the best efforts of her professional critics. So strong is this craving that it can have a reverse effect: some contemporary retellings, such as Patricia Rozema's 1999 film version of *Mansfield Park*, have sought to capitalize on the notoriety, even scandal, that a nonnostalgic version of Austen necessarily produces.

How might this knot be untied? How might nostalgia be understood without being entirely disowned – or, how could the nostalgic desires of Austen's readers and consumers be explained using the historicist tools of contemporary academic criticism? One possible route lies through the very absence of the word "nostalgia" in

Austen's work. From the late eighteenth century up to the late nineteenth century the word was undergoing what might be called a prolonged semantic slumber in English, in which its meaning was rapidly metamorphosing into its modern form out of an initially specialized medical use. The word was coined in 1688 by the Swiss physician Johannes Hofer, whose "Dissertatio medica de nostalgia" combined the Greek *nostos*, or homecoming, and *algia*, or pain, to develop a new kind of potentially fatal homesickness – a form of yearning for a return to home so severe that it could lead to the most severe pathological effects. Commonly found in the European medical taxonomies or nosologies of the eighteenth century, "nostalgia" was classed with forms of mental aberration such as melancholia, nymphomania, bulimia, and hypochondriasis, and the descriptions of its etiology sound nothing like the genial sentimentalism of the word's contemporary meaning. One such vivid description is offered by William Falconer, physician at Bath General Hospital from 1784 to 1819, his tenure there coinciding with Austen's own relocation from Hampshire. Falconer's 1788 *Dissertation on the Influence of the Passions Upon Disorders of the Body* describes the progress of nostalgia as starting with "melancholy, sadness, love of solitude, silence," but rapidly progressing to nausea, vomiting, and fever. When advanced, Falconer adds, "nothing avails but returning to their own country, which is so powerful an agent in the cure, that the very preparations for the return prove more effectual than anything else" (Falconer 1788: 90–1). In line with most European medical knowledge of the time, Falconer describes a disease of transplantation or forced mobility, in which the individual patient, confronted with a separation from a native home, either refuses or is unable to adapt psychically to the new milieu, resulting in mental and finally physical debility. The population most susceptible to the disease seems to have been the military, particularly in the late eighteenth century, when the mass mobilizations of the period of the French Revolution created enforced dislocations of a kind and scale previously unknown in European history. Accounts of epidemics of nostalgia can be found on board ships – the HMS *Endeavor*, sailing past the coast of New Guinea in 1770 under the command of James Cook, reported one such instance – and in armies: two separate waves of nostalgia swept French armies in 1793 and 1799.

These and other facts and illuminating anecdotes about eighteenth-century "nostalgia," and its relation to the contemporary use of the term, have recently come under the investigation of scholars such as Linda Austin, Svetlana Boym, Michael Roth, Jean Starobinski, and Susan Stewart. The collective work of uncovering the medical roots of nostalgia offers one important lesson: that the human personality, as imagined by eighteenth-century medical theorists, was incapable of sudden or prolonged mobility. It was, in fact, what I have elsewhere called an "unassimilable self" (Dames, 2001), safest when not detached from familiar physical surroundings and not then forced to brood on vanished sights. So specialized was the word "nostalgia" that it is almost never used by lay writers in the eighteenth century; it is notably absent from Samuel Johnson's 1755 *Dictionary* despite its frequent use in medical texts. Instead, vaguely appropriate synonyms perform the same work as the medical term, as in Johnson's

1750 description of "sorrow": "Sorrow is properly that state of the mind in which our desires are fixed upon the past, without looking forward to the future, an incessant wish that something were otherwise than it has been, a tormenting and harassing want of some enjoyment or possession which we have lost, and which no endeavors can possibly regain" (Bate and Strauss 1969: 254). This is precisely the condition described by doctors as "nostalgia": a backward-turned consciousness unable (either because of the passage of time, or the impossibility of spatial movement) to recover what is lost and therefore tending to the mind's fruitless yearnings against itself.

While it is worth recovering these forgotten origins of the term, it is also worth keeping in mind the term's remarkable passage into a nearly opposite signification. What was a harmful and pathologized form of memory in the eighteenth century turns, by the end of the nineteenth century, into a vague, pleasurable, and commercially exploitable kind of retrospect, available to everyone, not just to select sufferers. The "unassimilable self," unable to adjust to new surroundings or facts, turns into the thoroughly assimilable self, willing to fondly recollect what is gone as a genial indulgence rather than a dangerous fixation. Squarely in the midst of this conceptual and semantic shift is Austen. The biographical debate about her enforced move from Steventon – was it with intense regret, reluctance tempered by obedience, or even a desire for fresh scenes, that Austen met this change? – echoes this historical shift in unintentional fashion. Biographers are asking, in effect, whether Austen was an eighteenth-century nostalgic or a modern one. In general, literary critics have been far more willing to see her as the former: Tony Tanner speaks for most when he confidently asserts that "Jane Austen is no novelist of the pícaro, the unhoused and unhomed" (1986: 204). It is, oddly enough, historians who have been more capable of seeing the constant movements, geographically small by contemporary standards though they may be, that dot Austen's plots and that challenge her characters. Linda Colley (1987), and Leonore Davidoff and Catherine Hall (1987) have recently turned to *Northanger Abbey* and *Pride and Prejudice* to illustrate the increasing popularity of "internal tourism," or travel to picturesque or otherwise notable British locations, in the final decades of the eighteenth century. As a result, they point our attention to the catalogue of spatial dislocations in Austen: the Dashwoods, in *Sense and Sensibility*, forced to leave Norland Park, their family seat for several generations and the only home the girls had known; Fanny Price, in *Mansfield Park*, taken at a young age from her Portsmouth family; the Elliots, in *Persuasion*, forced by bad financial management to rent their estate and set up home in Bath; not to mention the latter novel's collection of sailors, whose unimaginably long voyages echo the case histories of eighteenth-century nostalgia. Austen's novels are full of movement and the correspondingly complex psychic attitudes that come with it. They are located at the moment when an older notion of nostalgia was beginning to yield to a new one, and it is possible that Austen registers that shift as part of her fictional practice, and that the forms of nostalgia critics have always read as either a happy or unfortunate part of her readers' pleasure may in fact be produced – if not wholly satisfied – by the novels themselves.

Tracing this connection requires turning back to the central question posed by both Austen's nineteenth-century nostalgic admirers and her contemporary denostalgizing critics: the value of detail within her work, particularly detailed recollection of the past. The importance of the theme of obsessive remembrance is evident as early as Austen's juvenilia, which continually lampoon characters afflicted with what Johnson called "sorrow." The comically melancholy Eloisa Lutterell, from "Lesley Castle," speaks for them all: "You must expect from me nothing but the melancholy effusions of a broken Heart which is ever reverting to the Happiness it once enjoyed and which ill supports its present wretchedness" (*MW*: 132). This is a purely literary joke, if an acute one: a jape poking fun at the fashion for ineradicable melancholia, particularly of the retrospective kind, that dominates British fiction in the second half of the eighteenth century, and which found its most canonical expression in Samuel Richardson's *Clarissa* (1747–8). With the beginning of Austen's publishing career, however, her novels work explicitly to both fully describe and completely cure this kind of subjectivity: they are invested in the canceling of obsessive nostalgic regret.

This investment works both thematically and formally. Its formal enactment is most obvious in Austen's relative lack of interest in flashback narrative; her novels tend to avoid prolonged explanatory narratives in favor of quick summaries. She is not unaware of this choice, as demonstrated by one of her more acerbic narratorial commentaries:

> This brief account of the family is intended to supercede the necessity of a long and minute detail from Mrs. Thorpe herself, of her past adventures and sufferings, which might otherwise be expected to occupy the three or four following chapters; in which the worthlessness of lords and attornies might be set forth, and conversations, which had passed twenty years before, be minutely repeated. (*NA*: 34)

The expressed distaste for narrative recollection works on several levels: it doubts the relevance of the past (how much do we care about "the worthlessness of lords and attornies"?), it doubts the accuracy of recollection (how could 20-year-old conversations be minutely recollected without invention?), and it doubts our interest in its details. Situated resolutely in the present, Austen's novels at least formally refuse the luxury of retrospection in favor of a mode of *summary*. As a narrative preference, Austen's dislike for flashback narration has been at least as influential as those other techniques – free indirect discourse, omniscient narration – with which she is so often credited.

Thematically, the cancellation of the past is even more patent, particularly in the therapeutic treatment given Marianne Dashwood, Austen's most prototypically eighteenth-century nostalgic. While the objects of her regret change – from Norland, her childhood home, to Barton Cottage, the scene of her failed courtship with the rake Willoughby – their manner is consistent: an attachment to the details of the past. "I love to be reminded of the past, Edward," she tells her sister Elinor's suitor, "and you will never offend me by talking of former times" (*SS*: 92). A catalogue of objects that tether her to the past – her piano, old drawings, remembered landscapes – become cherished occasions for indulging in what is clearly physically harmful as well as mentally enfeebling. Marianne's eventual, near-fatal disease is, after all, occasioned by her desire to walk alone, savoring her regret. Not "nostalgia" in the strict sense – it is never named by the novel – Marianne's disease nonetheless bears all the marks of its eighteenth-century, pathological character, including a climactic fever. Her recovery under the hands of her sister Elinor results in a remarkable self-chastening in regards to memory: "As for Willoughby," Marianne proclaims, "to say that I shall soon or that I shall ever forget him, would be idle. His remembrance can be overcome by no change of circumstances or opinions. But it shall be regulated, it shall be checked by religion, by reason, by constant employment" (*SS*: 347). This is a direct echo of Samuel Johnson's recommendation that "the safe and general antidote against sorrow, is employment" (Bate and Strauss 1969: 257). Moving the mind forward – toward the potential, toward work, toward the future-directed – is seen as a healthier mental process than retrospection, which requires "regulation."

This is not to say that recollection is entirely or always harmful in Austen's work. In fact, Austen's later novels are rife with prescriptions for the precise manner in which a debilitating concentration on the detail of the past – which might be called regret, sorrow, or medical "nostalgia" – might become a much more pleasurable, and vaguer, form of recollection, one that exemplifies the contemporary definition of "nostalgia." The most famous of these moments is from *Pride and Prejudice*, in a summarizing conversation between Elizabeth and Darcy, in which Darcy attempts to apologize in detail for his previous conduct to her, including the hurtful, if self-exculpatory, letter that he had sent her explaining his actions. Elizabeth forestalls his recourse to detail with a declaration of independence from the past:

> The feelings of the person who wrote, and the person who received it, are now so widely different from what they were then, that every unpleasant circumstance attending it, ought to be forgotten. You must learn some of my philosophy. Think only of the past as its remembrance gives you pleasure. (*PP*: 368–9)

Elizabeth's wisdom is the wisdom of contemporary nostalgia. Remembering the past fondly or pleasurably implies a complex combination of mental acts: invoking the past in order to cancel it, particularly its negative aspects; replacing forgiveness with forgetfulness; seeing oneself as standing on one side of an abyss which separates past from present. This is remembrance under the sign of oblivion. It is clearly a solution to the problem of "sorrow" as Johnson described it. It is also signally unconcerned with the "truth" of the past. Whether or not Darcy's letter was hurtful – even if, a skeptical reader might say, rereading the novel would show it clearly was – that past "truth" is less important than the exigency, in the present, of remembering it fondly and vaguely, of transforming the past into a mythic communal story. Thus, perhaps, the peculiar efficacy of Austen's endings, where happiness arising out of misunderstandings and conflict can be achieved with such seeming effortlessness. That effortlessness is in fact the effort of nostalgia, an effort whose greatest talent is the ability to hide itself.

Austen seems to use Elizabeth here to advocate a careful vagueness of recollection that neither Austen-Leigh's many details, nor Chapman's antique illustrations, nor the historical contextualization of contemporary critics would satisfy. If most historical work of late-twentieth-century academic criticism is, consciously or not, antinostalgic – motivated to reveal the hidden pains, sufferings, and errors that nostalgic readers would perhaps prefer to remain ignorant of – the kind of nostalgic supplement offered by Austen-Leigh or Chapman's editions are equally, if more surprisingly, distant from Austenian nostalgia. The version of memory recommended by Elizabeth posits a happy past but stops short of any desire to fully inhabit it; at the end of their conversation, "they found at last, on examining their watches, that it was time to be home" (*PP*: 370). Home, that is, in the present moment signified by those watches, away from the messy details of the past: nostalgia here is a "homesickness" whose purpose is creating present-tense homes. Delving into the detail of that past world, through the material objects and practices that surround so much of Austen's contemporary reception, courts regret and unhappiness in the present in the manner of Marianne. Academic historicization and popular supplementation both, it seems, court the details of the past, one to disenchant, the other to license, our desire to know a better world than the present one; Austen's novels themselves seem to warn us from either position, telling us to beware of what we will find in our efforts at recollection. This is not a consoling lesson for either the academic or popular reader: it would seem that Austen provokes a desire for getting at the detail of the past that she also strenuously rejects.

FURTHER READING

Austin, Linda (2007). *Nostalgia in Transition, 1780–1917*. Charlottesville: University of Virginia Press.

Boym, Svetlana (2001). *The Future of Nostalgia*. New York: Basic Books.

Dames, Nicholas (2001). *Amnesiac Selves: Nostalgia, Forgetting, and British Fiction*, New York: Oxford University Press.

Galperin, William (2003). *The Historical Austen.* Philadelphia: University of Pennsylvania Press.

Johnson, Claudia (2000). The divine Miss Jane: Jane Austen, Janeites, and the discipline of novel studies. In Deidre Lynch (Ed.), *Janeites: Austen's Disciples and Devotees* (pp. 25–44). Princeton, NJ: Princeton University Press.

Stewart, Susan (1993). *On Longing: Narratives of the Miniature, the Gigantic, the Souvenir, the Collection.* Durham, NC: Duke University Press.

37

Austen's European Reception

Anthony Mandal

As with her responses towards many things, Jane Austen's attitude towards Europe was an ambivalent one, and we can only speculate what her reaction to her 190-year-long presence on the mainland might have been. There is evidence of some excitement facetiously expressed by Austen at the potential passage of Alexander I of Russia through the Alton road in 1814, when she admonished her sister: "do not be trampled to death in running after the Emperor" (*Letters*: 263). The few direct comments she makes typically draw forth comparisons between the Continent and England, with Europe often found to be lacking. Having met a French nobleman in 1811, Austen commented that he had "quiet manners, good enough for an Englishman . . . if he wd but speak english *I* would take to him" (*Letters*: 185). Similarly, she singled out Sweden for praise, feeling it to be "so zealous in its Protestan[t]ism," "more like England than many Countries," "many of the names have a strong resemblance to the English" (*Letters*: 215). Towards the end of her life, Austen commented that her niece Anna's brother-in-law "is come back from France, thinking of the French as one cd wish, disappointed in everything" (p. 321).

Of course, the main litmus of Austen's perception of Europe is to be found in her novels, which amplify the opinions set down in her letters. The use of European words is shown to reveal modish affectation and moral vacuity: one need only think of Mrs Elton's "caro sposo" and its variants, Mr Parker's "cottage ornèe" (*sic*) and Knightley and Emma's discussion of Frank Churchill's being *"ami*able" or *"aim*able." In *Mansfield Park*, *Lovers' Vows*, the melodrama adapted from the play by the German radical August von Kotzebue, adumbrates familial unrest and inappropriate liaisons, culminating in the elopement of Henry Crawford and Maria Rushworth. And, lest we forget, the hero of Austen's last completed novel, *Persuasion*, makes *his* fortune at the expense of the French navy. More telling than any of these, however, is Austen's *Emma*, written at the climax of the Napoleonic wars, which juxtaposes the "true English gentleman," George Knightley, with the Francophilic interloper, *Frank* Churchill. In a crucial passage, Austen establishes a dichotomy between the liberality of England (metonymically realized as Donwell Abbey) and "Elsewhere" (in this context Napoleonic Europe), in her apostrophe to "English verdure, English culture, English comfort, seen under a sun bright, without being oppressive."

In this context, Austen is undoubtedly one of the few Anglophone writers whose quintessential "Englishness" encodes a vital element of her fiction. This Englishness has played a significant role in sustaining Austen's popularity for over two centuries, particularly in the "heritage market" that has bloomed in Britain and North America since the late twentieth century. While this Anglo-American "Austenmania" has been explored in depth, the effects of Austen's Englishness on her European reception have remained relatively underexamined, with scholars offering necessarily limited accounts of Austen's engagements with the mainland. In fact, a more complete image of her European reception is only now beginning to emerge, marked recently by a collection of essays anthologized in *The Reception of Jane Austen in Europe* (Mandal and Southam 2007). In many ways, the present chapter offers a distillation of the research contained within that volume, summarizing the findings in three key areas: translation activity, critical traditions, and the recent film and screen adaptations, which have had an impact not only in Britain and Hollywood, but as far afield as Bollywood.

Translations

Before moving on to a detailed account of European translations of Austen's works across 28 discrete cultural and linguistic boundaries, it might be useful to offer some broad brushstrokes of my own in order to contextualize the reception of this author's own "little bit (two Inches wide) of Ivory." Of course, translations are not the sole gauge of an author's reception, as evidenced by the various allusions to Austen's novels in texts as far removed from her England as Pushkin's *Eugene Onegin* (1823–31) and Tolstoy's *Anna Karenina* (1873–7). What quantifiable data regarding the translations can offer, however, are clear insights into the permeation, and therefore the popularity, of Austen's oeuvre among general readers in Europe.

The years 1813 to 2005 encapsulate the first translation of Austen's work (*Pride and Prejudice* into French) to the latest year for which there exists a complete enough bibliographical record. As Table 37.1 makes clear, *Pride and Prejudice* represents the most translated of Austen's works throughout this period. While Austen received only 16 translations during the nineteenth century, Figure 37.1 graphically illustrates the spectacular rise in translation activity surrounding Austen's works between 1905 and 2004. It becomes immediately apparent that there are two key moments in the translation of Austen's works. The first, centering on 1945–9, saw the issuing of 44 new translations, and can be seen principally as a result of the postwar restructuring of the mainland. The incipient formulation of a pan-European cultural identity drew attention towards Austen as a consequence of general interest in Britain among former wartime allies and opponents alike. Even more marked than this, however, is the proliferation of titles during 1995–9 that occurred in the wake of the various screen

Table 37.1 Translations of Austen's titles, by period

Title	1813–1900	1901–1945	1946–1990	1991–2005	1813–2005
Pride and Prejudice	4 (3.5%)	18 (15.7%)	67 (58.3%)	26 (22.6%)	115 (27.7%)
Emma	2 (12.5%)	8 (16.3%)	34 (16.8%)	24 (16.3%)	68 (16.4%)
Sense and Sensibility	2 (12.5%)	7 (14.3%)	25 (12.4%)	25 (17.0%)	59 (14.2%)
Persuasion	4 (25.0%)	8 (16.3%)	28 (13.9%)	17 (11.6%)	57 (13.7%)
Northanger Abbey	2 (12.5%)	5 (10.2%)	23 (11.4%)	14 (9.5%)	44 (10.6%)
Mansfield Park	2 (12.5%)	2 (94.1%)	13 (6.4%)	18 (12.2%)	35 (8.5%)
Other works	0 (0.0%)	1 (2.0%)	12 (5.9%)	24 (16.3%)	37 (8.9%)
Total translations	16	49	202	148	415

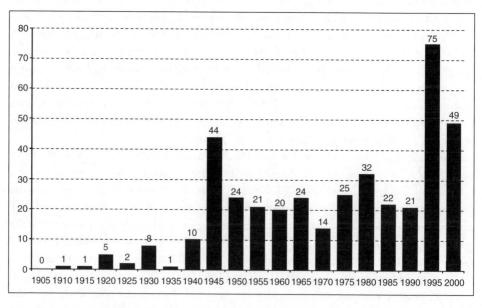

Figure 37.1 Output of new translations of Austen's works, 1905–2004 (excluding extracts, reprints, reissues)

adaptations. In contrast to the postwar period, this activity can be seen as a result of a direct interest in the author herself, particularly through the opening up of the borders of former Eastern Bloc countries, which constitute a large proportion of the 55 new translations published between 2000 and 2005 alone.

During the postwar period, the broader patterns that we recognize today in Austen's reception were established, with new translations of the six novels for 1946–90 quadrupling those of the preceding 45 years (202 to 49). As Figure 37.1 makes clear, however, it was during the mid-1990s that Austenmania profoundly affected Austen's European presence, with output of new translations of the novels during 1991–2005 (148) approaching that of the previous 45 years (202). Reflecting the influence of the film and screen adaptations, Table 37.1 quantifies the popular enthusiasm for *Pride and Prejudice*, followed by *Sense and Sensibility* and *Emma*. A significant factor of the last 15 years has been the heightened interest in Austen's minor works and correspondence, evidenced by the notable presence of translations of the juvenilia, *Lady Susan*, *The Watsons*, and *Sanditon* (24 translations). Such activity, which continues to produce increasingly nuanced editions of established favorites while simultaneously attending to the lesser-known works, suggests a long-lived and dynamic future for Jane Austen in Europe as the twenty-first century unfolds.

Translation activity on the Continent can also be considered through the treatment of Austen's novels across the individual nations: Table 37.2 summarizes the total number of new translations of Austen's works by language, along with details of first publication. Perhaps surprisingly, this most "English" of authors has found fertile ground principally in Mediterranean soil (Spain, Italy, France). Austen has been relatively well served in Germany, the Netherlands, and Portugal, while Romania and Poland evidence a slightly diminished presence. By contrast, Scandinavia, the Balkans, Russia, and the Baltic States have experienced rather limited encounters with Austen (despite early translations in Sweden and Denmark).

During the nineteenth century, Austen's European presence was relatively restricted, with her works being only translated into four languages (French, German, Danish, Swedish). Nevertheless, her works were circulated around Europe in Anglophone versions, both in editions with a British provenance and through enterprises such as Bentley's collaboration with the Parisian firm of Galignani in 1833, as well as Tauchnitz's German "Collection of British Authors" (1864–77). Furthermore, the complex polyglot interactions of the mainland ensured that translations were not confined to national boundaries, so that Francophone editions of Austen's works made their way to the Netherlands and Sweden, while Swedish-language versions themselves appeared in Finland. Similarly, Hungarian repositories hold various nineteenth-century copies of *Sense and Sensibility*, *Mansfield Park*, and *Emma* published in English and French, while Italian library catalogues list Tauchnitz's Anglophone editions amongst their holdings.

Austen's appearance in Europe occurred within her own lifetime, beginning with the translation of *Pride and Prejudice* in 1813, which was excerpted across four successive issues of the Swiss monthly periodical *Bibliothèque britannique*, less than six months

Table 37.2 Total Number of New Translations per European Language, 1813–2005

Language	Total	First title translated
Spanish	73	*Persuasion* (1919)
Italian	60	*Pride and Prejudice* (1932)
French	40	*Pride and Prejudice* (1813 extracts), *Sense and Sensibility* (1815)
German	32	*Persuasion* (1822)
Dutch	22	*Sense and Sensibility* (1922)
Portuguese	21	*Sense and Sensibility* (1943)
Greek	21	*Pride and Prejudice* (1950)
Romanian	19	*Pride and Prejudice* (1943)
Polish	16	*Sense and Sensibility* (1934)
Swedish	11	*Persuasion* (1836)
Czech	11	*Sense and Sensibility* (1932)
Danish	10	*Sense and Sensibility* (1835–6)
Estonian	10	*Pride and Prejudice* (1985)
Finnish	9	*Pride and Prejudice* (1922)
Serbian	9	*Persuasion* (1929)
Norwegian	8	*Pride and Prejudice* (1939)
Bulgarian	8	*Pride and Prejudice* (1980)
Hungarian	7	*Pride and Prejudice* (1934–6)
Russian	7	*Pride and Prejudice* (1967)
Slovak	6	*Pride and Prejudice* (1968)
Slovene	5	*Sense and Sensibility* (1951 extracts), *Sense and Sensibility* (1968)
Catalan	5	*Pride and Prejudice* (1985)
Latvian	5	*Pride and Prejudice* (2000)
Croat	3	*Emma* (1962)
Icelandic	2	*Pride and Prejudice* (1956)
Lithuanian	2	*Emma* (1997)
Basque	1	*Pride and Prejudice* (1996)
Galician	1	*Pride and Prejudice* (2005)

after its original British appearance that January. Further translations into French followed rapidly, so that by 1824 all six novels had been fully translated into at least one language. German translators followed suit fairly promptly (*Persuasion*, 1822; *Pride and Prejudice*, 1830), while a Swedish *Persuasion* appeared in 1836. Following this initial burst of activity, however, nineteenth-century translations of Austen became more drawn out: a Danish *Sense and Sensibility* and a Swedish *Emma* appeared at mid-century, to be followed towards the end of the century by two Francophone renditions (*Persuasion*, 1882; *Emma*, 1898). As Valérie Cossy and Diego Saglia note: "The main distorting factors in the early diffusion of her work were the relative marginalisation of women writers, but also the predominance of Walter Scott, whose name was synonymous with the 'English' novel for Continental readers" (2005: 170). This is borne out by the sheer weight of translation that Scott enjoyed, commencing in 1810 with the first translations of individual poems (Germany, 1810) and book-length pieces (France, 1813), and sustained throughout the nineteenth century with new translations appearing virtually on an annual basis (see Pittock 2006: xxiv–lxxiv).

Early translators of Austen enjoyed high literary reputations of their own and were popular novelists, whose own works had been translated into English. Most notable among them were Isabelle de Montolieu, the Swiss-French translator of *Sense and Sensibility* (*Raison et sensibilité*, 1815) and *Persuasion* (*La Famille Elliot, ou l'ancienne inclination*, 1821), and Wilhelm Adolf Lindau, German translator of *Persuasion* (*Anna, ein Familiengemählde*, 1822). Occasionally, however, these writers' sense of their own authorly credentials influenced their translations of Austen's originals. For instance, Montolieu's application of the same sentimental apparatus used in her own novels diminishes the polyvalent richness of *Sense and Sensibility*: not only are the more domestically inflected scenes cut from Austen's original, but episodes of a more "pathetic" nature are inserted or existing scenes are "heightened" emotionally, resulting in a text that more fully approximates the novel of sensibility – Austen's object of satire in the first place! Other translators, such as Carl Karup (who rendered *Sense and Sensibility* into Danish, as *Forstand og hjerte*, 1855–6) and Félix Fénéon (translator of *Northanger Abbey* into French, as *Catherine Morland*, 1898), were accomplished belletrists, who approached Austen from very different, but nevertheless erudite, perspectives. Karup was a Catholic propagandist and Fénéon an avant-garde anarchist: hardly the likeliest candidates for translators of Austen's domestic comedies. Yet both men prepared accurate renditions of Austen's originals. There is also the provenance of these translations to consider: for instance, Emilia Westdahl's Swedish translation of *Persuasion* (*Familjen Elliot: skildringar af engelska karakterer*, 1836) was based on Montolieu's *La Famille Elliot*, which itself contains a number of "heightened" and interpolated scenes. Hence, the question arises: to what extent can a translation of a translation render accurately the author's work?

The relative neglect of Austen in translation during the nineteenth century was redressed during the twentieth, which saw translations of Austen commence in earnest from the 1920s onwards. As Table 37.2 demonstrates, Austen was translated for the first time into a large number of languages during the interwar period. This period of activity culminated in the heightened output that followed World War II, decisively fixing Austen's presence on the mainland. A total of 44 new translations appeared during 1945–9 (20 of these in 1945 alone), with the majority published in Spanish (14) and French (12). As suggested earlier, a general postwar drift towards a pan-Europeanism (albeit a schismatic one that can be traced across the so-called "Iron Curtain") resulted in an increased interest in British culture and literature – particularly in the case of France, which sought a closer acquaintance with the literature of its former allies. Nevertheless, there were also more localized causes for the interest in Austen. In Finland, all six novels were published in new translations between 1947 and 1954, three of them as part of "The great novels of the world" series. In the partitioned Germany, Austen fulfilled East German ideological criteria regarding female emancipation and capitalist exploitation, which led to a more systematic approach to translation than in West Germany. The first introduction of Austen to Greece, *Pride and Prejudice* (*Perifania kai prokatalipsi*, 1950), resulted from collaboration between the Greek firm Ikaros and the British Council. Transformations in cultural attitudes also heralded an increased interest in Austen, when long-standing Danish Anglophobia was succeeded by postwar Anglophilia, which arose from a shared war against a common enemy and Denmark's desire to distance itself from German influences. In summarizing these developments, it seems fair to say that Austen's mid-century European appearance arose from a serendipitous combination of cultural circumstances, ideological imperatives and straightforward promotion.

The first full translations of Austen appeared across parts of Eastern Europe during the 1960s (Croatia 1962, Russia 1967, Slovenia 1968), while in 1975, the bicentenary of Austen's birth, Serbia issued a six-volume collected works, which ran to 10,000 copies that sold out by August 1977. Hungarian reprints of *Pride and Prejudice* (1979) and *Sense and Sensibility* (1980) were published in even larger numbers (75,000 and 65,000 respectively). The early 1980s were marked by French translations of the minor works, as well as increased Dutch activity. Although Russia had been a relative latecomer to Austen, by the end of the 1980s this oversight was addressed by the appearance of Ekaterina Genieva's *Complete Novels* (*Sobranie sochinenii v trekh tomakh*) in three volumes. In contrast to their antecedents in the nineteenth and early twentieth century, translations from this later period were more systematic, often the work of the same, skilled figures – typically academics or professional translators.

Between 1995 and 2004, no fewer than 124 new translations appeared across Europe, the increase in numbers matched by an increase in quality. For example, the French recognition of Austen as a literary "classic" is indicated by the inclusion of her collected works in Gallimard's prestigious Pléiade series (beginning in 2000), edited by the leading Austen scholar in France, Pierre Goubert. The Greek publishers Smili released translations of the six novels between 1996 and 2003, in a heavily annotated edition. Many recent versions have been prepared by the same translators with either an academic or personal interest in Austen, such as Elke Meiborg (Netherlands), Angelika Beck (Germany), Merete Alfsen (Norway), Ana Maria Rodríguez (Spain), and Stefania Censi (Italy). In the reunified Germany, where Austen was once the province of specialists and devotees, she now seems to be drawing attention from a wider readership through the large number of reissues that have appeared since the 1990s. The Danish mass-market publishers Lindhardt & Ringhof bought the copyrights to earlier translations of *Pride and Prejudice*, *Emma*, and *Persuasion*, repackaging them with covers bearing stills from the films. Austen's popularity is similarly evidenced in neighboring Sweden, in the sales figures for paperback translations issued by Månpocket, a budget publisher: *Pride and Prejudice* (1996), 18,988; *Emma* (1997), 14,025; *Northanger Abbey* (2001), 10,115 – a normal print run for classics at Månpocket is 7,000.

Nevertheless, popularity does not always guarantee quality: in Spain, for instance, the majority of translations seem hastily prepared works directed towards a mass readership, excepting three fresh translations issued by the Madrid publishers Cátedra. Similarly, Pierre Goubert's Pléiade edition is countered by a 1996 reprint of Madame de Montolieu's "free" translation of 1815, so that the film adaptation adheres more closely to Austen's original than the 1996 translation! Recent Italian translations, more rushed than their predecessors to meet a growing public taste, present hybrid texts that elide vital social distinctions of the time while utilizing archaic Italian grammar in order to supply a "period" feel. Despite such deficiencies, the quality of European translations is on the increase, and the commercial promise offered by Austen to the twenty-first-century market has secured her presence authoritatively throughout the European mainland.

Criticism

Of course, Austen was not only received in Europe through translations, but in a variety of other forums: brief reviews, surveys of literature, encyclopedia entries, and textbook anthologies. As early as 1816, early commentators in France, Germany, and Russia singled out Austen's "purity," "morality," and domestic focus as the paradigmatic components of her fiction. In France, where Austen received the most sustained critical attention, she garnered praise from commentators such as Philarète Chasles (1842) and Hippolyte Taine (1863–4) as "a new kind" of novelist for her pictures of domestic manners. Nonetheless, she remained overshadowed by Scott and, to a lesser extent, Burney, Edgeworth, and Radcliffe. Seen as a moralist, even a "puritan," the overarching image of Austen that emerges is blandly didactic and humorless. Later in the century, attention was drawn to her detailed psychological portraiture and use of dialogue (Boucher 1878), but critics continued to overlook her irony and humor. By the *fin de siècle*, however, Austen received more considered attention, especially for her use of language in rendering character, with Théodore Duret observing significantly that Austen "is now universally regarded as one of the great English writers" (1898: 278).

Despite these minor incursions into the European consciousness during the nineteenth century, Austen remained essentially unrecognized. As in Britain, a key reason for this neglect was the dominance of the historical novel pioneered by Sir Walter Scott. Another significant factor lay in the sociopolitical convolutions on the mainland, which often led to the Scottian model favored above other, more domestic fictional forms. For instance, in Flanders, Greece, Finland, and Slovenia, the desire to establish national and cultural sovereignty was articulated through more overtly polemical forms of fiction than *romans de moeurs*. It wasn't simply political convulsions *within* nations that preempted Austen's reception in nineteenth-century Europe: conflicts *between* nations also interrupted any meaningful interchange (for instance, nineteenth-century Danish Anglophobia). In other cases, aesthetic rather than ideological factors that interposed: for example, Austen's ironic perspective did not accord with Swedish perceptions of novels by "English lady novelists" – this in a country that saw two of her novels translated by 1857. Similarly, the partitioned Poland of the nineteenth century, which drew its aesthetic inspiration from France and held the novel in low esteem, hardly formed a theatre conducive to Austen's productions. Finally, Austen seems not to have reached some European shores (such as Croatia and Norway) during the nineteenth century simply because she was unknown.

During the twentieth century, however, Austen's status in Europe was consolidated by a number of studies penned by commentators from the mainland. Early in the century, discussions of Austen were typically influenced by Anglo-American approaches, with articles often translating Anglophone pieces verbatim (sometimes without acknowledgement). Nonetheless, as early as the 1910s, France and Italy began generating their own assessments, which drew meaningful attention to Austen's sense of irony and depth of characterization. For instance, Rague and Rague noted that Austen's "comparisons are rare, but exact. She does not shower adjectives on us: those she selects perfectly particularise their object" (1914: 148). This precision, however, should not be confused with miniaturism: an argument taken up by Emilio Cecchi, who rejected the paradigmatic correlation between Austen's writing and Flemish painting, arguing instead that "everything pulses with a clean dynamism that redeems minuteness" so that "a curious stylistic joy is never absent" (1915: 233–4). Danish commentators emphasized Austen's incisive social commentary as the defining trait of her fiction (Brusendorff 1928–30), while Dutch studies discussed Austen's literary style (rather than subject matter) and attempted to contextualize her against native literary traditions (De Haan 1935).

Nevertheless, Austen's early-twentieth-century critics fixed her writing within very restricted parameters, in paternalistic accounts that emphasized her "smallness," "grotesque" narrowness, and "innocent wit," as evidenced by responses in Norway (Bing 1929: 246–8), Italy (Caprin 1932: 8), and Hungary (Szerb 1973: 499). Nearly 20 years later, Austen's supposedly limited scope was seen as grounds for depreciation, so that one Polish commentator describes *Pride and Prejudice* as "a stereotypical romance . . . sprinkled with a tender, sentimental sauce" (Michalski 1957: 7). Even if Austen's ironic power had been acknowledged during the early twentieth century, critics often found it difficult to move beyond her benevolent humor, gentle comedy, and her miniaturist approach.

At mid-century, Austen's focus on decorum and her precise depictions of social hierarchies were sometimes perceived as antediluvian by egalitarian democracies such as 1950s Finland. By contrast, Greek scholarship welcomed Austen's arrival into the national literary consciousness, nevertheless modulating its praise with chauvinistic perspectives about women's writing. During the 1950s and 1960s, Austen was placed within an Augustan tradition by scholars writing in Hungary, Poland, Romania, and Slovenia, in studies which underscored her stylistic innovation and ironic sense. More generally, Communist analysis of Austen interpreted her through the prism of socialist realism, paradigmatically representing her as an author limited by her parochial, feminine focus and lack of social critique. In the 1970s, Italian scholarship analyzed Austen's stylistic methods and parodic approach in detail, whereas other European critics found Austen's position in literary history difficult to fix: as a Neoclassicist, a Romantic, a Victorian realist – and none of these. Often, the only response to such a paradox was to describe what Austen is *not*.

The later twentieth century witnessed a more sustained consideration of Austen's oeuvre, mainly as a result of wider ideological and cultural imperatives. For instance, East German, Hungarian, and Slovene scholarship perceived Austen's realism and focus on female marginalization as useful in promoting socialist policies and demonstrating the inadequacies of capitalist regimes. The rise of the women's movement from the 1960s onwards appears to have galvanized further translations and critical attention, culminating in a number of Danish and Norwegian reconsiderations of Austen's significance to both world literature and feminist issues. A key turning-point in Austen's Russian reception, coincidental with the height of *glasnost*, was signaled by the publication of Ekaterina Genieva's biobibliographial index of Austen (1986), which anticipated her single-handed translation of all six novels in 1988–9. The net result of these developments is a gradual increase in Austen's critical standing on, and a recognition of her broader sociocultural significance to, the Continent.

Discussions of Austen since the 1990s have underscored her status as an author of world classics, whose canonical position and popular appeal go hand in hand. In nations where she was relatively neglected until recently (for instance, Norway), she is now considered the most significant female novelist of the nineteenth century. Recent scholarship pays closer attention to the historical and literary contexts within which Austen wrote, as well as her use of language and, unsurprisingly, the issue of screen adaptation. More recently, a transgressive, carnivalesque Austen has been excavated by Spanish scholarship (Díaz Bild 1998), while Hungarian (Séllei 1999) and Polish criticism (Dobosiewicz 1997) observe how the Austenian obsession with marriage implicitly interrogates the marginalization of women.

Despite the influence of feminist criticism on European scholarship, a number of commentators still portray Austen's novels as escapist love stories, commonly comparing her writing to modern-day Harlequin/Mills and Boon romances. Nevertheless, other writers point to the ironized separation between the Austenian author and narrator/protagonist, which opens up her novels to polemical readings. As with Anglo-American perspectives, two views of Austen currently hold sway: she is either a conservative advocate of existing orthodoxies or a subversive critic of her world. A Janus-like figure, Austen draws us back to a bygone era of manners and morality, while propelling us forward towards continued female emancipation. In this context, a promising development is the sheer activity emanating from countries such as Italy, which recently hosted a groundbreaking international conference on Austen (Battaglia and Saglia 2004).

Influence of Films and Screen Adaptations

From the 1990s onwards, there has been a veritable explosion of "Austenmania," and this exponential growth in attention can be seen as arising undoubtedly from the phenomenal success of the screen adaptations of the mid-1990s. Nevertheless, other cultural stimuli can also be perceived as opening up previously restricted borders. The collapse of socialist ideology, which had dominated the Eastern Bloc since the end of

World War II, is a key factor in this. Postsocialist Croatia and Hungary offer useful examples, in which Austen's *classedness* (always a problem for socialist criticism) was transformed into *classiness*, framed by the newly reintroduced discourse of capitalism. As a result, an era of responsiveness towards Western European culture coincided with the remarketing of Austen through film and television, which extended her work to new audiences, and beyond the fringes of Anglo-American discourse.

The abundance of films and television serializations has accelerated Austen's status across the mainland, as well as generating a large number of fresh and reprinted translations. For instance, in the Netherlands, following the theatrical release of Douglas McGrath's *Emma* (1996), four translations were published in the same year, only two of which were new. In Germany, following the screening of Ang Lee's *Sense and Sensibility* in 1996, 10 editions appeared that year, with only two offering new translations. A number of editions employed stills from the films on their covers, in order to market the books. While the adaptations have generated dramatically increased interest in Austen, in some countries (such as Norway) this phenomenon seems to have been short-lived, while in others (Hungary) Austen has since been included in the top hundred "best reads." In the wake of McGrath's *Emma*, Croatian and Slovene readers were advised in the Slovene newspaper *Delo*, "If you've never read Austen's *Emma*, don't admit it in public," clearly emblematizing Austen as a legitimizing trope for cultural consumption.

The popularity of the screen adaptations is testified to by the repeated prime-time scheduling of the films on television channels over the past decade. Aside from the increased circulation of Austen in print, the main response to the films has appeared in newspaper reviews. Commentators are generally happy with the adaptations, although some refer to their "blandness," "vapidity," and lack of depth, advocating readers to return to the original texts. A number of reviews praise the accuracy and attractiveness of the sets, while others judge the psychological nuances of Austen's writing as lost in adaptation. In Sweden, the success of the films led to a televised interview with Elinor Wikberg in 1998, which asked: "Why is Jane Austen so popular?" Perhaps a more salient question is, now that the films have led to increased translations, have they led to Austen being *read* more, as opposed to being *watched* more? In many cases, the answer is no: since the screen adaptations are readily available, many younger viewers feel little urgency to acquaint themselves with the novels themselves. Despite the popularity of the films and serials (or perhaps because of them), Austen's typical readership in Europe remains relatively small, while the adaptations distill a less polyvalent version of the stories for a mass audience, a version which is absorbed by the mass-cultural category of "costume drama."

Conclusion

This chapter started by citing Austen's negative opinion towards Europe. Despite such prejudice, however, she surely would have taken some pride in witnessing the interest in her writing that has blossomed across the mainland over the last century. Over the years, Austen was circulated and received in a variety of different ways, in a variety of different climates. Following her nineteenth-century neglect, Austen's fortunes in Europe have steadily improved since the mid-twentieth century, culminating with the pan-European (not to mention, trans-Atlantic) "Austenmania" of the mid-1990s. At times, her reception has been a convoluted one, especially when Austen's ironic perspective and delicate characterization have been overlooked or misread. Nevertheless, as the years have progressed, European responses have become increasingly nuanced and attuned to the multivocal nature of her writing. Despite a meager presence during the nineteenth century, the attention given to Austen (at times, the Austenmania) on the Continent establishes that her "Englishness" – the issue with which this chapter began – has functioned less as a barrier than a point of interest for European readers and scholars. As the twenty-first century unfolds, more than any other single factor, the phenomenal success of the recent screen adaptations has played no small part in ensuring that Austen occupies a much-deserved position as one of the leading lights in today's canon of world literature.

FURTHER READING

Cossy, Valérie and Diego Saglia (2005). Translations. In Janet Todd (Ed.). *Jane Austen in Context* (pp. 169–81). Cambridge, UK: Cambridge University Press.

Garside, Peter and Anthony Mandal (1999). Jane Austen (1775–1817). In Joanne Shattock (Ed.). *The Cambridge Bibliography of English Literature, Volume IV: 1800–1900* (cols. 869–83). Cambridge, UK: Cambridge University Press.

Gilson, David (1997). *A Bibliography of Jane Austen*, Section C: Translations. Winchester, UK: St Paul's Bibliographies and New Castle, DE: Oak Knoll Press.

Gilson, David (2003). Jane Austen and Europe. *The Book Collector*, 23, 31–45.

Mandal, Anthony and Brian Southam (Eds) (2007). *The Reception of Jane Austen in Europe*. London and New York: Continuum.

Wright, Andrew (1975). Jane Austen abroad. In John Halperin (Ed.). *Jane Austen: Bicentenary Essays* (pp. 298–317). Cambridge, UK: Cambridge University Press.

38

Jane Austen and the Silver Fork Novel

Edward Copeland

The usual story, that Jane Austen's novels in the 20 years after her death were a taste for the discerning few alone, needs to be brought into line with a more provocative one – that within 10 years of her death in 1817 her near contemporaries, the novelists of the 1820s and 1830s, were using her novels as a source for wholesale plunder. The publisher Henry Colburn initiated the taste, the "mania" as John Sutherland calls it (1986: 70), for these novels about fashionable life in London by issuing a spate of them in the mid-1820s which became known derisively as "the silver fork school." William Hazlitt supplied the name in *The Examiner* (November 18, 1827) where he mocked Thomas Hook's admiration of the aristocracy in *Sayings and Doings* (1824) because, "they eat their fish with a silver fork."

Colburn, an aggressive advertiser of his publications, promoted the novels as aristocratic *romans à clef* written by authors who were themselves members of fashionable society. His assumption was that these new novels about contemporary "exclusives" would ride on the popularity of such earlier works of Regency scandal as Caroline Lamb's *Glenarvon* (1816), with its tale of her affair with Byron, or even the courtesan Harriette Wilson's more recent *Memoirs* (1825), in which she revealed liaisons with the Duke of Wellington and other well-known contemporaries. Paradoxically, Colburn's expensive new three-volume novels (31 shillings) were not aimed at an aristocratic readership at all, as Sutherland perceptively notes, but towards the much greater profits to be found in sales to the circulating libraries and the borrowing practices of their middle-class patrons (1986: 79). In fact, Colburn's novels were implicitly as interested in middle-class culture as they were in the aristocratic lives that appeared to be more directly in their sights. There is a good reason for this. Silver fork novels flourished in the years just before and after the passage of the Great Reform Bill of 1832. The emerging complicity – political, social, and economic – between the middle class and the aristocracy in these years, expressed with varying degrees of clarity and confusion in the silver fork novels, may explain the general bemusement with which they were greeted simultaneously by critics both as the unreliable "froth" of aristocratic decadence and as conduct manuals for those classes aspiring to ape the manners and consumer habits of the *ton*.

We read along in these now obscure works to hear echoes of Jane Austen's novels in the most unexpected places. Willoughby's slighting remark about Colonel Brandon in *Sense and Sensibility* (p. 50) reappears with little alteration in Lady Charlotte Bury's *The Devoted* (1836): ". . . what sort of person is she? I am curious to know, for hitherto I have only heard of her as a woman whom everybody praises, but nobody seems to care for" (vol. II: 180). Edmund Bertram's disapproval of home theatricals surfaces in Catherine Gore's *Women As They Are* (1830) in words much like Edmund's own: "I will frankly own to you, that I am sorry to find Lady Willersdale and yourself among the theatrical group," says Lord Forreston, "All English women act ill – they are encumbered by their natural decency" (vol. III: 190). In Gore's next novel, *Mothers and Daughters* (1831), Fanny Price's East Room retreat is on view with few alterations in its decor or in the character of its occupant: "Cousin Mary – surrounded by her books, her work, her music, her easel, her flowers, her birds! . . . sufficing to her own amusement – yet ever ready to lay aside her favourite pursuits and preoccupations in order to contribute to the happiness of others" (vol. III: 32). Marianne Spencer Hudson invokes the celebrated barouche landau from *Emma* in her novel *Almack's* (1826), now transferred to the status parade of a newly titled Lady Birmingham – "One has not great hopes from Birmingham," as Mrs Elton herself admits (*E*: 310) – "'I think, my dear,' said Lady Birmingham to her spouse, 'you had better go in the donkey curricle, as you feel a little gouty this morning . . . Or suppose we were all to walk down to the bridge, the barouche landau with four horses could meet us there'" (I: 189).

Nevertheless, in spite of the frequency with which these bits and pieces from Austen's novels come into view, changes in the political and cultural landscapes of the 1820s and of the 1830s, in both pre- and post-Reform Bill years, make the spoils lifted from Austen's novels, including her plots, dialogue, and characters, appear oddly unfamiliar. Austen's keen focus on the subjective identity of her characters, in particular, the very quality that attracts us to her novels, is a matter of almost complete indifference to silver fork novelists. For these writers the public world of objects, of collective identities, of media-worthy social phenomena takes center stage. In effect, silver fork novelists simply saw a different "Jane Austen" from ours as they prowled her novels for literary booty.

In the first place, their novels belong to a newly established print culture, one utterly different from the cottage industry of amateur and professional authors that was in operation when Austen began her career. The new system, according to Jon Klancher's *The Making of English Reading Audiences*, was a recognizably modern and professionalized order, mainly male, of daily newspapers, quarterly journals, monthly magazines, and a highly organized means of book production and distribution (1987: 43, 50). The daily newspaper in particular, argues Jonathan Mulrooney, promoted new reading habits with far-ranging consequences (2002: 353, 357). The silver fork novel, for example, trades on its pretension to currency with the *Morning Post*'s

"Fashionable World," a relationship that provokes bitter complaint from a character in Catherine Gore's *Women As They Are* (1830): "Oh, as to an English modern novel . . . I hold its vulgarity and bad taste as secondary only to that of the columns of your newspapers after a drawing-room; – which announce to admiring Europe, that Lady Alberville wore a train of Pomona green" (vol. II: 133). Deidre Lynch suggests that silver fork novels have their closest kinship with the professionally genteel sub-literature of annuals, picturesque sketches, and other "exhibitionary forms" of the period, "that rendered characters, classes, locales, and bodies adamantly visible" (1998: 150). Gary Kelly, most notably, consigns the literary company of silver fork novels to the "unrereadable" to distinguish it from the eminently "rereadable" fiction of Jane Austen (1993: 211).

Arguably, the political obsessions of the 1820s and 1830s replace subjective identity as the central activity of the contemporary novel. With their authors' focus on public concerns, silver fork novels are conceived for purposes where, according to Dror Wahrman, "collective identities count most" (1995: 9). In the 1820s, for example, as pressure for Catholic emancipation began to stir British politics, silver fork novelists combed Austen's novels for the "collective" figure that as Henry Brougham told Lord Grey, best fitted the tactical requirement for reform: gentlemen who "want and ought to think for themselves" (cited by Newbould 1990: 14). After the passage of the 1832 Reform Bill and the development of a modern party system, silver fork novelists found in Austen's *Mansfield Park* a useful collective figure in Fanny Price, her character now metamorphosed from anxious moralist to political partisan.

The question as to why this vigorous predation on Jane Austen's work has been so little recognized is a reasonable one. It may be that the Victorians ignored Austen's service to her late-Regency followers as an awkward stumbling block to the respectable place they intended for her in the literary canon (Sales 1994: 4–10). Our own neglect may well be explained by the general amnesia that has always afflicted the period between the last of the Romantics and the first of the Victorians. Nevertheless, Austen's ghost life among the silver fork novels exposes not only an unexplored field of kinship presumed by their authors, but also something fresh about Austen's work: its striking political and cultural relevance to the age of reform.

Austen's dialogue seems to be the main attraction as a model for T. H. Lister's aristocratic exclusives. The politically charged message in his act of appropriation, of course, lies in the implicit assumption, one that Lister also stresses explicitly, that aristocrats share the same social and moral values as the genteel, but lesser ranks of Austen's characters. But for the women writers, especially Catherine Gore and Lady Charlotte Bury, it is Austen's attention to distinctions of rank, especially in her last three novels, that provokes their raids on her works. The strains in the 1820s between the traditional power brokers of political life and the emergence of a politicized "polite society," one much akin to Jane Austen's pool of characters, gave Austen's work a new focus. Bury and Gore, along with Lord Normanby and Marianne Spencer Hudson, find plots and characters in *Mansfield Park*, *Emma*, and *Persuasion* that enable them to explore the social jockeying of this nascent political order.

The silver fork debt to Jane Austen, in short, belongs to an "overlapping of historicities" that Deidre Lynch describes in her essay "At Home with Jane Austen," in which Austen's novels are "reseen," she says, "as a cultural site supportive of new invention" (1996: 163). When, for example, Austen writes about gradations of *rank* in *Pride and Prejudice*, "He is a gentleman; I am a gentleman's daughter; so far we are equal" (p. 356), novelists of the 1820s and 1830s, in a mode of "overlap" and with much the same terminology, write about differences of *class*. In fact the terms "class" and "rank" are frequently in a state of negotiation in the silver fork novel, an activity that Stuart Hall (1995) argues is the condition of political identity itself: "By *identity*, or *identities*," he writes, "I mean the processes that constitute and continuously re-form the subject who has to act and speak in the social and cultural world" (p. 65). Thus the "politics" of silver fork novels seldom consist of logical political propositions, but rather possess a kind of "*discursive* logic, a way of connecting one statement to another," with, as Hall writes, "the capacity to condense and display contradictory symbolisations in the same space" (p. 63).

The task that silver fork novelists set themselves is the representation of such "symbolisations" in a period in which they are being actively and anxiously rearranged. Tories, Whigs, liberal-leaning spirits, and raging reactionaries circulate in their novels in common conversational company – at the opera, at Almack's, in the clubs, and in the drawing-rooms of Mayfair. The implications of rank and class "overlap" one another with frequent and unapologetic confusion. As David Cannadine reminds us, the limited political concessions actually granted by the landed classes to other classes in 1832, rather than diminishing their political role, actually "renewed, re-created, and re-legitimated" them under the cover of "reform" (1995: 36). Nevertheless, the social and political stakes for the various and contradictory groups of "polite society" below the aristocracy, especially its nonlanded members, could not have seemed more pressing. As Linda Colley argues passionately in *Britons: Forging the Nation*, "reform" as opposed to "revolution" was still the great accomplishment of the period and a "politically perilous" achievement at that (2005: 344). In this hard-won victory silver fork novelists took an active hand, almost universally on the side of reform.

Although silver fork novels of the 1820s and 1830s depicted aristocrats with their glittering goods and all their privileges of rank, it was, as Gary Kelly observes, seldom to their credit (1989: 223). The challenging task for those novelists sympathetic to political reform, just as for Whig politicians, lay in "diminishing the unacceptable face of aristocratic power," not in relishing its excesses (Cannadine 1999: 79). This did not imply a whitewashing of faults, though sometimes contemporaries wondered, but involved the more ambitious effort of imagining a renewed role for the traditional governing classes. Norman Gash in *Aristocracy and People* makes the political point, one especially true of silver fork novels, that the period was not interested in the politics of civic measures, but in power itself – who was to have it, and who not (1979: 168).

Silver fork novelists, in effect, imported probity into the aristocracy by expanding the net of the governing classes, a close mirror of the Whig party's political rhetoric as described by Wahrman: first, by reviving the traditional designation of the gentry as "middle," thus shading an older power group downwards into the language field of the new aspiring one (1995: 14–15); second, by engaging the "middle-class idiom" of respectability as a language of social power; and finally, by putting this socially marked idiom into the mouths of promising aristocrats as clear evidence that they were on the road to reformation (p. 46). As Klancher observes, contemporary writers for political reform, and this, excepting Theodore Hook, would include most silver fork novelists, took on a grandly paradoxical task: imagining a renewed aristocratic society in which the British middle class could be affirmed in its "natural" right to move in the company of the governing classes (1987: 49).

In a typical example from the 1820s, Thomas Lister's Caroline Jermyn and Vincent Trebeck in *Granby* (1826) are sent to follow in the footsteps of Austen's Catherine Morland and Henry Tilney in *Northanger Abbey* (1818). Each couple is of nearly equal rank: Catherine Morland, the daughter of a clergyman of respectable means, is a social match for Henry Tilney, a clergyman with an "income of independence and comfort" (*NA*: 250); Caroline Jermyn, the daughter of a provincial baronet, ranks comparably with Vincent Trebeck, "the only son of a gentleman of good family, and handsome, though not large independent fortune" (vol. I: 88). The two men even look the same: Henry Tilney is "rather tall, had a pleasing countenance, a very intelligent and lively eye, and, if not quite handsome, was very near it" (*NA*: 25); Vincent Trebeck is "neither plain nor handsome, but there was an air of intelligence and subdued satire, and an intuitive quickness in his eye" (vol. I: 89). Each sets a tone of "archness and pleasantry" in his first meeting with the respective heroine, addressing her with a teasing mock-instructional lecture on the social duties of the occasion. Trebeck's introductory remarks to Caroline Jermyn echo Henry's lively ballroom banter with Catherine Morland in both tone and subject:

> "I'm afraid you are not aware of the full extent of your privileges, and are not conscious how many things young ladies can, and may, and will do."
>
> "Indeed I am not – perhaps you will instruct me."
>
> "Ah, I never do that for anybody . . . But, however, for once I will venture to tell you, that a very competent knowledge of the duties of women may, with proper attention, be picked up in a ball room." (Lister 1826, vol. I: 94–5)

Both gentlemen also push their luck, each lady puzzled to find her escort "so – strange." Henry Tilney: "'What are you thinking of so earnestly?' said he, as they walked back to the ball-room; – 'not of your partner, I hope, for, by that shake of the head, your meditations are not satisfactory'" (*NA*: 29). Vincent Trebeck: "Yes, I see you do not know exactly what to make of me – and you are not without your apprehensions. I can perceive that, though you try to conceal them. But never mind. I am a safe person to sit near – sometimes. I am to-day. This is one of my lucid intervals" (vol. I: 96–7). Yet despite all this similarity there remains one great difference: Henry is the hero of Austen's novel and Trebeck is the villain of Lister's – rejected by the heroine out-of-hand: "Yet she did not like him, and often wondered by what fatality it should have come to pass that a sort of confidence should exist between them; as he was decidedly the last person to whom she would voluntarily entrust a secret, and whom she would dare to rely on as a friend" (vol. I: 161–2). It is the politics, dear reader – the political culture of 1826.

Unlike Henry Tilney, a man contented with his rank as a clergyman, Vincent Trebeck has ambitions to rise above the class into which he has been born, "a gentleman's son," to enter the "exclusive" aristocratic circles of power. Caroline's supposed fortune is her attraction – he needs the money. Trebeck is thus a figure of arch villainy in the 1820s, an uncommitted political entrepreneur, an unscrupulous social riser, a character repeated in Disraeli's *Vivian Grey* (1826) and Bulwer's *Pelham* (1828). The push for Catholic emancipation in the 1820s and the expectation that greater constitutional reforms lay ahead made it painfully evident to liberal factions within both the governing Tories and the out-of-power Whigs that the support (or myth) of "enlightened disinterestedness" was essential to any hope for political reform (Mandler 1990: 37). Caroline Jermyn's suspicion of Trebeck's character describes a consummate politician: "There was a heartlessness in his character, a spirit of gay misanthropy, a cynical, depreciating view of society, an absence of high-minded generous sentiment, a treacherous versatility, and deep powers of deceit, to which not all his agreeable qualities and fashionable fame could effectually blind her" (vol. I: 161–2). Granby, the hero of the novel, is in contrast exactly that liberal-minded, uncommitted gentleman most admired by novelists (and by political essayists) as the key to parliamentary reform: a man of tested principle, a successful professional man (an army officer), an aristocrat-in-waiting who in the final chapters is elevated (for the good of the nation) to the Upper House.

The next major silver fork raid on Austen's novels took place in the political heat of 1832 itself, when two novels appeared in that year – Thomas Lister's *Arlington* and Catherine Gore's *The Opera* – in which the amateur theatricals from *Mansfield Park* are pressed into service to address public anxieties concerning the controversial Reform Bill. Lister's home theatre, his trope in *Arlington* for a corrupt aristocracy, produces a fairly pedestrian echo of the seductive behavior of Henry Crawford and Maria Bertram during the *Lovers' Vows* rehearsals, even to the point of including, as a likely nod to Austen, a morally lax Lady Crawford in the cast of characters (Gilson 2003: 40). The hero, Lord Arlington, mortified by the betrayal of the woman to whom he is engaged, retreats to his estate in the remote "North of England" to nurse his ego and read political philosophy until he is persuaded to assume his duties in the House of Lords, convinced of the institution's value as a "protection against fluctuations and violence" (vol. III: 212). The lesson: "It is to be regretted," says Arlington, "that they [the aristocracy] have exhibited too much supineness, and too little liberality" (vol. III: 213).

The theatrical trope in Catherine Gore's *The Opera* is far more complex and politically ingenious. Her characters engage in the production of a pastoral opera by Charles Favart (1710–92), one composed specifically for aristocratic home performance: *Annette et Lubin* (1762), conflated in the novel with a similar Favart piece, *Ninette à la cour* (1755), both featuring the tale of young peasant lovers whose plain-spoken passions triumph brilliantly over the oppression of local authorities. The pressing threat of violence among the working classes in England in the year of this novel, together with the recent 1830 revolution in France, impart an unsettling political resonance to her amateurs' choice for home production.

The intersecting ironies of the Favart opera and Gore's novel are closely modeled on those set in motion between *Lovers' Vows* and the action of *Mansfield Park*, though rather more highly painted. The hero, Adrian Maldyn, raised in exile in the Bavarian Alps by his father (old Irish aristocracy), spends his childhood years as the playmate of a local peasant's daughter who, as they grow into adolescence, becomes his partner in a full-blown love affair. Adrian's father peremptorily separates the young lovers, sending Adrian to France and the girl to Italy where, unknown to either the father or the son, she becomes a famous opera singer, La Silvestra, who now plots her revenge on both Adrian and his father. As the greatest diva of the day, she arrives in London to be received into the most exclusive aristocratic drawing rooms in Mayfair. Her glittering social success, however, does not come without protest from more conservative observers: "How I do detest the modern custom of admitting these mountebanks into society!" says an old officer. "In a general point of view, I agree with you," replies her liberally inclined sponsor, the Duke of Cardigan, "but it is impossible to subject such a miracle of nature as La Silvestra to ordinary rules," adding by way of extenuation, "She is of irreproachable conduct, and honourable parentage. Her father, by whom she is always accompanied, is a veteran in the service of the King of Sardinia" (vol. II: 100). In truth, this so-called father is her business manager and cruelly abusive husband.

The Duke's justification of La Silvestra's presence in society through her "irreproachable conduct" marks a significant and contentious political possibility in 1832, that the "middle-class idiom" of respectability has become an unexamined passport for entrance into aristocratic society. The shocking revelation comes to Adrian, Gore's hero, during a performance at the King's Theatre in the Haymarket, London's Italian opera house – that La Silvestra is none other than Stephanine Haslinger, the peasant girl he had seduced in his youth. "Were those mellifluous accents which had recently so melted my soul, the same whose coarse Lower-Austrian dialect had breathed, that night, a tender farewell to her '*Schatzerl?*' – Was that fairy foot in its sandal of silvery satin, the same which had plodded away in its buckled hob-nailed shoe, on the announcement of Brother Remigius's approaching snuffle?" (vol. II: 113).

The diva accepts an invitation to attend rehearsals of the Favart opera at the Duke's country house, an episode producing close echoes of the Mansfield Park rehearsals. But Gore shows little genuine interest in the flirtations and embarrassments of her amateur actors. Instead, she shifts the dramatic focus of the home theatricals onto the audience itself. Like a fifth column insurgent, La Silvestra/Stephanine takes her seat in the attending circle of nobility to witness a group of British aristocrats playing at being peasants. Adrian, in the part of the peasant lover, must act out in excruciating detail the very role he had played in real life with Stephanine, leaving the reader (and Stephanine of course) to the pleasures of its bitter irony. The subversive implications of such plot ironies are present in *Mansfield Park* in Fanny Price's near hysteric refusal to challenge the power of the absent Sir Thomas, but the greater political threat of an enlarged audience in Austen's novel suggests the model for Gore's more inventive use of the trope. When Tom Bertram proposes that Charles Maddox, "a young man very slightly known to any of us" (*MP*: 153), be imported to join the players at the Park, Julia Bertram's perceptive taunt, that "the Mansfield Theatricals would enliven the whole neighbourhood exceedingly" (*MP*: 148–9), puts the finger on the seriousness of the situation. As Edmund well knows, Charles Maddox's presence, presumably with his friends in tow, would produce a public exposure that could call the Park's assumption of moral and social dominance in the neighborhood into question. "This is an end of all the privacy and propriety which was talked about at first," says Edmund, "But if I can be the means of restraining the publicity of the business, of limiting the exhibition, of concentrating our folly, I shall be well repaid" (*MP*: 155).

La Silvestra/Stephanine succeeds brilliantly in her double role as injured peasant and companion to aristocrats in Gore's novel, even receiving a proposal of marriage from the liberal-minded Duke. Political success in 1832, Gore suggests, goes to the class that seizes the role of power with the greatest confidence. La Silvestra is thus paradoxically both a political terror and an attractive revolutionary as she cuts a swath through the ranks of an enfeebled aristocracy. "Will nothing but an English peer satisfy the ambition of this opera singer?" cries an elderly female aristocrat, "We are none of us safe!" (vol. II: 277). The speaker is a reactionary old fool, but she has her point, and certainly not an uncommon one in 1832. In rejecting the Duke's proposal of marriage, La Silvestra sounds very much like Elizabeth Bennet refusing Mr Darcy in *Pride and Prejudice* (*PP*: 192–3), but appropriately worked up to operatic intensity and now infused with a bitter consciousness of class divisions:

> You say you love me; – you would prove it by outraging, for my sake, all the bonds of family union, all the claims of state and station, the prejudices of society . . . Infatuated, miserable man! – listen to my reply. – I loathe you! – There is not an atom of dust lying at my feet more worthless in my sight than yourself. (vol. III: 312–13)

Mrs Gore's antiheroine represents the great political conundrum of 1832, a puzzle shared equally by supporters and opponents of the Reform Bill.

The influence of *Mansfield Park* on silver fork novelists as a model for contemporary political anxieties can hardly be overestimated. After the eventual passage of the historic bill, the authors introduce characters with names like "Minnie" or "Bessy" to function very much as Clara Tuite argues for Fanny, as ombudsmen of "female subjectivity" designed to instruct the aristocracy in the "cultural, social and political complicity which enables class compromise for mutual gain" (Tuite 2002: 141). Bessy Grenfell in Gore's *The Cabinet Minister* (1839) shoulders this exemplary task. As the

patient and long-suffering companion to Lady Mary Woodbridge, an Aunt Norris-
style tyrant, Gore's heroine is sufficiently sidelined by her rich relations to develop a
moral identity of her own and, in this case, some specifically Whiggish opinions
concerning Lady Mary and company, Tories all, with their selfish, arrogant, and over-
bearing politics. In the final pages Bessy, like Fanny, also marries her cousin, Lady
Mary's son Sir Henry, who, obedient to his wife's high-principled political notions,
refuses the offer of a peerage: "But as my poor mother no longer lives to be troubled
by my refusal, and I have a wife above all paltry solicitude for coronation honours,
we have chosen to remain as we are" (vol. III: 286).

As strange as it may seem to us, Jane Austen's novels may have been exactly the
right place for silver fork novelists to look for inspiration. In fact, a mischievous question rises unbidden. Is it possible that Jane Austen is, well, a little bit silver fork
herself? Her letters register a scarcely suppressed delight at her brother Henry's invitation to the celebrated victory ball held by White's Club on June 20, 1814, where
he could be imagined rubbing shoulders with the Emperor of Russia, the King of
Prussia, the allied sovereigns and the greatest names of the British aristocracy (June
23, 1814, *Letters*: 264). More locally, the shopping records of the Austen family at a
Hampshire emporium, Ring Brothers of Basingstoke, show a determined effort to
keep the clerical Austens in consumer company with the local landed gentry (Copeland 1996). Moreover, *Sense and Sensibility* demonstrates knowledge of a topographical
grammar, the social declensions of Mayfair addresses, that she holds in common with
all silver fork writers in her revealing choice of Harley Street for the John Dashwoods'
London address, a street notorious for its reputation as the home of social parvenus
(Copeland 2001: 116–20).

More seriously in the silver fork mode, however, is their shared trope of aristocratic
reform from beneath. Mr Darcy, the most aristocratic of Austen's heroes, is destined
to be set right by Elizabeth Bennet whose origins in the lesser gentry so trouble his
titled aunt. In *Mansfield Park*, Sir Thomas Bertram achieves moral reformation through
his low-born niece Fanny. And if anything untoward should happen to his scapegrace
son Tom, the heir to the Park, Fanny and Edmund are prepared to step into the baronetcy already well-practiced in the "middle-class idiom" of respectability. In fact,
the most profound attraction of silver fork novelists to Austen's *Mansfield Park* may
lie in their common reliance on the mythology of the Glorious Revolution of 1688
as a template for reform. For silver fork novelists and for Whig statesmen of the 1820s
and 1830s, the seventeenth-century revolution is ever-present as the historical justification for change. In *Mansfield Park* the fact that Tom Bertram's continued health
and well-being is implicitly "left open to speculation," writes Tuite, offers "at once
the hope of reform, but also the hope that he might die" (Tuite 2002: 130).

Finally, the sense of "collective identity" that governs characterization in silver fork
novels is not really as foreign to Austen as we tend to think. In *Emma*, for example,
we find a society affirmed in collective terms through the rising Coles, the aspiring
Martins, the sinking Bateses and the permanently invasive Mrs Elton. In *Persuasion*
there is a beginning renegotiation of *rank* and *class* in a "foolish, spendthrift baronet"

(*P*: 248) who must resign his estate to representatives of a worthier class. There is also an observant servant in this novel, Nurse Rooke, who appraises her genteel clients with stinging accuracy – "Women of that class . . . may be well worth listening to," admits Anne Elliot (*P*: 155–6). Finally, in the unfinished *Sanditon* (1817), Austen creates "collective identities" that actually count far more than individual identities. Lady Denham, for example, rises from origins in petty trade to the tyrannical powers of a titled landowner. Her aristocratic step-children stand as models for the selfishness, greed, and corruption of their weakened class. If Austen shows such sensitivity to the changing social, economic, and political culture in this final fragment of 1817, it takes no great stretch of the imagination to see that silver fork novelists, less than 10 years later, might well find her published novels rich with "overlapping historicities." When all is said and done, Austen's novels are in fact steady in their general political direction: a contempt for fashionable aristocratic mores, respect for the gentry as the "middle" of society and a carefully judged enthusiasm for her genteel professional and mercantile ranks as proper company for the governing classes. Such principles alone make her, understandably, a ripe source for silver fork novelists in the age of reform.

FURTHER READING

Colley, Linda (1992). *Britons: Forging the Nation, 1707–1837*. New Haven, CT and London: Yale University Press.

Copeland, Edward (2001). Crossing Oxford Street: silverfork geopolitics. *Eighteenth-Century Life*, 25, 116–34.

Copeland, Edward (2004). Opera and the great reform act: silver fork fiction, 1822–1842. *Romanticism on the Net* <http://www.erudit.org/revue/ron/2004/v/n34–35/009440ar.html>.

Lynch, Deidre Shauna (1996). At home with Jane Austen. In Deidre Lynch and William B. Warner (Eds). *Cultural Institutions of the Novel* (pp. 159–92). Durham, NC and London: Duke University Press.

Mulrooney, Jonathan (2002). Reading the romantic-period daily news. *Nineteenth-Century Contexts*, 24, 351–78.

Wahrman, Dror (1995). *Imagining the Middle Class: The Political Representation of Class in Britain, c. 1780–1849*. Cambridge, UK: Cambridge University Press.

39

Jane Austen in the World:
New Women, Imperial Vistas

Katie Trumpener

The Book Code

Exiled from Mansfield Park, Fanny Price takes refuge in Portsmouth's circulating library. Its books provide mental escape, and materials to begin educating her ignorant sister. Even Fanny's unaccustomed freedom to choose her own reading imparts new confidence. Engaging long-standing debates about novels' effects on women, Jane Austen links reading habits to self-determination.

Like many young women, Elizabeth Bennet and her sisters educate themselves. The younger sisters became bad readers: Mary parrots moralistic literary excerpts with no sense of ethical complexity. Elizabeth, like her father, derives from books a witty, ironic mode of interpreting social life. Yet where Mr Bennett disappears into his library to evade familial responsibility, Elizabeth hones her reading skills to hold her own in the world. Novel reading, Austen insists, is no frivolous, narcissistic distraction. It trains women to draw inferences from details, parse interactions, fathom unspoken conversational subtexts, assess character, develop social intelligence, and make informed marital choices. Novels detailing women's emotional and domestic experience are particularly revelatory – counteracting the misogynist tendencies Anne Elliott notes in most older literature.

Many Austenite novelists consciously extend Austen's homage to the novel and brief for literary self-education. But what happens when Austen's "book code" and pedagogy of reading traverse the British Empire? How did the Austenian heroine, courtship plot, and ethnography function in radically different cultural settings? How did they shape readings of local conditions and history? Did Austen's book code become part of the psychic armature of empire, or an alternative analytic framework?

British travelers, settlers, and administrators often traveled with substantial libraries. When Ada Cambridge and her husband emigrated to Australia in 1870, a London friend seeing them off impulsively purchased a complete Dickens at the railway bookstall, tumbling volumes into their already moving carriage (Cambridge 1903: 7). Traversing the Himalayas, Austenite horticulturalist Reginald Farrer sent an illiterate native servant "thousands of feet" down a pass "to fetch *Northanger Abbey*," showing "little clemency" when the man struggled back with *Emma* (Shulman 2004: 102).

British novels shaped early colonial literatures and school curricula. Australia and Canada's celebrated nineteenth-century novels – John Richardson's *Wacousta* (1832), Thomas M'Combie's *Arabin* (1845), Marcus Clarke's *His Natural Life* (1870) – echoed Walter Scott's *Waverley* and Dickens's *David Copperfield* (Trumpener 1997). Austen's influence became visible later, in New Women novels written in Canada, Australia, and India, as in England, Scotland, and Ireland. This essay reconsiders such novels in light of recent Austen-influenced historical novels situating feminism in relation to war and decolonization. Read together, these novels demonstrate the global reach of Austen's paradigms.

They also challenge her old placement in a "great tradition" of nineteenth-century British realists. Instead they underscore her proximity both to the Scottian historical novel and to the Brontëan novel of female psychology and emancipatory struggle. *Mansfield Park* directly influenced Scott's *Guy Mannering* (1815) and Charlotte Brontë's *Jane Eyre* (1847). Scott's recasting of the historical novel grafted it onto the national tale, a female-dominated genre allegorizing transnational courtship (Ferris, 1991, Trumpener, 1997). Yet if Scott's (unsigned) 1815 *Emma* review celebrates the spirit, originality, and detail of her "sketches," his 1826 journal contrasts her "exquisite touch" to his own epic "Big Bow-wow strain" (Southam 1968: 63, 68, 106). Scott's description framed Austen's reception as a conservative apologist, her ahistorical, apolitical works self-consciously resisting contemporary pressures, achieving formal perfection at the cost of social relevance.

For Charlotte Brontë, Austen was "shrewd and observant" but "lacking sentiment" (Southam 1968: 126–8). Some female modernists found Austen sexually repressed. In the 1970s, feminists decried *Mansfield Park* as antifeminist; to them, the female novel tradition divided between Austen, satiric but smug, and the Brontës, fiery Romantics (Trumpener 2000). Twenty years of debate over Austen's relationship to sexuality and social history have challenged such distinctions. Many critics see Austen's marriage plots chronicling an important historical shift: the ascendancy of the mercantile middle class. In eighteenth-century "bourgeois tragedies," despotic nobles intervene in middle-class life, seducing burghers' girls or preventing cross-class marriages. Like these dramas, courtship novels champion companionate marriage, and women's rights to choose partners by compatibility, not caste. The haughty high-handedness of Darcy and Lady Catherine de Bourgh mark them as aristocratic despots, yet Darcy eventually wins unpropertied Elizabeth.

During the 1990s, feminist historicists explored nineteenth-century sexual codes, a "sexualization" of Austen that alarmed traditionalists. Eve Sedgwick's "Jane Austen and the Masturbating Girl" (1991) explicated social fears implicit in Romantic polemics against novel reading. Terry Castle read Austen's intense bond with her sister

Cassandra to exemplify a nineteenth-century mode of intimacy distinct from incest and conscious lesbianism (Castle 1995/2002). Claudia Johnson explored Austen's historical importance for gay and lesbian readers (Johnson 2000).

Edward Said's influential *Culture and Imperialism* (1993) read *Mansfield Park* as exemplifying British unconsciousness about empire. Yet feminist historicists were demonstrating Austen's attention to contemporary political debates over feminism, empire, and Jacobinism. The abolition of the slave trade threatened British plantation owners; the Napoleonic Wars created new fortunes; new mercantile classes built new communities: *Mansfield Park*, *Persuasion*, and *Sanditon* detail the ongoing, if subterranean effects of these recent upheavals on domestic life, courtship, and female self-perception (Johnson 1988, Ferguson 1993, M. A. Stewart 1993, Lynch 2004).

Nineteenth-century novelists underscored the confluence between the historical novel and the Austenian novel of manners. The bookish orphan in Catherine Spence's *Clara Morison: A Tale of South Australia during the Gold Fever* (1854) proves as long-suffering as Fanny Price or Jane Fairfax, as plucky as Jane Eyre. Heedless relatives ship her to Australia to find work as a governess; destitute, she becomes a servant. Yet Melbourne's egalitarianism and social fluidity, especially during the gold rush, militate against this irrevocable loss of gentility; Clara's book-conversations with a wealthy landowner end in marriage, despite her laboring past. One early champion, Australian New Woman novelist Miles Franklin, thought Spence "as sound a match-maker as Jane Austen, though not circumscribed to the idea of marriage as the only end of women" (Franklin 1945/2001: 193). Spence admired Austen, yet rued Austen's social world as even more constricted than her own: "The life of Austen's heroines, though delightful to read about, would have been deadly to endure" (p. 193).

In turn, Franklin rued the "ludicrous and impoverishing results" of the Romantic novel's "attempt to segregate men's and women's minds into watertight airtight compartments," into "feminized" and "masculinized" fiction, "the Fanny Burney and the Jane Austen" courtship novel and "the Sir Walter Scott" adventure story (Franklin 1933/2001: 112). For Franklin, *Clara Morison* undoes this dichotomy, expanding the Austenian frame of action, and thereby increasing Australian fiction's social scope and analytic depth. Louisa Atkinson's *Gertrude, the Emigrant: A Tale of Colonial Life* (1857) uses a Wickham/Darcy courtship plot to complicate anticonvict prejudices, extol serious reading over romances, and contrast the idle leisure of Markald Park, a would-be aristocratic estate, to New South Wales' rugged bush farms. Mary Theresa Vidal's *Bengala, or Some Time Ago* (1860), set in the same province, crosses *Emma* with *Mansfield Park*. Vidal's Austenian estate life – Mr Herbert's courtship of his young neighbor, Isabel Lang, over discussions of books and conduct; nostalgic Bath reminiscences; a fraught picnic; Isabel's attempted matchmaking, misguided given the minister's secret engagement to the governess; fortune hunting by libertine siblings – unfolds in relation to the 1843 Bank of Australia failure, shifts in the convict labor system, the anguish of convict bondage, and the specter of convict unrest.

In Britain, too, Mrs Gaskell's *Sylvia's Lovers* (1863), George Moore's *A Drama in Muslin* (1886), and Mrs Oliphant's *Kirsteen* (1890) showed recent history transforming social mores and horizons. Following *Persuasion*, Gaskell and Oliphant explore the Napoleonic Wars' effect on soldiers' fiancées, waiting at home. Decades after Oliphant rewrote *Emma* as *Miss Marjoribanks* (1866), *Kirsteen* adapted *Mansfield Park* plot devices to show Highland aristocrats' impoverishment, following the 1745 Jacobite Rebellion, shaping ballroom snobbery, marital alliances, and female bids for independence. Moore's Anglo-Irish gentry find political unrest curtailing their marital options. Alice Barton attends her first ball under the hostile gaze of Irish peasants, whose haggard faces line the windows of the makeshift hall; debutantes attending the Dublin season fear hostile crowds and bomb-throwing more than proving wallflowers.

Brontë herself amplifies Austen's political subtexts: despite obvious differences between Austen's "creepmouse" Fanny and Brontë's fiery Jane, *Jane Eyre* rewrites *Mansfield Park* as a meditation on domestic power relations. Long treated as a chattel by her Bertram cousins, Fanny struggles for psychic independence, even as British landowners like her uncle reorganize their Caribbean plantations, following the slave trade's abolition. Jane's opening outburst – denouncing her cousin as a slave driver – makes the connection explicit. *Mansfield Park* ends with the moral, *Jane Eyre* with the physical, collapse of the great house; once a downtrodden dependent, each heroine is elevated to an official source of moral authority (long after the novel's readers are under her sway). Both novels hinge, indeed, on the gap between the heroine's compelling inner life (available to readers through Austen's free indirect discourse, Brontë's first person confession) and the social world's repeated misreading, underestimation, or belittlement of her (given her low status and unprepossessing appearance).

Brontë's move from Austenian free indirect discourse into first-person narration implicitly makes her heroines writers as well as narrators. Austen's heroines learn from novels, without becoming novelists; Brontë's learn self-expression along with self-emancipation. New Women heroines conjoin Austenian moral insight with Eyrean imagination. The downtrodden Austenian heroines of Jane and Mary Findlater's *Crossriggs* (1906) and F. M. Mayor's *The Rector's Daughter* (1924) unexpectedly reveal themselves inspired artists, performing dramatic recitations or composing mystic poetry. Even the narrator of Daphne du Maurier's *Rebecca* (1938), so self-effacing she remains nameless, proves Jane Eyre as much as Fanny Price, suppressed passion channeled into narrative.

Jean Webster's *Daddy Long-Legs* (1912) rewards Brontëan self-discovery with Austenian happy ending. A foundling from a grim orphanage is sent to college by an anonymous benefactor, on condition she writes him letters about her experiences, and tries to become a writer. Like Brontë's *Jane Eyre* or *Villette* (1853), Webster's epistolary novel immerses readers in the heroine's consciousness, as she renames herself Judy and discovers, in college classroom and library, an unknown literary and intellectual legacy, weeping in identification over *Jane Eyre*. Webster's romantic resolution echoes *Pride and Prejudice*. Judy's benefactor proves identical to a wealthy suitor, on whose estate she spent a summer, exploring the grounds, hearing an old retainer's unsolicited testimonials, reading the master's childhood favorites, and composing her own first novel: Pemberton as writer's colony.

Like *Jane Eyre* and *The Rector's Daughter*, Elizabeth Taylor's *Palladian* (1946) and Cynthia Ozick's *Heir to the Glimmering World* (2004) adapt the Austenian book code to expose the domestic politics of knowledge. Mr Bennet's library is a retreat from (and weapon against) his family. St John Rivers teaches Jane Eyre Hindustani to bend her to his will. Already aficionados of Austen and Brontë, Taylor and Ozick's heroines become governess-amanuenses, in Gothic households haunted by family secrets. Their learned but difficult employers have long used books and learning to dominate their families. Yet the heroines' quixotic love partly tames these domestic tyrants. Still mourning her scholarly father, *Palladian*'s Cassandra prepares to love her elderly employer long before they meet. Their romance begins in his exquisite personal library, but rekindles in a second-hand bookshop, a more egalitarian meeting place for readers of different classes and generations.

In 1930s New York, Ozick's Rose is hired to tend the children of an irascible German-Jewish refugee and assist his research into the history of religious heresy. Initially incensed by Rose's stupidity, including how she packs and unpacks his library, Professor Mitwisser finally seeks solace in her arms. Meanwhile, channeling Grace Poole alongside Jane Eyre and Dorothea Brooke, Rose rooms in the attic with the professor's mad wife Elsa, a physicist traumatized by fascism. Yet Rose's Scheherazadian reading aloud of *Sense and Sensibility* arms Elsa, wooing her back to sanity, until, in a "seizure of concentrated intelligence" (Ozick 2004: 85), Elsa begins reading Austen on her own, opening herself to English, America, a life beyond Europe.

Rose haunts libraries and reads novels – *Jane Eyre*, *Middlemarch*, and especially Austen – to escape: from the provinces and the Depression, her father's misogyny, her dreary teachers' college, her unrequited crush on "my own Mr. Knightly" (p. 23), her manipulative distant cousin Bertram. Bertram's Leninist girlfriend Ninel denounces Rose's Austen-reading as a "provocation": all novels are opiates, Austen an advocate of social inequality, expressing "the pre-Marxist capitalist darkness of . . . wickedly imperialist times" (p. 83).

> "Do you realize," [Ninel] demanded, "how the servants in those big houses *lived*? . . . And where the money to keep up those mansions *came* from? From plantations in the Caribbean run on the broken backs of Negro slaves?". . . .
>
> "Mr. Knightly doesn't have a plantation," I said.
>
> "What do you think the British Empire is? The whole *thing*'s a plantation!" (Ozick 2004: 24)

Channeling Edward Said, Ninel damns Austen's historical unconscious. Yet Austen's materialist historical grounding restores Elsa's sanity. For Elsa as for Rose (Ozick's alter-ego, and clearly a future writer), Austen represents the capaciousness of the novelistic form and the immigrant dream, championing provincials and outsiders, promising intellectual mobility between worlds.

Into the Glimmering World: Empire as Escape

Retracing the narrative arc of eighteenth-century women's novels like Frances Burney's *Evelina* (1778), Austen repeatedly follows a young girl launched into the world, leaving a circumscribed social sphere to explore heterogeneous Bath or London. Anne Elliott, raised in aristocratic claustrophobia, embraces the British Navy's meritocratic culture – and determines to sail away with the Navy, leaving British high society for a more peripatetic, unanchored life, joining the floating military presence in parts unknown (Johnson 1988: Ch. 7).

New Women novelists aligned Anne's choice with Nora's slammed door in Henrik Ibsen's *A Doll's House* (1879). In her Edinburgh suburb, the long-suffering heroine of Findlater's *Crossriggs* endures Austenian domestic travails: tending her sister's children; nursing her invalid father; struggling to preserve gentility on insufficient money; suffering hopeless, if silently reciprocated, love for a married, fatherly neighbor; rejecting a boyish suitor and witnessing his tragic end. Elizabeth Bennet mourns Wickham but ends, much better matched, with Darcy; Emma marries Mr Knightly. *Crossriggs'* heroine realizes her independence in spinsterhood, sailing away with her father on a world voyage from which she may never return.

Oliphant's Highland clans and Moore's Ascendancy are inbred, politically doomed, survivable only by exile. Kirsteen flees Scotland and her father's marital plans, becoming a successful London businesswoman. Alice Barton escapes Ireland through marriage, becoming a housewife and bohemian writer in London's suburbs. Throughout the Empire, New Women novelists plotted similar escapes. Yet because their heroines already stem from remote, "new" places, they hesitate, in their passage through Austenian marriage plots, between seeking London's freedoms, or lingering to reform colonial society.

Such choices are political as well as personal and marital. The Australian New Women in Ada Cambridge's *The Three Misses King* (1891) and Miles Franklin's *My Brilliant Career* (1901) rescind or delay emigration. From their remote hamlet, the King sisters move to Melbourne to continue their education, studying every morning at the Public Library before exploring the city or the International Exhibition. Initially, their ignorance of social codes threaten their marriagability, but all find suitable husbands. The eldest marries an English lord and moves her sisters to his English estate, to which they prove the rightful heirs. Nonetheless, the family's Elizabeth Bennet moves back to Melbourne to wed a crusading journalist, a fellow provincial who shares her faith in Australia's meritocratic possibilities. Franklin's outspoken Sybylla revolts both against traditional womanly virtues and Australia's hardscrabble outback. Yet cultured gentility prove equally confining; Sybylla's quest for independence and authorship involves renouncing the Austenian marriage plot. *The End of My Career* (written 1902, published 1946) describes the controversial success of Sybylla's first novel, a disillusioning Sydney sojourn, and her resolve to seek real literary society in England.

Canadian-born novelist Sara Jeanette Duncan worked as a reporter in the United States and Britain, traveled the world, married a British civil servant, and settled in Calcutta. Her novels explore the Austenian marriage plot from different colonial perspectives. In *A Canadian Girl in London* (*Cousin Cinderella*, 1908) Canadian ingenue Mary Trent visits London with her aesthete brother Graham, Boer War hero and Canadian Member of Parliament. Initially a wide-eyed, conventional, self-effacing narrator, Mary blossoms into a self-possessed heroine, helped by her brother's sardonic yet idealistic reading of England. Catherine Morland becomes Elizabeth Bennet because Henry Tilney is already in residence to speed her education. As both siblings soon realize, their Canadian upbringing gave them more meritocratic values than their English hosts or their ambitious American friend (a gentler, wittier Isabelle Thorpe).

Yet Graham's reverence for tradition almost undoes him. Elizabeth Bennet's growing regard for Darcy deepened at Pemberton. Duncan underscores the consequences of falling in love with an estate: to save her parents' ancestral home, Graham chivalrously proposes to Barbara Pavisay. Although raised to expect alliances of honor and expedience, Barbara eventually breaks the engagement, convinced Graham deserves more than friendship. Barbara's impoverished brother made his own way as a colonial administrator in India. His love-marriage with Mary is cemented by their shared rejection of dynastic marriages; both embody an alternative logic of the colonies, where shared hardships shape a less stratified society.

Yet Duncan's earlier *The Imperialist* (1904) and *Set in Authority* (1906) challenged such colonial self-understanding. In *The Imperialist*, an Ontario Highbury, an Austenian town chronicle, are linked to a world economic system. Like *A Canadian Girl*, the novel centers on Canadian siblings, charismatic politician Lorne and bluestocking teacher Advena. His idealistic yet vague rhetoric of "imperialism" (favorable political and economic ties with Britain) wins Lorne a place in a Canadian trade delegation to London, a British aristocrat's friendship, and the chance to run for the Canadian parliament. Yet when the aristocrat visits Lorne in Canada, he steals Lorne's fiancée and wrecks his candidacy. The electoral district proves a rotten borough, corrupt since the disenfranchisement of local Indians, and the oligarchical governance of Upper Canada's Family Compact. Lorne's heartfelt "imperialist" rhetoric conceals a squalid history of misrule, massacre, and American-style commercialism.

Balancing this political plot – and incisive portrait of colonial hypocrisies – is an Austenian subplot, Advena's emancipation through courtship. Unconventional in her aestheticism and interest in Native life, Advena develops an intellectual friendship with a Scottish curate. Their duel of minds inadvertently develops into passionate courtship, complicated by his long-distance engagement, arranged by elderly relations. Here, as in *A Canadian Girl*, arranged marriages afflict men as much as women. Luckily, his Scottish fiancée elopes with someone else, enabling him to wed Advena. Colonial life has two facets, coded by gender. Anglophile idealism leads colonial men to overlook what is venal in Canada and London; they risk becoming political pawns. Thinking colonial women are less easily led; in settler colonies like Canada, looser social constraints aid the emergence of female freethinkers, reformers, and ethnographers, including Duncan herself.

Yet in British India, Duncan's colonial calculus breaks down. E. M. Forster was Duncan's houseguest in Simla, and her *Set in Authority* clearly inspired him. Like Forster's *Passage to India* (1924), Duncan's masterpiece turns on a miscarriage of colonial justice which threatens the stability of the Raj, and its hesitant appointment of native judges. Caught in adultery with a British soldier, an Indian woman is disfigured and killed by her husband. The soldier attacks the husband, and is sentenced to death. The sentence horrifies colonial society. Determined to uphold equality before the law as fundamental to British jurisprudence, the Chief Commissioner faces either native revolt or Army mutiny, his deliberations complicated by moral pressure from his wife's circle, his London family, and his best friend, a New Woman doctor, whose strong convictions about the case end their long platonic liaison.

Like *Emma*, Duncan's novel belatedly proves a mystery story. The Anglo-Indian doctor discovers herself wrong; she listened to the wrong people, drew the wrong conclusions about the case, because her relationships with her Indian servants and coworkers are unwittingly condescending; because she has forgotten they have lives, motivations, and allegiances unrelated to the English. Her emancipation has been self-centered, helping neither the man she loves nor the Indian community she thought she served. The effort to uphold an Austenian moral universe, a sphere of female resoluteness, only reinforced colonial prejudices. Men's intellectual and cultural labor in India's "civilizing," Duncan insists, are buttressed by colonial and London New Women, fully implicated in the failures of the imperial project.

In the Bookstore: The Postcolonial Jane Austen

The study of English literature, begun in Scottish universities, was adopted by schools in nineteenth-century British India, as a secular curriculum able to circumvent sectarian tensions (Crawford 1992, Viswanathan 1989). Across the Empire, generations of colonial students were raised on British literature. Yet along with a particular sensibility, and strong identification with Britain, this curriculum instilled an uneasy colonial cringe.

After decolonization, students and writers began questioning or rejecting British literary models. The irreverent Indian slacker in Upamanyu Chatterjee's *English, August* (1988, first published 2006), himself ironically nicknamed "English," wonders "What is Jane Austen doing in Meerut? Or *Macbeth* in Ulhasnagar, and Wordsworth in Azamganj . . .Why is some Jat teenager reading Jane Austen? Why does a place like Meerut have a course in English at all?" The curriculum persists, English concludes, solely because older Indian academics, having received PhDs in Jane Austen, "need a place where they can teach this rubbish" (2006: 191).

Yet Vikram Seth's *A Suitable Boy* (1993) argues for Austen's relevance to post-Independence India, and Shyam Selvadurai's *Cinnamon Gardens* (1999) argues her historical importance in preparing the ground for colonial independence struggles. Framed by a middle-class family's search for an appropriate husband for a self-possessed college student, Seth's novel offers a panoramic picture of Indian Hindu and Muslim society immediately following Partition. The courtship plot which begins, ends, and organizes the novel, repeatedly gives way to dramatic presentations of historical events, from sectarian riot to crowd stampede. Yet Seth is equally interested in social and intellectual life: family arguments over dating and marriage, childrearing, religious observance, encroaching consumerism, generational conflict over adding James Joyce to the syllabus of a provincial English department.

In portraying a domestic life constrained, disrupted, and transformed by civil violence, Seth draws on the nineteenth-century historical novels of Scott, Alessandro Manzoni, Theodore Fontane, and Leo Tolstoy. Yet *A Suitable Boy* most explicitly honors Austen, and presents domestic transformation as itself world-historical: shifts of courtship mores, the redefinition of family allegiances under new economic and social pressures, the new possibility, in India's fledgling democracy, of intellectual exchange, intermarriage, and hence kinship alliances across religious or caste lines.

Books and bookstores are crucial to Seth's new India. Lata, a Hindu English major and Kabir, a Muslim history major, begin a tentative love affair after meeting accidentally in the Imperial Book Depot. Located on a "fashionable street that was the last bulwark of modernity before the labyrinthine alleys and ancient, cluttered neighbourhoods of Old Brahmpur" (Seth 1994: 49), the bookstore itself is a bulwark of modernity, where male and female, Hindus and Muslims students mingle unchaperoned; noting each other's book choices, they glimpse each other's inner life.

Given India's long-standing sectarian and caste divisions, and the still-unassimilated violence of Partition, Lata and Kabir's attraction does not lead to marriage. Their love flourishes only within the bookstore and the secular university, not the messier reality of family and community. A thousand pages after their first meeting, they inadvertently meet again in the Imperial Book Depot, where Lata has come to buy herself "a Jane Austen" (p. 1406). Lata is crying when she leaves the bookstore and Kabir's life – so Kabir reminds her not to forget her book. "*Mansfield Park?* I haven't read that one. Tell me if it's any good" (p. 1407). Kabir upholds the fiction that they can keep meeting in the republic of letters, if not in the still riven India outside the bookstore. But book chat is not joint life.

Lata turns down a book-based match with her literary brother-in-law. Lata, who placed well on the Senior Cambridge exam, has just finished *Emma*; Amit is a writer and confirmed Janeite. At Oxford, he "remained faithful to Jane Austen"; back in Calcutta, he is "content to lead a life of contemplation" (p. 1019). His poetry makes him irresistible to women, his sisters tease, yet Amit remains "very peculiar . . . Jane Austen is the only woman in his life" (p. 415). A novel-reader as witty as Henry Tilney, Amit is also a monastic mandarin whose aesthetic sensibilities overshadow Lata's more robust character.

In the end, Lata freely chooses her mother's favored suitor, an intelligent, literate businessman who likes Thomas Hardy. In accepting a socially sanctioned partner,

Lata has not simply bowed to tradition or surrendered the effects of her (literary) education. Anne Eliot chooses Captain Wentworth rather than Captain Benwick, man of action over man of melancholy contemplation. Lata chooses an equally dynamic husband who will push her to engage in the new India. Novels, Seth suggests, should convey historical experience and prepare readers to live.

Selvadurais' *Cinnamon Gardens* (1999) draws heavily on *A Suitable Boy*, down to the bookstore where the unsuccessful suitor hands the novel-reading heroine a copy of *Mansfield Park*. But where Seth extends the nineteenth-century European novel into the postwar, postcolonial present, Selvadurai reconceives colonial history in light of recent critical debates over Austen's imperial and sexual consciousness. Selvadurai was raised in Colombo but now lives in Canada. His debut novel, *Funny Boy* (1994) describes a homosexual boy's coming-of-age during the Sri Lankan civil war. Reaching back to the 1920s, *Cinnamon Gardens* describes earlier civil strife and historical change in colonial Ceylon.

Tracking parallel paths of Austenian moral testing, Selvedurai splits the Austenian heroine's role between New Woman Annalukshmi and her gay uncle Balandran, both opposing family expectations, standing up to the repressive, hypocritical patriarch, and challenging patriarchal assumptions about arranged marriage. As a pupil at Colombo's preeminent British-run mission school, Annalukshmi places "first island-wide in English literature" on the Senior Cambridge, "to the discomfiture of every boys' school" (1999: 3). Staying on as a teacher at her old school, she declines to marry her father's choice, a dull distant cousin whom her practical sister Kumudini (like Charlotte Lucas) eagerly marries instead.

Dismissing arranged marriages as "cattle markets" (p. 80), Annalukshmi imagines meeting a husband while reading, he asking "what she was reading" and love arising from book discussion. From Austen, Annalukshmi internalizes fantasies of erotic choice and recognition, although Kumudini insists, "This is not *Pride and Prejudice* . . . Your Mr. Darcy isn't going to ride up on a horse" (p. 80). In fact, Annalukshmi meets Seelen, another distant cousin (fresh from English medical school) in a scenario much like her fantasized one. In Uncle Balendran's library, they discuss reading, he recommending *A Passage to India* (which she never reads). By chance, they meet again in a bookshop. She is perusing *Mansfield Park*. He is delighted – "dear Jane Austen" is "One of my favorite writers" (p. 317) – and insists on buying, then inscribing it for her: "May our joy of reading strengthen our regard for each other." Yet his impetuousness and indiscretion shock Annalukshmi. And the discovery of the book inscription horrifies the family patriarch, who bursts, with Annalukshmi's angry mother, into a follow-up tea party, just as the cousins discover a mutual interest in George Eliot.

Annalukshmi can brave family opprobrium. Yet despite their shared love of books, she and Seelen appear ill-matched. Perhaps she no longer needs a Darcy or a Knightley, given the library's – and her community's – unexplored riches. Reading Austen, she treasured moments where courtship expanded self-knowledge. Now she foregoes Austen's happy ending, lest marriage curtail such maturation.

For Annalukshmi, reading (or reading British-style: mission-school literature curriculum, Senior Cambridge exam, bookshop) focuses a new interiority, an alternative to the local middle-class family-based ethos. The English novel inaugurates a new sense of self, choices, and personal fate. Yet her new-found independence – and nationalist debates over Ceylon's future, and the selective extension of the franchise – push her to criticize British colonialism. Even once-beloved British teachers, she realizes, are animated by racism and paternalism alongside feminist enlightenment. Rejecting the mission-school's colonial curriculum, Annalukshmi considers transferring to a Hindu school in Jaffna.

Yet the impetus for feminism, gay liberation, universal franchise, the abolition of caste, and national independence are also, paradoxically, British inheritances. At home, Austen might be read as a conservative, guarding the status quo. Yet for native readers like Annalukshmi, Austen appears simultaneously as a harbinger of personal liberation – and a particularly acute manifestation of the cultural pressures of imperialism. Austen represents the "wedge" of British literature, reading practices, and social attitudes which rend the social fabric of Ceylonese society.

Balendran's narrative elucidates this contradiction. As a student in England, he lived with a gay lover, until his father harshly separated them. Years later, his lover visits Ceylon; now married and middle-aged, Balandran falls in love anew. Like Anne Elliott, he has a second chance to escape family life for erotic fulfillment. Yet he refuses to abandon his dependents. Selvedurai does not view "gay identity" as a Western import, imposition, or construct. Yet Balandran's historical circumstances force a choice not only between the closet and open homosexuality, but between metropolitan exile in London, and a life in his own culture, language, and religion. Balandran chooses family system over personal fulfillment partly in the hope that those remaining in Ceylon can topple both British and patriarchal rule. The choice, then, is not – or not only – between modern individualism and archaic communalism, but between personal happiness and political utility.

The collapse of despotism, as family members challenge the patriarch's authority: *Mansfield Park* augurs and enables liberation. Colonial New Women novelists sometimes celebrated Austen as a conduit for cultural imperialism. Yet for some postcolonial novelists, she is a prophet against empire.

FURTHER READING

Fraiman, Susan (2000). Jane Austen and Edward Said: gender, culture and imperialism. In Deidre Lynch (Ed.). *Janeites: Austen's Disciples and Devotees* (pp. 206–24). Princeton, NJ: Princeton University Press.

Makdisi, Saree (2008, forthcoming). Jane Austen, Empire and moral virtue. In Jillian Heydt-Steenson and Charlotte Sussman (Eds). *Recognizing the Romantic Novel: New Approaches to British Fiction*. Liverpool, UK: Liverpool University Press.

Nafisi, Azar (2003). Austen. In *Reading Lolita in Tehran: A Memoir in Books* (pp. 255–339). New York: Random House.

Park, You-me and Rajeswari Sunder Rajan (Eds). (2000). *The Postcolonial Jane Austen*. London: Routledge.

Perera, Suvedrini (1991). *Reaches of Empire: The English Novel from Edgeworth to Dickens*. New York: Columbia University Press.

Suleri, Sara (1989). What Mamma knew. In *Meatless Days* (pp. 151–69). Chicago: University of Chicago Press.

40
Sexuality

Fiona Brideoake

At the outset of her 1999 *The Friendly Jane Austen* ("A Well-Mannered Introduction to a Lady of Sense and Sensibility"), Natalie Tyler offers a quiz designed to determine whether one is a Janeite of the "Gentle," "Ironic," or "Subversive" School. Notable amongst the questions is one in which the reader is asked if she or he identifies with the sensibility of (a) Martha Stewart, (b) household advice columnist Heloise ("she of the Hints"), (c) etiquette advisor Miss Manners, or (d) Susie Bright, the queer writer, activist, and self-described "sexpert" (Tyler 1999: 9). Selection of the latter, alongside a penchant for vegetarian cooking, Tai Kwon Do, Annie Leibovitz, and poetry slams, reveals one to belong to the "School of Subversive Jane," whose adherents view Austen as a feminist bad girl "full of ribaldry and revolution" (Tyler 1999: 12–13).

The very notion of there being multiple Austens from whom to select may appear proof of the cultural *coup d'état* undertaken throughout the 1990s by the *"Tenured Radicals"* excoriated in the academic and popular press (Sedgwick 1993: 109). Notable amongst these are Eve Kosofsky Sedgwick, whose 1991 essay "Jane Austen and the Masturbating Girl" describes Marianne Dashwood, whose abstracted autoeroticism takes place under the constant gaze of her sister Elinor, as emblematic of the masturbatory subject Sedgwick identifies as the first minority sexual identity (Sedgwick 1993: 116–21). The primacy of sororal bonds within Austen's textual and biographical corpus was further foregrounded in Terry Castle's 1995 review of Deirdre Le Faye's edition of Austen's letters, published in the *London Review of Books* under the provocative headline, "Was Jane Austen Gay?" (Castle 1995:15). This moment in Austen studies elicited significant anxieties.[1] Sedgwick's and Castle's essays circulated widely, not only due to their titles, but often as no more than such designations (Berry 2004: 4), from which their subversive content was held to be immediately legible. Their scandalized iteration obscured the extent to which neither critic sought to ascribe a sexual identity to either Austen's characters or Austen herself. Rather, Sedgwick's essay offered a strategic occupation and rebuttal of the New Historical critical project, in particular the tension between its chastening accounts of the circulation of power and knowledge throughout literary and cultural texts and the disavowed pleasure taken in bringing such relations to light (Sedgwick 1993: 127, Berlant 1994: 128). The outrage occasioned by Sedgwick's intervention obfuscated her use of the term "queer" to describe both same-sex sexual object choice and a range of subject positions that confound the heteronormative alignment of gender, sex, sexuality, and desire without congealing into a fixed identity (see Sedgwick 1993: 6–9). Read on their own terms, such analyses revealed the ways in which the affective investments evident in Austen's life and work exceed the presumptive telos of the marital plot in ways neither straightforwardly oppositional, nor reducible to a stable set of significations.

This queer turn in Austen studies has been deemed a perverse denial of Austen's evident status as "one of those of the shelved and safe" (Henry James quoted in Miller 2003: 4). Such responses rely upon the productive ambiguity of the designation "Jane Austen," which denotes the biographical Austen, Austen the author or author-function, Austen's textual oeuvre, Austen the cultural and critical institution (Tuite 2004: 306–7); and the employment of Austen "as a byword for chastity" (Miller 2003: 4). The virulence of many of the responses to Austen's queering may be seen to endorse Sedgwick's claim that "homosexual panic" marks the cultural locations in which heteronormativity stands under the most strain (Sedgwick 1985: 201). The author of the aforementioned quiz is not immune from such anxieties; while Tyler reassures readers that Austen has "layer[ed] her novels with substantial material to keep everyone happy" (Tyler 1999: 13), she stresses her intention to "let other pens dwell on Lacan, Derrida, Foucault, political correctness, and cultural diversity" (Tyler 1999: xix), her litany of critical bogeys tellingly obscuring the "L-word." This demurral locates Tyler's text, as it does its "friendly" authoress, in a discursive space both different from and prior to the critical specters of the late twentieth century, in which aesthetic appreciation is unburdened by ideological freight.

As Claudia L. Johnson has demonstrated, the Austen incapable of cohabiting, at least conceptually, with a queer feminist in thigh-high boots is of relatively recent provenance. It was not until the 1960s that marriage and romantic love became identified as the structurally and thematically defining element of her "six perfect novels" (Johnson 1996: 158). Prior to this period, Austen's apparently minimal investment in her marriage endings engendered considerable unease, leading George Sampson to complain in 1924, "In her world there is neither marrying nor giving in marriage, but just the make-believe mating of dolls" (quoted in Johnson 1996: 149). Doubling the representational status of Austen's texts, Sampson figures her characters as childhood toys, bearing a fraught relation to the "real thing." Recent scholars of narrative identify Austen's marriage endings as the moral and teleological center of her works, yoking structural closure with an implicitly heterosexual model of maturity (Johnson 1996: 152: 157–8). Highly literal reading practices are nonetheless required to maintain this view. In *Northanger Abbey*, the narrator draws attention to the novel's fictive status, presenting Catherine Morland's errors of judgment as stemming from her inability to distinguish the interpretative conventions of life and art. Learning to read signs of narrative ambivalence, as does Catherine, one cannot fail to notice that she is initially as enamored of Eleanor as she is of Henry Tilney, her sight of the latter "leaning on her brother's arm" leading her to exclaim to John Thorpe, "I cannot go on. – I will not go on. – I must go back to Miss Tilney" (*NA*: 87). The conventionality of Henry's proposal is moreover underscored by the narrator's acknowledgement of "the tell-tale compression of the pages" (*NA*: 250) with which the impending nuptials are materially marked. As we are told, Henry's affection for Catherine "originated in nothing better than gratitude, or, in other words, [. . .] a persuasion of her partiality for him had been the only cause of giving her a serious thought" (*NA*: 243), a situation "dreadfully derogatory of an heroine's dignity" (*NA*: 243). The formulaic rendering of their union underscores the threat it poses to the verisimilitude of the novel's companionate ménage: "Henry and Catherine were married, the bells rang, and every body smiled" (*NA*: 252) – this perfunctory account attesting to Lauren Berlant's claim that love operates as "a conventional and historical mode of attachment to form" (2001: 433). The ambivalence of Catherine's marital maturation anticipates the chastening impulses evident in *Emma*, in which Austen's heroine attains adulthood not only through the renunciation of her investments in a variety of female love-objects, but by acknowledging her brother-in-law's assessment of "the good fortune of the engagement as [being] all on my side" (*E*: 464). Austen thus asserts both the banality of married domesticity (marked in *Sense and Sensibility* by Marianne's "submitting" to both a second match and Colonel Brandon's flannel waistcoat, *SS*: 379) and its compulsory nature, disclosed in the disciplinary force and formal structure of both novels.

Clara Tuite describes the way in which the identification of Austen's oeuvre with "almost parodically formulaic heterosexual romance" requires the exclusion of her final work *Sanditon* (1817), its lack of marital closure occasioned, not only by its fragmentary nature, but its deviation from Austen's "archetypal" plot of marital maturation and upward female mobility (Tuite 2002: 156–7). *Persuasion*, often identified as her last work, is notable for its failure to settle Anne and Wentworth in relation to property. This failure is even more apparent within Sanditon's unsettled landscape. In the place of England's landed green core, *Sanditon* depicts its speculative coastal fringe, the Parkers' movement from "the house of [their] forefathers" (*MW*: 379) to a modern cliffside dwelling emblematizing the circulation of landed property throughout a geographically peripheral market (Austen quoted in Tuite 2002: 159). Within this new familial figuration, the Parkers' "self-doctoring" is presented as a form of nonreproductive sexuality, with Diana's prescription of "friction alone steadily persevered in" for Mr Parker's sprained ankle suggesting a frenzied form of autoeroticism (Tuite 2002: 161–2). Lady Denham's establishment of Clara Brereton further displaces patriliny with a feminized mode of property transfer, her rivalry with Sir Edward Denham for Clara's affections threatening to instantiate herself as a financially productive, rather than biologically generative, marital supplement (Tuite 2002: 172–8).

Not even consigning *Sanditon* to the realm of "Austenuations"[2] is sufficient to secure the generic primacy of Austen's marriage plots. As Marilyn Butler notes, Edmund Wilson observed in 1950 that Austen more eloquently portrayed the affective bonds between women than she did the realm of "heterosexual passion [. . .] and plainly did not find this a merit" (Butler 1987: x). An initiation into the works of Austen acted in the latter decades of the twentieth century as a rite of passage into English-speaking young womanhood. Over a similar period, Austen has been conversely held to assert an enervating effect upon young men. The enduring effects of such emasculation were evoked in 1923 by Virginia Woolf, who declared, "Anyone who has the temerity to write about Jane Austen is aware . . . that there are twenty-five elderly gentlemen living in the neighbourhood of London who resent any slight upon her genius as if it were an insult to the chastity of their Aunts" (quoted in Miller 2003: 9). D. A. Miller argues that the éclat of Austen's dazzlingly impersonal "Style" is thereby displaced upon the homosexual scapegoat, whose "secret" desires for books and men are all too legible (Miller 2003: 8–9). E. M. Forster's declaration, "I am a Jane Austenite, and therefore slightly imbecilic about Jane Austen. [. . .] I read and re-read, the mouth open and the mind closed" (quoted in Castle 2002: 52) thus operates as "a coming-out statement" (Johnson 1996: 162) in which Forster's submission to Austen stands as a synecdoche for his putative sexual passivity. The "queer" figurations of Austen identified in the early 1990s as an "index of depravity in academe" (Sedgwick 1993: 109) thus possess an illustrious pedigree, rather than emerging fully formed from the prurient minds of contemporary critics.

Concerns as to the status of sexuality in Austen's texts often slide imperceptibly into those of Austen's own sexual practices. This concatenation of biographical and textual personae reflects Austen's hypercanonical status, akin to that of Shakespeare, whose heteronormativity is similarly asserted in troubled relation to his hermeneutically suggestive texts. As Johnson observes, the fact that Austen's heterosexuality was not guaranteed by marriage has led her to be figured as alternately asexual, frigid, and lesbian (Johnson 1996: 148–9). Like Fanny Price's ability to withstand Henry Crawford, deemed irresistible by the Bertram sisters and Mary Crawford's friends "all dying for him in their turn" (*MP*: 43), Austen's spinsterhood has been interpreted as "queer" and "prudish" (*MP*: 230). Upon closer examination, however, such pre-1960 anxieties appear peculiarly specific in nature. Writing of women's same-sex desire, Martha Vicinus notes the unevenly distributed burden of proof that assumes historical figures are heterosexual until proven otherwise, insisting that same-sex desire should not be held to a higher evidentiary standard than its implicitly unmarked other (Vicinus 1994: 59, Lanser 1999: 184). She also gestures towards the vexed question of what constitutes "evidence" of sexual acts in history, particularly those which their subjects had considerable reason to conceal. The prohibitive height of this evidentiary threshold is demonstrated by critical figurations of Austen's near contemporaries, Lady Eleanor Butler (c.1739–1829) and Miss Sarah Ponsonby (1755–1831), known as the Ladies of Llangollen. Despite eloping together from Ireland in 1778 and sharing 51 years of devotion in a North Welsh cottage, Butler and Ponsonby have been rendered emblematic of the "romantic friendship" model of emotionally intense, yet sexually chaste, female bonds (see Faderman 1981). Reflecting the particularity of mid-twentieth-century anxieties over Austen's spinster status, the denial of the evident queerness of Butler and Ponsonby's relationship has persisted in spite of Susan Lanser's acute observation that it makes no sense to think of them as either heterosexual or undesiring (Lanser 1999: 261). The implication that Austen's normativity would have been secured by marriage is further undermined by the case of Anne Damer (1749–1828), the sculptor and Whig socialite, whose marriage and widowhood failed to shield her from public accusations of sapphism, and private descriptions identifying her as "a Lady much suspected for liking her own Sex in a criminal Way" (Thrale 1942: 770).

The anxieties elicited by Austen's spinsterhood acknowledge elements of her textual and biographical corpus that exceed heteronormative bounds. The charge that it is anachronistic to ascribe same-sex desires to women of the late eighteenth and early nineteenth centuries was disproved by the 1988 publication of extracts from the journals of the Yorkshire gentlewoman, Anne Lister (1791–1840), detailing her seduction of an array of female friends and neighbors.[3] While the absence of marital "evidence" has proven unable to alleviate anxieties as to Austen's queerness, the evidence provided by Lister's synchronous archive has simultaneously proven insufficient to undermine the myth of the asexual "Gentle Jane" (Tyler 1999: 11). Noting the insistence upon the radical alterity of these figures, Tuite observes, "Both Austen and Lister occupy the same period, the early nineteenth-century, yet 'Jane Austen's world' is decisively not the same as 'Anne Lister's world'" (Tuite 2004: 203–4). The obduracy of this position is demonstrated by the biographical connections that unite these seemingly divergent domains. Lister and the Ladies of Llangollen are frequently figured as the mascots of competing models of women's same-sex desire in the Romantic period (Brideoake 2004–5). Lister pilgrimaged to Butler and Ponsonby's cottage in 1822, whereupon she quizzed them as to the precise nature of their affective bond (Lister 1988: 202–10). Austen's proximity to such queer encounters is revealed by Eleanor Butler's journal of July 1819, in which an incapacitated friend writes to request the loan of "Emma & any other light reading." Having remained committed to Emma Woodhouse's assertion, "If I were to marry, I must expect to repent it" (*E*: 84), Butler dispatched both Austen's novel and Charlotte Smith's "trumpery" *Emmeline* (1778) from her and Ponsonby's private library (Butler 1819, Butler quoted in G. H. Bell 1930: 113) which worked throughout their lives to assert their class-based distinction from the "ridiculous, disagreeable old maid[s]" of Emma and Harriet's fears (*E*: 85). Austen and Lister's apparently very different domains may thus be seen to be linked by textual and biographical associations, as they are by affective investments and anxieties.

Employing the term "queer" to indicate locations in which bodies and desires constitute matter out of place brings into focus the queerness of Austen's oeuvre. Since the 1990s, scholars have done much to demolish the perception that Austen's texts stand in an "almost extra-territorial" (Steiner quoted in Jones 1996: x) relationship to the turbulent period of their genesis.[4] The outcry with which Sedgwick and Castle's above-mentioned essays were greeted nonetheless suggests that Austen's "safety" depends on the excision of the sexualized body from her work, in spite of its central place in the political consciousness of the late eighteenth and early nineteenth centuries.

The denial of the body in Austen's fiction has necessitated the active assertion of the epistemic myopia that Sedgwick terms "unknowing" (Sedgwick 1993: 23–51). In *Pride and Prejudice*, the embodied exuberance that constitutes Elizabeth Bennet's beguiling charm also threatens to render her a monitory figure, her physical exertions and forthright wit potentially comprising her performance of genteel femininity. Walking three miles to Netherfield in order to attend to the ailing Jane, Elizabeth's physicality distinguishes her from the etiolated ideals of decorum endorsed by conduct literature, her "weary ancles [*sic*], dirty stockings, and [. . .] face glowing with the warmth of exercise" (*PP*: 32) rendering her contemptible to Miss Bingley and Mrs Hurst (Johnson 1988: 75). The questionable nature of her actions is indicated by the ambivalence of Darcy's response, "divided between admiration of the brilliance which exercise had given her complexion, and doubt as to the occasion's justifying her coming so far alone" (*PP*: 33). In an equally corporeal display, Miss Bingley invites Elizabeth to join her in strolling about the drawing room, thereby allowing Darcy to attend to her figure. The alluring intent of this contrivance is acknowledged by its intended audience. Refusing Miss Bingley's invitation to join them, Darcy remarks:

> "You either chuse this method of passing the evening because you are in each other's confidence and have secret affairs to discuss, or because you are conscious that your figures appear to the greatest advantage in walking; – if the first, I should be completely in your way; – and if the second, I can admire you much better as I sit by the fire."
> (*PP*: 56)

A reader of Tyler's School of "Gentle Jane" might echo Miss Bingley's response, "Oh, how shocking!" – perceiving the "abomination" of Darcy's speech to be constituted less by the acuity of his observation than the forthright nature of its expression (*PP*: 56). Elsewhere, however, it is the frankness of Elizabeth and Darcy's dialogue that constitutes the defiance and vulnerability that enables their eventual intimacy. The fact that their most affectively charged exchanges take place alone and in secret further pushes their courtship "to the verge of an impropriety unique in Austen's fiction" (Johnson 1988: 90).

Granting that Lydia Bennet's hat-shopping constitutes the Regency equivalent of a Jimmy Choo fetish is not to deny that Austen depicted both the pleasures and dangers of female sexuality (Swendson 2005: 66). Lydia is depicted imagining herself amidst the military finery of Brighton:

> She saw with the creative eye of fancy, the streets of that gay bathing place crowded with officers. She saw herself the object of attention, to tens and scores of them at present unknown. She saw all the glories of the camp, crowded with the young and the gay, and dazzling with scarlet; and to complete the view, she saw herself seated beneath a tent, tenderly flirting with at least six officers at once. (*PP*: 232)

Lydia's sensual reverie locates her within a teeming mass of the "young and gay" whose mobility recalls such dangerously alluring figures as Henry Crawford, with his "great dislike" of "any thing like a permanence of abode" (*MP*: 41) and Lady Susan, whose lack of fixed address signals her status as "the most accomplished Coquette in England" (*MW*: 248). Lydia's vision of "tenderly flirting" with an array of officers is characterized by a hyperbole that underscores her naïveté, her "tender" addresses reflecting the equal tenderness of her years. While gesturing towards the parental indulgence that enables Lydia's folly, Austen does not downplay the scandal of her elopement with Wickham. Through Darcy's moral and financial intervention, Lydia is spared the fate of the two Elizas who haunt *Sense and Sensibility*, the mother's disgrace repeated by the offspring of her "guilty connection" (*SS*: 208). She is nonetheless yoked to a demonstrable cad, whose affection for her "was just what Elizabeth had expected to find it; not equal to Lydia's for him" (*PP*: 318). Even in this "lightest and brightest" of Austen's novels, she neither shies from displaying the desiring body, nor the effects of its improper employment, allowing Lydia to absorb the potentially damning critique of Elizabeth's physical and psychological freedoms (Johnson 1988: 77).

The sexualized body is similarly apparent throughout *Persuasion*. At the novel's outset, Anne Elliot's beauty is described as having "vanished early" (*P*: 6), her "altered [. . .] youth and bloom" contrasting cruelly with Captain Wentworth's "more glowing, manly, open look" (*P*: 61). While Anne's reserve distinguishes her from the bodily preoccupations of Elizabeth and Sir Walter, her second courtship is highly corporeal. Anne's first encounter with the newly returned Wentworth is profoundly kinesthetic:

> Her eye half met Captain Wentworth's; a bow; a curtsey passed; she heard his voice – he talked to Mary, said all that was right; said something to the Miss Musgroves, enough to mark an easy footing: the room seemed full – full of persons and voices – but a few minutes ended it. (*P*: 59)

Anne's psychological vulnerability is marked by the overwhelming impact of Wentworth's presence, her consciousness flooded with acutely registered sense impressions. Austen offers a similarly impressionistic account of Wentworth's solicitude in releasing Anne from her nephew Walter, his unfastening of the child's "little sturdy hands" from her neck recognized only in retrospect (*P*: 80). Anne's climactic assertion of the tenderness and endurance of women's attachments is enabled by her embodied negotiation of public space, her assertion to Captain Harville of the endurance of women's attachments placing Wentworth in the position of physically and psychologically afflicted eavesdropper she has previously occupied. Having received Wentworth's avowal, "You pierce my soul. I am half agony, half hope," Anne is assailed at every moment by "fresh agitation" (*P*: 237–8). Their ensuing conversation occasions further sensory displacement, their mutual absorption leading them to proceed "seeing neither sauntering politicians, bustling house-keepers, flirting girls, nor nursery-maids and children" (*P*: 241). In this most compelling of Austen's marriage endings, sexual desire is both physically experienced and publicly negotiated, while Anne's assertion of women's steadfastness constitutes a bold assertion of the place of female subjectivity in the public sphere.

Critics have long acknowledged the same-sex desires evident in *Emma*, in which it is Harriet Smith's "soft blue eyes and all those natural graces" that render her a suitable candidate for Emma's notice (*E*: 23). Lisa L. Moore observes that it is relationships between women that allow the female body to be perceived as desirable within this text (Moore 1997: 123), from Harriet's prettiness to Emma's "perfect beauty [. . . of] face and figure," which is enthusiastically detailed by Mrs Weston and merely endorsed by Mr Knightley: "I think her all you describe" (*E*: 39). The nonnormativity of Emma's female friendships lies moreover in the blurring of class hierarchies constituted by her intimacy with Harriet, "the natural daughter of somebody" (*E*: 22) and her former governess, Mrs Weston, whose gentility occasions Mrs Elton such surprise.

Emma's relationship with Mr Knightley may also be described as queer insofar as it is characterized by age asymmetry and familial proximity. Knightley is introduced as "a very old and intimate friend of the family, but particularly connected to it as the elder brother of Isabella's husband" (*E*: 9). At the age of "seven or eight-and-thirty," he is at the far end of generational parity with the 20-year-old Emma, his age and authority indicated by his status as "one of the few people who could see faults in Emma Woodhouse, and the only one who ever told her of them" (*E*: 11). Their relationship thereby flirts with the dangers of both incestuous and cross-generational desire, located at the furthest reaches from Gayle Rubin's "charmed circle" of sexual normativity (Rubin 1993: 93). Like their familial intimacy, Emma and Knightley's age asymmetry enables their romantic relationship, with Knightley's declaring of Emma's youth, "I could not think about you so much without doating on you, faults and all; and by dint of fancying so many errors, have been in love with you ever since you were thirteen at least" (*E*: 462). The extent to which their adult relationship represents the continuation of this asymmetrical relation is demonstrated by Emma's stated refusal to refer to her future spouse as "any thing but 'Mr. Knightley'," a resolution she declares to set aside only once in deference to the Anglican marriage service (*E*: 463). Rather than enacting the expected trajectory of female mobility and gentry regeneration, Emma's marriage to Knightley thus stages the endogamous contraction of the family circle (Tanner 1986: 204). Sexuality is thus shown to suffuse cultural spaces from which it is ostensibly absent, notably the sanctified spaces of childhood and domesticity.

Nonnormative sexuality is similarly apparent throughout *Mansfield Park*. As the novel opens, the estate exists in a state of moral decline signaled by Lady Bertram's torpor, her maternal caretaking failing to extend beyond her "poor pug" (*MP*: 10). In departing for Antigua as his daughters enter the marriage market, Sir Thomas similarly neglects his parental duties, his rightful authority supplanted by the venal Mrs Norris. In his absence, the Mansfield household is threatened from without, its fragile integrity endangered by the Crawfords' arrival at the Parsonage, Mr. Yates's introduction of "the infection" of acting (*MP*: 184), and Edmund's acquiescence to participating in the production of *Lovers' Vows*, based on the presumptively greater danger of admitting strangers to their circle. Within this spatial economy, Fanny is characterized by a commensurately queer indeterminacy, her inhabitancy of the fireless East Room underscoring her liminal class, sexual, and familial location. Maria and Henry's adultery emblematizes the canker both within and without Mansfield Park. Their liaison, publicized in the nationally circulating print press, reflects Austen's engagement in political debates about sexual regulation. The union between Edmund and Fanny is nonetheless rendered possible by Maria and Henry's adultery, which deprives Edmund of a sibling in Maria and a potential wife in Mary (Pollak 2002: 185), and promotes Fanny to the status of his "only sister" (*MP*: 444), her simultaneous status as endogamous and exogamous kin marking the indeterminacy of both familial and heteronormative bounds.

The queerness of the Austen canon is manifest complexly throughout Austen's popular cultural presence. The immense success in 1995 of the Simon Langton/Andrew Davies *Pride and Prejudice* and Ang Lee and Emma Thompson's *Sense and Sensibility* affirmed the proper generic mode of the Austen adaptation as the picturesque heterosexual romance. Roger Mitchell's 1995 *Persuasion* was accordingly criticized for alleged aesthetic failings including "an unappealing Anne Elliot, a pockmarked Captain Wentworth, a greasy necked Benwick and a slovenly looking Lady Russell" (Brooke Allen quoted in Collins 1998: 86). Patricia Rozema's 1999 *Mansfield Park* occasioned outrage with its foregrounding of Sir Thomas's Antiguan slave holdings, Henry and Maria's adulterous coupling, and Mary Crawford's sexualized "fascination," to which Fanny herself falls sway. The 2006 Hodder Headline edition of *Mansfield Park* claims a heteronormative Austen as the godmother of chick-lit, its cover featuring a purple-tinged Regency couple, a backdrop of shooting stars and pale blue roses accentuating the teasing précis, "When the gorgeous Henry Crawford and his pretty sister Mary come to Mansfield Park, they've no idea what a disturbance they will cause." A similar Austen is installed as biographical fact in Julian Jarrold's 2007 film *Becoming Jane*. Jarrold's Austen retains the verve attributed, via Austen's juvenilia, to Rozema's Fanny Price, playing cricket and embarking upon an elopement with the roguish Irishman, Thomas Lefroy. Austen is depicted embracing the initially hesitant Lefroy, their lengthy clinch causing her to tremble and breathe audibly. The physicality of this scene recalls that of the passionate kiss, filmed in close-up, shared by the newlywed Elizabeth and Darcy in Langton's *Pride and Prejudice*. Standing as tropes of apparent lack in Austen's novels, such imagined and interpolated scenes endorse the corporeality of her fictional courtships, even as they elide the more excessive desires apparent in her work.[5] Jarrold's narrative further endorses the interrelation of Austen's life and work, her heroines' "incandescent marriages" standing in place of the marital fulfillment denied her and Cassandra.

The trade in normatively sexed-up Austen is apparent in the virtual gift "shoppe" of the *Republic of Pemberley* web community, in which Janeites may purchase "Elizabeth" and "Darcy" notebooks, tote bags, and t-shirts. The fictional personae celebrated by these products are represented by silhouettes of Colin Firth's Darcy (whose wet shirt sends Helen Fielding's Bridget Jones into an intertextual fit, 1999: 137–8), coupled with an Elizabeth embodied by the spectacularly bosomed Jennifer Ehle, also of Langton's production.[6] Such is the audience investment in this hypersexualized pair that critics of Joe Wright's 2005 *Pride and Prejudice* suggested that it was redundant, not only due to the tremendous affection for the 1995 miniseries, but because Keira Knightley, in the role of Elizabeth, possessed a comparatively gamine figure (Ditkoff 2005). Wright supplied the now-requisite earthiness through Austen's "Brontëfication," depicting a windswept Elizabeth overlooking the Derbyshire plains, and Darcy striding through a misty field, his long coat and brooding physicality only lacking Rochester's faithful dog. The physicality of Elizabeth's encounter with Darcy's portrait at Pemberley is emphasized by the transposition of Austen's scene to a black-and-white flagged sculpture hall, in which Elizabeth's fitness to be the house's mistress is marked by the echo between the monochromatic interior and her simple dress. The depiction of the text's portraits as three-dimensional objects echoes the physical charge of Elizabeth and Darcy's attraction, the camera lingering over pert marble bottoms before bringing Elizabeth face to face with Darcy's likeness in a sculptured bust. The film's ending also responds to audience expectations of romantic closure. The British release of Wright's film ends with Elizabeth and Darcy sharing a sunlit nuzzle before the camera cuts to a laughing Mr Bennet. The North American release, however, features an added scene in which Elizabeth and a bare-legged Darcy dine *al fresco* on the Pemberley balcony. Requesting that Darcy does not address her as "my dear" ("It is what my father always calls my mother when he's cross about something"), Elizabeth offers a range of romantically exaggerated alternatives. Darcy responds by asking whether he should address her as "Mrs Darcy" to indicate displeasure. Elizabeth responds, "You may only call me Mrs Darcy when you are completely and perfectly and incandescently happy," inciting him to fervently echo her marital patronym as they embrace.

Austen's contemporary cultural figuration may thus be seen to thematize the decisive rejection of her mythic sexual and textual purity. It might also be seen to reject any uneasiness over the oddity of her spinster status, the normativity of her most popular cinematic progeny demonstrating the triumphal endorsement of her marital plots. Upon closer reflection, these figurations also constitute a continuingly necessary insistence upon the sexuality inherent to the Austen canon, the recognition of her publicly staged bodies and potentially excessive desires representing an importantly queer critical mode. Like Wright's balcony scene, the emphatic normativity of such representations is moreover undone by their own supplementarity, their compulsive iterations evidencing the tension between narrative form and queer impulse so apparent throughout Austen's oeuvre.

NOTES

1 For accounts of the critical mêlée that greeted such publications, see Sedgwick (1993: 109–13), Castle's general Introduction (xi–xxiii) and Postscript to "Was Jane Austen Gay?" in Castle (2002: 125–36), Berlant (1994), Johnson (1996: 143–47), and Tuite (2004).

2 "Austenuations" is the title given to the section of *The Republic of Pemberley* website devoted to the discussion of "Jane Austen's minor works, comparisons among Jane Austen novels, and published sequels to Jane Austen novels" <http://www.pemberley.com/bin/aoa/aoa.cgi>.

3 See Anne Lister (1988, 1992).

4 Significant contributions to this revision include Said (1993) and Johnson (1998).

5 I am grateful to Gillian Russell for drawing my attention to this point.

6 See <http://www.cafepress.com/pemstore>.

FURTHER READING

Castle, Terry (1995). Sister-sister. *The London Review of Books* 17.15 (1995): 3–6. Reprinted in *Boss Ladies, Watch Out! Essays on Women, Sex, and Writing* (pp. 125–36). New York and London: Routledge, 2002.

Heydt-Stevenson, Jill (2000). "Slipping into the ha-ha": bawdy humor and body politics in Jane Austen's novels. *Nineteenth-Century Literature*, 55: 3, 309–39.

Johnson, Claudia L. (1996). The divine Miss Jane: Jane Austen, Janeites, and the discipline of novel studies. *boundary 2*, 23.3, 143–63.

Miller, D. A. (2003). *Jane Austen, or the Secret of Style*. Princeton, NJ and Oxford: Princeton University Press.

Sedgwick, Eve Kosofsky (1993). Jane Austen and the masturbating girl. In *Tendencies* (pp. 109–29). Durham, NC and London: Duke University Press.

Tuite, Clara (2002). *Romantic Austen: Sexual Politics and the Literary Canon*. Cambridge, UK: Cambridge University Press.

41

Jane Austen and Popular Culture

Judy Simons

In the Spring of 1814 Jane Austen was making one of her regular visits to her brother, Henry, who lived in Covent Garden, then, as now, the heart of theatreland. She was in the middle of reading *The Heroine, or Adventures of Cherubina* by Eaton Stannard Barrett, a "delightful burlesque on the Radcliffe style," which had appeared a few months earlier, and which she found tremendously entertaining, racing through the third volume after tea on Wednesday March 2 in order to get to the end (*Letters*: 261). By Saturday she had also finished the newest Lord Byron romance, *The Corsair*, and was starting to feel bored, with only sewing and letter-writing to occupy her. Her spirits picked up considerably that evening when she went to Drury Lane, having managed to get tickets for Edmund Kean as Shylock, all the rage since his London premiere in January that year. Two days later she was off to see the celebrated comic actress, Dora Jordan, in *The Devil to Pay* by Charles Coffey. Indeed by the end of the first week of her stay, she had been to the theatre three times to enjoy both classical and popular works, including the opera, *Araxerxes*, a farce, a pantomime, *The Farmer's Wife* – "a Musical thing in 3 Acts" – and was eagerly anticipating another Shake-spearean outing, this time to *Richard III,* starring the matinee idol, Charles Mayne Young (*Letters*: 261).

Austen's third completed novel, *Mansfield Park*, with its high moral tone and apparent critique of modern theatre, was already in press but Austen's appetite for metropolitan pleasures had lost none of its edge. Throughout her life she remained addicted to contemporary culture, and her trips to town were packed with visits to the theatre, galleries, exhibitions, musical soirees, and other crowd-pulling events, such as the Indian jugglers who gave daily performances in Pall Mall during the winter of 1813–14. Her taste was eclectic, her critical opinions uncompromising. She judged each piece on its merits; and could be as delighted by a sparkling performance of a low comedy as wearied by a classic if poorly acted. Reputation and intellectual weight proved no guarantee of approval, whether for text or performance. "Ought I to be very much pleased with Marmion? – as yet I am not," she grumbled in June

1808, searching for some glimmer of life in Sir Walter Scott's lackluster tale of Flodden Field (*Letters*: 131).

The divide between "high" and popular culture was not so sharp in Austen's day as in our own: a pantomime was considered an appropriate coda to a Shakespearean tragedy. Austen could read the Romantic poets and a spoof of the Gothic novel on successive days with equal pleasure. Yet she came to maturity as a writer during the period when questions about individual discernment and cultural hierarchies were being articulated and when artistic boundaries were being formulated in the public arena. These questions surface in her work with increasing insistence as her writing charts the transition from poking fun at some ludicrous aspects of popular literature to inquiring profoundly into reading and what we now term its cultural capital (Guillory 1996). What constitutes literary "value"? What factors determine the formation of a canon? And how do these reflect the prevailing educational system and its underlying political ideology?

The late eighteenth century witnessed a marked change in reading habits, concurrent with the growth of a consumer culture, and these together had a massive impact on the publishing industry. Private libraries became recognized as civilized accoutrements of a gentleman's residence, signaling the possession of a cultivated mind. Miss Bingley's manifestly shallow desire for an excellent library once she has a house of her own indicates the social cachet attached to book collecting. In contrast, Mr Bennet's Longbourn library, accumulated over years, is an extension of his personality and a haven from domestic trials. The very layout of a private library, with its idiosyncratic collection of volumes and styles, reflects the cultural miscellany which characterized the period. As Barbara M. Benedict has observed, a library provided "a transitional arena permitting a rich interchange between rival literary ideals. Here critical hierarchies vanish. Libraries juxtaposed current and classical, entertaining and technical, profiteering and pious texts. . . . This jumble elided the emerging distinction between literature as a class commodity and as popular entertainment" (Benedict 2000: 65).

Yet such a distinction was not without its problems. In 1793, John Burton objected that

> The Press daily teems with . . . publications, which are the trash to circulating Libraries. There are but few Novels, which have a tendency to give a right turn to the affections; or at least, are calculated to improve the mind. A perusal of them in rapid succession, is, in fact, a misemployment of time. (1793, vol. 1: 188)

Austen's novels were fueled by contemporary debates about taste and literary value, which linked artistic preference to moral judgment. Moreover, they intervene in those debates. "He does not read?" asks Emma of Harriet Smith about Robert Martin. The question is designed to damn the young farmer, and Emma is thrown off balance when Harriet's reply is not what she anticipates:

He reads the Agricultural Reports, and some other books that lie in one of the window seats – but he reads all *them* to himself. But sometimes of an evening, before we went to cards, he would read something aloud out of the Elegant Extracts – very entertaining. And I know he has read The Vicar of Wakefield. He never read the Romance of the Forest, nor the Children of the Abbey. He had never heard of such books before I mentioned them, but he is determined to get them now as soon as ever he can. (*E*: 29)

Harriet's catalogue sends a message to Emma and to contemporary readers, who would register that Martin is a literate and informed man, keen to keep his business knowledge up to date. But the list also reveals that his taste ranges from the practical to the improving, encompasses both verse and prose, and that he is open-minded in his approach to modern literature, prepared to follow up a young woman's recommendations.

Austen's concern with literary categorization emerges in different ways in virtually all her writings. From an early fascination with burlesque in "Love and Freindship" to *Persuasion's* exploration of reading as a guide to human character, her work is not just influenced by the expansion of popular fiction and drama during this period but itself becomes an agent in the argument as to what constitutes culture. Her novels, studded with allusions to specific novels, poems, and plays, comprise a response to mass-market literature and the emergence of a new type of consumer, while at the same time they offer a robust defense of cultural eclecticism.

The growth of a literate population coincided with Austen's formative years as an artist. The development of new modes of distribution of print culture, including the lending library, had resulted in a steep rise in the volume of publications, particularly of novels. One of the most successful of the new brand of booksellers to capitalize on this shift in consumerism was William Lane, whose Minerva Press, launched in 1790, catered to an undiscriminating readership and targeted women. Carefully marketed, frequently with anonymized authors, Minerva aimed its wares at female readers and was largely responsible for the bad name given to popular fiction by stern critics, who objected to the sensational and often licentious stories at which the Press excelled. Lane cannily exploited his notoriety and made it his trademark, proudly advertising Minerva as "now unrivalled in the public estimation, for Novels, Romances, Adventures." As E. J. Clery has pointed out, Minerva and the brand of fiction which it introduced helped to create the categories of classics and trash which led to the debate about literary value which has persisted to the present day (Clery 1995).

By the turn of the century the controversy had taken on a new dimension, energized by the irrefutable suspicion that literature was no longer an elite pursuit. High-minded detractors argued that mass consumption had lowered the standards of literary production as well as the standards of morality. The parameters of the debate about the quality of mass media, endemic in modern society nowadays, were articulated with particular clarity in 1805 by Hugh Murray's *Morality of Fiction*:

The invention of printing and consequent diffusion of books, has given birth to a multitude of readers, who seek only amusement, and wish to find it without trouble or
thought. Works thus conducted, supply them with one which is level to the lowest
capacities. How well they are adapted to the taste of this description of readers appears
plainly from the extraordinary avidity with which they are devoured. (Murray quoted
in Clery 1995: 150)

The reasoning is familiar to anyone who studies new genres, for example, modern-day
scholars of film or media studies, who must defend their subjects from the same sorts
of criticism today that the novel faced in Austen's time. The attack on novels as per-
nicious to the minds of vulnerable readers was by no means new. Forty years earlier,
John Fordyce's *Sermons to Young Women* (1766) severely lectured women about the risks
of novel reading.

We consider the general run of Novels as utterly unfit for you. Instruction they convey
none. They paint Scenes of Pleasure and Passion altogether improper for you to behold
even with the Mind's Eye. Their Descriptions are often loose and luscious in a High
Degree; their representations of Love between the sexes are almost universally over-
strained. (Fordyce quoted in Clery 1995: 96)

It is no accident that Mr Collins chooses Fordyce's *Sermons* as after-dinner entertainment for the Bennet sisters, nor that John Thorpe in *Northanger Abbey* has neither the
stamina nor the inclination to read a novel all the way through. They represent the
two arms of the opposition: the prig and the boor. Austen, both in literature and in
life, was vigorous in her defense of the novel. "*Our* family . . . are great Novel-readers
& not ashamed of being so," she boasted in 1798 (*Letters*: 26). That most erudite of
Austen heroes, Henry Tilney, proudly claims to have read "hundreds and hundreds"
of modern novels. "Do not imagine that you can cope with me in a knowledge of
Julias and Louisas," he teases Catherine Morland (*NA*: 107).

Coexistent with Austen's parody is the conviction that popular literature is a genus
to be taken seriously. The elopements and scandals, the standard stuff of the minor
novels of sensation and romance, haunt Austen's major work. Whilst they form the
core of the more uncontrolled juvenilia, they remain an oblique presence in the mature
fiction, referenced through second-hand accounts and confined to minor characters.
Lydia Bennet's seduction, the child abuse and abandonment of Eliza Brandon, Harriet
Smith's illegitimacy, Maria Rushworth's adultery, Mrs Smith's financial ruin: these
are the narrated disasters which form the sinister backdrop to the domestic scenarios
and psychological dramas of Austen's heroines. Thus Austen subverts the plot of the
popular novel and the parallel scenarios of sentimental drama, placing shady intrigue
and sexual threat in the background, whilst the routine fabric of daily life becomes
the stage for playing out the real horrors, the economic and social threats, which
confront young women in Regency England. As Kathryn Sutherland suggests, by
subsuming and inverting the expected patterns of popular narrative, Austen's work

does not discount the stock generic conventions but rather discloses their more disturbing propositions (Sutherland 2005: 354).

It is ironic that Austen's work, with its unashamed defense of popular culture, should have become the province of a select and refined readership. It is equally incongruous that at the start of the twenty-first century such a canonical writer has become reclaimed by a popular audience. Both the novels and the novelist have acquired a cult status, which offers a prime target for parody and invests them with an afterlife susceptible to modern scripting. Never best sellers in their author's lifetime, today Austen's six novels have consistently high sales and are available across the world in paperback and hard cover editions from dozens of publishing houses. Her books have proved sufficiently elastic to suit the full range of modern media. Recent film versions of *Sense and Sensibility*, *Pride and Prejudice*, and *Emma* have created new audiences for Austen, the movies playing to packed cinemas and nominated for major awards. Austen's work has changed social and cultural habits, acquiring a fresh generation of readers who find in the Regency scenarios unexpected correspondences with their own lives.

The popularity of her fiction and the impulse to perpetuate it started only a few years after their author's death with attempts by Austen's niece, Anna Lefroy, and her great-niece, Catherine Anne Hubback, to write continuations to the incomplete *Sanditon* and *The Watsons* respectively. But it is the adoption by a mass public of the sequel or revision as a discrete art form which has characterized Austenian reception in the last 25 years. The existence of the internet in particular, with its virtually global scope, has stimulated a new form of energetic fandom, and given rise to specialist websites devoted to Austen, her works, her life, and her milieu. The most extensive of these, "The Republic of Pemberley," styles its members "Janeites," a tribute to Kipling's 1924 story of that name, which shows how an enthusiasm for Austen secures admission into a privileged circle.

A section of "The Republic of Pemberley" website is devoted to listings and reviews of published sequels by professional writers. The list contains 49 modern sequels to *Pride & Prejudice* alone, many of which are fairly crude continuations of the original plot and character histories of the "what happened next?" variety, such as *Mr Darcy's Daughters* (2003) or *Postscript from Pemberley* (2000), whose authors have built careers out of this branch of the revitalized Austen industry. There are also more sophisticated transpositions, drawing heavily on other subgenres, such as Stephanie Barron's mystery series, starting with *Jane and the Unpleasantness at Scargrave Manor* (1996), and Paula Marantz Cohen's witty romp, *Jane Austen in Boca* (2003), which relocates the story to a Jewish retirement complex in Florida. In a reversal of the Jewish mother joke, Cohen neatly re-presents the Bennet sisters as a group of elderly widows with a managing daughter-in-law desperate to find them husbands from amongst the retired, eligible widowers who have made their fortunes on Wall Street. The novel is peppered with allusions to academia and the lit crit industry, including a seminar on *Pride and Prejudice*, which forms a wry, self-reflexive comment on Austenian reception and the academy.

Another subsection of "The Republic of Pemberley" encourages fans to produce their own sequels and circulate them electronically for others to contribute the next installment. The love of parody which features so brilliantly in Austen's writing has elicited a new generation of practitioners, who use the works of their favorite author as stimuli for their own comic inventions. Often unfinished, the fragments exhibit the same degree of joyful exuberance as the *Juvenilia*, whose author was supremely sensitive to the inspirational nature of popular texts. Today, the dominant forms of the Austenian continuation – burlesque, pastiche, and excess – are identical to those which captivated Austen. Her own six novels are now so embedded in contemporary reading cultures that they have become fair game for revision, whether on page or screen. Just as "Jack and Alice" travestied the traditions of the playhouse and the novel of sensibility, so *Bridget Jones's Diary* (1996) subsumes *Pride and Prejudice*, confident that its scenarios will have resonance with today's audiences. The unmarried protagonist of Helen Fielding's novel longs for a partner both comically and soulfully as she reflects on the fortunes of being a "singleton" woman in twentieth-century London, and her prejudices against Darcy melt when she visits his magnificent house (having been side-tracked en route to true romance by a duplicitous charmer à la Wickham). Starting out as a newspaper column, subsequently published in book form and adapted as a feature film, Fielding's text exemplifies what is becoming a familiar literary phenomenon, the textual portfolio career.

The start of the twenty-first century is thus witness to a resurgence of the Minerva Press phenomenon, with its amalgamation of theatrical and fictional styles, which provided such a rich imaginative resource for Austen. The rapid growth of the new media and the consequent development of diverse forms of dissemination have accelerated a change in modern reading habits, with an immediate impact on Austenian reception. The intimacy once associated with the act of reading has been displaced by a project of shared recovery. The iPod, the DVD, the audio book, the TV and cinema screen have taken over from print culture as major forms of cultural transmission. But it is print culture which supplies the urtext, and in reformulating its substance these new media engage directly with its interpretation. Furthermore, the wide appeal of audio versions of the novels signals a return to their original mode of transmission – reading aloud. Distinguished actors, famous for their classical roles, including Anna Massey and Juliet Stevenson, have found their métier as exceptionally insightful readers of Austen, restoring the dramatic power of the texts which spoke directly to their first audiences.

The integration of Austen's writing into the popular cultural imagination is overwhelmingly evident in the electronic shared reading and discussion groups which have spiraled into existence on the internet. The Group Reading section of the "Republic of Pemberley" invites members to read according to a strict weekly schedule and then to post personal views about the pages designated for each week's program. Suggestions for further reading extend far beyond the primary works. The on-line "Library" recommends Austen fans to other authors, based on a presumption of shared tastes and interests. Here, novels by Fanny Burney and Maria Edgeworth rub shoulders with the mid-twentieth-century Regency romances of Georgette Heyer and the detective novels of Elizabeth George. The construction of the site transcends hierarchical barriers in its fusion of highbrow and popular texts, scholarly editions, and pulp romances, so that it resembles nothing more than an eighteenth-century library in its assortment of titles and genres, making no claims other than expressions of personal taste.

Austen herself has become a frequent presence in modern fictional texts, and one with whom readers are expected to identify. *Becoming Jane*, a feature film based loosely on Austen's flirtation with Tom Lefroy, imagines Austen's emergence as a novelist even as it also incorporates variant reworkings of her novels on screen. The writer and her works have merged into a pop culture phenomenon whose treatment has advanced considerably from her appearance in Kipling's story "The Janeites" to studied use of the novels' plots and characters in a work such as Karen Joy Fowler's *The Jane Austen Book Club* (2004). Despite being published almost a century apart, these texts register a sense of cultural and social privilege conferred by being part of an elite coterie. Paradoxically they indicate Austen's assimilation into the popular imagination at the same time as they depict her exclusivity.

The distinction between "high" and "low" culture blurs in *The Jane Austen Book Club*, in part because it assimilates many of the critical issues which concern Austen scholars: ownership, status, reception, genre, and the postmodern. The novel offers a validation of the amateur reading association, and acquires its ironic force from the fact that each member of the eponymous club is simultaneously acting out her (or, in one case, his) own Austen scenario. The story works on a range of levels and comments on the act of reading for a responsive interpretative community, who learn from sharing their reading experiences. The novel skillfully deploys characteristic Austen techniques. It reinforces both Austen's provincial appeal – the six readers who form the club are small-town inhabitants, and as two members are a mother and daughter, a replica of Austen's "three or four families in a country village" – and her transatlantic portability. The setting, in an American suburb with a distinctively twenty-first century outlook and culturally specific environment, indicates Austen's ability to transcend geographical distance and national boundaries. It also explicitly acknowledges modern critical approaches in order to expose the nexus of possible readings. Gender boundaries, for example, become fluid in a twenty-first century reincarnation, with *Sense and Sensibility* played as a lesbian romance. Catherine Morland is envisaged as a male science-fiction addict, who attends a literary convention, where genres and interests collide. And in a particularly poignant episode, the visit to Northanger segues into a 1970s Gothic nightmare set in a mansion, which has been taken over by drug-taking hippies. An international bestseller, the novel is sold at airport bookstalls and is available as an audio book. In 2004 it featured in the *New York Times* 100 Notable Books of the Year and *The Australian*'s Book of the Year list and made *Good Housekeeping*'s Top 20 list of Christmas gifts.

Yet the widest circulation of Austen's work is not through the written word but through cinema and television. The 1980s and the 1990s saw a spate of screen renderings of Austen's novels, a trend which, with three serializations in ITV's 2007 Jane Austen Season, shows no signs of abating. As Roger Sales has noted, the more recent adaptations have become increasingly self-referential (Sales 2000). In 2005, Working Title, the production company responsible for screening *Bridget Jones's Diary*, returned to its source with a fresh cinematic version of *Pride and Prejudice*, which clearly drew on its screen predecessors. The movie is typical of the latter-day versions which presuppose a sophisticated reader, familiar not just with Austen's originals but with their successive filmic transformations. Deborah Moggach's screenplay allows Mrs Bennet a voice that often goes unheard in conventional interpretations of the text. Instead of the monstrous figure, as played in 1995 by Alison Steadman, Brenda Blethyn presents Mrs Bennet as a distressed mother in a household where the father (a louche Donald Sutherland impersonating an English squire) retreats to his library to evade his duty as paterfamilias. As Blethyn said in an interview,

> . . . she's the only one taking the problem seriously. Mr. Bennet's all right, they've got a roof over their heads all the time he's alive – it's when he dies that they've got the problem when the money goes down the male line. As it turned out, I think she's the only one speaking up for her daughters and trying to solve these problems. (Fischer 2000)

Contrasting Mrs Bennet's pragmatism with her husband's irresponsible strategies of avoidance, the film illustrates the potential of film to produce alternative, feminist, readings.

Working Title's 2005 *Pride and Prejudice* responds directly to the BBC serial. Matthew McFadyen's performance recalls the wet-shirted Darcy, emerging from the lake at Pemberley, itself a calculated contrast to Laurence Olivier's previously definitive portrayal in the 1940 movie, and develops the romantic ideal in Brontëan directions. In casting off the impact of the 1995 adaptation, it underscores the absorption of those images into the collective cultural imagination. That impact is also evident in films which pay only oblique reference to the original Austen text. *Bridget Jones's Diary* dexterously exploits its different media representations. The ingenious casting of Colin Firth as Darcy in *Bridget Jones's Diary* is a deliberate allusion to Firth's casting in the BBC serial. The palimpsestic nature of these products continue to resonate for the practiced Austen reader, aware of eighteenth-century literary conventions, the nuances of the original text, and the quirks of cinema and critical histories.

The impulse to read against the texts not only of Austen but of her representation in film motivates the most unconventional of these adaptations, Patricia Rozema's *Mansfield Park* (1999). Using the somewhat alarming tag line, "Jane Austen's Wicked Comedy," Rozema turns Austen's quiet heroine, Fanny Price, on her head in order to release an oppositional Austen, subversive and challenging in her resistance to social norms. Rozema's interpretation is profoundly influenced by late twentieth-century critical debates, including feminist critiques and postcolonial readings, which unearth a subtext of slavery and see the novel as a commentary on British power relations and the imperialist ethic in the early nineteenth century. It affords an opportunity for immediate bonding between two of the *Jane Austen Book Club*'s characters, united in their objection to Austen abuse. Unsurprisingly, the film lacks the popular appeal of those more integrative and benign versions which draw explicitly on the conventions of screen romantic comedy.

Of these, both *Clueless* (1995), Amy Heckerling's homage to *Emma*, and Gurinder Chadha's *Bride & Prejudice* (2004) skillfully recycle popular cinematic forms: the teen comedy and the Bollywood musical. The films abandon period fidelity in favor of the cultural hybridity which is both their subject and their tribute to Austen. Paradoxically, it is by discarding textual conformity that they recapture Austen's own "light, bright and sparkling" tone, frequently lost in the more plodding efforts of the heritage film industry. Their alien settings defamiliarize Austen and reinterpret the novels in ways that are at once more accurate and more consistent than many traditional versions.

Clueless's setting in a Beverly Hills high school resituates the narrative of *Emma* in a world which evokes both the innocence and the parochialism of a closed "village" community. From the opening credits, with their musical accompaniment of popular hit songs such as "Girls Just Wanna Have Fun," the mood of a high-spirited but thoughtless youth culture is established, brilliantly echoing the consummate poise of *Emma* itself. Precisely because *Clueless*'s central characters are adolescent, the viewer can be indulgent of their self-importance and inability to see beyond their own life-style. The society, with its own linguistic codes, its insouciance, and its arcane rules thinks itself self-sufficient but has yet to recognize the larger world picture, where, as in *Emma*, menace lurks beyond the margins of their privileged existence.

In *Bride & Prejudice*, Austen's novel is relocated to present-day Amritsar, drawing on the marked correspondences between Indian cultural traditions and the social conventions of eighteenth-century England. In addition to the send-up of the embedded hierarchical system and the social aspirations of the Indian middle class, the film exposes the cultural mix which defines twenty-first-century India, and the impact of the East/West divide. In *Bride & Prejudice*, the world has shrunk to a global village, with Will Darcy a sophisticated American millionaire contemptuous of the manners he finds in provincial India. The different locations used in the film mirror Austen's use of the voyage of discovery undergone by both Elizabeth and Darcy, and in a splendidly comic episode – with Mr Collins reinvented as a born-again adoptive citizen of LA – the superficiality of American excess is revealed as not entirely dissimilar to the Indian love of the extravagant. *Bride & Prejudice* integrates music into the action more overtly than does *Clueless*, featuring lavish set-piece musical numbers to reinforce the blend of cultures and styles which dominates an uncertain society in search of an identity in a rapidly changing world.

At the same time both films interrogate Austen's present-day reputation through their amalgamation of dissonant cultures and their depiction of the impact of the past on current attitudes. In their different ways they have fun with the concept of the "classic" and its status in modern culture. "Oooh, classic!" Cher in *Clueless* coos at the sight of her schoolteacher in love, congratulating herself on having made the perfect match. It is only one of a series of references the film makes to a recessive culture, where the line, "Rough winds do shake the darling buds of May" is attributable only as a famous quote from Cliff Notes, and where Cher's very name announces its debt to modern cultural icons. Cher pays tribute to her dead mother whose portrait hangs prominently in the foyer of her home, which, adorned with ersatz columns, dating "all the way back to 1972," contains an ironic homage to postbellum architecture, itself an imitation of Hellenic classicism; and in a delightful take on the portrait painting scene, she photographs Tai, noting admiringly that she resembles "one of those Botticelli chicks."

Glossy and glitzy in its appearance and mores, *Clueless* anticipates the brash *Bride & Prejudice*, which inflates its lavish production values as part of its satire of Bollywood excess. Here the casting of Aishwarya Rai, an ex-Miss World, as a postcolonial Elizabeth Bennet, together with a guest appearance by a celebrity pop star, Ashanti, carry cultural reverberations which have particular resonance for their cinema audiences – it is an accepted tradition in Bollywood films that a guest celebrity makes a cameo appearance to sing a song which has no direct relevance to the narrative. The very status of cinema as an art form in modern Indian culture itself encodes a cultural message about the configuration of the "classic" and its significance, and it is notable that the film was made in three simultaneous versions, in English, Punjabi, and Hindi, for transmission to its culturally diverse audiences. The powerful impact of the colonial inheritance affords the English classics a special status; the film's bold transposition of one of the most sacrosanct of English writers is thus iconoclastic in more ways than one, abandoning the imperial ethic as well as lampooning contemporary Indian mores. In their insistent modernity, these two movies come closer to appreciating the cultural subtleties of the novels than many of the more reverential adaptations, where Austen sometimes loses her comic edge.

No other English writer inspires the same intellectual rigor and irreverence as Austen. She has become a cultural icon, occupying a unique position in the modern world, her very name embodying a set of values which resonate even with those who have never read a word she wrote. Authors as varied as Samuel Beckett, Irvine Welsh, and Harper Lee have acknowledged her influence, and are designated "Friends of Jane" on a website whose members are on familiar first-name terms with their favorite novelist. Yet, despite the heterogeneity of her following, Austen's artistic integrity remains intact, recognized by readers outside as well as inside the academy. As Austen's First Law of Blogging states, "I could not sit seriously down to write a serious Blog under any other motive than to save my Life; and if it were indispensable for me to keep it up & never relax into laughing at myself or other people, I am sure I should be hung before I had finished the first post"[1] (http://www.austenblog. com/jane-austens-first-law-of-blogging).

NOTE

1   The parody recalls Austen's famously restrained letter to James Stanier Clarke, the Prince of Wales' librarian, who had suggested that her next novel might be in a style more suited to his Highness' taste.

FURTHER READING

Lynch, Deidre (Ed.) (2000). *Janeites: Austen's Disciples and Devotees*. Princeton, NJ: Princeton University Press.

MacDonald, Gina and Andrew MacDonald (Eds) (2003). *Jane Austen on Screen*. Cambridge, UK: Cambridge University Press.

Pucci, Suzanne R. and James Thompson (Eds) (2003). *Jane Austen & Co: Remaking the Past in Contemporary Culture*. Albany: State University of New York Press.

Simons, Judy (1998). Classics and trash: Jane Austen in the 1990s. *Women's Writing*, 5:1, 27–39.

Sutherland, Kathryn (2005). *Jane Austen's Afterlives: From Aeschylus to Bollywood*. Oxford: Oxford University Press.

Wiltshire, John (2001). *Recreating Jane Austen*. Cambridge, UK: Cambridge University Press.

42

Austenian Subcultures

Mary Ann O'Farrell

"For the truth is that every true admirer of the novels cherishes the happy thought that he alone – reading between the lines – has become the secret friend of their author."[1] When I have encountered in the past Katherine Mansfield's famous 1920 remark about the admiring reader's response to Austen's novels, my own response as reader has resonated with Mansfield's outline of a fantasized friendship with Austen, alluring in its secrecy and exclusivity, while also dangerous in its attaching power and in the near-escapability of the scary recognition that, reading between the lines, I may be making it all up. Rereading Mansfield today, though, I am struck by the condition of singularity that informs her account of what looks like a reader/writer dyad. Reading Austen à la Mansfield, although it promises the intimacies of a friendship between two (reader and writer), might instead be not merely (in being a fantasy) the solitary pleasure of one alone but indeed a dream of isolation, a pleasure in solitariness itself and in the identification even of "she" with the fierce accomplishment of being the exemplary "he alone." The victory over the others that constitutes secret friendship with the author is also an accession to a lonely place.

How extraordinary, then, that a writer with whom readers have so often imagined themselves in a private duality (Mansfield is not wrong) is in the twenty-first century as notorious for the production of reader communities devoted to her as for representing in the popular imagination the fantasy of authorial possession by a friendly reader. Even a work that takes as its task fictionalizing a sociable understanding of Austen's work in the world, Karen Joy Fowler's novel *The Jane Austen Book Club* (2004) cannot resist invoking possessiveness at its start. In a sentence surrounded by white space, isolated from others on the page, the voice of the group announces "Each of us has a private Austen" (Fowler 2004: 1), fantasizing a local truth about group members' authorial intimacies into one that could almost be subject to universal acknowledgment: a private Austen is a private self. Exploring their discrete Austens together, the participants in her Jane Austen Book Club, Fowler seems to suggest, make a society out of personal and private obsessions and demonstrate that society itself is so constituted. And thinking about the function of author-based communities for an Austenian readership that is attached to a sense of victorious and possessive oneness in friendship with Austen means recognizing a readership that, in the course of developing subcultures, embodies the tension and enacts the play between private obsession and public relations.

Fowler's suggestion about a reader-based society, though, and my own, are consequential upon Austen's articulation of social relations, particularly through her habit of writing as dialogue what readers recognize as simultaneous monologues. In *Emma*, for example, when Mr Weston arrives at an evening party at Hartfield bearing news of his son Frank Churchill's impending visit, he shares his happy-anxious news with Mrs Elton in an extended conversation that permits them both to indulge in favorite subjects. Mr Weston talks delightedly of Frank and nervously of Mrs Churchill's obstructive health and whims, while Mrs Elton turns all references (to the evils of distance, to the fineness of fine ladies, to the seclusion of the best estates, to the "horror of upstarts," *E*: 310) away from Mr Weston's news and toward her particular obsessions: herself and her associates, these latter living still the fine life she has been privileged to witness at Maple Grove. Readers may remember best the social self-interestedness of Mrs Elton; the novel teaches us to expect it, and it is everywhere to be found. But Mr Weston is, if genial, a genial bore, and the conversation is as much a record of his talky self-indulgences as of hers. Enthusiasts love a witness.

Austen is careful, too, though, to note that, in the singularity of their obsessions, Mr Weston and Mrs Elton form an effective duality. The union of their discursive disparities into a passable conversation is the product of some practiced social skill. Adept at spotting an opening ("Your description . . . made me think of them directly," *E*: 310), Mrs Elton is *attentively* inattentive, while, monologuing, Mr Weston responds to her needs with a generosity that suits his economic sense of social return. If Mrs Elton's oblique "call for a compliment" is, despite its indirection, "too loud . . . to be passed by," the "good grace" with which Mr Weston proffers a compliment on call facilitates his taking back his own: "He had done his duty and could return to his son" (*E*: 307–8). Austen the social theorist, that is, has shown sociability to be what it is: the caught references and the missed ones, the opportunities seized upon and let pass by, the ungracious exhibitions of and gracious yieldings to obsessions that, together, are narcissism in company. Shown through Mr Weston's and Mrs Elton's energetic tedium at its least attractive, sociability is not any less effective for that apparent unattractiveness at arranging us so that we may tolerate one another's narcissisms, the better to ensure the toleration of our own.

Still, while Austen's strict presentation of the insularity of Mrs Elton's self-attentions nudges readers towards knowing that our enthusiasms – whatever else their objects – are for ourselves, the novelist's kinder presentation elsewhere in *Emma* of an open-hearted and genuinely solicitous Mr Weston (he worries, for example, that by way of Frank he might have hurt Emma) indicates some authorial forgiveness of occasional social narcissism as a human inevitability. And the balance in this social accounting extends to a balanced and forgiving account of sociability itself: Austen's novels demonstrate sociability in action as both a condition of our being and its gift. In forming themselves around the social encounter, Austen's novels model as well as record the workings of sociability as an exercise in management of time, life, and world. Bonding: it's what we do. And Austen's balls and meetings, walks, talks, and meals, her theatricals and games, her excursions and tours, as well as her homecomings, all suggest that being in the world, if it is of necessity a succession of encounters, may yet be construable as a sequence of occasions.

No uncomplex gift, though, sociability *chez* Austen yields not only the warmth and satisfactions of the occasion but also its discomforts and demands. And what Austen's occasions look like in series are a course of bondings, breakings, and re-formings that, precisely in their ephemeral shapes and stabilities, are no less beautiful and no less contained than the colored bits in a child's kaleidoscope. When a ball ends in Austen, the social *monde* changes, regathering and reshaping itself through private intimacies forged in response to the public comings together. Austen's influential understanding of the workings of sociability – inclusive as it is of all there is in the social that makes it close and coercive, hot in its pressures, cool in its distances, relentless in its anxious comparisons – is powerful not just in rendering alongside its difficulties the attractions of sociability but in suggesting that those attractions can inhere precisely in the acts of rehearsal and examination with which one comes to understand and to manage the history of oneself among others. Readers of *Pride and Prejudice* may imagine that Elizabeth Bennet is never so lively, never so attractive, never so endearing, and never so wounded as when she repeats for her sisters and friends the story of a social slight. Sociability in Austen inheres not only in the party but in the sharp-eyed social criticism and scary self-examination, performed in company, of the party postmortem. Representing the attractions and the difficulties of the social life, Austen represents no less compellingly the means by which a second-order social function effects a handling of and a living with the self. The mortification rehearsed and performed as a *tour de force* – the public rearticulation of self that takes self as its indirect object – models for Austen's readers what sociability might achieve when put to private use. And, by extension, the fabled sociability of reading in indissoluble attachment to Austen's narrator makes clear the dependence of reading itself on a fantasy of company, most useful when – compelling yet ineluctably fantastic – it cannot exercise company's demands.

If, as I have been suggesting, sociability (in Austen's corpus and as we may learn from that corpus to consider and to experience it in the world) is a circuit of multiform excursions and retreats that follow, fuel, and reproduce one another, it then makes sense that a readership powerfully responsive to Austen might itself oscillate between attraction to social formation and removal from it to private readership. And the ways that Austen readers now find and speak to one another, considered collectively, bespeak a need for social adhesion alongside some ambivalence about that need.

Austenian subcultures, and the individuals constituting them, will engage variously the rigors and the comforts of an Austen-inspired sociability. From group to group, from person to person, and from moment to moment, the sociability that produces a community or a culture may seem to a reader welcoming, warming, stimulating, challenging, irritating, alienating. No account of reader communities can explain all such effects. But a set of readily identifiable Austenian subcultures, in the presentation of their public faces, may be mappable along a continuum from a barely broken isolation to companionship on full display.

The extent and constancy of physical presence in community may be determining of place on this continuum. The ability to tolerate others' private Austens – perhaps the eagerness of an Austen of one's own to be in company or to hold her ground among or against others' Austens – is what facilitates the formation of Austen societies, Austen tour groups, and even Austen classes. With their teas and balls, dance classes and conferences, the Jane Austen clubs and societies in both their most and least formal manifestations have long been organized around a celebration of face-to-face sociability. But the Jane Austen Society of the UK, the Jane Austen Society of North America (JASNA), and the Jane Austen Society of Australia (along with other societies organized regionally, nationally, and internationally) have also understood themselves as undertaking the public missions of education, preservation, archival development, and scholarship through conferences, lectures, tours, publications, and institutions (the preservation of Chawton Cottage, for example, which was the founding motive for the UK Society in 1940), as well as fostering the Austenian version of what would once have been called a "get-together." (JASNA memorializes its 1979 founding by reference to the *New Yorker*'s characteristically casualizing account of the society's beginnings: "Some people who like Jane Austen got together the other evening. . . ."[2]) Writers have sometimes responded defensively to stories about Austen-based gatherings that have dealt understatedly with the gatherings' public labors and serious purposes, emphasizing instead the lighter occasions on which readers of Austen met for social pleasures. Emily Auerbach, for example, complains with some justification that, in its article about the 2001 University of Wisconsin Center for the Humanities festival "Jane Austen in the Twenty-first Century," the *Chicago Tribune* "mentioned our sponsorship of an English country dance and a game show but not the fact that speakers included internationally acclaimed novelist and *Oxford Companion to {English} Literature* editor Margaret Drabble, distinguished BBC screenwriter Andrew Davies, or renowned Austen scholars Claudia Johnson, Juliet McMaster, Jan Fergus, Joseph Wiesenfarth, and others" (Auerbach 2004: 283). But a conference director's pride is also that of a host in those she has gotten together, and it may remind us that scholars, screenwriters, novelists, conference registrants, and society members in assemblage are readers engaging Austen's ideas no less (if less directly) when they are configuring social relations in talk and in dance than when they are lecturing or listening.

A middling relation to physical presence as a constituent part of an Austenian subculture is effected by Austen commodities. We know what these are: after buying DVDs of film and television adaptations of her novels, Austen shoppers can line mantles or bookshelves with porcelain heroine *objets* and plastic dolls (such as the Jane Austen Action Figure), lie on beach towels imprinted with a truth universally acknowledged, sleep on the Colin Firth pillowcase that would make them nocturnal Elizabeths, decorate refrigerators or file cabinets with Austen felt finger puppet magnets. We can play Austen's card games and novel-based board games (marriage their object), drink from Austen mugs we keep on Austen coasters, wear Austen aprons and t-shirts, carry her everywhere on tote bags, play tunes she may have known on our pianos or listen to them through some enabling technology; we can tell time by an Austen wall clock or calendar, thank others or invite them or console them with our Austen notecards. Books available for purchase hold out the possibility of taking tea with Jane Austen and cooking with her, consulting her on matters of etiquette and romance, walking in her footsteps on tours of England, designing and furnishing our homes in some relation to a style less Austenian than contemporary Regency suburban, wear jewelry that evokes hers or that is engraved with her words. The Jane Austen cuff bracelet, a recent catalogue tells us, "speaks Jane Austen's prayer of contentment eloquently in a simple script font"; not my Austen, the Austen of braceleted contentment takes on in nagging prayer the dilemma-resolving properties of the model Jesus, like him never answering the question that underwrites her beatification by t-shirt slogan – "What Would Jane Austen Do?".

Purchasers of Austen consumables participate in a subculture basing itself in materiality and communicating by means of *objet*-signs. The Austen mug and t-shirt advertise the bearer to a set of imaginary Austen friends, while announcing a set of tastes and attachments that, like all conspicuous personal advertisements (for teams and schools and vacations on which one was not invited), distance at least as often as they attract. But it is notable that, except for those in the gift shops in designated tourist locations, Austen objects are largely purchasable not through the companionable act of shopping in stores but through online and catalogue shopping. The Austen shopper shops alone, every late-night impulse buy at once calling for companionship and bespeaking a taste for isolation; imprinted with a range of slogans, all Austen objects might be construed to say with the bumper sticker, "I'd rather be reading Jane Austen."

Shoppers who make purchases from the site store that is part of the economy of the Republic of Pemberley, though, might not rather be reading Jane Austen. The extensiveness of their postings and the nature of their relations (which – like those on many long-established websites – extend beyond their ostensible subject to matters that, among acquaintances and friends, invite condolence or congratulation) have led to the production of objects that join the traditional Austen tableware and t-shirts in speaking as much to the sociability constituted by internet relations as to Austen and her works. Notably, the site's featured webstore offers articles that follow the exclamation "I blame Jane" with a parenthetical string of letters that is at first bewildering. But regular visitors to the Republic of Pemberley come to know that "(A.I.S.S.B.H.)" is shorthand for "(and I'm sure she blames herself)," a reading of what her sister Elizabeth describes as Jane Bennet's "sweetness and disinterestedness" that in a friendly way mocks and modernizes such generosity of spirit into a self-effacement reified by the teachings of self-help. Even the requisite parentheses reproduce typographically the modesty with which Jane might be understood to tuck herself away. The site's answer to a query about this language (it is a designated FAQ), which explains it as "a reference to Jane Bennet's irrational need to take too much upon herself, especially with regard to the matter of Wickham's character, and her pact with Lizzy to curb public knowledge of its true nature," refashions from its assessment of Jane Bennet a collective *self*-assessment the results of which it attributes to Jane Austen.[3] A.I.S.S.B.H., the site indicates, "may be extended to mean one blames Jane Austen for getting us all into this fine obsessive mess." The FAQ-writer's understanding of the online community and its obsessions as a "fine obsessive mess" is transparently, as it seems meant to be, a secret celebration of the indulged narcissisms in company that, no less than Mr Weston's and Mrs Elton's, produce a serviceable sociability that styles itself a Republic. The mugs, tiles, and t-shirts that are able to signify only for those who frequent the site celebrate not just Austen but particular readings of her coupled with a sharp-eyed self-awareness about the site itself as a locus of sociability. The purchaser of the A.I.S.S.B.H. mug, who might perhaps rather be reading Jane Austen, seems still more likely rather to be talking about her with online friends, and these Austen objects (like the objects produced for sale at Austen societies' meetings) memorialize a relation and give to a virtual sociability a physical presence in dailiness.

"We, all of us, remember only too well the great relief we felt upon discovering this haven for Jane Austen Addicts." The words greeting "newbies" on their earliest visits to the Republic of Pemberley website speak to the lure and the affect of a sociability that once – when we tended to call it virtual – might have seemed fictive. With their welcome, the site managers (the oligarchs?) of the Republic establish that this online community constitutes itself as an alternative to the world beyond. Self-consciously a "haven," the site calms and orders Austenian users rambling about in its discussion boards, its shopping district, its information pages, its illustrations, its advice center, and its for-the-nonce book clubs ("groupreads"), reminding us where we are by means of a boxed and bolded statement of reassurance frequently encountered: "No, you've not lost your way. You remain safe within the borders of The Republic of Pemberley." As if worried that a mad link could lead us astray, this web community constantly reconstitutes itself – and enlists us for its citizenry by enscripting us within its borders – through an oppositionality to the world outside its pages that is at once exaggerated and mild. Though the social relations regular site members enjoy seem powerfully binding, the site is self-consciously exclusive, even perhaps rebarbative. Answering an FAQ representatively imagined to ask "Why is this place so clubby?" the site reinforces the perception of clubbiness by responding, essentially, that it is because it is and that it is so because it wants to be so: "We do tend to be a little cliquey, don't we? . . . entry is open, but visitors who don't fit the profile either will elect not to join the community or will lose interest as they see it is not meant for them." Descriptive language ("visitors who don't fit the profile . . . will") masks a directive (visitors who don't fit the profile ought). The site points unhappy visitors elsewhere, to a place they might belong: "The attitude weeds out some people, and that's what we intend. If you resonate with the tone, visiting the site will be all the more fun for you. If you don't, just don't come; it's not your kind of place. You might want to give AUSTEN-L a try." The sneer is just visible.

Though other Austenians seem most obviously who and what is being weeded out by "attitude" from the civility of the Republic of Pemberley, that expressed sense of relief "upon discovering this haven," in preceding internecine rivalries, seems to radiate beyond such rivalries to express the discomfort with the world (with sex, with history, with embodiment, with contemporaneity) that is the essence of Janeitism in the cultural imagination.[4] Though much written on the site (as on AUSTEN-L and on numerous other sites wholly or partially devoted to Austen) is thoroughly engaged with all that cultural fantasy would deny the Austenian, Janeitism, expressed in the exhalation of relief upon arrival, is understandable in these terms as a beleaguredness and besiegedness in search of respite and refuge.

Suspicious as I am of the claim that the Austen reader really needs refuge – Austen's works are too available, too taught, too filmed, too commodified for her readers collectively to feel more culturally out-of-touch than we want to feel – I cannot help noticing nevertheless that the socialized Janeite is a figure of cultural fun. Written accompaniments to and comments upon Austen-related material on YouTube, for example, often create and rely upon a harassable Janeite. Austen's presence on YouTube, which might be unexpected, becomes less surprising and the YouTube Austen fan culture more familiar after surveying the hundreds of videos returned by searches on Austen's name and on words featured in her novel's titles. Some of the hits yield images of people dancing, memorializations and publications of Austen society events (the yearly Jane Austen Ball in Pasadena), or of personal events with Austen themes ("my coming-of-age 'Jane Austen Birthday'"). The bulk of the Austen YouTube videos consist of edited clips of favorite bits from Austen film and television adaptations set to a favorite and/or appropriate contemporary pop song. (Imagine a montage of Austen's men as portrayed in film and television set to "I'm Bringing Sexy Back" or a sequence of romantic clips with any of a number of songs recorded by Fall Out Boy serving as soundtrack.) Other videos are quirky variations on this project: the trailer to the most recent version of *Pride and Prejudice* is remade using characters from the Harry Potter films; a scene from *Emma* is recreated with images of celebrities cut in under film voices; a quick version of *Pride and Prejudice* is retold by means of scenes and characters from *Ouran High School Host Club*, a manga-inspired Japanese anime television series; a video reedits the end of *Persuasion* to deprive Anne Elliot and Captain Wentworth of a happy ending, its match-unmaking editor linking Anne with Mr Elliot and asking viewers, "plz don't hate me."

The Austen YouTube subculture is a subculture by implication, outlined in the overlappings and borrowings, the answers and echoes of videos alongside one another. It is a culture of engagement and of enthusiasms – for Austen, for actors, for mass culture's latest productions, for romantic love and pop songs – that may have as much to say about the permissions granted and the constraints imposed by internet culture itself as about Austen's presence in this culture. But it is also a subculture that sometimes forms itself against the Janeite and, as such, speaks beyond YouTube to suggest

the utility of the Janeite for the culture to which Austenian subcultures are subordi-
nated. The written matter surrounding the videos (the YouTube paratexts) sometimes
include invocations of, imprecations against, and offerings to the Janeite: "plz don't
hate me" (because I'm revising an ending); an announcement that a video will include
"all of my favorite jane austen adaptations (yeah the ones less liked by janeites but
like I care)"; a claim that a particular video will be "funny and manly" (it is set to a
raspy metal tune), unlike those "girly movies" made by "Natalie and a bunch of girls
on youtube." The plea offered by the "plz" that accompanies the revision of *Persuasion*
may be the least hostile of these. Reimagining the end of the novel's 2007 adaptation,
the composer of the video, which is set to a song called "Too Late," seems less invested
in one coupling over another than in the suffusing melancholy that loss offers opportunities to indulge. The spectral Austenian who might hate this remaker of Austen
is likely to recognize in the remaker a version of herself or himself – someone as deeply
involved in Anne's feelings and in Wentworth's. Begging the Janeite's negative favor
("don't hate me"), the author of the *Persuasion* video revision would respect and appease
the Janeite and is rewarded for that gesture; one viewer includes in a positive comment
the prediction that the revision of *Persuasion* "would have met with Jane Austen's
approval, too."

The maker of another video advises in paratext that the video is "made out of
boredom. Consider it a parody. It's not to be taken seriously . . . because if it were,
I'd have a legion of angry Jane Austen fans after me with pitch forks and other sharp,
shiny things." Resemblances to "plz don't hate me" are illusory. This note would not
appease but would enforce the maker's intentions: here's my video and how to take
it (not seriously), how to consider it (it's parody), how to contextualize it (it's better
than the videos those Janeites like), how to identify the maker (no Janeite). But pretending to ward off a mob of angry, witchy Janeites is a ruse, the invocation of the
mob an aggression in service of a self-aggrandizing self-image. The video that prompts
the note, which assembles dancing scenes and cuts them to a rhythm more contemporary than period, resembles rather than parodies the videos produced by more self-
conscious devotees of Austen and of the Austen adaptations. The paratextual Janeite
is a function of the videographer's imagination, allowing him or her to erect and to
maintain a fantasy that quick cuts are truly cutting and that they make one impressively bad, a slayer of sociability, a superantiheroic Violator of Conventions (albeit a
bored one); the Janeite-function permits the maker of the video an impossible not-
knowledge – that only a fan watches and cuts and scores with such attention.

In the nakedness of their fantasies and the relative unsophistication of their online
social skills as well as of their paratextual prosings, the YouTube videographers and
commentators who call upon the Janeite point beyond their YouTubean world toward
the utility of the Janeite for members of the professional media and thus for the culture
at large. How easily written for distancing laughs is the predictable film adaptation
story: find the Janeites. Entertainment journalist Kim Masters's NPR story about
the 2005 *Pride and Prejudice* film, for example, finds them (at JASNA's general
meeting) in a succession and sameness that it highlights: "There was Elaine Bander

of Montreal . . . Fredericka Jarrett of New York, who felt that the heroine's family was not portrayed correctly . . . There was Kimberly Brangwin of Seattle, who objected to the grooming" (Masters 2005). How could the particularity of the attendees' responses pass as anything but triviality given their introduction in the very language of passivity, endlessness, tedium? There was, then there was, and yet again there was. All set-up for the half wit of director Joe Wright ("They can, I don't know, all go jump in a lake") – his comment so reminiscent of YouTube commentary on Janeites (nearly as sophisticated as "like I care") – the JASNA Austenians are a laughably "tough crowd," without sharp, shiny pitchforks. Disgruntled about the pigs and the posture and disturbed by the messy hair, they are willing enough to oblige the interviewer as Janeites, taking their parts in the cultural script that asks them to serve as a location for prudery, nostalgia, and conservatism, as if the republic in which these flourish is bound by Pemberley's psychic borders. The weird isolato ostensibly made weirder by her pleasure or his in the company of like weirdos (surprise! the isolato loves company), the Janeite is, as a YouTuber suggests, a fan like other fans ("Think Trekkies") in being made a function of the culture as a whole – a culture for whom not only Jane Austen but her readers are made to mean. By their unseemly display of an enthusiasm and attachment so enlivening and so contagious as to become an adhesive identity, sociable Janeites – if they sometimes agreeably fulfill D. H. Lawrence's expectation of their old maidishness – nevertheless violate its cognate: the overwhelming expectation that they will embody the dismissible "knowing in apartness" that Lawrence attributed to Austen (see Lawrence 1973: 58). In their attachments not just to one another but to Austen in aloneness, Janeites enact a mixedness about the sociability that defines them and that, despite their enacted ambivalence about it, they treasure as a refuge. Representing sociability as a need (and not – as, say, sports fans do with fearful insistence – as nothing but fun), Janeites are an abject reminder to a culture that likes to think it knows it all already ("like I care") of the embarrassing generality of that need.

Notes

1   Mansfield's observation appeared first in 1920 in a review of M. Austen-Leigh's *Personal Aspects of Jane Austen* (Mansfield 1930) in its very existence testimony to the desire for a personal relationship with the author.

2   The brief mention of JASNA's foundational occasion quoted on its "About JASNA" page, <http://www.jasna.org/info/about.html>, appeared first in "Homage" in "Talk of the Town," *New Yorker*, November 5, 1979, pp. 41–2.

3   My thanks to Amanda Himes, who first introduced me to A.I.S.S.B.H.

4   Given Deidre Lynch's convincing assertion, made in the introduction to *Janeites*, that the term "Janeite" itself is "now used almost exclusively about and against other people," I have resisted using it so far, not wanting to engage its alienating properties. But as I continue thinking about the image of Austen's readers in the world, I mean to think about their function for the culture in occupying a place of alienation from it. The Janeite I discuss, then, is the Janeite of the public imagination.

FURTHER READING

Handler, Richard and Daniel Segal (1990). *Jane Austen and the Fiction of Culture*. Tucson: The University of Arizona Press.

Lynch, Deidre (Ed.) (2000). *Janeites: Austen's Disciples and Devotees*. Princeton, NJ and Oxford: Princeton University Press.

Margolis, Harriet (2003). Janeite culture: what does the name "Jane Austen" authorize? In Gina Macdonald and Andrew F. Macdonald (Eds). *Jane Austen on Screen* (pp. 22–43). Cambridge, UK and New York: Cambridge University Press.

Simon, Richard Keller (1999). *Trash Culture: Popular Culture and the Great Tradition*. Berkeley: University of California Press.

Russell, Gillian and Clara Tuite (Eds) (2002). *Romantic Sociability: Social Networks and Literary Culture in Britain, 1770–1840*. Cambridge, UK and New York: Cambridge University Press.

Wiltshire, John (2001). *Recreating Jane Austen*. Cambridge, UK and New York: Cambridge University Press.

Bibliography

Aczel, Richard (2001). Throwing voices. *New Literary History*, 32: 3, 703–5.

Agius, P. (text) and Jones, S. (introduction) (1984). *Ackermann's Regency Furniture and Interiors.* Marlborough, UK: Crowood Press.

Alexander, Christine and Juliet McMaster (Eds) (2005). *The Child Writer from Austen to Woolf.* Cambridge, UK: Cambridge University Press.

Allestree, Richard (1658/1784). *The Whole Duty of Man.* London: Printed for John, Francis, and Charles Rivington, Publishers for the Society for Promoting Christian Knowledge.

Anderson, Benedict (1991/1983). *Imagined Communities: Reflections on the Origin and Spread of Nationalism.* London: Verso.

Anderson, Chris (2006). *The Long Tail: How Endless Choice is Creating Unlimited Demand.* London: Random House.

Anon. (1816). *Brief Remarks on English Manners, and an Attempt to Account for Some of Our Most Striking Peculiarities.* London: John Booth.

Appadurai, A. (Ed.) (1986). *The Social Life of Things: Commodities in Cultural Perspective.* Cambridge, UK: Cambridge University Press.

Appadurai, Arjun (1996). *Modernity at Large: Cultural Dimensions of Globalization.* Minneapolis: University of Minnesota Press.

Aravamudan, Srinivas (2001). The return of anachronism. *Modern Language Quarterly*, 62, 331–53.

Armstrong, Nancy (1987). *Desire and Domestic Fiction.* Oxford: Oxford University Press.

Armstrong, Nancy (1990). The nineteenth-century Jane Austen: a turning point in the history of fear. *Genre XXIII*, 227–46.

Armstrong, Nancy (2005). *How Novels Think: The Limits of Individualism from 1719–1900.* New York: Columbia University Press.

Auerbach, Emily (2004). *Searching for Jane Austen.* Madison: The University of Wisconsin Press.

Auerbach, N. (1983). Jane Austen's dangerous charm. Feeling as one ought about Fanny Price. In Janet Todd (Ed.). *Jane Austen. New Perspectives* (pp. 208–33). Women and Literature, New Series, 3. New York and London: Holmes & Meier. Reprinted in Claudia Johnson (Ed.). *Mansfield Park* (pp. 445–57). New York: W. W. Norton, 1998.

Austen, Frank (1880). Letter. *The Times.* May 12.

Austen, James (1790). *The Loiterer,* 59, 13 March 1790; 58, March 6 1790.

Austen, Jane (1811/1932–4/1965–6). *Sense and Sensibility,* 3rd edn, R. W. Chapman (Ed.), revised by Mary Lascelles. *The Novels of Jane Austen,* vol. 1. London: Oxford University Press.

Austen, Jane (1813/1932–4/1965–6). *Pride and Prejudice,* 3rd edn, R. W. Chapman (Ed.), revised by Mary Lascelles. *The Novels of Jane Austen,* vol. 2. London: Oxford University Press.

Austen, Jane (1813/2003). *Pride and Prejudice,* Claudia L. Johnson and Susan J. Wolfson (Eds). London: Longman/Pearson.

Austen, Jane (1932–4/1965–6). *Mansfield Park,* 3rd edn, R. W. Chapman (Ed.), revised by Mary Lascelles. *The Novels of Jane Austen,* vol. 3. London: Oxford University Press.

Austen, Jane (1815/1932–4/1965–6). *Emma,* 3rd edn, R. W. Chapman (Ed.), revised by Mary Lascelles. *The Novels of Jane Austen,* vol. 4. London: Oxford University Press.

Austen, Jane (1818/1932–4/1965–6). *Northanger Abbey and Persuasion,* 3rd edn, R. W. Chapman (Ed.), revised by Mary Lascelles. *The Novels of Jane Austen,* vol. 5. London: Oxford University Press.

Austen, Jane (1954/1969). *Minor Works,* R. W. Chapman (Ed.), revised by B. C. Southam. The Works of Jane Austen. vol. 6. London: Oxford University Press.

Austen, Jane (1964). *Jane Austen's Letters to her Sister Cassandra and Others,* R. W. Chapman (Ed.). London: Oxford World's Classics University Press. 2nd edn. 1979.

Austen, Jane (1993). *Catharine and Other Writings,* Margaret Anne Doody and Douglas Murray (Eds). Oxford World's Classics. Oxford: Oxford University Press.

Austen, Jane (1995a). *Jane Austen's Letters,* Deirdre Le Faye (Ed.), 3rd ed. Oxford, New York: Oxford University Press.

Austen, Jane (1995b). *The History of England,* Jan Fergus et al. (Eds). Edmonton, University of Alberta Press. Also Deirdre Le Faye (Ed.). London: British Library, 1993.

Austen, Jane (2006). *Juvenilia,* Peter Sabor (Ed.). Cambridge, UK: Cambridge University Press.

Austen, Jane (forthcoming). *Later Manuscripts,* Janet Todd and Linda Bree (Eds). Cambridge, UK: Cambridge University Press.

AustenBlog. <www/austenblog.com/>.

AUSTEN-L Archives. <http://lists.mcgill.ca/archives/austen-l.html>.

Austen-Leigh, Caroline (1952). *My Aunt Jane Austen: A Memoir.* London: Jane Austen Society.

Austen-Leigh, James Edward (1870). *A Memoir of Jane Austen.* London: Richard Bentley. 2nd edn. 1871. Reprinted in *A Memoir of Jane Austen and Other Family Recollections,* Kathryn Sutherland (Ed.). Oxford: Oxford University Press, 2002.

Austen-Leigh, Mary Augusta (1920). *Personal Aspects of Jane Austen.* London: J. Murray.

Austen-Leigh, William and Richard Arthur Austen-Leigh (1913/1965). *Jane Austen: Her Life and Letters: A Family Record.* New York: Russell and Russell. Also 2006 New York: Barnes and Noble.

Austin, Linda (2007). *Nostalgia in Transition, 1780–1917.* Charlottesville: University of Virginia Press.

Armstrong, N. (2005). *How Novels Think: The Limits of Individualism from 1719–1900.* New York: Columbia University Press.

Bal, Mieke (2002). *Travelling Concepts in the Humanities: A Rough Guide*. Toronto: University of Toronto Press.

Balibar, E. and I. Wallerstein (1991). *Race, Nation, Class: Ambiguous Identities*, trans. Chris Turner. London: Verso.

Barker-Benfield, G. J. (1992). *The Culture of Sensibility: Sex and Society in Eighteenth-Century Britain*. Chicago: University of Chicago Press.

Barthes, Roland (1989). The death of the author. In *The Rustle of Language*, trans. Richard Howard (pp. 49–55). Berkeley and Los Angeles: University of California Press.

Barthes, Roland (1975). *The Pleasure of the Text*, trans. Richard Miller. New York: Farrar, Straus and Giroux.

Bate, W. J. and Albrecht B. Strauss (Eds) (1969). *The Yale Edition of the Works of Samuel Johnson*, vol. 3. New Haven, CT: Yale University Press.

Battaglia, Beatrice and Diego Saglia (Eds) (2004). *Re-Drawing Austen: Picturesque Travels in Austenland*. Naples: Liguori.

Baudrillard, J. (1996). *The System of Objects*, trans. James Benedict. London and New York: Verso.

Baum, L. Frank (1973). *The Wonderful Wizard of Oz*. In Michael Patrick Hearn (Ed.), *The Annotated Wizard of Oz*. New York: Clarkson N. Potter.

Becoming Jane (2007). Julian Jarrold (Dir.). Miramax.

Behrendt, S. C. (1997). Sibling rivalries: author and artist in the earlier illustrated book. *Word & Image*, 13:1, 23–42.

Bell, G. H. (1930). *The Hamwood Papers of the Ladies of Llangollen and Caroline Hamilton*. London: MacMillan.

Bell's Common Place Book for the Pocket. Formed Generally upon the Principle Recommended and Practised by Mr. Locke (1770). London: John Bell. Held by Eighteenth-Century Collections Online (ECCO).

Benedict, Barbara M. (2000). Sensibility by the numbers: Austen's work as regency popular fiction. In Deidre Lynch (Ed.). *Janeites: Austen's Disciples and Devotees* (pp. 63–86). Princeton, NJ: Princeton University Press.

Bennett, Jane (2001). *The Enchantment of Modern Life: Attachments, Crossings, and Ethics*. Princeton, NJ: Princeton University Press.

Berg, M. (2005). *Luxury and Pleasure in Eighteenth-Century Britain*. Oxford: Oxford University Press.

Berlant, Lauren (1994). Evidences of masturbation. In James Chandler, Arnold I. Davidson, and Harry Harootunian (Eds). *Questions of Evidence: Proof, Practice, and Persuasion Across the Disciplines* (pp. 125–31). Chicago and London: University of Chicago Press.

Berlant, Lauren (2001). Love, a queer feeling. In Tim Dean and Christopher Lane (Eds). *Homosexuality and Psychoanalysis* (pp. 432–51). Chicago and London: University of Chicago Press.

Berman, Russell A. (2001). Politics: divide and rule. *Modern Language Quarterly*, 62, 317–30.

Bermingham, A. (1995). Elegant females and gentlemen connoisseurs: the commerce in culture and self-image in eighteenth-century England. In A. Bermingham and J. Brewer (Eds). *The Consumption of Culture, 1600–1800: Image, Object, Text* (pp. 489–513). London and New York: Routledge.

Berry, Amanda (2004). Some of my best friends are romanticists: Shelley and the queer project in Romanticism. *Romanticism on the Net, 36–7*, 4.

Bettelheim, Bruno (1976). *The Uses of Enchantment: The Meaning and Importance of Fairy Tales.* New York: Alfred A. Knopf.

Bing, Just (1929). *Verdens-litteraturhistorie: grunnlinjer og hovedverker*, vol. 2. Oslo: Aschehoug.

Binhammer, Katherine (1996). The sex panic of the 1790s. *Journal of the History of Sexuality*, 6:3, 409–34.

Birkett, Mary (1792). *A Poem on the African Slave Trade. Addressed to her own Sex.* Part I online at <http://www.brycchancarey.com/slavery/mbc1.htm>; Part II <http://www.brycchan-carey.com/slavery/mbc2.htm>.

Blackwall, Anthony (1717/1725). *Introduction to the Classics*, 3rd edn. London: C. Rivington and W. Cantrell.

Blair, Hugh (1783). *Lectures on Rhetoric and Belles Lettres by Hugh Blair, D.D*, 3 vols. Dublin: Whitestone, Coles et al.

Booth. A. (2004). *How to Make It as a Woman: Collective Biographical History from Victoria to the Present*. Chicago: University of Chicago Press.

Boucher, Léon (1878). Le roman classique en Angleterre: Jane Austen. *Revue des deux mondes*, 3rd ser. 29, 449–67.

Bourdieu, Pierre (1996). *The Rules of Art: Genesis and Structure of the Literary Field*, trans. Susan Emanual. Stanford, CA: Stanford University Press.

Bowlby, R. (1985). *Just Looking: Consumer Culture in Dreiser, Gissing and Zola*. New York and London: Methuen.

Boym, Svetlana (2001). *The Future of Nostalgia*. New York: Basic Books.

Brabourne, Edward, Lord (Ed.) (1884). *Letters of Jane Austen*, 2 vols. London: Richard Bentley & Son.

Bray, J. (2003). *The Epistolary Novel: Representations of Consciousness*. London and New York: Routledge.

Bride & Prejudice (2004). Gurinder Chadha (Dir.). Miramax.

Brideoake, Fiona (2004–5). "Extraordinary female affection": the ladies of Llangollen and the endurance of queer community. *Romanticism on the Net, 36–7*.

Bridget Jones's Diary (2001). Sharon Maguire (Dir.). Working Title/Miramax.

Bromley, Eliza Nugent (1784). *Laura and Augusta*, 3 vols. London: W. Cass.

Brontë, Charlotte (1995). *Letters*, Margaret Smith (Ed.), 2 vols. Oxford: Clarendon.

Brophy, Brigid (1968). Jane Austen and the Stuarts. In Brian Southam (Ed.). *Critical Essays on Jane Austen* (pp. 21–38). London: Routledge and Kegan Paul.

Brown, Julia Prewitt (1975). *Jane Austen's Novels: Social Change and Literary Form*. Cambridge, MA: Harvard University Press.

Brown, Marshall (2001). Periods and resistances. *Modern Language Quarterly*, 62, 309–16.

Brown, P. (1981). *The Cult of the Saints: Its Rise and Function in Latin Christianity*. Chicago: University of Chicago Press.

Brownstein, Rachel (1997). Northanger Abbey, Sense and Sensibility, and Pride and Prejudice. In Edward Copeland and Juliet McMaster (Eds). *The Cambridge Companion to Jane Austen* (pp. 32–57). Cambridge, UK: Cambridge University Press.

Brunton, M. (1810/1986). *Self-Control*. London and New York: Pandora Press.

Brusendorff, Ebba (1928–30). *Stolthed og fordom*. Translation of *Pride and Prejudice*. Copenhagen: Gyldendal.

Burgett, Bruce (1998). *Sentimental Bodies: Sex, Gender, and Citizenship in the Early Republic*. Princeton, NJ: Princeton University Press.

Burke, Edmund (1782). *A Philosophical Enquiry into the Origin of our Ideas of the Sublime and Beautiful*, 9th edn. London.

Burke, Edmund (1790). *Reflections on the Revolution in France*, 2nd edn. London: J. Dodsley. Also Conor Cruise O'Brien (Ed.). Harmondsworth, UK: Penguin, 1983; Thomas H. D. Mahoney (Ed.). Bobbs-Merrill, 1955; C. C. O'Brien (Ed.). Harmondsworth, UK: Penguin, 1968.

Burke, Edmund (1989). *The Writings and Speeches of Edmund Burke*, L. G. Mitchell (Ed.), vol. 8, *The French Revolution*. Oxford: Clarendon Press.

Burney, F. (1972–84). *The Journals and Letters of Fanny Burney* (Madame D'Arblay), Joyce Hemlow et al. (Eds), 12 vols. Oxford: Clarendon Press.

Burney, F. (1796/1983). *Camilla: or a Picture of Youth*. Oxford: Oxford University Press.

Burney, F. (2001). *The Wanderer; or, Female Difficulties*, Margaret Anne Doody & Robert L Mack (Eds). Oxford: Oxford University Press.

Burton, A. (1995). "Invention is what delights me": Jane Austen's remaking of "English" history. In Devoney Looser (Ed.). *Jane Austen and Discourses of Feminism* (pp. 35–50). New York, St. Martin's Press.

Burton, John (1793). *Lectures on Female Education and Manners*. London.

Bury, Lady Charlotte (1836). *The Devoted*, 3 vols. London: Richard Bentley.

Butler, Eleanor (1819). *Journal*, July 18. Dublin: Wicklow Collection, National Library of Ireland.

Butler, J. (1993). *Bodies that Matter: On the Discursive Limits of "Sex."* New York: Routledge.

Butler, Marilyn (1975). *Jane Austen and the War of Ideas*. Oxford: Clarendon Press. Rev. edn. 1987.

Butler, Marilyn (1986). History, politics, and religion. In J. David Grey, A. Walton Litz, and Brian Southam (Eds). *The Jane Austen Companion* (pp. 190–208). New York: Macmillan.

Byrne, Paula (2002). *Jane Austen and the Theatre*. London: Hambledon and London.

Cafarelli, A. W. (1990). *Prose in the Age of Poets: Romanticism and Biographical Narrative from Johnson to De Quincey*. Philadelphia: University of Pennsylvania Press.

Cambridge, Ada (1903). *Thirty Years in Australia*. London: Methuen.

Cannadine, David (1995). *Aspects of Aristocracy: Grandeur and Decline in Modern Britain*. London and New York: Penguin.

Cannadine, David (1999). *The Rise and Fall of Class in Britain*. New York: Columbia University Press.

Caprin, Giulio (1932). *Orgoglio e prevenzione*. Translation of *Pride and Prejudice*. Milan and Verona: Mondatori.

Cardwell, Sarah (2002). *Adaptation Revisited: Television and the Classic Novel*. Manchester, UK: Manchester University Press.

Castle, Terry (1995). Sister-Sister. *The London Review of Books*, 17, 15. Reprinted as Was Jane Austen gay? In *Boss Ladies, Watch Out! Essays on Women, Sex, and Writing* (pp. 125–36). London: Routledge, 2002.

Castle, Terry (1998). Introduction. In Ann Radcliffe. *The Mysteries of Udolpho*. Oxford: Oxford University Press.

Castle, Terry (2002). Austen's *Emma*. In *Boss Ladies, Watch Out! Essays on Women, Sex, and Writing* (pp. 39–54). New York and London: Routledge.

Cecchi, Emilio (1915). *Storia della letteratura inglese nel secolo XIX*. Milan: Fratelli Treves Editori.

Chandler, James (1998). *England In 1819: The Politics of Literary Culture and the Case of Romantic Historicism*. Chicago: University of Chicago Press.

Chapone, Hester (1807). *Letters on the Improvement of the Mind*. Vol. 1 of *Works*, 4 vols. London: Murray.

Chasles, Philarète (1842). Du Roman en Angleterre depuis Walter Scott. *Revue des deux mondes*, 4th ser. 31, 185–214.

Chatterjee, Upamanyu (2006). *English, August: An Indian Story*. New York: New York Review of Books.

Chesterton G. K. (1913). *The Victorian Age in Literature*. New York: Henry Holt.

Chesterton G. K. (1922). Preface. In *Love & Freindship and Other Early Works by Jane Austen*. London: Chatto & Windus.

Clark, R. and G. Dutton (2005). Agriculture. In J. Todd (Ed.). *Jane Austen in Context* (pp. 185–93). Cambridge, UK: Cambridge University Press.

Clarkson, T. (1808). *The History of the Rise, Progress, and Accomplishment of the Abolition of the African Slave-Trade by the British Parliament*, 2 vols. London: Longman, Hurst, Rees, and Orme.

Clery, E. J. (1995). *The Rise of Supernatural Fiction 1762–1800*. Cambridge, UK: Cambridge University Press.

Clueless (1995). Amy Heckerling (Dir). Paramount Pictures.

Cohn, D. (1983). *Transparent Minds: Narrative Modes for Presenting Consciousness in Fiction*. Princeton, NJ: Princeton University Press.

Cole, Michael (1988). *The Pianoforte in the Classical Era*. Oxford: Clarendon Press.

Coleridge, Henry Nelson (1835). *Specimens of the Table Talk of the Late Samuel Taylor Coleridge*, 2 vols. London: John Murray.

Coleridge, Samuel Taylor (1907/1979). *Biographia Literaria*, 2 vols, J. Shawcross (Ed.). Oxford: Oxford University Press. Also London: J. M. Dent, 1993.

Coleridge, Samuel Taylor (1978). *The Collected Works of Samuel Taylor Coleridge. Vol. 3:II. Essays on his Times*, David V. Erdman (Ed.). London and Princeton, NJ: Routledge & Kegan Paul.

Coleridge, Samuel Taylor (1987). *Lectures 1808–1819: On Literature*, R. A. Foakes (Ed.). Princeton, NJ: Princeton University Press.

Colley, L. (1992). *Britons: Forging the Nation 1707–1837*. New Haven, CT and London: Yale University Press. 2nd edn. 2005.

Collingwood, R. G. (2005). Jane Austen (?1934). In *The Philosophy of Enchantment: Studies in Folktale, Cultural Criticism, and Anthropology*, David Boucher, Wendy James, and Philip Smallwood (Eds). (pp. 34–48). Oxford: Clarendon Press.

Collins, Amanda (1998). The pitfalls of postmodern nostalgia. In Linda Troot and Sayre Greenfield (Eds). *Jane Austen in Hollywood* (pp. 78–89). Lexington: University of Kentucky Press.

Collins, Irene (1994). *Jane Austen and the Clergy*. London: Hambledon Press.

Copeland, Edward (1986). Jane Austen and the consumer revolution. In J. D. Grey (Ed.). *The Jane Austen Handbook* (pp. 77–92). London: Athlone.

Copeland, Edward (1995). *Women Writing about Money: Women's Fiction in England 1790–1820.* Cambridge, UK: Cambridge University Press.

Copeland, Edward (1996). The Austens and the Elliots: A consumer's guide to *Persuasion.* In Juliet McMaster and Bruce Stovel (Eds). *Jane Austen's Business: Her World and Her Profession* (pp. 136–53). Basingstoke, UK: Macmillan.

Copeland, Edward (2001). Crossing Oxford Street: silverfork geopolitics. *Eighteenth-Century Life,* 25, 116–34.

Cowper, W. (1968). *Poetry and Prose.* Selected by Brian Spiller. London: Rupert Hart-Davis.

Cossy, Valérie and Diego Saglia (2005). Translations. In Janet Todd (Ed.). *Jane Austen in Context* (pp. 169–81). Cambridge, UK: Cambridge University Press.

Crawford, Robert (1992). *Devolving English Literature.* Oxford: Clarendon Press.

Cronin, R. (2005). Literary scene. In Janet Todd (Ed.). *Jane Austen in Context* (pp. 289–96). Cambridge, UK: Cambridge University Press.

Crusie, Jennifer (2005). *Flirting with Pride and Prejudice: Fresh Perspectives on the Original Chick-Lit Masterpiece.* Dallas, TX: Benbella Books.

Dant, T. (1996). Fetishism and the social value of objects. *The Sociological Review,* 44, 495–516.

Davidoff, Leonore and Catherine Hall (1987). *Family Fortunes: Men and Women of the English Middle Class,* 1780–1850. Chicago: University of Chicago Press.

De Haan, M. H. (1935). De Invloed van Richardson op Jane Austen en op Nederlandse Auteurs. *De nieuwe taalgids,* 29, 274–80.

Deresiewicz, W. (2004). *Jane Austen and the Romantic Poets.* New York: Columbia University Press.

De Rose, P. L. and S. W. McGuire (1982). *A Concordance to the Works of Jane Austen,* 3 vols. New York: Garland.

Derrick, S. (Ed.) (1761). *A Poetical Dictionary; or, the Beauties of the English Poets, Alphabetically Displayed,* 4 vols. London: John Newbery, George Kearsley, etc.

Deutsch, H. (2005). *Loving Dr. Johnson.* Chicago: University of Chicago Press.

Díaz Bild, Aída (1998). Jane Austen: artistic mastery as a means of rebellion. In Fernando Galván et al. (Eds). *Mary Wollstonecraft and her World.* Alcalá: University of Alcalá.

D'Israeli, I. (1822). *The Literary Character, Illustrated by The History of Men of Genius,* 2 vols, 3rd edn. London: John Murray.

Ditkoff, Anna (2005). She's a flat character; and the story in this threadbare Jane Austen adaptation is pretty dull, too. *Baltimore City Paper Online* <http://baltimorecitypaper.com/film/review.asp?rid=9522>.

Dobosiewicz, Ilona (1997). *Female Relationships in Jane Austen's Novels: A Critique of the Female Ideal Propagated in 18th-Century Conduct Literature.* Opole, Poland: Uniwersytet Opolski.

Doody, Margaret Anne (1980). George Eliot and the eighteenth-century novel. *Nineteenth-Century Fiction,* 35, 260–91.

Doody, Margaret Anne (2005). Jane Austen, that disconcerting "child." In Christine Alexander and Juliet McMaster (Eds). *The Child Writer from Austen to Woolf* (pp. 101–21). Cambridge, UK: Cambridge University Press.

Dowdall, William (1798). *The Press.* Dublin.

Drake, Judith (1696). *An Essay in Defence of the Female Sex.* London: A. Roper & E. Wilkinson; R. Clavel.

Duckworth, Alistair M. (1971). *The Improvement of the Estate: A Study of Jane Austen's Novels.* Baltimore, MD: Johns Hopkins University Press.

Duff, W. (1767). *An Essay on Original Genius and its Various Modes of Exertion in Philosophy and the Fine Arts, Particularly in Poetry.* London: Edward and Charles Dilly.

Duncombe, John (1981). *The Feminiad. A Poem* (1754). Augustan Reprint Society. Los Angeles: William Andrews Clark Memorial Library.

Dupuy, Jean-Pierre (1997). It may require another person to deceive oneself. In "Open peer commentary" to Alfred R. Mele, Real self-deception. *Behavioral and Brain Sciences* 20, 111.

Duret, Théodore (1898). Miss Austen. *La Revue blanche*, 16 (May–August), 278–82.

During, Simon (2002). *Modern Enchantments: The Cultural Power of Secular Magic.* Cambridge, MA: Harvard University Press.

Eagleton, Terry (1990). *The Ideology of the Aesthetic.* Oxford: Blackwell.

Eagleton, Terry (2003). Pork chops and pineapples. *London Review of Books*, 23 October. <http://www.lrb.co.uk/v25/n20/eagl01_.html>.

Eagleton, Terry (2005). *The English Novel.* Oxford: Blackwell.

Edgeworth, Maria (1801/1994). *Belinda.* K. Kirkpatrick (Ed.). Oxford: Oxford University Press.

Edgeworth, Maria (1814/1986). *Patronage.* London and New York: Pandora Press.

Edgeworth, Maria and Richard Lovell Edgeworth (1798). *Practical Education.* London: J. Johnson.

Elfenbein, A. (1999). *Romantic Genius: The Prehistory of a Homosexual Role.* New York: Columbia University Press.

Ellis, Markman (1996). *The Politics of Sensibility: Race, Gender and Commerce in the Sentimental Novel.* Cambridge, UK: Cambridge University Press.

Ellison, Julie (1999). *Cato's Tears and the Making of Anglo-American Emotion.* Chicago: University of Chicago Press.

Empson, William (1966). *Seven Types of Ambiguity.* New York: New Directions.

Emsley, C. (1979). *British Society and the French Wars, 1793–1815.* London: Macmillan.

Evelyn, J. (1955). *The Diary of John Evelyn*, E. S. de Beer (Ed.), 6 vols. Oxford: Clarendon.

Ezell, Margaret (forthcoming). Invisible books. In Pat Rogers and Laura Runge (Eds). *The Eighteenth-Century Book: New Perspectives on Writing and Publishing, 1650–1825.* London: Ashgate.

Faderman, L. (1981). *Surpassing the Love of Men.* New York: William Morrow.

Falconer, William (1788). *A Dissertation on the Influence of the Passions Upon the Disorders of the Body.* London: C. Dilly and J. Phillips.

Farrer, Reginald (1917/1987). Jane Austen, *ob. The Quarterly Review*, 228, 29. Reprinted in B. C. Southam (Ed.). *Jane Austen: The Critical Heritage, 1870–1940*, vol. 2 (pp. 240–4). London and New York: Routledge & Kegan Paul.

Favret, Mary A. (1993). *Romantic Correspondence: Women, Politics, and the Fiction of Letters.* Cambridge, UK: Cambridge University Press.

Favret, Mary A. (1996). War correspondence: reading romantic war. *Prose Studies*, 19:2, 173–85.

Favret, Mary A. (2005). Everyday war. *ELH*, 72:3, 603–33.

Felluga, D. (2005). *The Perversity of Poetry: Romantic Ideology and the Popular Male Poet of Genius.* Albany, NY: State University of New York Press.

Fergus, Jan (Ed.) (1995). Introduction. Jane Austen, *The History of England*. Edmonton, AB: Juvenilia Press.

Fergus, Jan (1997). The professional woman writer. In Edward Copeland and Juliet McMaster (Eds). *The Cambridge Companion to Jane Austen* (pp. 12–31). Cambridge, UK: Cambridge University Press.

Ferguson, Moira (1993). *Colonialism and Gender Relations from Mary Wollstonecraft to Jamaica Kinkaid*. New York: Columbia University Press.

Ferris, I. (1991). *The Achievement of Literary Authority: Gender, History, and the Waverley Novels*. Ithaca, NY: Cornell University Press.

Ferris, I. (2002). *The Romantic National Tale and the Question of Ireland*. Cambridge, UK: Cambridge University Press.

Ferris, Suzanne and Mallory Young (Eds). (2006). *Chick Lit: The New Woman's Fiction*. New York and London: Routledge.

Fielding, Helen (1996). *Bridget Jones's Diary*. London: Picador.

Fielding, Helen (1999). *Bridget Jones: the Edge of Reason*. Harmondsworth, UK: Penguin.

Fielding, Sarah (1744). *The Adventures of David Simple*. London.

Fingarette, Herbert (2000). *Self-Deception, with a New Chapter*. Berkeley: University of California Press.

Fischer, Paul. Brenda Blethyn interview: Jane Austin's [*sic*] *Pride and Prejudice*. <http://www.girl.com.au/brenda-blethyn-pride-prejudice-interview.htm>.

Fisher, Philip (1998). *Wonder, the Rainbow, and the Aesthetics of Rare Experiences*. Cambridge, MA: Harvard University Press.

Fleishman, Avrom (1967). Mansfield Park in its time. *Nineteenth-Century Fiction*, 22, 1–18.

Fletcher, L. (1998). Time and mourning. *Persuasion. Women's Writing*, 5, 81–90.

Flynn, Carol Houlihan (1997). The letters. In Edward Copeland and Juliet McMaster (Eds). *The Cambridge Companion to Jane Austen* (pp. 100–14). Cambridge, UK: Cambridge University Press.

Fordyce, James (1766). *Sermons to Young Women*, 3rd edn. London: Millar; 12th edn 1800. Reprinted in Janet Todd (Ed.). *Female Education in the Age of Enlightenment*, vol. 1. London: Pickering & Chatto, 1996.

Forster, E. M. (1924). Review of *The Novels of Jane Austen*, ed. R. W. Chapman. *Nation and Athaenaeum*, 34, 512–14. Reprinted in *Abinger Harvest* (pp. 45–8). London: Edward Arnold, 1936.

Foucault, Michel (1979). *Discipline and Punish*, trans. Alan Sheridan. New York: Vintage Books.

Fowler, Karen Joy (2004). *The Jane Austen Book Club*. New York: G. P. Putnam's Sons.

Fraiman, S. (2000). Jane Austen and Edward Said: gender, culture, and imperialism. In D. Lynch (Ed.). *Janeites: Austen's Disciples and Devotees* (pp. 206–23). Princeton, NJ: Princeton University Press.

Franklin, Miles (1933). The feminisation of literature. Reprinted in *A Gregarious Culture. Topical Writings of Miles Franklin*, ed. Jill Roe and Margaret Bettison (pp. 110–13). St. Lucia: Queensland University Press, 2001.

Franklin, Miles (1945). Clara Morison. Reprinted in *A Gregarious Culture. Topical Writings of Miles Franklin*, ed. Jill Roe and Margaret Bettison (pp. 191–4). St. Lucia: Queensland University Press, 2001.

Freud, Sigmund (1989). *The Future of an Illusion*, trans. James Strachey. New York: W W Norton & Co.

Fulford, Tim (2002). Sighing for a soldier: Jane Austen and military pride and prejudice. *Nineteenth-Century Literature*, 57:2, 153–78.

Galperin, William H. (2003). *The Historical Austen*. Philadelphia: University of Pennsylvania Press.

Garrod, H. W. (1928). Jane Austen: a depreciation. In Lawrence Binyon (Ed.). *Essays by Divers Hands, Transactions of the Royal Society of Literature*, New Series, 8 (pp. 21–40). London: Oxford University Press.

Garside, P. (1999). Walter Scott and the "common novel," 1808–1819. *Cardiff Corvey: Reading the Romantic Text* 3, January 9, 2007, <http://www.cf.ac.uk/encap/corvey/articles/cc03_n02.html>.

Garside, Peter, James Raven, and Rainer Scholwerling (Eds). (2000). *The English Novel 1770–1829*. Oxford: Oxford University Press.

Garside, P. D., J. E. Belanger, and S. A. Ragaz (2004). Contemporary reviews for *The Wanderer*. British Fiction, 1800–1829: A Database of Production, Circulation & Reception. <http://www.british-fiction.cf.ac.uk/titleDetails.asp?title=1814A017>.

Gash, Norman (1979). *Aristocracy and People: Britain 1815–1865*. Bungay, UK: Edward Arnold.

Gassert, Imogen (2002). In a foreign field: what soldiers in the trenches liked to read. *Times Literary Supplement*, May 10, 2002, 17–19.

Gay, Penelope (2002). *Jane Austen and the Theatre*. Cambridge, UK: Cambridge University Press.

Gay, Penelope (2005). Pastimes. In J. Todd (Ed.). *Jane Austen in Context* (pp. 337–45). Cambridge, UK: Cambridge University Press.

Genieva, Ekaterina (1986). *Dzheĭn Osten: biobibliograficheskiĭ ukazatel'*. Moscow: Kniga.

Gerard, A. (1774). *An Essay on Genius*. London: Cadell.

Gibbons, Stella (1938). *Cold Comfort Farm*. Harmondsworth, UK: Penguin.

Gilbert, Sandra and Susan Gubar (1979). *The Madwoman in the Attic: The Woman Writer and the Nineteenth-Century Literary Imagination*. New Haven, CT: Yale University Press.

Gilson, D. (1997). *A Bibliography of Jane Austen*. Winchester, UK: St Paul's Bibliographies.

Gilson, David (2003). Jane Austen, the aristocracy and T. H. Lister, a supplement. *The Jane Austen Society: Report for 2003*, 39–41.

Gilson, D. (2005). Later publishing history, with illustrations. In J. Todd (Ed.). *Jane Austen in Context* (pp. 121–59). Cambridge, UK: Cambridge University Press.

Gisborne, Thomas (1797/1799). *An Enquiry into the Duties of the Female Sex*. London: Cadell.

Gore, Catherine (1830). *Women As They Are; or, The Manners of the Day*, 2nd edn, 3 vols. London: Henry Colburn and Richard Bentley.

Gore, Catherine (1830). *Mothers and Daughters; a Tale of the Year 1830*, 3 vols. London: Henry Colburn and Richard Bentley.

Gore, Catherine (1832). *The Opera, A Novel*, 3 vols. London: Henry Colburn and Richard Bentley.

Gore, Catherine (1839). *The Cabinet Minister*, 3 vols. London: Richard Bentley, 1839.

Goring, Paul (2005). *The Rhetoric of Sensibility in Eighteenth-Century Culture*. Cambridge, UK: Cambridge University Press.

Guest, Harriet (2000). *Small Change: Women, Learning, Patriotism, 1750–1810*. Chicago and London: University of Chicago Press.

Guillory, John (1996). *Cultural Capital: The Problem of Literary Canon Formation*. Chicago: University of Chicago Press.

Habermas, Jürgen (1989). *The Structural Transformation of the Public Sphere*, trans. Thomas Burger with Frederick Lawrence. Cambridge, MA: MIT Press.

Halévy, Elie (1960). *England in 1815*, trans. E. I. Watkin & D. A. Barber. London, Ernest Benn.

Hall, Stuart (1995). Fantasy, identity, politics. In Erica Carter, James Donald, and Judith Squires (Eds). *Cultural Remix: Theories of Politics and the Popular* (pp. 63–9). London: Lawrence & Wishart.

Halperin, John (1983). Jane Austen's anti-romantic fragment: some notes on *Sanditon. Tulsa Studies in Women's Literature*, 2: 2, 183–91.

Harding, D. W. (1980). Regulated hatred: An aspect of the work of Jane Austen. In Monica Lawlor (Eds). *Regulated Hatred and Other Essays on Jane Austen* (pp. 5–26). London: Athlone Press.

Hardy, B. (1975). The objects in *Mansfield Park*. In J. Halperin (Ed.). *Jane Austen: Bicentenary Essays* (pp. 180–96). Cambridge, UK: Cambridge University Press.

Harris, J. (1989). *Jane Austen's Art of Memory*. Cambridge, UK: Cambridge University Press.

Hassall, J. (1986). Illustrating Jane Austen. In J. David Grey (Ed.). *The Jane Austen Handbook: With a Dictionary of Jane Austen's Life and Works* (pp. 215–22). London: Athlone.

Hawkins, Laetitia Matilda (1801). *Letters on the Female Mind, Its Powers and Pursuits; Addressed to Miss H M Williams, With Particular Reference to Her Letters from France*. London: J and T Carpenter.

Hazlitt, Willliam (1827). The Dandy school. *The Examiner*. November 18, 1827. In *The Complete Works of William Hazlitt* (vol. 20, pp. 143–9). London and Toronto: J. M. Dent and Sons, 1934.

Heydt-Stevenson, Jill (2000). "Slipping into the ha-ha": bawdy humor and body politics in Jane Austen's novels. *Nineteenth-Century Literature*, 55:3, 309–40.

Heydt-Stevenson, Jill (2005). *Austen's Unbecoming Conjunctions: Subversive Laughter, Embodied History*. New York and Basingstoke, UK: Palgrave Macmillan.

Hibbert, Christopher (1959). *King Mob: The Story of Lord George Gordon and the London Riots of 1780*. Cleveland, OH: World Publishing.

Holly, Grant (1989). *Emmagramatology. Studies in Eighteenth-Century Culture*, 19, 39–51.

Holmes, John (1739). *The Art of Rhetoric made Easy: or, The Elements of Oratory. Briefly Stated and Fitted for the Practice of the Studious Youth of Great-Britain and Ireland*. London: A. Parker.

Homage. (1979). *New Yorker*, November 5, 1979, 41–2.

Hudson, Glenda (1989). Precious remains of the earliest attachment: sibling love in Jane Austen's *Pride and Prejudice. Persuasions*, 11, 125–31.

Hudson, Glenda (1992). *Sibling Love and Incest in Jane Austen's Fiction*. New York: St. Martin's Press.

Hudson, Marianne Spencer (1826). *Almack's, a Novel*, 2nd edn, 3 vols. London: Saunders and Otley.

Hume, David (1978). *The Treatise of Human Nature*, L. A. Selby-Bigge (Ed.), 2nd edn. Oxford: Clarendon Press.

Irvine, Robert P. (2002). Introduction. *Pride and Prejudice*. Peterborough, ONT: Broadview.

Iacuzzi, Alfred (1932). *The European Vogue of Favart: The Diffusion of the Opéra-Comique*. New York: Publications of the Institute of French Studies, Inc.

In other news essay (2003). Online Newshour. 6 May 2003. <http://www.pbs.org/newshour/essays/jan-june03/rosenblatt_05-06.html.>.

Isbell, John Claiborne (1994). *The Birth of European Romanticism*. Cambridge, UK: Cambridge University Press.

James, Henry (1905). The lesson of Balzac. Boston: Houghton Mifflin. Reprinted in *Literary Criticism: French Writers, Other European Writers, the Prefaces to the New York Edition*, ed. Leon Edel and Mark Wilson (pp. 115–39). New York: Library of America, 1984.

James, Henry (1909). Preface. *The Golden Bowl*. New York: Charles Scribner's Sons.

James, Henry (1962). *The Art of the Novel*. New York: Charles Scribner's Sons, 1962.

Jane Austen's first law of blogging (2005). Jane in the news, November 27, <http://www.austenblog.com/jane-austens-first-law-of-blogging/>.

JASNA, Homepage of the Jane Austen Society of North America, <http://www.jasna.org/>.

Jerinic, Maria (1995). In defense of the Gothic: rereading *Northanger Abbey*. In Devoney Looser (Ed.). *Jane Austen and the Discourses of Feminism* (pp. 137–49). New York: St. Martin's Press.

Johnson, Claudia L. (1988). *Jane Austen: Women, Politics, and the Novel*. Chicago and London: University of Chicago Press.

Johnson, Claudia L. (1995a). *Equivocal Beings: Politics, Gender, and Sentimentality in the 1790s*. Chicago: University of Chicago Press.

Johnson, Claudia L. (1995b). "Not at all what a man should be!": remaking English manhood in *Emma*. In *Equivocal Beings* (pp. 191–203). Chicago: University of Chicago Press.

Johnson, Claudia L. (1997). Austen cults and cultures. In Edward Copeland and Juliet McMaster (Eds). *The Cambridge Companion to Jane Austen* (pp. 211–26). Cambridge, UK: Cambridge University Press.

Johnson, Claudia L. (1996/2000). The divine Miss Jane: Jane Austen, Janeites, and the discipline of novel studies. *boundary 2*, 23:3, 143–7. Reprinted in Deidre Lynch (Ed.). *Janeites: Austen's Disciples and Devotees* (pp. 25–44). Princeton, NJ: Princeton University Press.

Johnson, Claudia L. (2002). Introduction. *Sense and Sensibility*, Ed. Claudia L. Johnson (pp. ix–xviii). New York: Norton.

Johnson, Claudia L. (2003). Introduction. *Northanger Abbey, Lady Susan, The Watsons, Sanditon*. Oxford: Oxford University Press.

Johnson, Samuel (1959). *Johnson on Shakespeare*, Ed. Walter Raleigh. London: Oxford University Press.

Jones, Vivien (1996). Introduction. In *Pride and Prejudice* (pp. vii–xxiv), Vivien Jones (Ed.). Harmondsworth, UK: Penguin.

Jones, Vivien (Ed.) (2004). *Jane Austen. Selected Letters*. Oxford: Oxford University Press.

Jones, Vivien (2005). Reading for England: Austen, taste, and female patriotism. *European Romantic Review*, 16:2, 221–30.

Joyce, James (1963). *Ulysses*. London: Bodley Head.

Kames, Henry Home, Lord (1778/2007). *Sketches of the History of Man*, 2 vols. Indianapolis, IN: Liberty Fund.

Kaplan, Deborah (1988). Representing two cultures: Jane Austen's letters. In Shari Benstock (Ed.). *The Private Self: Theory and Practice of Women's Autobiographical Writings* (pp. 211–29). London: Routledge.

Kaplan, Deborah (1992). *Jane Austen Among Women*. Baltimore, MD and London: Johns Hopkins University Press.

Karlinsky, Simon (1984). Russian comic opera in the age of Catherine the Great. *19th-Century Music*, 7, 318–25.

Keen, Paul (1999). *The Crisis of Literature in the 1790s*. Cambridge, UK: Cambridge University Press.

Keen, Paul (Ed.) (2004). *Revolutions in Romantic Literature: An Anthology of Print Culture, 1780–1832*. Peterborough, ONT: Broadview Press.

Kelly, Gary (1989). *English Fiction of the Romantic Period, 1789–1830*. London and New York: Longman.

Kelly, Gary (1993). *Women, Writing, and Revolution, 1790–1827*. Oxford: Clarendon Press.

Kelly, Gary (1995). Jane Austen, Romantic feminism, and civil society. In Devoney Looser (Ed.). *Jane Austen and the Discourses of Feminism* (pp. 19–34). New York: St. Martin's Press.

Kelly, Gary (2005). Education and accomplishments. In Janet Todd (Ed.). *Jane Austen in Context* (pp. 252–61). Cambridge, UK: Cambridge University Press.

Kent, Christopher (1989). Learning history with, and from, Jane Austen. In J. David Grey (Ed.). *Jane Austen's Beginnings: The Juvenilia and Lady Susan* (pp. 59–72). Ann Arbor, MI: UMI Research Press.

Kent, C. (1981). "Real solemn history" and social history. In D. Monaghan (Ed.). *Jane Austen in a Social Context* (pp. 86–104). London: Macmillan.

Kermode, Frank (2000). *The Sense of an Ending: Studies in the Theory of Fiction*. Oxford: Oxford University Press.

Kinderman, William (1987). *Beethoven's Diabelli Variations*. Oxford: Clarendon Press.

Kirkham, Margaret (1983). *Jane Austen, Feminism and Fiction*. Brighton, UK: Harvester Press and Totowa, NJ: Barnes & Noble.

Kirkham, Margaret (1993a). Romantic fiction. In Stuart Curran (Ed.). *The Cambridge Companion to British Romanticism* (pp. 196–215). Cambridge, UK: Cambridge University Press.

Kirkham, Margaret (1993b). *Women, Writing, and Revolution, 1790–1827*. Oxford: Clarendon Press.

Klancher, Jon P. (1987). *The Making of English Reading Audiences, 1790–1832*. Madison: University of Wisconsin Press.

Knox-Shaw, Peter (2004). *Jane Austen and the Enlightenment*. Cambridge, UK: Cambridge University Press.

Kollar, Dom Rene (1983). The Oxford Movement and the heritage of Benedictine monasticism. *Downside Review*, 101, 281–90.

Kroeber, K. (1990). Jane Austen as an historical novelist. *Sense and Sensibility. Persuasions*, 12, 10–18.

Kruger, Loren (2003). History plays (in) Britain: dramas, nations, and inventing the present. In W. B. Worthen and Peter Holland (Eds). *Theorizing Practice: Redefining Theatre History* (pp. 151–76). New York: Palgrave.

Kucich, Greg (2000). The re-gendering of historical memory. In Matthew Campbell, Jacqueline M. Labbe, and Sally Shuttleworth (Eds). *Memory and Memorials 1789–1914* (pp. 15–29). London: Routledge.

Lane, Maggie (1984). *Jane Austen's Family: Through Five Generations*. London: Robert Hale.

Lane, Maggie (1995). *Jane Austen and Food*. London and Rio Grande: Hambledon Press.

Lanser, Susan S. (1999). Befriending the body: female intimacies as class acts. *Eighteenth-Century Studies*, 32:2, 179–98.

Lawrence, D. H. (1973). *A propos of* Lady Chatterley's Lover. New York: Haskell House Publishers.

Leavis, F. R. (1973). *The Great Tradition*. New York: New York University Press. Also Harmondsworth, UK: Penguin, 1972.

Le Faye, Deirdre (2002). *Jane Austen: The World of her Novels*. London: Frances Lincoln.

Le Faye, Deirdre (2004). *Jane Austen: A Family Record*. Cambridge, UK: Cambridge University Press.

Le Faye, Deirdre (2005). *A Chronology of Jane Austen and Her Family*. Cambridge, UK: Cambridge University Press.

la Roche, S. von (1933). *Sophie in London in 1786, being the Diary of Sophie v. la Roche*, trans. Clare Williams. London: Jonathan Cape.

Levine, George (1981). *The Realistic Imagination: English Fiction from Frankenstein to Lady Chatterley*. Chicago: University of Chicago Press.

L'Estrange, A. G. L. (1870). *The Life of Mary Russell Mitford*. London: Richard Bentley.

Levinson, Marjorie (2007). What is new formalism? *PMLA*, 122:2, 558–69.

Lister, Anne (1988). *I Know My Own Heart: The Diaries of Anne Lister 1791–1840*, Helena Whitbread (Ed.). London: Virago.

Lister, Anne (1992). *No Priest but Love: The Journals of Anne Lister from 1824–1826*, Helena Whitbread (Ed.). New York: New York University Press.

Lister, Thomas H. (1826). *Granby. A Novel*, 3 vols. London: Henry Colburn.

Lister, Thomas H. (1832). *Arlington. A Novel*, 3 vols. London: Henry Colburn and Richard Bentley.

Litvak, Joseph (1992). The infection of acting: theatricals and theatricality in *Mansfield Park*. In *Caught in the Act: Theatricality in the Nineteenth-Century English Novel* (pp. 1–26). Berkeley, Los Angeles and Oxford: University of California Press.

Litvak, Joseph (1996). Charming men, charming history. In Ann Kibbey, Thomas Foster, Carol Siegel, and Ellen E. Berry (Eds). *On Your Left: Historical Materialism in the 1990s* (pp. 248–74). New York: New York University Press.

Litvak, Joseph (1997). *Strange Gourmets: Sophistication, Theory, and the Novel*. Durham, NC and London: Duke University Press.

Litz, A. Walton (1961). *The Loiterer*: A reflection of Jane Austen's early environment. *Review of English Studies*, 12, 251–61.

Litz, A. Walton (1965). *Jane Austen: A Study of Her Artistic Development*. New York: Oxford University Press.

Locke, John (1963). *Two Treatises of Government*, Peter Laslett (Ed.). New York: Cambridge University Press.

Locke, John (1975). *An Essay Concerning Human Understanding*, Peter H. Nidditch (Ed.). Oxford: Clarendon Press. Also Roger Woolhouse (Ed.). London: Penguin, 1997.

Locke, John (1989). *Some Thoughts Concerning Education*, John W. and Jean S. Yolton (Eds). Oxford: Clarendon Press.

Locke, John (1999). *The Reasonableness of Christianity as Delivered in the Scriptures*, John C. Higgins-Biddle (Ed.). Oxford: Clarendon Press.

Lockhart, J. G. (1821/1947). *John Bull's Letter to Lord Byron*, A. L. Strout (Ed.). Norman: University of Oklahoma Press.

Loesser, Arthur (1955). *Men, Women and Pianos: A Social History*. London: Victor Gollancz.

Looser, Devoney (Ed.) (1995). *Jane Austen and the Discourses of Feminism*. New York: St. Martin's Press.

Looser, Devoney (2000). *British Women Writers and the Writing of History, 1670–1820*. Baltimore, MD: Johns Hopkins University Press.

Lootens, T. (1996). *Lost Saints: Silence, Gender, and Victorian Literary Canonization*. Charlottesville: University Press of Virginia.

Lukács, Georg (1937/1962). *The Historical Novel*, trans. Hannah and Stanley Mitchell. London: Merlin Press.

Loudon, J. C. (1822). *The Different Modes of Cultivating the Pine-Apple*. London: Longman, Hurst, Rees, Orme, and Brown.

Lynch, Deidre S. (1996). At home with Jane Austen. In Deidre Lynch and William B. Warner (Eds). *Cultural Institutions of the Novel* (pp. 159–92). Durham, NC and London: Duke University Press.

Lynch, Deidre S. (1998). *The Economy of Character: Novels, Market Culture, and the Business of Inner Meaning*. Chicago: University of Chicago Press.

Lynch, Deidre S. (Ed.) (2000). *Janeites: Austen's Disciples and Devotees*. Princeton, NJ and Oxford: Princeton University Press.

Lynch, Deidre S. (2003). *Clueless*: about history. In Suzanne R. Pucci and James Thompson (Eds). *Jane Austen and Co.* (pp. 71–92). Albany: State University of New York Press.

Lynch, Deidre S. (2004). Introduction. In Jane Austen, *Persuasion* (pp. vii–xxxiii). Oxford: Oxford University Press.

Macaulay, T. (1982). *Selected Letters*, T. Pinney (Ed.). Cambridge, UK: Cambridge University Press.

Mack, Robert L. (2006). Introduction. *The Loiterer: A Periodical Work in Two Volumes Published at Oxford in the Years 1789 and 1790 by the Austen Family* (pp. xv–xx, xxxv–xlvi). Lampeter, UK: The Edwin Mellen Press Ltd.

Macpherson, C. B. (1962/1964). *The Political Theory of Possessive Individualism: Hobbes to Locke*. New York: Oxford University Press.

Magee, W. H. (1975). The happy marriage: the influence of Charlotte Smith on Jane Austen. *Studies in the Novel*, 7, 120–32.

Mandal, Anthony and Brian Southam (Eds). (2007). *The Reception of Jane Austen in Europe*. London and New York: Continuum.

Mandler, Peter (1990). *Aristocratic Government in the Age of Reform: Whigs and Liberals, 1830–1852*. Oxford: Clarendon Press.

Mannings, David (1984). Reynolds, Garrick, and the choice of Hercules. *Eighteenth-Century Studies*, 17: 3, 259–83.

Mansfield, Katherine (1930). Friends and foes. In John Middleton Murry (Ed.). *Novels and Novelists* (pp. 314–16). New York: Alfred A. Knopf.

Mansfield Park (1999). Patricia Rozema (Dir.). Miramax/BBC.

Masters, Kim (2005). Profile: new version of *Pride and Prejudice*. *Morning Edition*. NPR, November 11.

McGann, Jerome (1983). *The Romantic Ideology*. Chicago: University of Chicago Press.

McKenzie, D. F. (1986). *Bibliography and the Sociology of Texts*. London: British Library.

McKillop, Alan D. (1956). *The Early Masters of English Fiction*. Lawrence: University of Kansas Press.

McLuhan, Marshall (2003). *Understanding Media: The Extensions of Man*, W. Terrence Gordon (Ed.). Corte Madera, CA: Gingko.

McMaster, Juliet (1996). From *Laura and Augustus* to "Love and Freindship." *Thalia: Studies in Literary Humor,* XVI: 1–2, 16–26.

McMaster, Juliet (2006). Your sincere freind, the author. *Persuasions On-Line*, 27: 1. <http://www.jasna.org/persuasions/on-line/vol27no1/mcmaster.htm>.

McRobbie, Angela (2004). Post-feminism and popular culture. *Feminist Media Studies*, 4, 255–64.

Mee, Jon (2000). Austen's treacherous ivory: female patriotism, domestic ideology, and empire. In You-Me Park and Rajeswari Sunder Rajan (Eds). *The Postcolonial Jane Austen* (pp. 74–92). London and New York: Routledge.

Mele, Alfred R. (1997). Real self-deception [followed by "Open peer commentary"]. *Behavioral and Brain Sciences*, 20:1, 91–136.

Michalski, Hieronim (1957). Klasyka zniesiona ze strychu. *Nowe ksi ki*, 6, 6–8.

Midgley, C. (1992). *Women against Slavery: The British Campaigns, 1780–1870*. London and New York: Routledge.

Midgley, C. (1998). Anti-slavery and the roots of "imperial feminism." In C. Midgley (Ed.). *Gender and Imperialism* (pp. 161–79). Manchester, UK: Manchester University Press.

Miles, R. (2002). The 1790s: the effulgence of gothic. In J. E. Hogel (Ed.). *The Cambridge Companion to Gothic Fiction* (pp. 41–62). Cambridge, UK: Cambridge University Press.

Miles, Robert (2003). *Jane Austen*. Writers and Their Work series. Tavistock, UK: Northcote House Publishers.

Miller, Christopher R. (2005). Jane Austen's aesthetics and ethics of surprise. *Narrative,* 13: 3, 238–60.

Miller, D. A. (1989). *The Novel and the Police*. Berkeley: University of California Press.

Miller, D. A. (1990). The late Jane Austen. *Raritan*, 10:1, 55–79.

Miller, D. A. (1995). Austen's attitude. *The Yale Journal of Criticism*, 8: 1, 1–5.

Miller, D. A. (2003). *Jane Austen, or The Secret of Style*. Princeton, NJ and Oxford: Princeton University Press.

Milton, John (1931). Of reformation touching church-discipline in England. In Harry Morgan Ayres (Ed.). *The Works of John Milton*, vol. 3 New York: Columbia University Press.

Modert, Jo (Ed.) (1990). *Jane Austen's Manuscript Letters in Facsimile*. Carbondale and Edwardsville: Southern Illinois University Press.

Modleski, Tania (1991). *Feminism Without Women*. New York and London: Routledge.

Monaghan, David (1978). *Mansfield Park* and evangelicalism: a reassessment. *Nineteenth-Century Studies*, 33, 215–30.

Montag, W. (2005). On the function of the concept of origin: Althusser's reading of Locke. In S. H. Daniel (Ed.). *Current Continental Theory and Modern Philosophy* (pp. 148–61). Evanston, IL: Northwestern University Press.

Montagu, M. W., Lady (1965). *The Complete Letters of Lady Mary Wortley Montagu*, 3 vols, Ed. R. Halsband. Oxford: Clarendon Press.

The Monthly Review (1798). 27, 205–10.

The Monthly Review (1824). Review of *Saint Ronan's Well*, 103, 61–75.

Moody, Ellen (1999). A calendar for *Sense and Sensibility*. *Philological Quarterly*, 78, 301–34.

Moody, Jane (2000). *Illegitimate Theatre in London, 1770–1840*. Cambridge, UK: Cambridge University Press.

Moody, Jane (2007). "Dictating to the empire": performance and theatrical geography in eighteenth-century Britain. In Jane Moody and Daniel O'Quinn (Eds). *The Cambridge Companion to British Theatre, 1730–1840* (pp. 21–41). Cambridge, UK: Cambridge University Press.

Moore, Lisa L. (1997). *Dangerous Intimacies: Toward a Sapphic History of the British Novel.* Durham, NC: Duke University Press.

More, Hannah (1782). *Sacred Dramas.* London: Cadell.

More, Hannah (1799/1996). *Strictures on the Modern System of Female Education*, 2 vols, 2nd edn. London: Cadell and Davies. Reprinted in R. Hole (Ed.). *Selected Writings of Hannah More.* London: William Pickering.

More, Hannah (1805/1818/1996). *Hints Towards Forming a Bill for the Abolition of the White Female Slave Trade.* Reprinted in R. Hole (Ed.). *Selected Writings of Hannah More.* London: William Pickering.

Moretti, F. (1998). *Atlas of the European Novel 1800–1900.* London and New York: Verso.

Motooka, Wendy (1998). *The Age of Reasons: Sentimentalism, Quixotism and Political Economy in Eighteenth-Century England.* London: Routledge.

Mozart, W. A. (1985). *The Letters of Mozart and his Family*, Emily Anderson (Ed.), 3rd edn. London: Macmillan.

Mudrick, Marvin (1952). *Jane Austen: Irony as Defense and Discovery.* Princeton, NJ: Princeton University Press.

Mullan, John (1988). *Sentiment and Sociability: The Language of Feeling in the Eighteenth Century.* Oxford: Clarendon.

Mulrooney, Jonathan (2002). Reading the romantic-period daily news. *Nineteenth-Century Contexts*, 24, 351–78.

Nachumi, Nora (2001). Seeing double: theatrical spectatorship in *Mansfield Park*. *Philological Quarterly* 80.3, 233–52.

National Gazette and Literary Register (1832). Philadelphia, September 8.

The Naval Chronicle (1799), 2 vols.

Negra, Diane (2004). Quality postfeminism? Sex and the single girl on HBO. *Genders, 39*, <http://www.genders.org/g39/g39_negra.html>.

Neill, Edward (2003). "Found wanting?" Second impressions of a famous first sentence. *Persuasions, 25*, 76–84.

New European Magazine (1824). Review of *Saint Ronan's Well*. 4, 54–61.

A New Riddle-Book (1778). London: T. Carnan and F. Newbery.

Newbould, Ian (1990). *Whiggery and Reform, 1830–41.* Stanford, CA: Stanford University Press.

Nokes, David (1997). *Jane Austen. A Life.* Berkeley and Los Angeles: University of California Press.

O'Farrell, Mary Ann (2006). Missing Jane Austen: Henry James considers the old maid. *The Henry James Review* 27, 1–9.

Oliphant, M. (1899/1990). *The Autobiography of Margaret Oliphant: The Complete Text*, E. Jay (Ed.). Oxford and New York: Oxford University Press.

Olsen, K. (2005). *All Things Austen: An Encyclopedia of Austen's World*, 2 vols. Westport, CT and London: Greenwood Press.

Ozick, Cynthia (2004). *The Heir to the Glimmering World.* Boston: Houghton Mifflin.

Page, Norman (1972). *The Language of Jane Austen.* Oxford: Blackwell.

Palter, R. (2002). *The Duchess of Malfi's Apricots, and Other Literary Fruits*. Columbia: University of South Carolina Press.

Parker, J. A. (1998). *The Author's Inheritance: Henry Fielding, Jane Austen and the Establishment of the Novel*. Dekalb: Northern Illinois University Press.

Pascal, R. (1977). *The Dual Voice*. Manchester, UK: Manchester University Press.

Pascoe, Judith (1997). *Romantic Theatricality: Gender, Poetry, and Spectatorship*. Ithaca, NY and London: Cornell University Press.

Patten, R. L. (2004). Bentley, Richard (1794–1871). In *Oxford Dictionary of National Biography* (article 2171). Oxford: Oxford University Press.

Paulson, Ronald (1983). *Representations of Revolution, 1789–1820*. New Haven, CT: Yale University Press.

Peacham, Henry (1577). *The Garden of Eloquence, Conteyning the Figures of Grammar and Rhetoric, From Whence Maye Bee Gatherd Al Manner of Flowers*. London: H. Jackson.

Perry, Ruth (2004). *Novel Relations: The Transformation of Kinship in English Literature and Culture 1748–1818*. Cambridge, UK: Cambridge University Press.

Pevsner, Nikolaus (1968). The architectural setting of Jane Austen's novels. *Journal of the Warburg and Courtauld Institutes*, 31, 404–22.

Phillips, Mark Saber (2000). *Society and Sentiment: Genres of Historical Writing in Great Britain, 1740–1820*. Princeton, NJ: Princeton University Press.

Piggott, Patrick (1980). Jane Austen's Southampton piano. *Jane Austen Society Reports*, 6–9.

Pinch, Adela (1996). *Strange Fits of Passion: Epistemologies of Emotion, Hume to Austen*. Stanford, CA: Stanford University Press.

Pittock, Murray (Ed.) (2006). *The Reception of Sir Walter Scott in Europe*. London and New York: Continuum.

Plantinga, Leo (2004). The piano and the nineteenth century. In Larry Todd (Ed.). *Nineteenth-Century Piano Music* (pp. 1–15). New York: Routledge.

Plasa, C. (2000). *Textual Politics from Slavery to Postcolonialism: Race and Identification*. New York: St. Martin's.

Pollak, Ellen (2002). *Incest and the English Novel, 1684–1814*. Baltimore: Johns Hopkins University Press.

Polwhele, Richard (1798). *The Unsex'd Females: A Poem*. London: Cadell and Davies.

Poovey, Mary (1984). *The Proper Lady and the Woman Writer*. Chicago: University of Chicago Press.

Pride & Prejudice. (2005). Joe Wright (Dir.). Universal Pictures.

Prins, Y. (1999). *Victorian Sappho*. Princeton, NJ: Princeton University Press.

Pritchett, V. S. (1970). *George Meredith and English Comedy*. London and New York, Knopf.

Prospectus of a New Periodical Work, Dedicated, By Permission, to the Right Honourable Earl Spencer, Entitled, The Naval Chronicle (n.d.), 2. London.

Proust, Marcel (1988). *A la Recherche du temps perdu*, vol. III. Paris: Gallimard. *The Prisoner and the Fugitive. The Prisoner*, trans. Carol Clark. London: Allen Lane, 2002.

Radcliffe, Ann (1998). *The Mysteries of Udolpho*. Oxford: Oxford University Press.

Raff, S. (forthcoming). Blame Austen: *Emma*, Janeism, and the betrayal of Fanny Knight. *The Eighteenth-Century Novel*, 8.

Rague, Kate and Paul Rague (1914). *Jane Austen*. Paris: Bloud et Gay.

Raven, James (1992). *Judging New Wealth: Popular Publishing and Responses to Commerce in England, 1750–1800*. Oxford: Clarendon.

Rawson, C. J. (1958). The sentimental hero in fiction and life: a note on Jane Austen and Fanny Burney. *Notes and Queries*, n.s. 5.6, 253–4.

Rawson, Claude (1994). *Satire and Sentiment 1660–1830: Stress Points in the English Augustan Tradition*. Cambridge, UK: Cambridge University Press.

Reade, B. (1953). *Regency Antiques*. London: B. T. Batsford.

Renan, E. (1882/1990). What is a nation?, trans. M. Thom. In H. K Bhabha (Ed.). *Nation and Narration* (pp. 8–22). London and New York: Routledge.

The Repository of Arts, Literature, Commerce, Manufactures, Fashions and Politics (1809). vol. 2, 11, November.

Repton, Humphry (1816). *Fragments of the Theory and Practice of Landscape Gardening*. London.

The Republic of Pemberley Discussion Groups and Information Pages. <http://www. pemberley.com/>.

Ribeiro, A. (1986). *Dress and Morality*. London: B. T. Batsford.

Richardson, Alan (2001). *British Romanticism and the Science of the Mind*. Cambridge, UK: Cambridge University Press.

Richardson, Samuel (1748–9/1985). *Clarissa; or the History of a Young Lady*, Angus Ross (Ed.). New York: Viking and Penguin.

Richardson, Samuel (1804). *Correspondence of Samuel Richardson*, Anna Barbauld (Ed.), 6 vols. London: Phillips.

Richmond, Hugh M. (1994). *King Henry VIII*. Manchester, UK: Manchester University Press.

Roberts, W. (1979). *Jane Austen and the French Revolution*. New York: St. Martin's.

Robinson, Kathryn (2003). Why I heart chick lit. *Seattle Weekly*, October 22.

Robinson, Terry F. (2006). "A mere skeleton of history": Reading relics in Jane Austen's *Northanger Abbey. European Romantic Review*, 17:2, 215–27.

Romilly, Anne and Maria Edgeworth (1936). *Romilly-Edgeworth Letters 1813–18*, Samuel Henry Romilly (Ed.). London: John Murray.

Rooney, Ellen (2000). Form and contentment. *MLQ*, 61, 17–40.

Rosenfeld, Sybil (1978). *Temples of Thespis: Some Private Theatres and Theatricals in England and Wales, 1700–1820*. London: The Society for Theatre Research.

Roth, Michael (1991). Dying of the past: medical studies of nostalgia in nineteenth century France. *History and Memory*, 3, 5–29.

Rousseau, George S. (2004). *Nervous Acts: Essays on Literature, Culture and Sensibility*. Basing-stoke, UK: Palgrave.

Rubin, Gayle (1993). Thinking sex: notes for a radical theory of the politics of sexuality. In Henry Abelove, Michèle Aina Barale, and David M. Halperin (Eds). *The Gay and Lesbian Studies Reader* (pp. 3–44). London and New York: Routledge.

Russell, Gillian (1995). *The Theatres of War: Performance, Politics and Society, 1793–1815*. Oxford: Clarendon Press.

Russell, Gillian (2007). Private theatricals. In Jane Moody and Daniel O'Quinn (Eds). *The Cambridge Companion to British Theatre, 1730–1840* (pp. 191–204). Cambridge, UK: Cambridge University Press.

Ryle, Gilbert (1968). Jane Austen and the moralists. In B. C. Southam (Ed.). *Critical Essays on Jane Austen* (pp. 106–22). London: Routledge and Kegan Paul.

Saglia, D. (1999). The dangers of over-refinement: the language of luxury in romantic poetry by women, 1793–1811. *Studies in Romanticism*, 38, 641–72.

Said, Edward (1993). *Culture and Imperialism.* New York: Alfred Knopf.

Sales, Roger (1994/1996). *Jane Austen and Representations of Regency England.* London: Routledge.

Sales, Roger (2000). In face of all the servants: spectators and spies in Austen. In Deidre Lynch (Ed.). *The Janeites: Austen's Disciples andf Devotees* (pp. 188–205). Princeton, NJ: Princeton University Press.

Sampson, George (1924). Review of Chapman edition. *Bookman.* January.

Scott, Sir Walter (1890). *The Journal of Sir Walter Scott, 1825–1832,* David Douglas (Ed.), 2 vols. Edinburgh: David Douglas.

Scott, Sir Walter (1968). Review of *Emma.* In B. C. Southam (Ed.). *Jane Austen: The Critical Heritage.* London: Routledge and Kegan Paul.

Scott, Sir Walter (1981). *Waverley,* C. Lamont (Ed.). Oxford: Clarendon Press. Also P. D. Garside (Ed.). Edinburgh: Edinburgh University Press, 2007.

Sedgwick, Eve Kosofsky (1985). *Between Men: English Literature and Male Homosocial Desire.* New York: Columbia University Press.

Sedgwick, Eve Kosofsky (1991). Jane Austen and the masturbating girl. *Critical Inquiry,* 17.4, 818–37. Reprinted in *Tendencies* (pp. 109–29). Durham, NC and London: Duke University Press, 1993. Also reprinted in Frank Lentricchia and Andrew DuBois (Eds). *Close Reading: The Reader* (pp. 301–20). Durham, NC: Duke University Press, 2003.

Sedgwick, Eve Kosofsky (1993). *Tendencies.* Durham, NC and London: Duke University Press.

Séllei, Nóra (1999). *Lánnyá válik, s írni kezd: 19. századi angol írónők.* Debrecen: Kossuth University Press.

Selvadurai, Shyam (1999). *Cinnamon Gardens.* Toronto: McClelland & Stewart.

Selvadurai, Shyam (1994). *Funny boy: A Novel in Six Stories.* Toronto: McClelland & Stewart.

Selwyn, D. (1999). *Jane Austen and Leisure.* London: Hambledon Press.

Selwyn, D. (2005). Consumer goods. In J. Todd (Ed.). *Jane Austen in Context* (pp. 215–24). Cambridge, UK: Cambridge University Press.

Senner, Wayne, William Meredith, and Robin Wallace (Eds). (1999). *The Critical Reception of Beethoven's Compositions by His German Contemporaries.* Lincoln: University of Nebraska Press.

Seth, Vikram (1994). *A Suitable Boy.* New York: Harper.

Shaftesbury, Earl of (1713). *A Notion of the Historical Draught or Tablature of the Judgement of Hercules.* London.

Shaw, Harry E. (1999). *Narrating Reality: Austen, Scott, Eliot.* Ithaca, NY: Cornell University Press.

Shera. F. H. (1939). *The Amateur in Music.* Oxford: Oxford University Press.

Shulman, Nicole (2004). *A Rage for Rock Gardening: The Story of Reginald Farrer, Gardener, Writer and Plant Collector.* Boston: David Godine.

Siegel, J. (2000). *Desire and Excess: The Nineteenth-Century Culture of Art.* Princeton, NJ: Princeton University Press.

Siskin, Clifford (1988). *The Historicity of Romantic Discourse.* New York and Oxford: Oxford University Press.

Siskin, Clifford (1999). *The Work of Writing: Literature and Social Change in Britain 1700–1830.* Baltimore, MD: Johns Hopkins University Press.

Smiles, Samuel (1891). *A Publisher and His Friends: Memoir and Correspondence of the Late John Murray,* 2 vols. London.

Smith, C. (1791/2005). *Celestina*. In *The Works of Charlotte Smith*, vol. 4, K. Straub (Ed.). London: Pickering and Chatto.

Solinger, Jason (2006). Jane Austen and the gentrification of commerce. *Novel: A Forum on Fiction* 38: 2/3, 272–90.

Sonneck, O. G. (1926). *Beethoven: Impressions of Contemporaries*. New York: Schirmer.

Southam, B. C. (1964). *Jane Austen's Literary Manuscripts*. London: Oxford University Press.

Southam, Brian (Ed.) (1968). *Jane Austen: The Critical Heritage*, vol. I. London: Routledge and Kegan Paul.

Southam, Brian (Ed.) (1987). *Jane Austen: The Critical Heritage,* vol. II. London: Routledge.

Southam, Brian (2001). *Jane Austen's Literary Manuscripts*, 2nd edn. London: Athlone.

Southam, Brian (2000/2003). *Jane Austen and the Navy*. London: Hambledon and London. 2nd edn. 2005.

Southam, Brian (2002). *"Rears"* and *"vices"* in *Mansfield Park*. *Essays in Criticism,* 52:1, 23–35.

Southam, Brian and Anthony Mandal (Eds). (2007). *The Reception of Jane Austen in Europe*. London and New York: Continuum.

Southey, R. (1951). *Letters from England*, J. Simmons (Ed.). London: Cresset Press.

Spacks, Patricia (2003). *Privacy: Concealing the Eighteenth-Century Self*. Chicago: University of Chicago Press.

Spacks, P. M. (2006). *Novel Beginnings: Experiments in Eighteenth-Century English Fiction*. New Haven: Yale University Press.

Spectator (1711). 1, March 1.

Spectator (1711). 4, March 5.

Spectator (1711). March 11, 13.

Spielmann, M. H. and W. Jerrold. (1931). *Hugh Thomson: His Art, His Letters, His Humour and His Charm*. London: A & C Black.

Spring, David (1983). Interpreters of Jane Austen's social world: literary critics and historians. In Janet Todd (Ed.). *Jane Austen: New Perspectives* (pp. 53–72). New York and London: Holmes and Meier.

Starobinski, Jean (1966). The idea of nostalgia. *Diogenes*, 54.3, 81–103.

Stanhope, Philip Dormer (1774). *Letters Written by the Late Right Honourable Philip Dormer Stanhope, Earl of Chesterfield, to His Son*, 2nd edn, 4 vols. London: J. Dodsley.

St Clair, W. (2004). *The Reading Nation in the Romantic Period*. Cambridge, UK: Cambridge University Press.

Steele, R. (1793). *An Essay Upon Gardening, Containing a Catalogue of Exotic Plants*. York: Printed for the Author by G. Peacock.

Sterne, L. (1760). *The Life and Opinions of Tristram Shandy, Gentleman*. 9 vols. Reprinted 1767. London: T. Becket and P. A. Dehondt. Also James A. Work (Ed.). New York: Odyssey Press, 1940.

Sterne, L. (1768). *A Sentimental Journey Through France and Italy. By Mr. Yorick*, 2 vols. London: T. Becket and P. A. De Hondt.

Stewart, Maaja A. (1993). *Domestic Realities and Imperial Realities. Jane Austen's Novels in Eighteenth Century Contexts*. Athens: University of Georgia Press.

Stewart, Susan (1993). *On Longing: Narratives of the Miniature, the Gigantic, the Souvenir, the Collection*. Durham, NC: Duke University Press.

Stokes, Myra (1991). *The Language of Jane Austen*. Basingstoke and London: Macmillan.

Subotnik, Rose Rosengard (1991). *Developing Variations: Style and Ideology in Western Music*. Minneapolis: University of Minnesota Press.

Sulloway, Alison G. (1989). *Jane Austen and the Province of Womanhood*. Philadelphia: The University of Pennsylvania Press.

Sutherland, Kathryn (Ed.). (2002). *J. E. Austen Leigh: A Memoir of Jane Austen and Other Family Recollections*. Oxford: Oxford University Press.

Sutherland, Kathryn (2004). Jane Austen and the invention of the serious modern novel. In T. Keymer and J. Mee (Eds). *The Cambridge Companion to English Literature 1740–1830* (pp. 244–62). Cambridge, UK: Cambridge University Press.

Sutherland, Kathryn (2005). *Jane Austen's Textual Lives: From Aeschylus to Bollywood*. Oxford: Oxford University Press.

Sutherland, Kathryn (2006). Letters to the editor: Jane Austen editions. *Times Literary Supplement*, February 3, 15.

Sutherland, Kathryn (2006). On looking into Chapman's *Emma*. *Times Literary Supplement*, January 13, 12–13.

Sutherland, Kathryn (2006). Review of The Cambridge Edition of *Mansfield Park* and *Emma*. *Review of English Studies*, 57:232, 833–8.

Sutherland, John (1986). Henry Colburn, publisher. *Publishing History*, 19, 59–84.

Swendson, Shanna (2005). The original chick-lit masterpiece. In Jennifer Cruise (Ed.). *Flirting with Pride and Prejudice: Fresh Perspectives on the Original Chick-Lit Masterpiece* (pp. 63–70). Dallas, TX: BenBella Books.

Sykes, Norman (1959). *From Sheldon to Secker: Aspects of English Church History, 1660–1768*. Cambridge, UK: Cambridge University Press.

Szerb, Antal (1941/1973). *A világirodalom története*, 5th edn. Budapest: Magvető.

Tadmor, Naomi (1996). "In the even my wife read to me": women, reading, and household life in the eighteenth century. In James Raven, Helen Small and Naomi Tadmor (Eds). *The Practice and Representation of Reading in England* (pp. 162–74). Cambridge, UK: Cambridge University Press.

Taine, Hippolyte (1863–4). *Histoire de la littérature anglaise*, 4 vols, vol. 4. Paris: Hachette.

Tandon, Bharat (2003). *Jane Austen and the Morality of Conversation*. London: Anthem Press.

Tanner, Tony (1986). *Jane Austen*. Basingstoke, UK: Macmillan.

Tanner, Tony (1969/1995). Introduction. *Sense and Sensibility* (355–83), Ros Ballaster (Ed.). London: Penguin.

Tave, Stuart M. *Some Words of Jane Austen*. Chicago and London: University of Chicago Press.

Taylor, A. (1769). *A Treatise on the Ananas or Pine-Apple*. Devizes, UK: Printed by T. Burrough for the Author.

Temperley, Nicholas (1981). Ballroom and drawing-room music. In Nicholas Temperley (Ed.). *Music in Britain: The Romantic Age, 1800–191* (pp. 109–34). Oxford: Blackwell.

Thompson, E. P. (1971). The moral economy of the English crowd in the eighteenth century. *Past and Present*, 50, 76–136.

Thompson, J. (1986). Jane Austen and history. *Review*, 8, 21–32.

Thrale, Hester Lynch (1942). *Thraliana: The Diary of Mrs. Hester Lynch Thrale (Later Mrs. Piozzi) 1776–1809*, Katherine C. Balderston (Ed.), 2 vols. Oxford: Clarendon Press.

Tillotson, John (1702). *Fifteen Sermons on Several Subjects*. London.

Todd, Janet (1986). *Sensibility: An Introduction*. London: Methuen.

Todd, Larry (2004). *Nineteenth-Century Piano Music*. New York: Routledge.

Tomalin, Claire (1997). *Jane Austen: A Life*. Harmondsworth, UK: Viking. New York: Alfred A. Knopf. Also Harmondsworth: Penguin, 2000.

Trevelyan, G. M. (1926). *History of England*. London: Longmans & Green.

Trilling, Lionel (1955). Mansfield Park. In *The Opposing Self: Nine Essays in Criticism* (pp. 206–40). New York: Viking.

Trilling, Lionel (1957/1965). Emma and the legend of Jane Austen. Introduction to the Riverside edition of *Emma*. Reprinted (in slightly different form) in *Beyond Culture* (pp. 28–49). New York: Harcourt Brace Jovanovich. Also reprinted in David Lodge (Ed.), *Jane Austen: Emma: A Casebook* (148–70). London: Macmillan, 1991.

Trilling, Lionel (1976/1979). Why we read Jane Austen. In *The Last Decade: Essays and Reviews, 1965–75* (pp. 204–25). New York: Harcourt Brace Jovanovich.

Trumbach, Randolph (1978). *The Rise of the Egalitarian Family: Aristocratic Kinship and Domestic Relations in Eighteenth-Century England*. New York: Academic Press.

Trumpener, Katie (1997). *Bardic Nationalism: The Romantic Novel and the British Empire*. Princeton, NJ: Princeton University Press.

Trumpener, Katie (2000). The Virago Jane Austen. In Deidre Lynch (Ed.). *Janeites: Austen's Disciples and Devotees* (pp. 140–65). Princeton, NJ: Princeton University Press.

Tucker, George Holbert (1983). *A Goodly Heritage: A History of Jane Austen's Family*. Manchester, UK: Carcanet New Press.

Tuite, Clara (2000). Decadent Austen entails: Forster, James, Firbank, and the "queer taste" of *Sanditon*. In Deidre Lynch (Ed.). *Janeites: Austen's Disciples and Devotees* (pp. 115–39). Princeton, NJ: Princeton University Press.

Tuite, Clara (2000). Domestic retrenchment and imperial expansion: the property plots of *Mansfield Park*. In You-me Park and Rajeswari Sunder Rajan (Eds). *The Postcolonial Jane Austen* (pp. 93–115). London and New York: Routledge.

Tuite, Clara (2002). *Romantic Austen: Sexual Politics and the Literary Canon*. Cambridge, UK: Cambridge University Press.

Tuite, Clara (2004). Period rush: queer Austen, anachronism and critical practice. In Beatrice Battaglia and Diego Saglia (Eds). Re-Drawing Austen (pp. 294–311). Naples: Ligouri.

Tuite, Clara (2005). Austen, Jane 1775–1817. In Mary Spongberg, Ann Curthoys, and Barbara Caine (Eds). *Companion to Women's Historical Writing* (pp. 40–2). New York: Palgrave Macmillan.

Tyler, Natalie (1999). *The Friendly Jane Austen: A Well-Mannered Introduction to a Lady of Sense and Sensibility*. Harmondsworth, UK: Penguin.

Van Sant, Ann Jessie (1993). *Eighteenth-Century Sensibility and the Novel: The Senses in Social Context*. Cambridge, UK: Cambridge University Press.

Veblen, T. (1899/1934). *The Theory of the Leisure Class: An Economic Study of Institutions*. New York: The Modern Library.

Vicinus, Martha (1994). Lesbian history: all theory and no facts or all facts and no theory? *Radical History Review*, 60, 57–75.

Viswanathan, Gauri (1989). *Masks of Conquests: Literary Study and British Rule in India*. New York: Columbia University Press.

Wahrman, Dror (1995). *Imagining the Middle Class: The Political Representation of Class in Britain, c. 1780–1849*. Cambridge, UK: Cambridge University Press.

Waldron, Mary (1994). The frailties of Fanny: *Mansfield Park* and the evangelical movement. *Eighteenth-Century Fiction*, 6, 259–82.

Waldron, M. (1999). *Jane Austen and the Fiction of her Time*. Cambridge, UK: Cambridge University Press.

Walpole, H. (1996). *The Castle of Otranto: A Gothic Story*, W. S. Lewis (Ed.). New York: Oxford.

Walsh, John and Stephen Taylor (1993). Introduction: the church and Anglicanism in the "long" eighteenth century. In John Walsh, Colin Haydon, and Stephen Taylor. *The Church of England c. 1689–1833: From Toleration to Tractarianism* (pp. 1–64). Cambridge, UK: Cambridge University Press.

Watt, Ian (1957). *The Rise of the Novel*. Berkeley and Los Angeles: University of California Press.

Wells, Juliette (2004). "In music she had always used to feel alone": Jane Austen, solitude, and the artistic woman. *Persuasions*, 26, 98–110.

Whatley, Richard (1821). Review. *Quarterly Review*, 24, 356–57, 360.

White, Hayden (1987). *The Content of Form: Narrative Discourse and Historical Representation*. Baltimore, MD: Johns Hopkins University Press.

Williams, C. (1933). Introductory essay. In S. v. la Roche, *Sophie in London in 1786, being the Diary of Sophie v. la Roche*, trans. C. Williams. London: Jonathan Cape.

Williams, Carolyn D. (1998). General Tilney and the maidens all forlorn: typecasting in *Northanger Abbey*. *Women's Writing*, 5:1, 41–62.

Williams, Raymond (1970). *The English Novel: From Dickens to Lawrence*. London: Chatto & Windus.

Williams, Raymond (1973). *The Country and the City*. London: Chatto & Windus; New York: Oxford University Press.

Williams, Raymond (1983). *Keywords: A Vocabulary of Culture and Society*, rev. edn. New York: Oxford University Press.

Wilson, F. (1999). Introduction: Byron, Byronism and Byromaniacs. In F. Wilson (Ed.). *Byromania: Portraits of the Artist in Nineteenth- and Twentieth-Century Culture* (pp. 1–23). Basingstoke, UK: Macmillan Press and New York: St. Martin's Press.

Wilt, Judith (1980). *The Ghosts of the Gothic*. Princeton, NJ: Princeton University Press.

Wiltshire, John (1992). *Sanditon*: the enjoyments of invalidism. In *Jane Austen and the Body* (pp. 197–221). Cambridge, UK: Cambridge University Press.

Wiltshire, John (2005). Introduction. *Mansfield Park*. Cambridge, UK: Cambridge University Press.

Wiltshire, J. (2006). *Jane Austen: Introductions and Interventions*. London: Palgrave Macmillan.

Wollstonecraft, Mary (1787). *Thoughts on the Education of Daughters*. London: J. Johnson.

Wollstonecraft, M. (1792). *A Vindication of the Rights of Woman*. London: J. Johnson. Also in Janet Todd and Marilyn Butler (Eds). *The Works of Mary Wollstonecraft*, 7 vols (vol. 5, 61–266). London: William Pickering, 1989; and Anne K. Mellor and Noelle Chao (Eds). London: Longman/Pearson, 2006.

Wollstonecraft, Mary (1993). *Political Writings: A Vindication of the Rights of Men; A Vindication of the Rights of Woman; An Historical and Moral View of the French Revolution*, Janet Todd (Ed). London: W Pickering.

Wollstonecraft, Mary (1995). *A Vindication of the Rights of Men, with A Vindication of the Rights of Women, and Hints*, Sylvana Tomaselli (Ed.). Cambridge, UK: Cambridge University Press.

Woolf, D. R. (2004). Jane Austen and history revisited: the past, gender, and memory from the Restoration to *Persuasion*. *Persuasions, 26*, 217–36.

Woolf, Virginia (1925). Jane Austen. *Collected Essays* (vol. 1, pp. 144–54), 4 vols, Leonard Woolf (Ed.). New York: Harcourt, Brace &World.

Woolf, Virginia (1925/1937). *The Common Reader*. London: Hogarth.

Woolf, Virginia (1984). Jane Austen. In Andrew McNeillie (Ed.). *The Common Reader: First Series* (pp. 137–49). San Diego, New York, and London: Harcourt Brace Jovanovich.

Woolf, Virginia (1986). *The Essays of Virginia Woolf*, A. McNeillie (Ed.). 4 vols. London: Hogarth.

Yeazell, R. B. (1984). The boundaries of *Mansfield Park*. *Representations, 7*, 133–52.

Young, B. W. (1998). *Religion and Enlightenment in Eighteenth-Century England: Theological Debate from Locke to Burke*. Oxford: Clarendon Press.

Young, E. (1759). *Conjectures on Original Composition*. London: A. Millar and R. and J. Dodsley.

Zimmerman, Everett (1996). *The Boundaries of Fiction: History and the Eighteenth-Century British Novel*. Ithaca, NY: Cornell University Press.

Index

Note: Page numbers in italic type indicate illustrations.